Affirming Diversity

The Sociopolitical Context of Multicultural Education

Third Edition

Sonia Nieto

 LONGMAN

An imprint of Addison Wesley Longman, Inc.

New York • Reading, Massachusetts • Menlo Park, California • Harlow, England
Don Mills, Ontario • Sydney • Mexico City • Madrid • Amsterdam

For Angel

Editor-in-Chief: Priscilla McGeehon
Acquisitions Editor: Arthur Pomponio
Development Editor: Phil Herbst
Marketing Manager: Wendy Albert
Full Service Production Manager: Denise Phillip
Project Coordination, Text Design, and Electronic Page Makeup: WestWords, Inc.
Cover Designer/Manager: Nancy Danahy
Cover Illustration/Photo: Gigi Kaeser
Senior Print Buyer: Hugh Crawford
Printer and Binder: The Maple-Vail Book Manufacturing Group
Cover Printer: Coral Graphics Services, Inc.

Library of Congress Cataloging-in-Publication Data

Nieto, Sonia.
    Affirming diversity : the sociopolitical context of multicultural
education / Sonia Nieto. — 3rd ed.
        p.   cm.
    Includes bibliographical references (p.) and index.
    ISBN 0-8013-3104-8 (pbk.)
    1. Multicultural education—United States—Case studies.
I. Title.
LC1099.3.N54   2000
370.117—dc21   99-24481
                                                        CIP

Copyright © 2000 by Addison Wesley Longman, Inc.

All rights reserved. No part of this publication may be reproduced,
stored in a retrieval system, or transmitted in any form or by any
means, electronic, mechanical, photocopying, recording, or
otherwise, without the prior permission of the publisher.

Please visit our website at http://www.awlonline.com

ISBN 0-8013-3103-X

2 3 4 5 6 7 8 9 10-MA-02010099

SER MAESTRO

Angel Nieto Romero

Ser maestro es
ser padre, hermano, amigo, compañero,
confidente, enfermero, constante consejero.

Ser maestro es:
    Amar, apreciar, dar exemplo
respetar.
    Perseverar, tener paciencia (y perderla),
perdonar.
    Aconsejar, empujar, dar amistad,
escuchar.
    Explicar, aplicar, no dejarse derrotar,
apreciar.

Tener caridad y compasión,
firmeza y determinación,
alegría y pasión,
mucha pasión y
amor a esa locura
que implica la creación.

Ser maestro es:
    Repetir, corregir, dar orgullo,
exigir.
    Estimular, animar, ser humilde,
admirar.
    Comprender, reprender, ser atrevido,
imponer.
    Imaginar, moldear, tener ganas,
realizar.
    Insistir, sufrir, tener humor,
requerir.

Hacer reglas y romperlas,
no confiar en lo obvio
descartar lo cómodo
escapar de la rutina.
Contestar y preguntar,
siempre preguntar.
No hacer caso al qué dirán.

(continúa)

TO BE A TEACHER

Angel Nieto Romero

To be a teacher means
to be a parent, a friend, a companion,
a confidant, a nurse, a constant counselor.

To be a teacher means:
    To love, to cherish, to set an example
to respect.
    To push, to have patience (and to lose it),
to forgive.
    To advise, to persevere, to befriend,
to listen.
    To explain, to apply, to not give up,
to appreciate.

To have charity and compassion,
strength and determination,
joyfulness and passion,
passion and love
for that madness
which implies creation.

To be a teacher means:
    To repeat, to correct, to instill pride,
to require.
    To stimulate, to encourage, to be humble,
to reprimand.
    To fulfill, to impose, to laugh
to admire.
    To imagine, to mold, to care
to demand.
    To persist, to struggle, to dare,
to understand.

To make rules and to break them,
to mistrust the obvious
to reject the comfortable
to escape routine.
To answer and to ask,
always to ask.
Not paying attention to what people might say.

(continued)

Dormir poco y soñar mucho,
soñar dormido, despierto soñar,
siempre soñar y
lo imposible buscar.
Aprender, compartir, enseñar
y aprender una vez más.
Descubrir, formar, lograr
y luego volver a empezar.

To sleep a little and dream a lot,
to dream asleep, and dream awake,
always to dream and
reach for the impossible.
To learn, to share, to teach
and to learn again.
To discover, to shape, to achieve
and then to start all over again.

Contents

List of Case Studies

Foreword

It is common these days to hear corporate leaders talk positively about "globalization" and the economic opportunities that have arisen (for some) from the rapid integration of world markets and the explosion of information, estimated to be doubling every two years. Corporations are increasingly multinational and ply their trade in countries around the world. The ease and efficiency of telecommunications, together with unprecedented population mobility, has made the *global village* a reality only three decades after Marshall McLuhan first coined the phrase.

The implications for education of this technological and social change might appear obvious. Domestically and internationally, cross-cultural contact is the norm, so surely we should prepare students to function effectively in a multicultural global society. Racism and other forms of discrimination are not only repugnant from a social justice perspective but also, in the long run, counterproductive to all sectors of society insofar as they squander the cultural and intellectual resources of the society.

In principle, this orientation appears consistent with various corporate pronouncements and government reports about both education and globalization. Corporate America wants people whose heads are not stuffed with soon-to-be-obsolete information, but rather people who know how to get access to information, who can critically interpret this information to discover what is relevant and useful, and who can work cooperatively across cultural, linguistic, and racial boundaries to solve problems using this information. It might appear obvious then that our schools should be aiming to produce critical and creative thinkers who are knowledgeable about and sensitive to other cultural perspectives. Any student who emerges into our culturally diverse society speaking only one language and with a monocultural perspective on the world can legitimately be considered educationally ill prepared and perhaps even "culturally deprived." Historian Robert Hughes expressed it well when he said: "...in a globalized economy, the future lies with people who can think and act with informed grace across ethnic, cultural, linguistic lines."* In light of these considerations, one might imagine that multicultural education and effective teaching of additional languages would be educational priorities.

Unfortunately, this is not the case. On the contrary, even mention of the terms *multicultural education* and *bilingual education* arouses anger and volatile debate. Multicultural education is interpreted as an attack on the foundations of western civilization. The self-appointed protectors of the "canon of western civilization"

*Hughes, R. *Culture of Complaint: A Passionate Look into the Ailing Heart of America.* (New York: Warner Books, 1993).

label multiculturalism as "the cult of ethnicity" focused only on "ethnic redress" for the alleged injustices of the past. They see the federal government's support of bilingual education for students of bilingual/bicultural heritage as exemplifying a "death wish" that is pushing the nation toward fragmentation and disunity. The integrity of the United States is seen as now being threatened by "revisionist" interpretations of history and demands to expand the canon to include the voices of previously excluded communities.

These "culture wars" are being waged in every classroom, not only in the United States, but around the world.

Every country has erected its symbolic myths of nationhood and identity; school curricula reconstruct national histories to highlight what is consistent with these myths and to eliminate or sanitize what is inconsistent. The attempt by previously subordinated groups to include their histories in school curricula is interpreted by some as threatening to undermine the foundations of nationhood. Why expose to the light of critical scrutiny our past and current failure to live up to our constitutional ideals of justice and human rights? Surely this will weaken our sense of unity and the patriotic impulses of our youth?

Those who argue against multicultural education respond to the imperatives of globalization and the realities of increasing cultural diversity by agreeing that we want our schools to develop creative and critical thinkers, but these thinking skills should be focused only on solving technical problems related to the production of wealth. They should never be focused on uncovering social injustice and attempting to resolve inequities of opportunity in our society. Issues related to power relations should be out of bounds for educators and students, and consequently invisible in approved curricula.

Opponents of multicultural and bilingual education will also agree that knowledge of additional languages is a worthwhile educational goal. However, the imperatives of national unity dictate that the souls of five-and six-year-old children who enter schools capable of expressing their identities, hopes, and dreams only in foreign tongues should be purged from allegiance to these languages. The language of belonging, acceptance, and opportunity is English, and other languages can be admitted as "foreign languages" only after "the language of equal opportunity" has been imprinted.

In short, multicultural education is controversial because it insists that awareness of issues of social justice and power relations in our society, past and present, are crucially relevant to the future of our society and the priorities and values of the next generation. It highlights the fact that the languages and cultures that children bring to school are resources for them as individuals, their families, and the entire society. It insists that these resources be valued and affirmed in contrast to the experience of previous generations whose identities were frequently brutalized in the schools.

This third edition of *Affirming Diversity* addresses these issues in a lucid and powerful way that speaks to every educator who is committed to drawing out the inherent potential that all children bring to school. Sonia Nieto challenges us, as educators, to make explicit the image of our students and of our society that is implied in our interactions in the school context. What kind of people do we hope our students will grow up to be? What kinds of abilities and knowledge are we giving them the opportunity to acquire? What kind of society do we hope they will create? The answers to all these questions are written in the daily record of our interactions with our students. Our interactions with students and communities constitute a moral enterprise, whether we define it as such or not.

Students' voices occupy a central place in this book. They complement and illustrate the theoretical analyses and remind us that the interactions between educators and students dramatically affect not only the acquisition of knowledge and skills, but the creation of both student and teacher identity.

Unfortunately, in many classrooms the curriculum has been sanitized such that opportunities for critical reflection on personal and collective identity and on issues of social justice are minimized. The image of our students and society implied by this pedagogical orientation is an image of compliant consumers who will gratefully accept their place within the existing power structure and who can easily be manipulated to exercise their democratic rights to preserve that power structure.

A radically different image is implied by the pedagogical orientations articulated in *Affirming Diversity*. Students are viewed as critical thinkers capable of, and responsible for, creating change through action both in their own lives and in the broader society. Their interactions in school provide opportunities to collaborate across cultural and linguistic boundaries in the generation, interpretation, and application of knowledge. The curriculum orients students toward critical reflection on issues of social justice and of identity (both personal and collective).

The image of students and society implied in these educational interactions is an image of individuals who have developed respect both for their own cultural identity and for the identities of others; who are capable of collaborating with others in the democratic pursuit of social justice; and who see themselves as members of a global community with shared economic, scientific, and environmental interests. As such, the directions highlighted in *Affirming Diversity* respond much more adequately to the challenges of the twenty-first century than the introverted xenophobic focus of those who argue, explicitly or implicitly, for a monolingual monocultural education.

Affirming Diversity not only constitutes an eloquent and forceful statement about the importance of multicultural education to our society, it also affirms the central role that individual educators play in nurturing and shaping the lives and identities of our youth. To be a teacher is to be a visionary—as we interact with our students we envisage what contributions they will play in shaping a better society and we orchestrate our classroom interactions to enable them to realize these possibilities. This book encourages us to recognize that power relations in the broader society, and particularly the negative discourse about diversity and multicultural education, often operate to constrict our vision of what we can achieve with our students. *Affirming Diversity* challenges us to make choices in our classrooms that will resist the perpetuation of coercive relations of power. It affords both the insight and the inspiration to enable us to create interactions with our students that are respectful, intellectually challenging, and empowering for both them and us.

Jim Cummins
Ontario Institute for Studies in Education

Preface

To The Third Edition

When *Affirming Diversity* was first published in 1992, someone asked how long it had taken me to write it. After thinking about it for a moment, I answered, "All my life." Although the actual writing had taken me just about two years of research, reflection, and writing, the ideas expressed in the book had been percolating for many years.

My life is as much a part of this book as is my educational philosophy. Because my life experiences have influenced my thinking deeply, it is inevitable that they should be woven into the fabric of this book. These experiences include being born and raised in the United States of Puerto Rican-born working-class parents; attending New York city public schools and learning English as my second language; being one of the first members of my family, along with my sister, to graduate from high school and go to college; teaching poor children of many backgrounds in impoverished urban school; living through the maelstrom of the political struggle for self-determination in the early 1970s when I was a young faculty member in the Puerto Rican Studies Department at Brooklyn College; and then becoming a professor at the University of Massachusetts preparing teachers for the tremendous diversity they would face in their classrooms. Even more than any of these experiences, becoming a mother changed forever how I would think about children, education, and fairness.

Much has happened in my life since *Affirming Diversity* was first published. For one thing, I have seen my daughters grow up and I have become a grandmother. Since 1992, I have also had the opportunity to speak with many thousands of educators around the country and I have taught hundreds of future and current teachers. In the intervening years, the conditions in which teachers work have become in some ways more difficult and stifling than ever. Poverty, racism, and the decreasing support for public education—issues that are not unrelated—have worsened in the past decade. All these changes, both in my own life and in the conditions in the nation and its public schools, have fueled the urgency I feel to make schools more affirming and caring places for all students. This third edition reflects that urgency.

WHAT'S NEW IN THE THIRD EDITION?

Although my fundamental ideas about education have not changed since I first wrote *Affirming Diversity*, they have developed as I have continued to study and learn. A number of changes in the third edition are a direct result of the evolution in my thinking.

Some changes are apparent throughout the text. I thoroughly updated the references, reflecting the newest research in multicultural education. I also linked the case studies much more closely to the chapters with which they are associated. I believe the reason for placing particular case studies in the context of specific chapters will now be more evident to readers. I also added more concrete examples and anecdotes to illustrate abstract concepts more clearly. Most of all, I rewrote a good deal of the text, working at making the writing more accessible.

Specific chapters were significantly revised. In particular, I expanded Chapter 1 (Why the Case Study Approach?) to include more information about the research I did concerning the case study students. Because many readers over the years have requested advice on how to do case studies, Chapter 1 also includes guidelines for developing them. In addition, I thoroughly revised Chapter 6 (Linguistic Diversity in Multicultural Classrooms) to reflect the current condition in which linguistic minority children are educated. The vast majority of children who speak a language other than English are *not* in bilingual classrooms. More are in either ESL-only programs, or in mainstream classes. Given this reality, the focus of Chapter 6 is on what teachers who are not specialists in ESL or bilingual education can do to be more effective with language minority students. All teachers, even if they do not speak the students' languages, can find ways to promote students' acquisition of English while at the same time affirming the use of their native languages. My support for bilingual education remains as strong as ever, and this support is reflected in the chapter. But because most teachers at all levels will at some point be responsible for teaching language minority students, they need to know what they can do in all classrooms, not simply in bilingual programs.

Readers of the previous two editions will notice that the book currently has 11 rather than 12 chapters. Because of some duplication, and because the issues addressed in Chapters 10 and 11 were related, I combined them to create the new Chapter 10. For purposes of readability, I removed the list of multicultural resources and literature in the last chapter (previously Chapter 12), and placed them in the new Appendix.

A final change in the third edition is the *Epilogue*. Given the keen interest so many readers have expressed about the case study students since the book was first published, I intended to include updated information on where they were and what they were doing. I asked the original interviewers to find and interview the students again. As you will see in the short *Epilogue* at the end of the book, we were able to find only three of them. At any rate, I decided to include those we found because I knew that many readers were curious to find out what had become of them.

ACKNOWLEDGMENTS

No book ever writes itself, and no author writes a book alone, even if her name in the one on the cover. I am deeply appreciative of the many individuals who have helped me with the third edition of *Affirming Diversity*.

First, I owe a debt of gratitude to the many readers who have communicated with me through mail, phone, email, and in person in the years since the second edition was published. Readers have been uniformly gracious and supportive, even when they do not always agree with my ideas. Their insights and analysis have helped me to think more critically about my work. I trust that their feedback is evident in the third edition.

Paula Elliott, Diane Sweet, and Carlie Tartokov were able to locate and reinterview the young people they first interviewed a decade ago, and I am very thankful to them for doing so. I also appreciate the efforts made by the other interviewers—Haydée Font, Maya Gillingham, Beatriz McConnie Zapater, Mac Lee Morante, and Carol Shea—who tried valiantly to find the students they had originally interviewed. I am especially indebted to Linda Howard, Avi Abramson, and Fern Sherman for taking the time to let us know how they are doing after so many years.

I am also grateful to the reviewers of the manuscript for Longman Publishers:

John McFadden, CSU-Sacramento

Lilian Vega-Castaneda, CSU-San Marcos

Becky Kirschner, Ohio State University

Patricia Weibust, University of Connecticut

C. Garn Coombs, Brigham Young University

Their detailed comments and suggestions for improving the book were enormously helpful. I know that the third edition is better as a result.

For help with references, I thank Elizabeth Capifali, Denise Gaskin, and Lori Mestre. Their cheerful assistance made the sometimes laborious task of locating difficult resources much easier. The entire staff at Longman, but particularly Art Pomponio and his assistant Cori Gabbard, were consistently accommodating and encouraging every step of the way. Richard Saunders and the staff of WestWords did a fine job with copy editing and getting the book into final production.

If *Affirming Diversity* is more readable and engaging, Phil Herbst, the development editor for the book, is largely responsible. He read every word I wrote and was a careful teacher. Thanks to his precision, I believe I have become a better writer. Finally, a heartfelt thank you to Jim Cummins, a scholar of rare genius as well as a wonderful friend. Jim has been a consistent and enthusiastic supporter of this book and of my work in general. His willingness to write the new foreword for this third edition means a great deal to me.

My most important support, and the reason for my work, is my family. My daughters Alicia and Marisa and their husbands Celso and John, my granddaughters Jazmyne and Monique, along with nephews, nieces, stepgrandchildren, as well as my sister Lydia, a caring educator, are always in my mind as I think and write about the meaning of education and other public endeavors. My husband, Angel, to whom I dedicate this third edition, has been a constant and loving soul mate for the past 33 years.

THE THIRD EDITION AS A TOOL IN AFFIRMATION

The labels commonly used to describe some students—*at risk, disadvantaged, deprived*—are accepted by some educators as if they told the whole story. But the whole story is a much more complicated one. Our students do not come to school fully formed, nor do they come to us simply as walking sets of deficiencies. All students have talents and strengths that can be used in the service of their learning.

Our schools reflect the sociocultural and sociopolitical context in which we live, and this context is unfair to many young people and their families. The ideologies underlying many school policies and practices are based on flawed ideas about intelligence and difference. If we want to change the situation, it means changing the curriculum and pedagogy in individual classrooms, as well as the school's practices and the ideologies undergirding them. That is, we need to create not only affirming classrooms, but also an affirming society in which racism, sexism, social class discrimination, and other biases are no longer acceptable. This book is a small contribution toward that effort.

Having been a classroom teacher myself, I have a profound respect and admiration for teachers. The work they do is noble, although rarely cherished. At the same time, I recognize that many teachers have not been given the time or support to help them teach the most educationally abused students in our schools. I hope that *Affirming Diversity* is one tool educators can use to help them think deeply about the children in our schools and our society's responsibility to educate them all well.

Sonia Nieto

Introduction

As a young child growing up in Brooklyn, New York, during the 1940s, I experienced firsthand the effects of relative poverty and discrimination. In the schools I attended, a common perception was that my culture and language were inferior. I spoke only Spanish when I entered first grade, and I was immediately confronted with the arduous task of learning a second language while my developed native language was all but ignored. Almost 50 years later, I still remember the frustration of groping for English words I did not know to express thoughts I could say very capably in Spanish. Equally vivid are memories of some teachers' expectations that my classmates and I would not do well in school because of our language and cultural differences. This explains my fourth-grade teacher's response when mine was the only hand to go up when she asked whether anybody in the class wanted to go to college. "Well, that's okay," she said, "because we always need people to clean toilets."

I also recall teachers' patronizing attitudes about students who spoke a language other than English. "Is there anybody in this class who started school without speaking English?" my tenth-grade homeroom teacher asked loudly, while filling out one of the endless forms that teachers are given by the central office. By this time, my family had moved to a middle-class neighborhood of mostly Jewish, Italian, and Irish families. My classmates watched in hushed silence as I, the only Puerto Rican in the class, raised my hand timidly. "Are you in a special English class?" he asked in front of the entire class. "Yes," I said. "I'm in Honors English." My teacher looked surprised, and I was secretly pleased that I could respond in this way. Certainly there is nothing wrong with being a second language learner, or being in an ESL (English as a Second Language) class, but I had learned to feel ashamed of speaking Spanish and I wanted to make it very clear that I was intelligent *in spite of it.*

Those first experiences with society's responses to cultural differences did not convince me that something was wrong with the *responses.* Rather, I assumed, as many of my peers did, that there was something wrong with *us.* We learned to feel ashamed of who we were, how we spoke, what we ate, and everything else that was different about us. "Please," I would beg my mother, "make us hamburgers and hot dogs for dinner." Luckily, she never paid attention and kept right on cooking rice, beans, *plátanos* (plantains), and all those other good foods that we grew up with. She and my father also continued speaking Spanish to us in spite of our teachers' pleas to speak to us in English only. And so, alongside the messages at school and in the streets that being Puerto Rican was not something to be proud of, we learned to keep on being who we were. As the case studies in this book point out, a great many young people still face negative messages about their language and culture in school, even while their families attempt to teach them to see diversity in a positive light.

DIVERSITY: THE VIEWS OF SCHOOLS AND TEACHERS

Negative beliefs about diversity leave their imprint not only on students but on teachers and schools as well. Although I have been fortunate to work with many talented and caring teachers who welcome their students' identities and view them as assets, I have met others who accept the notion that differences get in the way of learning. Even many well-meaning teachers who care about their students hold this belief. This has become evident to me through the scores of presentations on multicultural and bilingual education I have made in many different school systems, colleges, and universities over the years. After each session, a few teachers invariably approach me with the same concern: Why do some of their students (usually African American, Latino, or American Indian students and very often poor European American students) fail no matter what they, their teachers, do, whereas other students (usually middle-class European American and some Asian American students, as well as middle-class students of other ethnic groups) succeed?

A small number of these teachers may believe that their unsuccessful students are genetically or culturally inferior. But I am convinced that the vast majority of teachers do not harbor such racist and classist beliefs. I have found that some teachers who were committed and idealistic when they began teaching have simply tired of facing hostile and nonachieving students in their classrooms every day. Still other teachers who have not been able to reach students of diverse backgrounds may start to believe that children from some groups may indeed be inherently "better" students than others. The cause for failure, they may reluctantly conclude, must be within the children, their families, or their culture. After all, the schools have tried everything from compensatory education to free lunch and breakfast programs. Nothing seems to work, and the same young people keep dropping out and failing. How can multicultural education help?

WHAT GOOD CAN MULTICULTURAL EDUCATION DO?

Educational failure is too complex and knotty an issue to be "fixed" by any single program or approach. To view multicultural education as "the answer" to school failure is simplistic because other important social and educational issues that affect the lives of students would be ignored. Multicultural education does not exist in a vacuum but must be understood in its larger personal, social, historical, and political context. However, if it is broadly conceptualized and implemented, multicultural education *can* have a substantive and positive impact on the education of most students. That is the thesis of this book.

I have come to this understanding as a result of many experiences, including my childhood and my life as a student, teacher, researcher, and parent. I believe that to be effective, multicultural education needs to move beyond diversity as a passing fad. It needs to take into account our history of immigration as well as the inequality and exclusion that have characterized our past, our present, and our educational record. These issues are too often ignored in superficial treatments of multicultural education.

For example, immigration is not a phenomenon of the past. In fact, the experience of immigration is still fresh in the minds of a great many people in the United States. It begins anew every day that planes land, ships reach our shores, and people on foot make their way to our borders. Many of the students in our schools who themselves are not immigrants have parents or grandparents who are. Not just a nation of past immigrants, often romantically portrayed, the United States is a nation of immigrants even today.

Although almost all of us have an immigrant past, very few of us know or even acknowledge it. But because schools have traditionally perceived their role as that of an assimilating agent, the isolation and rejection that accompany immigration have simply been left at the schoolhouse door. The rich experiences of millions of our students, and of their parents, grandparents, and neighbors, have been lost. Rather than using students' experiences as a foundation, curriculum and pedagogy have been based on the myth of a painless and smooth assimilation.

U.S. history is also steeped in slavery and conquest. Millions of descendants of Africans, American Indians, Mexicans, Puerto Ricans and others colonized within and beyond U.S. borders have also experienced disparagement of their native cultures and languages. But the history of racism and exploitation experienced by so many of our people, including their children, is rarely taught.

The research reported in this book suggests to me that we need to make the history of all these groups visible by making it part of the curriculum, instruction, and schooling in general. The words of the students in the case studies in this book provide eloquent testimony for the need to do so. For instance, Manuel Gomes, the young man who is the subject of one of the case studies following Chapter 6, claims that he "cannot be an American" because it would mean forsaking his Cape Verdean background. Vanessa Mattison, a young woman fiercely devoted to social justice and equality but with little awareness of the U.S. history of racism and inequity, knows nothing about her European American past and even feels uncomfortable discussing it. James Karam, whose case study is presented at the end of Chapter 5, is a Lebanese Christian student whose culture is totally missing in the school's curriculum and extracurricular activities. James has learned to appreciate any references to his background, even if negative.

The immigrant and colonization experiences are a significant point of departure for our journey into multicultural education. This journey needs to begin with teachers, who themselves are frequently unaware of or uncomfortable with their own ethnicity. By reconnecting with their own backgrounds, and with the suffering as well as the triumphs of their families, teachers can lay the groundwork for students to reclaim their histories and voices.

No child should have to make the painful choice between family and school, which inevitably becomes the choice between belonging or succeeding. The costs of such a choice are too high, from becoming a "cultural schizophrenic" to developing doubts about one's worth and dignity. This is nowhere more poignantly described than in Richard Rodriguez's painful recollection of growing up as a "scholarship boy," an academically promising student doomed to lose his family and native culture and language in the process. His conclusion is that the public and private worlds of immigrant children cannot be reconciled:

> My awkward childhood does not prove the necessity of bilingual education. My story discloses instead an essential myth of childhood—inevitable pain. If I rehearse here the changes in my private life after my Americanization, it is finally to emphasize the public gain. The loss implies the gain.[1]

Because of the wrenching experience of the loss of his native language and culture, Rodriguez decided that policies such as bilingual education, multicultural education, and affirmative action do not work because they only delay the inevitable loss. My conclusion is quite the opposite: Losing one's culture and language is too high a price to pay for academic success and social acceptance. I am not calling here for cultural separation or "ethnic purity"; these notions are not only unrealistic but also undesirable and impossible in a pluralistic nation. But because culture and language help define the very soul of a people, to insist on wiping them out is both an unusually cruel strategy and, in the end, a counterproductive one.

I am not suggesting that multicultural education simply concerns the affirmation of language and culture. Multicultural education is a transformative process that goes far beyond cultural and linguistic maintenance. In the final analysis, multicultural education needs to confront issues of power and privilege in society. This means challenging racism and other biases as well as the structures, policies, and practices of schools.

As you will see in this book, affirming language and culture can help students become successful and well-adjusted learners. But unless language and cultural issues are approached through a critical lens based on equity and social justice, they are unlikely to have a lasting impact in promoting real change.

SOME ASSUMPTIONS

There are a number of assumptions in the text that I want to clarify. The first concerns who is included in my idea of multicultural education. My framework is broad and inclusive: multicultural education is for everyone regardless of ethnicity, race, language, social class, religion, gender, sexual orientation, ability, and other differences. But although I refer to many kinds of differences, this text is primarily concerned with race, ethnicity, and language. I use these as the major lenses to understand multicultural education. Both multicultural and bilingual education were direct outgrowths of the civil rights movement and they developed in response to racism, ethnocentrism, and language discrimination in education. These inequities continue to exist, especially for Native American, Latino, and African American youngsters.

Other lenses with which to view inequality in education include gender, social class, sexual orientation, religion, and exceptionality. But because one book cannot possibly give all of these topics the central importance they deserve, my focus is on race, ethnicity, and language. Other books emphasize differences that are equally meaningful and necessary for all teachers to know about. I encourage you to become aware of all the differences that are not the main focus of this book because they provide valuable insights into how students who are not considered part of the "mainstream" are also marginalized in schools.[2]

Having a broad definition of multicultural education raises another dilemma, however. One reason it is easier for some educators to embrace a very inclusive and comprehensive framework of multicultural education is that they have a hard time discussing and facing racism. For example, whenever I bring up racism with a group of predominantly White teachers, I find that too often they want to go immediately to, say, sexism or classism without spending much time on racism. Sexism and classism are certainly worthy of study and attention; in fact, they must be part of a multicultural agenda. But the discomfort that many White teachers feel in talking about racism is very evident in incidents such as these. Racism is an excruciatingly difficult issue for most of us. Given our history of exclusion and discrimination, this is not surprising. But it is only through a thorough exploration of discrimination based on race and other differences related to it that we can understand the genesis as well as the rationale for multicultural education.

Another assumption that guides this book is that teachers cannot be singled out as the villains in the failure of students. Although some teachers do bear responsibility for having low expectations, being racist and elitist in their interactions with students and parents, and providing educational environments that discourage many students from learning, most do not do so consciously. Most teachers are sincerely concerned about their students and want very much to provide them with the best education. But because of their own limited experiences and knowledge, they may know very little about the students they teach. As a result, their beliefs about students of diverse backgrounds may be based on spurious assumptions and stereotypes. Further, teachers are often at the mercy of decisions made by others far removed from the classroom; they generally have little to do with developing the policies and practices in their schools, and frequently they do not even question them.

Teachers are also the products of educational systems that have a history of racism, exclusion, and debilitating pedagogy. Hence their practices reflect their experiences and they may unwittingly perpetuate policies and approaches that are harmful to many of their students. We cannot separate schools from the communities they serve or from our society in general. Oppressive forces that limit opportunities in the schools reflect such forces in the society at large. But the purpose of this book is not to point a finger but to provide a forum for reflection and discussion so that teachers take responsibility for their own actions, challenge the actions of schools and society that affect their students' education, and help bring about positive change.

ABOUT THIS BOOK

Why students succeed or fail in school has been the subject of much research and debate, particularly for students whose racial, ethnic, linguistic, or social class backgrounds differ from that of the dominant group. Programs in bilingual and multicultural education have been two responses to the dilemma of school failure, and both have been viewed as controversial because they challenge the status quo. But in the final analysis, even bilingual and multicultural education by themselves will not substantially change the outlook for most students because the issue is more complicated than implementing a specific program or approach. The complex interplay among personal, social, political, and educational factors helps explain students' academic success or failure. In this book, I will consider these links in exploring the benefits of multicultural education. I will also use case studies because it is especially by listening to students that we can learn how they experience school, how social and educational structures affect their learning, and what we can do to provide high-quality education for them.

Educators frequently rely on their own experiences and common sense when they teach. However, educational research (i.e., the systematic and careful study of how and why students learn) generally provides a better source for educational practice. Rather than relying on convention or tradition or what seems to work, it is more effective to look to research for ways to improve teaching. This book is grounded in research because research gives us a way to understand what happens in classrooms, with implications for improving education.

I do not mean to imply that research is always neutral and fair. As human beings, we approach each endeavor with a set of assumptions and a philosophical and political outlook. No research can be entirely free of biases, no matter how neutral it may claim to be. Even the decision to study a particular phenomenon is not impartial and may have unstated agendas. Moreover, research findings are seldom neat and tidy, and often contradictory. But research nonetheless contributes to our understanding of education by sharpening our awareness of complex issues.

This book explores the meaning, necessity, and benefits of multicultural education for students from all cultural backgrounds through the following:

1. An investigation of how schooling is influenced by
   a. racism and other biases and expectations of students' achievement.
   b. school organization and educational policies and practices.
   c. cultural and other differences such as ethnicity, race, gender, language, and social class.
2. A rationale for multicultural education based on that investigation.

3. Case studies—in the words of a selected group of students from a variety
   of backgrounds—about home, school, and community experiences and
   how these have influenced the students' school achievement.

This book presents data on the multicultural nature of schools and society, including information about different cultural and linguistic groups, their experiences in
schools, and the issues and challenges they face. Relevant research on the success
or failure of students in schools is also presented.

The book consists of 11 chapters organized in three parts. In Part I, I describe
the case study approach and summarize the terminology used in the book. In Part
II, I present a conceptual framework for multicultural education in a sociopolitical
context, emphasizing institutional and cultural factors in schooling and individual and group responses to education. This section explores the multiple forces
that may affect the school achievement of students from a variety of backgrounds.

To provide insights into the interrelated roles that discrimination, school policies and practices, and culture play in the education of students in the classroom, I
present 12 case studies. Incorporated throughout Part II, the case studies highlight
the salient issues discussed in particular chapters, and they provide a concrete
means for addressing issues of diversity and success or failure in the schools. I
hope that the case studies will help you more fully understand the lives and school
experiences of a variety of young people and that they reflect what social justice in
schools might look like. The case studies can be read in their entirety, in conjunction with the chapter in which they are located, or in short selections, depending
on the particular focus of the course, the racial and ethnic groups under study, and
the context of the school system or university.

Part III focuses on the implications of the case studies for teaching and learning in a multicultural society such as ours. I use themes that emerge from the case
studies to review factors that may affect learning for different students. This leads
to defining multicultural education as a way to equalize education, a definition
that emerges organically from the conceptual framework developed in Part II.
Chapters 10 and 11 focus on areas in which further collaboration between home,
school, and community can be developed for positive student achievement and on
ways to remove barriers that inhibit learning. Suggestions for developing environments that foster high-quality education, concentrating on multicultural education as a process, are offered in Ch. 10. In addition, I propose a model of
multicultural education to affirm all students. Finally, in Chapter 11 I recommend
strategies that teachers and schools can use to implement multicultural education,
with a focus on collaborative projects.

Each chapter concludes with a series of problems or situations for readers to
think about. There are no immediate or easy answers to many of the dilemmas
teachers face with their students every day. The purpose of posing these problems
is to suggest that careful attention needs to be paid to the many manifestations of
inequality in our schools, and that productive resolutions can come about when
teachers, students, and parents reflect critically about these problems and work
together to solve them.

THE COMPLEX NATURE OF SCHOOLING

Writing a book that might offer useful insights into education in a highly complex and diverse society is an exceedingly difficult task. The major pitfall in writing a book about multicultural education is that the information presented can be over-generalized to the point that it becomes just another harmful stereotype. For example, after reading the case study of Hoang Vinh, the Vietnamese student whose case study follows Chapter 5, one may reach the conclusion that Vietnamese students are always successful in school because their culture reinforces academic success. But this explanation is neither complete nor wholly satisfactory because it neglects issues such as the effect of societal expectations on school achievement, as well as many other factors. Or one may conclude that all Chicanos are gang members, as is the case with Paul Chavez, whose story follows Chapter 7, or that all Jewish students are religious, as is true of Avi Abramson, whose case study follows Chapter 4. None of these conclusions is warranted by the case studies, yet that is the danger of using individual examples.

In this book I have tried to consider schooling as a dynamic process in which competing interests and values are at work every day in complex and contradictory ways: Expectations of students and the community are often pitted against expectations of teachers and schools; the organization and policies of schools are sometimes diametrically opposed to what is developmentally appropriate for young people; and racial, gender, class, and language stratification are frequently used to explain the success or failure of students. Through the study of the many complex forces that influence young people, we can begin to understand the lives of the students who comprise our multicultural society.

● *NOTES*

1. Richard Rodriguez, *Hunger of Memory: The Education of Richard Rodriguez* (Boston: David R. Godine, 1982), 27.
2. See, for example, Ellen Brantlinger, *The Politics of Social Class in Secondary School: Views of Affluent and Impoverished Youth* (New York: Teachers College Press, 1993); Simi Linton, "Reshaping Disability in Teacher Education and Beyond." In *Teaching Education*, 6, 2 (Fall 1994), 9–20; and the Special Issue on Lesbian, Gay, Bisexual, and Transgender People and Education, *Harvard Educational Review*, 66, 2 (Summer 1996).

part one

Setting the Stage
Approaches and Definitions

———•———

Multicultural education cannot be understood in a vacuum. Yet in many schools it is approached as if it were divorced from the policies and practices of schools and from society. The result is a "fairyland" multicultural education disassociated from the lives of teachers, students, and communities. The premise of this book is quite different: *No educational philosophy or program is worthwhile unless it focuses on two primary concerns:*

- Raising the achievement of all students and providing them with an equitable and high-quality education.
- Giving students an apprenticeship in the opportunity to become critical and productive members of a democratic society.

Let me begin by defining a number of terms and explaining the approach used in this book. Helping students get along, teaching them to feel better about themselves, or "sensitizing" them to one another may be meaningful goals of multicultural education. But these goals can turn into superficial strategies that only scratch the surface of educational failure if they do not tackle the far more thorny questions of stratification and inequity. Simply wanting our students to get along with and be respectful of one another makes little difference in the options they will have as a result of their schooling. Because students' lives are inexorably affected by social and political conditions in schools and society, we need to consider these conditions in our conception of multicultural education. Decisions made about education are often treated as if they were politically neutral. Such decisions are *never* politically neutral, but rather tied to the social, political, and economic structures that frame and define our society. This book is predicated on the *sociopolitical context* of multicultural education.

Two terms often associated with multicultural education are *equality* and *equity*, and although they are sometimes used interchangeably, they are in fact different. *Equal education* does not just mean providing the same resources and opportunities for all students (although this alone would afford a better education for a wide

9

range of students). Equal education also means considering the skills, talents, and experiences that all students bring to their education as valid starting points for further schooling. *Equity* is a more comprehensive term because it suggests fairness and the real possibility of *equality of outcomes* for a broader range of students. Throughout this book, both equal education and equity are considered fundamental to multicultural education.

Our public schools are unsuccessful with many students, primarily those from racially, culturally, and linguistically diverse and poor families. Why schools fail to meet their mission to provide all students with an equal and high-quality education has been the subject of educational research for some time. Theories about cultural deprivation and genetic inferiority are once again being used to explain differences in intelligence and achievement, and the implications of these deficit theories continue to influence educational policies and practices. *Deficit theories* assume that some children, because of genetic, cultural, or experiential differences, are inferior to other children; that is, they have a deficit. One problem with such hypotheses is that they place complete responsibility for children's failure on their homes and families, effectively reducing the responsibility of the school and society. Whether the focus is on the individual or the community, the result remains largely the same: blaming the victims of poor schooling rather than looking in a more systematic way at the schools in which they learn (or fail to learn) and the society at large. All these factors need to be explored together.

Another problem with deficit theories is their focus on conditions that are out of the control of most teachers, schools, and even students. Deficit theories tend to foster despair because students' problems are thought to be determined, with no hope for changing the circumstances that produced them in the first place. But teachers and schools cannot alleviate the poverty and other oppressive conditions in which students may live. It is more realistic to tackle the problems that they *can* do something about, among them, providing educational environments that encourage all students to learn. That is why school policies and practices and teachers' attitudes and behaviors, rather than the supposed shortcomings of students, are the basis for the kinds of transformations suggested in this book.

Part I sets the stage for understanding the approach used in this text. Chapter 1 begins with the rationale for using case studies, then describes the case study approach and briefly introduces the students in the case studies. Chapter 2 underscores the connection between terminology and multicultural education by exploring how groups of people are identified in the text.

Why the Case Study Approach?

[Teachers should] not think of a lesson as a lesson. Think of it as not a lesson just being taught to students, but a lesson being taught to one of your own family members, you know? 'Cause if it's like that, they get more deep into it, and that's all it takes. Teach a lesson with heart behind it and try to get your kids to understand more of what's going on.

Paul Chavez (Interviewee, Chapter 7)

*E*ducational researchers, teachers, and policy makers have all had their say about what causes school achievement or failure. Students, however, are rarely included in the conversation, and the voices of students from disempowered and dominated communities such as Paul Chavez's are even more silent. As you will see when you read his case study, Paul has a lot to teach us about school success and failure. Case studies provide a useful vehicle for understanding classroom dilemmas, whether they be cases of teachers, schools, or individual students.[1] In the case studies in this book, young people speak freely about school, family, and identity.

The case studies, 12 in all, are placed at the ends of Chapters 3 through 7 to highlight particular issues discussed in those chapters. In the case studies, students "think out loud" about what they like and dislike about school, about teachers who have made a difference in their lives, about the importance of culture and language in their lives, and about what they expect to get out of school. I hope you will hear not only the students' pain and conflict but also their determination and hope. The fervor with which these youths speak of their families and communities, their eloquence in discussing missed opportunities at such tender ages, and the feelings they convey when talking about their future are a confirmation of their ideals and aspirations.

DEFINING THE CASE STUDY APPROACH

The case study approach fits within the general framework of qualitative research. Sharan Merriam defines the case study as "a thing, a single entity, a unit around which there are boundaries." She goes on to state that "The case then, could be a person such as a student, a teacher, a principal; a program; a group such as a class, a school, a community; a specific policy; and so on."[2] She describes the essential characteristics of a qualitative case study as *particularistic* (focusing on one person or social unit), *descriptive* (because the result is a rich, thick portrait), *heuristic* (because it sharpens the reader's understanding and leads to discovering new meanings). The case study is also *inductive* (because generalizations and hypotheses emerge from examination of the data). Case studies can help us look at specific examples so that solutions for more general situations can be hypothesized and developed. According to Frederick Erickson, practitioners can learn from a case study even if the circumstances of the case do not match those of their own situation.[3]

Case studies have earned a solid reputation in research over the past several years because of the sense of empathy they help to promote. In the words of Elliot Eisner, researchers "have begun to realize that human feeling does not pollute understanding."[4] The thoughts and insights of the students in the case studies help us to understand how the presence or absence of multicultural education, as broadly defined in Chapter 9, might affect the education of those students and of others. They are *ethnographic case studies;* that is, they use a sociocultural analysis of each of the students, all of whom are presented contextually within their cultural and social environment.[5] The students are described within a variety of settings— home, school, community, and city or town in which they live—because by looking at each of these settings we gain a more complete picture of their lives.

The purpose of the case studies is not to generalize to all students within U.S. schools. No research, whether qualitative or quantitative, can expect to do so. The issue of *sampling* provides one of the major differences between qualitative and quantitative research. The students in the case studies in this book represent not a *sample,* as might be the case with quantitative research, but *examples* of a wide variety of students. This type of research provides the possibility of generating sound hypotheses from even a small number of case studies. For example, James Karam, the Lebanese Christian student whose case study follows Chapter 5, does not reflect the experiences of all Lebanese students in U.S. schools. But describing James's experience within its sociocultural framework can help us understand other Lebanese students. Whereas quantitative methods may yield some important data about Lebanese students in general (e.g., their numbers in the United States or their relative levels of achievement), it is only through a qualitative approach that one can explore more deeply, for example, the impact of "invisible minority" status on James.

Qualitative approaches render very distinct but equally crucial data to influence educational practice, but no case study of a single individual can adequately or legitimately portray the complexity of an entire group of people. Not all Mexican Americans learn cooperatively, and not all African Americans perceive school success as "acting White" (these issues will be discussed further in Chapters 5 and 7). To reach such conclusions contradicts one of the very purposes of case studies, which is to challenge stereotypes.

CHALLENGING STEREOTYPES

The case studies are meant to challenge you to ask questions rather than to make assumptions about what it means to be Vietnamese, African American, Cape Verdean, or anything else. It is far easier to pigeonhole people according to our preconceptions and biases, but the deeper struggle is to try to understand people on their own terms. Some of the experiences, feelings, and statements of the young people in the case studies may surprise you and shake some deep-seated beliefs. So much the better if they do. On the other hand, they may reflect some of your own experiences or your knowledge of young people of diverse backgrounds. In either case, what these students say should be understood within the context of their particular school, family, and community experiences.

The students in the case studies are both typical and atypical of their ethnic, racial, or linguistic group. This is as it should be because in this way, they may challenge and even shatter commonly held stereotypes. The issues and perspectives that these students bring up are probably similar to those of other young people of their background. At the same time, each of their experiences is singular and should be understood as such. None of these students is a walking stereotype. The purpose of the case studies is not to understand "the Black experience" or "the Puerto Rican experience" as an isolated and hypothetical phenomenon, but instead to expose us to *one* of the many experiences within that broader context.

CASE STUDIES: A MOSAIC OF STUDENTS IN U.S. SCHOOLS

The case studies have been developed to give you a glimpse into the mosaic of the student body in U.S. classrooms, the citizens of the twenty-first century. These students are young men and women from a number of racial, ethnic, linguistic, and social class groups. They live in various geographic locations, in large cities and in small rural areas. They are first-, second-, or third-generation Americans, or their ancestors may have been here for many hundreds or even thousands of years. Some are from economically poor families, others from struggling working-class or middle-class families. They range in age from 13 to 19. When first interviewed, two of them were almost graduating from high school, two were in junior high school, and the others were at various levels of high school. They range from monolingual English-speaking youths to fluent bilinguals. Their families vary from very large (11 children) to very small (one child), in both one- and two-parent households. Their parents' educational backgrounds vary as well, from no high school education to doctorate.

The stories in these case studies provide valuable insights into contemporary U.S. life. Our increasingly diverse society demands that all of us, but especially those of us who interact with students every day, "tune in" to the voices of those who are different from ourselves. Maxine Greene explains why we need to hear from all the people who make up our newly acknowledged diversity: "What is crucial," she says, "is the provision of opportunities for telling all the diverse stories, for interpreting membership as well as ethnicity, for making inescapable the braids of experience woven into the fabric of America's plurality."[6] The need for schools to do this is particularly urgent.

In spite of the vast differences in their experiences and backgrounds, most of the students in these case studies share one characteristic: They are successful in school. Although there may be disagreements about what it means to be successful (research by Fine, for example, has suggested that in some ways the most "successful" students are those who drop out of school),[7] most of the students in these case studies have been able to develop both academic skills and positive attitudes about themselves and about the value of education. They generally have good grades, most have hopes (but not always plans) of attending college, and most have fairly positive perceptions of school.

A focus on academic success is a good way to think about what works well in schools, but we also need to pay attention to what can cause academic failure. For this reason, I have also included the case studies of two students who have had problems in school. Their voices, as eloquent and intelligent as the others, need to be heard if schools are to become places in which all students belong and can learn. Also, adolescents of secondary school age were selected because they generally are able to think about and articulate their experiences in a more reflective and analytic manner than younger students. They can also discuss both present and past experiences, providing an important continuity. Many books on multicultural education have been designed with an elementary school population in mind, and this has unwittingly reinforced perceptions that multicultural education is for younger children only, that it cannot be included in the more "rigorous" requirements of the high school, and that it is a frill unrelated to basic curriculum. The focus on secondary school students challenges these perceptions.

The case studies were chosen to reflect the changing demographics in U.S. society. We need to understand these changes as we prepare to teach the students of the future. For example, between 1981–1990 alone, more than 7,300,000 people immigrated to the United States, increasing the immigrant population by 63 percent over the previous decade.[8] By 1995, 35 percent of all students enrolled in grades 1–12 in public schools were considered to be part of a "minority" group, an increase of 11 percent from 1976. This increase was largely due to the growth in the percentage of immigrant students.[9] Furthermore, 50 of the largest urban school systems had student populations that were more than 76 percent students of color in 1992, and this percentage was expected to increase notably over the next several years.[10] Among the population of youths 5 to 17 years of age, about 6,323,000 spoke a language other than English, and about two-thirds of this number speak Spanish.[11] In addition, rather than decreasing, racial and ethnic segregation has been on the rise: The largest backward movement toward segregation for Blacks since the *Brown v. Board of Education* decision occurred between 1991–1995. For Latinos, the situation is even more ominous: by 1995, 74 percent of Latinos were attending predominately "minority" schools, also among the most high-poverty schools in the nation. Latinos now hold the dubious distinction of being the most segregated of all ethnic groups in our schools.[12]

The students in our country's public schools are also experiencing more poverty than has been the case in the recent past. For instance, the percentage of persons living below the poverty level was 12.6 percent in 1970, 13 percent in 1980, 13.5 percent in 1990, and 14.5 percent in 1994.[13] Poverty is especially grim among people of color: 33.1 percent of all African Americans, 30.6 percent of Latinos, and

18.8 percent of other people of color live in poverty, as compared to 9.9 percent of White residents.[14] At the same time that the number of students of color, those who speak languages other than English, and those who live in poverty has increased, the nation's teachers have become more monolithic, monocultural, and monolingual. For example, the percentage of White teachers grew from 88 percent in 1971 to 90.7 percent in 1996, while the number of Black teachers decreased from 8.1 percent to 7.3 percent and the number classified as "other" has decreased from 3.6 percent to 2.0 percent during the same time.[15]

Being aware of such demographics is crucial if we are serious about designing schools to help all students learn.

SELECTION OF STUDENTS

The students in the case studies were selected in a number of ways, as explained next. Those doing the interviews usually attempted to find students through community or informal channels rather than through schools, although in some cases teachers or counselors were consulted. Most students were interviewed at home or in a community setting away from school. The only requirement in selecting students was that they be of varied backgrounds to give us the diversity we were seeking. To maintain confidentiality, we used pseudonyms for the students and for most towns or cities, except for large urban areas such as Boston or Los Angeles. The names of schools, teachers, and family members also have been changed. All the students and their families gave us permission to tape their interviews and to use the results in this book.

As it turned out, a number of the students were chosen serendipitously. In one case, for example, interviewer Haydée Font, a graduate student at the University of Massachusetts at the time, asked the director of a university tutoring program for linguistic minority students to suggest a Vietnamese student to interview. When Haydée called Information to get the student's telephone number, the operator gave her the number for *another* Vietnamese family in town, obviously confusing the last name. The young girl who answered informed Haydée that she had reached the wrong number, but then suggested that her older brother, *also* a student at the local high school, would be happy to talk with Haydée. This is how Vinh was found. In the case of James, Diane Sweet went to a local Arab American bakery. After speaking informally with the proprietor, she was able to get the name of a local Lebanese family with a son who was studying at a nearby high school. The owner called James's mother, who agreed instantly to have James speak with Diane. Paula Elliott, an educator and also a musician, found Linda and Rich, both young musicians, through a music department at a high school in Boston.

RESEARCHING AND DEVELOPING THE CASE STUDIES

Each case study begins with a contextual description of the individual under study: a sketch of the student's family, school, community, and ethnic group, along with other information that I thought was relevant to include. Following are the students' words, categorized according to the three or four themes that were suggested by the interviews.

I directed the research team, which included doctoral students and colleagues. The primary responsibility of the team members was to locate and interview one or more students of diverse backgrounds; some team members also transcribed the interviews. The interviewers were Dr. Carlie Collins Tartakov, Dr. Paula Elliott, Haydée Font, Maya Gillingham, Dr. Mac Lee Morante, Diane Sweet, Carol Shea, and Beatriz McConnie Zapater. It was my responsibility to review the interviews, determine themes, and write the case studies based on the interviews as well as on further research concerning the students' ethnic background, city or town, and experience in school.

The themes, sometimes quite similar across several students, concern family, language, culture, and community. The guiding questions we used for the interviews centered on these particular issues to determine how they might affect the students' schooling. We tried to make the interviews themselves informal, and we used the questions primarily as a guide and springboard for further dialogue. We interviewed most students several times for a total of two to four hours, although some were interviewed for shorter periods of time. Questions focused on their experiences in school as young children and at present, including their thoughts about how schools might be improved so that more young people could succeed academically. We also asked them about their identity and whether it was important to them. Finally, we asked them about their families and their experiences at home and in their communities.

When the interviews were transcribed, I clustered the students' words according to the themes that emerged. I used ellipses to show that one statement was not said immediately after another, and new paragraphs generally indicate related statements made at separate points in time. For example, when Yolanda Piedra discussed family, all her thoughts on this topic were placed together in the case study even though she may have said them at different times. This method makes clear the concerns each student emphasized.

After I had listened carefully to each tape several times, I determined the primary themes by the issues the student seemed to return to time after time. I then wrote the case study. I omitted most common interjections such as *well, um, you know, and,* and *but* statements, as well as false starts. I gave the case study to the member of the research team who had done the interviews for review and corroboration of the data and themes and to share with the interviewee. When the interviewer felt that the student had been portrayed appropriately and that we had caught the essence of the student's message, the case study was complete. Members of the research team also made a number of suggestions for revision, inclusion, or removal, most of which I accepted. Although I am most grateful for their recommendations and insights, I myself must take final responsibility for the case studies, especially for any errors or oversights.

In this regard, I am especially aware of how my interpretations may differ from those of the students, those who interviewed them, and readers of this book. I could not agree more with the comments of Kathy Carter, who wrote,

Despite our fondest wishes, we cannot escape the problems of interpretation and meaning, either by ignoring them or by claiming to overcome them. We can only deal with them self-consciously and directly, using whatever tools we can to track their influence on our thinking and resisting as strenuously as possible the impulse by ourselves and others to elevate a particular interpretation to the status of doctrine.[16]

I present these case studies with the hope of motivating critical thought and careful dialogue, not rigid doctrine or simplistic solutions.

ACADEMIC SUCCESS AND FAILURE

After reviewing the preliminary interviews and transcripts, we discovered that all 10 of the students we had originally interviewed for the first edition of this book could be classified as successful. We thought more carefully about what it means to be a successful student and determined that we would consider them to be so if they met most of the following conditions:

- They were still in school and planning to complete high school, or had recently graduated.
- They had good grades, although they were not necessarily at or near the top of the class.
- They had thought about the future and made some plans for it.
- They generally enjoyed school and felt engaged in it.
- They were critical of their own school experiences and those of their peers.
- Most important, they described themselves as successful.

Although most of the students had thought about continuing their education, I did not consider definite college plans essential for classifying them as successful students. For example, Manuel Gomes was graduating from high school and had thought vaguely about college, but he had no actual plans. Just the fact that he was the first in his large family to graduate from high school, the pride he felt in this accomplishment, and the importance he ascribed to education were enough to classify him as successful.

However, although I do not consider college attendance the primary criterion for being a successful, intelligent, or well-adjusted student, I thought it was a necessary consideration because so many students of color and students from low-income families have been effectively denied the opportunity to receive a high-quality education or even to dream of college. That many of the students in these case studies have done so in spite of expectations to the contrary is vital to explore if we are serious about providing educational equity to all students. The hope for college or another form of higher learning is one indication that students believe that they are capable and worthy of the very best education, and this is apparent even in the cases of Ron and Paul, the two students who have not felt successful in school. That is why I thought it was meaningful to explore students' hopes for college.

It was also clear that all the students felt that they were *entitled* to a good education, and they were eager to talk about problems with school. They felt free to critique their education, whether or not they considered themselves to be successful in school. They were anxious to suggest ways to make school a better and more rewarding experience for all students.

The focus on academically successful students was not an intentional objective of the research but emerged as a result of the original interviews. In fact, it was surprising to us that all the students whom we originally sought out and who agreed to speak with us were successful. On closer reflection, it seemed logical that students who are successful in school are more likely to want to talk about their experiences than those who are not. To explore what it was about these specific students' experiences that helped them learn, I began concentrating on issues such as home, school, and community resources, attitudes, and activities. Because the students reflect a great deal of diversity, these issues may be different for each student. Notwithstanding these differences, you will see that most of the successful students report similar conditions, albeit within a broad range of environments, that have helped them learn.

The focus on academic success is a counterpoint to much of the research over the past several decades that has focused on "failure." The result has been an entire industry of researchers who have made their living by documenting how and why students fail. The "failure of failure" has been characterized thus:

> Once the threat of failure and the pressures of success are pushed aside, once we recognize that the task of schooling is not to explain which students do or do not learn, learning becomes easy for most. This will require the dismantling of the elaborate apparatus we have erected for documenting the failures of our children and redirecting the energies taken by that enterprise into organizing more learning. . . . We must instead confront the very idea of school failure, seeing it for what it is, manifestations of classism and racism.[17]

In spite of the problems that emerge with a focus on failure, emphasizing only successful students also has its drawbacks, including a tendency to overlook the legitimate problems that many students have in school. Students who do not succeed academically can too easily become casualties of educational systems that cannot "see" them because their problems remain invisible. We can learn as much from those who do not benefit from a particular institution as from those who do. For this reason, Ron Morris and Paul Chavez, two students who had not been successful in school, were included in the second edition. They might have been considered classic failures in the educational literature, but they were now striving to succeed. For example, when they were interviewed both Ron and Paul were attending alternative schools designed specifically for young people who have not been able to benefit from traditional school settings.

An unexpected outcome of participating in the project was that the interviews themselves were empowering for the students. In every case, they enjoyed and looked forward to being interviewed. They eagerly accepted the opportunity to discuss their families, school experiences, and cultures. More than one mentioned that it was the first time anyone had ever bothered to ask them these kinds of questions. The questions became sources of dialogue and awareness for the students. When Carlie Tartakov, who interviewed Fern Sherman, the young Native American student whose case study follows Chapter 4, asked her what was special about being Native American, Fern answered, "Getting picked for things like this." After her first interview, Linda Howard, whose case study follows Chapter 3, said that she couldn't wait for the next one. Some of the students had not thought deeply about some of the issues that emerged through the interviews: James Karam clearly became more aware of the exclusion of Arab Americans from the multicultural fair at his school and Vanessa Mattison, the only European American student interviewed, began to think more about White privilege. These are good examples of what Concha Delgado-Gaitán and Henry Trueba have termed the "ethnography of empowerment," that is, using ethnographic research methods to frame educational reform and empower teachers and students.[18]

The fact that empowerment can take place through dialogue should not be lost on teachers. Not only can we learn something from students about their cultures and languages through interviews, but dialogue of this kind can and should become a useful pedagogical strategy in itself. This also has implications for using oral histories in the development of literacy and fostering family and community involvement in the schools.[19]

PLACEMENT AND BRIEF DESCRIPTION OF THE CASE STUDIES

Each case study has been placed at the end of a particular chapter in order to explain related problems from the perspective of students who have experienced them. This is not to suggest that these young people's lives focus on only one issue. In fact, the interviews revealed an intricate interplay of factors that can contribute to academic success or failure. But placing each case study following a particular chapter highlights the major issues addressed in that chapter.

Following Chapter 3, you will read three case studies. Linda Howard and Rich Miller speak eloquently about how racism, discrimination, and teacher expectations have affected them. This does not mean that they were unconcerned about other issues, but both expressed more than other students the pain, distress, and other consequences of racism and discrimination. You will also find Vanessa Mattison's case study included here for quite a different reason. In her case, the issues of race, culture, and diversity were so removed from her experience that they were almost invisible to her, although she was not unconcerned about them.

The case studies of Fern Sherman and Avi Abramson follow Chapter 4, in which we explore how school organization, policies, and practices can help or hinder students' achievement. Both Fern and Avi reflected carefully on these issues although their concerns were different. Avi focused on school structures based on values profoundly different from his own and Fern talked about the isolation she felt by being the only Native American student in her school. In Chapter 5, the impact of culture on learning is explored. Here, the stories of James Karam, Marisol

Martinez, and Hoang Vinh are included. The invisibility of James's culture is crucial in understanding his story. How Marisol's culture has been maligned or denied and her ambivalence toward it is apparent in her case study. Vinh[20] poignantly describes the impact of immigration, separation from family, and cultural clash on his life. How all three of them were nevertheless able to counteract negative messages is essential for teachers to know.

The tremendous influence of language and linguistic diversity in learning is considered in Chapter 6. The cases of Manuel Gomes and Yolanda Piedra are included here. Manuel's case is compelling because of the role that bilingual education and Cape Verdean teachers had in his school success. Yolanda's story focuses on how her language was seen in a positive light within the school, even though she was not in a bilingual program. Finally, the cases of Ron and Paul, students for whom educational success had been elusive, follow Chapter 7. This chapter, which concerns school failure and some of the many theories offered over the past several decades to explain it, seemed a fitting place to consider two specific examples of how students are failed by schools.

LEARNING FROM THE CASE STUDIES

Although the students in all these case studies are wonderful and engaging, they are not exceptional in the sense that they are totally unlike other young people. We did not have to go to extraordinary measures to find them. Young people such as these are all around us. They are the young people in our local urban, rural, or suburban schools; they can be found on our sports teams, in our communities, and in our places of worship. They are in our English and math classes, bilingual and monolingual programs, and special education and gifted and talented programs. All we have to do is speak to them and listen to what they have to tell us. You will probably find the stories of the students in your own classrooms, whether they are succeeding in school or not, just as fascinating as the stories in the case studies.

I hope that you will read each of these stories critically and with the goal of understanding how the experiences and thoughts of young people can influence classroom discourse and strategies, as well as school policies and practices in general. These 12 students challenge us to believe that all students in our nation's classrooms are capable of learning. Although their stories prove the indomitable strength of youth, they also demonstrate the tremendous fragility of academic success—so easily disrupted by a poor teacher, a negative comment, or an environment that denies the importance of one's experiences. In the end, all their voices challenge us as teachers and as a society to do the very best we can to ensure that educational equity is not an illusion but an achievable goal.

GUIDELINES FOR DEVELOPING CASE STUDIES

Over the years, professors who use this book have told me of the many ways in which they make use of the case studies: They assign particular students to study and in effect "become" the young people in the case studies; they ask students representing each of the young people to have a dialogue about identity, school, and family; they suggest that students keep a journal focused on their reactions to the case studies; and they ask the students to develop a case study of a young person in their own school or community. The last assignment has been especially powerful for many students because it helps to ground their understanding of diversity in a concrete way.

Some readers have asked me to suggest specific guidelines for creating their own case studies. Following are some of my recommendations:

- Select a young person of the approximate age that you will be (or are currently) teaching. It would probably be best not to select a student whom you know well.
- Choose a young person from a background with which you are not very familiar. The assignment should provide a rich learning experience for you, and this is most likely to occur when you interact with and do additional research about a person from a different background.
- As a class, develop and agree on a list of questions. What most interests you about young people? What do you most want to know? Think about issues related to identity, culture, school success, and the role of teachers and family in their lives.
- Decide how many times you will meet to interview the young people. It is generally better to meet for several short sessions of one hour or less than for one long session of 90 minutes or more. Dividing the questions by topic also makes sense.
- Make certain to meet the parents or guardians of the young people you plan to interview. Speak to them about the purpose and scope of the interviews and assure them of their child's confidentiality. Secure written and oral permission (on an audiotape), and let them know that they have the right to pull out at any time. Also tell them how you will be using the interview, and how you will share it with the family when it's completed.
- Get as much information from the family as you will need to develop the case study, but be sensitive to the family's privacy and feelings. Do not impose yourself on them, and be discreet.
- Select a comfortable, quiet, stress-free environment for the interviews. I would suggest meeting away from school, either in a community center, their home, the park, or a place where you can have a soda and relax.
- Try to make the interviews as comfortable as possible. Ask the young person for permission to audiotape, as that will give you the most accurate record of the interviews. Don't ask questions in a rushed way as if you're trying to get through an assignment; give your interviewee time to respond completely and then follow up with additional relevant questions. Ask the interviewee if he/she has any questions or concerns.
- Transcribing all the tapes is very time consuming and labor intensive, and it may not be realistic to expect complete transcriptions for a one-semester course. But you can still develop effective case studies. First, listen to the

tapes several times. Then try to determine the most important themes that keep cropping up. Once you have done this, you can transcribe those parts that seem to be the most intriguing or relevant for the student you interviewed.

- Do some research on the context in which the student lives: find out about his or her ethnic group and their history in this country; look for information concerning the city or town in which they live; try to get some data on the school system they go to (number of students, types of programs, and so on). Also ask interviewees if they would like to share writing samples such as poems, letters, or essays with you.
- Write up the case study. Begin with an introduction to the young person, including pertinent information about them, their family, community, cultural group, and school experience. Then let the young people speak for themselves by creating a narrative based on the most salient themes that you heard them address. Include any other information such as their writings or other material they may have given you.

Each case study is different, and there is no ideal model to follow. The guidelines will get you started on creating a convincing case study of a young person. The process may also help you develop important insights about the lives of young people. As you will see throughout this book, students can teach educators many things, and entering into a dialogue with young people through the development of a case study can be one way to begin to learn from them.

• *NOTES*

1. See, for example, Rita Silverman, William M. Welty, and Sally Lyon, *Multicultural Education Cases for Teacher Problem Solving* (New York: McGraw-Hill, 1994); and Mary A. Lundeberg, Barbara B. Levin, and Helen Harrington (eds.), *Who Learns What From Cases and How? The Research Base for Teaching with Cases* (Mahwah, NJ: Lawrence Erlbaum Associates, 1999).
2. Sharan B. Merriam, *Case Study Research in Education: A Qualitative Approach* (San Francisco: Jossey-Bass Publishers, 1998), p. 27.
3. Frederick Erickson, "Qualitative Methods in Research on Teaching." In *Handbook of Research on Teaching,* 3rd ed., edited by Merlin C. Wittrock (New York: Macmillan, 1986).
4. Elliot Eisner, "The Promise and Perils of Alternative Forms of Data Representation." *Educational Researcher,* 26, 6 (1997), 4–10, p. 8.
5. Merriam, *Case Study Research in Education.*
6. Maxine Greene, "The Passions of Pluralism: Multiculturalism and the Expanding Community." *Educational Researcher,* 22, 1 (February 1993), 17.
7. Michelle Fine, *Framing Dropouts: Notes on the Politics of an Urban High School* (Albany, NY: State University of New York Press, 1991).
8. U.S. Bureau of the Census, *Statistical Abstract of the United States* (114th ed.) (Washington, DC: U.S. Government Printing Office, 1994) 11.

9. *The Condition of Education. . . Elementary and Secondary Students.* http://nces.ed.gov/pubs98/c9843a01.html

10. Council of the Great City Schools, *National Urban Education Goals: 1992–1993 Indicators Report* (Washington, DC: Author, 1994).

11. U.S. Bureau of the Census, *1990 Census of Population and Housing Data Paper Listing* (Washington, DC: U.S. Government Printing Office, 1990).

12. Gary Orfield, Mark D. Bachmeier, David R. James, and Tamela Eitle, *Deepening Segregation in American Public Schools* (Cambridge, MA: Harvard University Project of School Desegregation, 1997).

13. U.S. Bureau of the Census, *Current Population Reports, Series P–60, No. 188.* (Washington, DC: U.S. Government Printing Office, 1995).

14. Cynthia Taeuber (editor and compiler), *The Statistical Handbook on Women in America*, 2nd ed. (Phoenix, AZ: Oryx Press, 1996).

15. National Education Association, *Status of the American Public School Teacher, 1995–96* (Washington, DC: Author, 1997).

16. Kathy Carter, "The Place of Story in the Study of Teaching and Teacher Education." *Educational Researcher,* 22 (1993), 10.

17. David Smith, Perry Gilmore, Shelley Goodman, and Ray McDermott, "Failure's Failure." In *Minority Education,* edited by Evelyn Jacob and Cathie Jordan (Norwood, NJ: Ablex, 1993), 210–211, 213.

18. Concha Delgado-Gaitán and Henry Trueba, *Crossing Cultural Borders: Education for Immigrant Families in America* (London: Falmer Press, 1991).

19. I have expanded further on this idea in the article, "Lessons from Students on Creating a Chance to Dream." *Harvard Educational Review,* 64, 4 (Winter 1994), 392–426.

20. The Vietnamese use family names first, given names second. In this case, Vinh is the given name and Hoang is the family name.

chapter **2**

About Terminology

*L*anguage is always changing. Because it mirrors social, economic, and political events, it is an important barometer of a society at any given time. Language also becomes obsolete; it could not be otherwise because it is a reflection of societal changes. The shift in terminology over the years, for example, from *Negro* to *Black* to *Afro-American* and more recently to *African American,* is a case in point. Such changes often represent deliberate attempts by a group to name or rename itself. This decision is political as well as linguistic, and it responds to the need for group self-determination and autonomy. Terms also evolve as an attempt to be more precise and correct. In this sense, the term *African American* is more comprehensive than *Black* because it implies culture rather than simply color. This term recognizes that the notion of "race," in spite of its overarching importance in a society rigidly stratified along these lines, does not define the complexity of a people.

Terminology is particularly important in multicultural education. In our society we have not always been appropriate or sensitive in our use of words to describe people. In its most blatant form, this insensitivity is apparent in the racial and ethnic epithets that even our youngest children seem to know. It is also evident in more subtle examples, such as observations made by Allport many years ago: (a) that the refusal of southern newspapers to capitalize *negro* was meant to diminish the stature of Blacks, and (b) that certain words develop stereotypical ethnic connotations (e.g., *inscrutable* is almost automatically associated with Asians, *rhythm* with African Americans).[1] Although these words are not negative in and of themselves, they can become code words for simplifying the experience of an entire group of people, and hence are disparaging.

MAKING CHOICES ABOUT WHAT TERMS TO USE

To be both sensitive and appropriate in the use of language, I prefer particular words or terms over others. I am not suggesting that these terms are "politically correct" or that they are the only ones that should be used, nor do I want to impose my usage on others. Rather, I will explain my own thinking to help others determine what terminology is most appropriate for them.

24

My choice of terms is based generally on two major criteria:

1. What do the people themselves want to be called?
2. What is the most accurate term?

I have answered these questions by talking with people from various groups, reading current research, and listening to debates regarding the use of terms. Language is always tentative, and so are the choices made here. New terms evolve every day. Such is the inexactitude of language that it can never completely capture the complexity of our lives.[2]

In some cases, I have chosen to use two terms or more, sometimes interchangeably, because each may have meanings important in particular contexts. My choices change over the years because of changing usage. For example, for years I used the term *Native American* exclusively for the many indigenous nations in the Western Hemisphere. During the late 1960s this seemed to become the preferred term because it reflected a people's determination to name themselves and to have others recognize them as the original inhabitants of these lands.

During the late 1980s and 1990s, the use of this term declined, so I decided to use the terms *American Indian, Indian,* and *Native people* more often. I did so because I noted that people from this group generally used the term *Indian*. Also, a number of students explained to me that it is not so much that the term *Native American* has been *abandoned,* but rather that some of their communities had never really adopted it. Another student told me that this term had become confusing because it was often used to mean a citizen of the United States whose early ancestors came from Europe (i.e., who is now *native* to this land). Because *Indian* also refers to people from India, I usually add the qualifier *American* or *Native*. More recently, the term *Native American* has again become common among the group itself.[3] Fern, one of the young women in the case studies, deliberately refers to herself in this way, thus reminding us that even among people from the same group, different terms are used.

Chicano, a term popular in the late 1960s and early 1970s, is also making a comeback. An emphatically self-affirming and political term reflecting the culture and realities of urban, economically oppressed Mexican Americans in U.S. society, *Chicano* grew out of the Brown Power Movement in the 1960s. It was never wholly accepted in the general community. Although used by many scholars and activists, the more descriptive but less political term *Mexican American* has been more common in many segments of the community. *Mexican,* on the other hand, is used generally to refer to first generation immigrants. I have decided to use all these terms within their appropriate contexts because each has connotations that must not be lost.

I have used the terms *Hispanic* and *Latino* more or less interchangeably to refer to people of Latin American and Caribbean heritage. Although I generally prefer the term *Latino*—because its connotation includes the African and indigenous heritage as well as the Spanish heritage of these groups—*Hispanic* is more widespread and well known.[4] Unlike *European, African, Latin American,* or *Asian,* however, it does not refer to a particular continent or country (i.e., there is no continent named *Hispania*). *Latino,* on the other hand, has the disadvantage of having a sexist connotation when used to refer to groups that include both genders. I use neither term, however, when the more specific ethnic name is available. For example, none of the Latino students in the case studies refer to themselves as either Latino(a) or Hispanic: Marisol defines herself as Puerto Rican; Yolanda is Mexican; and Paul uses both *Chicano* and *Mexican American.* Whenever possible, these distinctions need to be made because otherwise fundamental differences in ethnicity, national origin, self-identification, and time in this country are easily overlooked.

White people, as the majority in U.S. society, seldom think of themselves as *ethnic*—a term they tend to reserve for other, more easily identifiable groups. Nevertheless, the fact is that we are all ethnic, whether we choose to identify ourselves in this way or not. This is one of the reasons I have opted to use the term *European American* rather than *White* in most cases in this book. Although Whiteness is an important factor, it hides more than it reveals: There is a tremendous diversity of ethnic backgrounds among Whites, and this is lost if race is used as the only identifier. The term *European American* also implies *culture,* something that many European Americans lament they do not have. This is nonsense, of course. Everybody has a culture, whether clearly manifested in its more traditional forms or not.

The term *European American,* just as all terms, has its drawbacks. For one, although it is more specific than *White,* it is still overly inclusive of a great many ethnic backgrounds that may have little in common other than "race." A similar criticism applies to terms such as *African, Asian,* or *Latin American.* For another, many European Americans are a mixture of several European ethnic groups: A person may be German, Irish, and Italian and not speak any of the languages or follow any of the rituals associated with any of these cultures. It is reasonable to ask, in such cases, why they should be called *European American* when in effect they are "as American as apple pie." They may never have even visited Europe, for example, or may not at all identify with a European heritage. I have chosen to use the term because the habits, values, and behaviors of White Americans are grounded in European mores and values. Although these may be quite distant, and adapted and modified within the U.S. context, their roots are still European. Because Whites in U.S. society tend to think of themselves as the "norm," they often view other groups as "ethnic" and therefore somewhat exotic and colorful. By using the term *European American,* I hope to challenge Whites also to see and define themselves in ethnic terms.

I do not use the terms *Anglo* and *Anglo-American,* except when speaking specifically of those with an English heritage, because it is inaccurate as a general term to refer to Whites in the United States. Many Whites are not English in origin but represent a wide variety of ethnic groups from European societies; classifying all of them as Anglos is a gross overgeneralization. If used to contrast English speakers from speakers of other languages, *Anglo-American* is equally inaccurate because African Americans, among others whose native language is English, are not included in this classification. Finally, it is a term rejected by some, not the least of whom are many Irish Americans, who are often understandably offended at being identified with an English heritage.

Race as a notion is dubious at best, as I will explain. But the problem with using terms that emphasize *culture* only is that the very real issue of racism in our society is then obscured. My use of terminology is in no way meant to do so but rather to stress that the notion of race alone does not define people. For example, African Americans and Haitians are both Black. They share some basic cultural values and are both subjected to racist attitudes and behaviors in the United States. But the particular experiences, native language usage, and ethnicity of each group is overlooked or even denied if we simply call them both Black rather than also identifying them ethnically.

I have decided to use terms that refer specifically to so-called racial groups when they are warranted. In speaking of segregated schools, for example, it makes sense to refer to Black and White students rather than to African American and European American students because color is the salient issue. In this way, I also hope to underscore the fact that there are always differences of opinion about the use of various terms.

I have capitalized the terms *White* and *Black*. I do so because they refer to groups of people, as do terms such as *Latino, Asian,* and *African*. As such, they deserve to be capitalized. Although these are not the scientific terms for so-called racial groups, terms such as *Negroid* and *Caucasian* are no longer used in everyday speech or are rejected because of their negative connotations. Because I treat the more commonly used words *Black* and *White* as the terms of preference, I capitalize them.

The concept of "race" itself has come in for a great deal of criticism because, in a strictly biological sense, race does not exist at all. There is no scientific evidence that so-called racial groups differ biologically or genetically in significant ways. Differences that do exist are primarily social; that is, they are based on one's experiences within a particular cultural group. There is really only one "race". In the words of Linda Howard, one of the interviewees in the case studies that follow Chapter 3, "I'm human. That's my race; I'm part of the human race." Linda identified as Black American and White American, but she saw herself primarily as a member of her family rather than a race: "My culture is my family," she explained. She knew that, historically, the concept of race has been used to oppress entire groups of people for their supposed differences.

It is now generally accepted that the very concept of race is a social construction, that is, a racial group is socially and not biologically determined. Many scholars who write about race have made the decision to use it only in quotation marks to underscore its social construction ("race").[5] I have decided not to do so for a couple of reasons. First, it can be reasonably argued that *all* differences are socially constructed (social class, gender, ethnicity, sexual orientation, and so on) and to separate race from the others seems arbitrary. The second reason is for the sake of convenience: Given the many times that race, gender, social class, ethnicity, and other differences are discussed in this text, readers would find it disconcerting to trip over entire paragraphs about "race," "gender," "social class," and so on.

I generally use terms related to specific ethnic backgrounds, but if an overarching term is needed, I prefer either *people of color* or *bicultural* rather than *minority*. First, *minority* is a misnomer; it is never used to describe groups such as Swedish Americans, Albanian Americans, or Dutch Americans. Yet strictly speaking, these groups, which represent numerical minorities in our society, should also be referred to in this way. Historically, the term has been used to refer only to *racial minorities*, implying a status less than that accorded to other groups.

Even when these groups are no longer a "minority," there seems to be in the dominant discourse a tenacious insistence on maintaining the "minority" status of some groups. The result is convoluted language that maintains a pejorative classification. For example, schools in which African American students become the majority are called "majority minority" schools rather than "primarily Black" schools. The connection between name and low status in the use of this term is quite clear. Given this connotation, the word is offensive.

The term *people of color* encompasses those who have been labeled "minority," that is, American Indians, African Americans, Latinos, and Asian Americans, and it emerged from these communities themselves. It also implies important connections among the groups and underlines some common experiences in the United States. But in spite of the acceptance of *people of color* and its use by many people (and in this book), I find it increasingly unsatisfactory on several counts. One problem is the implication of a common historical experience among all those included under this designation. Aside from a mutual history of oppression at the hands of those in power—not an insignificant commonality—a shared historical experience among all people of color is an illusion. Moreover, a presumed common experience suggests that there is no conflict among these groups. As we know, such conflicts not only exist but they have resulted in periodic outbreaks of serious interethnic violence. These emanate not only from a shared oppression and the competition for scarce resources that results from political domination, but also from deep-seated cultural and social differences among the groups themselves.

People of color is also inaccurate when referring, for example, to Latinos of European background, as is the case with many Argentinians and Cubans, and light-skinned Latinos in general. When these Latinos refer to themselves in this way, it might imply that they have experienced the same level of virulent racism as their dark-skinned compatriots, and this may be entirely false. I am thus not wholly comfortable with its use.

In the case of *bicultural*, I am following the lead of Antonia Darder, who has argued that this term is preferable to "minority" because it emphasizes the fact that students from these groups must contend with two cultural systems that are often at odds with one another and with a vastly different educational experience from that of majority-group students.[6] I like the term because it emphasizes what students from these groups *have* rather than what they are *missing*, as is usually the case when terms such as *minority, disadvantaged, at risk,* or even more consciously politically charged words such as *disempowered* or *dominated*—terms that are accurate although incomplete because they emphasize only victimization—are used.

At the moment, there is no completely adequate language for such a huge con-glomeration of groups. Whenever possible and for the sake of clarity, I prefer to identify people by their specific ethnic or racial group to avoid lumping people of different groups together.

LUMPING GROUPS TOGETHER

Overarching terms cause a number of problems. The term *European American,* for example, implies that all those who are White are also European American. This is not always true, as in the case of many Jews, but language remains imprecise in capturing these differences. Although some groups, such as Latinos, share a great many cultural attributes, they are also quite different from one another. A Guatemalan and a Dominican, for example, may both speak Spanish, practice the Catholic religion, and share deeply rooted family values. But the native language of some Guatemalans is not Spanish, and Dominicans have an African background not shared by most Guatemalans. These differences, among many others, often go unacknowledged when we speak simply of *Latinos* or *Hispanic Americans.* Within the context of the U.S. experience, Latinos differ in many respects, including race, social class, level of education, and length of time in this country. Each of these may make a dramatic difference in the school achievement of children from dis-tinct groups.

The same discussion applies to the terms *Native Americans* and *Asian Americans*, each of which includes groups with tremendously distinct histories and cultures. Again, although they may share some basic cultural values and historical experiences, specific ethnic characteristics and historical frames of reference are lost when we lump these people all together. For this reason, I try to refer to each group by national origin. Besides being more accurate, it is ordinarily how people prefer to be called. A Bolivian, for example, refers to herself first as a Bolivian and then as a Latina; the same can be said for a Navajo, who identifies first with his Nation and second with Indians as a larger group.

But it is also true that there are many commonalities among all indigenous groups, as there are among most Latino groups. These may include a worldview, a common historical experience, and shared conditions of life in the United States. Where such commonalities exist, I sometimes refer to the groups by the more gen-eralized term. In addition, I am restricted by the fact that much of the literature of both American Indian and Hispanic groups does not distinguish the ethnic groups within them. As a result, I am sometimes obliged to use the generic term in spite of my preference to disaggregate along ethnic lines.

A similar argument can be made for Asian and Asian American ethnic groups. These classifications include an incredibly diverse array of groups, such as Chinese, Japanese, Vietnamese, Filipino, Native Hawaiian, Pakistani, and Indian. To believe that one designation could possibly be sufficient to cover them all is foolhardy, because they differ not only in history and culture, but also in language—unlike Latinos, most of whom share at least a common language. Asians also differ in social class, length of time in the United States, immigrant experience, and educational background and experiences, and these differences invariably influence the educational achievement of the children in these groups.[7] The term *Pacific Islander* now is used together with *Asian* to provide a more specific term for a number of groups. It is preferred to the outdated and exotic *Oriental* by most Asians and Pacific Islanders, but this term also fails to account for all differences.

Finally, a word about the terms *America* and *American*. Because *America* refers to the entire Western Hemisphere, whenever possible I will refer to our country as the *United States*. Also, although *American* has been limited by common use to mean U.S. citizens, this is not only inaccurate but also offensive to millions of North, Central, and South Americans who consider themselves as much Americans as people living within the confines of the United States. Nevertheless, because the term is in common use in the United States, I have decided to use it at times to refer to citizens and residents of the United States.

● CONCLUSION

The language choices made throughout this book are meant first and foremost to *affirm diversity*. I have attempted to identify people as they would want to be identified. I have also used terms that emphasize what people *are* rather than what they *are not* (e.g., I have avoided terms such as *non-White* and *non-English-speaking*). Readers familiar with the first and second editions of this text will note that I have made some changes in my terminology for this third edition, and I expect to continue to do so. Language that refers to human beings is inaccurate and imprecise, and although I have strived to be both precise and sensitive, my choices are certainly open to debate. Language can capture only imperfectly the nuances of who we are as people but, like multicultural education itself, it is in constant flux. We therefore need to pay close attention to the connotations and innuendos of its daily use.

● NOTES

1. Gordon W. Allport, *The Nature of Prejudice* (Reading, MA: Addison-Wesley, 1954).
2. Zoë Anglesey has written a helpful guide on the need to change offensive and dehumanizing terms: see "Moving From an Obsolete Lingo to a Vocabulary of Respect." In *Multicultural Review*, 6, 3 (September, 1997), 23–28; for a useful dictionary on the evolution of ethnic and racial terms and the biases they contain, see *The Color of Words* by Philip H. Herbst (Yarmouth, ME: Intercultural Press, Inc., 1997).
3. This was pointed out by Deirdre A. Almeida in "The Hidden Half: A History of Native American Women's Education." *Harvard Educational Review*, 67, 4 (1997), 757–771. For a helpful discussion about "real Indians," see Cornel Pewewardy, "Will the 'Real' Indians Please Stand Up?" *Multicultural Review*, (June, 1998), 36–42.
4. See the discussion by Murguia on the different connotations of each of these terms. Edward Murguia, "On Latino/Hispanic Ethnic Identity," *Latino Studies Journal*, 2, 3 (1991), 8–18.
5. Anthony Appiah, "Identity, Authenticity, Survival: Multicultural Societies and Social Reproduction." In *Multiculturalism*, edited by Amy Gutmann (Princeton, NJ: Princeton University Press, 1994), 149–163.

6. Antonia Darder, *Culture and Power in the Classroom: A Critical Foundation for Bicultural Education* (New York: Bergin & Garvey, 1991).
7. For specific examples of the great differences among Asian Americans and the influence of these differences on student learning, see the report by Heather Kim, *Diversity Among Asian American High School Students* (Princeton, NJ: Educational Testing Service, 1997).

part two

Multicultural Education in a Sociopolitical Context
Developing a Conceptual Framework

—●—

Part II looks at the sociopolitical context of multicultural education. It considers such things as racism and other biases, school organization and educational policies and practices, and cultural and linguistic differences. Although we cannot say whether any of these factors always leads to students' success or failure, these elements need to be considered to understand how they may influence the educational experiences of a wide variety of students.

The 12 case studies in Chapters 3 to 7 highlight how these factors can influence academic success or failure. Although I have grouped the case studies with particular chapters because of common themes, each case study raises numerous issues discussed in other chapters as well. For example, Linda's case study is placed after Chapter 3 because it highlights the impact that racism can have on school achievement, but it also concerns questions of teacher expectations and school climate.

Chapter 3 also explores the influence of the expectations of teachers and schools on students, and this is followed by three case studies that underscore these issues. Chapter 4 considers how school organization, policies, and practices—including tracking, testing, pedagogy, and curriculum—may affect student learning. Two case studies that emphasize curriculum and other school-related factors follow this chapter. The relationship of cultural issues to the education of students of diverse backgrounds is explored in Chapter 5, and Chapter 6 focuses on linguistic diversity and schools' responses to it. These chapters are followed by case studies that consider the influence of cultural and linguistic diversity on student learning. The final chapter in Part II presents a synopsis of current theories and provides a comprehensive view for understanding student learning. The case studies at the end of the chapter provide two vivid examples of students whose educational achievement has been negatively influenced by conditions both in school and out.

chapter 3

Racism, Discrimination, and Expectations of Students' Achievement

> *[Racists have power] only if you let them! We'll stick with [the example of]*
> *striped shirts: If I go where everyone is wearing solids, and I'm wearing a*
> *stripe, and someone comes up to me and tells me, "You don't belong here;*
> *you're wearing stripes," I'll say, "I belong anywhere I want to belong." And*
> *I'll stand right there! But there are some people who just say, "Oh, okay," and*
> *will turn around and leave. Then the racist has the power.*

Linda Howard, Interviewee

*L*inda Howard is a young woman who has been directly harmed by racism in and out of school, and she has a highly evolved understanding of it on both an individual and an institutional level. As you will see in her case study, Linda has thought very deeply about racism. Many teachers and other educators, however, have not. In this chapter, we will explore the impact that racism, other biases, and expectations of student abilities may have on achievement. We will focus on *racism* as an example of bias, but I will also point out other kinds of personal and institutional discrimination when appropriate. These include discrimination on the basis of gender (sexism), ethnic group (ethnocentrism), social class (classism), language (linguicism)[1] or other perceived differences. I will also mention anti-Semitism, discrimination against Jews; anti-Arab discrimination, directed against Arabs; ageism, discrimination based on age; heterosexism, discrimination against gay men and lesbians; and ableism, discrimination against people with disabilities.

DEFINITIONS OF RACISM AND DISCRIMINATION

Discussions of prejudice and discrimination tend to focus on the biases and negative perceptions of individuals toward members of other groups. For example, Gordon Allport, in his groundbreaking work on the nature of prejudice, quotes a United Nations document defining discrimination as "any conduct based on a distinction made on grounds of natural or social categories, which have no relation either to individual capacities or merits, or to the concrete behavior of the individual person."[2] This definition is helpful but incomplete because it fails to describe the harmful effects of such conduct. More broadly speaking, *discrimination* denotes negative or destructive behaviors that can result in denying some groups life's necessities as well as the privileges, rights, and opportunities enjoyed by other groups. Discrimination is usually based on *prejudice,* that is, the attitudes and beliefs of individuals about entire groups of people. These attitudes and beliefs are generally, but not always, negative.

Our society, among many others, categorizes people according to both visible and invisible traits, uses such classifications to deduce fixed behavioral and mental traits, and then applies policies and practices that jeopardize some and benefit others.[3] Classifications based on race, ethnicity, gender, social class, and other physical or social differences are all around us. Frequently, they result in gross exaggerations and stereotypes: Girls are not as smart as boys; African Americans have rhythm; Asians are studious; Poles are simple-minded, Jews are smart; and poor people need instant gratification. Although some of these may appear to be "positive" stereotypes, both "negative" and "positive" stereotypes have negative results because they limit our perspective of an entire group of people. There are two major problems with categorizing people in this way: First, people of all groups begin to believe the stereotypes; and second, both material and psychological resources are doled out accordingly.

We see a clear example of the implications of such categorizations in the case study of Rich Miller. Rich was quite severe in his criticism of other African Americans, whom he characterized as "settling for the easiest way out," "lazy," and "tacky." He had internalized the myth of success based completely on individual endeavor rather than as also influenced by structural issues such as institutional racism and lack of opportunity. It is easy to understand how this happens: In our society, the metaphor of "pulling yourself up by your bootstraps" is powerful indeed; it allows little room for alternative explanations based on structural inequality.

Racism and other forms of discrimination are based on the perception that one ethnic group, class, gender, or language is superior to all others. In the United States, the conventional norm used to measure all other groups is European American, upper-middle class, English-speaking, and male. Discrimination based on perceptions of superiority is part of the structure of schools, the curriculum, the education most teachers receive, and the interactions among teachers, students, and the community. But discrimination is not simply an individual bias; it is above all an *institutional* practice.

Most definitions of racism and discrimination obscure the institutional nature of oppression. Although the beliefs and behaviors of *individuals* may be hurtful, far greater damage is done through institutional discrimination, that is, the systematic use of economic and political power in institutions (such as schools) that leads to detrimental policies and practices. These policies and practices have a harmful effect on groups that share a particular identity (be it racial, ethnic, gender, or other). The major difference between individual and institutional discrimination is the wielding of *power,* because it is primarily through the power of the people who control institutions such as schools that oppressive policies and practices are reinforced and legitimated. Linda Howard, one of our young interviewees, already understood this distinction. In her case study, she distinguished between prejudice and racism in this way: "We all have some type of person that we don't like, whether it's from a different race, or from a different background, or they have different habits." But she went on to explain, as we saw in the quote at the beginning of this chapter, that a racist is someone who has *power* to carry out his or her prejudices.

Let me give another example: Let's say that I am prejudiced against tall people. Although my bias may hurt individual tall people because I refuse to befriend them or because I make fun of them, I can do very little to limit their options in life. If, however, I belonged to a group of powerful "non-talls" and we limited the access of tall persons to certain neighborhoods, prohibited them from receiving quality health care, discouraged intermarriage with people of short or average height, developed policies against their employment in high-status professions, and placed all children who were the offspring of "talls" (or who showed early signs of becoming above average in height) in the lowest ability tracks in schools, then my bias would have teeth and its institutional power would be clear. In the discussion that follows, we will be concerned primarily with institutional discrimination.

Institutional discrimination generally refers to how people are excluded or deprived of rights or opportunities as a result of the normal operations of the institution. Although the individuals involved in the institution may not be prejudiced or have any racist intentions or even awareness of how others may be harmed, the result may nevertheless be racist. In this sense, intentional and unintentional racism are different. But because they both result in negative outcomes, in the end it does not really matter whether racism and other forms of discrimination are intentional. Rather than trying to figure out whether the intent was to do harm or not, educators would do better to spend their time addressing the effects of racism.

When we understand racism and other forms of discrimination as a *systemic* problem, not simply as an individual dislike for a particular group of people, we can better understand the negative and destructive effects it can have. Vanessa Mattison, whose case study is one of those that follows this chapter, provides a good example of a young person struggling to reconcile our country's lofty ideals of equality and fair play with the reality of the injustice she saw around her. Vanessa was committed to social justice, but she saw it primarily as working to change the attitudes and behaviors of *individuals*. She had not yet made the connection between racism and *institutional* oppression, and she did not grasp that institutional racism was far more harmful than individual biases or acts of meanness. But she was beginning to see that certain norms existed that were unfair to Blacks, women, and gays and lesbians. In her words: "There's all these underlying rules that if you're not this, you can't do that."

This is meant neither to minimize the powerful effects of individual prejudice and discrimination, which can be personally painful, nor to suggest that discrimination occurs only in one direction, for example, from Whites toward Blacks. There is no monopoly on prejudice and individual discrimination; they happen in all directions, and even within groups. However, interethnic and intraethnic biases and personal prejudices, while negative and hurtful, simply do not have the long-range and life-limiting effects of institutional racism and other kinds of institutional discrimination.

As an illustration of institutional racism, let us look at how testing practices are sometimes used in schools: Students from dominated groups may be stigmatized and labeled because of their performance on standardized tests. What places these students at a disadvantage is not that particular teachers have prejudiced attitudes about them; teachers may, in fact, like the students very much. What places the students at jeopardy is the fact that they may be labeled, grouped, and tracked, sometimes for the length of their schooling, because of their score on an ethnocentric and biased test. In this case, it is *institutions*—schools and the testing industry— that have the major negative impact on students from culturally dominated groups.

Prejudice and discrimination, then, are not just personality traits or psychological phenomena; they are also a manifestation of economic, political, and social power. The institutional definition of racism is not always easy to accept because it goes against deeply held notions of equality and justice in our nation. According to Beverly Tatum, "An understanding of racism as a system of advantage presents a serious challenge to the notion of the United States as a just society where rewards are based solely on one's merits."[4] Racism as an institutional system implies that some people and groups benefit and others lose. Whites, whether they want to or not, benefit in a racist society; males benefit in a sexist society. Discrimination always helps somebody—those with the most power—which explains why racism, sexism, and other forms of discrimination continue.

According to Meyer Weinberg, racism is a system of privilege and penalty. That is, one is rewarded or punished in housing, education, employment, health, and so on, by the simple fact of belonging to a particular group, regardless of one's individual merits or faults. He goes on to explain, "Racism consists centrally of two facets: First, a belief in the inherent superiority of some people and the inherent inferiority of others; and second, the acceptance of distributing goods and services—let alone respect—in accordance with such judgments of unequal worth." In addressing the institutional nature of racism, he adds, ". . . racism is always collective. Prejudiced individuals may join the large movement, but they do not cause it." According to this conception, the "silence of institutional racism" and the "ruckus of individual racism" are mutually supportive.[5] It is sometimes difficult to separate one level of racism from the others, as they feed on and inform one another. What is crucial, according to Weinberg, is understanding that the doctrine of White supremacy is at the root of racism.

THE HISTORY AND PERSISTENCE OF RACISM IN U.S. SCHOOLS

As institutions, schools respond to and reflect the larger society. It therefore is not surprising that racism finds its way into schools in much the same way that it finds its way into other institutions such as housing, employment, and the criminal justice system. Overt expressions of racism may be less frequent in schools today than in the past, but racism does not just exist when schools are legally segregated or racial epithets are used against Black students. Racism is also manifested in rigid ability tracking, low expectations of students based on their identity, and inequitably funded schools.

Racism and other forms of discrimination—particularly sexism, classism, ethnocentrism, and linguicism—have a long history in our schools and their effects are widespread and long lasting. The most blatant form of discrimination is the actual withholding of education, as was the case with African Americans and sometimes with American Indians during the nineteeth century. To teach enslaved Africans to read was a crime punishable under the law and it became a subversive activity that was practiced by Blacks in ingenious ways.[6] Other overt forms of discrimination include segregating students, by law, according to their race, ethnicity, or gender, as was done at one time or another with African American, Mexican American, Japanese, and Chinese students, as well as with females; or forcing them into boarding schools, as was done with American Indian students. In such groups, children have been encouraged to adopt the ways of the dominant culture in sundry ways, from subtle persuasion to physical punishment for speaking their native language.[7] This, too, is a bitter reminder of the inequities of U.S. educational history.

Unfortunately, the discrimination that children face in schools is not a thing of the past. School practices and policies continue to discriminate against some children in very concrete ways. Recent studies have found that most students of color are still in schools that are segregated by race and social class, and the situation is worsening rather than improving.[8] At the impetus of the civil rights movement, many school systems throughout the United States were indeed desegregated. But less than rigorous implementation of desegregation plans, "White flight," and housing patterns have succeeded in resegregating many schools. Segregation invariably results in school systems that are "separate and unequal" because segregated schools are differently funded, with fewer resources provided to schools in poor communities and vastly superior resources provided to schools in wealthier communities.

Segregation often results in students receiving differential schooling on the basis of their social class, race, and ethnicity. In addition, schools that serve students of color tend to provide curricula that are watered down and at a lower level than schools that serve primarily White students. Also, teachers in poor urban schools tend to have less experience and less education than colleagues who teach in schools that serve primarily European American and middle-class students.[9] Even when they are desegregated, many schools resegregate students through practices such as rigid ability tracking. Consequently, desegregating schools in and of itself does not guarantee educational equity.

Manifestations of Racism and Discrimination in Schools

Racism and discrimination are manifested in numerous school practices and policies. Policies most likely to jeopardize students at risk of educational failure are most common precisely in the institutions in which those students are found. For example, many studies have found that rigid tracking is most evident in poor communities with large numbers of African American, Latino, and American Indian students.[10]

It is sometimes difficult to separate what is racist or discriminatory from what appear to be neutral school policies and practices or behaviors of individual teachers. An early study cited by Ray McDermott[11] can help illustrate this point. Through filmed classroom observations, he found that a White teacher tended to have much more frequent eye contact with her White students than with her Black students. Was this behavior the result of racism? Was it because of cultural and communication differences? Or was poor teacher preparation responsible for her behavior?

David and Myra Sadker cite many anecdotes in their powerful report on sexism in schools that bring up similar questions. They found that well-intentioned and otherwise excellent teachers often treat their female students far differently from their male students, interacting with them less frequently, asking them fewer questions, and giving them less feedback than they give male students. Because boys are expected to be more verbal and active and are both praised and reproached more often by their teachers, girls become invisible in the classroom. Girls are singled out neither for praise nor for disciplinary action. They are simply expected, as a group, to be quiet, attentive, and passive.[12] Is this because of inherent sexism? Are teachers simply unaware of how such practices may jeopardize girls and, in a different way, boys as well?

In another example of how difficult it is to separate racism from individual teachers' behaviors or seemingly neutral policies, Patricia Gándara found in a study of 50 low-income and high-achieving Mexican Americans that most were either light-skinned or European-looking. Few of the sample, according to Gándara, looked "classically Mexican in both skin color and features."[13] Does this mean that teachers intentionally favored them because of their light skin? Did teachers assume that their light-skinned students were smarter?

These questions are impossible to answer in any conclusive way; it is probable that institutional racism and teachers' biases both play a role in negative outcomes such as those described in the studies. The results, however, are very clear: In the study by McDermott, the Black children had to strain three times as hard to catch the teacher's eye, looking for approval, affection, and encouragement. In the Sadker and Sadker report, the researchers concluded that girls are frequently denied an equal education simply because of their gender, rather than because of any personal talents or deficits. In Gándara's study, the light-skinned students were able to derive more benefits from their schooling than their darker-skinned peers.

Thus students' educational success or failure cannot be explained solely by their family circumstance, social class, race, gender, or language ability. Racism and other forms of institutional discrimination also play a part. African American, Latino, American Indian, and poor children in general continue to achieve below grade level, drop out in much greater numbers, and go to college in much lower proportion than their middle-class and European American peers. Two concrete examples illustrate this point: Black students are chronically underrepresented in programs for the gifted and talented, being only half as likely to be placed in a class for the gifted as are White students, even though they may be equally gifted. Latino students drop out of school at a rate higher than any other major ethnic group; and in some places, the rate has been as high as 80 percent.[14] If educational failure were caused only by students' background and other social characteristics, it would be difficult to explain why similar students are successful in some classrooms and schools and not in others. For instance, students at Central Park East High School in East Harlem, one of the most economically impoverished communities in New York City, have reached unparalleled levels of success compared to their peers in other neighborhood schools who are similar to them in every way.[15]

School structures have also proved to be sexist in organization, orientation, and goals. Most schools are organized to meet best the needs of White males; that is, the policy and instruction in schools generally reflect what is most effective for the needs of their male students, not the needs of either females or students of color.[16] This organization includes everything from the curriculum, which follows the developmental level of males more closely than that of females, to instructional techniques, which favor competition as a preferred learning style, although it is not necessarily the best learning environment for either females or most students of color. The effect of such discrimination on female students is to reinforce the persistent message that they are inferior. In fact, high-achieving female students tend to receive the least attention of all from their teachers.[17]

Discrimination based on social class is also prevalent in our public schools. In a study of affluent and low-income youth in a secondary school, Ellen Brantlinger found that students' social class was highly correlated with their academic placement, with most low-income students in special education or low tracks and *all* the high-income students in college preparatory classes. This was the case in spite of the fact that two of the high-income students were classified as "learning disabled."[18] Using data from 1993, the National Center for Education Statistics also found a significant correlation between social class and dropping out of school: While only 6 percent of high-income students dropped out, over 40 percent of low-income students did so.[19]

The *hidden curriculum,* that is, subtle and not-so-subtle messages that are not part of the intended curriculum, may also have an impact on students. These messages may be positive (e.g., the expectation that all students are capable of high-quality work) or negative (e.g., that children of working-class backgrounds are not capable of aspiring to professional jobs), although the term is generally used to refer to negative messages. These frequently unintentional messages may contradict schools' stated policies and objectives. For instance, Carolyn Persell found that, in spite of schools' and teachers' stated commitment to equal education, social class is repeatedly related to how well students do in school.[20] In fact, she found that students are more different from one another when they *leave* school than when they *enter* it, thus putting to rest the myth of school as the "great equalizer." Persell found that differences in academic achievement experienced by students of different economic and cultural backgrounds are due primarily to a number of specific factors: the kinds of schools the students attend, the length of time they stay in school, the curriculum and pedagogy to which they are exposed, and societal beliefs concerning intelligence and ability.

Rather than eradicate social class differences, then, it appears that schooling reflects and even duplicates them. This finding was confirmed by Samuel Bowles and Herbert Gintis in their ground-breaking class analysis of schooling.[21] They compared the number of years of schooling of students with the socioeconomic status of their parents and found that students whose parents were in the highest socioeconomic group tended to complete the most years of schooling. They concluded that schooling in and of itself does not necessarily move poor children out of their parents' low economic class. More often, schooling maintains and solidifies class divisions.

Intentional or not, racism, classism, and other forms of discrimination are apparent in the quality of education that students receive. A graphic example of discrimination based on both race and class is found in the differential resources given to schools. As is evident in Jonathan Kozol's searing indictment of the funding of public education, the actual money spent on schools is very often directly correlated with the social class and race of the student body. Furthermore, a review of relevant literature by Carol Ascher and Gary Burnett reported that disparities in funding between rich and poor states, and between rich and poor districts in the same state, has actually grown in the recent past.[22]

In the case of African American youth, Angela Taylor found that to the extent that teachers harbor negative stereotypes about them, African American children's race *alone* is probably sufficient to place them at risk for negative school outcomes.[23] Of course, many teachers and other educators prefer to think that students' lack of academic achievement is due solely to conditions inside their homes or inherent in their cultures. But the occurrence of racism in schools has been widely documented. In a report about immigrant students in California, more than half of the students interviewed indicated that they had been the victims of teachers' biases, citing instances where they were punished, publicly embarrassed, or ridiculed because of improper use of English. They also reported that teachers had made derogatory comments about immigrant groups in front of the class.[24] Most of the middle and high school students interviewed in a study by Mary Poplin and Joseph Weeres also had witnessed incidents of racism in school.[25] And in a study in an urban high school in the Northeast, Karen Donaldson found that an astounding 80 percent of students surveyed said they had experienced or witnessed racism or other forms of discrimination in school.[26]

Studies focusing specifically on Latino youth have reported similar results. Marietta Saravia-Shore and Herminio Martínez interviewed Puerto Rican youths who had dropped out of school and were currently participating in an alternative high school program. These youths keenly felt the discrimination of their former teachers, who they said were "against Puerto Ricans and Blacks." One young woman said that a former teacher had commented, "Do you want to be like the other Puerto Rican women who never got an education? Do you want to be like the rest of your family and never go to school?"[27] In Virginia Zanger's study of high-achieving Latino and Latina high school students in Boston, one young man described his shock when his teacher called him "spic" right in class. Although the teacher was later suspended, the incident had clearly affected how this young man perceived school and his teachers.[28] If we keep in mind that these are successful students, who are apt to hear far fewer of such damaging comments than other students, we can begin to grasp the enormity of the problem confronted by young people who are not as successful in school.

The effect of discrimination on students is most painfully apparent when students themselves have the opportunity to speak. Their thoughts concerning their education are revealing. In her study, Karen Donaldson found that students were affected by racism in three major ways: White students experienced guilt and embarrassment when they became aware of the racism to which their peers were subjected; students of color sometimes felt they needed to compensate and overachieve to prove they were equal to their White classmates; and at other times, students of color said that their self-esteem was badly damaged.[29] However, self-esteem is a complicated issue that includes many variables. It does not come fully formed out of the blue, but is *created* in particular contexts and responds to conditions that vary from situation to situation. Teachers' and schools' complicity in creating negative self-esteem cannot be discounted. This point was illustrated by Lillian, a young woman in a study of an urban high school by Nitza Hidalgo. Lillian commented, "That's another problem I have, teachers, they are always talking about how we have no type of self-esteem or anything like that. . . . But they're the people that's putting us down. That's why our self-esteem is so low."[30]

RACISM, DISCRIMINATION, AND SILENCE

Many times, unintentional discrimination is practiced by well-meaning teachers who fear that talking about race will only exacerbate the problem. As a consequence, most schools are characterized by a curious absence of talk about differences, particularly about race.[31] The process begins with the preparation of teachers. In one study, Alice McIntyre interviewed a group of White female student teachers working in urban schools in order to understand how they made meaning of their Whiteness in relation to teaching.[32] She found that these preservice teachers were reluctant to discuss racism or to consider their individual or collective role in perpetuating it. Because they saw their students primarily as victims of poverty and parental neglect, these student teachers preferred to place themselves in relationship to their students as protective "White Knights." This patronizing stance facilitated their denial of racism.

Silence and denial about racism are still quite prevalent when student teachers become teachers. In a follow-up study to her initial research concerning students' experiences with racism, Karen Donaldson had a hard time recruiting White teachers to take part in an antiracist education teacher study because most White teachers were not aware (or claimed not to be aware) of racial biases in schools and of how these biases could influence students' achievement.[33] In another study, Julie Wollman-Bonilla found that a sizable proportion of the teachers in her children's literature courses explicitly rejected children's books about race and racism for use with their students. Whether it was to shield their students from unpleasant realities, or to uphold particular societal myths, Wollman-Bonilla concluded that many teachers lack the courage to present views that differ from the mainstream perspective. As a result, their role becomes one of maintaining the status quo rather than helping children question social inequality and injustice.[34] That this attitude can be taken to an extreme is evident in research by Ellen Bigler: When she asked a middle school librarian in a town with a sizable Puerto Rican community if there were any books on the Hispanic experience, the librarian answered that carrying such books was inadvisable because it would interfere with the children's identification of themselves as "American"![35]

Silence pervades even schools committed to equity and diversity. This was a major finding in a study by Kathe Jervis of the first year of a New York City middle school consciously designed to be based on these principles.[36] Although she had not originally intended to focus her study on race, Jervis found that there was an odd silence on the part of most teachers to address it. Their reluctance to discuss race resulted in their overlooking or denying issues of power that are imbedded in race. Jervis concluded that "even in the 'best' schools, where faculty try hard to pay attention to individuals, Whites' blindness to race clouds their ability to notice what children are really saying about themseles and their identities."[37]

Failure to discuss racism, unfortunately, will not make it go away. As you will see in her case study, Linda Howard's close relationship with Mr. Benson, her English teacher, was no doubt partly due to the fact that they were able to talk openly about racism and other biases. Racism, classism, and other forms of discrimination play a key role in setting up and maintaining inappropriate learning environments for many students. A related phenomenon concerns the possible impact of teachers' expectations on student achievement.

EXPECTATIONS OF STUDENTS' ACHIEVEMENT

Much research has focused on teachers' interactions with their students, specifically teacher expectations. The term *self-fulfilling prophecy,* coined by Robert Merton in 1948, means that students perform in ways that teachers expect.[38] Student performance is based on both overt and covert messages from teachers about students' worth, intelligence, and capability. The term did not come into wide use until 1968, when a classic study by Robert Rosenthal and Lenore Jacobson provided the impetus for subsequent extensive research on the subject.[39] In this study, several classes of children in grades one through six were given a nonverbal intelligence test (the researchers called it the "Harvard Test of Influenced Acquisition"), which researchers claimed would measure the students' potential for intellectual growth. Twenty percent of the students were randomly selected by the researchers as "intellectual bloomers," and their names were given to the teachers. Although the students' test scores actually had nothing at all to do with their potential, the teachers were told to be on the alert for signs of intellectual growth among these particular children. Overall these children, particularly in the lower grades, showed considerably greater gains in IQ during the school year than did the other students. They were also rated by their teachers as being more interesting, curious, and happy, and thought to be more likely to succeed later in life.

Rosenthal and Jacobson's research on teacher expectations caused a sensation in the educational community, and controversy surrounding it continues to the present. From the beginning, the reception to this line of research has been mixed, with both supporters and detractors.[40] But one outcome was that the effect of teachers' expectations on the academic achievement of their students was taken seriously for the first time. Before this research, students' failure in school was usually ascribed wholly to individual or family circumstances. Now, the possible influence of teachers' attitudes and behaviors and the schools' complicity in the process had to be considered as well. The most compelling implications were for the education of those students most seriously disadvantaged by schooling, that is, for students of color and the poor.

Early research by Ray Rist on teachers' expectations is also worth mentioning here. In a ground-breaking study, he found that a kindergarten teacher had grouped her class by the eighth day of class. In reviewing how she had done so, Rist noted that the teacher had already roughly constructed an "ideal type" of student, most of whose characteristics were related to social class. By the end of the school year, the teacher's differential treatment of children based on who were "fast" and "slow" learners became evident. The "fast" learners received more teaching time, more reward-directed behavior, and more attention. The interactional patterns between the teacher and her students then took on a "castelike" appearance. The result, after three years of similar behavior by other teachers, was that teachers' behavior toward the different groups influenced the children's achievement. In other words, the teachers themselves contributed to the creation of the "slow" learners in their classrooms.[41]

In the research by Rist, all the children and teachers were African American but represented different social classes. But similar results have been found with poor and working-class children of any race. Persell, in a review of relevant research, found that expectations for poor children were lower than for middle-class children *even when their IQ and achievement scores were similar.*[42] Teachers' beliefs that their students are "dumb" can become a rationale for providing low-level work in the form of elementary facts, simple drills, and rote memorization. Students are not immune to these messages. On the other hand, a study by Diane Pollard found that the academic performance of African American students is enhanced when they perceive their teachers and other school staff to be supportive and helpful.[43]

Some of the research on teacher expectations is quite old. Although it is reasonable to expect that, with the increasing diversity in our schools, it no longer holds true, there are still numerous examples of teachers' low expectations of students. A recent study by Francisco Ríos underscores the problem. Ríos studied teachers in an urban city in the Midwest to determine what principles of practice they used for teaching in culturally diverse classrooms.[44] Among the 16 teachers he studied, he found that most of the comments they made about their students were negative; further, *none* of the teaching principles that they identified focused on academic achievement and only *one* teacher said that her students wanted to learn.

These findings are particularly problematic when we consider the impact that such beliefs can have on students. Given the increasing diversity in our public schools, the problem is even more acute because many teachers know little or nothing about the background of their students. Consequently, teachers may consider their students' identity to be at fault. This was the result found by Bram Hamovitch in an ethnographic study of an urban after-school program for adolescents at risk of dropping out of school. In his study, Hamovitch concluded that the program failed to meet its objective of motivating students to continue their education because "it allegorically asks them to dislike themselves and their own culture."[45]

Teachers' attitudes about the diversity of their students develop long before they become teachers, however. In a review of recent literature, Kenneth Zeichner found that teacher education students, who are mostly White and monolingual, by and large view diversity of student backgrounds as a problem.[46] He also found that the most common characteristics of effective teachers in urban schools are a belief that their students are capable learners, and an ability to communicate this belief to the students. Martin Haberman reached a similar conclusion, identifying a number of functions of successful teachers of the urban poor. Most significant, he found that successful teachers did not blame students for failure and they had consistently high expectations of their students.[47] Rich Miller, whose case study follows this chapter, offers compelling evidence of this reality. According to Rich, standards would be higher in his high school if there were more White students. But the reason was not because White students are smarter, but because *White teachers don't push the Black students* as much as they push White students. On the other hand, Black teachers, Rich said, have "expectations [that] are higher than White teachers. . . because they know how it was for them."

What happens when teachers develop high expectations of their students? In a wonderful example of how changing the expectations of students can influence achievement in a positive direction, Rosa Hernandez Sheets recounted her own experience with five Spanish-speaking students who had failed her Spanish class.[48] Just one semester after placing them in what she labeled her "advanced" class, the very same students who had previously failed passed the AP Spanish language exam, earning college credits while just sophomores and juniors. A year later, they passed the AP Spanish Literature exam. As a result of the change in her pedagogy, over a three-year period, Latino and Latina students who had been labeled "at risk" were performing at a level commonly expected of honors students.

The issue of labeling is key in this situation. In a similar case, Rubén Rumbaut found that the self-esteem of immigrant students is linked to how they are labeled by their schools. Specifically, he found that students' self-esteem is diminished when they are labeled "Limited English Proficient."[49] If this is the case with a seemingly neutral term, more loaded labels no doubt have a much greater impact. But explicit labeling may not even be needed. According to Claude Steele, the basic problem that causes low student achievement is what he terms "stigma vulnerability" based on the constant devaluation faced by Blacks and other people of color in society and schools.[50] In schools, this devaluation occurs primarily through the harmful attitudes and beliefs that teachers communicate, knowingly or not, to their students. Steele maintains, "Deep in the psyche of American educators is a presumption that black students need academic remediation, or extra time with elemental curricula to overcome background deficits."[51]

Although disadvantage may contribute to the problem, Steele contends that Blacks underachieve *even* when they have sufficient material resources, adequate academic preparation, and a strong value orientation toward education. To prove his point, he reviewed a number of programs that have had substantial success in improving the academic achievement of Black students without specifically addressing either their culturally specific learning orientations or socioeconomic disadvantage. What made the difference? In these programs, student achievement was improved simply by treating students as if they were talented and capable. Steele concludes, "That erasing stigma improves black achievement is perhaps the strongest evidence that stigma is what depresses it in the first place."[52]

Research on teachers' expectations is not without controversy. First, it has been criticized as unnecessarily reductionist because, in the long run, what teachers expect matters less than what teachers do.[53] Second, the term itself and the research on which it is based imply that teachers have the sole responsibility for students' achievement or lack of it. This is both an unrealistic and an incomplete explanation for student success or failure. The study by Rosenthal and Jacobson, for example, is a glaring indication of the disrespect with which teachers have frequently been treated and raises serious ethical issues in research. Blaming teachers, or "teacher bashing," provides a convenient outlet for complex problems, but it fails to take into account the fact that teachers function within contexts in which they usually have little power.

There are, of course, teachers who have low expectations of students from particular backgrounds and who are, in the worst cases, insensitive and racist. But placing teachers at the center of expectations of student achievement shifts the blame to some of those who care most deeply about students and who struggle every day to help them learn. The use of the term *teachers' expectations* distances the school and society from their responsibility and complicity in student failure. That is, teachers, schools, communities, and society interact to produce failure.

Low expectations mirror the expectations of society. It is not simply teachers who expect little from poor, working-class, and culturally dominated groups. Garfield High School in East Los Angeles, a school made famous by the extraordinary efforts of Jaime Escalante and other teachers in propelling an unprecedented number of students to college in spite of poverty and discrimination, was visited by George Bush when he was running for U.S. president. Rather than build on the message that college was both possible and desirable for its students, Bush focused instead on the idea that a college education is not needed for success. He told the largely Mexican American student body that "we need people to build our buildings. . . people who do the hard physical work of our society."[54] It is doubtful that he would even have considered uttering these same words at Beverly Hills High School, a short distance away. The message of low expectations to students who should have heard precisely the opposite is thus replicated even by those at the highest levels of a government claiming to be equitable to all students.

THE COMPLEX CONNECTIONS BETWEEN DIVERSITY AND DISCRIMINATION

Because societal inequities are frequently reflected in schools, institutional racism and other biases are apparent in inequitable school policies and practices in complex ways. Let us take the example of language. The fact that some children do not enter school speaking English cannot be separated from how their native language is viewed by the larger society or from the kinds of programs available for them in schools. Each of these programs—whether ESL, immersion, or two-way bilingual education—has an underlying philosophy with broad implications for students' achievement or failure, as we will see in Chapter 6. As a consequence, each approach may have a profound influence on the quality of education that language minority children receive. But linguistic and other differences do not exist independently of how they are perceived in the general society or by teachers; there is a complex relationship between students' race, culture, native language, and other differences with institutional discrimination, school practices, and teachers' expectations.

Social class provides another example of the complex links between difference and discrimination. In spite of the firm belief in our society that social class mobility is available to all, classism is a grim reality because *economic inequality is now greater in the United States than in any other industrial or postindustrial country in the world*; in fact, social class inequality has actually *increased* in the past 20 years.[55] Related to this reality is the widely accepted classist view among many educators that poverty *causes* academic failure. Yet although poverty may have an adverse effect on student achievement, the belief that poverty and failure go hand-in-hand is questionable. Research by Denny Taylor and Catherine Dorsey-Gaines provides evidence that by itself poverty is not an adequate explanation for the failure to learn. In their work with Black families living in urban poverty, they found inspiring cases of academically successful students. They discovered children who consistently did their homework, made the honor roll, and had positive attitudes about school. The parents of these children motivated them to learn and study, had high hopes for their education, were optimistic about the future, and considered literacy an integral part of their lives—this in spite of such devastating conditions as family deaths; no food, heat, or hot water; and a host of other hostile situations.[56]

Similarly, an in-depth study by David Hartle-Schutte of four Navajo students who might be identified as "at risk" by their teachers because of poverty and culture found that these students came from homes where literacy was valued. But their school failed to recognize and build on the many literacy experiences they had in their homes to help them become successful readers.[57] These cases point out that home background can no longer be accepted as the sole or primary excuse for the school failure of large numbers of students.

Examples such as these demonstrate that although poverty is certainly a disadvantage, it is not an insurmountable obstacle to learning. The economic condition of African American and other poor students has often been used as an explanation for academic failure, but as Kofi Lomotey, in a review of the education of African American youths, states: ". . . there are clear examples of environments that have, over long periods of time, been successful in educating large numbers of African-American students. These models can be replicated; the situation is not hopeless."[58] In fact, one major explanation for students' lack of academic achievement lies in the lack of equitable resources given to students of different social classes and cultural backgrounds. For instance, one of the most disturbing patterns found in the 1997 national *Condition of Education* report was that, compared with middle-class White children, children of color and low-income students were much more likely to be taught by teachers who had little academic preparation for their teaching field. Furthermore, the skills differentials that result from this inequity will lead to earnings differentials as adults to a much greater extent than was the case even 20 years ago.[59]

In the ideal sense, education in the United States is based on the lofty values of democracy, freedom, and equal access. Historically, our educational system proposed to tear down the rigid systems of class and caste on which education in most of the world was (and still is) based and to provide all students with an equal education. Education was to be, as Horace Mann claimed, "the great equalizer." On the other hand, some educational historians have demonstrated that the common school's primary purposes were to replicate inequality and to control the unruly masses.[60] Thus the original goals of public school education were often at cross purposes.

Mass public education began in earnest in the nineteenth century through the legislation of compulsory education and its most eloquent democratic expression is found in the early-twentieth-century philosophy of John Dewey.[61] The commitment that Dewey articulated for educational equity continues today through policies such as desegregation and nonsexist education and through legislation and policies aimed at eradicating many existing inequalities. But the legacy of inequality also continues through policies and practices that favor some students over others, including unequal funding, rigid tracking, and unfair tests. As a result, schools have often been sites of bitter conflict.

Race is another pivotal way in which privilege has been granted on an unequal basis. Based on his research, the historian David Tyack asserts that the struggle to achieve equality in education is nothing new, and that race has often been at the center of this struggle. He adds: "Attempts to preserve white supremacy and to achieve racial justice have fueled the politics of education for more than a century."[62] But resistance on the part of parents, students, and teachers has been crucial in challenging the schools to live up to their promise of equality. That is, schools were not racially desegregated simply because the courts ordered it, and gender-fair education was not legislated only because Congress thought it was a good idea. In both cases, as in many others, educational opportunity was expanded because many people and communities engaged in struggle, legal or otherwise, to bring about change.

Although in theory education is no longer meant to replicate societal inequities but rather to reflect the ideals of democracy, we know that such is not always the reality. Our schools have consistently failed to provide an equitable education for all students. The complex interplay of student differences, institutional racism and discrimination, teachers' biases that lead to low expectations, and unfair school policies and practices all play a role in keeping it this way.

● *CONCLUSION*

Focusing on the persistence of racism and discrimination and low expectations is meant in no way to deny the difficult family and economic situation of many poor children and children of color, or its impact on their school experiences and achievement. Drug abuse, violence, and other social ills, as well as poor medical care, deficient nutrition, and a struggle for the bare necessities for survival harm children's lives, including their school experiences. The fact that poor children and their parents do not have at their disposal the resources and experiences that economic privilege would give them is also detrimental.

But blaming poor people and people from dominated racial or cultural groups for their educational problems is not the answer to solving societal inequities. Teachers can do nothing to change the conditions in which their students may live, but they can work to change their own biases as well as the institutional structures that act as obstacles to student learning. As we have seen, racism and other forms of discrimination play a central role in educational failure, as does the related phenomenon of low expectations.

● *TO THINK ABOUT*

1. Let's say that you are a high school teacher and you are having a discussion with your students about the benefits of education. This is your dilemma: Horace Mann's claim that education is "the great equalizer" has been criticized as simplistic or unrealistic. On the other hand, a focus on racism, discrimination, and teachers' expectations can be criticized as being overly deterministic in explaining school failure. What is the appropriate approach to take? Do you say to students, "You can do anything you want! You can become president of the United States. The sky's the limit, and all you need to do is work hard"; or do you say, "No matter what you do, it is almost impossible to accomplish anything if you are [Navajo, African American, Mexican, female, etc.]"? Try role playing this situation in which you, as the teacher, try to find the most beneficial stance.

2. Think about schools with which you are familiar. Have you seen evidence of racism or other forms of discrimination? Was it based primarily on race, gender, class, language, sexual orientation, or other differences? How was it manifested?

3. Observe a classroom for a number of days to see if you can find some examples of the hidden curriculum. How does it work in that classroom? What are the messages, unintended or not, that children pick up?

4. There has been some controversy about research on teachers' expectations. Review some of the debate in the sources cited in this chapter. Think about your own experiences as a student: Describe a time when teachers' expectations did or did not make a difference in your life.

Case Study: Linda Howard

"Unless you're mixed, you don't know what it's like to be mixed."

Jefferson High School is a large, comprehensive high school in Boston. It has a highly diverse population of students from throughout the city, including African American, Puerto Rican and other Latino, Haitian, Cape Verdean, Vietnamese, Cambodian, Chinese American, other Asian American, and European American students. This is the high school from which Linda Howard,[1] a 19-year-old senior, is just graduating. Linda is the class valedictorian, has been awarded a four-year scholarship to a prominent university in New England, and is looking forward to her college education. She is already thinking about graduate school, and although she has not yet decided what she wants to study, she is contemplating majoring in education or English.

Frequently taken for Puerto Rican or Cape Verdean because of her biracial background (her father is African American, and her mother is European American), she resents these assumptions by those who do not know her. Linda's insistence about being recognized as biracial and multicultural sometimes puts her in a difficult situation, especially with friends who pressure her to identify with either her Black or her White heritage. She remains steadfast in proclaiming her biracial identity in spite of the difficulty it has caused her. Her friends represent the varied backgrounds of her school and of the community in which she lives. Her best friend is Puerto Rican, and her boyfriend is West Indian.

Linda has had an uneven academic career. At Tremont School, a highly respected magnet elementary school in the city, she was very successful. The school's population was quite mixed, with children from diverse backgrounds from all over the city. She loved that school and has good memories of caring teachers there. By the time she reached junior high, she was held back twice, in both seventh and eighth grades. There were two major reasons for this: She had been in an accident and had to be absent from school a great deal during her recuperation; and she disliked the school, Academic High, one of the most prestigious public schools in the city. After the eighth grade, Linda transferred to her present school, which she attended for two years, including summer school. By the end of her second eighth grade, she had improved her grades significantly. She has been a highly successful student ever since, although she feels that Jefferson High is "too easy." The normal load for most students is four academic courses and two electives, but Linda has taken six academic courses per semester.

Linda is recognized as a gifted student by her teachers. She is a talented singer and hopes someday to make a living as a musician. She inherited her love of music from her father, who gave up a career in music. The entire family sings together, and Linda claims to be the best singer when her father is not around. She has been a member of the school choir and also studies music on her own. Music gives her great solace and motivates her to do her best. In addition to her musical talent, Linda is also gifted in language. She frequently writes poems to express her feelings.

Linda lives with her mother, father, one older brother, and two younger brothers in a middle-class, predominantly Black community in Boston. Her family moved from a public housing project 14 years ago and bought their first home two years later. She still calls the housing project and neighborhood where she grew up "part of my community, part of my heritage." Both of Linda's parents are working professionals, although that was not always the case. She is proud of the fact that her father started in the telephone company as a lineman some 20 years ago. He now has a white-collar job. Her mother is a human services administrator.

Being both outgoing and personable, Linda has a great many friends. When showing her more playful side, she says she and some of them frequently "cruise around, find cute guys, and yell out the window, 'Yo, baby!' That's how we hang!" Tyrone is her "very best friend." They have known each other for 17 years and were actually engaged when she was 15. She broke off the engagement because she felt that she had her life ahead of her and needed to plan for college and a career. One month ago, they broke up completely but are still good friends. Linda says that she would do anything in the world for Tyrone. Both of them think that they may end up getting married to each other in the future.

Linda is very aware of her values and of the role her family plays in their formation. Her interviews highlighted a number of issues that are central to understanding these values: her struggle around identity and racism, the importance of teachers' caring and their role in students' learning, and the great value of education in her life and her parents' influence over this factor.

Identity, Racism, and Self-Determination

My parents are Black and White American. I come from a long heritage. I am of French, English, Irish, Dutch, Scottish, Canadian, and African descent.

I don't really use race. I always say, "My father's Black, my mother's White, I'm mixed." But I'm American; I'm human. That's my race; I'm part of the human race.

After all these years, and all the struggling (because when [my parents] got married it was a time right before desegregation), people from all sides were telling them, "No, you'll never make it. You'll never make it. White and Black don't belong together in the same house." And after 20 years, they're still together and they're still strong. Stronger now than ever, probably. That's what I like the most about them. They fought against all odds and they won.

It's hard when you go out in the streets and you've got a bunch of White friends and you're the darkest person there. No matter how light you are to the rest of your family, you're the darkest person there and they say you're Black. Then you go out with a bunch of Black people and you're the lightest there and they say, "Yeah, my best friend's White." But I'm not. I'm *both*.

I don't always fit in—unless I'm in a mixed group. That's how it's different. Because if I'm in a group of people who are all one race, then they seem to look at me as being the *other* race. . . . whereas if I'm in a group full of [racially mixed] people, my race doesn't seem to matter to everybody else. . . . Then I don't feel like I'm standing out. But if I'm in a group of totally one race, then I sort of stand out, and that's something that's hard to get used to.

It's hard. I look at history and I feel really bad for what some of my ancestors did to some of my other ancestors. Unless you're mixed, you don't know what it's like to be mixed.

My boss, who was a teacher of mine last year, just today said something about me being Puerto Rican. I said, "We've been through this before. I am *not* Puerto Rican. I am Black and White." I may look Hispanic, but this is what I mean. And this is a person who I've known for a whole year and a half now. [I felt] like I was insignificant. If, after all this time, he didn't know and we discussed it last year. . . . It was insulting. I usually don't get insulted by it. I say, "Oh, no, I'm not Spanish. I'm Black and White." And people say, "Oh really? You *are*? I thought you were Spanish."

[Teachers should not] try to make us one or the other. And God forbid you should make us something we're totally not. . . . Don't write down that I'm Hispanic when I'm not. Some people actually think I'm Chinese when I smile. . . . Find out. Don't just make your judgments. And I'm not saying judgment as insulting judgments. But some people, they don't realize that there are so many intermarried couples today. You have to ask people what they are. If you really want to know, you have to ask them. You don't just make assumptions. 'Cause you know what happens when you assume. . . . If you're filling out someone's report card form and you need to know, then ask. . . . Like I said, race isn't important to me. But if you need it for paperwork, or if you need it for something important, then ask. When people are misjudged, especially after you've known them for a while, and you write down the wrong thing about them, it's kind of insulting.

I don't know how to put this. . . race hasn't really been a big factor for me. Because in my house, my mother's White, my father's Black; I was raised with everybody. Sometimes I don't even notice. I see people walking down the street, I don't care what they are; they're people.

My culture is my family. I have an enormous family. I have three brothers, two parents, and my father has 10 brothers and sisters, and all of my aunts and uncles have children. That to me is my culture. . . . I was born and raised in America. I'm fourth-generation American, so it's not like I'm second generation where things were brought over from a different country or brought and instilled in me. I'm just American and my culture is my family and what we do as a family. Family is very important to us. . . . My family is the center of my life.

I've had people tell me, "Well, you're Black." I'm not Black; I'm Black and White. I'm Black and White American. "Well, you're Black!" No, I'm not! I'm both. It's insulting, when they try and. . . bring it right back to the old standards, that if you have anybody in your family who's Black, you're Black. . . . I mean, I'm not ashamed of being Black, but I'm not ashamed of being White either; and if I'm both, I want to be part of both. And I think teachers need to be sensitive to that.

I would say I have more Black culture than White. . . because I know all about fried chicken and candied yams and grits and collard greens and ham hocks and all that because that's what we eat. . . . My father had to teach my mother how to cook all that stuff [*laughs*]. But that's just as far as food goes. . . . But as far as everything else, my family is my culture.

See, the thing is, I mix it at home so much that it's not really a problem for me to mix it outside. But then again, it's just my mother and my grandmother on the "White side," so it's not like I have a lot to mix.

My [Black] grandmother, I don't think she means to do it, when she talks, she refers to people, she describes them. If she's telling you, "Oh, you know that girl, the White one, with the blond hair and the blue eyes?" Why not "the thin girl with the long hair"? Instead, they have to get you by the color. I don't notice [color] too much. But it is unusual, because a lot of people I know do it. And I just say, what's that got to do with it?

I don't think [interracial identity is] that big of a problem. It's not killing anybody, at least as far as I know, it's not. It's not destroying families and lives and stuff. It's a minor thing. If you learn how to deal with it at a young age, as I did, it really doesn't bother you the rest of your life, like drugs. . . .

In the city, I don't think there's really much room for racism, especially anymore, because there's just so many different cultures. You can't be a racist. . . . I think it's *possible,* but I don't think it's logical. I don't think it was *ever* logical. It's possible, it's very possible, but it's sort of ridiculous to give it a try.

I think we're all racist in a sense. We all have some type of person that we don't like, whether it's from a different race, or from a different background, or they have different habits.

But to me a *serious racist* is a person who believes that people of different ethnic backgrounds don't belong or should be in *their* space and shouldn't invade *our* space: "Don't come and invade *my* space, you Chinese person. You belong over in China or you belong over in Chinatown."

Racists come out and tell you that they don't like who you are. Prejudiced people [on the other hand] will say it in like those little hints, you know, like, "Oh, yes, some of my best friends are Black." Or they say little ethnic remarks that they know will insult you but they won't come out and tell you, "You're Black. I don't want anything to do with you." Racists, to me, would come out and do that.

Both racists and prejudiced people make judgments, and most of the time they're wrong judgments, but the racist will carry his one step further. . . . A racist is a person that will carry out their prejudices.

[Racists have power] only if you let them! We'll stick with [the example of] striped shirts: If I go where everyone is wearing solids, and I'm wearing a stripe, and someone comes up to me and tells me, "You don't belong here; you're wearing stripes," I'll say, "I belong anywhere I want to belong." And

I'll stand right there! But there are some people who just say, "Oh, okay," and will turn around and leave. Then the racist has the power.

I wrote a poem about racism. I despise [racism]. . . .

Why do they hate me?
I'll never know
Why not ride their buses
In the front row?
Why not share their fountains
Or look at their wives?
Why not eat where they do
Or share in their lives?
Can't walk with them
Can't talk with them unless I'm a slave
But all that I wonder is who ever gave
them the right to tell me
What I can and can't do
Who I can and can't be
God made each one of us
Just like the other
the only difference is,
I'm darker in color.

I love to write. I do a lot of poetry. . . . Poetry is just expression. You can express yourself any way you want; it doesn't have to be in standard English.

I had a fight with a woman at work. She's White, and at the time I was the only Black person in my department. Or I was the only person who was *at all* Black in my department. And she just kept on laying on the racist jokes. At one point, I said, "You know, Nellie, you're a racist pig!" And she got offended by *that*. And I was just joking, just like she'd been joking for two days straight—all the racist jokes that she could think of. And we got into a big fight over it. She threw something at me, and I was ready to kill her. . . . There's only so far you can carry this. . . . She started to get down and dirty. . . . She was really getting evil. . . . They locked her out of the room, and they had to hold me back because I was going to throttle her.

She thought I was upset because she tossed the water at me. I said, "You know, Nellie, it's not the water. It's all these remarks you've been saying. And you just don't seem to have any regard for my feelings."

I remember one thing she was talking about. She said, "I'm not racist, just because I was jumped by eight Black girls when I was in the seventh grade, I'm not racist." After [30] years, why was she still saying they were eight *Black* girls? That to me was insulting. That was then; this is now. I didn't do it to you, I didn't jump you. It wasn't my father who jumped you; it wasn't my aunt who jumped you. . . . I told her I didn't want it taken out on me, that's the thing. I don't want anybody's racism taken out on me.

I've got a foot on both sides of the fence, and there's only so much I can take. I'm straddling the fence, and it's hard to laugh and joke with you when you're talking about the foot that's on the other side.

She couldn't understand it. We didn't talk for weeks. And then one day, I had to work with her. We didn't say anything for the first like two hours of work. And then I just said, "Smile, Nellie, you're driving me nuts!" and she smiled and laughed. And we've been good friends ever since. She just knows you don't say ethnic things around me; you don't joke around with me like that because I won't stand for it from you anymore. We can be friends; we can talk about anything else—except race.

Teachers, Role Models, and Caring

My first-grade teacher and I are very close. . . . As a matter of fact, she's my mentor. I'm following in her footsteps. I'm going to study elementary education. . . . She's always been there for me. After the first or second grade, if I had a problem, I could always go back to her. Through the whole rest of my life, I've been able to go back and talk to her. . . . She's a Golden Apple Award winner, which is a very high award for elementary school teachers. . . . She keeps me on my toes. . . . When I start getting down. . . she peps me back up and I get back on my feet.

All of my teachers were wonderful. I don't think there's a teacher at the whole Tremont School that I didn't like. . . . It's just a feeling you have. You know that they really care for you. You just know it; you can tell. Teachers who don't have you in any of their classes or haven't ever had you, they still know who you are. . . . The Tremont School in itself is a community. . . . I love that school! I want to teach there.

I knew [Academic High] would be a hard school, but I didn't know it would be so. . . they're just so *rigid*. The teachers, there's no feeling. . . . Like I said, the Tremont was a community for me and I loved it. I'm that type of person; I'm an outgoing person and I like to be able to talk to anybody and not feel that I can't talk to someone. If I have to spend six hours a day in school, I want to feel that I can talk to my teachers. At Academic, I didn't feel that at all. I *hated* it, absolutely hated it. They let me know that I wasn't high anymore. I was average. They slapped me with it. My first report card, *oh goodness,* it was terrible. I don't remember exactly what grades they were; I just do remember it was the first time in my life I had seen an *F* or a *D* under my name.

I think you have to be creative to be a teacher, you have to make it interesting. You can't just go in and say, "Yeah, I'm going to teach the kids just that; I'm gonna teach them right out of the book and that's the way it is, and don't ask questions." Because then you're gonna lose their interest. . . . Because I know there were plenty of classes where I lost complete interest. But those were all because the teachers just [said], "Open the books to this page." They never made up problems out of their head. Everything came out of the book. You didn't ask questions. If you asked them questions, then the answer was, "In the book." And if you asked the question and the answer *wasn't* in the book, then you shouldn't have asked that question!

Mr. Benson, he cared; he was the only one of the two Black teachers [at Jefferson High School]. He was not enough. . . . The other Black teacher, he was a racist, and I didn't like him. I belonged to the Black Students' Association, and he was the advisor. And he just made it so obvious. . . he was all for Black supremacy. . . . A lot of times, whether they deserved it or not, his Black students passed, and his White students, if they deserved an A, they got a B. . . . He was insistent that only Hispanics and Blacks be allowed in the club. He had a very hard time letting me in because I'm not all Black. . . . I just really wasn't that welcome there.

He never found out what I was about. He just made his judgments from afar. He knew that I was Black and White and I looked too White for him, I guess. But we never discussed it.

At Jefferson, just about the whole school is like a big community. There are very few White, Caucasian, whatever you want to call them, *us* [laughing]. There are very few, but they don't cluster together. It's all integrated. . . . Nobody gets treated differently. We're all the same.

I've enjoyed all my English teachers at Jefferson. But Mr. Benson, my English Honors teacher, he just threw me for a whirl! I wasn't going to college until I met this man. . . . He was one of the few teachers I could talk to. . . . Instead of going to lunch, I used to go to Mr. Benson's room, and he and I would just sit and talk and talk and talk. . . . My father and Mr. Benson share a lot of the same values. And every time I've heard Mr. Benson talk, all I could think about was Daddy: "Oh, that's exactly what my father says!" . . . "Education, get your education and go far." "Whether you're flipping burgers at the local joint or you're up there working on Wall Street, be proud of yourself."

'Cause Mr. Benson, he says, I can go into Harvard and converse with those people, and I can go out in the street and rap with y'all. It's that type of thing, I love it. I try and be like that myself. I have my street talk. I get out in the street and I say "ain't" this and "ain't" that and "your momma" or "wha's up?" But I get somewhere where I know the people aren't familiar with that language or aren't accepting that language, and I will talk properly. . . . I walk into a place and I listen to how people are talking, and it just automatically comes to me.

Mr. Benson is the same as I am. Well, his mother was Black and his father was White, so Mr. Benson and I could relate on all the problems that you face in the world. Like when you go to fill out any kind of form and they ask you, "Black, White, Chinese, Hispanic, Other." I check off "Other" and I'll write it down. And then Mr. Benson told me that he found out that when you write it down, they put you under "Black" because it all comes back to the old laws about if you had any Black blood in you, you were Black.

I wrote a poem about it. It was just a bunch of questions: "What am I?" I had filled out a whole bunch of college essays, and I was tired of having to write out "Other: Black American and White American." And I went to him and I said, "Mr. Benson, what do you do when you get all these forms and they ask you "Black, White, or Other?" And he said, "You might as well just fill out "Black" because that's what they'll do to you." That just drives me nuts! And we got on this big conversation about it. . . . But no other teacher ever. . . .

He came from the lower class in Chicago and worked his way, and he studied every night, six hours a night. He got into Harvard and he went to Harvard, and now he's back helping the people who needed help. Because the way he sees it, he could go and he could teach at Phillips Academy and he could teach at Boston Latin, which he did for awhile. But those people don't need his help. That's how he sees it. They're gonna learn with or without him. He wanted to come back to a small community, the underprivileged community, and help those people. That's what made me admire him the most because I like to help people.

The teacher who didn't really help me at all in high school. . . was my computer lit. teacher. Because I have no idea about computer literacy. I got A's in that course. Just because he saw that I had A's, and that my name was all around the school for all the "wonderful things" I do, he just automatically assumed. He didn't really pay attention to who I was. The grade I think I deserved in that class was at least a C, but I got A just because everybody else gave me A's. But everybody else gave me A's because I earned them. He gave me A's because he was following the crowd. He just assumed, "Yeah, well, she's a good student." And I showed up to class every day. . . . He didn't help me at all because he didn't challenge me. Everybody else challenges me; I had to earn their grades. I didn't have to earn his grade. I just had to show up.

I'd do what I've seen teachers who I like or enjoyed do: make the classroom fun; make it exciting. If I were to teach math, I'd turn all the math problems into games. I had a teacher who did that. I hated math up until the second time I was in the seventh grade. . . . I *hated* math; I despised math until I met Ms. Morgan. And from that point on, I have never received less than a B in math. She turned every math problem, every type of math problem was a game.

So that school is never, "This is the way it is, and that's just it. Just learn it." I'd make everything exciting and fun, or I'd try to. That makes school enjoyable.

Family Values and Education

In the Tremont and in the Williams [schools], I was the top of my class, well, not top of my class, but I was very high up in the ranks. . . . That all comes from family. My mother's been reading me books since probably the day I was born, up until school age. . . . Any book with a serious message for children. . . . My mother's always been very big on that, to make sure that reading was important. I still love to read. . . mysteries, human interest stories. . . . It made a difference in elementary school, it really did. And, actually, it made a difference in high school, after I left Academic High, because I graduated first in my class.

My parents know that the further I go in school, the better life I'll have. Because they had to struggle to get where they are today. They had to struggle to make themselves comfortable. Going to school is going to be a struggle. But as long as I'm in school, my parents will always be there for me.

The first five years of your life, that's when you develop the most. Before you go to school, you've already got your personality. If you have parents who are showing you the right values (not *"the* right values" because everybody's values to them are right. . .), whatever values they've given you are what you carry for the rest of your life.

That's the way my family has raised me. . . . They really taught me not to judge. . . . You just accept [people] the way they are. . . . With my family, if you go to church, you go to church; if you don't, you don't. My grandmother says, "Jesus still loves you and I still love you, whether you go to church or not. . . ." It's that kind of thing. You just learn to accept people.

Sexuality—I don't judge, I try not to, anyway. I'm sure subconsciously I do. . . . I don't come out and say, "Ugh, he's gay." My neighborhood is thoroughly mixed and sexually open. And they're my neighbors. I don't differentiate them. And that's something I wish a lot of people would do. Because I think it's wrong. Because if you were to take people and differentiate because of their preferences, be it sexual or anything, *everybody's* different. I prefer a certain type of music; you prefer a different type of music. Does that mean we have to hate each other? Does that mean you have to pick on me and call me names? That's the way I see it.

I'm not going to be exactly like my parents. I grew up with basic values. And I follow those basic values. And if you think about it, the choices I make have something to do with my values. And the only place I got my values from was [home]. . . . So, I may change things around, flip them over, just adjust them a bit. But they still come down to my home values, my basic values, and my basic values came from home.

[My parents] have always taken good care of me. . . . They're always there for me, all the time, if I need to talk. And they make it so obvious that they love me, you know, with these ridiculous curfews that I have [*laughs*]. I know it's for the better, although I can't stand it; I know there's a reason behind it, some twisted reason! . . . Just a regular night out, I have to be in at midnight. If it's a party, I don't have to be in till two. All my friends stay out till three and four in the morning. But that's because their parents can go to sleep. My parents can't sleep if I'm not home. That's what I like the most about them.

I was reading an article the other day about how the family dinner has sort of been tossed out the window in today's society. My family sits down to dinner together four out of seven nights a week, all six of us. Dinner's at six. If it's late, then everybody waits. You don't just eat on your own. . . . I've noticed a lot of people, my boyfriend, for one, they never eat together. I've had all kinds of friends who always say. . . "Your family *eats* [together]?" And that's different from other families.

It's very important to my parents and it'll be important to me. Because that's the time when we sit down and say, "How was your day? What'd you do? How are you feeling? Do you have a headache? Did you have a rough day? Did you have a good day?" You know? And that's about the only time the whole family can sit together and talk and discuss. . . . It's different from other families, because a lot of families, they sort of miss each other. And they say, "Oh, *you* were supposed to pick Johnny up today?". . . My family never has that problem because we always sit down together and talk.

I have wonderful parents, although I don't tell them [*laughing*]. [*Do they know?*] Probably.

My father and my mother had to work up. . . . My father has been working for the telephone company for 20 years. He started off cutting lines and working underground. Now he sits in his office. . . . He's a businessman these days, and he had to work his way up. Whereas if I go and get myself a college education, I'm not going to have to start splicing lines if I want to work at the telephone company. I'm going to start with the knowledge that I don't have to splice a line. I could start in the office with my father.

A lot of us [Black kids] just don't have the home life. I really do think it begins when you're a baby! My mother, like I said, I believe she read to me from the day I was born; I'm sure of it. A lot of people just didn't have that. Their parents both had to work; they didn't have anybody at home to read to them. They just sat in front of the tube all day. When they came home from school, their homework was just tossed aside and they sat in front of the television until Mom and Dad came home. Then Mom and Dad rushed them through dinner, got them to bed, and this and that. A lot of them just didn't come from the right background to have—not the smarts, but to be educated enough to pass that test [to get into Academic High]. Because the Academic test isn't a test of how much you know; it's more of a test of how well can you solve problems. . . . The Black population wasn't very high there.

I blew two years. . . . I learned a lot from it. As a matter of fact, one of my college essays was on the fact that from that experience, I learned that I don't need to hear other people's praise to get by. . . . All I need to know is in here [*pointing to her heart*] whether I tried or not.

It's not the school you go to, it's what you want to get out of it and what you take from it.

If I know I did my hardest, if I know I tried my very best and I got an F, I'd have a beef with the teacher about it, but if that's what I got, that's what I got. If that's seriously what I earned after all my efforts, then I'll have to live with it.

[Grades] are not that important. To me, they're just something on a piece of paper. . . . [My parents] feel just about the same way. If they ask me, "Honestly, did you try your best?" and I tell them yes, then they'll look at the grades and say okay. . . . The first thing my father always looked at was conduct and effort. If all the letter grades in the academic grades said F's, and I had A's in conduct and effort, then my father would just see the F's, and say "Oh, well. . . ."

I love music. Music is life. I sing at the top of my lungs every morning. . . . I'm always going to keep this in my mind: After school, after I go to college, after I get my degrees in what I want to get my degrees in, maybe I'll put all of that on hold. Even if I have a teaching degree, I may never teach. I want to be a singer. I just want to go out there, and I want to make myself known, and I want to sing to my heart's content. It's just what I love to do! But I always want to have something to fall back on. Singing is not my main career goal because I realize it's a far-fetched dream to become a world-famous singer. It's not *too* far-fetched, but it is far-fetched. . . . Oh, I can do it. I have no doubts I can do it. I just know it's a lot of work. . . . I do eventually want to be a singer. . . . I can become more famous, and you can read about me in the papers, and you can see my videos on television, and you can see me in interviews on "Good Morning, America". . . [*laughing*].

[The reason for going to school is] to make yourself a better person. To learn more, not only about the world and what other people have gathered as facts, but to learn more about yourself.

The more that there are opportunities for you to learn, you should always take them. . . . I just want to keep continuously learning, because when you stop learning, then you start dying.

I've got it all laid out. I've got a four-year scholarship to one of the best schools in New England. All I've gotta do is go there and make the grade.

If I see the opportunity to become a leader, I'll do it. I'll just go and take over. . . . I like the recognition.

I'm ready now. I can face the challenge. . . . I'm ready to go out in the world and let [that] university know who I am!

COMMENTARY

Issues of identity are clearly at the core of Linda's striving to carve out a place for herself in her family, community, and school. Although she has reached quite a sophisticated understanding of race, racial awareness, racism, and identity, some feelings of ambivalence, conflict, and pain are still apparent. Being "mixed," to use Linda's term, is the reality of more and more students in U.S. schools. In an ethnographic study of an alternative urban public school in East Harlem, for instance, Linda Levine found that almost two-thirds of the children in the classroom she observed were members of biracial or interethnic families.[2] Yet many schools are unaware of the strains and dilemmas that biracial identity poses for children. A recent study concerning the self-concept of biethnic and biracial students found that the school environment was hostile to them through an insistence that these students deny part of their heritage. Moreover, the students who were interviewed felt that their schools did not promote the inclusion of biethnic and biracial students, and in fact, hindered their self-identification.[3]

Many people in the United States are probably a mixture of several racial heritages, but this is either not known or not readily acknowledged. According to some estimates, Blacks in the United States are on average about 20 percent

White, and Whites are about 1 percent Black.[4] Although this assertion is impossible to prove, *miscegenation,* or racial mixing, is far more common than generally admitted in our society. Discomfort with this issue is understandable, given the history of rape and subjugation forced on African and African American women, especially during slavery. This is an example of the legacy of racism, as is the "one-drop" rule—the law that one drop of Black blood makes a person Black—to which Linda alluded. In fact, the "one-drop" rule was reaffirmed as late as 1982 in a court decision in Louisiana, in which 1/32 African ancestry was sufficient to keep "Black" on an individual's birth certificate.[5]

This classification has not been practiced in other societies and was not always the case in the United States, either. Rather, it emerged sometime in the early eighteenth century.[6] The classification was to the benefit of the institution of slavery because with this logic, people could still be enslaved even if they were mostly White. As is the case with race itself, this was a social construction rather than a biologic one. By the beginning of the twentieth century, the vast majority of those of mixed African and European ancestry were identifying as Black rather than as White or mixed. Horace Mann Bond, the renowned sociologist and educator—and himself a light-skinned Black—wrote of a blue-eyed and seemingly Anglo-Saxon man who spoke fervently at a meeting about "the necessity that all of us black men in America and the world stand together."[7]

Although interracial marriages in the United States had declined dramatically during the first half of the twentieth century from earlier times, they began to increase after the civil rights movement. Between 1970 and 1980, the number of interracial marriages doubled, from 310,000 to 613,000, and by 1991, the number had climbed to 994,000. As documented in *Of Many Colors,* a recent book of portraits and interviews of multiracial and multiethnic families, it is estimated that there are now over a million interracial marriages. However, this still represents a small percentage of all marriages in the United States.[8]

Given the racist underpinnings of group and self-identification in the United States, the dilemmas Linda faces are difficult indeed. According to Robin Lin Miller and Mary Jane Rotheram-Borus, the biracial child may be even more vulnerable to racism than monoracial adults: "This is because the biracial child represents an affront to the racial divide; biracial persons must often cope with reactions reflecting the internalized racism of society."[9] The pressure to identify as one race or the other is something that Linda has lived with since birth. In *Of Many Colors,* Ifeoma Nwokoye, a young adult of Nigerian/White American heritage, writes, "In America, people are often unwilling to accept the idea of a biracial person. In our everyday lives we are constantly confronted with situations in which we must define who we are. We check the boxes marked *"white," "black,"* on our college forms, but there is no space marked *'multiracial'* yet. There is no place for me."[10]

Linda is adamant in claiming both her heritages. But she is certain that although she goes to the trouble of writing "Mixed—Black and White" on college applications and other forms, she is automatically placed in the "Black" category anyway. (Like Linda, the national movement Interracial Pride—or

"I-Pride"—advocates the elimination of "check only one" forms; they also object to current census categories.[11]) But Linda identifies most strongly with her family. As she says, "My culture is my family." And because her family is mixed, so is her culture. Hers is an extraordinarily courageous stand in a society that either forces you to choose one over the other, or fits you into one that you have not necessarily chosen yourself. The simple act of naming herself has been a powerful experience.

Except for her time at Academic High, where she was made to feel unintelligent, Linda has for the most part loved school. Having teachers who have understood and cared has also been meaningful for Linda. Fortunately, there have been a number of such teachers in each of her schools. Of course, Linda does not expect all her teachers to be biracial like herself, but she expects them all to be sensitive and accepting of who she is, rather than imposing their own identity on her. Her strong family background has been her first and most significant support system. This is evident from what she calls "family jam sessions," in which everybody takes part; the key role of reading in the family; and the centrality of family dinners. Friends are Linda's second strongest support. Her schools have come in a distant third, although she has had some stellar teachers. The teachers who have stood out have been not only those with whom she could identify culturally but also those who have made learning fun, engaging, and challenging.

Linda Howard is an extraordinary young woman who is full of ambition, certain of her talents, and ready for the future. Her strong family bonds, love of learning, and steadfast identification as Black and White no doubt all contribute to her academic success. Her teachers and schools have not always been able to understand or support her, emphasizing the importance of a school's social context and the degree to which it can insulate students from racism and influence self-esteem.

TO THINK ABOUT

1. Linda Howard insists on identifying herself as biracial. She also says that she is just "a member of the human race" and that race is not that important to her. Nevertheless, she obviously has spent a great deal of time thinking about race, as some of her anecdotes and poems make clear. Are these assertions contradictory? Why or why not?
2. If you were one of Linda's teachers, how might you show her that you affirm her identity? Give specific suggestions.
3. What kind of teachers have most impressed Linda? Why? What can you learn from this in your own teaching?
4. Linda's family is, as she says, "the center of my life." How do you think this has helped Linda become a successful student? Does this mean that students whose families are different from hers cannot be successful? Give some examples of academically successful students you have known.
5. Can issues of race and identity be handled by the school? Or are these issues too complicated for schools? What skills do you think teachers need if they are to face these concerns effectively?

Case Study: Rich Miller

"Self-respect is one gift that you give yourself."

Speaking slowly and deliberately, Rich Miller[1] is a young man who thinks carefully about life, education, and the key role of family. Rich is 17 years old and is just graduating from high school. He is Black and has lived in a racially and ethnically mixed community in Boston since he was born. Rich says that the neighborhood "isn't bad" but laments that it was once much nicer than it is now.

The youngest of three children, Rich lives with his mother, brother, and sister. Both of his siblings are in college—his brother in a public college in the South studying engineering, and his sister in a private liberal arts college in New England. All three are close in age, the oldest being 20. Rich's mother is a nursery and kindergarten teacher. She did not attend college until she was an adult, and she has had to struggle to get an education and develop her professional career. Consequently, she feels very strongly about the need for her children to get a college education. This is a major value in their family. Rich is clearly devoted to his mother and considers himself lucky to be part of his family. But he is also quick to point out that at times he feels that his mother is overbearing, "getting on his case."

Rich feels that he has had a good basic education. He has always gone to desegregated schools that have "a good mix" and are, he recalls, free of racial tension. At present, he attends a comprehensive high school that he describes as "pretty good." He decided not to go to his neighborhood school because his high school offers a number of special programs, including one in music. Almost three-quarters of the students in his school are African American, about 10 percent Latino, 15 percent White, and a small number of Asians. Rich will be graduating this year, and although he feels that he has had a very good education there, he points out that the teachers' expectations are often based on their students' race and background. He plans to study pharmacology and has been accepted into a respected program at a good college.

Because he has been studying music (both violin and piano) since fourth grade, Rich has been very involved in the music program at school. He played at graduation and other occasions, and he has conducted workshops for other students. Music is a big part of Rich's life outside of school, too: He plays the organ at his church, and he and his family frequently take part in church activities. Thus his church is also a significant part of his life. Rich is contemplating combining a profession as a pharmacist with teaching music to private students.

Three themes emerged through interviews with Rich. One is his great sense of personal responsibility and independence; another focuses on the expectations and pressures he feels from society and teachers and some of the attitudes he has developed as a result. The third relates to family lessons that he has learned along the way.

Personal Responsibility

I'm more or less an independent person. I don't depend on anyone to do any-thing for me. . . . I don't let dependence stand in the way of anything that has to get done. . . . I don't depend on anyone learning for me or making deci-sions for me or anything. I just want to see how far I can carry myself and what I can achieve on my own. I'm not saying that I wouldn't accept the aid of others, but just see what Rich can do.

The first year [of high school] was real heavy . . . because I was in that transition going from junior high to high school, and at that particular time, when you have that homework—I had never had this much homework before! . . . My mother stayed on me about that, but then it was *my* decision. That first semester of my first year was, oh, it was terrible. It actually opened my eyes up that it was left up to me; it's up to me to go and get that education.

I'm looking at the future as long as I can just continue right into educa-tion and not wait until the latter part of my life. I believe that "business before pleasure," so take care of this now and later I can enjoy the time off; I can enjoy the finer things in life that one wants earlier. . . . Many of us want to go out and get cars, but some things have to give and some things come first. I feel that if I involve myself in a lot of things now within the world, then that may hinder me from getting my education. . . . My future is getting that edu-cation. Whatever else happens after that, I won't have that problem or worry about getting a job.

I decided on pharmacy. . . . That's next to being a doctor, so it's just as hard. I decided that I wanted to go into a career that would give me guaran-teed bacon. . . . Like with music, there's so much competition out here and no matter how much or how hard you study, there's always somebody better than you are. . . . So I figured there's enough room out here for pharmacists.

I always liked music, but when I was little I never felt there was a place for me in music. Other people are talented, and they can just sit down and just actually play. Well, I started from scratch, so I didn't know that there was a place for me. . . . So I began taking lessons. . . and I have stuck with that.

There was a time that I had decided to go into music education. Now, I am going to pursue this career in pharmacy, but I also want to be a music teacher. . . . Now, as far as performance, that's something that has to be worked with. I feel there *can* be a slot for me in music education.

I plan on keeping my music up. I really don't have hobbies and I don't play too many sports or anything like this, so I really think this keeps me going. It gives me something to go for from day to day. And you learn some-thing new all the time.

I'm always looking to learn something new. The music I like playing the most is, well, I like playing between the classical and the gospel music. I learned the classical and I always feel that it's a challenge. That's the first music that I really got into before I began the gospel music. . . . I like gospel music because I like to play for the church.

Getting ahead in life, not letting anyone discourage you in any way [is important]. Say, "Well, I want to go forth and do this. . . ." And then someone might say, "Well, I don't think you can do it; I don't think you can make it." And because of someone saying something, then you decide, "Well, no, I'll leave it alone. . . ." I think no matter what anyone says, if you feel that within yourself you can achieve something, go for it!

I was fairly comfortable in school. I'll admit, I mainly kept to myself. Now, it's not saying that I didn't have any friends or anything like that. I had friends, but I knew how to take relationships up to how far. So I've maintained trust and loyalty to friends. So it's not like I was totally alone. . . . I know how I want my friends to treat me, and I treat them how they would expect to be treated.

Friends won't let you down. Friends will be around. My closest friends are there. . . more so to offer encouragement to get that education. . . . Many of my friends are encouraging me to go on to college. I've had that kind of push from outside just as much as I have from inside.

There's just things that I just want to fulfill for myself, and if it takes the rest of my life, eliminating [plans for a] family and whatever, then so be it. . . . I don't want to take on a million responsibilities at once.

Expectations, Pride, and Shame

I went to the Robert Jennings School, where we had an Advanced Work Class. Advanced Work Class was more like an exam school for elementary students [*Note:* Students need to take an examination to be admitted].. . . That's when I first became familiar with music. We had a teacher to come in to teach violin and cello and those string instruments. So that's where I first started with music and I began taking violin. My mother asked me did I want to take piano lessons, so that's also when I started taking piano lessons.

I was a good student in the average class, the normal, basic class that everyone has to go through. Now, getting into the Advanced Work Class, *there* there are students who fall behind. And I think that I wasn't really looking to be there. I managed to get myself there, but I don't think I really wanted to be there. And I think that's more what the problem was.

I did act out, as I didn't want to be there. But between my mother and the faculty, I never did get out! So, I managed to be in there up until the end of eighth grade. I was trying to get out by acting out, but they didn't go for that because it was just a show that I was putting on that could be stopped. It wasn't a real disability of not being able to do the work.

There are certain teachers that challenge you to think. There are students who say, "School is really tough and I can't do this and I can't do that, and this is just too hard for me. . . ." Some students get through high school; that's it for education for them. They don't pursue college. They take a trade because they might be better at working with their hands. . . . Then there is a part that helps you to think. Some people like challenging problems. . . . I believe there are parts of school that can promote you to think.

[Chemistry class] was just totally interesting. When I first heard of it, you know, my brother and sister, they had chemistry before I did. . . . To hear them tell it, chemistry was hard and I just knew I couldn't do it. . . . But I did it. . . . I still didn't understand it like I understand music. You can tell me something about music and I can understand it; I can see how you go about it. There were some things in chemistry that I couldn't. I myself personally feel like I need to take it all over again. . . . That's what made up in my mind that anything that you want to do, it can be done. Because I just had in my mind that I couldn't do it. . . I kept at it, I didn't give up. . . . The teacher just constantly told us that it's not difficult. The only difficult thing is getting that understanding. Once you understand how you do something, you can in fact go on with it.

There were games that go on. Like math classes, when we had math competitions that actually help you to learn. You'd win little prizes, candy prizes, or whatever. It actually made school a bit more interesting. It made learning a lot easier because it was a game.

I would put more activities into the day that can make it interesting. . . . It's up to you what you think you might be interested in. If you think that you're interested in dance, which they had, that would be fun to you, so then you would not look at it as being a math class. Who likes a math class? There are people who do, but who really likes a math class that would go there because they like being there? But for people who like to dance or the physical education class, they would break their neck practically to get into that class.

I believe a teacher, by the way he introduces different things to you, can make a class interesting. Not like a normal teacher that gets up, gives you a lecture, or there's teachers that just pass out the work, you do the work, pass it in, get a grade, good-bye!

I didn't know what I wanted to do; I had no *idea*. At least the majority of students graduating have some idea of what they want to do. I didn't have the faintest. So [my guidance counselor] put in front of me many different brochures about dental hygienist or pharmacy and other different careers. . . . Well, I didn't hear of too many people in the career of pharmacy, so it's something that I want to try. I feel that if I put forth that effort, there's a chance for me. . . . She was more like you would say a fellow classmate. There's always somebody who knows just a little bit more that can help you out. It wasn't about "Well, make an appointment to come and see me." She was always glad to help, so when she offered or presented you with different things or different ideas, or careers, it was from the heart more so than from "doing my job." It made a difference, because she has a general idea of what you're about and what you might like.

This particular guidance counselor. . . I had her for my sophomore year in high school. And till the end of June, even after graduation, I was still seeing her. . . . We still keep in touch. She's White. . . . She'd probably have in the range of 200 [students].. . . . She gave me ideas. . . . If I didn't have the guidance counselor that I had, then I really don't know what direction I would be in.

I don't think that we [Black folks] do enough to stick out like a sore thumb. I don't think we do enough to put us on top or put us up in a higher league. I don't think many of us are working to the ability that we can. We are settling for the easiest way out as far as working, as far as education. We feel that after high school, that's it for us; we don't have to go on with it. As far as getting a job, some of us even would resort to selling drugs (not only the Black race, but specifically speaking on the Black race); we would even go to sell drugs just to make it easier for us. I mean, selling drugs, you can make more that day than the average person makes a week. We always oftentimes, we set up the limits rather than going on to higher expectations.

It's important to me because I believe that I am no different from anyone else. I believe there is a space for me. And it's up to me as an individual; it's up to others in the Black race, to take on those opportunities to further ourselves education-wise and as far as living is concerned.

I'm not saying that there's not enough of us out there. I mean, let's take a household, for example. Nine times out of ten, out of a family, there may be at least one person that succeeds in life. Well, why can't *everyone* succeed in life? That's the question that I'm asking: Why can't everyone?

We're somewhat tacky. We don't act professional at anything. I'm not saying everyone, but there are some of us who just don't want to be professional. We rely on welfare to take care of us. I don't believe that even those that are on welfare, I don't believe that anyone should have to touch welfare. . . . You know, there are some of us who are smart or some of us who are able to either further our education or get a job, and we don't even want to do that much. . . . Lazy. I think lazy, and we get too comfortable. . . . "Well, I won't go today, I'll go tomorrow." And tomorrow never comes. And I think too many of us are just too comfortable at home, comfortable with the way things are, not really struggling, getting this check every month.

See, I believe that you can take a rich White and put him in a poor Black neighborhood, and he would [be] somewhat immune to it. But if you take a Black and put him in a rich White neighborhood, how do you think that Black would act? There are some of us who are classy, but then there are some who like to have those parties, and have everyone over and being loud. . . . They just really can't fit in.

I feel that's something that Black people are doing to themselves. Like, for instance, I find that a White can move anywhere, and a Black, if he wants to get out in a highly suburban area where there are rich White doctors, something like that, and for instance, if that house is $300,000, it might go up $100,000 just so you can't get in there. Because it is known for Blacks to, not necessarily true, but it is known for Blacks to pull down an area.

I believe that we can do something about it as Blacks. Because we buy homes, very nice homes and so forth, but we don't seem to be upkeeping our homes. We just let it fall down to the ground completely. And then we say, "Oh, look at them! They're not taking care of the house," and whatever.

With [my] school being predominately Black, well, it's natural that you're going to have quite a bit of top Black students. However, if you were to take those top Black students, say you have two top Black students, and you put them in a classroom with 20 top White students, where would you rank? . . .

Just how educated do you think you are? You know some of us, because we sit in this class, and we say, "Well, I'm the smartest," just how educated are you?

Most people think it's not being top [because it's a Black school]. . . . I think if we had more White students, Black students would go further. I find that White students want to learn. Most White students wanted to learn as much as they can get. I think standards would be higher [if there were more White students].

Many of the White teachers there don't push. . . . Their expectations don't seem to be as high as they should be. I mean, work that I feel myself, being a teacher, I would give them to promote any kind of high standards. I know that some Black teachers, their expectations are higher than White teachers. . . . They just do it, because they know how it was for them. . . . Actually, I'd say, you have to be in Black shoes to know how it is.

Black teachers. . . want to impress you more about getting an education, you know; they're your own race, more so than the opposite race. Because of back then, segregated times or times when you weren't able to get that education. But I think that it is just important to all teachers and to all students just to teach the curriculum as they would in an all-White school or as they would any other student.

My only thing to make it better is just to encourage the teachers to push the curriculum, that's about it.

Family Lessons

I have one brother, one sister, and my mother. And we're just a happy-go-lucky family. My brother is the oldest; my sister is the second to the last in line. It's okay, because the parent and first-child relationship has broken the barrier for the second and the last child. So things that they did, they can expect from the second and the third. So it's not like it's tougher on me.

[My mother] didn't go to college right away. . . so she felt that a lot of what she's doing now, she could've been doing back then. But by not going to school right away, by prolonging that time, "Well, I won't go this year, but I'll go next year," has turned into a matter of years. And she feels that if you go right after school, then things will look up. And then you'll say, "Well, I'm glad I went to school now rather than wait." You see, we don't want to go to school (going to college, I should say) because we've had it with 12 years of school! It's hard; it's dull; it's boring; we don't like the teachers! So this is our option, whether we want to go on to college. And many of us feel that "Well, I'm not going to go right away. . . ." And she didn't want the same thing to happen to us. . . . Even today, she's wondering, "Well, what are you going to do about school? All I want is you kids to go to college and get an education and live a halfway decent life."

It mattered to me, because I used to say to myself, and probably still do, back in my mind, "Well, what's the big deal about going to school?" I'm not going to find a job without going to college.

I like the goals and objectives that she set for herself being a single parent. Things that I would change: She's really bossy. I should say bossy *to her children,* not to everyone else. Because she desires those things for us to go on and gradually be pharmacists and nurses and engineers. So, she's very persistent. . . . It's out of love, but it's really aggravating [*laughs*]. . . . Actually, it is out of love and persistence, so I'm trying to bear with it.

It's wonderful being a member of my family. We have our ups and downs, but every day, I have fun. I enjoy being with my mother, my sister, and my brother. And I don't think I can compare her. I wouldn't exchange her for anyone else's parents. . . . I mean, look at us, we're not out roaming the streets or anything like that.

My sister's going into nursing, so it's the same [field], medicine. So I'm looking to actually learn with her. Because some classes, she already had that I'm going to be taking in the fall. And then some classes we're going to be having together. So I feel that this will be an excellent benefit for the both of us.

I don't want to be a letdown to my family, personally, and to myself. But I feel that if I tried and then failed, then that's a different story. At least I did put forth that effort. But you never know until you've tried. You don't know what you can do or what you cannot do unless you've tried.

I've learned from my family, I could say how to survive. Now you say, how do you survive? I know I've learned how to work a job, how to stay on the job.

I've learned about being Black. . . that Blacks have to work harder at things. Some things are just harder than others. What I mean by working hard, I say if you work hard now, it'll pay off later, it definitely will. Something good will come in your life. But let's not look at life as a piece of cake, because eventually it'll dry up, it'll deteriorate, it'll fall, it'll crumble, or somebody will come gnawing at it. . . . But we want to build *solid* foundations for ourselves and for our future generations, for our future children.

We find many students saying, "Well, Mom, you didn't go to college. How come you're making me go?" But let's not look at it that way. Let's look at it, "Well, you have the opportunity; you can get scholarships; you can get financial aid." And just pursue it. Do something for yourself. You know, it might be hard trying to help with your parents, but that'll make them happy, by you prospering.

Grades are very important to my family. My mother is the most influential on that, and my sister. . . . At all times, I just look out for what Rich can do, what he can accomplish, how well he can do it. Because I find that when you are competing, sometimes if you're trying just a little too hard, sometimes we try just a little too hard and we end up messing things up for ourselves. So I feel that, don't take it easy, but you know how much you can take and when to let go. . . . I'm comfortable setting my own standards.

I mean, I feel that there's a thing with "very well," "good," "average," and "poor" and "inferior." I believe that everyone should at least be "average." It's all right to come out "good" and it's all right to come out "excellent," but you should try to at least be average.

I'm just looking forward to all of us to be graduates of some college. Even if not my brother and sister, I at least want to do something for myself. . . . As they say, self-respect is one gift that you give yourself. And I feel that I'll be doing something for myself if I go to college. Nobody can't go to college for you; nobody can't get that knowledge and understanding for you but yourself. So I think I'm going to be doing something for myself.

My mother won't always be there. . . . So that's where it's left for you to decide: "Well, what am I going to do? How am I going to avoid this situation?"

I think the only thing that's holding me back from getting a good education might be me. I just have to be ready to accept it. . . . I want to pursue a future the right way. . . and not find myself in a graveyard or in jail somewhere.

COMMENTARY

The three themes revealed here are inextricably linked. Independence and responsibility, for example, are major values in Rich Miller's life. He has learned these by being the son of a strong mother who is deeply concerned about the education of her children. But the expectations held for him by teachers and society sometimes counteract this message. What emerges in this case study is a portrait of a highly complex young man who is independent, resourceful, mature; at once proud, and critical of his culture; and always appreciative of his family for their pressure and support. Through the messages of family, school, and community, Rich has also learned that Blacks have to work harder to get anywhere and that White teachers have lower expectations of Black students than of White.

The sociopolitical context in which Rich has developed his values and learned these lessons cannot be underestimated. For example, Rich's enrollment in an Advanced Work Class placed him with a minority of African American students. Data collected by the U.S. Office for Civil Rights support the contention that African American students do not receive equal educational opportunities but in fact are subjected to what has been called "second generation school discrimination" through practices such as ability grouping, differential disciplinary practices, and lower graduation rates. They are grossly overrepresented in classes for the mentally retarded and grossly underrepresented in classes for the gifted and talented.[2] Although racism may be manifested differently from before, it still exists.

Another way messages are communicated to students is through the social status of students and staff in schools. Rich, for example, has concluded that the presence of more White students would raise standards for all students. It is not simply the *presence* of these students that would raise standards, however, but rather teachers' expectations of them. The issue he raises is one of teachers' perceptions as well as of student responsibilities. Even the percentage of Black teachers in a school may make a crucial difference (in his case, for instance, Rich feels that Black teachers have higher standards for Black students). By stressing what Michele Foster calls "the paradox of desegregation," that is, the contrast between the ideology and the reality of equal educational opportunity in desegregated schools, African American teachers help to challenge the status quo.[3] Yet, the number of teachers of color in public schools is diminishing.[4]

In Rich's case, we can see that the relationship among students, teachers, and communities can influence both student achievement and the perceptions they may have of themselves and their people. Organizational arrangements in schools such as tracking, discriminatory disciplinary policies, and testing can also have an impact. All of these factors in combination may send damaging messages to young people about themselves, their families, and their cultural groups.

Rich has benefited academically from school, but in the process he has picked up some disabling messages: that Blacks are lazy, unproductive, and too ready to take "the easy way out." Rich has no doubt had experiences in his own community that reinforce these perceptions, but by presenting the problem in such broad strokes, it becomes an indictment not against *particular* Blacks but against Blacks *as a class*. Rich has learned to "blame the victim," although he himself becomes one of them.

The issue is not this simple, however. Although Rich may be demonstrating some negative perceptions of his community, he is also tremendously proud of his culture: He loves gospel music and is involved in his church; he wants to "build solid foundations" for future generations; and most important, he feels that Blacks can take control of their lives ("I believe we can do something about it as Blacks"). His ideas are influenced by expectations from schools and society and point to their complex role in helping young people develop their self-concepts.

The issue of Black self-esteem has been studied by many scholars. Research by William Cross on African American identity may help us to understand the many and seemingly contradictory statements made by Rich about his culture, family, and teachers. Cross points out that diversity is at the very core of Black psychology. Although most African Americans have healthy personalities, they may have different ideologies. Cross also challenges the view that "Negro self-hatred" is a thoroughly documented finding or that it explains everything. He proposes that it is a complex, layered, multidimensional construct. In what he calls "The Pre-Encounter Stage" of Black identity, Cross describes several characteristics and attitudes that are clearly evident in Rich: social stigma attitudes (race is seen as a problem or stigma); anti-Black attitudes (a "blame the victim" prism); and spotlight, or race image, anxiety (anxiety about being "too Black," and hence too conspicuous).[5] This anxiety is evident when Rich talks about Blacks being loud or not taking care of their property. Cross points out what is apparent in Rich: "A great deal of pain and sorrow can be associated with such behaviors."[6]

The role of parents and family in building strong character and motivating children to succeed in school is equally important. Rich's mother and siblings have provided strong motivation for him to succeed and go on to higher education. But Rich's mother is not unlike other parents in this regard. What makes her different is that *she knows how to help her children get the education they need.* Because she herself went to college, albeit several years after graduating from high school, she is convinced that a college education is necessary to her children's welfare. Her involvement with her children's education, starting with elementary school, is evident every step of the way. Rich talks of how instrumental she was in keeping him in the advanced class. He also complains, although lovingly, that she is too "bossy." She came from an economically oppressed family, and she learned the hard lesson of the value of an education and passed it on to her children. The fact that she may have been poor or that she is a single parent have not been viewed by her as insurmountable roadblocks.

These family lessons are not always easy to teach. In fact, some of them run counter to the reality that Rich confronts every day and that he will continue to face in the future. The role that a strong family takes on in teaching its children to struggle against societal constraints becomes much more crucial in the lives of students like Rich, who must constantly buck the tide of low expectations and negative images.

Rich Miller is, like all of us, a product both of his environment and of his own doing. He has learned about his worth and about the value of an education from his mother. He has learned about his culture from his family and his church. He has learned about the expectations of Blacks from his teachers and from society in general. And he has learned the important lesson that "self-respect is one gift that you give yourself." We are left with the portrait of a young man who defies easy categorization and who challenges us as educators to look beyond stereotypes of students, their families, and communities for the more subtle but complex issues that help explain student achievement.

TO THINK ABOUT

1. What does Rich Miller mean when he says, "Self-respect is one gift that you give yourself"?
2. What do you think has helped Rich become a successful student?
3. How is Rich's determination to get ahead apparent to you? How might it be related to his criticisms of other Blacks?
4. Rich says that most teachers "just pass out the work, you do the work, pass it in, get a grade, good-bye." What are the implications for teachers? How might you design curriculum to appeal to Rich?
5. Think of some of the Black students you teach or have known. How are they different from Rich? How are they the same? What did you learn from reading this case study?

Case Study: Vanessa Mattison

"A good education is like growing, expanding your mind and your views."

Vanessa Mattison[1] is 17 years old and European American, and her family has been in the United States for generations. Vanessa lives in a small, rural hill town in western New England, but she has had a number of experiences that have helped make her far more worldly than others in her circumstances. By 17, she had traveled to Africa, the Caribbean, and Mexico. Her travels opened her eyes to some of the realities beyond Welborn Hills, the town where she lives.

Welborn Hills is a small community made up of several diverse groups of people: farming families, who have lived in the area for generations; more educated and liberal families who have come from urban areas; and working-class families, who make their living in the retail and light industry of the surrounding towns and small cities. Although Vanessa's family does not fit neatly into any category, it is probably closest to the second group. For example, they read not only *Newsweek* but also *Greenpeace;* they are vegetarians; they listen to Bob Dylan, Joan Baez, and reggae and blues music; and they have traveled from time to time. A number of the other families from Welborn Hills routinely travel outside the United States, but others have never even been to Boston or New York, both just a few hours away by car. In the town's only elementary school, as well as in the regional secondary school that the town's students attend, the class conflict between the more liberal and educated families and the families that have lived here for generations is almost palpable.

Only a tiny minority of the residents of Welborn Hills are people of color. The same is true of Hills Regional High School, a grades 7 to 12 school with a population of approximately 700 students, which serves a number of rural towns including Welborn Hills. For many of the European American students, access to understanding cultural differences and to meeting and being friends with people different from themselves depends on class and educational privilege. Only students who have had the privilege of traveling—as Vanessa has—have any inkling of the influence of racism or cultural differences on those different from themselves. Both their social class background and rural, White New England culture have influenced their perceptions of people of other cultures.

Currently taking classes in Spanish, calculus, sociology, humanities, art, and "contemporary problems," Vanessa is in an academic track. She is looking forward to being the first in her family to go to college and is successful and engaged in school. She is socially active, involved in sports, and quite self-confident and open to new ideas. She has many friends, both male and female, from a variety of cultural backgrounds. She enjoys spending time with her friends and describes a good time as laughing and talking with them. Very soft-spoken and thoughtful in all her replies, Vanessa has deeply held beliefs about the value of all people, peace, social justice, and environmental issues.

At present, there are just three people at home: Vanessa and her parents. Her sister, age 21, lives in a nearby town. Her father, who was raised in this area, is a craftsperson; her mother is a paralegal. Although both parents finished high school, neither went to college. Vanessa sees her family as different from others because her parents are still together and everyone is happy and gets along. She takes pride in the fact that her parents stand up for what they believe in. At the time she was interviewed, their courage of conviction was taking the shape of protest against the Gulf War, which had just begun. Vanessa and her family live in a modest home and are economically lower middle class. She works after school in a local store.

Having never needed to identify ethnically or racially because she has always been considered the "norm," it became clear from the outset that Vanessa was embarrassed and uncomfortable with the issue of self-identification and culture. In spite of her probable greater awareness of culture and cultural differences than the majority of her peers, it nevertheless was a difficult issue for her. She did want to grapple with it, however. In fact, she agreed to be interviewed precisely because the project sounded "interesting and important," and she made time for it in her busy schedule. Discomfort with issues of cultural, racial, and linguistic differences is the major theme that emerged with Vanessa. The other issues focused on the promise, sometimes unfulfilled, of education and on what teachers can do to make school more fun for students.

The Discomfort of Differences

[*How do you describe yourself?*]: I generally don't. . . . Wait, can you explain that? Like, what do you want to know?

Well, I would [describe myself as White], but it doesn't matter to me, so that's why I said it's a tough question. 'Cause I usually just describe myself as like what I believe in or something like that. Rather than like what culture I am, whether I'm Black or White. 'Cause that doesn't matter.

[I'm]. . . well, Scottish, French, and German, I guess. My family all speak English at home, though I'm taking Spanish. I guess I'm middle class or lower class. It depends on how you think of it. I guess the German part might have come in the twentieth century. I'm not really sure, that's just a general guess. . . . I wasn't really interested. I don't really know if we have that many connections back to who was where when and what happened.

I don't have any [religious beliefs]. I've never gone to church. We never like read the Bible as a family or anything. I think both of my parents used to go to church. I think they were Catholic. . . . They probably didn't think it was as important to their life as the people who had wanted them to go. . . . I don't really know much about it. But if I had a choice, I probably wouldn't want to go to church because I think that I'd rather formulate my own ideas than being told that the earth was created in seven days and God did this and He did this. I don't know, He seems like just too almighty of a person to me. I just don't believe it.

I guess obviously I just made it seem like [culture] wasn't [important]. It's just that like all the stuff that's happened to people because of their culture, like the slaves and Jewish people. Culture, what you look like, whether you're

Black or White could matter less to me. It's the person who you are. . . it's not what your appearance depicts.

The American society has always been. . . you had more opportunities and stuff. But I don't really see that as good 'cause it's not fair. You have more opportunities and just more of an equal chance. But I guess "equal" can't really be used there. Less of a struggle.

I don't think it's fair. I don't think that one person should have an easier time just because of the color of their skin, or their race, or 'cause they belong to a particular church or something.

People like Blacks still don't have as many rights as the White man. I'm saying "man" because women don't have their rights either. The "superiority game. . . " 'Cause people just have it stuck in their head that that's the way it is and. . . I don't really know how to change it. I try and change it, speak out against it.

[Other cultures] are not that well represented [in my school] because there's not that many people who live around here. The majority is probably White. But they're represented in a small margin. . . . We've read books and we've seen movies. I think we saw part of the freedom marches in the South and stuff like that. And we saw *Gandhi,* although that isn't really to this culture.

Each of us that go there is important to our school because it adds what you could say would be a *culture.* Just like our community, the school community. . . . Well, I guess people's backgrounds *do* [matter] because that's what makes them what they are.

[Culture] is like a conglomeration of language, the way you speak, the way you are. . . things that are important to you. . . . Well, the culture of the United States is kind of like norms, things that happen a lot. Like if you were to go to another country, it might strike you as weird because you don't do it at home that way.

Well, people in Central Africa, if you go into a store you need to say "hi" to the person who's working there and acknowledge them. Because if you don't acknowledge them, they're not going to acknowledge you and they won't help you, and that's really important to them. . . . Like when a woman has a child, they go off with their mother and their aunts and their sisters and stay with them for three months to start to raise the child. Which I don't know if I completely agree with, because it leaves the husband away and detaches him at the very start.

In Mexico, I was in a really big city, quite the change. There's lots of rules there about what women can wear. I know at one time, they couldn't wear shorts. I don't really think that's true anymore. It was weird. . . . The way people did things was really different. . . . Like in Central Africa, people sweep their houses and their yards every day, but then they'll just throw their junk right off the edge of their property. Which here, it's a little bit more discreet because you throw it at the dump.

I don't agree with a lot of our culture. I don't agree with how it's so rushed and how if you're Black, you're supposedly not as good or you're not as fit for the job or something like that. And if you're a woman, it's the same thing. And like you can't be gay without being put down. I don't know, there's all these underlying rules about if you're not this, you can't do that.

It seems weird. . . because people came over from Europe, and they wanted to get away from all the stuff that was over there. And then they came here and set up all the stuff like slavery, and I don't know, it seems the opposite of what they would have done. It was probably like burned into their head already from where they were: If you were lower class, then you usually weren't taught to read or educated. . . . They might not have come over thinking that's what they had in mind, but since that's what they had always known, that's what they did.

When I see racism, I often think that I wish I was Black or I wish I was the group that was being discriminated against. You know how some women say, "I hate men"? I don't know, but I'm sure that Black people said this, when they were slaves, like "I hate White people." I don't want to be thought of like that because I'm not against them. I think they're equal. And also after they've been put through so much awfulness, I think that every White person should be in their shoes.

Like [President] Bush says in his speech a little while ago that "We're doing all we can to fight racism" and blah, blah, blah, when the Supreme Court just made the ruling about schools and busing, which was basically turning back a decision they had made a long time ago.

When I was in second grade, there was somebody coming into our class who was going to be Black. He was like a new student and somebody said something about it, and me and a couple of my other friends got really mad at him. "It doesn't matter what color they are. They could be orange or yellow or brown. It doesn't matter, they're just a person."

For strength and inspiration, I usually look to Martin Luther King, Jr.

I like Gandhi too, because I believe in nonviolence. And I believe they helped to strengthen the basis for my belief and they gave specific examples of how it could work. I just believe in nonviolence as a way to get what you want and peace. I don't believe if you punch somebody, then, yeah, they may do what you want them to do, but they're not going to be doing it because they want to. They're just going to be doing it because of fear. I don't think fear is a good policy.

Education and Values

Supposedly education is what this country is built on, but there's no money for it.

Money is being cut out of all the schools. We lost a bunch of programs. We don't have as many teachers. We're going to lose more money, and it seems like the government's always promoting it as this great big deal. Then, where's the money for it? They're not supporting it. . . . They still have, for seventh and eighth grade, sewing and cooking and art. Music is still there, and sports was supported by the public this year through bottle drives and a big fund-fest. I don't know what's going to happen next year. I hope it's still supported.

[My parents] feel the same way, that the government needs to step in and help and that it's sad that it's going downhill. I think they think it's important to learn. Because they want me to be able to do what I want to do, and not, as I said before, get locked in a corner.

I've learned a lot of my morals [from my parents], like nonviolence and expressing myself, and striving for what I want, being able to have the confidence to reach what I want.

They're caring and they're willing to go against the norm. They're willing to protest, that's a good word for it, for what they believe in.

I think [Dad] values being able to survive on his own. Like moving away from your family and growing up and having your own job and supporting yourself and being able to get around, and not always having to have people do things for you. . . . He's fun and supportive.

[Mom] also strives for what her goals are and believes in self-support, working for what's yours.

[I would like] a little less pressure. . . like around college and school.

It's not a broken-up family. My parents are together and they're happy and there isn't any fighting. Everybody gets along. A lot of my friends [are from divorced families]. There's a lot of support that I don't see in other families. . . . We don't always go with the flow. You know, like most people supposedly right now are for the Gulf War. We're not, so we stand in the minority. . . . I personally don't believe in violence to solve things. I don't think that killing a zillion million people for oil is a good reason either. And you can't bring peace to somewhere that's not your culture and has a different government, and you especially can't do it through war. That's not going to solve things. And it would take a lot of talking and rearranging their entire society to get them to be like us, which I don't think is what they should be, 'cause they're not and they never have been and probably won't be. . . . People drive by the [peace] vigils and give us the finger.

[My parents want me to go to school] so I can be educated and get a job. So I can have options and not get stuck. . . . Probably because they didn't go to college and they'd like me to. That's just a guess.

[I want to] go to college to help people. I want to be a psychologist or do social work, work with the environment. I'm not sure. . . . There's a guidance counselor, but my parents have done more of that with college. I'm not sure what help I need.

I guess [grades are important] because they've kind of become that way. Once you get into the cycle of being in one place, you kind of stay there. . . . I think education is if you learn *personally*. That's not what the school thinks. It's not like if you get an A or an F, but if you learn. It's not just for the grades. . . . If I get grades that aren't real good, [my parents] are not real excited. And they always make sure that I'm doing my homework. They tell me to get off the phone.

I'm happy. Success is being happy to me, it's not like having a job that gives you a zillion dollars. It's just having self-happiness.

A good education is like when you personally learn something. . . . like growing, expanding your mind and your views.

Making School More Fun

[In elementary school I liked] recess, 'cause it was a break between doing stuff. Everything wasn't just pushed at you. And art, which was really fun. . . . It was a safe place and I liked the teachers and the people that went there. . . . I liked that on Valentine's Day and Christmas and birthdays they had [parties] for us. They mixed school and fun.

I did the work, I understood it, and I was interested.

My favorite [subject] is art because of the freedom to express myself, to paint and draw. Humanities is my worst 'cause it's just lectures and tests.

I play field hockey and I've done track and I've done tennis, because it's a way of releasing energy and feeling good about yourself and being in shape. And working with other people. . . . I play sports and I'm in a peer education group. It's a group of 18 seniors who set up programs to educate the other students in the school on issues like alcoholism, drunk driving, stereotyping, a bunch more. It's kind of like, since they're students and they're projecting to a student audience, it's easier for some people to relate.

We did a skit on [stereotyping]. We had jocks, hippies, snobs, burnouts, and a nerd. And we did these little scenarios like the snob liked this guy who was a hippie and all her friends were like, "Oh, my God! You like *him?!* He's such a hippie!" And then like the hippie friends said the same thing about the snob, and then like everything stopped and the two people who liked each other got up and said, "I wish my friends would understand. . . ." And then the person who was narrating said, "Well, here's one way in which the situation could be fixed." So they went back where they were and said, "Okay, yeah, well, I guess we should give them a chance." Most of the ideas came from us except for the one I just explained to you. Me and two other people basically wrote the whole skit. We just did it for the seventh and eighth grade. We thought that would be the most effective place 'cause that's where it basically starts. They liked it.

It's important for teachers to get to know all the students and know where they're coming from and why they may react a certain way to certain things because then it'll be easier to get through. And there won't be as many barriers because they'll already know. . . . Maybe if school didn't just start off on the first day with homework, maybe if it started off with just getting to know each other, even if you're in a class that's already known each other.

Have games, more free time. . . . You could have games that could teach anything that they're trying to teach through notes or lectures. Well, like if you're doing Spanish, you can play hangman or something. You can play word games where you have to guess the word. Like they give you a definition and it makes you remember the words. Or if somebody acts out a word, you remember it better than someone just looking it up or writing it down.

Make it more entertaining 'cause people learn a lot from entertainment. If you see a play, you'll probably remember it more than a lecture, if you see a movie, play a game, or something. Work those more into what they're doing. . . . I think that some books should be required just to show some points of view.

Some [teachers], based on [students'] reputation, may not be as patient with some people. [Students get reputations] basically through grades and troublemaking, like if you get in trouble with the system and get detentions.

[Unhelpful teachers are] ones that just kind of just move really fast, just trying to get across to you what they're trying to teach you. Not willing to slow down because they need to get in what they want to get in.

[Most teachers] are really caring and supportive and are willing to share their lives and are willing to listen to mine. They don't just want to talk about what they're teaching you; they also want to know you.

COMMENTARY

Coming face-to-face with racial, class, cultural, and other differences was diffi-cult for Vanessa because she had not often needed to consider these things. One gets the sense that for her, "culture," "ethnicity," and "race" are what *other* peo-ple have and Vanessa sometimes seemed offended at having to talk about them. It was almost as if it were rude to broach questions of race and culture, that dis-cussing them meant you were a racist. In this, Vanessa is similar to other young people of European descent: In one study assessing the salience of identity for young people of various backgrounds, the researcher found that most African American, Mexican American, and Asian American youngsters rated ethnicity as important to their identity, but only one quarter of White students did.[2]

Vanessa took the approach that cultural and racial differences are not sig-nificant, that it "couldn't matter less to me." In this, she is simply reflecting the value of being color-blind, which we all have been led to believe is both right and fair. In this framework, differences are seen as a *deficit* rather than as an *asset.*[3] Being White and Christian, she rarely has been confronted with her cul-tural identity. She considers herself the "norm," "just a person." As is the case for most White Americans, she has the privilege of seeing herself as just an indi-vidual, an opportunity not generally afforded to those from dominated groups.

Because Vanessa, as well as others from dominant (and dominating) groups, associates culture, race, and other differences with oppression and inequality, the subject becomes difficult to address. For one, she sees cultural and other differences as *causing* oppression ("like all the stuff that happened to people because of their culture, like the slaves and the Jewish people"). For another, she is offended by the unfairness with which differences are treated: The fact that some people are penalized for being who they are, while others are rewarded for it, makes it difficult for her to confront differences.[4] Not wanting to benefit from racism, Vanessa finds it easier to avoid or downplay the issue. Her growing awareness of sexism, revealed through comments such as, "I'm saying 'man' 'cause women don't have their rights either" may help her make the connection between the two issues.[5]

Vanessa is struggling to understand the contradictions between the ideals she has been taught and the discrimination she sees around her. She is beginning to forge links among issues such as peace, social justice, and racism and other biases. Although she associates herself with her race only when confronted with the example of other White people being racist, it is at such times that Vanessa sees clearly the need for Whites to stand up and take responsibility. She also understands that being White means having more opportunities, which she resents as unfair.

Through dialogue with Vanessa, it became clear that few of these issues have ever been addressed in any of her classes. When asked if she learns history and other subject matter in school from the perspectives of different groups of people, she answered that everything was taught from what she called "a general perspective." Because the viewpoints of others are invisible in the curriculum, students begin to think of the one reality that is taught as the "general" reality, whereas the experiences of others become little more than ethnic add-ons to "real" knowledge.

In spite of her lack of awareness of diverse perspectives, Vanessa is becoming keenly aware of and committed to social issues. For example, she says that she speaks out against discriminatory statements and in that way tries to change things. This quality was already apparent in second grade. Even in that incident, however, she and her friends thought that by *overlooking* racial differences, they would be helping the new boy in class. Being color-blind was, in their understanding, the moral imperative.

Vanessa is quite involved in a peer education group and has taken the issues of drug abuse, alcoholism, and others seriously. To make the skits they developed for young audiences more accessible to their experiences, they centered on social class types in the school (e.g., "nerds," "hippies") rather than race or culture.

Vanessa believes that education should be a major priority in our society if we want to give all students an equal education; yet she is aware that the societal commitment simply is not there. The promise of education for advancement and rewards is important but "not as important as society makes out," she is quick to add. "They want me to go and I have to," she says, supporting the idea that although education is compulsory it often is not engaging. Related to the value of education are the other values that Vanessa has learned from her parents: self-reliance, self-confidence, and independent thought. These values obviously have helped her develop her own persona in a school setting that may be both conformist and conservative.

The role that her parents play in supporting her personal choices and her academic success is very clear. Vanessa's parents value education beyond high school for their daughter, understanding very well that it will give her options they themselves did not have. They are involved in school activities (her mother served on the local school committee, and both parents have volunteered time to the schools) and have demonstrated their concerns in many other ways as well. Their involvement, in Vanessa's words, "shows that they care."

Vanessa sees education as crucial, but she is not getting as much out of it as she thinks she should. She wishes it were more interesting and interactive. Her perceptions on the boring and "flat" nature of schooling, especially at the secondary level, corroborate what has been found concerning many schools around the United States,[6] and her suggestions for teachers emphasize making school more entertaining and fun for all students. She is particularly concerned about students who want to drop out because they feel so disconnected from school. In relation to this, Vanessa also suggests that clubs, sports, and other activities be continued. She is dismayed that so many of these activities have been removed because of budgetary constraints. In her own case, involvement in a school club and in several sports, as well as her part-time job, seems to have helped her develop in more than just academic ways.

A strong and forthright young woman with deeply held values and beliefs, Vanessa Mattison views education as a vital part of every person's growth and development. Although still uncomfortable with issues of diversity in any comprehensive way, she is committed to struggling with them. The interviews themselves seemed to have served as a catalyst to her thinking more extensively about diversity, racism, and identity. For example, after thinking about how *unimportant* race and culture are to her, she quietly admitted, "Well, I guess people's backgrounds *do* [matter] because that's what makes them what they are." Given the strength and support of her family, her searching soul, and her grounding in peace and social justice, she is a wonderful example of a young person ready to, in her words, "expand my mind and my views."

TO THINK ABOUT

1. Why do you think that White people in the United States in general do not identify with any particular racial or ethnic group? Who might be exceptions?
2. What kinds of school experiences might have made Vanessa more comfortable with diversity?
3. As a teacher, what is your responsibility in introducing your students to diversity? What strategies and activities might you use? How would these differ in a primarily White school from a more culturally and racially heterogeneous school?
4. What is the role of values in education? Should schools teach values? Why or why not? Would some of the values that Vanessa's family believes be included? Why or why not?
5. Vanessa gave several suggestions to make school more entertaining and fun. What do you think of these? Do they contradict the purpose of school?
6. In a group, develop suggestions for teachers that would make school more interesting and engaging for students. Focus on a particular grade level and subject area.

● *NOTES TO CHAPTER 3*

1. According to Tove Skutnabb-Kangas, *linguicism* can be defined as "ideologies and structures which are used to legitimate, effectuate and reproduce an unequal division of power and resources (both material and non-material) between groups which are defined on the basis of language (on the basis of their mother tongues)." See "Multilingualism and the Education of Minority Children." In *Minority Education: From Shame to Struggle,* edited by Tove Skutnabb-Kangas and Jim Cummins (Clevedon, England: Multilingual Matters, 1988), 13.

2. Gordon Allport, *The Nature of Prejudice* (Reading, MA: Addison-Wesley, 1954), 52.

3. See, for example, Stephen Jay Gould, *The Mismeasure of Man* (New York: Norton, 1981), for a history of racism in intelligence measurement; Joel Spring in *The American School, 1642–1993,* 3rd ed.(New York: McGraw Hill, 1994) does a good review of racial thought in the eighteenth and nineteenth centuries.

4. Beverly Daniel Tatum, "Talking about Race, Learning about Racism: The Application of Racial Identity Development Theory in the Classroom," *Harvard Educational Review,* 62, 1 (Spring 1992), 6.

5. Meyer Weinberg, "Introduction." In *Racism in the United States: A Comprehensive Classified Bibliography,* compiled by Meyer Weinberg (New York: Greenwood Press, 1990), xii–xiii.

6. Weinberg, *Racism in the United States.*

7. Weinberg, *Racism in the United States.* See also the history of segregated schooling by Spring in *The American School* and the documentation of educational discrimination against Mexican Americans in Rubén Donato, *The Other Struggle for Equal Schools* (New York: State University of New York Press, 1997); for the history of educational discrimination against Native Americans, see Donna Deyhle and Karen Swisher, "Research in American Indian and Alaska Native Education: From Assimilation to Self-Determination." In Michael W. Apple, ed. *Review of Research in Education,* v. 22. (Washington, DC: American Educational Research Association, 1997); for the history of gender-segregated schooling, see Myra Sadker and David Sadker, *Failing at Fairness: How America's Schools Cheat Girls* (New York: Charles Scribner's Sons, 1994).

8. For example, Gary Orfield and his associates found that the period from 1991–1994 saw the largest backward movement toward segregation for Blacks since the 1954 *Brown* v. *Topeka Board of Education* decision. They also reported that Latino students have become the most segregated of all groups. See Gary Orfield, Mark D. Bachmeier, David R. James, and Tamela Eitle, *Deepening Segregation in America's Public Schools* (Cambridge, MA: Harvard University Project of School Desegregation, 1997). See also *Latino Youths at a Crossroads* (Washington, DC: Children's Defense Fund, 1990); and Richard R. Valencia, ed., *Chicano School Failure and Success: Research and Policy Agendas for the 1990s* (London: Falmer Press, 1991).

9. Linda Darling-Hammond, *The Right to Learn: A Blueprint for Creating Schools That Work* (San Francisco: Jossey-Bass Publishers, 1997).

10. See, for example, Caroline Hodges Persell, "Social Class and Educational Equality." In *Multicultural Education: Issues and Perspectives,* 3rd ed., edited by James A. Banks and Cherry A. McGee Banks (Boston: Allyn & Bacon, 1997); Jeannie Oakes, Amy Stuart Wells, Makeba Jones, and Amanda Datnow. "Detracking: The Social Construction of Ability, Cultural Politics, and Resistance to Reform." *Teachers*

College Record, 98, 3 (1997), 482–510.; and Carol Ascher and Gary Burnett, *Current Trends and Issues in Urban Education* (New York: ERIC Clearinghouse on Urban Education, Teachers College, Columbia University, 1993).

11. Cited by Ray P. McDermott, "The Cultural Context of Learning to Read." In *Papers in Applied Linguistics: Linguistics and Reading Series 1,* edited by Stanley F. Wanat (Washington, DC: Center for Applied Linguistics, 1977).

12. Myra Sadker and David Sadker, *Failing at Fairness.*

13. Patricia Gándara, *Over the Ivy Walls: The Educational Mobility of Low-Income Chicanos* (Albany, NY: State University of New York Press, 1995).

14. See Donna Y. Ford, *Reversing Underachievement Among Gifted Black Students: Promising Practices and Programs* (New York: Teachers College Press, 1996); Eugene E. García, "Educating Mexican American Students: Past Treatment and Recent Developments in Theory, Research, Policy, and Practice" and Sonia Nieto, "A History of the Education of Puerto Rican Students in U.S. Mainland Schools: 'Losers,' 'Outsiders,' or 'Leaders'?" Both in James A. Banks and Cherry A. McGee Banks (eds.), *Handbook of Research on Multicultural Education* (New York: Macmillan, 1995).

15. Deborah Meier, *The Power of Their Ideas: Lessons for America From a Small School in Harlem* (Boston: Beacon Press, 1995).

16. See the extensive report issued by the Wellesley College Center for Research on Women, *How Schools Shortchange Girls: The AAUW Report* (Washington, DC: American Association of University Women Educational Foundation, 1992); and Sadker and Sadker, *Failing at Fairness.*

17. Ibid.

18. Ellen Brantlinger, *The Politics of Social Class in Secondary School: Views of Affluent and Impoverished Youth.* (New York: Teachers College Press, 1993).

19. National Center for Education Statistics, *Dropout Rates in the United States: 1993.* (U.S. Department of Education, 1993).

20. Persell, "Social Class and Educational Equality."

21. Samuel Bowles and Herbert Gintis, *Schooling in Capitalist America: Educational Reform and the Contradictions of Economic Life* (New York: Basic Books, 1976).

22. Jonathan Kozol, *Savage Inequalities: Children in America's Schools* (New York: Crown Publishers, 1991). Also see Carol Ascher and Gary Burnett, *Current Trends and Issues in Urban Education.*

23. Angela R. Taylor, "Social Competence and the Early School Transition: Risk and Protective Factors for African-American Children," *Education and Urban Society,* 24, 1 (November 1991), 15–26.

24. Laurie Olsen, *Crossing the Schoolhouse Border: Immigrant Students and the California Public Schools* (San Francisco: California Tomorrow, 1988).

25. Mary Poplin and Joseph Weeres, *Voices from the Inside: A Report on Schooling from Inside the Classroom* (Claremont, CA: The Institute for Education in Transformation, Claremont Graduate School, 1992).

26. Karen B. McLean Donaldson, *Through Students' Eyes: Combating Racism in United States Schools* (Westport, CT: Praeger Publishers, 1996).

27. Marietta Saravia-Shore and Herminio Martínez, "An Ethnographic Study of Home/School Role Conflicts of Second Generation Puerto Rican Adolescents." In *Cross-Cultural Literacy: Ethnographies of Communication in Multiethnic Classrooms,* edited by Marietta Saravia-Shore and Steven F. Arvizu (New York: Garland Publishers, 1992), 242.

28. Virginia Vogel Zanger, "Academic Costs of Social Marginalization: An Analysis of Latino Students' Perceptions at a Boston High School." In *The Education of Latino Students in Massachusetts: Research and Policy Considerations,* edited by Ralph Rivera and Sonia Nieto (Boston: Gastón Institute, 1993).

29. Donaldson, *Through Students' Eyes.*

30. Nitza M. Hidalgo, *"Free Time, School Is Like a Free Time": Social Relations in City High School Classes.* (Unpublished Doctoral Dissertation, Graduate School of Education, Harvard University, 1991) 95.

31. See, for example, Fine, *Framing Dropouts*; Christine E. Sleeter, "White Racism." *Multicultural Education,* 1, 4 (Spring, 1994), 5–8, 39; and Frances E. Kendall, *Diversity in the Classroom: New Approaches to the Education of Young Children,* 2nd ed. (New York: Teachers College Press, 1996).

32. Alice McIntyre, "Constructing an Image of a White Teacher." *Teachers College Press,* 98, 4 (Summer, 1997), 653–681.

33. Karen B. McLean Donaldson, "Antiracist Education and a Few Courageous Teachers." *Equity and Excellence in Education,* 30, 2 (September, 1997), 31–38.

34. Julie E. Wollman-Bonilla, "Outrageous Viewpoints: Teachers' Criteria for Rejecting Works of Children's Literature." *Language Arts,* 75, 4 (April, 1998), 287–295.

35. Ellen Bigler, *American Conversations: Puerto Ricans, White Ethnics, and Multicultural Education* (Philadelphia: Temple University Press, 1999).

36. Kathe Jervis, "'How Come There Are No Brothers on That List?': Hearing the Hard Questions All Children Ask." *Harvard Educational Review,* 66, 3 (Fall, 1996), 546–576.

37. Ibid., p. 573.

38. Robert Merton, "The Self-Fulfilling Prophecy." *Antioch Review,* 8 (1948), 193–210.

39. Robert Rosenthal and Lenore Jacobson, *Pygmalion in the Classroom* (New York: Holt, Rinehart & Winston, 1968).

40. See, for instance, Richard E. Snow, "Unfinished Pygmalion." *Contemporary Psychology,* 14 (1969), 197–200; Samuel S. Wineburg, "The Self-Fulfillment of the Self-Fulfilling Prophecy: A Critical Appraisal." *Educational Researcher,* 16, 9 (December 1987), 28–37; Robert Rosenthal, "Pygmalion Effects: Existence, Magnitude, and Social Importance." *Educational Researcher,* 16, 9 (December 1987), 37–44; Jacquelynne Eccles and Lee Jussim, "Teacher Expectations II: Construction and Reflection of Student Achievement." *Journal of Personality and Social Psychology,* 63, 6 (December 1992), 947–961.

41. Ray C. Rist, "Student Social Class and Teacher Expectations: The Self-Fulfilling Prophecy in Ghetto Education." In *Challenging the Myths: The Schools, the Blacks, and the Poor,* Reprint Series no. 5 (Cambridge, MA: Harvard Educational Review, 1971).

42. See the review of this research in Persell, "Social Class and Educational Equality."

43. Diane Pollard, "A Profile of Underclass Achievers." *Journal of Negro Education,* 58 (1989), 297–308.

44. Francisco A. Ríos, "Teachers' Principles of Practice for Teaching in Multicultural Classrooms." In *Teaching Thinking in Cultural Contexts,* by Francisco A. Ríos, ed. (Albany, NY: State University of New York Press, 1996).

45. Bram A. Hamovitch, "Socialization Without Voice: An Ideology of Hope for At-Risk Students." *Teachers College Record,* 98, 2 (Winter, 1996), 286–306, p. 302.

46. Kenneth Zeichner, "Educating Teachers To Close the Achievement Gap: Issues of Pedagogy, Knowledge, and Teacher Preparation." In *Closing the Achievement Gap:*

A Vision to Guide Changes in Beliefs and Practice by the Urban Education National Network (Washington, DC: United Stated Department of Education, Office of Educational Research and Improvement, 1995).

47. Martin Haberman, "Selecting 'Star' Teachers for Children and Youth in Urban Poverty." *Phi Delta Kappan,* 76, 10 (June, 1995), 777–781.

48. Rosa Hernandez Sheets, "From Remedial to Gifted: Effects of Culturally Centered Pedagogy." *Theory into Practice,* 34, 3 (Summer, 1995), 186–193.

49. Rubén G. Rumbaut, "The Crucible Within: Ethnic Identity, Self-Esteem, and Segmented Assimilation Among Children of Immigrants." In *Origins and Destinies: Immigration, Race, and Ethnicity in America,* edited by Silvia Pedraza and Rubén G. Rumbaut (Belmont, CA: Wadsworth Publishing Co., 1996).

50. Claude M. Steele, "Race and the Schooling of Black Americans." *The Atlantic Monthly* (April 1992), 68–78.

51. Ibid., p. 77.

52. Ibid., p. 77

53. Claude Goldenberg, "The Limits of Expectations: A Case for Case Knowledge About Teacher Expectancy Effects." *American Educational Research Journal,* 29, 3 (Fall 1992), 514–544.

54. As quoted in the *Newsletter* of the Tomás Rivera Center, 2, 4 (Fall 1989), 9.

55. Carolyn Hodges Persell, "Social Class and Educational Equality."

56. Denny Taylor and Catherine Dorsey-Gaines, *Growing Up Literate: Learning from Inner-City Families* (Portsmouth, NH: Heinemann, 1988).

57. David Hartle-Schutte, "Literacy Development in Navajo Homes: Does It Lead to Success in School?" *Language Arts,* 70, 8 (December 1993), 643–654.

58. Kofi Lomotey, ed., *Going to School: The African-American Experience* (Albany, NY: State University of New York Press, 1990), 9.

59. See Richard J. Murnane and Emiliana Vega, "The Nation's Teaching Force." *Teachers College Record,* 99, 1 (Fall, 1997), 36–41.

60. Michael B. Katz, *Class, Bureaucracy, and the Schools: The Illusion of Educational Change in America* (New York: Praeger, 1975).

61. John Dewey, *Democracy and Education* (New York: Free Press, 1916).

62. David Tyack, "Schooling and Social Diversity: Historical Reflections." In Willis D. Hawley and Anthony W. Jackson, eds. *Toward a Common Destiny: Improving Race and Ethnic Relations in America* (San Francisco: Jossey Bass Publishers, 1995), 4.

NOTES TO LINDA HOWARD'S CASE STUDY

1. I appreciate the work of Paula Elliott in conducting and analyzing the extensive interviews that were the basis for this case study. Paula is a teacher educator whose research interests focus on the experiences of educators of color in preservice and inservice programs that explicitly address racism, racial identity development, and the process of teaching and learning.

2. Linda Levine, "'Who Says?': Learning to Value Diversity in School." In *Celebrating Diverse Voices: Progressive Education and Equity,* edited by Frank Pignatelli and Susanna W. Pflaum (Newbury Park, CA: Corwin Press, 1993).

3. Marta I. Cruz-Janzen, *Curriculum and the Self-concept of Biethnic and Biracial Persons.* (Unpublished doctoral dissertation, College of Education, University of Denver, April, 1997).

4. Joel Williamson, *New People: Miscegenation and Mulattos in the United States* (New York: Free Press, 1980).

5. Robin Lin Miller and Mary Jane Rotheram-Borus, "Growing Up Biracial in the United States." In *Race, Ethnicity, and Self: Identity in Multicultural Perspective,* edited by Elizabeth Pathy Salett and Diane R. Koslow (Washington, DC: National Multicultural Institute, 1994).

6. Williamson, *New People.*

7. Horace Mann Bond, "Two Racial Islands in Alabama," *American Journal of Sociology,* 36 (1930–1931), 554.

8. Rita J. Simon and Howard Alstein, *Transracial Adoptees and Their Families* (New York: Praeger, 1987); Miller and Rotheram-Borus, "Growing Up Biracial;" and Gigi Kaeser and Peggy Gillespie, *Of Many Colors: Portraits of Multiracial Families* (Amherst, MA: University of Massachusetts Press, 1997).

9. Miller and Rotheram-Borus, "Growing Up Biracial," 148. Other good resources on the topic of biracial children and adults is *Black, White, Other: Biracial Americans Talk About Race and Identity* by Lise Funderburg (New York: William Morrow & Co., 1994); Kaeser and Gillespie, *Of Many Colors.*

10. Kaeser and Gillespie, *Of Many Colors,* 137.

11. Miller and Rotheram-Borus, "Growing Up Biracial."

NOTES TO RICH MILLER'S CASE STUDY

1. I am grateful to Paula Elliott for doing the interviews with Rich and providing me with many insights about his case.

2. For more data on this phenomenon, see Ford, *Reversing Underachievement Among Gifted Black Students.*

3. Michele Foster, "The Politics of Race: Through the Eyes of African-American Teachers," in *What Schools Can Do: Critical Pedagogy and Practice,* edited by Kathleen Weiler and Candace Mitchell (Albany, NY: State University of New York Press, 1992).

4. Ibid.; see also *Diversity in Teacher Education: New Expectations,* edited by Mary E. Dilworth (San Francisco: Jossey-Bass Publishers, 1992).

5. William E. Cross, Jr., *Shades of Black: Diversity in African-American Identity* (Philadelphia: Temple University Press, 1991).

6. Ibid., 195.

NOTES TO VANESSA MATTISON'S CASE STUDY

1. I am grateful to Maya Gillingham for the interviews and the background for Vanessa's case study. At the time of the interviews, Maya was completing her undergraduate degree at the University of Massachusetts. She is currently a massage therapist and also an educator in massage therapy and health education in the San Francisco Bay area.

2. See Jean D. Phinney, "A Three-Stage Model of Ethnic Identity Development in Adolescence." In *Ethnic Identity Formation and Transmission Among Hispanics and Other Minorities,* edited by Martha E. Bernal and George P. Knight (Albany, NY: State University of New York Press, 1993).

3. For a more detailed discussion of this topic, see Sonia Nieto, "We Speak in Many Tongues: Linguistic Diversity and Multicultural Education." In *Multicultural*

Education for the Twenty-first Century, edited by Carlos F. Díaz (Washington, DC: National Education Association, 1992).

4. See Beverly Daniel Tatum, *"Why Are All the Black Kids Sitting Together in the Cafeteria?" and other Conversations About Race* (New York: HarperCollins, 1997).

5. See Peggy McIntosh, *White Privilege and Male Privilege: A Personal Account of Coming to See Correspondences through Work in Women's Studies,* Working Paper no. 189 (Wellesley, MA: Wellesley College Center for Research on Women, 1988).

6. See, for example, Patricia Phelan, Ann Locke Davidson, and Hanh Cao Yu, *Adolescents' Worlds: Negotiating Family, Peers, and School* (New York: Teachers College Press, 1998).

chapter 4

Structural and Organizational Issues in Schools

Many years ago, John Dewey warned that "Democracy cannot flourish where the chief influences in selecting subject matter of instruction are utilitarian ends narrowly conceived for the masses, and, for the higher education of the few, the traditions of a specialized cultivated class."[1] As Dewey feared, our public schools, as currently organized, are not fulfilling the promise of democracy. Certain school policies and practices exacerbate the inequality that exists in society.

Ironically, some of these policies and practices have evolved in an attempt to deal more equitably with student diversity. This is true of tracking, which often is meant to help those students most in academic need. Others are so integral to the schooling experience that they are hardly disputed; this is the case with traditional pedagogy and the compartmentalization of knowledge, especially at the secondary school level. Some may not be official policies at all but unquestioned practices that can lead to disempowerment. This is the case with the limited roles that teachers, students, and parents have in school.

In the case studies that follow this chapter, you will see other examples of organizational practices and policies that can harm students. Avi Abrahamson, for example, was adamant that teachers' pedagogy can either motivate or turn off students. For Fern Sherman, the content of the curriculum sometimes made her feel alienated and angry. As these cases demonstrate, all school policies and practices need to be critically evaluated if we are serious about developing the kind of public education that Dewey deemed necessary.

It is legitimate to ask how structural and organizational issues such as school policies and practices are related to multicultural education. When multicultural education is thought of as simple additions of ethnic content to the traditional curriculum, a discussion of school policies and practices may seem irrelevant. But when thought about comprehensively, multicultural education questions the total context of education, including curriculum, student placement, physical structure of schools, pedagogical strategies, assumptions about student ability, hiring of staff, and parent involvement, among other issues. In this sense, organizational structures are central to the development of a comprehensive multicultural education and the reason why they are considered in this chapter.

The following discussion provides classroom and school-based examples of policies and practices that may reinforce social inequities by inhibiting the educational success of some students. But because the focus is on the classroom and school rather than society, the impression may be that issues such as school governance and financing are not as important. On the contrary; they are all implicated in school failure. I urge you to keep these societal issues in mind to understand how they also directly influence inequities at the classroom and school levels.[2]

Each of the following will be briefly described and examined:

- Tracking
- Testing
- The curriculum
- Pedagogy
- Physical structure
- Disciplinary policies
- Limited role of students
- Limited role of teachers
- Limited family and community involvement

TRACKING

One of the most inequitable and, until recently, relatively undisputed practices in schools is tracking. *Tracking* is the placement of students into groups that are perceived to be of similar ability (*homogeneous groups*), within classes (e.g., reading groups in self-contained classes), or by subject areas (e.g., a low-level math group in seventh grade), or by specific programs of study at the high school level (e.g., academic or vocational).[3] In most schools, some kind of tracking is as much a part of school as are bells and recess. Tracking often begins at the very earliest grades.

In the classic study mentioned in Chapter 3 concerning teachers' expectations, Ray Rist reported on one class of poor Black children during their first three years of schooling. On the eighth day of school, the kindergarten teacher in this study classified the children into three groups that she placed at different tables. These groups remained almost intact two years later.[4] Of all the data used by the teacher to make grouping decisions, none related directly to academic ability. Instead, she used social indices such as information provided by preregistration forms, initial interviews with mothers, and her own prior knowledge of which families received public assistance. The results were also social: Most students at table 1 (the so-called high achievers) wore cleaner clothes that were relatively new and pressed, had no body odor, spoke more standard English, were generally lighter skinned, and were more likely to have processed (straightened) hair.

As we can see, grouping decisions are often made on tenuous grounds. Furthermore, research over many years has confirmed that tracking has frequently been linked with racial, ethnic, and social-class differences.[5] For example, the Massachusetts Advocacy Center found that in Boston public schools, African American, Latino, and some Asian students were most likely to be categorized by their supposed "deficits" in the early grades, whereas White and other Asian students were most likely to be placed in programs emphasizing their "abilities" or "gifts," especially after the elementary grades.[6] In a more recent study, Jeannie Oakes and Gretchen Guiton found similar results: In three high schools they studied, economically advantaged Whites and Asians had much greater access to high status and academically rigorous courses than Latinos *whose achievement was similar*.[7]

In middle schools also, tracking is implicated with race, ethnicity, and social class. A study by Jomills Braddock found that widespread whole-class tracking was particularly prevalent in middle schools with high concentrations of African American and Latino students.[8] Another study of the grouping policies of an urban middle school found that low-income students and students of color were almost always in the bottom tracks.[9]

What are the consequences of tracking? First, students at impossibly young ages are expected to make program choices that can virtually chart the course of their lives. As adolescents, some students must decide among vocational school, an academic track, a secretarial or "business" track, or what is sometimes called a "general" track. Through these choices, they may pursue a college education, a low-paying job, or almost certain joblessness. Young people of 13 or 14 years of age are hardly prepared to make such monumental decisions on their own, and most schools lack adequate staffs to help them. The families of many students may be unable to assist with these decisions, and students may base their choices on what their best friends do or on what is perceived as relevant by their peers.

Another consequence of tracking is that students develop enduring classroom personalities and attitudes. They may begin to believe that their placement in these groups is natural and a true reflection of whether they are "smart" or "dumb." Although students may feel that they themselves are deciding which courses to take, these decisions may actually have been made for them years before by the first teacher who placed them in the "Crows" rather than the "Blue Jays" reading group. The messages children internalize from grouping practices are probably more destructive than we realize, and their effects more long lasting than we care to admit.

Another result of tracking may be more subtle: In one study of 25 schools that tracked eighth and ninth graders according to ability, researchers found that the rates of student participation and discussion were higher in honors classes than in "regular" or remedial classes, thereby further contributing to the learning gaps between groups.[10] Researchers concluded that ability grouping divides students on social as well as cognitive characteristics.

Tracking leaves its mark on pedagogy as well. Students in the lowest levels, for example, are the most likely students to be subjected to rote memorization and worn methods, as their teachers often feel that these are the children who most need to master the "basics." Until the basics are learned, the thinking goes, creative methods are a frill that these students can ill afford. Poor children and those most alienated by the schools are once again the losers. The cycle of school failure is repeated: The students most in need are placed in the lowest level classes and exposed to the drudgery of drill and repetition, school becomes more boring and senseless every day, and the students become discouraged and drop out.

This is not to imply that students at the top ability levels always receive instruction that is uplifting, interesting, and meaningful. They too are exposed to similar methods and materials as those students at the bottom levels. But if innovative methods and appealing materials exist at all, they tend to be found at the top levels. Knowledge becomes yet another privilege of those who are already privileged.

The effectiveness of tracking is questionable. In her classic 1985 research study of 25 junior and senior high schools around the country, Jeannie Oakes found that the results of tracking were almost exclusively negative for most students. Many other studies since her research was first released have been consistent with this finding.[11] In a recent analysis, Oakes concluded that tracking as a practice is largely grounded in ideologies that maintain race and social class privilege.[12] If the purpose of tracking is to provide access to opportunity for those who most have been denied this access, it has failed badly. Actually, it has had the opposite effect.

Despite the extensive evidence that it does not work for most students, tracking is in place in most schools throughout the United States. Many educators sincerely believe that it helps to individualize instruction, that is, that it *promotes* equality. Although its effects may be contrary to its stated intended outcomes, tracking has been an immutable part of the culture of middle and secondary schools for many years. The culture of the school is resistant to change: Once an idea has taken hold, it seems to develop a life of its own, regardless of its usefulness or effectiveness. Moreover, schools respond poorly to pressure for change, particularly if it comes from those most jeopardized but least powerful.

If tracking were unanimously acknowledged as placing all students at risk, it would have been eliminated long ago. The truth is that powerful vested interests are crucial in explaining why tracking persists. Although tracking affects most students negatively, it may actually help a few. The evidence is mixed, but there is some indication that high-achieving students benefit from being tracked in honors and high-level classes. It is not surprising, then, that it is frequently the parents of high-achieving students who are most reluctant to challenge it because they perceive tracking to be beneficial to their children. In addition, as mentioned previously, tracking decisions and race are often linked. This was found to be the case in a three-year longitudinal case study by Oakes and her colleagues. In their review of 10 racially and socioeconomically mixed secondary schools participating in detracking reform, the researchers concluded that one of the greatest barriers to detracking was the resistance of powerful parents, most of whom were White. Through strategies such as threatening to remove their children from the school, the parents of students who traditionally benefited from tracking made detracking difficult if not impossible.[13]

As we have seen, tracking is propped up and sustained by class interests. Because it sorts and classifies students, it helps prepare them for their place in the larger society. Students in the top tracks generally end up attending college and becoming professionals; those in the bottom tracks frequently drop out or, if they do finish high school, become unskilled workers. Without falling into a mechanistic explanation for a complex process, it is nevertheless true that some students benefit and others lose because of tracking. Teachers and schools may compound the problem by seeing tracking as the only alternative to handling student differences and as a "natural" and even "neutral" practice.

However, grouping in and of itself is not always a negative practice. Good and experienced teachers have always understood that short-term and flexible grouping can be very effective in teaching a particular skill, or teaching intensively a missing piece of social studies or math or science. In fact, grouping in such instances can be effective in meeting temporary and specific ends. But because tracking is tied with and supported by particular classist and racist ideologies, grouping of any kind needs to be done with care.

What are the alternatives to tracking? One approach is to "detrack," but simple detracking will do little unless it is accompanied by a change in the school's culture and norms.[14] Detracking combined with strategies such as cooperative learning, peer tutoring, multilevel teaching, shared decision making with students, and de-emphasizing the use of textbooks, while challenging racist and classist notions of ability, can also result in inspired stories of improved learning and intergroup relations. Successes achieved with such strategies have been documented, and they provide a positive incentive for considering alternatives to tracking.[15]

Although students differ from one another in many ways, and such differences need to be understood in order to provide students with a high-quality education, tracking in and of itself has not proved to be the answer.

STANDARDIZED TESTING

Another practice that impedes equity in our schools is norm-referenced and standardized testing, particularly when used to sort students rather than to improve instruction. Originally designed to help identify mentally retarded children, the use of standardized tests expanded greatly after the beginning of the twentieth century. Influenced by the tremendous influx of new immigrants into the country at that time, the original aims of standardized tests were subverted to include rationalization of racist theories of genetic inferiority. An extensive review of how test use changed during this period is not called for here. But it should be pointed out that tests, particularly intelligence tests, have frequently been used as a basis for segregating and sorting students, principally those whose cultures and languages differ from the mainstream. Moreover, the relationship between IQ tests and repressive and racist social theories and policies is not a historical relic; even recent texts document this fact.[16]

Testing and tracking have often been symbiotically linked. Lewis Terman, a psychologist who experimented with intelligence tests at the turn of the twentieth century, was able to state with absolute conviction after testing just two Native American and Mexican children, "Their dullness seems to be racial, or at least inherent in the family stock from which they came. . . . Children of this group should be segregated in special classes . . . they cannot master abstractions, but they can often be made efficient workers."[17] The same reasoning was used on other occasions to "explain" the inferior intelligence of Blacks, Jews, and Italians; practically every new ethnic group to the United States has fared badly on standardized tests.[18]

The situation today is not as blatant, but the kind and number of standardized tests to which we continue to subject our students are staggering. FairTest, an organization that monitors the use of standardized testing, has conservatively estimated that about 100 million standardized tests are given to the 40 million students in our schools yearly. This is an average of 2.5 tests per student per year.[19] A decade ago, it was suggested that annual costs for developing and scoring tests under local and state mandates ran between 70 and 107 million dollars.[20] Given the tremendous increase in testing mandates since then, the amount is no doubt quite a bit more now. This is money that could be better spent on direct instruction and other support services for students.

Much of the standardized testing frenzy is a result of the educational reform movement of the 1980s and 1990s when "accountability" became a major buzz word. As a result, students' academic achievement was directly linked to their test scores. Yet in a 1996–1997 evaluation of standardized tests throughout the states, FairTest found that the testing programs in most states need a complete overhaul, or at least major improvements, to actually achieve what they claim to be doing.[21] Although most states claim that they use the results of tests to improve curriculum and pedagogy, the vast majority of states use predominantly multiple choice tests that may not achieve these aims.

Goals 2000, the federal education strategy to raise national standards, is also based on the dubious reasoning that more tests will somehow lead to more learning and higher standards.[22] A new and dizzying round of tests for all fourth-, eighth-, and twelfth-grade students in the nation in all five core subjects is proposed, with standards developed by an appointed National Education Goals Panel. The plan has focused little attention, however, on changes in curriculum or instructional practices, or on improvements in teacher education.

A concern for equity is a common reason cited for "high stakes" testing, that is, for linking test scores to the success of schools, teachers, and students. Certainly equity is a significant concern because, as we have seen, schools for poor children of diverse backgrounds are often inferior in quality. However, there is evidence that standardized testing has not appreciably improved learning. In fact, tests may have had largely damaging effects. A review of testing legislation in terms of equity and diversity concluded that instead of improving learning outcomes, such legislation is likely to have a detrimental impact on students of color because gross inequities in instructional quality, resources, and other support services are ignored.[23] Moreover, standardized test scores correlate very highly with family income. Even the president of the College Board, Donald Stewart, admitted that SAT scores "reflect the socioeconomic split between the well-educated of all races and the rest of society."[24] Also, because more states are now requiring that students pass a standardized test before they graduate from high school, tests may actually result in increasing the urban dropout rate.

Testing affects other practices that can impede equity. For example, testing may have a harmful effect on curriculum by limiting teachers' creativity. This is because teachers in schools in which children have poor test scores may be forced to "teach to the test" rather than create curricula that respond to the real needs of learners. The result may be "dumbing down" or restricting the curriculum to better reflect the content and approach of tests. This is precisely the conclusion of a study on the impact of statewide testing in Maryland and Pennsylvania. There, researchers found that the new testing mandates narrowed the curriculum and created conditions hostile to learning; in additon, teacher motivation was reduced.[25]

Pedagogy is affected by testing as well. Linda Darling-Hammond found a decline in the use of teaching and learning methods such as student-centered discussions, essay writing, research projects, and laboratory work when standardized tests were required.[26] This in turn affects teacher autonomy, for it removes curriculum decision making from the teacher to the school, district, city, or even state level. The further the curriculum is from the teacher and the school, the less it will reflect the culture of the students in that school.

Although standardized tests ostensibly are used to provide teachers and schools with information about the learning needs of students, in fact they are often used to sort students further. John Dewey minced no words concerning his views of rigid assessments: "How one person's abilities compare in quantity with those of another is none of the teacher's business. It is irrelevant to his work," Dewey wrote. He went on to suggest instead, "What is required is that every individual shall have opportunities to employ his own powers in activities that have meaning."[27]

Regrettably, the concern for engagement in meaningful activities is missing in many state-mandated testing programs, and students who are most vulnerable are once again the major victims. In a vicious cycle of failure, students who are perceived as needing more help are placed in classes in which the curriculum is diluted and higher levels of thinking are not demanded, and in which instruction is bland and formulaic. As a result, the academic achievement of students may fall even further behind. Because of the harmful ways in which test results have been used, some researchers have suggested that all norm-based assessment be abandoned, particularly for linguistically and culturally diverse students.

In spite of the shortcomings of standardized testing, there is a real need to have reliable and effective assessment of student learning. Teachers and schools must be held accountable for what students learn or fail to learn, especially in the case of those who have received low-quality schooling. But standardized tests do not necessarily provide the kind of assessment that is needed. Even supporters of assessment insist that it needs to be concerned primarily with improving classroom instruction.[28]

Some educators and policy makers have responded to the need to have reliable assessment by developing a code for equitable testing. The *Principles and Indicators for Student Assessment Systems*, developed and organized by the National Forum on Assessment and signed by more than 80 national education and civil rights organizations, include seven ideals:

1. The primary purpose of assessment is to improve student learning.
2. Assessment for other purposes also supports student learning.
3. Assessment systems are fair to all students.
4. Professional collaboration and development support assessment.

5. The broad community participates in assessment development.
6. Communication about assessment is regular and clear.
7. Assessment systems are regularly reviewed and improved.[29]

Another response has been to promote alternative assessments. Since the late 1980s there has been a movement to replace norm-referenced tests with *performance-based assessments,* also called *authentic assessments.* More educators and communities are calling for schools to put into place practices such as portfolios, performance tasks, and student exhibitions as a more appropriate way of documenting student learning.[30] But whether performance-based assessments are positive alternatives to norm-referenced assessments, they are not necessarily more equitable, especially if they are used in the same way as externally developed and mandated tests.[31] Once again, *how* assessment is used is just as important as *what kind* of assessment is used.

In terms of high-stakes tests that act as gatekeepers to higher education, a recent publication from FairTest found that highly selective colleges that use alternatives to SAT and ACT scores in their admissions decisions end up having more diverse applicant pools *without any loss in academic quality.*[32] The alternative assessment movement represents an important shift in thinking about the purpose and uses of tests, from sorting and separating students toward ensuring more equitable opportunities for all children to learn at high levels of achievement.

THE CURRICULUM

The curriculum in many schools is also at odds with the needs of learners. This mismatch is evident in the irrelevance of the content to the lives and lifestyles of many students and their families. In many places, schools are fortresses separated in more than physical ways from their communities. The life of the school is separate and distinct from the life of the community in ways that are abundantly clear as soon as one steps inside. As an example, it is not unusual to see classrooms in which young children learn about "community helpers" without ever studying about the real people in their communities. They learn about police officers, fire fighters, and mail carriers, all of whom may live outside their immediate neighborhood. Students may learn about doctors and lawyers and business people but may never have met one of them in their neighborhood. Yet the owner of the corner "bodega," the local factory worker, and community service staff are rarely mentioned as "community helpers." In like manner, the curriculum rarely includes the study of non-Christian holidays or history, and this fact helps explain why Avi Abramson, whose case study follows this chapter, had a hard time adjusting to public school.

When studying the "four food groups," children learn to make up fictitious breakfasts in order to satisfy their teachers, for to admit to having eaten bread and butter and coffee or cold noodles for breakfast is to admit that they are doing something wrong, at least in the eyes of the school. Similarly, a teacher with a mandate to teach her second graders about Holland may struggle to find relevant ways to describe the lives of Dutch children, while at the same time neglecting to include the heritage and backgrounds of some of the children who are sitting in her own classroom. Or there may be the incongruous situation of Mexican American, Puerto Rican, and other Latin American children who are fluent in Spanish being forced to learn "Castilian Spanish" because their teachers have accepted the premise that it is more "correct." Yet these same students are often prohibited from speaking Spanish outside of Spanish class. Lamentably, some children learn early in their academic experience that what goes on in school is irrelevant to their lives.

This is not meant to suggest that children should study only about themselves and their communities. This would fly in the face of one of the major objectives of education, that is, to broaden students' worlds outside their own particular experiences. One of my very favorite books when I was a child was *Heidi*, a story that was as distinct from my own experience as night is from day. What could a relatively poor, Puerto Rican child growing up in New York City possibly get out of the story of a Swiss orphan sent to live in the mountains with her cantankerous grandfather? I knew nothing about Switzerland, I had spent little time outside of urban Brooklyn, and I didn't even have a grandfather! But I understood Heidi because hers was a story of close family relationships and resilience in the face of considerable obstacles, and I could relate to these things. It was precisely because I could identify with these issues on a personal level that I was able to benefit from *Heidi*: after reading it, I could picture the mountains of Switzerland and I could imagine what it would be like to have a grandfather. My point is that curriculum needs to *build on* rather than neglect the experiences with which students come to school in order to broaden their worlds.

Curriculum is the organized environment for learning what is thought to be important knowledge. But because only a tiny fraction of the vast array of available knowledge finds its way into textbooks and teachers' guides, the curriculum is never neutral. It represents what is perceived to be consequential and necessary knowledge by those who are dominant in a society. The problem is that it is often presented as if it were the whole, unvarnished, and uncontested truth. But if we think of curriculum as a decision-making process, we realize that *somebody* made decisions about what to include. Furthermore, curriculum decisions are generally made by those furthest from the lives of students, namely, central and state boards of education, with little input from teachers, parents, and students.

The curriculum lets students know whether the knowledge they and their communities value has prestige within the educational establishment. For example, students who speak Black English and are constantly corrected by their teachers pick up the powerful message that the language variety they speak has little status or power in our society. On the other hand, if teachers use students' language as a bridge to standard English, or to discuss critical perspectives about the role that language and culture play in their lives, the value of students' identity is affirmed.[33] But talk about such issues is frequently silenced. In this way, curriculum serves as a primary means of social control. Students learn that what is meaningful at home is often negated in school.

Research on the link between what students learn at school and their lives at home demonstrates that the curriculum further alienates many young people from schooling. A study of four highly diverse public schools in southern California by Mary Poplin and Joseph Weeres found that students frequently reported being bored in school and saw little relevance of what is taught in their lives and for their future.[34] The authors also reported that students became more disengaged as the curriculum became more standardized and less relevant to their experiences. Although young people may believe that cultural diversity is valuable, they also learn that in school it is not as valuable as is the dominant culture.

Children who are not in the dominant group have a hard time finding themselves or their communities in the curriculum. When they do see themselves, it is often through the distorted lens of the dominant group. Native American children read about themselves as "savages" who were bereft of culture until the Europeans arrived; African Americans read sanitized versions of slavery; Mexican Americans read of the "westward expansion," with no indication that their ancestors were already living on the land onto which Europeans were expanding; working-class children learn virtually nothing of their history, except perhaps that the struggle for the eight-hour workday was a long one; and females may be left wondering how it is that half of humanity has consistently been left out of the curriculum. Little wonder, then, that school curricula and real life are often at polar extremes. Henry Louis Gates makes a cogent argument for a more inclusive curriculum by explaining: "Common sense says you don't bracket 90 percent of the world's cultural heritage if you really want to learn about the world."[35]

Sometimes the curriculum is "watered down" by teachers who believe that such accommodations will better meet the needs of diverse learners. On the face of it, this practice may seem equitable, but the truth is that it may reflect teachers' lower expectations of some students. That is, all children can benefit from high expectations and a challenging curriculum, but some students are regularly subjected to diluted, undemanding, and boring educational programs because teachers and schools do not tap into their strengths and talents. For instance, Luis Moll maintains that students for whom English is a second language have many unacknowledged resources available to them outside of school, and that these resources, which he calls "funds of knowledge," can be used to enhance instruction. Working with 30 Mexican American families, Moll found that the families possessed impressive knowledge and skills from fields as diverse as agriculture to medicine, and that these can contribute to the intellectual and academic development of their children. Moll documented a number of classrooms where students' funds of knowledge formed the basis of the curriculum and resulted in an education that far exceeded what working-class students generally receive.[36]

Another example of using students' experiences and identities as an appropriate foundation for the curriculum is a collaborative action research project in which two university researchers, Judith Solsken and Jerri Willett, worked with a teacher researcher, Jo-Anne Wilson Keenan. The project was based on the premise that parents and other family members of children from widely diverse backgrounds can enhance their children's learning. Although projects in which parents are invited to speak about their culture and to share food or teach youngsters particular crafts are not new, the research by Solsken, Keenan, and Willett focused instead on how parents' talents and skills can be used to actually promote student learning. The researchers explained how the visits of students' families to their second-grade classroom "changed the nature of the conversation in Room 8." They added that the families "opened the conversation to many aspects of the children's language and lives that had not previously had a place in the classroom, and they created many different opportunities for everyone to connect to one another and to the academic discourse of school."[37]

Another aspect of the curriculum that helps separate students' school and home lives is teachers' resistance to bring up difficult, contentious, or conflicting issues, even though these may be central to students' lives. In Chapter 3, we saw how teachers and prospective teachers are socialized in this attitude. Michelle Fine has called this "silencing," that is, determining "who can speak, what can and cannot be spoken, and whose discourse must be controlled."[38] One topic that seems to hold particular saliency for many young people, regardless of their background, is that of biases and discrimination. But teaching about these things is staunchly avoided in most classrooms. This may be due to several factors: Most teachers are unaccustomed to, afraid of, or uncomfortable discussing discrimination and inequality; they feel pressure to "cover the material" and these topics are not included in the traditional curriculum; they are used to presenting information as if it were free of conflict and controversy; and they may feel that bringing up issues concerning conflict will create or exacerbate animosity among students. In the words of one of the teachers in Michelle Fine's study, discussing such issues would be a mistake because "it would demoralize the students, they need to feel positive and optimistic—like they have a chance."[39] Racism and discrimination and other "dangerous" topics, students quickly find out, are not supposed to be discussed in school.

But these issues do not simply vanish because they are excluded from the curriculum. On the contrary, squashing them reinforces students' feelings that school life is separate and unrelated to real life. In spite of teachers' reluctance to broach issues such as racism, slavery, inequality, genocide, and so on, a number of studies suggest that discussing them can be tremendously beneficial to students if they are approached with sensitivity and care. This is the case with Melinda Fine's description of the "Facing History and Ourselves" (FHAO) curriculum, a model for teaching history that encourages students to reflect critically on a variety of contemporary social, moral, and political issues. Using the Holocaust as a case study, students learn to think critically about scapegoating, racism, and personal and collective responsibility.[40] Curriculum can result in what María Torres-Guzmán has called "cognitive empowerment," that is, a process to help students recognize the potential benefits and power of knowledge on both an individual and a collective level.[41] In one of the cases Torres-Guzmán describes, a teacher used racism and discrimination as themes for a dialogue, and the discussion helped validate students' experiences rather than heighten their alienation.

The relationship between curriculum and democracy is also significant. In a description of how his 11-year-old daughter, Rachel, and her friend Petra challenged the practice of reciting the Pledge of Allegiance in their classroom by doing research on case law and then starting a petition that they presented to their principal, David Bloome links literacy and access to information with strategies that are crucial to democracy.[42] Although the girls were successful in bringing up the issue, it was not because it was included in the curriculum but rather because they had highly educated parents who could give them access to information they needed to practice the skills of democracy. Bloome pointedly asked: "How successful can we claim our reading and writing programs to be if they don't give students access to the genres of writing (like petition writing or reading state laws and court decisions and rulings) needed for a democracy?"[43]

Donaldo Macedo wrote about a similar incident in the case of David Spritzler, a 12-year-old student in Boston who was faced with disciplinary action for his refusal to recite the Pledge of Allegiance, which he considered "a hypocritical exhortation to patriotism."[44] This case demonstrates the chasm that often exists between expounding on democracy and the lack of democratic actions in schools. Macedo mused, "This inability to link the reading of the word with the world, if not combatted, will further exacerbate already feeble democratic institutions and the unjust, asymmetrical power relations that characterize the hypocritical nature of contemporary democracies."[45] Issues such as these are at the center of curriculum transformation if we believe that one of the basic purposes of schooling is to prepare young people to become productive and critical citizens of a democratic society.

Democratic principles are thwarted by the lack of access to knowledge in other ways as well. As we saw in reviewing the effect of rigid ability grouping on access to knowledge, curriculum and tracking are frequently connected. That is, whether students have access to high-status and high-level knowledge, and consequently to higher education and more options in life, is often related to their race, class, or gender. In this way, curriculum differentiation regularly results in stratifying knowledge to reflect societal inequality.[46] In reviewing statistics that documented patterns of disproportionately low achievement and participation in science and math by female students, students of color, and students of low-income families, Jeannie Oakes found that by secondary school the educational experiences of these students were "strikingly different" from those of middle-class, male, and dominant-group students in general.[47] As a result, low-income students and students from the inner city had few opportunities to learn math and science. They also had fewer material resources, less engaging learning activities in their classrooms, and less qualified teachers.

Textbooks, a considerable component of the curriculum in most schools, may also be at odds with democratic and pluralistic values. Textbooks tend to reinforce the dominance of the European American perspective and to sustain stereotypes of groups outside the cultural and political mainstream. This situation is not new. A 1949 comprehensive analysis of 300 textbooks revealed that many of them perpetuated negative stereotypes of "minority" groups.[48] This has been found time and again in more recent years. In a historical overview of the image of ethnic groups in U.S. textbooks since the 1800s, Jesús García found that although textbooks have become more representative and include more content about the experiences of immigrants of diverse backgrounds, the increase in quantity has not necessarily been accompanied by an improvement in quality.[49]

Even in recent textbooks, the lack of adequate representation of women and people of color is striking; critical and nondominant perspectives are also largely missing. In a thorough examination of textbooks used in grades 1 through 8, for instance, Christine Sleeter and Carl Grant found that the presence of Whites was still dominant, both in story line and in lists of accomplishments. They also found that women and people of color had much more limited roles than did White males. Equally troubling was the fact that most textbooks contain very little information about contemporary race relations, and they convey an image of harmony among various groups that contrasts sharply with reality. Similar findings have been reported concerning Latinos and Latin Americans.[50] As you will see, Fern Sherman, whose case study follows this chapter, was very aware of the limitations of textbooks: As the only Native American student in her school, she often felt a tremendous obligation to tell her teachers what was wrong in the history textbook, whether it was about scalping or Geronimo. This is too burdensome a responsibility for such a young woman.

According to James Loewen, most history textbooks are filled with half-truths or myths. In an extensive study, Loewen points out how textbooks perpetuate the myths that are the basis for much of the U.S. history taught in school.[51] Commenting on the increased multicultural content of school textbooks, Michael Apple explains that although *items* relating to the experiences of subordinated groups may be mentioned (a concession to demands from underrepresented groups that they be included), they are rarely developed in depth, and in this way, the dominance of powerful groups in society is maintained.[52] A similar situation has been documented in children's literature, which until recently largely omitted or stereotyped the lives and experiences of African American, Latino, Asian American, American Indian, and other groups.[53]

PEDAGOGY

The observation that schools are tedious places where little learning takes place and where most students are not challenged to learn is hardly new. It is particularly true of secondary schools, where subject matter dominates pedagogy and classes are too often driven by standardized tests as gatekeepers to promotion and/or accreditation. Both Avi Abramson and Fern Sherman provide enlightening examples of pedagogy that is engaging or boring. Avi contrasts teachers that "teach from the point of view of the kid" with those who "just come out and say, 'All right, do this, *blah, blah, blah*." Fern mentioned that she would like more "involved activities" in which more students take part, "not making only the two smartest people up here do the whole work for the whole class."

Avi and Fern's impressions are confirmed by research. In his far-reaching and classic study on secondary schools, John Goodlad found that textbooks were used frequently and mechanistically, whereas other materials were used infrequently if at all; that teaching methods varied little from the traditional "chalk and talk" methodology common 100 years ago; and that routine and rote learning were favored over creativity and critical thinking.[54] Larry Cuban's comprehensive historical study of teachers' pedagogy in the past century reached similar conclusions, although he found that teachers' lack of creativity was more often than not due to the severe structural limits placed on them because of decisions made outside their classrooms. Notwithstanding these limits, Cuban suggests that teachers have generally had a "margin of choice" about their pedagogy.[55]

Pedagogy does not simply mean, however, the techniques or strategies that teachers use to make learning more fun or interesting. Pedagogy also refers to how teachers perceive the nature of learning and what they do to create conditions that motivate students to learn and to become critical thinkers. Most classrooms, for example, reflect the belief that learning can best take place in a competitive and highly charged atmosphere. Techniques that stress individual achievement and extrinsic motivation are most visible. Ability grouping, testing of all kinds, and rote learning are the result. Although learning in such classrooms can be fun or interesting, students may learn other unintended lessons as well: that learning equals memorization, that reciting what teachers want to hear is what education is about, and that critical thinking has no place in the classroom.

Teachers' pedagogy is also influenced by their lack of knowledge concerning the diversity of their students and how cultural and language differences may affect learning. Many teacher education programs still function within a monocultural framework, and because of this few teachers are prepared for the numerous cultures, languages, lifestyles, and values they will face in their classrooms. The result is that many teachers attempt to treat all students in the same way, reflecting the unchallenged assumption that "equal means the same." The same methods and approaches perceived as appropriate for students from mainstream backgrounds, whether or not they were ever effective, are used for all students.

Students from subordinated groups are the primary casualties of this thinking. Martin Haberman uses the term "pedagogy of poverty" to refer to a basic urban pedagogy that encompasses a body of specific strategies that are limited to asking questions, giving directions, making assignments, and monitoring seatwork. Unsupported by research, theory, or even the practice of the best urban teachers, the "pedagogy of poverty" is based on the dubious assumption that children of disempowered backgrounds cannot learn in creative, active, and challenging environments. Suggesting instead that exemplary pedagogy in urban schools actively involves students in real-life situations and allows them to reflect on their own lives, Haberman finds that good teaching is taking place when, among other things:

- students are involved with issues they perceive as vital concerns (e.g., rather than avoid such controversies as censorship of school newspapers or dress codes, students use these opportunities for learning).
- students are involved with explanations of differences in race, culture, religion, ethnicity, and gender.
- students are helped to see major concepts, big ideas, and general principles rather than isolated facts.

- students are involved in planning their education.
- students are involved in applying ideals such as fairness, equity, and justice to their world.
- students are actively involved in heterogeneous groups.
- students are asked to question commonsense or widely accepted assumptions.[56]

Expanding pedagogical strategies, however, will not in itself change how and what students learn in school. Let us take the example of cooperative learning, generally praised as a useful instructional strategy. Eugene García, in fact, found it to be tremendously effective. In the high-achieving schools with large numbers of language minority children that he studied, cooperative learning was a powerful instructional approach because students engaged in higher order cognitive and linguistic discourse during peer interactions. Students were more likely to ask *each other* hard questions than to engage in this level of discourse with their teachers.[57] In spite of its commendable qualities, however, cooperative learning should be viewed no more than as a means to an end.

Cooperative learning is premised on the idea that using the talents and skills of all students is key to designing successful learning environments. But if it is viewed unproblematically as the answer to all manner of ills, then cooperative learning will have little chance of changing the fundamental climate of learning in the classroom. In this regard, research by Mary McCaslin and Thomas Good found that small-group work too often allowed students to become even more passive and dependent learners than if they were in whole-class settings.[58] This is a good reminder that particular methods can become, in the words of María de la Luz Reyes, "venerable assumptions" that take on a life of their own, disconnected from their educational purposes or sociopolitical context.[59] Instead of devotion to a particular instructional strategy, Lilia Bartolomé has suggested that teachers need to develop a "humanizing pedagogy" that values students' cultural, linguistic, and experiential backgrounds.[60] To underscore the secondary place of particular strategies, Jim Cummins cautions, "good teaching does not require us to internalize an endless list of instructional techniques. Much more fundamental is the recognition that human relationships are central to effective instruction."[61]

PHYSICAL STRUCTURE

The physical structure of schools also gets in the way of educational equity. It is not unusual in poor urban areas to find schools with police officers standing guard. In some, students are frisked before entering. Teachers sometimes feel afraid unless they lock their classrooms. In many schools, desks are nailed to the ground; halls and classrooms are airless and poorly lit; and shattered glass can be found in courtyards where young children play. Add the lack of relevant and culturally appropriate pictures, posters, and other instructional materials as well as the lifeless and institutional colors of green and gray on the walls, and we are left with environments that are scarcely inviting centers of learning.

Many times, of course, schools are uninviting fortresslike places because school officials are trying to protect schools, students, and teachers against vandalism, theft, and other acts of violence. Frequently it is students from these very schools who do the damage. Boredom and rage are implicated in these actions, particularly when schools show little regard for students by silencing their voices and negating their identities in the curriculum.[62] Destructiveness and violence by students sometimes represent a clear message that some school structures are incompatible with students' emotional and physical needs. For instance, in a report on the middle grades that has been a major catalyst for the restructuring of many middle schools in the past decade, the Carnegie Council on Adolescent Development concluded that there is a volatile mismatch between the organization and curriculum of middle-grade schools and the intellectual, emotional, and social needs of young adolescents.[63] But schools alone are not to blame. Violence in our society is reflected in the violence that takes place in schools, and teachers and administrators often struggle heroically to contain it and to make schools places of learning and joy.

The resemblance of some schools to factories or prisons has been mentioned many times over the years.[64] The size of schools alone is enough to give them this institutional look: High schools hold sometimes two, three, and even four thousand students, and it is easy to understand the feelings of alienation and insecurity that can result. These characteristics are not true of all schools: In general, the farther away from urban, inner-city schools or poor rural schools, the less institutional the appearance of the school. Suburban schools or schools in wealthy towns tend to look strikingly different from schools that serve the poor. Not only do the former usually have more space, bigger classrooms, and more light, but they also have more material supplies and generally are in better physical condition, partly because the level of financing for the education of poor students is lower than for children in more affluent districts.[65] Wealthier schools tend to have smaller classes as well, another condition that is related to higher quality education for students.[66]

The physical environment of schools can reflect expectations that educators have of the capabilities of students. If students are perceived to be "deficient," then the educational environment will reflect a no-nonsense, back-to-basics, drill orientation. However, if they are perceived as intelligent and motivated young people with an interest in the world around them, then the educational environment will tend to reflect an intellectually stimulating and academically challenging orientation, a place where learning is considered joyful rather than tedious.

We might well ask what would happen if the schools attended by youngsters in poor urban and rural areas were to miraculously become like the schools that middle-class and wealthy youngsters attend. Might there be a change in educational outcomes if all students had access to generously endowed, small, and more democratically run schools? We cannot know the answer to that question until we try it, but one thing is for certain: The physical environment in many schools provides a stark contrast to the stated purposes of teaching and learning. When schools are not cared for, when they become fortresses rather than an integral part of the community they serve, and when they are holding places instead of learning environments, the contradiction between goals and realities is a vivid one. This chasm between ideal and real is not lost on the students.

DISCIPLINARY POLICIES

Disciplinary policies, especially in middle and secondary schools, may be at odds with the developmental level of students and as a result can aggravate the sense of alienation felt by some students. Research that supports this hypothesis is compelling. Using longitudinal data from the national *High School and Beyond* study, Gary Wehlage and Robert Rutter found that certain conditions in the schools themselves can *predict* the dropping-out behavior of students.[67] Conditions that encourage students to leave include disciplinary policies that are perceived by students to be unfair and ineffective, especially those that are imposed rather than negotiated. Consequently, there is a serious problem with what Wehlage and Rutter call the "holding power" of school for some students. They conclude that certain student characteristics *in combination with* certain school conditions are responsible for students' decision to drop out.

Interpretations of student behavior may be culturally or class biased, and this poses an additional barrier to enforcing disciplinary policies fairly. For example, students in poor schools who insist on wearing highly prized leather jackets in class may be doing so out of a well-founded fear that they will be stolen if left in the closet. Latino children who cast their eyes downward when being scolded probably are not being defiant but simply behaving out of respect for their teachers, as they were taught at home. African American students are especially vulnerable when following particular styles. For example, in a study of an urban school undergoing restructuring, Pauline Lipman described the case of an African American male student who was given a 10-day, in-school suspension for wearing his overall straps unsnapped, a common style among African American males, whereas White students who wore their pants with large holes cut in the thighs, a widespread style among their group, were not even reprimanded.[68]

In another example, Rosa Hernandez Sheets documented major differences in perception among students and teachers of diverse backgrounds concerning racism and disciplinary policies. While students and teachers alike felt that racism was a factor in disciplinary actions, most Whites felt it was unintentional, whereas most people of color felt it was purposeful. She also found that there was inadequate understanding among teachers concerning the cultural behavior of students.[69]

Poor students and students of color are also more likely to be suspended and to be victims of corporal punishment. This inequity is frequently related to poor communication among administrators, teachers, and students. But discipline can be an issue even among more economically privileged students who are culturally different from the mainstream. For instance, in one of the case studies that follows this chapter, Avi Abramson pointed out how he was the subject of several anti-Semitic incidents. Because teachers were uncertain how they should respond, Avi felt that he had to take matters into his own hands. In one case, he said, "I went up to the teacher and I said to her, 'I'm either gonna leave the class or they leave.'"

A lack of awareness of cultural and social factors on the part of teachers and schools can lead to misinterpretations and faulty conclusions. Although it is usually students who experience the least success in school who bear the brunt of rigid school policies, all students who differ from the cultural mainstream are jeopardized.

LIMITED ROLE OF STUDENTS

That many students are alienated, uninvolved, and discouraged by school is abundantly clear. This fact is most striking, of course, in dropout rates, the most extreme manifestation of disengagement from schooling. Students who drop out are commonly uninvolved and passive participants in the school experience.

Schools are not usually organized to encourage active student involvement. Although school is a place where a lot of talk goes on, it is seldom student talk, and teachers and other staff lose out on an opportunity to learn firsthand from students about their educational experiences and what could make it better. Students and teachers who spend the most time in schools and classrooms often have the least opportunity to talk about their experiences.

Although it is true that students are nominally represented in the governance structure of many schools, often this representation is merely window dressing that has little to do with the actual management of the school. Rather than being designed to prepare students for democratic life, most schools are more like benign dictatorships in which all decisions are made for them, albeit in what schools may perceive to be "their best interests." They are more often organized around issues of control than of collaboration or consultation.

Dick Corbett and Bruce Wilson have accurately pointed out that there is a stark contradiction between the passivity that is expected of students in school reform and the constructivist expectations teachers have for their learning.[70] In many cases, however, constructivist notions of learning are invisible in classrooms too. Even there, students are expected to learn what is decided, designed, and executed by others. Often, it is not the teacher or even the school that determines the content, but some mythical "downtown," school board, or state education department. When everybody in the school is disempowered, frustration and alienation are the result. This kind of situation was the impetus for a project designed by Suzanne Soo Hoo to enlist middle-school students as coresearchers in investigating the question, "What are the obstacles to learning?" According to her, this question "electrified the group," and the result of the project was empowering to all of them: "Their initial feelings of powerlessness and inadequacy transformed into conviction about alternatives and notions of reform, which prompted the development of an action plan, a plan to move beyond the meeting room and do something about the obstacles they had identified in their schooling environment."[71]

In the classroom itself, the pedagogy frequently reflects what Paulo Freire called "banking" education, that is, a process by which teachers "deposit" knowledge into students, who are thought to be empty receptacles. It is education for powerlessness. In a characterization of what happens in most schools, Freire contrasted the expected roles of the teacher and the students:

a. the teacher teaches and the students are taught;

b. the teacher knows everything and the students know nothing;

c. the teacher thinks and the students are thought about;

d. the teacher talks and the students listen—meekly;

e. the teacher disciplines and the students are disciplined;

f. the teacher chooses and enforces his choice, and the students comply;

g. the teacher acts and the students have the illusion of acting through the action of the teacher;

h. the teacher chooses the program content, and the students (who were not consulted) adapt to it;

i. the teacher confuses the authority of knowledge with his own professional authority, which he sets in opposition to the freedom of the students;

j. the teacher is the subject of the learning process, while the pupils are mere objects.[72]

What impact does involvement of students have on their school experiences and achievement? Little research has been done on this issue. But Jim Cummins, in a review of a number of programs that include the goal of student empowerment, concluded that students who are empowered to develop a positive cultural identity through interactions with their teachers experience a sense of control over their own lives and develop the confidence and motivation to succeed academically.[73] In a project focusing on students' perspectives regarding school in which more than 50 students of diverse backgrounds in California were interviewed over a two-year period, researchers Patricia Phelan, Ann Davidson, and Hanh Cao Yu found that the students' views on teaching and learning were notably consistent with those of contemporary theorists and educators: Students wanted (a) classrooms that were caring communities where they could feel safe and respected; (b) active rather than passive learning environments; (c) a reliance on teachers rather than textbooks for learning; (d) to work in small groups; and (e) an environment where differences were valued rather than feared.[74]

Schools that restructure do not automatically promote student involvement. But when they do encourage involvement, the results can be empowering. In documenting what it meant for teachers and students to develop a small charter school within a larger public school, Jody Cohen described the impact on students: "When schooling is about building participatory communities, students learn to make themselves heard—to occupy speaking and acting roles in their education, to co-construct with teachers what knowledge, whose knowledge, and how knowledge is produced in school."[75] The message should not be lost on teachers and schools: When students are involved in directing their own education in some way, they are more enthusiastic learners.

LIMITED ROLE OF TEACHERS

Teachers as a group are shown little respect by our society and they are usually poorly paid and infrequently rewarded. In school, they are sometimes the victims of physical and verbal threats and attacks, and they feel a lack of parental support and involvement. Moreover, teachers are traditionally discouraged from becoming involved in decision-making processes in the schools. In some ways teachers have become even more alienated in the late-century climate of "reform" because more decisions about curriculum and instruction are being made by others. Alienated and discouraged teachers can hardly be expected to help students become empowered and critical thinkers. For example, Michelle Fine reported research findings that teacher disempowerment correlates highly with disparaging attitudes toward students; that is, the more powerless teachers feel, the more negative they are toward their students as well.[76] In contrast, teachers who feel that they have autonomy in their classrooms and with their curriculum generally also have high expectations of their students.[77]

New structures such as teacher-led schools, weekly released time for professional development and other activities, or job sharing may help make teachers more active players in the schools, but this is only one aspect of a larger problem. Teachers are disempowered for many reasons, and these do not correspond simply to school structures. Their condition has much more to do with their perceived status. For example, a study of 24 schools undergoing restructuring found that the single most important element in developing a sense of community was the finding that *respect* was at the core of a positive school culture.[78] As in the case of student involvement, restructuring and greater teacher efficacy by themselves are no guarantee that schools will become more effective learning environments for students. In research of a restructuring school, Pauline Lipman found that some policies remained largely untouched: For example, tracking was never challenged, disciplinary practices continued to jeopardize students of color primarily, and the school was pervaded by a general silence concerning issues of racism and inequality.[79]

Structural changes to broaden the roles, responsibilities, and status of teachers need to be accompanied by changes in (a) the general public's attitudes about teachers' professionalism, (b) teachers' beliefs about their own capabilities, and (c) the dynamic possibilities for learning that students' diversity creates.

LIMITED FAMILY AND COMMUNITY INVOLVEMENT

The research is clear on the effectiveness of family and community involvement: In programs with strong family involvement components, students are consistently better achievers than in otherwise identical programs with less family involvement. In addition, students in schools that maintain frequent contact with their communities outperform students in other schools. These positive effects persist well beyond the short term. For example, research has demonstrated that when they reached senior high school, low-income bicultural children whose families participated in preschool programs were still outperforming their peers whose families were not involved.[80]

But how parent and family involvement is defined differs depending on the context. Although it is true that involvement through activities such as attendance at parent–teacher conferences, participation in parent–teacher associations (PTAs), and influence over their child's selection of courses help predict student achievement, involvement of this kind is becoming more and more scarce. In a society increasingly characterized by one-parent families or two-parent families in which both work outside the home, defining involvement in traditional ways is problematic. PTA meetings held during the day, parent–teacher conferences during school hours, and the ubiquitous cake sale are becoming relics of the past. Most families nowadays, regardless of cultural or economic background, find it difficult to attend meetings or to otherwise be involved in the governance of the school or in fundraising.

Cultural and economic differences also influence family involvement. Families of linguistically and culturally diverse communities and from working-class neighborhoods frequently have a hard time with the kind of parent involvement expected by the school, such as homework assistance and family excursions. Not taking part in these activities should not be interpreted as noninvolvement or apathy, however. One study of Mexican American and European American families found that everyday learning activities in the home and families' aspirations for children's futures were crucial resources that could provide cultural school-home linkages. But there was a general lack of awareness among school staff concerning these resources. Further, although the Mexican American families' aspirations for their children were as high as those of European American families, the former often had little comprehension of how to help their children attain those aspirations. Similar conclusions have been reached with Puerto Rican families.[81]

More promising practices have been highlighted in programs stressing effective family and community involvement. In an analysis of such programs, it was found that all of them shared, among others, the following components: They all had a commitment to involve low-income families, frequently the most reluctant to become involved; family empowerment was a major goal; and they had a strong commitment to reducing the gap between home and school cultures by designing programs that respond to and build on the values, structures, languages, and cultures of the home.[82]

But family involvement is a complex issue and unless teachers and schools really understand the cultural meanings underlying different families and the goals that parents have for their children, typical involvement strategies may further estrange families who already feel disconnected from the school. This was one of the conclusions reached by Guadalupe Valdés in a study of 10 Mexican immigrant families in the Southwest. She found that although the beliefs and practices of the families were perfectly reasonable in their former contexts, they did not always work in their new setting. Schools do not always know how to negotiate these different worlds, and common strategies such as "parenting classes" tend to worsen the situation. In the words of Valdés, "Relationships between parents and schools do, in fact, reflect the structural locations of these individuals in the wider society. Simply bringing parents to schools will not change the racist or classist responses that teachers may have toward them and their behaviors. Parenting classes alone will not equalize outcomes."[83]

In spite of its shortcomings—especially when it comes to poor and immigrant families—parent involvement still represents a potential avenue for bringing community values, lifestyles, and realities into the school. When families become involved, it also means that their language and culture and the expectations they have for their children can become a part of the dialogue. And it is through dialogue that true change can begin to happen.

• SUMMARY

The organization and structures of schools often are contrary to the needs of students, the values of their communities, and even to one of the major articulated purposes of schooling—to provide equal educational opportunity for all students. The result is that policies and practices in schools more often than not reflect and maintain the status quo and the stratification of society. How it could be otherwise will be the subject of subsequent chapters.

• TO THINK ABOUT

1. Observe a number of similar classrooms, some that are tracked and others that are not. What are the differences in these classrooms? Be specific, citing student engagement with work, expectations of student achievement, level of academic difficulty, and teacher–student and student–student relationships.
2. The *nature versus nurture* argument in explaining intelligence has been raging for many years. While some people believe that intelligence is primarily dependent on genetic makeup, others believe that the environment plays a more important role. What are your thoughts on this debate? Why? On what do you base your conclusions?
3. Think about the curriculum in classrooms where you have been a student. How have your experiences and culture and those of your classmates been included? If they have not, what do you think the effect has been on you and others? In a journal, write to a former teacher and tell her or him what changes in the curriculum would have made you a more enthusiastic and engaged student.
4. Get some evaluation checklists for textbooks at your library or, working with colleagues, design your own. Review and evaluate the textbooks used in your local school. Do they discriminate against students of any group? How? Give specific examples based on the checklists you have used.
5. Observe a classroom and indicate the kind of pedagogical strategies used by the teacher. Are all students engaged in learning? Who are not, and what might help engage them?
6. If you believe that the physical structure of most schools is not an appropriate environment for learning, design a school for either the elementary or secondary level that would be. State the primary objectives you might have for this school.
7. The criticism has been made that because schools do not provide opportunities for either teachers or students to exercise critical thinking or leadership, they subvert the very purpose of education as preparation for civic life and democratic participation. Discuss some ways in which schools might provide more opportunities for teachers and students to be more fully engaged.

Case Study: Avi Abramson

"Some teachers teach from the point of view of the kid. They don't just come out and say, "All right, do this, blah, blah, blah." They're not so one-tone voice."

Talbot is a small, quiet, and aging working-class town in eastern Massachusetts a few miles from the busy metropolis of Boston. Its total area is a mere 1.6 square miles, and it has a population of approximately 20,000. With the exception of salt marshes and surplus federal installations, there is little vacant land in Talbot.

One gets a sense of the community's aging by its housing: More than half of the dwellings are at least 50 years old, and this is partly due to the nature of the population. In recent years, the number of youths has been declining, with younger adults and families moving to more prosperous settings. The older residents remain, continuing to live in homes that long ago lost their newness and modern veneer. Both public and parochial school enrollment have been dwindling over the past two decades. From 1975 to 1986 there was a particularly dramatic decline: Student enrollment plummeted from 4,128 to 2,163. One of the three elementary schools has been turned into condominiums. The one high school in town, Talbot High School, has approximately 700 students.

People from a great many ethnic groups, primarily European and Catholic in origin, make up the population. Talbot is home to many Italians and Irish, and to smaller concentrations of other European American immigrants. The percentage of people of color is quite low—only a handful of families. The number of Jewish families is also very small, although there was a thriving community here just a generation ago. As evidence, there are two synagogues in town, one known as the "big synagogue" and the other as the "small synagogue." Many Jewish families have moved to other communities, and the remaining Jews are mostly senior citizens; many of them are observant and go to temple regularly. According to Avi Abramson,[1] the subject of this case study, many people in his community are close to 85 years of age. At the high school there are no more than 10 Jewish students in all.

Avi has lived in Talbot almost all his life, except for a year when his family moved to North Carolina. He went to first and second grade in public school, before going to a Jewish day school until eighth grade. He is now 16 years old and a senior at Talbot High School. As he explained during his interviews, Avi was not always a successful student and he had a hard time adjusting to public school because the curriculum was so different from what he had experienced in the Jewish day school. He plans on going to college next year, and he has given some thought to becoming either a history teacher or a graphic designer. Since both his parents have been teachers and drawing is one of his hobbies, these choices are not unexpected. Currently Avi is studying English, basic trigonometry, marine science, and psychology. He has already finished all the requirements for his favorite subject, history.

Avi lives on the water tower hillside of this quaint old town in a quiet neighborhood of single and multifamily homes. During the Christmas season, his house is easily spotted: It is the only one on the street without Christmas lights. He describes his town as peaceful, and he enjoys living here. Avi and his family have developed good relationships with their neighbors, whom he describes with fondness ("Everybody looks out for each other," he says). Nevertheless, he clearly longs to live in a community where he is not perceived as being so "different."

Avi lives with his mother and brother, who is 10 years his elder. His older sister lives in New York City with her husband and two children. Avi's father came from Israel originally, met his Jewish American wife in the United States, and stayed here to live. He died six years ago after a long illness. Although he was 10 when his father died, Avi remembers little about him, probably because he was sick for so long. Before his illness, he was a much loved teacher in various Hebrew schools. Avi's mother was also a Hebrew teacher, and although she loved teaching, there is not much call for Hebrew teachers in the area now. Recently she began studying computers to prepare for a new career.

There is a warm glow of familiarity and old, comfortable furniture in Avi's home. The house is filled with the aroma of latkes (potato pancakes) during the Hanukkah season, and of many other Jewish foods at other times of the year. Books and artifacts are everywhere, reflecting the family's respect for tradition and history. Avi is a typical American teenager in many ways. He has a girlfriend and enjoys frequent telephone conversations with his friends. His bedroom is crammed with posters, comic books, encyclopedias, track team gear, woodworking projects, Star Trek memorabilia, drawing pads full of his own comics, and underneath it all, bunk beds.

Avi is also different from many other American youths. His serious, wise demeanor is evident in the profound respect and love that he has for his culture and religion. Few young people of any religion would dedicate every Saturday, as he does, to leading the last elderly remnants of his community in their Sabbath prayers at the small synagogue (what one might call a "role model in reverse"). He enjoys speaking Hebrew, loves the Jewish holidays, and devotes a great deal of time to religious and cultural activities. He is an energetic and thoughtful young man who enjoys school as well as sports and other hobbies. But Avi is not what one would call a "nerd." Although he is serious about his studies, he has not always excelled in school and he does not spend an inordinate amount of time studying.

Three basic themes were revealed in Avi's interviews. One is his sense of responsibility—to himself, his family, and his community—as well as his persistence in fulfilling this responsibility. This trait is especially evident in the care with which he treats his culture and religion. The joy and pain of maintaining them is another theme frequently discussed by Avi. The role of positive pressure, from peers and family, and through activities such as track, is the third.

Independent Responsibility and Persistence

I usually do my homework on my own and study for my tests on my own. That way, I can just do it on my own. I won't be able to have people around me to help me all the time, so I might as well learn how to do it myself.

If you don't go to school, then you can't learn about life, or you can't learn about things that you need to progress [in] life.

I think that anybody that goes to school tries, at least. Accomplishes something. . . . It helps you with your life. 'Cause if you don't go to school, you probably won't get a good job someplace.

What am I getting out of school? I'm learning to be with people . . . learning to work with people.

I admire a lot of people 'cause I look at people and I see all kinds of things in them, in all kinds of people. . . . I admire my mother 'cause she's been through a lot and she's held on. . . . I admire people in school that in freshman and sophomore years just goofed off and did nothing and now they can be in Level One and really . . . prove themselves. . . . I admire people who can get off drugs. People like that. Nobody I knew, I just admire people who can do that.

I got the willpower. I don't give up so easy on some things. Some things I give up, though. But if I really want something, I usually try to work as hard to get it.

[To be successful, you have to] work hard and have confidence in yourself.

I'm currently working, or helping out, in Temple Solomon. With their services. . . . A lot of people here too, they come to temple but . . . some of them don't understand exactly what they're doing. They come, and if there weren't certain people here, they wouldn't know what to do and they wouldn't come at all, probably. . . . So, I guess one of the reasons why I probably do what I'm doing is well, I enjoy it 'cause I enjoy doing the services. I enjoy being that kind of leader. To help them.

I was going to temple every Saturday. . . . when I was little. I didn't follow along, but I just listened to them every time, and I got the tune and everything. And it wasn't as hard for me. It wasn't hard for me at all to learn the service for my Bar Mitzvah 'cause I already knew half of it in my head. . . . Yeah, it's fun, it is.

I'm fairly religious. I mean, I work in a temple on Saturdays, so I keep myself Orthodox. . . . I try to keep the law, you know, for Shabbos [Yiddish for *Sabbath*], 'cause I'm reading the Torah [holiest book for Jews], so it would be nice if the person who's reading at least [should follow it] . . . if you're reading the law, then you might as well follow it. . . . Set an example, in a way. Try to. . . . Again, I don't know how much of a role model I can be to 85-year-olds [*laughs sadly*].

The Price of Maintaining Language and Culture

There were more [Jews] years ago. Yeah, and now everybody has aged and all the young ones are gone and left. So, there's not too many young ones coming up, 'cause there's not too many families—young families. . . . The average age is probably 50s.

[In school] I'm the only, really, person that I guess follows the laws. So I wouldn't go out on a Friday night or something like that. . . . Right now, most people know that I don't usually come out on a Friday night. . . . But when I started high school, people used to say sometimes, "Ya coming out tonight?" I'm like, "No, I can't . . . ." In a way, it brought me away from those people. . . . I mean, I have different responsibilities than most people.

If I miss track and say, "'cause it's not exactly the holiday, it's the day before and I have to go home and prepare," most people won't understand. "What do you mean, you have to prepare?" or, "I thought the holiday was tomorrow?"

Most other religions don't have so many holidays during the year. So there's not that much preparation that they have to do, I guess.

[*How would you feel if you lived in a place where everybody was Jewish?*] [I'd] have a good feeling every day, 'cause everybody knows there's a holiday. . . . It would be fun, 'cause I mean, it wouldn't be boring on Shabbos 'cause when you can't . . . really do anything, there's always somebody around. . . . That's why I go to [Jewish] camp, too.

There's not too many other Jewish children around [here]. I'm sure there's some families. I know there are a few families that live in Talbot. But they aren't religious or they . . . just don't have time to send their children to temple.

We just had Simchas Torah here the other day. . . . It was really pathetic. I mean, on Thursday night, there were four little kids there and there were less than 20 people all together. . . . And then, Friday morning, there was 11 men at the big shul [temple] and there were 10 at the little shul.

When I have kids, I want to bring them up in a Jewish community. And from the looks of it here, there might be a Jewish community. I mean, there is one now, but it's dwindling away, or starting to rebuild itself. But it will probably take a while before it actually becomes a large Jewish community again, when people start coming and bringing their children to the temple and actually doing something. . . .

And I'd like to be in a place myself, even if I'm not married, I'd like to be in a place where I could walk to the temple on Saturday, or I could just go down the street and I won't have to travel so far to where I could get some good kosher meat. Or things like that. Some place where I can always, where there's always something to do, [so] you don't have to travel too far.

If the other people that are out there, if the reason that they don't come is also probably 'cause their parents [don't]. . . .'Cause I remember, I was just speaking to a friend of mine last week who's Jewish, and I said to him . . . "When was the last time you were in temple? I'm just curious." I was just joking around with him, of course. And, he was like, "Yeah, I haven't been there in a while, you know. It's pretty sad. My parents don't follow anything, so I don't," he basically said.

A couple of years ago, I had some anti-Semitic things happen. . . . But that was cleared up. I mean, it wasn't cleared up, but they, I don't know. . . . There's a few kids in school that I still know are anti-Semites. Basically Jew haters.

I was in a woods class, and there was another boy in there, my age, and he was in my grade. He's also Jewish and he used to come to the temple sometimes and went to Hebrew school. But then, of course, he started hanging around with the wrong people, and some of these people were in my class, and I guess they were . . . making fun of him. And a few of them started making swastikas out of wood. . . . So I saw one and I said to some kid, "What are you doing?" and the kid said to me, "Don't worry. It's not for you. It's for him." And I said to him, "What?!" And he walked away. And after a while, they started bugging me about it, and they started saying remarks and things and. . . . Finally, it got to a point where I had them thrown out of class . . . . 'Cause I just decided to speak up.

And there was one kid that I didn't have thrown out because I didn't think he was as harmful as they were. But it turned out, as the year went on, I had a little incident with him, too.

It was one of the last days of school, and I was wearing shorts, and it was hot out, you know. . . . And I came into the class and I said to myself, "This is it. If he says something to me today, I'm gonna go hit him." So I walked in there and I was just walking around, and he started bugging me again, so I did the same thing. I just went up to him and I pushed him, and he must've been 300 pounds. . . . And I just started pushing him and I said, "Come on, let's go already. I'm sick of you . . . ." I don't remember exactly what happened, but I know I got pulled away. . . . And he walked by me again and he goes, "You ready for the second Holocaust?"

And then I think I had him thrown out. . . . Yeah, you see, I went up to the teacher and I said to her, "I'm either gonna leave the class or they leave."

It was funny 'cause one of the kids I got thrown out actually wasn't that harmful. . . . I don't know, he was just like a little follower on the side. And it turns out last year, I was on the track team and he decided to do track, and I became friends with him. And I got to know him, and . . . apparently his grandfather had converted to Judaism before he died. . . . This year, I'm pretty good friends with him, and every time I'm talking to him, he's always mentioning Judaism. . . . And he's very interested in Judaism and he told me that he would like to convert himself. . . . He just asked me last week if he could come to the temple.

He understands a lot now. . . . So, I mean, he was hanging around with the wrong [crowd]. . . . They didn't care. I mean, they weren't doing anything in the class, anyways. They were just sitting around. . . . Yeah, druggies basically.

[*Do your teachers understand your culture?*] Yeah, when I tell them I'm gonna be out of school for the holidays and they say, "Okay, don't worry. Make up, don't worry." They know about Rosh Hashanah and Yom Kippur [major Jewish holidays], but they don't know about Succos. There's the first day and the last day. After Yom Kipper I say I'm gonna be out these other days and they go, "Oh, I thought the holidays were over with," and I go, "No, there's a few more." But they're nice about it, anyway. I mean, sometimes, once in a while, someone gets a little frustrated. You know, if I come in the next day after a holiday and I'm not ready for the test 'cause I couldn't write or do anything to study for it, but I make up my work in pretty good time. And I don't usually have any trouble.

I knew who was [Jewish at school] . . . I knew them from [an] early age. Some of those kids used to go to the temple, to the junior congregation on Saturdays. But . . . I don't really know 'cause, for example, a history teacher I had in ninth grade—I didn't know he was Jewish. Last year somebody told me he was Jewish. . . . I mean, I don't know why I just didn't want to believe he was Jewish. I mean, he never really mentioned anything to me or said anything about being Jewish or whatever.

[*How do you celebrate holidays with your family?*] With pride and tradition! . . . [*laughs*] I usually have to stay around here 'cause I work in the temple. . . . But if we can, we invite somebody over for the seder [Passover dinner]. . . . It's nice to have people over for the holidays. It makes the holiday more enjoyable.

I like the taste of chicken on a Friday night. That I've waited for all week long. It's just not the same on Wednesday night. . . . You can't even smell it the same. It's different. I like deli stuff: corned beef, a nice sandwich, a little pickle, you know. . . . I like kugel too. . . . All the Jewish food's good. . . . On like Shavuos or Pesach or Succos, we usually get special fruits, like the new spring fruits, the first fruits of the harvest.

[Pesach, or Passover] is my favorite holiday. . . . I love the preparation for it. I don't like it after the third day because there's no more seders, and there's nothing left to do except for waiting it out. I mean, it wouldn't be so bad. . . . You see, if I have to go to school, I have to go to school in the middle. But if I didn't have to go to school, then I could sit home and kind of enjoy it. But I have to go to school, and I just say it's not the same when you see other food that you can't eat. I mean, it would be a whole different feeling if you saw so many other people eating matzoh or whatever.

When I went to day school, it was nice to have people who were Jewish around you. . . . I mean, it made you understand. I mean, it was a Hebrew day school so you obviously did things that involved the religion. . . . So, it gave you a good background, is what they did.

There wasn't anybody in my town that went to the school I went to, so like, I had friends here but like when I had a holiday, no one would understand. "Why can't you come out?" You know, "Why can't you come out on a Friday night? . . ." I still get asked that same question today [*chuckles*]. . . . People know today that when I say it's a holiday, I can't come out, can't do anything.

When I came in the ninth grade, it was hard 'cause I didn't hardly know anybody, and I didn't know what to expect 'cause it was such a different curriculum. . . . I didn't know anybody, like I said, and you just walked around, you know, tried to speak to people, see who you could make friends with, who was right to make friends with.

I have a few [non-Jewish] friends around here. . . . I think this year I'm just starting to become better friends with them 'cause everybody's matured more and they're starting to go their different ways. . . . They're starting to realize that [*smiles*] they've gone wrong all these years. . . . I mean, it's our last year in high school, so I guess we're all just becoming better friends now, 'cause we're not gonna see each other again.

The Role of Positive Pressure

[Good grades] give you confidence, show you what you're doing. . . . And [help you] keep on going.

I haven't done really bad in a while. . . . I mean occasionally, I'll do bad on a test or something, but I'll just bring it back up after. 'Cause I'll feel bad after. "Ugh, I really did bad. I should have done really well." And I just try and do it better the next time. . . . Let myself slip a little bit and then I'll go back. I'll take a break and go on.

If [parents] see you're . . . having good grades, hopefully they'll trust you more and they won't nag you about this and that, and know you can function on your own.

Growing up at an early age, [my parents taught me] like what was right and wrong and the basics of Judaism.

One summer, my mother was teaching me Hebrew. My mother actually taught, sat me down and actually taught me.

She's fair. . . . She doesn't keep me bound, keep me in. You know, "Stay here; don't go anywhere. You can't go out if you have to." She trusts me. . . . Most of the time, I can see why she wouldn't want me to do something.

Most [teachers] are understanding. I mean, if you don't know how to do something, you can always just go ask them. And ask them again and again and again.

[*He singles out one particular teacher, a math teacher he had in ninth grade*] 'Cause I never really did good in math till ninth grade and I had him. And he showed me that it wasn't so bad, and after that I've been doing pretty good in math and I enjoy it.

There's some teachers that understand the kids better than other teachers. . . . They teach from the point of view of the kid. They don't just come out and say, "All right, do this, *blah, blah, blah.*" I mean, in a way, they like, sometimes joke around with the kid. They try to act like the student. . . . They're not so *one-tone voice.*

[A bad teacher is] one who just . . . for example, some student was doing really bad on his tests, test after test after test. The teacher would just correct them and that's it. Wouldn't say anything to the student. . . . I mean, you can't expect a teacher to come up to that kid every day or whatever. I mean, the teacher will say, "You know, I'm here after school. Come and get help . . . ." Instead of just walking in, writing on the board, erasing, and leaving.

[My classes are] challenging in some cases, but it's fun.

I try to run [track] as often as I can. I mean, during the season you kinda have to run every day just to keep in shape. But I like to run anyways, 'cause when you run you think about everything and just . . . it gives you time, in a way, [to] relax, and just get your mind in a different place. . . . It takes up most of my time, 'cause after that, you know you're tired. Come home from school, just go do your homework, whatever. And speak to your friends on the phone that are far away.

I do a lot of drawing. I've been drawing for years. Just sometimes—it's nothing special. Sometimes it's just doodling or drawing strange designs or things like that. But I enjoy it. It relaxes me to sit down, flip on my radio, anything I want to listen to and just draw away. . . . It just puts you away from the rest of the world.

During the week, you know, I come home late, it's after track . . . tired, don't usually go out and do something. And on the weekends, I like to relax. . . . [Shul on Saturday] tires me out for the rest of the day. . . .

I take a Hebrew course [at the Hebrew College on Sunday], and I'm taking some other course . . . about the first Jews that came to America.

Some of my friends have an influence on me, too, to do well in school. . . . My friends from camp . . . I mean, they all do pretty good in school and we're all close friends. . . . Whenever one of us gets in, if we ever got into some sort of trouble, we'd bail each other out of it. . . . Because, well, I mean, we all trust each other, basically. . . . We keep in touch a lot. . . . We'll always be friends.

I run up my phone bill talking to them 'cause they're all out of state. . . . [My mother] tells me to write letters [*laughs*]. But sometimes it's hard 'cause sometimes, in a way, I live off my friends. . . . They're like a type of energy . . . like a power source.

COMMENTARY

When asked to describe himself, Avi said he was "fun loving and religious," adjectives that might not ordinarily be juxtaposed in this way. Yet curiously, his description is an apt one. He is deeply involved in his religion, as is apparent from his earnest and responsible attitude and the dedication he gives to his work at the synagogue. He is also a gregarious and playful teenager who enjoys camp, sports, and practical jokes. A little digging may reveal how Avi has been able to develop these seemingly divergent qualities.

Avi is the youngest of three children, and his siblings are quite a bit older. Because of his father's illness, Avi's mother has been his major role model. Avi grew up watching her care for his ill father and then adjust to the loneliness and demands of widowhood. She taught him the need to be responsible, which in his family's context meant taking his studies seriously. Avi's sense of responsibility is evident in his desire to be independent, and when he makes up work after holidays or makes up his mind to bring up his grades after a slip. It is equally evident in his persistence and self-confidence. His admiration for people who have the strength to overcome adversity, whether it be drugs or failing grades, is a further indication of his belief in sheer willpower to triumph.

Because both of his parents were teachers, and given the immensely important role of scholarship within religious education in the Jewish culture, it is no surprise that Avi has done well in school. What is surprising, however, is the enormous commitment he has developed to his religious community in the "small synagogue." Avi speaks Hebrew and works hard at it. He relishes Friday night Shabbos at home and services in the temple on Saturday. He studies the Torah and is open about the love he feels for his culture and religion.

But the price Avi pays for upholding his religion and culture is often steep. It is apparent that he has thought deeply about the dilemmas of being a minority. The mismatch of his own culture with that of the school is evident in many ways, especially when it comes to organizational policies and practices. For example, during his interviews, Avi said that he had accepted that most of his teachers and classmates did not pronounce his name correctly. He appreciated that most of them tried to be understanding about the Jewish holidays, although they usually did not understand what holiday observance meant within his religious context. His days off are always at odds with those of the other students, and the curriculum is at odds with his experience.

Other problems he talks about focus on his social life and the lack of friends in this community. For a teenager, making the decision between staying home on Friday evening with family or going out with friends can be difficult. Incidents of anti-Semitism in school are even more painful reminders that being different from the majority can still be dangerous in our society. The decisiveness with which he handled these particular incidents reveals his self-confidence and desire to take control of his life (by "having them taken out of the class"), although in his hesitant explanation, it was also evident that he felt powerless ("But that was cleared up. I mean, it wasn't cleared up, but they, I don't know . . ."). The incidents also revealed his own stereotypes and class biases about those he calls "druggies."

Because remaining somewhat unassimilated is a hard choice, Avi's desire to move from Talbot when he has his own family is not unanticipated. Right now, he maintains his Jewish culture and religion by going to temple, Hebrew college, and Jewish summer camp. He has made some non-Jewish friends at school this year and alludes to the rejection he has felt in the past by joking about how they're "starting to realize that they've gone wrong all these years." And although he may smile as he says it, there is more sadness than joy in the words. Avi does not even enjoy the solidarity of the few Jewish teachers in school, whom he believes are trying to hide their Jewishness.

Combined with all of this distress is the joy of his culture and religion, which help to ground him. He relishes being "that kind of leader" within his community. It is ironic that he refers to his service in the temple as "work," given the prohibition of work on the Sabbath for observant Jews. Yet this too is an indication of the gravity with which he takes his responsibilities. As a 16-year-old, he feels the burden of keeping his community alive, even if it means being a "role model for 85-year-olds." He loves his language, his holidays, being with his family, and being religious. Family traditions such as chicken on Friday evening and preparing for Pesach are some of his favorite things.

Straddling two worlds as he does, Avi is constantly confronted with the need to accommodate the outside world. This is not a new challenge but one historically faced by most immigrants. As expressed by Stephan Brumberg in describing the experience of Jewish immigrants in New York City at the turn of the century, "In the immigrant world, learning to live simultaneously in two worlds may have been required for successful adaptation."[2] What is new in Avi's case is that this balancing act is increasingly taking place with those who have been here for more than one generation, not simply with new arrivals.

Positive pressures to be successful in school are apparent in several areas of Avi's life: high expectations at home; support from friends at camp, school, and Hebrew school; and positive reinforcement from his involvement in sports. Although his mother has never been involved in school in any significant way, Avi knows that she has great hopes for him. He describes both parents as "very educated, hard working, dedicated," adjectives that could be used to describe him as well.

At school, Avi's teachers also have high expectations for him. It is probably easy for his teachers to accommodate his religious observance since they know that he will make up his missing work in no time. Yet the perception that all Jewish children are good students, what has often been called a "positive stereotype," has placed an undue burden on many youths. Like the "model minority" myth surrounding the academic achievement of Asian students, this stereotype may result in holding Jewish students as a point of reference for all other "minorities" and influencing teachers to have unrealistic expectations for all of their Jewish students. Like the "model minority" myth, the consequences of this "positive stereotype" are negative in that they treat a whole class of students in the same way without allowing for individual differences. The historic context of education in Jewish history has influenced the educational experiences of Jews in the United States, but perceiving the Jewish community as monolithic is unfair to individual students as well as to the entire group.[3]

Avi is very involved in track. He specializes in distance running and currently participates in three seasons—cross-country, indoor, and spring track—which keeps him busy most of the school year. His team won the championship two years ago. Involvement in this activity has been the one way that Avi has been able to develop friendships outside of his culture. Because the team focuses on common goals, it is a positive environment in which to develop solidarity with others who are different from oneself. And because involvement in sports is regarded positively by most students, track has given Avi a "hook" with which to relate to others in school.

Another source of positive pressure are Avi's Jewish friends, who are, in his eloquent phrase, "a type of energy . . . like a power source." They influence him through their own academic success and their involvement with the religion and culture. That peers can have this kind of influence on young people is often overlooked by schools and parents. Yet it is the very reason for the existence of such institutions as Portuguese American schools, Hebrew camps, and Saturday culture schools in the Chinese community.

Jewish culture is intertwined with religion and tradition, rather than with nationality as in other groups, and this may make maintaining cultural ties more difficult. Although our society claims to be secular, clearly it is not. Rather, it is openly a Christian nation, as can be seen in the abundance of Christian symbols and artifacts, from the daily prayer in Congress to the crèches that adorn small towns in New England, where Avi comes from, at Christmas. Added to this is the weight of centuries of oppression, minority status, and marginality to which Jews have been subjected. Even in societies where they have been assimilated, Jews have often been victimized and treated as scapegoats.[4] Given this long history of oppression, Jews throughout the world have had to think long and hard about the balance between the degree of accommodating to host societies and maintaining their cultural traditions. The results have ranged all the way from becoming completely assimilated and losing all traces of their roots, to remaining within religious and cultural enclaves removed from any but the most basic and necessary exchanges with non-Jews.[5]

Pressure toward assimilation and the accommodations made to it are only one reflection of the diversity in the Jewish community in the United States, which has often been portrayed in a unidimensional manner. Yet Jews differ in religiosity, tradition, political viewpoints, language, and social class, among other characteristics. The religious tenets in Judaism itself—that is, Orthodox, Reform, and Conservative elements—reflect this diversity. In addition, some Jews who are not religious at all, secular Jews, are still profoundly Jewish. Some Jews speak Hebrew, others speak Yiddish, and still others speak neither. Jews differ in their viewpoints on relations with the Arab world and on Zionism.

Racist stereotypes depict Jews as wealthy merchants who control the banking industry and the media, and as landlords, moneylenders, and chiselers. *Jew down,* meaning to bargain downward, is a phrase still used almost casually in many quarters and is a reflection of this racist stereotype. Yet although Jews as a group have a higher average income than other groups, they also have higher education levels. Rather than wealthy, most Jews in the United States are middle class in income and profession, and a substantial number of Jews live in poverty.[6]

These are some of the dilemmas faced by Avi Abramson, who is trying to be both an American and a Jew. He is maintaining a difficult balancing act between complete assimilation into the mainstream of U.S. life and holding onto his religion and culture. This is not easy, even for seasoned adults. For Avi, it means not giving in to assimilationist forces while also accommodating those parts of his life to U.S. society that will not compromise his values. With the help of his family, friends, and religious community, and with the support of his non-Jewish community, he may just be able to do it.

TO THINK ABOUT

1. What, in your view, keeps Avi Abramson so involved in his synagogue?
2. Do you think Avi's school life would be different if he were not on the track team? How? What implications can you draw from this for schools?
3. The United States officially supports "separation of church and state," but is it possible for teachers to affirm Avi's culture and background without bringing religion into the school? Think about some ways this might be done. If you do not believe it is possible, then list some of the ways that the separation of church and state is violated by schools. What is the alternative to this practice?
4. Friends are, in Avi's words, "like a power source." How can teachers use this power source to good advantage? Think of strategies that teachers and schools might develop to build on positive peer pressure.
5. It is obvious that Avi has little respect for those he calls "the druggies." Do you think schools perpetuate stereotypes such as these? If you were a teacher in his school, what might you do about this problem?

Case Study: Fern Sherman

"If there's something in the history book that's wrong, I should tell them that it is wrong."

Springdale, a small city in Iowa, is surrounded by farm country. With a population of close to 50,000, the city is a haven from the problems of more populated midwestern cities, yet it affords the advantages of a large university and other cultural activities. Springdale is not very ethnically diverse. Most of its residents of European heritage identify themselves as "American," with no ethnic classification. Many have been here for several generations. The African American community numbers just over 1,000, and there are fewer than 800 Latinos. There are slightly more than 3,000 Asians, the largest non–European American group. The number of Native Americans in the entire city is minuscule, totaling only about 60.

Fern Sherman[1] is 14 years old and an eighth grader in the middle school in town. With Chippewa, Ponca, Norwegian, German, and English heritage, Fern identifies herself as Native American. She and her sisters are registered as both Turtle Mountain Chippewa and Northern Ponca, an Indian Nation that was reinstated after being "terminated" (no longer recognized by the federal government) in 1966. Tribal affiliation designations are so complex and bureaucratic that Fern and her sisters have been classified as 237/512, or slightly over half Indian. This kind of identification is arbitrary and clearly a social construct, having little to do with self-identification. American Indians are unique in having a legal definition in the United States.[2]

The Indian community is extremely heterogeneous. It numbers almost 2 million, more than double the 1970 U.S. Census. About 500 Nations are recognized by the federal government, over 200 of which have a land base or reservation. There are others that are not officially recognized.[3] About two-thirds of all Indians now live away from reservations in other communities, primarily in urban areas. Although a growing number of American Indians speak only English, one-third regularly speak another language as well. Currently more than 200 languages are spoken and many are still vigorously maintained. For example, over 70 percent of Navajo children enter school speaking Navajo as their native language. Several Indian Nations have declared their languages to be official, designating English as a "foreign language."[4] American Indians are also very diverse in cultural traditions, physical appearance, religion, and lifestyle. In spite of these vast differences, a pan-Indian identity has been emerging in the past generation, probably the result of several factors: the many values shared by most Native peoples; the need to develop greater political strength; and intermarriage among Native groups, as is the case in Fern's family.

Fern says she is the only Native American in her entire school and she wishes there were more. Before moving to Springdale, she attended a tribal reservation school for kindergarten and first grade and later a public school where there were a large number of Indian students. In that school, there were some Indian teachers, an Indian Club, an Indian education program with special tutors, and other support services. In both of those schools, Fern and her sisters felt comfortable and accepted, which is not always the case now.

Fern lives with her father, two sisters, and young nephew, although at present both sisters are away. Her father is a professor of political science at the local university, and her mother, who lives in another city, is a truck driver. Her parents have been separated for years, and Fern and her sisters rarely see their mother, who has taken little responsibility for their upbringing and education. She has two other sisters who live with their mother. Instrumental in raising her nephew, Daryl, now two years old, Fern knows firsthand what raising a child is like and wants to delay having children of her own for a long time. She says, "I want to get my life started and on the go before I have a family."

Fern's sisters, Juanita and Rose, are 16 and 17 years old. They are actually stepsisters, sharing the same mother. Despite not being their biological father, Mr. Sherman has taken responsibility for raising Juanita and Rose as well as his own daughter. Both of the older girls have a history of alcohol and drug abuse. Rose is in an out-of-state treatment center and she is expected to move back home in a few months; Juanita is living at an alcohol and drug abuse residential center. She began drinking a number of years ago because, according to her father, "she just never fit in." Isolated and alone at school, she sought relief through alcohol.

Drug abuse and alcoholism are tearing many Indian communities apart. Mr. Sherman's ex-wife and three daughters have all been affected. The girls' mother has been in four treatment centers for drug and alcohol abuse and has served a prison term of over two years for offenses related to her addiction. Even Fern, a successful student who loves school and is thoroughly involved in sports and other extracurricular activities, has not been spared: She has tried marijuana and alcohol but is not addicted, probably having learned a difficult lesson from the experiences of her sisters.

Mr. Sherman has been instrumental in helping Juanita and Rose overcome their addiction. He has seen the results of drug and alcohol abuse and he is convinced that they are linked to poor self-esteem and lack of success in school. As a result, he pushes his daughters to excel in school. Having lived through the nightmare of addiction with his family, he thinks about the role that schools should be playing. "Do we have to intervene in every Indian kid's life that goes into these school systems in such drastic manners?" he asks ruefully. Although he does not place the blame entirely on teachers for his children's problems, he thinks that there are too many misunderstandings in school that can lead to failure. Getting a good education is an essential that he feels his children cannot afford to neglect. He is tireless in his pressure on them to study, get good grades, and prepare for college. Fern is only in eighth grade and doing very well academically, and her father is keeping his fingers crossed that she will continue to do so. His agonizing experiences with his other daughters have tempered his optimism.

Becoming aware and proud of their heritage is the other message that Mr. Sherman gives his daughters. They do not speak a language other than English at home, but he sometimes teaches them words in Ponca. They perceive his pressure on them to succeed and to identify themselves as Native American as sometimes overwhelming, but they also appreciate him for giving them strength in their culture and determination to get ahead.

Fern and her family live in a middle-class neighborhood close to the university. It is a friendly and close-knit community but, like many suburbs, provides little recreation for youths. She and her family live in a block of condominiums. Although they are the only Native American family in the area, Fern describes her community as a "really nice neighborhood" and "one big happy family." She says that her neighbors are always there to help one another out and that they are understanding and kind.

Saying that the middle school she attends is "kinda stuck on itself," Fern nevertheless acknowledges that it is a good school, and she loves going. She is taking classes in science, math, English, home economics, art, physical education, and family and consumer science, her favorite subject because it includes experiences in child care. Her grades are very good, although they do not necessarily reflect her interests accurately: Her highest grade was in English, her least favorite subject; and her worst grade, C, was in her favorite subject, science. The grades, however, are a reflection of the particular teachers who taught these subjects this year. Fern is very active in school activities such as chorus, cooking club, and sports, and in out-of-school activities such as dance.

Aware of the role of teachers' expectations on her achievement, Fern spoke about her reaction to different teachers and schools. Family pressures and responsibilities, the isolation she feels as the only Native American student in her school, and identifying as a successful student are the other themes that highlight Fern's interviews.

The Role of Teachers' Expectations

I'd rather go through school and get A's and B's than D's and F's. . . . In Springdale, I've noticed if you're getting D's and F's, they don't look up to you; they look down. And you're always the last on the list for special activities, you know?

Most of my friends were from the same culture or background [in former school in South Dakota] 'cause there are a lot of Native Americans there. And you weren't really treated different there. . . . You were all the same and you all got pushed the same and you were all helped the same. And one thing I've noticed in Springdale is they kind of teach 25 percent and they kinda leave 75 percent out. . . . [Teachers] really push us hard, but if we're getting bad grades, they don't help us as much.

Being at the top of my class, always being noticed as a top person, gradewise [made me feel good]. I mostly got straight A's and B's until I moved to Springdale. And I got like a C and D the first semester, in science and math here because they just push you to your limits. I mean, it's just incredible the way they think you're like "Incredible Woman" or something.

I don't like being pushed to my limit. I mean, I think you should have a little bit of leeway. . . . Like, this past week, I had three different reports due in three different classes. . . . I think [teachers] should have at least a little bit of communication, not to give you three reports due in the same week.

I like going to math or like science to do different experiments. I've always liked science, but it's not really my best subject. I like American history because sometimes I'll know more than the teacher, just because my dad has taught me stuff.

I don't really like English . . . because I hate when they make you cut off at 400 words. . . . If you can't write what you're gonna write, why write it?

In science, if you don't understand something, and the science teacher doesn't get in until 8:00 and the bell rings at 8:10. . . . In 10 minutes, you can't learn something. . . . Like if you don't have your assignment done, and you need help on it, you have 10 minutes to go in, get help, get it done. Because if it's not done by class time, you'll have detention. . . . That really holds me back. Because if they're not gonna take time to teach you and you're the one that's taking time to come in and let them teach you.

[*What would you do to make school more interesting?*] More like involved activities in class, you know? . . .'Cause like when you're sitting in class, and the teacher is lecturing, I usually feel like falling asleep, 'cause it's just blah. And in chorus, there's like this rap about history, you know? It's really fun. . . . More like making the whole class be involved, not making only the two smartest people up here do the whole work for the whole class.

Family Pressure, Expectations, and Responsibilities

I [try to do well in school] for my dad, but I mostly do it for myself.

[My sisters] are always like, "Yeah, you're daddy's girl, just 'cause you get A's and B's . . . ." It's how they put me down for what I'm doing, for how I'm succeeding.

He's always involved in what's happening in school, unlike most parents. . . . My dad is just always [at school]. He's always been there, every school activity, I mean, unless our car breaks down. . . . I sure remember, we were having a musical and it was set up with like 300 kids. And our car had a flat tire. And so my dad put this air stuff in so he could get me to the musical [*laughing*]. And he went and got the tire fixed and he made the guy give him a ride back to school so he could see it! . . . He's always been involved, so I really don't know what it's like to not be involved.

He thinks [school] is heaven! . . . When he was young, he only got A's and B's . . . C was an F to him. And I sometimes have to stop him and say, "Hey, I'm not you!" But I'm glad he's pushing me.

Just from my family breaking up so many times . . . I've learned to always stick with it. . . . I've learned really to stick with my family. I've always been told to love everybody the same in your family, but sometimes that's really hard for me because I've always been so close to Juanita. . . .

So, I really feel that Juanita's my mom. . . . My dad's probably the first person I go to, and Juanita's probably someone I can go to, you know, for "woman help."

My dad is more or less a brick wall that you can't get through [*laughing*]. He's really set, like you always get those stupid lectures: "Well, my dad did it this way . . . ." But, Dad, *you're* not your dad. I know I might grow up and treat my children a little bit the same way as my dad, but knowing how much it hurts me inside when he says, "Well, you know, I was a straight A student when I was little . . ." I'm not gonna do that to my kids because it just makes them want to fail more. . . . When you're mad at your parents, you try to find something to get them back with. And I think grades are a very good way to get them back with.

He's a kid at heart. He doesn't try to be "Macho Parent" or "Mercedes Man." He doesn't try to fit in with people. He's himself, and he's always been himself. And if people don't like the way he is, tough sherlock!

He's a one-of-a-kind dad. I'll always love him for what he is.

I've really not known [my mother] that much. From just what my dad's told me and what I've seen, she is really hard to get along with. She's like very emotional. . . . She makes all these excuses, of "Yeah, my phone bill's really high, I'm sorry I can't call you." Well, if the stupid boyfriend's more important than calling her own daughter, you know, that's not my fault. She's always been mean, in my eyes, but nice when she's face to face with me.

I think I'm gifted to have a family like this. But I'm glad we're not a Leave-it-to-Beaver-Cleaver family. I've got friends that their families are perfect, no problems. But I'm sure there are problems inside the locked doors, but not really showing it. But in my family, if I'm angry, I'm going to go out and tell them. . . . I hate people who try to hide it.

You know how counselors say "dysfunctional" and "functional" families? I think every family's dysfunctional, in their own way. I mean, every family is gonna have a fight about what they're gonna eat for supper, or who gets the family car tonight, or whatever.

[Dad] always tries to comfort me, telling me that he's always there for me. He can always arrange for me to talk to somebody if I'm hurting. But I try to explain to him that he's the only person I really need. . . . He's always been understanding. . . . [When things go bad], I talk to my dad.

The Isolation of Being Native American

[South Dakota] was more like everybody was a family. . . . You would go to your backyard and have a banquet with the whole neighborhood, you know? It was like the whole town was one big family.

Sometimes I get sick of hearing about [being Native American]. . . . I mean, like my dad just goes on and on, and finally, I just space out and pretend like I'm listening to him. . . . Because I've already heard all of it. . . . And he always tries to make me what I'm not, make me more Native American.

And since I'm the only Native American in the Springdale school district almost, he tries to make me go to the principal and say, "We need this." There's no use, because there's no other Native Americans to help me!

I'm really not noticed as a Native American until something . . . like the ITBS test. . . . The woman was giving us our codes. . . . She called "Native Americans," and she goes, "Well, I don't think there is any." And the whole auditorium goes, "Fern!" I think it's really neat. . . . I don't hide it. I express it.

[My teachers don't understand my culture.] Like if I say, "This isn't done in my culture. This isn't the way it's done . . . ." Like talking about abortion in history or something. For Native Americans, abortion is just . . . like you should really put the mother in jail for it. Because . . . the baby is alive, just like we are. And that's the way I feel. And when they sit there and say, "It's the mother's right to do it," well, I don't think it's the mother's right because it's not the baby's fault the mother doesn't want it. And so, when I try to tell them, they just, "Oh, well, we're out of time." They cut me off, and we've still got half an hour! And so that kinda makes me mad.

If there's something in the history book that's wrong, my dad always taught me that if it's wrong, I should tell them that it is wrong. And the only time I ever do is if I know it's *exactly* wrong. Like we were reading about Native Americans and scalping. Well, the French are really the ones that made them do it so they could get money. And my teacher would not believe me. I finally just shut up because he just would not believe me. . . . Just my arguments with them, they just cut it off.

[Other people] are not going to understand me as much, if I start talking about spirituality. . . . But I don't feel like people put me down or put me up for being Indian. . . . I always get good praises from people, you know. "I'm glad you're sticking in there, not being ashamed of being Native American."

We do have different values. . . . We do have different needs and we do have different wants. I mean, I'm sure every family needs love. Love is a very, very top thing in our list of needs. . . . For White people, it's usually shelter over their heads. For Native Americans, usually number one, family love.

It can be different. Like my family sits down and eats corn soup and fried dough. It would be different from, "Well, my family goes out for pizza."

I don't know why . . . other Native Americans have dropped out of Springdale schools. Maybe it's because I just haven't been in high school yet. But I remember one time, my sister came home and she was just mad. They said that . . . "Geronimo was a stupid chief riding that stupid horse," and my sister got mad!

I've always been taught to be kind to elders, to always look up to them. And my dad's always taught me that everybody's really the same. I mean, there's no difference between Black and White. . . . Really everybody's the same to me, because we're all the same blood, you know?

It really disgusts me when somebody with brown hair wants blond hair. I mean, it's what God wanted you to have, you know? . . . It just makes me sick. . . . It really never made sense to me.

Identifying as Successful

I found school fun. . . . I liked to do homework. I got moved: I didn't go to kindergarten, I went straight from Head Start to first grade because I was too bored in the classes, and I wouldn't do the work because I fought with the teachers and told them I already did it because I had done it the year before. And so my dad made them move me out because there was no use for me to stay back if I wasn't gonna learn anything new.

I like sports a lot, volleyball and basketball. . . . I like sports and I'm just glad they offer them 'cause some schools don't have enough funding. . . . But basketball is mostly my sport. . . . I compare it to stuff, like, when I can't get science, or like in sewing, I'll look at that machine and I'll say, "This is a basketball; I can overcome it . . . ."

One [of my friends], she's really understanding. If I have family problems, she's always there to talk to. We're really close. . . . We're like involved in the same sports, and we love basketball. . . . Natalie, I can always talk to. . . . I mean, she's like free counseling!

I've like always wanted to be president of the United States, but I figured that was too hard [*laughs*]. . . . I don't know, I kinda wanna be a fashion lawyer.

I've always wanted to be president and I think it's just because like, I'll see so many mess-ups and . . . I don't know, just George Bush right now. . . . I was infatuated with Ronald Reagan the whole time he was in office. . . . And like I'd make posters for Dad and tell him, "Yeah, this is me." And I just like the idea of being head honcho!

[*What is the reason for going to school?*] To learn and make something out of yourself when you're older, so you're not just, I don't know, a person on welfare or something.

I sure remember the day I got my first B; I started crying. Most of my friends, you know, get A's and B's, and everything. And it's not to impress them; it's to show them that I'm just as good, you know? It's mostly just for me, to make me know that I'm just as good as anybody else and that I can really do it.

I'm ambitious. I always want to get things done. Like say I'm running for copresident for the school, I want to get my campaign done ahead, not the day before.

I succeed in everything I do. If I don't get it right the first time, I always go back and try to do it again.

COMMENTARY

Fern Sherman is a successful student, although the dropout rate for Native American students as a whole is estimated to be among the highest of any other group, over 25 percent.[5] This percentage is misleading, however, because many students drop out before even reaching high school, as early as elementary school.

Teachers' expectations of Indian students' achievement play an important role. They certainly have had an impact on Fern's school achievement.

Although she says that she does not like to be pushed, it is obvious that when teachers hold high expectations, she is able to live up to them. What most distresses her is teachers with low expectations or who teach only to the high achievers (what Fern calls "the top 25 percent"). She believes that all students can learn if the instruction is meaningful to them.

Fern's father, who pushes academic achievement and ethnic pride and awareness, is obviously the major influence in her life. Having been a successful student himself, he knows the value of education. And as an American Indian, he is convinced that the only way to progress, both individually and for the community, is by having a good education. These are the messages Fern has been listening to since early childhood, and they have had a profound impact on her. She says that she tries to be successful for herself, her father, and her friends ("to show them that I'm just as good"). The need to excel on an individual basis contradicts a deeply held cultural value of collective progress in American Indian communities. Striving to excel for one's family, Nation, or community is a much better way of motivating children, which is why Fern's father stresses "making Grandmother proud." Providing a learning environment that emphasizes cooperative learning rather than individual competition is one important culturally appropriate strategy for schools to consider. Others include using traditional ways of knowing in constructing the curriculum and providing meaningful activities that build on and affirm students' culture.[6]

Being the only American Indian student in school is a theme that came up repeatedly during Fern's interviews. At times, the pressure of being the only one is unbearable, especially when she feels that her father expects her to confront every issue dealing with Native people head-on. At other times, being the only one means being unique and special (she identified being singled out for this kind of interview as one of the benefits). Although some teachers, such as her English teacher, make accommodations in their content and structure, most others do not. For example, when giving writing assignments about their families, her English teacher allows each student ample flexibility to discuss differences. And although Fern loves science, she feels that her teacher is not very helpful and probably the "last person for me to go talk to."

Being the only Native American in her school also means always being different. Fern is an extremely strong young woman, but this kind of pressure is exceedingly difficult for adolescents experiencing the traumas of identification and peer acceptance. Her feeling that a Native American perspective is missing from school curricula is likely correct. Her perception that it is not welcome (e.g., in the discussion about abortion) also may be true, but this perception is likely influenced by her feelings of isolation. We need to understand the history of American Indian education in the United States to understand the legacy of resentment and suspicion with which Native people often view U.S. schooling.[7]

Education has often been used to separate children physically, emotionally, and culturally from their families. A particularly graphic example of this practice is the 1895 *Annual Report* of the Indian commissioner to the secretary of the interior, in which the government's intent in educating Indian children was described as "to free the children from the language and habits of their untutored and oftentimes savage parents."[8] Such blatant expressions of racism probably would not be found today, but many of the patronizing attitudes stemming from this belief are still apparent in the curriculum and texts used in schools.

Being Native American brings with it other benefits that Fern is quick to point out. She has a very strong sense of her culture and is proud of it. Although she may sometimes feel marginalized, she has developed the mature belief that being Native American means accepting yourself for who you are. The fact that it disturbs her to see people dye their hair is her reaction to the self-rejection felt by many young people of culturally dominated groups. During her interviews, it was clear that Fern was beginning to enjoy the tangible expressions of her culture, from corn soup to powwows.

Unlike other young people her age, Fern is astute in understanding cultural differences. She has to be since she is usually the one who has had to accommodate to the majority. She is quite sophisticated in identifying differences between her ethnic group and the dominant culture. These are both concrete (e.g., differences in food) and intangible (such as Native American spirituality and her preference for some activities over others in school). When asked what she would like to see more of in schools, she is explicit: "more like involved activities, you know?" she says, capturing the general tendency of Indian students to do better in tests and activities requiring ability in observation, memory, and attention to detail than those emphasizing language and verbal expression.[9]

The fact that Fern has a hard time in science as it is taught in her school may be an indication of this difference. According to Sharon Nelson-Barber and Elise Trumbull Estrin, a majority of teachers do not recognize the knowledge or learning strategies that American Indian students bring to science and math; because of this, teachers lose out on ways to involve students more meaningfully in their learning. Yet ironically, traditional American Indian ways of knowing, such as modeling and providing time for observation and practice, are consistent with constructivist notions of learning.[10]

Staying in school, studying hard, and being successful are important to Fern in spite of—or perhaps because of—what she knows about the experiences of other Native American students. She knows the dropout problem is significant and correctly asserts that it is likely she has not faced it because she has yet to go to high school. Her sister Juanita's experience, sadly, is not that unusual. But underachievement and illiteracy have not always been the norm. When schools are culturally aware and make sense to students, the students tend to succeed. Fern's father's assertion that her former school was a better environment for learning is based on the support system that was in place for Indian students there. Even having Indian teachers, for example, has an impact on students' feelings of belonging and consequently on their achievement. One study found that Indian students who have Indian teachers do better on standardized achievement tests in reading and language arts.[11] Yet in 1990, Indian teachers in the United States represented only 0.6 percent of all teachers in the profession, and the number was expected to decrease in the years ahead.[12]

American Indian children are faced with other difficult situations as well: Suicide is much more prevalent among reservation Indians than in the general population and the rate of adult unemployment is extraordinary, reaching as high as 50 percent; health care, particularly on reservations, is either absent or completely inadequate; infant mortality is above the national average and there are widespread nutritional deficiencies; and alcoholism may affect the lives and functioning of more than 60 percent of all Native children.[13] Struggling against these odds is an awesome responsibility; school sometimes takes a back seat. Fern has developed a number of successful strategies to deal with these overwhelmingly negative barriers to success. She is unabashedly ambitious. She wants to succeed in school and beyond and is quite certain that she will ("I succeed in everything I do," she says confidently). When asked who she most admires, she mentions President Bush (who was president at the time she was interviewed)—not necessarily the man, but "his power and success, and I just wish I could be as successful." This ambition spurs her on to do her best both in and out of school. In fact, when asked what she likes most about herself, she is quick to single out her ambition.

In helping to raise her nephew, supporting her sister Juanita during this difficult time, adjusting to a school where she is evidently different from all her peers, and confronting the dual challenges of academic success and parental pressures, no matter how positive they may be, Fern Sherman has to contend with tremendous responsibilities at an early age. Despite the obstacles, she has identified a goal: to become president of the United States. She is determined and courageous enough to try.

TO THINK ABOUT

1. Fern's feeling of isolation in a city with so few American Indians affects her life in a great many ways. When have you been the only ___ (fill in the blank) in a particular setting? What impact did this have on you? Describe how you felt in school, at home, and in your community. What might have made you feel less isolated? What are the implications of this situation for you as a teacher?
2. What is meant by the statement that tribal affiliation is a *social construct?* Who determines what a person is? Why has that been done for some but not others in our society?
3. From Fern's case study, what do you think are some of the pressures that can lead to alcohol and drug abuse for young people? What specific situations in the Indian community can exacerbate this problem? What can schools do to help alleviate it?
4. If you could talk with Fern about remaining a successful and confident student, what would you say?
5. What approaches might work to lower the dropout rate of Indian students? What can schools, communities, and families do together to help?
6. Work together with a small group of your colleagues and plan a science lesson in which you incorporate some American Indian ways of knowing (you may want to read the article by Nelson-Barber and Estrin first). How might it

differ from another science lesson? Would Indian students be the only ones to benefit from such lessons? Why or why not?

● *NOTES TO CHAPTER 4*

1. John Dewey, *Democracy and Education* (New York: The Free Press, 1916), 175.
2. See, for example, Jonathan Kozol, *Savage Inequalities* (New York: Crown, 1991).
3. In the discussion that follows, the term *tracking* rather than *ability grouping* is generally used. Ability grouping may differ from tracking both in intent and structure. Ability groups may be temporary and ad hoc strategies used in particular situations, whereas tracking generally implies rather rigid placement of students in groups that change very little over time.
4. Ray Rist, "Student Social Class and Teacher Expectations: The Self-Fulfilling Prophecy in Ghetto Education." In *Challenging the Myths: The Schools, the Blacks, and the Poor,* Reprint Series no. 5. (Cambridge, MA: Harvard Educational Review, 1971).
5. Jeannie Oakes, Amy Stuart Wells, Makeba Jones, and Amanda Datnow, "Detracking: The Social Construction of Ability, Cultural Politics, and Resistance to Reform." *Teachers College Record,* 98, 3 (1997), 482–510.
6. *Locked In/Locked Out: Tracking and Placement Practices in Boston Public Schools* (Boston: Massachusetts Advocacy Center, March 1990).
7. Jeannie Oakes and Gretchen Guiton, "Matchmaking: The Dynamics of High School Tracking Decisions." *American Education Research Journal,* 32, 1 (Spring, 1995), 3–33.
8. Jomills H. Braddock, II, "Tracking the Middle Grades: National Patterns of Grouping for Instruction." *Phi Delta Kappan,* 71, 6 (February 1990), 445–449.
9. Ruth B. Ekstrom, "Six Urban School Districts: Their Middle-Grade Grouping Policies and Practices." In *On the Right Track: The Consequences of Mathematics Course Placement Policies and Practices in the Middle Grades.* Report to the Edna McConnell Clark Foundation (Princeton, NJ, and New York: ETS and the National Urban League, 1992).
10. Adam Gamoran, Martin Nystrand, Mark Berends, and Paul Le Pore, "An Organizational Analysis of the Effects of Ability Grouping." *American Educational Research Journal,* 32, 4 (Winter, 1995), 687–715.
11. Jeannie Oakes, *Keeping Track: How Schools Structure Inequality* (New Haven, CT: Yale University Press, 1985). See also Massachusetts Advocacy Center, *Locked In/Locked Out;* Thomas Hoffer, "Middle School Ability Grouping and Students' Achievement in Science and Math." *Educational Evaluation and Policy Analysis,* 14, 3 (Fall 1992), 205–227; Hugh Mehan and Irene Villanueva, "Untracking Low Achieving Students: Academic and Social Consequences." *Focus on Diversity* (Newsletter of the National Center for Research on Cultural Diversity and Second Language Learning), 3, 3 (Winter 1993), 4–6.
12. Oakes, *et al.,* "Detracking."
13. Ibid.
14. *Harvard Education Letter,* xiii, 1 (January/February, 1997). Special issue on detracking.
15. See, for example, Anne Wheelock, *Crossing the Tracks: How "Untracking" Can Save America's Schools* (New York: New Press, 1992); Mara Sapon-Shevin, "Ability Differences in the Classroom: Teaching and Learning in Inclusive Classrooms." In *Common Bonds: Anti-Bias Teaching in a Diverse Society,* edited by Deborah A. Byrnes and Gary Kiger (Wheaton, MD: Association for Childhood Education International, 1992).

16. A recent example of how IQ tests are used to "prove" the social and intellectual inferiority of some groups is *The Bell Curve: Intelligence and Class Structure in American Life,* by Richard J. Herrnstein and Charles Murray (New York: Free Press, 1994). The book has been repudiated by numerous social scientists: See the special issue of *American Behavioral Scientist:* The Bell Curve: Laying Bare the Resurgence of Scientific Racism, 39, 1 (September/October, 1995).

17. Lewis Terman, *The Measurement of Intelligence* (Boston: Houghton Mifflin, 1916).

18. See reviews of the connection between IQ testing and eugenics in Gould, *The Mismeasure of Man.* Also see Richard A. Figueroa and Eugene García, "Issues in Testing Students from Culturally and Linguistically Diverse Backgrounds." *Multicultural Education,* 2, 1 (Fall 1994), 10–19.

19. Noe Medina and D. Monty Neill, *Fallout from the Testing Explosion,* 3rd ed. (Cambridge, MA: FairTest, 1990).

20. Carol Ascher, *Testing Students in Urban Schools: Current Problems and New Directions* (New York: ERIC Clearinghouse on Urban Education, Teachers College, Columbia University, 1990).

21. FairTest, *Tables on State Testing* (Cambridge, MA: Author, 1997).

22. For a review and analysis of the 1990s national curriculum standards movement, see the special issue of *Educational Forum* (Sonia Nieto, guest editor) devoted to this topic (vol. 58, no. 4, Summer 1994); and Michael W. Apple, "The Politics of Official Knowledge: Does a National Curriculum Make Sense?" *Teachers College Record,* 95, 2 (Winter 1993), 222–241.

23. See, for example, research reported by Ascher, *Testing Students in Urban Schools.* See also Linda Winfield and Michael Woodard, *Assessment, Equity, and Diversity in Reforming America's Schools* (Los Angeles: National Center for Research on Evaluation, Standards, and Student Testing, UCLA Graduate School of Education, 1994); Carol Ascher and Gary Burnett, *Current Trends and Issues in Urban Education* (New York: ERIC Clearinghouse on Urban Education, Teachers College, Columbia University, 1993).

24. Pat Ordovensky, "SAT Scores Show Signs of Recovery." *USA Today,* August 27, 1992, p. 1D.

25. H. Dickson Corbett and Bruce L. Wilson, *Testing, Reform and Rebellion* (Norwood, NJ: Ablex, 1991).

26. Linda Darling-Hammond, "The Implications of Testing Policy for Quality and Equality." *Phi Delta Kappan,* 73, 3 (November 1991), 220–225.

27. Dewey, *Democracy and Education,* p. 172.

28. Figueroa and García, "Issues in Testing Students from Culturally and Linguistically Diverse Backgrounds"; W. James Popham, "Farewell, Curriculum: Confessions of an Assessment Convert." *Phi Delta Kappan,* 79, 5 (January, 1998), 380–384.

29. Monty Neill, "Transforming Student Assessment." *Phi Delta Kappan,* 79, 1 (September, 1997), 34–40, 58; p. 35.

30. See Elise Trumbull Estrin, *Alternative Assessment: Issues in Language, Culture, and Equity,* Knowledge Brief no. 11 (San Francisco: Far West Laboratory, 1993).

31. Linda Darling-Hammond, "Performance-Based Assessment and Educational Equity." *Harvard Educational Review,* 64, 1 (Spring, 1994), 5–30.

32. Charles Rooney, *Test Scores Do Not Equal Merit: Enhancing Equity and Excellence in College Admissions by Deemphasizing SAT and ACT Results* (Cambridge, MA: FairTest, 1998).

33. Lisa Delpit, *Other People's Children* (New York: The New Press, 1995).

34. Mary Poplin and Joseph Weeres, *Voices from the Inside: A Report on Schooling from Inside the Classroom* (Claremont, CA: The Institute for Education in Transformation, Claremont Graduate School, 1992).

35. Henry Louis Gates, Jr., *Loose Canons: Notes on the Culture Wars* (New York: Oxford University Press, 1992).

36. Luis C. Moll, "Bilingual Classroom Studies and Community Analysis: Some Recent Trends." *Educational Researcher,* 21, 2 (March 1992), 20–24.

37. Judith Solsken, Jo-Anne Wilson Keenan, and Jerri Willett, "Interweaving Stories: Creating a Multicultural Classroom through School/Home/University Collaboration." *Democracy and Education* (Fall 1993), 16–21, p. 21.

38. Michelle Fine, *Framing Dropouts: Notes on the Politics of an Urban Public High School* (Albany, NY: State University of New York Press, 1991), 33.

39. Ibid., 37.

40. Melinda Fine, "'You Can't Just Say that the Only Ones Who Can Speak Are Those Who Agree with Your Position': Political Discourse in the Classroom." *Harvard Educational Review,* 63, 4 (1993), 412–433.

41. María E. Torres-Guzmán, "Stories of Hope in the Midst of Despair: Culturally Responsive Education for Latino Students in an Alternative High School in New York City." In *Cross-Cultural Literacy: Ethnographies of Communication in Multiethnic Classrooms,* edited by Marietta Saravia-Shore and Steven F. Arvizu (New York: Garland Publishers, 1992).

42. David Bloome with Rachel Bloomekatz and Petra Sander, "Literacy, Democracy, and the Pledge of Allegiance." *Language Arts,* 70, 8 (December 1993), 655–658.

43. Ibid., 658.

44. Donaldo P. Macedo, "Literacy for Stupidification: The Pedagogy of Big Lies." *Harvard Educational Review,* 63, 2 (Summer 1993), 183–206.

45. Ibid., 187.

46. For an excellent analysis of this phenomenon, see Chapter 6 in Kathleen Bennett, *The Way Schools Work,* 3rd. ed. (New York: Longman, 1999).

47. Jeannie Oakes, *Multiplying Inequalities: The Effects of Race, Social Class, and Tracking on Opportunities to Learn Mathematics and Science* (Santa Monica, CA: Rand, 1990), vi.

48. Study by the American Council on Education in 1949; cited by Gordon Allport, *The Nature of Prejudice* (Reading, MA: Addison-Wesley, 1954), 202.

49. Jesús García, "The Changing Image of Ethnic Groups in Textbooks." *Phi Delta Kappan,* 75, 1 (September 1993), 29–35.

50. Christine E. Sleeter and Carl A. Grant, "Race, Class, Gender and Disability in Current Textbooks." In *The Politics of the Textbook,* edited by Michael W. Apple and Linda K. Christian-Smith (New York: Routledge & Chapman Hall, 1991); see also Bárbara C. Cruz, "Stereotypes of Latin Americans Perpetuated in Secondary School History Textbooks." *Latino Studies Journal,* 1, 1 (January, 1994), 51–67.

51. James W. Loewen, *Lies My Teacher Told Me: Everything Your American History Textbook Got Wrong* (New York: New Press, 1995).

52. Michael W. Apple, "The Text and Cultural Politics." *Educational Researcher,* 21, 7 (October 1992), 4–11, 19.

53. See, for example, Rudine Sims, *Shadow and Substance: Afro-American Experience in Contemporary Children's Fiction* (Urbana, IL: National Council of Teachers of English, 1982); Violet J. Harris, ed., *Using Multiethnic Literature in the K–8 Classroom* (Norwood, MA: Christopher-Gordon, 1997); Arlette Willis, ed., *Teaching*

and Using Multicultural Literature in Grades 9–12: Moving Beyond the Canon (Norwood, MA: Christopher-Gordon, 1998).

54. Goodlad, *A Place Called School.*
55. Larry Cuban, *How Teachers Taught: Constancy and Change in American Classrooms, 1880–1990,* 2nd ed. (New York: Teachers College Press, 1993).
56. Martin Haberman, "The Pedagogy of Poverty versus Good Teaching." *Phi Delta Kappan,* 73, 4 (December 1991), 290–294.
57. Eugene E. García, *Education of Linguistically and Culturally Diverse Students: Effective Instructional Practices* (Santa Cruz, CA: National Center for Research on Cultural Diversity and Second Language Learning, 1991).
58. Mary McCaslin and Thomas L. Good, "Compliant Cognition: The Misalliance of Management and Instructional Goals in Current School Reform." *Educational Researcher,* 21, 3 (April 1992), 4–17.
59. For a discussion of these issues, see María de la luz Reyes, "Challenging Venerable Assumptions: Literacy Instruction for Linguistically Different Students." *Harvard Educational Review,* 62, 4 (Winter 1992), 427–446.
60. Lilia I. Bartolomé, "Beyond the Methods Fetish: Toward a Humanizing Pedagogy." *Harvard Educational Review,* 64, 2 (Summer 1994), 173–194.
61. Jim Cummins, *Negotiating Identities: Education for Empowerment in a Diverse Society* (Ontario, CA: California Association for Bilingual Education, 1996), 73.
62. For an analysis of the interaction of violence in school and society, see Christine Clark, Morris Jenkins, and Gwendolyn Stowers, *Fear of Da' Gangsta': The Social Construction, Production, and Reproduction of Violence in Schools for Corporate Profit and the Revolutionary Promise of Multicultural Education* (Westport, CT: Greenwood, Bergin & Garvey, 1999).
63. Carnegie Council on Adolescent Development, *Turning Points: Preparing American Youth for the Twenty-First Century* (Washington, DC: Task Force for the Education of Young Adolescents, 1989).
64. David B. Tyack, *The One Best System: A History of American Urban Education* (Cambridge, MA: Harvard University Press, 1974); Michael B. Katz, *Class, Bureaucracy, and the Schools: The Illusion of Educational Change in America* (New York: Praeger, 1975).
65. Kozol, *Savage Inequalities.*
66. Jeremy Finn and Charles Achilles, "Answers About Class Size: A Statewide Experiment." *American Educational Research Journal* (Fall, 1990).
67. Gary G. Wehlage and Robert A. Rutter, "Dropping Out: How Much Do Schools Contribute to the Problem?" In *School Dropouts: Patterns and Policies,* edited by Gary Natriello (New York: Teachers College Press, Columbia University, 1986).
68. Pauline Lipman, "Restructuring in Context: A Case Study of Teacher Participation and the Dynamics of Ideology, Race, and Power." *American Educational Research Journal,* 34, 1 (1997), 3–37.
69. Rosa Hernandez Sheets, "Urban Classroom Conflict: Student-Teacher Perception." *The Urban Review,* 28, 2 (1996), 165–183.
70. Dick Corbett and Bruce Wilson, "Make a Difference *With,* Not *For,* Students: A Plea to Researchers and Reformers." *Educational Researcher,* 24, 5 (June/July, 1995), 12–17.
71. Suzanne Soo Hoo, "Students as Partners in Research and Restructuring Schools." *The Educational Forum,* 57, 4 (Summer 1993), 386–393, 389.
72. Paulo Freire, *Pedagogy of the Oppressed* (New York: Seabury Press, 1970), 59.

73. Cummins, *Negotiating Identities.*

74. Patricia Phelan, Ann Locke Davidson, and Hanh Cao Yu, *Adolescents' Worlds: Negotiating Family, Peers, and School* (New York: Teachers College Press, 1998).

75. Jody Cohen, "'Now Everybody Want To Dance': Making Change in an Urban Charter." In *Chartering Urban School Reform: Reflections on Public High Schools in the Midst of Change* by Michelle Fine, ed. (New York: Teachers College Press, 1994).

76. See Michelle Fine, *Framing Dropouts.*

77. Valerie E. Lee, Anthony A. Bryk, and Julia B. Smith, "The Organization of Effective Secondary Schools." In *Review of Research in Education, 19th Yearbook of the American Educational Research Association,* edited by Linda Darling-Hammond (Washington, DC: AERA, 1993).

78. Karen Seashore Louis, Helen M. Marks, and Sharon Kruse, "Teachers' Professional Community in Restructuring Schools." *American Educational Research Journal, 33,* 4 (Winter, 1996), 757–798.

79. Lipman, "Restructuring in Context."

80. Anne T. Henderson and Nancy Berla, *A New Generation of Evidence: The Family is Critical to Student Achievement* (Washington, DC: Center for Law and Education, 1995).

81. Margarita Azmitia, Catherine R. Cooper, Eugene E. García, Angela Ittel, Bonnie Johanson, Edward Lopez, Rebeca Martinez-Chavez, and Lourdes Rivera, *Links Between Home and School Among Low-Income Mexican-American and European-American Families* (Santa Cruz, CA: National Center for Research on Cultural Diversity and Second Language Learning, 1994); see also Moll, "Bilingual Classroom Studies and Community Analysis" and Carmen I. Mercado and Luis Moll, "The Study of Funds of Knowledge: Collaborative Research in Latino Homes." *Centro Bulletin,* ix, 9 (1997), 26–42.

82. Norm Fruchter, Anne Galletta, and J. Lynne White, "New Directions in Parent Involvement." *Equity and Choice,* 9, 3 (Spring 1993), 33–43.

83. Guadalupe Valdés, *Con Respeto: Bridging the Distance Between Culturally Diverse Families and Schools* (New York: Teachers College Press, 1996), 39.

NOTES TO AVI ABRAMSON'S CASE STUDY

1. I appreciate Diane Sweet's work in finding and interviewing Avi, and in providing extensive background information for this case study. Diane describes herself in this way: "I am a granddaughter, daughter, and mother. I am, and will always be, under-standing of others' stories, subtexts, contexts; I always try to see!" She is an adjunct professor at Newbury College, where she teaches courses in world literature, creative writing, and ESL, among others.

2. Stephan F. Brumberg, *Going to America, Going to School: The Jewish Immigrant Public School Encounter in Turn-of-the-Century New York City* (New York: Praeger, 1986), 2.

3. For a documentation of this historic context, see Brumberg, *Going to America.*

4. See Meyer Weinberg's extensive history of anti-Semitism in 12 countries, *Because They Were Jews: A History of Anti-Semitism* (Westport, CT: Greenwood Press, 1986); Chapter 12 deals with the United States. See also Leonard Dinnerstein, *Anti-Semitism in America* (New York: Oxford University Press, 1994).

5. For an examination of the pressure Jews feel to assimilate in U.S. society, see Seymour Martin Lipset and Earl Raab, *Jews and the New American Scene* (Cambridge, MA: Harvard University Press, 1995).

6. Data from a 1991 study found that 14 percent of Jewish households had annual incomes below $20,000 (as cited in *Teaching Strategies for Ethnic Studies,* 6th ed., edited by James A. Banks, Boston: Allyn & Bacon, 1997, p. 310).

NOTES TO FERN SHERMAN'S CASE STUDY

1. I would like to thank Carlie Collins Tartakov for the extensive interviews with Fern Sherman, her sister Juanita, and their father. We both especially appreciate the time, perspectives, and hope that Juanita gave to Carlie. Dr. Tartakov is an assistant professor in the College of Education at Iowa State University in Ames.
2. Cornel Pewewardy, "Will the 'Real' Indians Please Stand Up?" *Multicultural Review* (June 1998), 36–42.
3. U.S. Bureau of the Census, *We, the First Americans* (Washington, DC: U.S. Government Printing Office, 1993).
4. The Northern Ute Nation, for example, declared English a foreign language in 1984; see Jon Reyhner, "Native American Languages Act Becomes Law." in *NABE News,* 14, 3 (1 December 1990); for data on the Indian population, see U.S. Bureau of the Census, *We, the First Americans* (Washington, DC: U.S. Government Printing Office, 1993).
5. See Donna Deyhle and Karen Swisher, "Research in American Indian and Alaska Native Education: From Assimilation to Self-Determination." In *Review of Research in Education,* vol. 22, by Michael W. Apple, ed. (Washington, DC: AERA, 1997). Also see Richard St. Germaine, "Drop-out Rates Among American Indian and Alaska Native Students: Beyond Cultural Discontinuity." *Eric Digest* (Charleston, WV: Clearinghouse on Rural Education and Small Schools, November, 1995).
6. See, for example, Deyhle and Swisher, 1997; Sharon Nelson-Barber and Elise Trumbull Estrin, "Bringing Native American Perspectives to Mathematics and Science Teaching." *Theory into Practice,* 34, 3 (Summer, 1995), 174–185; and Donna Deyhle, "Navajo Youth and Anglo Racism: Cultural Integrity and Resistance." *Harvard Educational Review,* 65, 3 (Fall, 1995), 403–444.
7. See Deyhle and Swisher, 1997; K. Tsianina Lomawaima, "Educating Native Americans." In *Handbook of Research on Multicultural Education,* by James A. Banks and Cherry A. McGee Banks, eds. (New York: Macmillan, 1995).
8. As cited in John Reyhner, "Bilingual Education: Teaching the Native Language." In *Teaching the Indian Child: A Bilingual/Multicultural Approach,* edited by John Reyhner (Billings: Eastern Montana College, 1992), 39.
9. Nelson-Barber and Estrin, 1995; Carlos J. Ovando, "Teaching Science to the Native American Student." In *Teaching the Indian Child: A Bilingual/Multicultural Approach,* edited by Jon Reyhner (Billings: Eastern Montana College, 1992).
10. Nelson-Barber and Estrin, 1995.
11. Reyhner, "Bilingual Education."
12. Quality Education for Minorities Project, *Education That Works: An Action Plan for the Education of Minorities* (Cambridge, MA: Massachusetts Institute of Technology, 1990).
13. U.S. Bureau of the Census, *We, the First Americans*; and Lomawaima, "Educating Native Americans."

chapter *5*

Culture, Identity, and Learning

Young people whose languages and cultures differ from the dominant group must often struggle to sustain a clear image of themselves because differences are commonly treated as deficiencies by schools and teachers. The case studies of Marisol Martínez, James Karam, and Hoang Vinh that follow this chapter provide moving examples of how students' cultures are devalued in school. In spite of being very proud of their heritage, all three of these young people felt the need to hide or deemphasize their culture and language in school.

Many teachers and schools, in an attempt to be color-blind, do not want to acknowledge cultural or racial differences. "I don't see Black or White," a teacher will say, "I see only *students.*" This statement assumes that to be color-blind is to be fair, impartial, and objective because to see differences, in this line of reasoning, is to see defects and inferiority. Although it sounds fair and honest and ethical, the opposite may actually be true. When used in a conventional sense, being color-blind can mean being *nondiscriminatory* in attitude and behavior, and in this sense, color blindness is not a bad thing. But color blindness may result in *refusing to accept differences* and therefore accepting the dominant culture as the norm. It may result in denying the very identity of our students, thereby making them invisible.

A good example was provided by the U.S. Supreme Court in the *Lau* decision of 1974.[1] The San Francisco School Department was sued on behalf of Chinese-speaking students who, parents and other advocates charged, were not being provided with an equal education. The school department countered by claiming that they were providing these students with an equal education because they received *exactly the same teachers, instruction, and materials as all the other students*. The U.S. Supreme Court, in a unanimous decision, ruled against the school department. The Court reasoned that giving non-English speaking students the same instruction, teachers, and materials as English-speaking students flew in the face of equal educational opportunity because Chinese-speaking students could not benefit from instruction provided in English. The dictum "Equal is not the same" is useful here. It means that treating everyone in the same way will not necessarily lead to equality; rather, it may end up perpetuating the inequality that already exists. Learning to *affirm* differences rather than deny them is what a multicultural perspective is about.

What are the educational implications of "Equal is not the same"? First, it means *acknowledging the differences that children bring to school,* such as their gender, race, ethnicity, language, and social class, among others. The refusal to acknowledge differences often results in schools and teachers labeling children's behavior as deficient. In other cases, it results in making students invisible, as happened with James Karam, one of the students in the case studies you will read following this chapter.

Second, it means *admitting the possibility that students' identities may influence how they learn.* This should in no way devalue children's backgrounds or lower our expectations of them, yet this is precisely why so many educators have a hard time accepting "Equal is not the same." That is, they are reluctant to accept this notion because they may feel that in doing so, they must lower their expectations or water down the curriculum so that all children can learn. Yet neither of these practices is necessary.

Third, *accepting differences also means making provisions for them.* When students' cultural and linguistic backgrounds are viewed as a strength on which educators can draw, pedagogy changes to incorporate students' lives. This approach is based on the best of educational theory, that is, that individual differences must be taken into account in teaching. The truth of this assertion is often overlooked when it comes to cultural and linguistic differences. The fact that Marisol Martínez, whose case study immediately follows this chapter, is fluent in two languages has rarely been viewed as anything but a liability by most of her teachers. But if we are serious about providing all students with educational equity, then students' cultures and identities need to be seen not as a burden, a problem, or even a challenge, but rather as assets upon which to build.

This chapter explores the influence that cultural differences may have in student learning, and it reviews a number of promising pedagogical and curricular adaptations that teachers and schools have made. But before we can ask schools to change in order to teach all students, we need to understand the differences students bring with them to school. Culture is one of those differences, and I define it as follows: *Culture consists of the values, traditions, social and political relationships, and worldview created, shared, and transformed by a group of people bound together by a common history, geographic location, language, social class, and/or religion.* Culture includes not only tangibles such as foods, holidays, dress, and artistic expression, but also less tangible manifestations such as communication style, attitudes, values, and family relationships. These features of culture are often more difficult to pinpoint, but doing so is necessary if we want to understand how student learning may be affected.

Power is implicated in culture as well. That is, members of the dominant group in a society traditionally think of dominant cultural values as "normal" while they view the values of subordinated groups as deviant or wrong. The difference in perception is due more to the power of each of these groups than to any inherent goodness or rightness in the values themselves. For instance, U.S. mainstream culture stresses the necessity for youngsters to become independent at an early age, whereas other cultures emphasize interdependence as a major value. Neither of these values is innately right or wrong; each has developed as a result of the group's history and experiences. However, people with a U.S. mainstream frame of reference may view as abnormal, or at the very least curious, the interdependent relationships of Latino children and parents, for instance. They may characterize Latino children as overly dependent, too attached to their parents and siblings, and needing more attention than other children. Although Latina mothers may view U.S. mainstream culture as strange and cold for its insistence on independence at what they consider too young an age, their values do not carry the same weight or power as those of the dominant group.

We are always on shaky ground when considering cultural differences. It is vital to examine how culture may influence learning and achievement in school, but the danger lies in overgeneralizing its effects. Overgeneralizations can lead to gross stereotypes, which in turn may lead to erroneous conclusions about individual students' abilities and intelligence. We have all seen some of the more disastrous consequences of this line of thought: checklists of cultural traits of different ethnic groups, the mandate to use certain pedagogical strategies with students of particular backgrounds, and treatises on immutable student behaviors. Culture, in such instances, is treated as a product rather than a process, and it is viewed as unchanging and unchangeable. In the heart-rending words of Hoang Vinh, a Vietnamese student who is the subject of one of the case studies that follow, teachers sometimes "just understand some things outside, but they cannot understand something inside our hearts."

According to Frederick Erickson, one harmful implication of a static view of culture is directly linked to educational practice. He writes ". . . when we think of culture in education as aesthetic and/or relatively fixed we derive educational practice that supports the status quo. When we think of culture and social identity in more fluid terms, however, we can find a foundation for educational practice that is transformative."[2] A major premise of this book is that to be effective, multicultural education *must be* transformative; a static view of culture contradicts the very basis of multicultural education as presented here.

Culture is integral to the learning process, but it affects every individual differently. For instance, it may be true that Appalachian people share a rich heritage that includes a strong sense of kinship, but the culture may not have the same effect on every child.[3] Given differences in social class and family structure, psychological and emotional differences, birth order, residence, and a host of individual distinctions, it would be folly to think that culture alone accounts for all human differences. Anyone who has children can confirm this truth: Two offspring from the same parents, with the same culture and social class, and raised in substantially the same way, can turn out to be as different as night and day. Culture is neither static nor deterministic; it gives us just one way in which to understand differences among students. The assumption that culture is the primary determinant of academic achievement can be oversimplistic, dangerous, and counterproductive because, while culture may *influence*, it does not *determine* who we are.

Notwithstanding these caveats about overdetermining its significance, I want to emphasize that culture *is* important. One reason for insisting on the significance of culture is that some people, primarily those from dominated and disenfranchised groups within society, have been taught that they *have no culture*. This has resulted in, among other things, what Felix Boateng has called *deculturalization*, that is, a process by which people are first deprived of their own culture and then conditioned into other cultural values.[4] This is how a term such as *cultural deprivation*—which in reality means that some people do not share in the culture of the dominant group—came to mean that a group was without culture *altogether*. This, of course, is absurd because everybody has a culture, that is, everybody has the ability to create and re-create ideas and material goods and to affect their world in a variety of ways. Multicultural education is one way of counteracting the notion that culture is held by only the privileged.

Although everyone has a culture, many times members of the culturally dominant group of a society may not even think of themselves as cultural beings. For them, culture is something that other people have, especially people who differ from the mainstream in race or ethnicity. The problem with conceptualizing culture in this way is that it exoticizes those people who are not in the cultural mainstream. It also marginalizes multicultural education. According to Sandy Kaser and Kathy Short, university- and classroom-based researchers who explored culture with children in the classroom, "When culture is defined as ethnicity and race, many people view culture as a characteristic of particular groups and as outside of the experience of everyone else. From this perspective, multicultural curriculum remains a separate unit or book, not a characteristic of the learning environment."[5]

Although Vinh was only 18 years old when he was interviewed, his understanding of culture was more sophisticated than that of most adults. As you will see in his case study, Vinh described Vietnamese cultural values, behaviors, and expectations without falling into mechanical explanations for complex phenomena. He was also very accurate in pointing out cultural differences between his teachers in Vietnam and the United States: He said that one of his teachers, Ms. Mitchell, expected all students to do things in the same way. But people from other countries "have different ideas, so they might think about school in different ways. . . . So she has to learn about that culture." As one example, he described how his English teachers praised him about his English, although he felt that instead they should have been telling him to study more. He concluded, "But that's the way the American culture is. But my culture is not like that."

Much of the research reported here, and from which part of the conceptual framework for multicultural education is developed, is *ethnographic research,* that is, educational research based on anthropological constructs that include methods such as fieldwork, interviews, and participant observation. Over two decades ago, Ray McDermott defined ethnography as "any rigorous attempt to account for people's behavior in terms of their relations with those around them in different situations."[6] This area of research, that was beginning in earnest at that time, has profoundly affected educational thinking in the past 30 years. This is especially the case in educational settings distinguished by cultural diversity. As Henry Trueba and Pamela Wright have suggested, ethnographic research can lead to a better understanding of the educational process in multicultural settings because it has numerous implications for policy and practice in schools.[7]

Cultural differences in learning may be especially apparent in three areas: *learning styles* or *preferences, interactional* or *communication styles,* and *language differences.* Examples of the first two areas are explored next. Language and language issues will be considered in Chapter 6 (although it should be understood that language is a major component of culture).

LEARNING STYLES AND PREFERENCES

Learning style is usually defined as the way in which individuals receive and process information.[8] Some of the early research in this field concentrated on ethnic and racial differences in learning, a perspective that can skirt dangerously close to racist perceptions of differences in IQ. As such, it has been the subject of some controversy and criticism. Exactly how culture influences learning is unclear. Early learning style research maintained that mothers' (or primary caregivers') child-rearing practices were primarily responsible for the learning styles that children develop. The case was made that the values, attitudes, and behaviors taught at home became the basis for how children learned to learn.[9] The direct process implied by this theory is not entirely convincing, however. There are vast differences among learners *within* ethnic groups, and these differences may be due not just to culture but to social class, language spoken at home, number of years or generations in the United States, and simple individual differences.

Social class, for example, has been proposed as equally or more important than ethnicity in influencing learning. Because membership within a particular social group is based on economic factors as well as cultural values, the working class may differ from the middle class not only in particular values and practices but also in economic resources. The reasoning behind the hypothesis that social class is a more important influence on learning than is ethnicity is that the intellectual environment and socialization of children in the home may be due more to economic resources than to cultural resources.

I prefer the term *learning preferences* because it is a more flexible way of approaching this concept. A focus on rigid learning styles is problematic because of a tendency to dichotomize learning (see footnote 8). It is doubtful that a process as complex as learning can be characterized with only two poles. As many as 14 learning styles and 13 different learning style theories have been suggested. Some studies have focused on differences in visual or verbal emphasis and they point out the potential pitfalls in static learning classifications.[10] A good example is the case of Hoang Vinh, who loved working in cooperative groups, a learning preference that is not usually associated with Vietnamese students. Thus although learning style research can be helpful in identifying learning differences that may be related to ethnicity and culture, it also runs the risk of oversimplification and stereotyping and can be used as a rationale for poor or inequitable teaching.

A graphic example of the misapplication of learning style theories can be found in research by Flora Ida Ortiz that teachers used the "cooperative" attribute from the learning style literature concerning Hispanics to justify a number of clearly discriminatory pedagogical decisions.[11] For example, in integrated classrooms in which Hispanic children were present, teachers seldom granted them solo performances in plays or leadership activities in other situations. Teachers placed them in activities the students themselves had not chosen, whereas other children were allowed choices; and teachers had them share books when there were not enough to go around, whereas the non-Hispanic students could have individual copies. The result of these actions was that the Hispanic students tended to receive a lower quality education than others. Teachers rationalized that Hispanics would be more likely to feel uncomfortable in the limelight or in leadership roles (see footnote 9). They also reasoned that Hispanic children liked to share books because of their preference for working cooperatively. Consequently, any negative preconceived notions of children's ability that teachers may have had were reinforced by faulty interpretations of research. It is a good example of the truism, "A little knowledge is a dangerous thing."

Similarly, in a comprehensive review of research in American Indian and Alaska Native education, Donna Deyhle and Karen Swisher concluded that learning style research can point to meaningful adaptations that can improve the educational outcomes of these students. But they also warned of the detrimental consequences of viewing research on learning styles uncritically. Specifically, they pointed out that the depiction of the "nonverbal" Indian child is reinforced when teachers read that American Indian students prefer observation to performance. Deyhle and Swisher conclude, "The power relations in the classroom, rather than the Indian child as culturally or inherently 'nonverbal,' are central to understanding the nonparticipatory behavior observed in many Indian classrooms. In these 'silent' classrooms, communication is controlled by the teacher, who accepts only one correct answer and singles out individuals to respond to questions for which they have little background knowledge."[12]

An example of debilitating power relations can be seen in the case study of James Karam: Although the Arabic language and Lebanese culture were very important to James, they were virtually invisible in his school. As a result, he learned to deemphasize them in the school setting. Thus child-rearing practices alone, although they may be considerable in influencing children's learning preferences, do not offer a sufficient explanation. Other circumstances such as power relationships and status differentials are at work also, and these may be even more substantial than child-rearing practices.

Although not specifically related to cultural differences, Howard Gardner's work on "multiple intelligences" has implications for culturally compatible education.[13] According to this theory, each human being is capable of several relatively independent forms of information processing, and each of these is a specific "intelligence." These intelligences include logical-mathematical, linguistic (the two most emphasized in school success), musical, spatial, bodily kinesthetic, interpersonal, and intrapersonal. *Intelligence* is defined by Gardner as the ability to solve problems or develop products that are valued in a particular cultural setting.

The salience of cultural differences in intelligence is evident. Gardner's research has demonstrated that individuals differ in the specific profile of intelligences that they exhibit, and these differences may be influenced by what is valued in their culture. Because a broader range of abilities is acknowledged in this conception of intelligence, talents of individuals that previously have been discounted may be considered in a new light.

The theory of multiple intelligences may have significant implications for multicultural education because this theory goes beyond the limited definition of intelligence valued in most schools. In Gardner's words, it breaks out of the "hegemony of a single intelligence."[14] As a result, it may be particularly helpful in challenging current assessment practices that focus almost exclusively on logical-mathematical and linguistic intelligence. The danger, as always, lies in extrapolating from individual cases to an entire group. Although it may be true, for example, that certain cultures are highly developed in bodily kinesthetic intelligence, we should not conclude that all its members will manifest this intelligence equally. Nor should educators assume that individuals from this culture are *primarily* or *only* intelligent bodily-kinesthetically, and therefore unable to manipulate language, for example.

COMMUNICATION STYLE

Cultural influences can also be found in interactional or communication styles, that is, the ways individuals interact with one another and the messages they send, intentionally or not, in their communications. Ray McDermott, for instance, hypothesized that for many children from culturally subordinated groups, school failure is best explained by the cultural makeup of the classroom rather than by biologic, psychological, or linguistic deprivation.[15] He suggested that in environments where culturally subordinated students are taught by culturally dominant teachers, communication breakdowns happen simply by virtue of each group behaving in ways their subcultures sees as "normal." The result of the cultural conflict that ensues may be school failure. According to this explanation, school failure is actually "achieved" because it is the product of miscommunication between teachers and students and a rational adaptation by students who are devalued by schools. Unless changes are made in these environments, school failure is almost inevitable.

Roland Tharp has suggested at least four cultural variables that may be at odds with the expectations and structures of schools: *social organization, sociolinguistics, cognition,* and *motivation.*[16] An example or two will suffice to demonstrate the complex and fascinating interplay among them. Social organization, for instance, refers to the ways classrooms are organized. Tharp suggests, for instance, that the traditional U.S. whole-class organization, with "rank-and-file" seating and a teacher/leader who instructs or demonstrates, is not necessarily the best arrangement for all children. For example, Melvin Williams's ethnographic work in an inner-city school almost two decades ago suggested that African American students' skill at manipulating the dynamics of their classrooms was often interpreted, especially by European American teachers, as "acting out." But rather than devaluating behaviors such as staging spontaneous "dramas," some teachers have used them successfully in their instruction.[17]

In the area of sociolinguistics, Tharp explains how short "wait times" may disadvantage American Indian students, who take longer to respond to teachers' questions because their culture emphasizes deliberate thought. The cultural expectation here is that one can make informed and appropriate choices only when considering all possible ramifications and implications of a decision. The value of careful consideration may influence the classroom behavior of many American Indian students. Another example of sociolinguistics has to do with "rhythm." For example, African American mothers and their children often use a "contest" style of speech that approximates the call-and-response patterns found in Black music. Using such rhythms in classroom instruction by teachers of African American students has had positive results in the research.[18] On the basis of his extensive review of culturally compatible education, Tharp concluded that when schools become more attuned to children's cultures, children's academic achievement improves.

How relationships between students and teachers can be either improved or damaged by their interactions is another pertinent area of research. As an example, students and teachers from the same background are often on the same wavelength simply because they have an insider's understanding of cultural meanings and therefore they do not have to figure out the verbal and nonverbal messages they are sending. An example of this congruency can be found in Marisol Martínez's case study: Although she was not in a bilingual class, one year her homeroom teacher was a bilingual teacher, and Marisol felt proud of herself and her culture just by being in the same room and seeing the displays he put up on the bulletin board.

In this regard, Michele Foster examined how a shared cultural background or shared norms about how language is used in African American communities can benefit classroom interactions. She found that in classrooms of African American students taught by African American teachers, there are subtle but significant interactional differences from other classrooms. For example, she documented the positive classroom effect of one African American teacher who used standard English to regulate student behavior, but "performances" (i.e., what Foster described as stylized ways of speaking that resemble African American preaching style) to relate everyday life experiences of her students to more abstract concepts.[19]

Cultural differences probably influence students in more ways than we can imagine. I remember the case many years ago of a new teacher who was attending a workshop of mine. Susan was a young teacher of English as a second language (ESL) to Puerto Rican students. Although she was sincerely committed to her students' achievement, she was unaware of many aspects of their culture. The Puerto Rican children, most of whom had recently arrived in the United States, used the communication style typical of their culture. For example, many Puerto Ricans use a nonverbal wrinkling of the nose to signify "what?" When Susan would ask the children if they understood the lesson, some would invariably wrinkle their noses. Not understanding this gesture, Susan simply went on with the lesson, assuming that their nose wrinkling had no meaning.

Two years after first being exposed to this behavior, while attending a workshop in which we discussed Puerto Rican gestures and the work of Carmen Judith Nine-Curt, Susan learned that nose wrinkling among Puerto Ricans was a way of asking "What?" or "What do you mean?" or of saying, "I don't understand."[20] From then on, Susan understood that when they used this gesture, her students were asking for help or for further clarification. We all laughed about it that day in the workshop, but this humorous anecdote is not without its serious consequences: Students whose culture, verbal or nonverbal, is unacknowledged or misunderstood in their classrooms are likely to feel alienated, unwelcome, and out of place.

In Alaska Native cultures, we find a similar example of nonverbal gestures: Raised eyebrows are often used to signify yes, and a wrinkled nose means no. Because many teachers look for verbal rather than nonverbal responses, teachers might interpret these as rude nonresponses to their questions. The result may be communication problems between Alaska Native students and their non–Alaska Native teachers. Promoting teachers' familiarity with communication differences would go a long way in helping them to transform their curriculum to address their students' backgrounds more adequately.[21]

The communication styles explored here are only the tip of the iceberg, but they help to point out the sometimes subtle ways that culture, if not understood, can interfere with learning.

CULTURAL DISCONTINUITIES AND SCHOOL ACHIEVEMENT

Cultural discontinuities, that is, the lack of congruence between home and school cultures, have been identified as causing numerous problems for students from culturally dominated groups. A review of some of the literature on culture-specific educational accommodations can pinpoint how discontinuities between schools and students can lead to negative academic outcomes.

Research by Shirley Brice Heath in the Piedmont Carolinas during the 1970s is a classic example.[22] In exploring the language of Black children at home and at school, she found that different ways of using language resulted in tensions between the children and their mostly White teachers in the classroom. For example, the children were not accustomed to answering questions concerning the attributes of objects (color, size, shape, and so on), the kinds of questions typically found in classroom discourse. Instead, the children generally used language at home for storytelling and other purposes. The result was a communication breakdown, with teachers believing that many of the students were "slow," and students perceiving a lack of support from teachers. Through research coordinated by Heath, the teachers began to experiment with different ways of asking questions. The result was that teachers helped children bridge the gap between their home and school experiences and the children's language use in the classroom was enhanced.

In the case of American Indian children, Susan Philips' research on the Warm Spring Reservation is another powerful example.[23] Core Indian values of respect and value for the dignity of the individual, harmony, internal locus of control, and cooperation and sharing inevitably influence students' reactions to their educational experiences. That a teacher's best intentions may be ineffective if students' cultural differences are neglected in curriculum and instruction is underscored by Philips's ethnographic research. She found that students performed poorly in classroom contexts that demanded individualized performance and emphasized competition. But their performance improved greatly when the context did not require students to perform in public and when cooperation was valued over competition. In this case, cooperative learning, which is compatible with many values of Indian families, is an approach worth exploring. It may be helpful in other settings as well.[24]

A very different example might come from the experiences of a newly arrived Vietnamese immigrant attending a U.S. school. Such a child might feel extremely off balance and uncomfortable in a classroom environment in which teachers are informal and friendly, students are expected to ask questions and speak in front of the class, and group work is the order of the day.[25] The cultural discontinuity from an educational environment in which teachers are revered and have a formal relationship with their students, and where learning is based on listening and memorizing, can be a dramatic one. Nevertheless, as we shall see in Hoang Vinh's case study, not all Vietnamese students will react in this way because there are countless differences among people from the same cultural group.

An example from a field unrelated to schoolchildren can illustrate dramatically how communication breakdown happens. In her ethnographic research in the Yucatán region of Mexico, Brigitte Jordan described the participation of Mayan midwives in government-sponsored training courses. She found that the courses, for all their good intentions, generally failed. Although the midwives were exposed to years of training, their day-to-day practice did not change as a result, partly because of the culturally inappropriate teaching strategies employed in the government-sponsored courses. Specifically, Jordan mentions the teachers' imperialist view of the world and their dismissal of the local culture and its solutions.

Official training sessions, in Jordan's words, "render midwives' praxis and discourse deficient and without import."[26]

It is not far-fetched to apply this description of cultural imperialism in the Yucatán to the way children's cultures and lifestyles are devalued every day in U.S. classrooms. Although the settings are different, the process is unfortunately very familiar. The miscommunication that can result when schools and homes have radically different values, objectives, and practices is a similar process.[27] The culture and language children bring to school are often disregarded and replaced.

Discontinuities, however, do not develop simply for reasons of differing cultural values among groups. There is often a direct connection between culture and the *sociopolitical context of schooling*. A study by Kathleen Bennett is another good example. Bennett found that even a teacher who was considered excellent by her principal and peers was unable to make a significant difference in the reading achievement of her students, a group of Appalachian first graders. Bennett concluded that there were several reasons for this, including (a) a sharp dissonance between the expressed philosophy of the district and the actual reading program offered in the classroom and (b) the ideology of ability group stratification that permeated the entire reading program. The fact that the culture of the classroom was in stark contrast to the culture, natural language, and experiences of the children was not the only reason for the children's poor academic achievement.[28]

Another example of the connection between sociopolitical context and culture concerns the remarkable academic success of South Asian students. The prevailing explanation for their success is that the cultural values of South Asian students are congruent with the academic culture of schools. While this may be true, it alone is not sufficient to explain their success. The fact that the parents of South Asian students are highly educated is also a factor. For instance, Heather Kim has documented that an extraordinary 87 percent of South Asian fathers and 70 percent of South Asian mothers have a college degree or higher. This compares with 31 percent of United States parents as a whole. The Asian American students who perform best on tests are those whose parents have the most education. They are also the highest proportion born in this country compared to other immigrants.[29] As we can see, culture cannot so easily be separated from other issues such as social class and access to higher education.

Another example that highlights this sociopolitical link concerns Alaska Native and American Indian students. Going to high school in distant boarding schools often meant that the students were physically separated from their parents. The dropout rate among these students was very high because of the school-related social and emotional problems that they experienced. Although the dropout rate remains high in some areas, it has been reduced dramatically in cases where secondary education has been returned to local communities.[30] Deyhle and Swisher, in fact, have expressed the concern that educators sometimes use the cultural discontinuity theory to argue *only* for a culturally compatible curriculum to solve the dropout problem.[31] In so doing, educators may neglect to confront other more pressing problems in Native American and Alaska Native schools, problems such as the lack of equitable financing and appropriate resources. The same caution needs to be mentioned in the case of students of other nonmainstream backgrounds.

These examples demonstrate that cultural incompatibilities are varied and complex. Research concerning them is vital if we are to grasp how children from different cultural backgrounds respond to teachers' behaviors and what teachers can do to change how they teach. But no single solution will bridge the gap between the school and home cultures of all students.

CULTURE-SPECIFIC EDUCATIONAL ACCOMMODATIONS

Various programs have been designed to provide for the specific educational needs of students from particular groups, and some of these programs have proven to be extremely successful. A number of examples of modifications to make instruction more culturally appropriate can reveal the reasoning behind the approach known variously as *culturally compatible, culturally congruent, culturally appropriate, culturally responsive,* or *culturally relevant instruction.*[32] Cornel Pewewardy has called schools that are based on the culture of a particular culture "ethnic specific schools."[33] The Kamehameha Elementary Education Program (KEEP) in Hawaii described by Lynn Vogt and others is a particularly striking example.[34] Cultural discontinuities in instruction were identified as a major problem in the poor academic achievement of Native Hawaiian children, and KEEP was begun as a result. A privately funded, multidisciplinary educational research effort, the purpose of KEEP was to explore remedies for Hawaiian children's chronic academic underachievement by changing certain educational practices: from a phonics approach to one emphasizing comprehension; from individual work desks to work centers with heterogeneous groups; and from high praise to more culturally appropriate praise, including indirect and group praise. The KEEP culturally compatible K–3 language arts program has met with great success, including significant gains in reading achievement.

What explains the success of this program? The changes in instructional style, which more closely matched the children's cultural styles, is generally acknowledged as the reason. The move from phonics to comprehension, for instance, allowed the students to contribute in a speech style called the "talk-story," which is a familiar linguistic event in the Hawaiian community. The other instructional changes, including a preference for cooperative work and group accomplishment, were also compatible with Native Hawaiian culture.

The logic of KEEP was also used as the basis for the KEEP–Rough Rock Project, a collaborative project with the Rough Rock Demonstration School on the Navajo Reservation. It was not simply a replica of KEEP, however. Several of the features of KEEP had to be modified to be more culturally compatible with the Navajo culture because the instructional approaches in KEEP were not appropriate for other cultural settings. For example, Navajo children preferred working in same-sex groups, a preference that is culturally congruent. As a result, same-sex groups became a feature of KEEP–Rough Rock. Moreover, it became clear that Navajo children were more comfortable with holistic thinking than with linear thinking. The preference for holistic thinking among American Indians had been documented before, but now an entire school was organized that purposely used these data as a basis for the comprehensive modification of curriculum and pedagogy. Once these adaptations were made in the Navajo program, it proved to be more compatible with the cultural values and learning preferences of the students.

Recent research in the pedagogy of teachers—both African American and those of other backgrounds—of African American students provides other convincing illustrations of how teachers use cultural knowledge and experiences to overcome some of the debilitating and negative messages to which students are subjected in schools and society. Some studies document, for instance, how successful teachers use students' culture as a bridge to the dominant culture. Furthermore, the pedagogy of effective teachers is empowering because rather than simply teach students blind acceptance of the inherent values of the dominant culture, these teachers encourage students to think critically and work actively for social justice.[35] In addition to describing the competencies of teachers who are successful with African American students, these studies document additional effective practices, including teachers' use of interactive rather than didactic methods and the high standards they set for students.[36]

In a case study of a Yup'ik Eskimo teacher teaching Yup'ik students, Jerry Lipka documents how adapting the social interactions, knowledge, and values toward the students' culture is a potentially significant way to improve schooling. Lipka found that conflict was substantially reduced when there is cultural congruence in teaching, and he concluded, "When Yup'ik teachers are teaching Yup'ik children and relating in culturally compatible ways in village settings, many of the so-called factors of minority school failure may be dismissed."[37] In effect, a major finding of his ethnographic study was that relationships are at the center of any culturally responsive pedagogy. But Lipka is not suggesting that Yup'ik students are successful learners only when taught by Yup'ik teachers. According to him, ethnicity is not the central classroom variable here; rather, success is created by the teacher's interactional style and the relationship between the students and teacher. The good news is that teachers of any background can learn to be culturally responsive.

Another illustration in which the cultural identity of the teacher and his students is not the same is found in research by Jeannette Abi-Nader. Her description of the program for Latino youth in a large, urban high school in the Northeast focuses on the adaptations made by the teacher, Dan Bogan, to make the classroom culturally congruent. For example, interactions between him and his students were based on Latino cultural values of *familia:* The program was imbued with a sense of caring and support; the teacher acted as a father, brother, and friend to students; he held high expectations for them; students learned to develop collective responsibility for one another through activities such as peer tutoring and mentoring; and there was a commitment to extending the life of "the family." Unlike the dismal dropout statistics in so many other Latino communities, up to 65 percent of the high school graduates of this program have gone on to college. The youth attribute their academic success to their participation in the program, making enthusiastic comments about it, such as this one from a written survey: "The best thing I like about this class is that we all work together and we all participate and try to help each other. We're family!"[38]

Although the teacher in the classroom described by Abi-Nader was not Latino, there were a number of characteristics that made his pedagogy particularly effective with Latino students. For one, he was thoroughly immersed in Latino culture; he had spent several years as a Peace Corps volunteer in a Spanish-speaking country; and he was fluent in Spanish. He was, according to Abi-Nader, a great motivator. Research such as this that focuses on culturally compatible education is helpful because it points out that all children can learn if appropriate modifications in instruction are made.

Many teachers intuitively and consistently make such modifications, both in their curriculum and in their instructional practices. A good example is provided by Frederick Erickson and Gerald Mohatt in research concerning social relationships in two classrooms of culturally similar American Indian children, one taught by an Indian and the other by a non-Indian.[39] Although the classroom organizations differed substantially at the beginning of the year, both teachers had adapted their instructional practices by the end of the year in the direction of *greater cultural congruence*. The non-Indian teacher, for example, ended up by seating children in table groups, rather than individually in rows, and he also began to spend more time on small-group lessons and tutoring than on whole-group lessons. This teacher used what Erickson and Mohatt call "teacher radar," and the result was a culturally congruent classroom, apparently arrived at intuitively.

This dramatic example focuses on one particular cultural group, but changes in instruction and curriculum that reflect the *multicultural* character of schools are also possible. For example, most schools favor a highly competitive and individualistic instructional mode. In this environment, dominant-culture children and males are more likely to succeed, whereas students from other cultural groups and females may be at a distinct disadvantage. By combining this style with a more cooperative mode, the learning and cultural styles of all children can be respected and valued. The lesson is that although all schools cannot become *culturally compatible*, they can become *multiculturally sensitive*.

A CRITICAL APPRAISAL OF CULTURE-SPECIFIC ACCOMMODATIONS

In spite of their usefulness, culture-specific accommodations are limited by several factors. First, the diversity of the student population in most schools mitigates against culturally specific modifications. Many schools are multicultural, with students from a diversity of ethnic, social class, and linguistic backgrounds. There are few totally homogeneous schools, and designing a school to be culturally compatible with just one group of students might jeopardize students of other backgrounds. As a result, schools can change their instructional strategies to be compatible with students from one ethnic group, but these same strategies might be the opposite of what students from other backgrounds need.

Another problem with making educational choices that are solely culturally compatible is that segregation is posited as the most effective solution to educational failure. Although segregation might sometimes be warranted, the truth is that history has amply demonstrated that it often leads to inequality. When speaking of culturally dominated groups, "separate but equal" is rarely that; on the contrary, segregation generally means that powerless groups end up with an inferior education because they receive the least material resources with which to educate their children. Nevertheless, although recent U.S. history has upheld integration as a good to be strived for because it purportedly leads to increased educational equality, we know that this is not always the result. Sometimes desegregated schools end up being segregated in other ways, especially through tracking in gifted and talented, special education, and other such programs.

We need to distinguish between segregation of different kinds. The segregation that is imposed by a dominant group is far different from the self-segregation demanded by a subordinated group that sees through the persistent racism hidden behind the veneer of equality in integrated settings. This is the case, for instance, with Afrocentric, Native American, Latino, or other culturally based schools. Even in these cases, however, culturally separate schools may effectively isolate themselves from receiving some of the benefits of the public school system that might help them meet the needs of the children they serve. Thus although qualitatively different from segregated schools because they are developed by disempowered communities, culturally homogeneous schools are not always effective. Furthermore, there are also numerous cases of students of culturally diverse backgrounds who have been successfully educated in what might be considered culturally incompatible settings. Other factors unrelated to cultural conflict must be involved.

A further problem with culturally congruent education is the implication that all students from a particular group learn in more or less the same way. This assertion is problematic because it *essentializes* culture, that is, it ascribes particular immutable characteristics to it. Essentializing can lead to generalizations and stereotypes that get in the way of viewing students as individuals as well as of members of groups whose cultures are constantly evolving.

● SUMMARY

In this chapter, we have seen how culture can influence learning in crucial ways. Using learning style research, educators began to understand how students of different backgrounds might differ in their learning preferences. More recent methodologies of ethnographic investigation have yielded important findings that can also help teachers and schools recognize the possible impact of culture on learning. Modifications can be made in communicaton style, program design, and instruction to support the learning of students of diverse backgrounds. But because using only a cultural analysis concerning learning is limited, the chapter ended with a critical analysis considering some of the problems with cultural-specific accommodations.

In the final analysis, culture *does* matter. Learning cannot take place in settings where students' cultures are devalued and rejected. Teachers who want to provide all students with a caring and stimulating environment for learning have to take into account their identities. In the words of Gloria Ladson-Billings, "How can academic success and cultural success complement each other in settings where student alienation and hostility characterize the school experience?"[40]

● *TO THINK ABOUT*

1. What are the advantages of being color-blind? What are the disadvantages? Give some examples of each related to classrooms or schools.

2. What do we mean when we say "Equal is not the same"? To help you consider this question, think about some of the students you know.

3. Observe three different students in a classroom. How would you characterize their learning preferences? How do they differ? Do you think these differences have something to do with their gender, race, ethnicity, or social class? Why or why not? What are the implications for teaching these children?

4. Can you identify any pedagogical strategies that have seemed to be successful with particular children? How can you use these with students of different cultures?

5. Numerous educators have suggested that traditional seating in rows and conventional "chalk-and-talk" strategies are not appropriate learning environments for a great number of students. What do you think? What does this mean for classroom organization? Is there a difference in their effect between elementary and secondary schools? Suggest some alternatives to the traditional classroom organization and pedagogy that might give more students an equal chance to learn.

6. Given the contradictory messages between home and school received by children of various backgrounds, children may end up rejecting their parents' culture and way of life. What can teachers and schools do to minimize this situation?

7. Think about a culturally pluralistic school with which you are familiar. What steps could be taken by the school to make it more culturally compatible with its student body? Consider changes in curriculum, organization, use of materials, and pedagogical strategies.

Case Study: Marisol Martínez

"I'm proud of myself and my culture, but I think I know what I should know."

Marisol Martínez was born and raised in the United States, living first in New York City and later in Milltown, a small industrial city in the Northeast. Both of her parents were born in Puerto Rico but have raised most of their eight children in this country. Marisol's first language was Spanish, but because she learned English before going to school she was never in a bilingual program. She is still fluent in both languages and uses both when talking with bilingual speakers, and Spanish when addressing her parents. In language use, she is typical of Puerto Ricans in the United States: An impressive 91 percent still speak Spanish at home, higher than any other Latino group. An almost equal percentage speak English too.[1]

Marisol lives in a city housing project. It is a small brick town house, two stories high, in the middle of a row of exact replicas along the length of a city block. There is a patch of ground in front of each and a larger one in back, which some families have enclosed for a small vegetable or flower garden during spring and summer. The neighborhood is active and noisy with the sounds of children, music (both rap and salsa), and traffic. The living room of the Martínez apartment is very small, crowded with furniture and many family pictures and religious figures on tables and walls. Upstairs are three bedrooms and a bath. Marisol lives here with one brother, three sisters, and her parents. Her older siblings are married or living on their own. She is 16 years old and the fifth oldest of the children. The oldest daughter is 31.

The Martínez family is very close-knit. Marisol's parents are older than most of her friends' parents, and because of medical problems, neither her mother nor her father work. Both seem to have a firm hold on their children and are involved in their lives, particularly in educational matters. All of Marisol's older siblings have managed to graduate from high school, quite a feat in view of the dropout rate among Latinos, which has for many years fluctuated between 40 and 80 percent.[2] The success of Marisol and her siblings can no doubt be explained partially by the stability of the Martínez family: Research by Javier Tapia among low-income Puerto Ricans found that family stability was the most important factor influencing the academic performance of low-income students.[3] Marisol's parents also graduated from high school, although two-thirds of Latino adults in this city do not have a high school diploma.

Over the past two decades, the demographics of the small city where Marisol and her family live have changed dramatically. Nowhere is this more evident than in the schools, where the proportion of Puerto Ricans is now over 50 percent. African Americans make up a small percentage of the total, and the remainder of the students are European Americans, primarily Irish and French Canadians. In the city as a whole, however, Puerto Ricans make up just over a third of the population. The substantially higher percentage in the schools is due to several factors, including the larger family size in the Puerto Rican community and the considerable "White flight" that has taken place since the schools were desegregated in the early 1980s. Almost 60 percent of all Puerto Ricans in Milltown live in poverty, four times higher than the poverty rate of Whites.

The change in demographics has also been felt in town politics. Puerto Ricans in the schools and in town in general have often been the object of discrimination and stereotypes. There have been frequent newspaper articles and editorials about the rising crime rate, drug abuse, and the subsequent disintegration of the city from an overidealized past, all with not-so-subtle implications that Puerto Ricans are responsible. Puerto Ricans are not the first group to suffer this kind of treatment. Milltown is a city of immigrants, and each new group has had to struggle with similar conditions of discrimination and rejection.

Marisol is a sophomore in the city's public comprehensive high school. She is following an academic course of study, and her grades are all A's and B's. She likes all of her classes, especially biology and geometry, and she expects to go to college, although her plans are still relatively uncertain. Right now, she is fluctuating between the seemingly disparate goals of wanting to be a model or a nurse. If she does go to college, she will be the first in her family to do so.

Until fourth grade, Marisol went to school in New York City. She remembers being "very smart" in school and doing well there. But because her family considered the neighborhood too violent for the children, they moved to Milltown, where they have lived for about 10 years. This pattern of migration is not unusual for Puerto Ricans, who frequently first settle in New York and later move to other urban areas in the Northeast. About half of all Puerto Ricans living in the United States are in New York, but this percentage has decreased considerably in the past 50 years. In fact, one of the most significant findings of the 1990 Census concerning Puerto Ricans was that they were increasingly living in relatively small cities in the Northeast such as Milltown.[4] Estimated census figures for 1998 documented a dramatic increase in the number of Puerto Ricans in the United States: There were approximately 3.1 million Puerto Ricans in the United States, nearly the same as the number of residents on the island of Puerto Rico.[5] Between 1940 and 1970 alone, about 835,000 Puerto Ricans moved to the United States, reflecting one of the most massive outmigrations in the century.[6]

Puerto Rico became a colony of the United States in 1898, which helps explain some of the differences between Puerto Rican migration, or (im)migration, and other immigrations.[7] Taken over by the United States as a result of the Spanish-American War, since 1952 Puerto Rico has officially had "commonwealth" status, although some people maintain that this is a camouflage for what is in reality a colony.[8] After 1900, U.S. absentee landlords and later large corporations dominated the economy, displacing small farmers and creating economic and political dependence for the island. Puerto Ricans were made U.S. citizens in 1917 (some say, to coincide with the need for soldiers in the armed forces during World War I, for which Puerto Rican men were recruited en masse). Consequently, they do not need passports or special permission to migrate to the United States. In addition, "back and forth" or circulatory migration is a major characteristic of the Puerto Rican community in the United States. This kind of movement is based primarily on the economic dependence of Puerto Rico on the United States; it is estimated that there were as many as 130,000 circular migrants during the 1980s.[9] To explain the formidable economic subordination of the island, it is often said that "when the United States sneezes, Puerto Rico catches cold."

Although the economic situation of Marisol's family did not improve substantially after the move from New York, the family feels safer in this small city. But the problems of urban living, including drug abuse and crime, are apparent here as well. There are frequent drug raids by police in this neighborhood and others throughout the city. The signs of gang activity are also increasingly apparent. But there is also a "small town" atmosphere in this city that makes it feel more comfortable than large urban areas.

Marisol was shy but eager to discuss her experiences in school and at home. She seems to be very aware of her academic success as compared with the situation of many of her friends. It is a source of both pride and pressure. Three major themes emerged from interviews with Marisol: the desire "to be someone"; a keen awareness of peer pressure and her attempts to deal with it; and a contradictory cultural identity, which ranged from pride to lack of awareness or even embarrassment.

"I Want To Be Someone"

[When I was younger] I wanted to be a good student. I wanted to be someone when I grew up. . . . I wanted to have a future. I want to be someone, you know? Have work and be someone people can look up to, not be out in the streets doing nothing.

I was [a good student] because I respected the teachers, and I did my work, and I behaved. . . . Well, I go to school to learn. If I know I'm trying and my grades are down, the point is I tried.

[*What would you tell a new student in your school about what it means to be successful?*] I would say not a nerd, actually. I would just say that he has to keep up with the grades and the books and things like that, but then again, watch yourself in the school because if you're gonna stay quiet and be behaving, they're gonna take advantage of you, the bigger ones, you know, and the tougher ones. I would just say not take things.

I think I can make it, I think I wanna make it, I think I'm successful. . . . I'm still going to school, and I don't plan to drop out, and I'm still keeping on with everything, not like others that will quit and that have quit. . . . I don't think there's anything stopping me. I don't think there *should* be anything stopping me. If I know I can do it, I should just keep on trying. Of course, no one can stop me, and there's nothing that can get in the way of me wanting to do what I want to do.

I just think of that, you know. I wouldn't want to see myself like [my friends on the street or in prison or with babies]. So that's what keeps me going.

[My friends who are still in school] want to make it, just the way I want to make it. They *plan* to make it, and they have faith in themselves. They want to go to college, the same way I want to. They don't want to be in the streets. They want to be someone too.

[My parents] want me to be someone, I guess. . . . They talk to me, you know? They're open with me and they tell me what's right for me and what's not right. I do things to please them. . . . They like school and they encourage you to keep going. I think they're proud of us 'cause my sisters and brothers, they all have nice report cards; they never stood back, you know, and usually we do this for my mother. We like to see her the way she wants to be, you know, to see her happy.

I think if I believe in being something and if I believe that I want to do something, I think I should do my best in doing it. . . . I would take it on my own. I wouldn't go to teachers or counselors. I mean, I would talk to my friends about it, but I would take it on my own.

[*What will it take to make you successful in the future?*] I don't know . . . I guess never quit . . . and . . . have my hopes up. That's about it. I don't know . . . I mean, keep up with what I'm doing now and just keep on going.

Peer Pressure and Defenses Against It

[My family and I] talk about mainly things that are happening nowadays, such as drugs and teen pregnancy and, you know, things that are important to us. They really care about us and just tell us the rights from the wrongs. She prefers, and he prefers, us to be open to them, you know, and never keep things from them.

My parents are really beautiful people. They're peaceful, you know; they don't like problems. They like to share with other people. But one thing, if people come giving them problems, they will not stay shut, their temper will rise like this [*snaps her fingers*]. They're really nice people to get along with. . . . They understand us. They take time out to stay with us and talk to us, you know. Not too many parents do that. . . . I like living with these people, and I like being with them.

[*Would you change anything about them?*] Nope. Not a thing, absolutely nothing.

[At the teen clinic], we answer questions, for instance, students have. You know, they're free to ask us because we're students like them. We put up, like, the questions they might ask with the answers. We all get together and talk about topics and make fliers and give them out. . . . We also have like a "Dear Abby" sort of thing. . . . They do write letters, and we do read them and we keep it up because I guess they enjoy it.

There's a lot of girls out there getting pregnant and dropping out of school. I don't want one of those girls to be me, you know? I just want to stay away, you know? And I want to advise the ones that are not pregnant as to why they shouldn't get pregnant at an early age and how to prevent from doing that. . . . I would like the kids such as myself to realize what's happening out in the streets and not to put everything to waste. . . . If they're really interested in going to school and having a nice future, I think they should read things and take time to think about it and learn about it. . . . I think there are students out there that need this information and would take time to read it and know more about it.

Cultural Identity: Pride and Embarrassment

I'm proud of [being Puerto Rican]. I guess I speak Spanish whenever I can. . . . To me, it's important, you know, because I have to stand up for Puerto Ricans, to say like for the Whites probably it's more important for them too, just like the Blacks.

I used to have a lot of problems with one of my teachers 'cause she didn't want us to talk Spanish in class, and I thought that was like an insult to us, you know? Just telling us not to talk Spanish, 'cause [we] were Puerto Ricans and, you know, we're free to talk whatever we want. . . . I could never stay quiet and talk only English, 'cause sometimes, you know, words slip in Spanish. You know, I think they should understand that.

[*Are there any differences between Puerto Rican students and others?*] [No,] 'cause you know you can't say that Puerto Ricans act one way and the Whites act the other. . . . [But] I know that Puerto Ricans are way, way badder than the Whites. . . . You know, the way they act and they fight. . . . You know, but everybody's the same, everyone's human, and I don't know, I think they should understand everyone just the way they are.

I think [teachers] should get to know you, and whatever they don't like about Puerto Ricans, or they feel uncomfortable with, you know, just talk to you about it, and you can teach *them* things that probably they're confused about and they don't understand. That way we can communicate better.

I don't think [having a class in Puerto Rican history] is important. . . . I'm proud of myself and my culture, but I think I know what I should know about the culture already, so I wouldn't take the course. . . . No, 'cause [teachers] would have to know about Black and White and Irish [too]. . . . I think they should treat us all the same, you know?

[*Do you admire people in your community, for example?*] Admire them? No! I admire my mother, that's it.

COMMENTARY

This case study of Marisol Martínez brings up several dilemmas facing a great many young people from dominated cultures. One of these is wanting to be successful while also trying to maintain one's culture. This strain is evident in Marisol's determination to "be someone," also a major theme in Marcelo Suarez-Orozco's ethnographic study of Central American high school students.[10] The differences between Central American and Puerto Rican communities in the United States are substantial, including both historical and cultural differences. Yet in the case of Marisol, there is the same insistence on "making it," challenging the assumption that only "voluntary minorities" (as opposed to Puerto Ricans, who would be considered "involuntary minorities") have the drive to succeed academically.

To "be somebody," Marisol has had to be a good student. When she talks about what it takes to be a good student, her focus is not so much on grades as on behavior and attitudes. To be *educado* in the Latino sense of the word means being polite, respectful, and obedient, and it is how many Latino parents define a "good student."[11] This multiple definition of *educado* has a profound effect on many Latino children, who learn that to be a good student also means to be quiet and reserved, a departure from how intellectually curious children are defined in mainstream U.S. culture.

Marisol is caught in the classic struggle between what her parents and teachers want her to strive for and what her peers, including some of her close friends, have experienced. This dilemma was described poignantly by Marisol on several occasions. She virtually absolved the school of any responsibility and when she mentioned it at all, it was to say that students dropped out simply because they did not like school. The fact that certain school policies and practices might jeopardize some students was not taken into account by Marisol. She believes that youths must accept complete responsibility for their own success, that only their own determination will help them get an education.

The role of family is evident in Marisol's determination and academic success. Her efforts to please her parents and make them happy is a primary motivating factor in her academic success, and in this Marisol is similar to other Puerto Rican youngsters.[12] She says that her parents do not pay attention to grades as much as to their children "trying." What makes them angry is lack of effort or good behavior from their children. They have taught their children to "want to be someone," and this concern is reflected in Marisol. Her parents are involved in the children's education in ways that might not be evident to the school but may in the long run be even more meaningful in their children's academic success. When she was asked if her parents participated in school, Marisol was quick to answer that they did not because they do not visit the school or go to parent meetings or volunteer. But the strong influence they have on them seems to be even more significant in their children's drive to do well in school.

Although Marisol has a dogged determination not to drop out and succumb to the many negative pressures around her, she is unclear about how to plan for her future. The experiences of some of her friends (one is in prison, others are home with babies, some are on drugs, some live on welfare) have clearly made an impact on her determination. Their lives, as she puts it, are "down the drain." Yet she neither seeks nor receives help from teachers or counselors, and her parents are unable to give her the kind of information she needs for choosing a college or even for the kinds of classes she should be taking to prepare for college. She has no idea of how to go about fulfilling her dream of becoming a model. Even the choice of modeling as a possible profession indicates how she has internalized the limited role of women within society. Nursing, definitely a far second in her life choices, is only a backup if modeling fails. Although she does well in school, particularly in the sciences, she has apparently not even considered a career as a physician.

The school needs to play a role in opening the horizons of students such as Marisol. The kind of assistance teachers and schools provide for middle-class students in other settings is missing in her case, including nonsexist and nonracist career counseling, college admissions information, and advice on financial aid. Marisol has learned to rely on herself and does not expect help, but the incongruence between wanting success and the vague notion of how to achieve it is quite striking. Her desire to make it on her own is a powerful indication of her determination to succeed. Unfortunately, it is seldom enough.

Still, Marisol's strength and resoluteness to continue in school and to do well seem shatterproof. She has convinced herself, with the support of her close-knit family, that she can succeed and that she is worthy of success. Although the role models she has around her, especially her peers, are not always positive, she has developed strategies for confronting tough situations and temptations. Like other young people her age, Marisol is faced with the pressures of conforming to values and behaviors of other teenagers. In an urban setting, especially in a poor economic environment, these pressures are compounded.

The rate of teenage pregnancy in Milltown is one of the highest in the state. In explaining why she has been so concerned about this issue, Marisol seems to imply that she sees her work at the clinic almost as a vaccine against pregnancy. She is not involved in any other school activities: She does not participate in sports and is not interested in the few clubs that are available. Fortunately, one outlet for her is the teen clinic. Her work there supports and affirms her desire to be a good student and to persist in her education.

Marisol is fighting a constant battle to "make it" in this society while maintaining her heritage. Yet she also obviously has picked up the message that she needs to abandon her heritage to be successful. These contradictory sentiments are evident in many of Marisol's beliefs. Negative messages about cultural and linguistic differences and how they are devalued in society are evident not just in school but also in the media and in the everyday life of the community.

The attitudes young people develop about their culture and heritage cannot be separated from the sociopolitical context in which they live. In this particular city, for example, there have actually been proposals to limit the number of Puerto Ricans coming into town, based on the argument that they are a drain on the welfare rolls. (The Puerto Rican population of the city increased by 227 percent from 1970 to 1980, and by 120 percent from 1980 to 1990. Given the unemployment rate of 22 percent in the Puerto Rican community, the proposal was positively received by some segments of the non–Puerto Rican population.) In addition, the "English only" furor found its way here about a decade ago when municipal workers were told they could not speak Spanish on the job (this order was later revoked). Some Puerto Rican residents have mentioned seeing signs reading "No Puerto Ricans" on apartments for rent. That these incidents might profoundly affect young people is not surprising; what is surprising is that young people retain any pride at all in their culture.

Because she cannot resolve the challenge posed by the pluralism of her school and society, Marisol repeats what she has learned throughout her education: that *equal means the same,* that treating everyone the same is the fairest way. This is why she does not believe that a course in Puerto Rican history is necessary or even desirable. It was clear from her interview that she knew practically nothing of Puerto Rican history, but she was reluctant to want a course in it because somehow that would seem to be "special treatment." That European American students are accorded this special treatment every day probably has not occurred to her: It happens in the curriculum through courses on "world" (primarily European) history and American (primarily White) history.

Marisol is uncertain about the distinction between cultural and individual differences and she seems uncomfortable talking about these things in anything but a superficial way. This is no doubt related to how these issues are treated in school. For example, Marisol has never learned anything in her classes about being Puerto Rican. In social studies classes, she remembers studying about Spain, "but not to the point of studying about Puerto Ricans." One of her homeroom teachers in junior high school, Mr. Pérez, a Puerto Rican teacher of bilingual classes, stands out as the only one who ever bothered teaching his students anything about Puerto Rican history and culture. Marisol remembers seeing reports that students in his classes had done on the bulletin boards, along with books and other exhibits that were available in his classroom. She was interested in many of the things he taught, and although he was never her teacher, she says she learned a lot from him simply by looking through the materials he kept in the classroom. She used to feel, she says, "quite proud of myself" when she saw these things.

Marisol's tastes are typical of many young people. Her favorite foods are seafood and pizza, she likes to cook lasagna, and her favorite music is hip hop and rap. She never mentioned Puerto Rican food, music, holidays, or famous people. She says that her parents listen to "old-fashioned" music, referring to Puerto Rican music, which she is very clear about not liking ("Nope, I want them to hear me: NO.") There seems to be nothing, at least in her stated tastes, that would identify her as Puerto Rican.

Yet Marisol is obviously Puerto Rican in intangible but fundamentally more important ways: her deep feelings for her family, respect for parents, and desire to uphold important traditions such as being with family rather than going out with friends on important holidays. She is also respectful, *humilde* (humble), and soft-spoken but also strong. The last quality is evident, for example, in her uncompromising determination to maintain her native language. At home, she is spontaneously affectionate, rushing over to her mother to hug her tightly and kiss her. She also bears a larger share of family obligations than a great many young people from other cultural backgrounds. This is what is referred to in Hispanic culture as *capacidad,* or a combination of maturity, sense of responsibility, and capability. It is a trait that is very valued in the culture and that parents work hard to inculcate, particularly in their daughters.

In spite of the veneer of U.S. cultural traits she displays, Marisol is also very much a product of Puerto Rican culture, at least as it is manifested in the United States. The features of her native culture that she maintains can be compared to the "deep structure" of language. Marisol, and many young people like her of various immigrant backgrounds, have created a new culture, one that has elements of the native culture but is also different from it.

Both the peer culture and the demands of living in a community where her ethnic group is disparaged rather than admired have an effect on Marisol. Her definition of success—being a model or even a nurse (rather than a physician)—is evidence that she has internalized the sexist and limiting roles of women in our society. But her strong family network has helped Marisol counteract some of these negative effects by providing role models, at least within the family, that Marisol admires deeply. This admiration unfortunately has not spread to others in the community. When asked whom she admired, she answered "all them cute actresses," but was quick to say she did not admire people in her own community except her mother.

On one hand, Marisol has learned the lessons of this assimilationist society very well. On the other, she is hard at work at holding onto what is clearly meaningful for her: a culture and language that the people whom she most loves speak and maintain. The dilemma is a genuine one for this bright young woman who "wants to be someone."

TO THINK ABOUT

1. What do you think is responsible for Marisol's success in school?
2. How can teachers and schools take advantage of Marisol's (and other students') desire to "be someone"?
3. Why do you think Marisol says that "Puerto Ricans are way, way badder than Whites"?
4. Think of some students of various backgrounds whom you know. Do they struggle with a similar conflict of pride and embarrassment about their culture, and if so, how?
5. Marisol is divided about wanting to be a model or a nurse. What do you think has influenced this decision? If you were her school counselor, what would you say to her?

Case Study: James Karam

"I'd like to be considered Lebanese."

James Karam [1] is 16 years old and a junior in high school. His dark eyes are serious but animated when he speaks. He thinks he has a big nose and jokes that it is one of the characteristics of being Lebanese. Poised between childhood and adulthood, James is that pleasing combination of practical, responsible, wise adult and refreshing, spirited, eager kid. His maturity is due in no small part to his role as the "responsible" male in the household. His mother and father are separated and he is the oldest of three children, a position he generally enjoys, although he admits it can be trying at times.

James is Lebanese Christian, or Maronite. His father was born and raised in the United States. He met James's mother while visiting Lebanon and he brought her back here as his bride. She has been in this country for almost 20 years and is now fluent in English. Although James's parents are separated, both are close to their children and continue to take an active part in their upbringing and education.

According to the Census Bureau, Arab Americans are people who can trace their heritage to countries in North Africa and western Asia. The 1990 Census counted about 870,000 Arab Americans, but according to some, this represents a severe undercount.[2] The Lebanese community in the United States is little known to the general population. It is, in this sense, an "invisible minority," about which more will be said later. There are scattered communities of Lebanese throughout the United States, with large concentrations in several cities, including Springfield, Mass., where James lives. In a participant-observer study of the Arab community in this city three decades ago, it was reported that the first Arab settlers arrived in the 1890s from Lebanon. Most were laborers and worked in the city's factories, on the railroad, or in peddling businesses. They were both Christian and Muslim Lebanese, and there generally was little animosity between them. On the contrary, there was a genuine sense of solidarity and cohesiveness in the entire community.[3]

James went to a Catholic school from kindergarten until third grade but he has been in public school ever since. Although he was held back in third grade because his family moved out of the state and he lost a good deal of school time (this still bothers him a lot), James is a successful student who has given much thought to his plans after high school. He works at keeping his grades high so that he can get into a good college and is fairly certain that he wants to be a mechanical engineer. His real dream, however, is to become a professional bike racer. But even if he is able to pursue this dream, he wants a college education. Education is very important to James, as it is to his family. In fact, Arab Americans in general are better educated than the average American: 62 percent have been to college, compared with 45 percent of all Americans.[4]

Springfield is a midsize metropolitan city. It is culturally, racially, and economically diverse. James attends one of the high schools in the city, which he describes as almost "a little college," and he likes all of his classes. His class-mates represent many of the cultures and languages of the world, and the school system has been intent on incorporating this cultural diversity into the curriculum in many ways, some more successful than others. It offers a number of bilingual programs (for the Spanish-speaking, Portuguese, Russian, Vietnamese, and Khmer communities). Some of the other activities, such as cultural festi-vals and international fairs, although a promising start, are somewhat superficial attempts at acknowledging the rich cultural diversity of the city.

James is fluent in both English and Arabic. He has never studied Arabic formally in school, but the language is important to him and he means to main-tain it. The Maronite church in the city was established in 1905 and has been influential in encouraging the use of Arabic and the maintenance of other cul-tural values in the community. Indicative of the church's role, the Reverend Saab, pastor for over 50 years, made the following statement concerning his parishoners during his investiture as monsignor: "I did not want them to forget their Lebanese heritage because this is a wonderful thing."[5] Even when assimi-lation was generally perceived to be a great value in U.S. society, the Lebanese community was definitely bucking the tide. This is apparent even today in the large percentage of second and even third generation Lebanese in Springfield, both Christian and Muslim, who still speak Arabic. In the case of the Maronites, the church's role is not merely to provide a place for worship; rather, it contin-ues to serve as a haven for cultural pride and maintenance.

In other ways, however, the Arab American community has undergone great changes and has acculturated to the U.S. mainstream. In Springfield, Arabic surnames are now almost nonexistent because most family names have been Anglicized. Actually, were it not for the influence of the church and to a lesser extent other social and religious organizations and clubs, assimilation might have proceeded much more rapidly. The social class structure has changed as well. The Lebanese community in the city started out as working class but is now primarily middle class. In the first decades of the century, the Arab community was similar to many other immigrant communities: It was characterized by large families (an average of 10 children), overcrowded flats, congested sidewalks and doorsteps, and dirty and unpaved streets. Now three-quarters of Arabs in Springfield own their own homes and live in middle-class communities.[6]

This is true of James and his family as well. He, his mother, 14-year-old brother, and 9-year-old sister live in a quiet residential neighborhood in the city. His community is much more homogeneous than the city itself, primarily European American. He says the difference between his neighborhood and the city proper is that there are many trees ("Believe me, I know! I have to rake the leaves every year"). He enjoys living here and would probably want to live in a community just like it when he has his own family.

James's perception of himself as a good student, as "smart," is an important theme, which will be explored further. In addition, his role as "apprentice" will be discussed. The most important theme to emerge, however, is the invisibility of James's culture, which will be considered first.

The Invisible Minority

[My elementary school teacher, Mr. Miller] I just liked him. . . . He started calling me "Gonzo" 'cause I had a big nose. He called me "Klinger"—he said 'cause Klinger's Lebanese. You know, the guy on "M.A.S.H." . . . And then everybody called me Klinger from then on. . . . I liked it, kind of . . . everybody laughing at me. Yeah, it doesn't bother me. I don't care if somebody talks about my nose.

We had a foreign language month in school. They had posters and signs and everything. Spanish, French, Spain, Italy—they had all these signs and posters and pictures and stuff all over the school. . . . There was Chinese; they had Japanese; they had Korean. They had lots of stuff.

[*Why didn't they have Arabic?*] I don't know. . . .

[Another time] they made this cookbook of all these different recipes from all over the world. And I would've brought in some Lebanese recipes if some-body'd let me know. And I didn't hear about it until the week before they started selling them. . . . They had some Greek. They had everything, just about. . . . I asked one of the teachers to look at it, and there was nothing Lebanese in there.

[Another time, at the multicultural fair], there was . . . Poland, there was Czechoslovakia, there was Spain, there was Mexico, there was France. There was a lot of different flags. I didn't see Lebanon, though.

I guess there's not that many Lebanese people in. . . . I don't know; you don't hear really that much. . . . Well, you hear it in the news a lot, but I mean, I don't know, there's not a lot of Lebanese kids in our school. There's about eight or nine at the most.

I don't mind, 'cause I mean, I don't know, just, I don't mind it. . . . It's not really important. It *is* important for me. It would be important for me to see a Lebanese flag. . . . But you know, it's nothing I would like enforce or like, say something about. . . . If anybody ever asked me about it, I'd probably say, "Yeah, there should be one." You know, if any of the teachers ever asked me, but I don't know. . . .

Some people call me, you know, 'cause I'm Lebanese, so people say, "Look out for the terrorist! Don't mess with him or he'll blow up your house!" or some stuff like that.

But they're just joking around, though. . . . I don't think anybody's serious 'cause I wouldn't blow up anybody's house—and they know that. . . . I don't care. It doesn't matter what people say. . . . I just want everybody to know that, you know, it's not true.

On Being a Good Student

I'm probably the smartest kid in my class. . . . It's just like, usually I can get really into the work and stuff. But everybody else, you know, even the people that do their homework and assignments and stuff, they just do it and pass it in. You know, I like to get involved in it and *learn* it.

If you don't get involved with it, even if . . . . you get perfect scores and stuff . . . it's not gonna like really sink in. You'll probably forget it. . . . You can memorize the words you know, on a test. . . . But you know, if you memorize them, it's not going to do you any good. You have to *learn* them, you know?

I want to make sure that I get my college education. I want to make sure of that. Even if I do get into the career that I specialize in in college, I still want to get a college education.

[I think I didn't do well in school one year] just because I didn't try. . . . I thought it was too easy so I didn't try. . . . I don't think [Mom] liked that too much. . . . I said, "Mom, I wanna go to summer school, you know, just to bring up my grade." So she paid for it.

In a lot of the things that I do, I usually do good. . . . I don't like it when I don't finish something or when I do real bad. It makes me want to do better. . . . If I ever get a bad grade on a test, it makes me want to do better next time.

I have a counselor, but she's never in. She's always out with some kind of sickness or something. She helps figuring out my schedule and stuff like that. . . . I don't really talk to my counselor, you know, as personal talks and stuff like that.

Some teachers are just . . . they don't really care. They just teach the stuff. "Here," write a couple of things on the board, "see, that's how you do it. Go ahead, page 25." You know, some teachers are just like that.

Maybe it's not that they don't care. It's just that they don't put enough effort into it, maybe. . . . I don't know.

I like going over it with the class, and you know, letting . . . everybody know your questions. And you know, there could be someone sitting in the back of the class that has the same question you have. Might as well bring it out.

[James describes his favorite teacher, his geometry teacher, and her role in the Helping Hand Club at school.] The people send her letters and brochures and stuff. And, you know, she says, "This is a good idea." You know, she brings it up at the meeting. And we say, "Okay" and then figure out. . . . She's like the head of it. She's the one that's really thoughtful and helpful.

[Teachers should] make the classes more interesting. . . . Like not just sit there and say, "Do this and do this and do this." You know, just like explain everything, write things on the board.

I'd love to be an engineer, but my real dream is to be a bike racer. . . . Yeah, it's my love. I love it.

When things go bad, I go ride my bike. . . . That's what I did [once] in the middle of the night. . . . The faster I ride, the harder I pushed, the more it hurt. It made me keep my mind off [things].

Apprenticeship within the Family

I speak a mixture of both [Arabic and English]. Sometimes it's just like, some words come out Arabic and some words come out English. . . . Whichever expresses what I want to say the best, I guess, at the time.

[My parents] basically taught me to be good to people. You know, I've never really been mean to anybody. I don't like fighting. My mother taught me that, mostly.

We go to a lot of Lebanese parties and, you know, gatherings and stuff. . . . We go to Catholic-Lebanese church every week. . . . I always want to go to church. . . . Most of my friends don't go to church. . . . A lot of them do but most of them don't.

My mother's really proud to be Lebanese, and so am I. . . . First thing I'd say is I'm Lebanese. . . . I'm just proud to be Lebanese. If somebody asked me, "What are you?" . . . everybody else would answer, "I'm American," but I say "I'm Lebanese," and I feel proud of it.

Even though somebody might have the last name like LeMond or something, he's considered American. But you know, LeMond is a French name, so his culture must be French. His background is French. But, you know, they're considered Americans. But I'd like to be considered Lebanese.

My mother's really old-fashioned. "You gotta be in early." "You gotta be in bed at a certain time." That kind of stuff. . . . I guess it'll pay off. When I'm older, I'll realize that she was right, I guess. But right now, I wish I could stay out like a little later. . . . I don't mind it, 'cause I don't think I'm really missing much. . . . There must be a reason why.

I know a lot of kids that can stay out and, you know, they go out till 12 o'clock, 1 o'clock in the morning. They don't come back home and their mothers don't even ask them, you know, where they've been or whatever. [My parents are] really loving and caring. . . . [I] wouldn't want to be a part of any other family, put it that way.

COMMENTARY

James's experiences in school have reinforced the fact that Arab Americans are an invisible minority in the United States. This became clear not only through discussions with James but also through a review of the literature. Whereas much has been written about numerous other ethnic groups in the United States—even those fewer in number—very little is available about Arab Americans, their culture, school experiences, or learning styles. This situation is changing. In the past decade, more information and research have become available. An informative article by Mahmoud Suleiman, for example, includes essential data for teachers about the Arab American community and also describes implications of the growing presence of Arab Americans for multicultural education.[7] But compared with most other groups, for whom volumes of information are available (although not necessarily understood or used appropriately), Arab Americans represent in this sense a unique case of invisibility.

The reasons for this invisibility are probably varied. For one, the majority of Arabs did not come in a mass influx as the result of famine, political or religious persecution, or war, as have other refugees. Although many indeed have come under these circumstances in the recent past, their numbers have not been conspicuous. Consequently, their immigration to the United States has been a relatively quiet one, given scant attention by the media. Also, their problems of adjustment, although no doubt difficult, have not caught the public imagination as have those of other immigrants. Theirs has been an apparently smooth transition. Likewise, their children have not faced massive failure in the schools, as is true with other groups. For this reason, they have not been the focus of study as others have been. Finally, they are not always a racially visible minority, as is usually the case with Asians, Caribbeans, or most Latinos. They are much more apt to "blend in" with the European American population, even if they choose to maintain their cultural heritage.

Nonetheless, the lack of information is astonishing in light of the number and diversity of Arabs in the United States. The simple fact that Lebanon and the Middle East have been involved in a long-standing conflict and have frequently been in the news is reason enough for more information about Arab Americans. Beyond the issue of conflict, the reality of the diverse histories and cultures of the approximately 150 million Arabs worldwide deserves some mention on its own merit.[8]

Representing different religions, socioeconomic classes, and national origins, the Arab community is one of the most heterogeneous in the United States. It is also one of the most misunderstood, shrouded in mystery and consequently in stereotypes. According to Mahmoud Suleiman, "Although Arab Americans are less visible than other minorities, the anti-Arab perception in the media makes them more visible in a negative way."[9] The popular images of Arabs as rich sheikhs, religious zealots, or terrorists are gross stereotypes that do little to stir pride in Lebanese and other Arab Americans. Yet this is sometimes the only "information" the general public has. These are also the images that James and other Arab American children have to struggle against every day. In a poignant account of how this stereotyping affected his own children when they decided not to use their ethnic clothes for a multiethnic festival at school, James Zogby, a Lebanese American, concluded, "Confusion and perhaps fear made them resist any display of pride. What for other students was the joy of ethnicity had become for my Arab-American children the pain of ethnicity."[10] Racist stereotypes of Arabs as barbaric, treacherous, and cruel persist. Yet, according to an article based on actual census figures, "Real Arab Americans don't fit into media stereotypes"[11] because the vast majority are citizens, well educated, and highly diverse.

James has either felt invisible or his culture has been referred to in only negative ways. Because Mr. Miller, the teacher who called him "Gonzo," joked in the same way with many of the other students, and because he allowed them to "make fun" of him too, James liked this attention. It made him feel special and meant that his background was at least being acknowledged, but James also mentioned many ways in which his culture was not acknowledged. The stereotypes about his background have, in spite of what he says, probably taken their toll on James. Although he is quite active in school activities, he does not want to belong to student government. "I hate politics," he said simply.

James is conscious of being a good student. He is very confident about his academic success, and his perception of being a successful student is important to him. He is proud, for example, of being persistent, a quality that he believes is his best characteristic. But it goes beyond just thinking of himself as a good student; he demonstrates persistence through his actions as well. For example, during his sophomore year his grades were all A's and B's, except for a D+ in English. On his own, he decided to attend summer school (a decision his mother supported), and he did very well.

When he began his junior year after summer school, James broke his foot while playing sports. It required surgery, and he was on crutches for several weeks. Because he had missed two weeks of school, he stayed after school every day for a number of weeks, making up labs and quizzes and other assignments. He was struggling with both schoolwork and crutches, but his attitude was positive. "I can't wait to be done with all my makeup work," he said, with a touch of frustration. He got through it, though, as with everything else that he has to do.

James's family has played a significant role in the value he places on education and the need to persevere. Although his family is not typical of the majority of recent immigrants to the United States, who are overwhelmingly Asian and Hispanic, it nevertheless shares some fundamental characteristics. For example, faith in the rewards of education is common among immigrant families, as Laurie Olsen found in her ethnography of recent immigrants in a comprehensive high school in California.[12] James appreciates his parents' efforts and explains that his mother is not involved in school, at least not in terms of going to parent meetings and such. As James made clear, her involvement is most evident in the support and encouragement she gives him.

Perhaps because of his persistence and self-motivation—or perhaps because the services in his school are inadequate—James has not counted on anyone at school to help him plan for the future. He is intent on going to a good college, but it is unclear where he will get the advice he needs to make appropriate decisions about college. James's favorite teacher is his geometry teacher, the one who "takes the time" and goes over everything in class. She is also the faculty adviser for the Helping Hand Club, a community service group in the school and neighborhood. James is quite involved in this group, which helps raise funds for individuals in need and for charitable organizations. "I like doing that kind of stuff," he says, "helping out."

He is involved in other activities as well, and these seem to give him the energy and motivation he needs to keep up with schoolwork. He plays soccer and baseball and is on the swim team. He becomes most enthusiastic, however, when talking about his favorite activity, biking. This sport gives James great support in many ways. He was in a biking accident last year and still has not been able to have his heavily damaged bicycle repaired. He is thinking of organizing a biking team and has contemplated seeking financial support from neighborhood shop owners. Biking has given him the opportunity to learn about many things: how "practice makes perfect," how to develop and use leadership skills, how it feels to have a setback and not let it be a permanent loss, how to use a hobby to help relieve stress, and how to hone his interpersonal skills. Biking is not only a physical challenge, but also an important motivation. James's room is filled with biking magazines. The person he most admires is Greg LeMond, the only U.S. racer who has ever won the Tour de France and the world championship. "I want to be just like him," he says.

Like other parents, James's parents teach him the values and behaviors they believe most important for his survival and success. In the case of a family culturally different from the mainstream, this role becomes even more crucial. Teaching children their culture can be called an "apprenticeship." It is a role that is particularly evident among immigrant families who attempt, often against great odds, to keep their native culture alive. For families of the dominant culture, their apprenticeship is usually unconscious, for their children are surrounded by and submerged in the culture every day. They hear the dominant language, see dominant culture behaviors, and take part in all the trappings of what is to them *the* culture. For immigrant families, or even for third- or fourth-generation families who have chosen to maintain their native culture in some way, the task of their children's apprenticeship is appreciably more difficult. The language they speak at home is not echoed in the general population; their values, traditions, and holidays are often at odds with those of the dominant culture; and even the foods they eat or the music they listen to are absent in the dominant culture. Because their culture in many ways is simply unacknowledged, these families are engaged in an impossibly difficult balancing act of cultural adaptation without complete assimilation.

Although certainly not immune from the difficulties inherent in this role, James has been quite successful at this balancing act. He has a strong and healthy self-image, not only as a student but also as a Lebanese. The house is filled with Lebanese artifacts, and James displays them proudly. A Lebanese pennant is prominently displayed in his room, and his bike racing helmet has a Lebanese flag on it. James has never been to Lebanon but he definitely plans to go "when this war is over." He also says that he and his family talk about the situation in Lebanon. James loves Lebanese food, and he has even learned to cook some of it. The only thing he seems to dislike, in fact, is Lebanese music, which he calls "boring."

Being a part of a family out of the mainstream is not without its problems, however, particularly for adolescents. For James, it means having different rules than his friends (e.g., the demand that he attend church regularly). The church provides a particularly strong link with his culture, and as long as he can remember, James has been going to church every Sunday. He never misses, and he still goes to catechism. He is the oldest in the church class because everyone else his age feels too old to continue but James still enjoys it.

He does not feel, however, that this practice makes him particularly different from other youths. For the most part, James feels comfortable in two worlds. His apprenticeship has been a largely successful one. He is proud of his culture; he is bilingual; he is not usually embarrassed or ashamed about appearing "different." He considers his family to be "the average American family" in some ways and he would probably consider himself to be an "all-American kid." He likes to do what he calls "normal teenager stuff."

James Karam has been successful in forging his family, culture, language, hobbies, church, friends, and schoolwork into a unique amalgam, which has resulted in a strong self-image and a way of confronting a society not always comfortable with or tolerant of diversity. This achievement has not made him immune, however, to being an ethnic minority and to the different and distressing issues that arise because of it. The price James pays for being from an invisible culture is sometimes steep. He has learned, for example, to hide hurt feelings when his culture is disparaged and to treat everything "as a joke." He has learned to be quiet, preferring to accept invisibility rather than risk further alienation or rejection. He has also learned not to demand that his culture be affirmed. Nevertheless, the uncompromising strength of his family, the support he gets from his extracurricular activities, and his enduring faith in himself can help to make the difference between surviving the tension or succumbing to it.

TO THINK ABOUT

1. What other invisible minorities are you aware of? Why would you classify them in this way?
2. Why do you think James is reluctant to bring up his feelings of exclusion in school activities?
3. How would you characterize the role that biking has played in James's life? What can teachers and schools learn from this?
4. What advice do you think James would give new teachers about being successful teachers? Why?
5. If a teacher knew about James's apprenticeship within the family, how might he or she use this information?

Case Study: Hoang Vinh

"They just understand some things outside, but they cannot understand something inside our hearts."

Hoang Vinh's[1] hands move in quick gestures as he tries to illustrate what he has to say, almost as if wishing that they would speak for him. Vinh[2] is very conscious of not knowing English well enough to express himself how he would like and he keeps apologizing, "My English is not good." Nevertheless, his English skills are quite advanced for someone who has been in the United States for just a short time.

Vinh is 18 years old. He was born in the Xuan Loc province of Dong Nai, about 80 kilometers from Saigon. At the time he was interviewed, he had been in the United States for three years and lived with his uncle, two sisters, and two brothers in a midsize New England town. They first lived in Virginia but moved here after a year and a half. Vinh and his family live in a modest house in a residential neighborhood of a pleasant, mostly middle-class college town. The family's Catholicism is evidenced by the statues of Jesus and the Virgin Mary in the living room. Everyone in the family has chores and contributes to keeping the house clean and making the meals. In addition, the older members make sure that the younger children keep in touch with their Vietnamese language and culture: They have weekly sessions in which they write to their parents; they allow only Vietnamese to be spoken at home; and they cook Vietnamese food, something that even the youngest is learning to do. When they receive letters from their parents, they sit down to read them together. Their uncle reinforces their native literacy by telling them many stories. Vinh also plays what he calls "music from my Vietnam," to which they all listen.

Because Vinh's father was in the military before 1975 and worked for the U.S. government, he was seen as an American sympathizer and educational opportunities for his family were limited after the war. Vinh and his brothers and sisters were sent to the United States by their parents, who could not leave Vietnam but wanted their children to have the opportunity for a better education and a more secure future. Vinh and his family came in what has been called the "second wave" of immigration from Indochina[3]; that is, they came after the huge exodus in 1975. Although Vinh and his family came directly from Vietnam, most of the second-wave immigrants came from refugee camps in Thailand, Malaysia, and elsewhere. This second wave has generally been characterized by greater heterogeneity in social class and ethnicity, less formal education, fewer marketable skills, and poorer health than previous immigrants. During the 1980s, when Vinh and his family came to the United States, the school-age Asian and Pacific Islander population between the ages of 5 and 19 grew by an astounding 90 percent. About half of the 800,000 Southeast Asian refugees who arrived between 1975 and 1990 were under 18 years of age.[4]

Vinh's uncle works in town and supports all the children. He takes his role of surrogate father very seriously and tries to help the children in whatever way he can. He discusses many things with them; Vinh speaks with gratitude of the lengthy conversations they have. Mostly, he wants to make sure that all the children benefit from their education. He constantly motivates them to do better.

Vinh's older brother makes dried flower arrangements in the basement and sells them in town. During the summers, Vinh works to contribute to his family here and in Vietnam, but during the school year he is not allowed to work because he needs to focus on his studies ("I just go to school, and after school, I go home to study," he explains). He uses the money he makes in the summer to support his family because, he says, "we are very poor." They rarely go to the movies, and they spend little on themselves.

Vinh will be starting his senior year in high school. Because the number of Vietnamese speakers in the schools he has attended has never been high, Vinh has not been in a bilingual program. He does quite well in school, but he also enjoys the opportunity to speak his native language and would no doubt have profited from a bilingual education. He is currently in an English as a second language (ESL) class at the high school with a small number of other Vietnamese students and other students whose first language is not English. Some teachers encourage Vinh and his Vietnamese classmates to speak Vietnamese during the ESL class to improve their understanding of the curriculum content. But other teachers discourage the use of their native language. All of Vinh's other classes are in the "mainstream program" for college-bound students: physics, calculus, French, music, and law. Vinh's favorite subject is history because he says he wants to learn about this country. He is also interested in psychology.

Homework and studying take up many hours of Vinh's time. He places great value on what he calls "becoming educated people." His parents and uncle constantly stress the importance of an education and place great demands on Vinh and his brothers and sisters. He also enjoys playing volleyball and badminton and being with his friends in the gym. Because he loves school, Vinh does not enjoy staying home. He is a good student and wants desperately to go to college, but even at this late date he had not received any help or information about different colleges, how to apply, how to get financial aid, and admission requirements. He does not want to bother anyone to ask for this information. Added to his reluctance to ask for assistance is the economic barrier he sees to getting a college education. Because he wants to make certain that his brothers and sisters are well cared for, housed, and fed, he may have to work full time after graduating from high school.

Vinh is very concerned about becoming a good student. His explanation of what this means is explored further. Three other themes that surface are the stringent demands he places on himself, wanting to understand other cultures, and the strength he derives from his culture and family.

On Becoming "Educated People"

In Vietnam, we go to school because we want to become educated people. But in the United States, most people, they say, "Oh, we go to school because we want to get a good job." But my idea, I don't think so. I say, if we go to school, we want a good job *also,* but we want to become a good person.

[In Vietnam] we go to school, we have to remember *every single word.* . . . We don't have textbooks, so my teacher write on the blackboard. So we have to copy and go home. . . . So, they say, "You have to remember all the things, like all the words . . . ." But in the United States, they don't need for you remember all the words. They just need you to *understand.* . . . But two different school systems. They have different things. I think in my Vietnamese school, they are good. But I also think the United States school system is good. They're not the same. . . . They are good, but good in different ways.

When I go to school [in Vietnam], sometimes I don't know how to do something, so I ask my teacher. She can spend *all the time* to help me, anything I want. So, they are very nice. . . . My teacher, she was very nice. When I asked her everything, she would answer me, teach me something. That's why I remember. . . . But some of my teachers, they always punished me.

[Grades] are not important to me. Important to me is education. . . . I [am] not concerned about [test scores] very much. I just need enough for me to go to college. . . . Sometimes, I never care about [grades]. I just know I do my exam very good. But I don't need to know I got A or B. I have to learn more and more.

Sometimes, I got C but I learned very much, I learned a lot, and I feel very sorry, "Why I got only C?" But sometimes, if I got B, that's enough, I don't need A.

Some people, they got a good education. They go to school, they got master's, they got doctorate, but they're just helping *themselves.* So that's not good. . . . If I got a good education, I get a good job, not helping only myself. I like to help other people. . . . I want to help other people who don't have money, who don't have a house. . . . The first thing is money. If people live without money, they cannot do nothing. So even if I want to help other people, I have to get a good job. I have the money, so that way I can help them.

In class, sometimes [students] speak Vietnamese because we don't know the words in English. . . . Our English is not good, so that's why we have to speak Vietnamese.

In school, if we get good and better and better, we have to work in groups. Like if we want to discuss something, we have to work in groups, like four people. And we discuss some projects, like that. And different people have different ideas, so after that we choose some best idea. I like work in groups.

Sometimes, the English teachers, they don't understand about us. Because something we not do good, like my English is not good. And she say, "Oh, your English is great!" But that's the way the American culture is. But my culture is not like that. . . . If my English is not good, she has to say, "Your English is not good. So you have to go home and study." And she tell me what to study and how to study to get better. But some Americans, you know, they don't understand about myself. So they just say, "Oh! You're doing a good job! You're doing great! Everything is great!" Teachers talk like that, but

my culture is different. . . . They say, "You have to do better . . . ." So, sometimes when I do something not good, and my teachers say, "Oh, you did
great!" I don't like it. . . . I want the truth better.

Some teachers, they never concerned to the students. So, they just do
something that they have to do. But they don't really do something to help the
people, the students. Some teachers, they just go inside and go to the
blackboard. . . . They don't care. So that I don't like.

I have a good teacher, Ms. Brown. She's very sensitive. She understands
the students, year to year, year after year. . . . She understands a lot. So when
I had her class, we discussed some things very interesting about America. And
sometimes she tells us about something very interesting about another culture. But Ms. Mitchell, she just knows how to teach for the children, like
10 years old or younger. So some people don't like her. Like me, I don't like
her. I like to discuss something. Not just how to write "A," "you have to write
like this." So I don't like that. . . . She wants me to write perfectly. So that is
not a good way because we learn another language. Because when we learn
another language, we learn to discuss, we learn to understand the word's
meaning, not about how to *write* the word.

I want to go to college, of course. Right now, I don't know what will happen for the future. . . . If I think of my future, I have to learn more about psychology. If I have a family, I want a perfect family, not really perfect, but I
want a very good family. So that's why I study psychology. . . . When I grow
up, I get married, I have children, so I have to let them go to school, I have
good education to teach them. So, Vietnamese want their children to grow up
and be polite and go to school, just like I am right now. . . . I just want they
will be a good person.

I don't care much about money. So, I just want to have a normal job that
I can take care of myself and my family. So that's enough. I don't want to
climb up compared to other people, because, you know, different people
have different ideas about how to live. So I don't think money is important to
me. I just need enough money for my life.

Demanding Standards

I'm not really good, but I'm trying.

In Vietnam, I am a good student. But at the United States, my English is
not good sometimes. I cannot say very nice things to some Americans,
because my English is not perfect.

Sometimes the people, they don't think I'm polite because they don't
understand my English exactly. . . . I always say my English is not good, because
all the people, they can speak better than me. So, I say, "Why some people, they
came here the same year with me, but they can learn better?" So I have to try.

When I lived in Vietnam, so I go to school and I got very good credit
[grades], but right now because my English is not good, sometimes I feel very
sorry for myself.

[My uncle] never told me, "Oh, you do good," or "Oh, you do bad." Because every time I go home, I give him my report card, like from C to A, he don't say nothing. He say, "Next time, you should do better." If I got A, okay, he just say, "Oh, next time, do better than A! . . ." He doesn't need anything from me. But he wants me to be a good person, and helpful. . . . So he wants me to go to school, so someday I have a good job and so I don't need from him anymore.

He encourages me. He talks about why you have to learn and what important things you will do in the future if you learn. . . . I like him to be involved about my school. . . . I like him to be concerned about my credits.

Some people need help, but some people don't. Like me, sometime I need help. I want to know how to . . . apply for college and what will I do to get into college. So that is my problem.

I have a counselor, but I never talk to him. Because I don't want them to be concerned about myself because they have a lot of people to talk with. So, sometimes, I just go home and I talk with my brother and my uncle.

If I need my counselor every time I got trouble, I'm not going to solve that problem. . . . So, I want to do it by myself. I have to sit down and think, "Why did the trouble start? And how can we solve the problem? . . ." Sometimes, I say, I don't want them to [be] concerned with my problem.

Most American people are very helpful. But because I don't want them to spend time about myself, to help me, so that's why I don't come to them. One other time, I talked with my uncle. He can tell me whatever I want. But my English is not good, so that's why I don't want to talk with American people.

I may need my counselor's help. When I go to college, I have to understand the college system and how to go get into college. . . . The first thing I have to know is the college system, and what's the difference between this school and other schools, and how they compare. . . . I already know how to make applications and how to meet counselors, and how to take a test also.

Sometimes I do better than other people, but I still think it's not good. Because if you learn, you can be more than that. So that's why I keep learning. Because I think, everything you can do, you learn. If you don't learn, you can't do nothing.

Right now, I cannot say [anything good] about myself because if I talk about myself, it's not right. Another person who lives with me, like my brother, he can say something about me better than what I say about myself. . . . Nobody can understand themselves better than other people.

I don't know [if I'm successful] because that belongs to the future. . . . I mean successful for myself [means] that I have a good family; I have a good job; I have respect from other people.

Trying To Understand Other Cultures

Some [Black] people very good. . . . Most Black people in [this town], they talk very nice. . . . Like in my country, some people very good and some people very bad.

I am very different from other people who are the same age. Some people who are the same age, they like to go dancing, they like to smoke, they want to have more fun. But not me. . . . Because right now, all the girls, they like more fun [things] than sit down and think about psychology, think about family. . . . I think it's very difficult to find [a girlfriend] right now. . . . If I find a girlfriend who not agree with any of my ideas, it would not be a good girlfriend. . . . I don't need [her to be] very much like me, but some . . . we would have a little in common. . . . It is not about their color or their language, but their character. I like their character better.

I think it's an important point, because if you understand another language or another culture, it's very good for you. So I keep learning, other cultures, other languages, other customs.

I have Chinese, I have Japanese, I have American, I have Cambodian [friends]. Every kind of people. Because I care about character, not about color.

Strength from Culture and Family

Sometimes I think about [marrying] a Vietnamese girl, because my son or my daughter, in the future, they will speak Vietnamese. So, if I have an American girlfriend, my children cannot speak Vietnamese. Because I saw other families who have an American wife or an American husband, their children cannot speak Vietnamese. It is very hard to learn a language. . . . In the United States, they have TV, they have radio, every kind of thing, we have to do English. So, that why I don't think my children can learn Vietnamese.

When I sleep, I like to think a little bit about my country. And I feel very good. I always think about . . . my family . . . what gifts they get me before, how they were with me when I was young. . . . Those are very good things to remember and to try to repeat again.

I've been here for three years, but the first two years I didn't learn anything. I got sick, mental. I got mental. Because when I came to the United States, I missed my fathers, my family, and my friends, and my Vietnam.

So, every time I go to sleep, I cannot sleep, I don't want to eat anything. So I become sick.

I am a very sad person. Sometimes, I just want to be alone to think about myself. I feel sorry about what I do wrong with someone. Whatever I do wrong in the past, I just think and I feel sorry for myself.

I never have a good time. I go to the mall, but I don't feel good. . . . I just sit there, I don't know what to do.

Before I got mental, okay, I feel very good about myself, like I am smart, I learn a lot of things. . . . But after I got mental, I don't get any enjoyment. . . . I'm not smart anymore.

After I got mental, I don't enjoy anything. Before that, I enjoy lots. Like I listen to music, I go to school and talk to my friends. . . . But now I don't feel I enjoy anything. Just talk with my friends, that's enough, that's my enjoyment.

My culture is my country. We love my country; we love our people; we love the way the Vietnamese, like they talk very nice and they are very polite to all the people.

For Vietnamese, [culture] is very important. . . . I think my country is a great country. The people is very courageous. They never scared to do anything. . . . If we want to get something, we have to get it. Vietnamese culture is like that. . . . We work hard, and we get something we want.

If I have children, I have to teach them from [when] they grow up to when they get older. So, when they get older, I don't have to teach them, but they listen to me. Because that's education, not only myself, but all Vietnamese, from a long time ago to now. That's the custom. So that's why I like my customs and my culture.

Every culture . . . they have good things and they have bad things. And my culture is the same. But sometimes they're different because they come from different countries. . . . America is so different.

[My teachers] understand some things, just not all Vietnamese culture. Like they just understand some things *outside*. . . . But they cannot understand something inside our hearts.

[Teachers should] understand the students. Like Ms. Mitchell, she just say, "Oh, you have to do it this way," "You have to do that way." But some people, they came from different countries. They have different ideas, so they might think about school in different ways. So maybe she has to know why they think in that way. . . . Because different cultures, they have different meanings about education. So she has to learn about that culture.

I think they just *think* that they understand our culture. . . . But it is very hard to tell them, because that's our feelings.

When I came to United States, I heard English, so I say, "Oh, very funny sound." Very strange to me. But I think they feel the same like when we speak Vietnamese. So they hear and they say, "What a strange language." Some people like to listen. But some people don't like to listen. So, if I talk with Americans, I never talk Vietnamese.

Some teachers don't understand about the language. So sometimes, my language, they say it sounds funny. And sometimes, all the languages sound funny. Sometimes, [the teacher] doesn't let us speak Vietnamese, or some people speak Cambodian. Sometimes, she already knows some Spanish, so she lets Spanish speak. But because she doesn't know about Vietnamese language, so she doesn't let Vietnamese speak.

[Teachers] have to know about our culture. And they have to help the people learn whatever they want. From the second language, it is very difficult for me and for other people.

I want to learn something good from my culture and something good from American culture. And I want to take both cultures and select something good. . . . If we live in the United States, we have to learn something about new people.

[To keep reading and writing Vietnamese] is very important. . . . So, I like to learn English, but I like to learn my language too. Because different languages, they have different things, special. [My younger sisters] are very good. They don't need my help. They already know. They write to my parents and they keep reading Vietnamese books. . . . Sometimes they forget to pronounce the words, but I help them.

At home, we eat Vietnamese food. . . . The important thing is rice. Everybody eats rice, and vegetables, and meat. They make different kinds of food. . . . The way I grew up, I had to learn, I had to know it. By looking at other people—when my mother cooked, and I just see it, and so I know it.

Right now, I like to listen to my music and I like to listen to American music. . . . And I like to listen to other music from other countries.

We tell [our parents] about what we do at school and what we do at home and how nice the people around us, and what we will do better in the future to make them happy. Something not good, we don't write.

They miss us and they want ourselves to live together. . . . They teach me how to live without them.

COMMENTARY

Hoang Vinh's experiences in the United States closely parallel those of other Southeast Asian refugees in some respects, but they are quite different in others. His case study gives us many lessons about teachers' expectations, demands on Asian students, and the anguish of cultural clash and language loss. Vinh is emphatic about wanting to become "educated people," which he explains as wanting to know about other people and about the world and wanting to be able to get along with and help others. Grades are not as important to Vinh as doing "the best you can." He is convinced that there is a big difference—not only a semantic one but a cultural one as well—in what it means to "be educated" in the Vietnamese sense and in the United States. His explanation is a good example of what many Asians believe to be one of the main differences between U.S. and Asian cultures: Although U.S. culture is rich materially, it often lacks the spirituality so important in most Asian cultures.[5]

This attitude was developed in Vinh early in life. He was brought up in a strict home where he learned the meaning of responsibility and hard work. He was not allowed to play soccer with his friends until his room was clean and he had finished all his chores. He was expected to go to school and then study for many hours afterward. In school, he remembers his teachers as being very "difficult." He says they expected him to be well behaved and polite, to come to school with clean hands, and to study.

Vietnamese and other Indochinese immigrants generally have a substantially higher level of education than other groups, even well-established ones.[6] The high literacy rate has an impact on their schooling in this country as well. Southeast Asians in U.S. schools typically spend much more time on homework than other groups, and literacy and educational activities are part of the home as well as the school. The effects of Vinh's family background and early school experiences are evident in his attitudes toward school and in his study habits.

Although Vinh remembers his teachers in Vietnam with some fear because they were strict and demanding, he also recalls them with nostalgia. He seems to long for the extra attention and help they provided. He particularly remembers that they spent a great deal of time with each child until all of the children had learned. Vinh notices many differences in the educational system in the United States, some positive, others negative. He appreciates, for example, being allowed to use his native language in class and the individual help he receives from teachers. But he also thinks that teachers need to learn to explain *why* the subject they teach is important. Mostly he talks about how he loves working in groups. He particularly mentions one ESL teacher, his favorite teacher, who often has students working in groups, talking among themselves and coming up with their own solutions and answers. Most of the themes they discuss are related to their lives here, their culture, and their adaptation.

Much of the literature about the traditional learning styles of Vietnamese students emphasizes their passivity and reliance on rote memorization, but Vinh's case dramatizes how important it is to interpret such literature cautiously.[7] For one, there is great diversity among all Asian groups and even within groups. Vinh's predilection for group work, for example, may demonstrate how the *form* of education is not as important as the *content.* That is, group work in this case is the *means* used to facilitate dialogue, so important in learning a second language and in learning in general. But the content is what may be the crucial factor here because it is based on the students' own experiences and engages them meaningfully in their own education. Vinh also talks about things that are *not* helpful. He does not like what he considers being treated like a child, with boring and repetitive seat work or work that has to be copied from the board without follow-up. He also sees through the false praise that teachers give him and other students, praise that is meant to motivate but that has the opposite effect.

Lest we get the impression that all Vietnamese students are as concerned as Vinh with educational success, he is quick to point out that one of his best friends, Duy, is "very lazy." He does all of his homework, but only at school and in a haphazard way. Although Duy is very smart and has a "very good character," he does not care about learning in the same way as Vinh. He has long hair and spends many hours listening to music or thinking about girls. Duy likes to be "cool" and tries to think in what Vinh calls "an American way." Unlike Vinh, he has a job after school and likes to spend his money at the mall.

Both Duy and Vinh, in different ways, shatter the "model-minority" stereotype. According to this image, all Asian students excel in school, have few adjustment problems, and need little help. This stereotype is widely resented by many Asians and Asian Americans. It is not only inaccurate, but can also lead teachers to believe that all Asian American students are cut from the same cloth; yet the Asian American community in the United States is extremely heterogenous.[8] The model-minority myth is often used as a standard against which all other groups are measured. This, what Schaefer calls "praising the victim,"[9] may contribute to the interethnic hostilities already common in schools that are occurring with more frequency in communities as well. This myth also helps to discredit the very legitimate demands for social justice made by other, more vocal groups. The model-minority myth also overlooks the great diversity among Asian Americans, a diversity apparent in ethnicity, class, and language, as well as reasons for being in the United States and history here.[10] It may place severe demands on students, through teachers who have unreasonable expectations of their academic abilities. Furthermore, the myth is used to assuage the guilt of some cities and towns that do little to help Asians and Pacific Americans with social problems of adaptation, because it perpetuates the belief that these communities "take care of their own" and do not need any help.

Vinh too is very self-reliant, rarely seeking help outside the family. For example, although he is certain he wants to go to college, he has neither received nor sought help with making the important decisions to get him there. The help he has received, he says, is advice from teachers on studying hard and being a good student, advice that reinforces that of his family. He attends what is considered an excellent public school with an adequate number of counselors and good student services, but he has not taken advantage of them. He does not want to bother other people or have them worry about him.

But rigid self-sufficiency also leads to isolation, and this in turn can lead to being too self-critical if things don't work out as planned. Vinh is extremely hard on himself, and much of this self-assessment is tied to his English. The use of the English language as a standard by which to measure one's intelligence is not unusual among immigrant students, who often feel frustrated and angry by the length of time it may take to learn the language. Vinh does not consider himself to be a successful student, and he often contrasts his success in Vietnam with his struggles as a student now.

The tremendous traumas refugees suffer when leaving their country and facing the challenges of a new society are well known. One of the results has been a dramatic incidence in mental health problems. Moreover, there is evidence that unaccompanied minors, as was Vinh, have been especially at risk: They have experienced more depression and other problems such as withdrawal or hyperactivity. These problems are often caused by guilt, depression, alienation, and loneliness, and they are sometimes aggravated by the hostility and discrimination immigrants face.[11] Given the pivotal role of the family in Vietnamese culture, particularly the importance of parents and elders in general, Vinh was bound to suffer mental distress. At the improbable age of 15, he had the formidable task of relocating his family and acting as one of the "elders" in dealing with a new society. The result was almost inevitable. He became sick. He talks about this period of missing his family and "my Vietnam" with great melancholy.

Vinh's relationship with his uncle supports and affirms his commitment to school and education. In his case, culture and education are tied together inextricably. Although his uncle rarely goes to school, Vinh considers him to be very involved in his schooling: He checks Vinh's report card, encourages him to do better, makes sure that his friends are appropriate and "polite," and in general oversees Vinh's life so that he remains on the right track. "Because he love us, that's why he involved," Vinh says, although he is quick to add that his uncle rarely attends school meetings or visits the school. His uncle is "very smart," he says, but is intimidated by not speaking English well and by the unfamiliar and impersonal bureaucracy. Traditional respect for teachers along with structural barriers in schools discourage many guardians from attending school meetings and otherwise being involved in school matters. Vinh's uncle is similar to many Asian parents who demonstrate their concern for their children's education at home rather than at school.

Although his culture and family have provided tremendous emotional support for Vinh, they are largely unacknowledged by the school. Vinh appreciates his school and his teachers, but he feels that teachers need to learn about his culture and be sensitive to the difficulty of learning a second language at an older age. Adjusting to his new country has posed many challenges for Vinh: learning a new language and writing system; becoming familiar with a new and very different culture; and grieving the loss of parents who, although still living, are no longer with him. In such cases, even an apparent adjustment may be deceiving. For example, a study of a group of Cambodian refugee children found that as they became more successful at modeling the behavior of U.S. children, their emotional adjustment worsened. In addition, the feeling of being different from other children increased with time in this country.[12] As we can see, the problems of adolescence are aggravated by immigrant and minority status. Young people like Vinh have a double and sometimes triple burden compared with other youths. Continuing to rely on his culture is one way in which Vinh is trying to survive this difficult adjustment.

Newcomers must also learn to live in a country that is extremely pluralistic, at times uncomfortably so. The result can be confusion and uncertainty about other cultures outside the mainstream. Immigrants are quick to pick up messages about the valued and devalued cultures in the society. Their preconceived notions about racial superiority and inferiority may also play into this dynamic. The lack of awareness and knowledge of other cultures and their experiences in the United States can worsen the situation. Given no guidance by schools, through appropriate curricula or other means, new students are left on their own to interpret the actions of others. Moreover, immigrants are often the target of racist attitudes and even violence by other students.

All of these factors help explain how some attitudes brought by immigrants and then nurtured by prevailing racist attitudes and behaviors in society are played out in schools and communities. Vinh is no exception. His experience with African American children is an example. He explains that on several occasions he was jumped and robbed when he first lived in Virginia. Being a newcomer to the United States, he was perplexed and frustrated by these behaviors and came to his own conclusion about why they occurred. In spite of some of these negative experiences, he made friends with some of the students in that school ("Some of them is very cool and very nice").

Vinh sees a difference between the Black students from that first school and those in the mostly middle-class town in which he now lives. The former, he says, were "very dirty, smoked a lot, and played their music very loud." When asked why he thought this was so, he reflected, "I think that depend on the culture. . . . I don't understand much about Black culture." He added, "Not all Black people [are dirty and loud]. . . . There are good and bad in every group," a cliché often used to soften the impact of gross stereotypes. Vinh is obviously grappling with the issue and tries very hard to accept all people for "their character" rather than for the color of their skin or the language they speak.

Schools are expected to take the major responsibility of helping children confront these difficult issues, but often they do not. Given the changing U.S. demographics and the large influx of new immigrants, the rivalry and negative relationships among different groups of immigrants and native-born students will likely be felt even more. Interethnic hostility needs to be confronted directly through changes in curriculum and other school policies and practices. Students such as Vinh clearly need this kind of leadership to help them make sense of their new world.

Hoang Vinh is obviously on a long and difficult road to adaptation, not only in cultural and linguistic terms but also, and probably not coincidentally, in terms of his mental health. Many of his issues are based on the traumas he has endured as an immigrant. Whether or not his school is able to help him solve these problems is certain to have an impact on his future.

TO THINK ABOUT

1. Does Vinh's definition of "educated people" differ from yours? If so, how?
2. Vinh resents the false praise he receives from some of his teachers. Some students, however, seem to need more praise than others. What does this situation imply for teaching in culturally diverse schools?
3. What does Vinh mean when he says, "I'm not really good, but I'm trying"?
4. Vinh has trouble asking his teachers and counselors for help. Knowing this, what can schools do to help students like Vinh?
5. After reading Vinh's case study, what do you think of the conventional wisdom surrounding the "model minority"?
6. Given Vinh's interethnic experiences and the perceptions he has developed about other cultures, what can schools do to help students from different ethnic and racial groups understand one another better?
7. Because Vinh has never been in schools with high numbers of Vietnamese students, he has been unable to participate in a bilingual program. Do you think this is an advantage or a disadvantage? Why?

● *NOTES TO CHAPTER 5*

1. *Lau* v. *Nichols,* 414 U.S. 563 (St. Paul, MN: West Publishing, 1974).
2. Frederick Erickson, "Culture, Politics, and Educational Practice." *Educational Foundations,* 4, 2 (Spring, 1990), 21–45.

3. See Kathleen P. Bennett, "Doing School in an Urban Appalachian First Grade." In *Empowerment Through Multicultural Education,* edited by Christine E. Sleeter (Albany, NY: State University of New York Press, 1991). See also Rebecca Eller-Powell, "Teaching for Change in Appalachia." In *Teaching Diverse Populations: Formulating a Knowledge Base,* edited by Etta R. Hollins, Joyce E. King, and Warren C. Hayman (Albany, NY: State University of New York Press, 1994).

4. Felix Boateng, "Combating Deculturalization of the African-American Child in the Public School System: A Multicultural Approach." In *Going to School: The African-American Experience,* edited by Kofi Lomotey (Albany, NY: State University of New York Press, 1990).

5. Sandy Kaser and Kathy G. Short, "Exploring Culture Through Children's Connections." *Language Arts,* 75, 3 (March, 1998), 185–192, 189.

6. R. P. McDermott, "Social Relations as Contexts for Learning in School." *Harvard Educational Review,* 47, 2 (May 1977), 198–213.

7. Henry T. Trueba and Pamela G. Wright, "On Ethnographic Studies and Multicultural Education." In *Cross-Cultural Literacy: Ethnographies of Communication in Multiethnic Classrooms,* edited by Marietta Saravia-Shore and Steven F. Arvizu (New York: Garland, 1992).

8. For excellent overviews of different categories of learning styles and an analysis of each, see Christine I. Bennett, *Comprehensive Multicultural Education: Theory and Practice,* 4th ed. (Boston: Allyn & Bacon, 1999). See also Karen Swisher, "Learning Styles: Implications for Teachers." In *Multicultural Education for the 21st Century,* edited by Carlos Díaz (Washington, DC: National Education Association, 1992); and Jacqueline Jordan Irvine and Eleanor Darlene York, "Learning Styles and Culturally Diverse Students: A Literature Review." In *Handbook of Research on Multicultural Education,* edited by James A. Banks and Cherry A. McGee Banks (New York: Macmillan, 1995).

9. Witkin, an early theorist in this field, suggested that people are either *field independent* or *field dependent* in their learning (see Herman A. Witkin, *Psychological Differentiation* [New York: Wiley, 1962]). According to this theory, the former tend to learn best in situations that emphasize analytic tasks and with materials void of a social context. Individuals who favor this mode generally prefer to work alone and are self-motivated. According to this theory, field-dependent learners tend to learn best in highly social settings. Manuel Ramirez and Alfredo Castañeda applied Witkin's theory to ethnic groups (see Manuel Ramirez and Alfredo Castañeda, *Cultural Democracy, Bicognitive Development and Education* [New York: Academic Press, 1974]). In research with children of various cultural backgrounds, they concluded that European American students tend to be the most field-independent learners. Mexican American, American Indian, and African American students, by contrast, tend to be closer to *field sensitive* (their substitution for *dependent,* which may have negative connotations), with Mexican Americans closest to this pole.

10. For a review of holistic versus analytic thought processes and implications for educational practice, see Patricia M. Greenfield and Rodney R. Cocking, eds., *Cross-Cultural Roots of Minority Child Development* (Hillsdale, NJ: Lawrence Erlbaum Associates, Publishers, 1994). For a review of different learning style theories, see Lynn Curry, *Learning Styles in Secondary Schools: A Review of Instruments and Implications for Their Use* (Madison, WI: National Center on Effective Secondary Schools, University of Wisconsin, 1990).

11. Flora Ida Ortiz, "Hispanic-American Children's Experiences in Classrooms: A Comparison Between Hispanic and Non-Hispanic Children." In *Class, Race and Gender in American Education,* edited by Lois Weis (Albany, NY: State University of New York Press, 1988).
12. Donna Deyhle and Karen Swisher, "Research in American Indian and Alaska Native Education: From Assimilation to Self-Determination." In *Review of Research in Education,* vol. 22, by Michael W. Apple, ed. (Washington, DC: American Educational Research Association, 1997), 153.
13. See his update on the theory of multiple intelligences: Howard Gardner, *Multiple Intelligences: The Theory in Practice* (New York: Basic Books, 1993).
14. Ibid., 66.
15. Ray McDermott, "Achieving School Failure: An Anthropological Approach to Illiteracy and Social Stratification." In *Education and Cultural Process: Anthropological Approaches,* 2nd ed., edited by George D. Spindler (Prospect Heights, IL: Waveland Press, 1987).
16. Roland G. Tharp, "Psychocultural Variables and Constants: Effects on Teaching and Learning in Schools." *American Psychologist,* 44, 2 (February 1989), 349–359.
17. Melvin D. Williams, "Observations in Pittsburgh Ghetto Schools." *Anthropology and Education Quarterly,* vol. 12 (1981), 211–220.
18. Tharp, "Psychocultural Variables and Constants."
19. Michele Foster, "Sociolinguistics and the African-American Community: Implications for Literacy," *Theory into Practice,* 31, 4 (Autumn 1992), 303–311.
20. Carmen Judith Nine-Curt, *Nonverbal Communication,* 2nd ed. (Cambridge, MA: Evaluation, Dissemination, and Assessment Center, 1984).
21. For an example of a curriculum based on using nonverbal communication, see Virginia Vogel Zanger, *Face to Face: Communication, Culture, and Collaboration,* 2nd ed. (Boston: Heinle & Heinle, 1993).
22. Shirley Brice Heath, *Ways with Words* (New York: Cambridge University Press, 1983).
23. Susan Urmston Philips, *The Invisible Culture: Communication in Classroom and Community on the Warm Springs Indian Reservation* (Prospect Heights, IL: Waveland Press, 1993, reissued with changes).
24. Sharon Nelson-Barber and Elise Trumbull Estrin, "Bringing Native American Perspectives to Mathematics and Science Teaching." *Theory into Practice,* 34, 3 (Summer, 1995); Deyhle and Swisher, 1997.
25. Tam Thi Dang Wei, *Vietnamese Refugee Students: A Handbook for School Personnel* (Cambridge, MA: National Assessment and Dissemination Center, 1980).
26. Brigitte Jordan, "Cosmopolitan Obstetrics: Some Insights from the Training of Traditional Midwives." *Social Science and Medicine,* 28, 9 (1989), 925–944.
27. For an excellent review of related examples of cultural discontinuity, see Kathryn H. Au and Alice J. Kawakami, "Cultural Congruence in Instruction." In *Teaching Diverse Populations: Formulating a Knowledge Base,* edited by Etta R. Hollins, Joyce E. King, and Warren C. Hayman (Albany, NY: State University of New York Press, 1994).
28. Kathleen P. Bennett, "Doing School in an Urban Appalachian First Grade."
29. Heather Kim, *Diversity Among Asian American High School Students* (Princeton, NJ: Educational Testing Service, 1997).
30. See Quality Education for Minorities Project, *Education That Works: An Action Plan for the Education of Minorities* (Cambridge, MA: Massachusetts Institute of Technology Press, 1990); and Deyhle and Swisher, 1997.
31. Deyhle and Swisher, 1997.

32. See Kathryn H. Au and Alice J. Kawakami, "Cultural Congruence in Instruction"; Gloria Ladson-Billings, "Toward a Theory of Culturally Relevant Pedagogy." *American Educational Research Journal,* 33, 3 (Fall, 1995), 465–492; and Jacqueline Jordan Irvine, ed., *Critical Knowledge for Diverse Teachers and Learners* (Washington, DC: American Association of Colleges for Teacher Education, 1997).

33. Cornel Pewewardy, "Our Children Can't Wait: Recapturing the Essence of Indigenous Schools in the United States." *Cultural Survival Quarterly,* (Spring, 1998), 29–34.

34. Lynn A. Vogt, Cathie Jordan, and Roland G. Tharp, "Explaining School Failure, Producing School Success: Two Cases." In *Minority Education: Anthropological Perspectives,* edited by Evelyn Jacob and Cathie Jordan (Norwood, NJ: Ablex, 1993).

35. See, for example, Gloria Ladson-Billings, *The Dreamkeepers: Successful Teachers of African American Children* (San Francisco: Jossey-Bass Publishers, 1994); and Michele Foster, *Black Teachers on Teaching* (New York: The New Press, 1997).

36. For an excellent review of these, see Jacqueline Jordan Irvine, "Making Teacher Education Culturally Responsive." In *Diversity in Teacher Education: New Expectations,* edited by Mary E. Dilworth (San Francisco: Jossey-Bass Publishers, 1992).

37. Jerry Lipka, "Toward a Culturally Based Pedagogy: A Case Study of One Yup'ik Eskimo Teacher." In *Transforming Curriculum for a Culturally Diverse Society,* by Etta R. Hollins, ed. (Mahwah, NJ: Lawrence Erlbaum Associates, 1996), 207.

38. Jeannette Abi-Nader, "Meeting the Needs of Multicultural Classrooms: Family Values and the Motivation of Minority Students." In *Diversity and Teaching: Teacher Education Yearbook 1,* edited by Mary John O'Hair and Sandra J. Odell (Fort Worth, TX: Harcourt Brace Jovanovich, 1993).

39. Frederick Erickson and Gerald Mohatt, "Cultural Organization of Participation Structures in Two Classrooms of Indian Students." In *Doing the Ethnography of Schooling: Educational Anthropology in Action,* edited by George Spindler (New York: Holt, Rinehart & Winston, 1982).

40. Ladson-Billings, "Toward a Theory of Culturally Relevant Pedagogy." 469.

NOTES TO MARISOL MARTÍNEZ'S CASE STUDY

1. As cited in Clara E. Rodriguez, *Puerto Ricans: Born in the U.S.A.* (Boulder, CO: Westview Press, 1991).

2. Sonia Nieto, "A History of the Education of Puerto Rican Students in U.S. Mainland Schools: 'Losers,' 'Outsiders,' or 'Leaders'?" In *Handbook of Research on Multicultural Education,* edited by James A. Banks and Cherry M. Banks (New York: Macmillan, 1995). See also Sonia Nieto, "Fact and Fiction: Stories of Puerto Ricans in U.S. Schools." *Harvard Educational Review,* 68, 2 (Summer, 1998), 133–163.

3. Javier Tapia, "The Schooling of Puerto Ricans: Philadelphia's Most Impoverished Community." *Anthropology and Education Quarterly,* 29, 3 (1998), 297–323.

4. Francisco L. Rivera-Batiz and Carlos E. Santiago, *Island Paradox: Puerto Rico in the 1990s* (New York: Russell Sage Foundation, 1996).

5. Institute for Puerto Rican Policy, "Puerto Ricans and Other Latinos in the United States." (February, 1998) *IPR Datanote, 19.*

6. Rivera-Batiz and Santiago, 1996.

7. Because Puerto Rico is under the political control of the United States, the term *migration* rather than *immigration* is ordinarily used to refer to the movement of Puerto Ricans to the United States. But this term is not quite accurate either because it refers to movement within the same cultural and political sphere. Some writers have suggested that the term (im)migration is more suitable. See Roberto Marquez, "Sojourners, Settlers, Castaways, and Creators: A Recollection of Puerto Rico Past and Puerto Ricans Present." *Massachusetts Review,* 36, 1 (1995), 94–118.

8. The Decolonization Committee of the United Nations has termed Puerto Rico a colony and has consistently called on the United States to hand over sovereignty to the island. See Clara E. Rodriguez, *Puerto Ricans.*

9. Rivera-Batiz and Santiago, 1996.

10. Marcelo M. Suarez-Orozco, "'Becoming Somebody': Central American Immigrants in U.S. Inner-City Schools." *Anthropology and Education Quarterly,* 18, 4 (December 1987), 287–299.

11. See Catherine E. Walsh, *Pedagogy and the Struggle for Voice: Issues of Language, Power, and Schooling for Puerto Ricans* (New York: Bergin & Garvey, 1991).

12. See research by Nitza M. Hidalgo, "A Layering of Family and Friends: Four Puerto Rican Families' Meaning of Community." *Education and Urban Society,* 30, 1 (November, 1997), 20–40.

NOTES TO JAMES KARAM'S CASE STUDY

1. I want to thank Diane Sweet for the interviews with James, as well as for transcripts and other extensive information she was able to find about the Arab American community.

2. Samia El-Badry, "The Arab-American Market." *American Demographics,* (January, 1994).

3. Naseer H. Aruri, "The Arab-American Community of Springfield, Massachusetts." In *The Arab-Americans: Studies in Assimilation,* edited by Elaine C. Hagopian and An Paden (Wilmette, IL: Medina University Press International, 1969).

4. El-Badry, 1994.

5. Aruri, 1969.

6. Ibid.

7. Mahmoud F. Suleiman, "Empowering Arab American Students: Implications for Multicultural Teachers." In *1996 Proceedings of the National Association for Multiculural Education Conference,* edited by Carl A. Grant (San Francisco: Caddo Gap Press, 1997).

8. Educational resources concerning Arab Americans are available from the following organizations: The American-Arab Anti-Discrimination Committee, 4201 Connecticut Avenue, N, Washington, DC, 20008; AWAIR (Arab World and Islamic Resources and School Services), 2095 Rose Street, Berkeley, CA 94709; and AMIDEAST, 1100 17th Street, NW, Washington, DC, 20036.

9. Suleiman, "Empowering Arab American Students," 60.

10. James J. Zogby, "When Stereotypes Threaten Pride," *NEA Today* (October, 1982), 12.

11. El-Badry, 22.

12. Laurie Olsen, *Made in America: Immigrant Students in Our Public Schools* (New York: The New Press, 1997).

NOTES TO HOANG VINH'S CASE STUDY

1. I am grateful to Haydée Font for the interviews and transcripts for this case study. When she did these interviews, Haydée was a graduate student in multicultural education at the University of Massachusetts; currently she works in the development office at Wheelock College in Boston, Mass.

2. The Vietnamese use family names first, given names second. The given name is used for identification. In this case, Vinh is the given name and Hoang is the family name. According to *A Manual for Indochinese Refugee Education, 1976–1977* (Arlington, VA: National Indochinese Clearinghouse, Center for Applied Linguistics, 1976), whereas in U.S. society John Jones would be known formally as Mr. Jones and informally as John, in Vietnam, Hoang Vinh would be known both formally and informally as Mr. Vinh or Vinh.

3. See Ronald Takaki, *Strangers from a Different Shore: A History of Asian Americans* (New York: Penguin Books, 1989); "Meeting the Educational Needs of Southeast Asian Children." *Digest,* ERIC Clearinghouse on Urban Education, vol. 68, (1990).

4. Peter N. Kiang and Vivian Wai-Fun Lee, "Exclusion or Contribution? Education K–12 Policy." In *The State of Asian Pacific America: Policy Issues to the Year 2020* (Los Angeles: LEAP Asian Pacific American Public Policy Institute and the UCLA Asian American Studies Center, 1993), 25–48; *Digest,* 1990.

5. "A very rich man without a good education is not highly regarded by the Vietnamese," says Tam Thi Dang Wei, in *Vietnamese Refugee Students: A Handbook for School Personnel* (Cambridge, MA: National Assessment and Dissemination Center, 1980).

6. Heather Kim, *Diversity Among Asian American High School Students* (Princeton, NJ: Educational Testing Service, 1997).

7. See, for example, Stacey J. Lee's critique of these notions in *Unraveling the 'Model Minority' Stereotype: Listening to Asian American Youth* (New York: Teachers College Press, 1996).

8. Ibid.; see also Valerie Ooka Pang, "Asian Pacific American Students: A Diverse and Complex Population." In *Handbook of Research on Multicultural Education,* by James A. Banks and Cherry A. McGee Banks, eds. (New York: Macmillan, 1995).

9. Richard T. Schaefer, *Racial and Ethnic Groups,* 3rd ed. (Glenview, IL: Scott Foresman, 1988).

10. Kim, 1996; Pang, 1995.

11. See *Digest,* 1990.

12. Rubén G. Rumbaut, *Immigrant Students in California Public Schools: A Summary of Current Knowledge* (Baltmore, MD: Center for Research on Effective Schooling for Disadvantaged Students, 1990).

chapter 6

Linguistic Diversity in Multicultural Classrooms

*M*y daughter Marisa spoke Spanish fluently by the time we placed her in day care shortly before she was three years old, but she did not yet speak a word of English. My husband and I had planned this intentionally: Our reasoning was that she would quickly pick up English, which was all around her, but we could not be certain that she would speak Spanish if we did not make a conscious effort to use it. We were right: Three months after starting day care, she was as fluent in English as she was in Spanish. But on the day she started day care, one of the student teachers said, "Oh, I see she doesn't have language" when she heard us speaking together in Spanish. "She *has* language," I said, "but her language is not English." After all, Marisa was perfectly capable of making herself understood. She spoke fluently with many children and adults; she was familiar with stories in Spanish; and she was creative in using language to tell her own stories.

The notion that children who do not yet speak English lack language altogether is a prevalent one in the United States, and it is linked with the mainstream perception that cultures other than the dominant one lack importance. My husband and I have never regretted our decision to speak Spanish to our daughters because now both of them are able to function in two languages (our daughter Alicia is actually trilingual and a teacher of French). Even more critical is the fact that they are proud of their language abilities and they are richer as a result.

Language is intimately linked to culture. It is a primary means by which people express their cultural values and the lens through which they view the world. This link is described by Henry Trueba in the following way:

> Whatever knowledge we acquire, it is always acquired through language and culture, two interlocked symbolic systems considered essential for human interaction and survival. Culture and language are so intricately intertwined that even trained scholars find it impossible to decide where language ends and culture begins, or which one of the two impacts the other the most.[1]

The language practices that children bring to school inevitably affect how and what they learn. Yet native language issues are frequently overlooked in multicultural education, where race and ethnicity have been emphasized.[2] That language issues often go unaddressed in multicultural education is apparent in the lack of relevant terms concerning linguistic diversity. Terms that describe discrimination based on race, gender, and class are part of our general vocabulary: *Racism, sexism, ethnocentrism, anti-Semitism, classism,* and others are widely understood. But until recently, no such term existed for language discrimination, although this does not mean that language discrimination did not exist. Tove Skutnabb-Kangas, by coining the term *linguicism* to refer to discrimination based specifically on language, has helped to make the issue more visible.[3]

In this chapter, the impact of linguistic differences on student learning will be explored. How teachers and schools view language differences, whether and how they use these differences as a resource in the classroom, and different approaches to teaching *language minority students,* that is, those whose first language is other than English, will all be reviewed.

LINGUISTIC DIVERSITY IN U.S. SCHOOLS: A BRIEF OVERVIEW AND HISTORY

The number and variety of language minority students has escalated tremendously in the past two decades. By 1994, their number was estimated at 9.9 million.[4] Moreover, the number of students classified as having *limited English proficiency*— that is, those whose lack of facility in the English language may have negative consequences for their academic achievement in monolingual English classrooms—also has grown dramatically. For example, by 1996, 3,184,696 students were classified as having limited proficiency in English, almost a 5 percent increase in just one year. Students of limited English proficiency currently represent about 7.3 percent of all public school students, and the vast majority spend most or part of their days in monolingual English classrooms.[5]

The demographic changes indicated by these statistics are part of a larger trend of immigration to the United States, which since the late 1970s has been responsible for a remarkable change in our population. The reasons for this trend are varied, from a rise in the number of refugees from countries where the United States was involved in aggression (as was the case in Central America and Southeast Asia) to the loosening of immigration restrictions for some parts of the world. Legal immigration alone between 1980 and 1990 was 19.8 million and it nearly equaled that of 1900 to 1910 (although the percentage of the foreign-born population was far lower, just 7.9 percent in 1990, than the 14.7 percent it was in 1910).[6]

Unlike the earlier massive wave of immigration, the largest numbers of new immigrants are now from Asia and Latin America. For example, in 1980, the percentage of Hispanic origin residents in the United States was just 6.4 percent, but by 1990 it had grown to 9 percent and by 1996 to 10.7 percent. It is estimated that Hispanics will make up a quarter of the U.S. population by 2050. The Asian population has also increased substantially, from just under 400,000 in 1980 to over 740,000 in 1990 and nearly 1,000,000 in 1996.[7] Not coincidentally, the total number of people who speak a language other than English increased from 23 million (11 percent) in 1980 to almost 32 million (14 percent) in 1990.[8]

These changes in the population of the United States have profound implications for education. For one, approaches and programs to teach language minority students need to be expanded. Yet most students needing special language services are not enrolled in federally funded bilingual programs; about one-third are not receiving *any* language assistance in either local or federal programs. By far the largest number (over 51 percent) are receiving only Chapter 1 services in which their native language is not used at all. In addition, the percentage of students in bilingual programs has actually declined since 1980, although the number of language minority students has increased.[9] The reasons for the decline vary from an ideological resistance to approaches based on native language instruction, to poor enforcement of state and federal mandates. Finding qualified personnel has been another major problem, and it has become even more serious because fewer bilingual people are entering the teaching profession.

In U.S. classrooms, linguistic diversity has commonly been viewed as a temporary, if troublesome, barrier to learning. Once students learn English, the thinking goes, then learning can proceed unhampered. Forgetting their native language is seen as a regrettable but necessary price to pay for the benefits of citizenship. As a result of this thinking, the traditional strategy in most classrooms has been to help students rid themselves as quickly as possible of what is perceived as the "burden" of speaking another language. Joel Spring provides many compelling historical examples of the strategy of linguistic "deculturalization" used in the schooling of Native Americans, Puerto Ricans, Mexican Americans, and Asian Americans.[10]

Entire communities have been denied the use of their native language, not only for instruction in schools but also for social communication of all kinds. Throughout our history, the language rights of substantial numbers of people have been violated, from prohibiting enslaved Africans from speaking their languages to the recent imposition of "English Only" laws in a growing number of states.[11]

But U.S. language policies and practices have by no means been uniform. Rather, they have ranged all the way from "sink or swim" policies (i.e., immersing language-minority students in English-only classrooms to fend on their own), to the imposition of English as the sole medium of instruction, to allowing and even encouraging bilingualism. By 1900, for example, at least 600,000 children, or about 4 percent of students enrolled in public and parochial elementary schools, were being taught in bilingual German/English bilingual schools. Smaller numbers were taught in Polish, Italian, Norwegian, Spanish, French, Czech, Dutch, and other languages.[12]

The zigzag of support and rejection of languages other than English demonstrates the ambivalence with which language diversity has been viewed in the United States. Misgivings concerning native language maintenance are still true today, particularly with regard to bilingual education. The public remains deeply divided over bilingual education. In a recent Gallup poll, for instance, respondents were almost equally divided among the three options of native language instruction, ESL alone, and minimal tutoring until students learn English.[13] The fact that bilingual education has as one of its fundamental goals the learning of English often goes unmentioned by opponents, who focus instead on their ideological opposition to using students' native language in instruction because they perceive it to be a threat to national unity. But the myth that English has been a unifying force is just that. In the words of James Crawford, who has exhaustively researched language policies in the United States, "Such notions obscure a multilingual tradition that is unsurpassed in its variety and richness, while inventing for English a unifying role that it rarely enjoyed."[14]

Where language issues are concerned, everyone has gotten into the fray. President Theodore Roosevelt, a spokesperson for the restrictive language policies at the beginning of the nineteenth century that were a response to the huge influx of primarily East European immigrants to the United States, said: "We have room for but one language here, and that is the English language; for we intend to see that the crucible turns our people out as Americans, of American nationality, and not as dwellers in a polyglot boardinghouse."[15] Roosevelt's views were widely shared by many people who felt threatened by the new wave of immigrants.

In the United States, language use and patriotic loyalty have often been linked and patriotism has been measured by how quickly one has abandoned a native language and replaced it with English. Somehow being fluent in another language, even if one is also fluent in English, has been viewed with suspicion, at least in the case of immigrants. Some three-quarters of a century after Theodore Roosevelt spoke of a "polyglot boardinghouse," another president, Ronald Reagan, answered in response to a reporter's question about support for bilingual education: "It is absolutely wrong and against American concept to have a bilingual education program that is now openly, admittedly dedicated to preserving their native language and never getting them adequate in English so they can go out into the job market."[16]

Restrictive views of language have at times resulted in counterproductive policies that inhibit the learning of foreign languages as well as the understanding of other peoples. In 1998, the latest cycle of controversy surrounding native language use resulted in the passage of California's Proposition 227 in which bilingual education was virtually wiped out. That our society continues to be ignorant of other languages and cultures is self-evident. That it is now jeopardized by this monolingualism and monoculturalism in a world becoming increasingly interdependent is also becoming more and more apparent.

LINGUISTIC DIVERSITY AND LEARNING

One's native language is a foundation for future learning. If we think of language development as the concrete foundation of a building, it makes sense that it needs to be strong to sustain the stress of many tons of building materials that will be placed on top of it. This is generally what takes place when students who speak English as a native language enter school in the United States: They use the language they know to learn the content of the curriculum. For language minority students, however, not knowing English is a tremendous disadvantage, not because their native language is ineffectual for learning but because it is not usually viewed by their teachers and schools as a resource for learning. Extending the metaphor further, it would be as if the strong foundation that had been created were abandoned and the building materials were placed on top of a sand lot across the street. Needless to say, the building would crumble in short order. Yet this is precisely what happens to most students who enter our schools with limited proficiency in English: We expect them to devote all their time to learning English, we neglect to teach them any other content, and then we wonder why they haven't learned anything else.

All good teachers know that learning needs to be based on prior learning and experiences. But in the case of language minority students, we seem to forget this as we effectively rob students of access to their prior learning. This contradicts how learning takes place and the crucial role of language in the process. According to Jim Cummins, "There is general agreement among cognitive psychologists that we learn by integrating new input into our existing cognitive structures or schemata. Our prior experience provides the foundation for interpreting new information. No learner is a blank slate."[17]

As a rule, however, teachers and schools disregard language minority students' native languages and cultures for what they believe to be good reasons. Schools often link students' English-language proficiency with their prospective economic and social mobility. Students who speak a language other than English are viewed as "handicapped," and they are urged, through both subtle and direct means, to abandon their native language. The schools ask parents to speak English to their children at home, they punish children for using their native language, or they simply withhold education until the children have mastered English, usually in the name of protecting students' futures. The negative impact of this strategy on language minority students is incalculable. David Corson, for example, has suggested that when educators routinely repress and disempower language minority users because their practices differ from mainstream language norms, students quickly pick up the message that they speak a low-status language. Corson goes on to say, "The members of some social groups, as a result, come to believe that their educational failure, rather than coming from their lowly esteemed social or cultural status, results from their natural inability: their lack of giftedness."[18]

Devaluation can also result in students' deciding that their native language is the *cause* of their misfortunes. In her memoir *Silent Dancing*, Judith Ortiz Cofer recounts her experience with a teacher who struck her on the head because she thought Judith was being disrespectful; in actuality, she did not understand English and therefore was unable to respond to the teacher. The author summarized the painful but quickly learned lesson as follows: "I instinctively understood then that language is the only weapon a child has against the absolute power of adults."[19] In her case, it led to mastering the English language as well as maintaining Spanish. Many other cases do not end as happily.

Even if they have gifted and caring teachers, language minority students may experience trauma when learning their new language. No doubt the stress of immigration and the reasons for leaving their home countries play a part in this trauma. But just learning a new language can in itself be a devastating experience for many. In recounting her extensive experience teaching immigrant children,

Cristina Igoa suggests that sheer weariness is one consequence: "A recurring theme regarding the inner world of the immigrant child is a feeling of exhaustion, not only from the sounds of a new language but also from the continual parade of strange sights and events in a new culture."[20]

The fact that students speak a language other than English is treated by many teachers as a problem, but lack of English skills alone cannot explain the poor academic achievement of language minority students. It is tempting to point to English "sink or swim" programs as the solution to the problem of academic failure. But confounding English language acquisition with academic achievement is simplistic at best. For example, one study focusing on the academic achievement of Mexican American and Puerto Rican students in five cities concluded that contrary to the conventional wisdom, Spanish was *not* an impediment to achievement. In fact, the researchers found that in some cases, *better English proficiency meant lower academic performance.*[21] The researchers theorized that peer pressure might act as a "counterforce" against the traditional relationship between English proficiency and academic performance.

In contrast to negative perceptions of bilingualism, a good deal of research confirms the positive influence of knowing another language. Native language maintenance might act as a buffer against academic failure by simply supporting literacy in children's most developed language. This was the conclusion reached by researchers studying the case of Black English, also called *Black dialect*: dialect-speaking four-year-olds enrolled in a Head Start program were able to recall more details with greater accuracy when they retold stories in their cultural dialect rather than in standard English.[22] In the case of Spanish, Lourdes Díaz Soto's research among 30 Hispanic families of young children with low and high academic achievement found that parents of the higher achieving children she studied favored a native language environment to a greater extent than those of lower achieving youngsters.[23] Patricia Gándara, in analyzing the impressive academic achievements of 50 Mexican American adults who grew up in poverty, found that only 16 percent of them came from homes where English was the primary language. The largest percentage of these successful adults grew up in households where *only* Spanish was spoken, and a remarkable two-thirds of them began school speaking *only* Spanish.[24]

That students' native language is an asset that can enhance their academic achievement was also found to be true by Ana Celia Zentella in a study of 19 families in El Barrio, a low-income predominantly Puerto Rican community in New York City. In her research, the most successful students were enrolled in bilingual programs and were also the most fluent bilinguals.[25] In their review of several research studies concerning the adaptation and school achievement of immigrants of various backgrounds, Alejandro Portes and Rubén Rumbaut came to a striking conclusion: Students with limited bilingualism are far more likely to leave school than those fluent in both languages. Rather than an impediment to academic achievement, bilingualism can act to promote learning.[26]

Conclusions such as these contradict the common advice given to language minority parents to "speak English with your children at home." Challenging the prevailing wisdom of this advice, Virginia Collier has suggested that practicing English at home among students who are more proficient in another language can actually slow down cognitive development because it is only when parents and their children speak the language they know best that they are working at their "level of cognitive maturity."[27] Catherine Snow, another respected researcher in literacy and language acquisition, goes even further. She suggests that "the greatest contribution immigrant parents can make to their children's success is to ensure they maintain fluency and continue to develop the home language."[28] This makes sense, of course, and it leads me to reflect on the innate wisdom of many immmigrant mothers, including my own mother, who ignored teachers' pleas to speak to my sister and me in English. Had it not been for my mother's quiet but obstinant resistance, I would probably be a monolingual English speaker today.

The problem of language minority children has often been articulated as a problem of not knowing English. But the real problem may be what Luis Moll has labeled the "obsession with speaking English,"[29] as if learning English would solve all the other difficulties faced by language minority students, including poverty, racism, poorly financed schools, and lack of access to excellent education. Rather than supporting the suppression or elimination of native language use at home and school, the research reviewed here supports promoting native language literacy. If this is the case, then the language dominance of students is not the real issue; rather, *the way in which teachers and schools view students' language may have an even greater influence on their achievement.*

Language diversity needs to be placed within a sociopolitical context to understand why speaking a language other than English is not itself a handicap. On the contrary, it can be a great asset to learning, as we have seen. How language and language use are perceived by the schools and whether modifications in the curriculum are made as a result are crucial issues to keep in mind. The prevailing view is that among culturally dominated groups, bilingualism is a burden; yet among middle-class and wealthy students, it is usually seen as an asset. It is not unusual to find in the same high school the seemingly incongruous situation of one group of students having their native language wiped out while another group of students struggles to learn a foreign language in a contrived and artificial setting. There are more affirming approaches to teaching language minority students, and they need to be used more widely than is currently the case.

APPROACHES TO TEACHING LANGUAGE MINORITY STUDENTS

Given the dramatic increase in the number of language minority students in our country in the past three decades, every classroom in every city and town has already been, or will soon be, affected. The responsibility for educating language minority students can no longer fall only on those teachers who have been trained specifically to provide bilingual education and English as a Second Language (ESL) services. This responsibility needs to be shared by *all* teachers and *all* schools. Yet most teachers have had little training in language acquisition and other language-related issues.

Even in bilingual classrooms, only 10 percent of teachers serving English language learners are certified in bilingual education.[30]

What do all classroom teachers need to know to help them be better teachers of language minority students? How can they best prepare to teach students of different language backgrounds and varying language abilities? In what follows, I suggest a number of steps that teachers and schools can take to effectively educate their language minority students. Before doing so, however, let me emphasize that I am not suggesting that by simply following a set of prescribed strategies, teachers will automatically make a difference in the achievement of language minority students. While learning new approaches and techniques may be very helpful, teaching language minority students successfully means above all changing one's attitudes toward the students, their languages and cultures, and their communities. Anything short of this will result in repeating the pattern of failure that currently exists.[31] As Jim Cummins has eloquently stated, "Fortunately, good teaching does not require us to internalize an endless list of instructional techniques. Much more fundamental is the recognition that human relationships are central to effective instruction."[32] David Corson adds simply that, "Working with minority children is often more than a skill; it is an act of cultural fairness."[33]

Understanding Language Development, Second Language Acquisition, and the Sociopolitical Context of Education

All teachers need to understand how language is learned, both native and subsequent languages. This knowledge is often reserved for specialists in bilingual and ESL education, but it should become standard knowledge for all teachers. For example, Stephen Krashen's theories of second language acquisition and his recommendations that teachers provide students for whom English is a second language with *comprehensible input*—that is, interesting and contextualized cues in their instruction—is useful for all teachers who have language minority students in their classrooms.[34] Likewise, related knowledge in curriculum and instruction, linguistics, sociology, and history are all helpful for teachers of language minority students. Consequently, all teachers should be familiar with the following kinds of knowledge related to their language minority students:

- familiarity with first and second language acquisition
- awareness of the sociocultural and sociopolitical context of education for language minority students
- awareness of the history of immigration in the United States, with particular attention to language policies and practices throughout that history
- knowledge of the history and experiences of specific groups of people, especially those who are residents of the city, town, and state where they are teaching
- ability to adapt curriculum for students whose first language is other than English

- competence in pedagogical approaches suitable for culturally and linguistically heterogeneous classrooms
- experience with teachers of diverse backgrounds and the ability to develop collaborative relationships will colleagues that promote the learning of language minority students
- ability to communicate effectively with parents of diverse language, culture, and social class backgrounds [35]

Because many teachers have not had access to this kind of knowledge during their teacher preparation, they may need to acquire it on their own. They can do this by attending conferences in literacy, bilingual education, multicultural education, and ESL; participating in professional development opportunities in their district and beyond; subscribing to journals and newsletters in these fields; setting up study groups with colleagues to discuss and practice different strategies; and returning to graduate school to take relevant courses or seek advanced degrees.

Developing an Additive Bilingual Perspective

Additive bilingualism refers to a framework for understanding language acquisition and development as *adding* a new language rather than *subtracting* an existing one.[36] This perspective is radically different from the traditional expectation that immigrants need to exchange their native language for their new language, English. The terrible psychological costs of abandoning one's native language, not to mention the incredible loss of linguistic resources to the nation, is now being questioned. An additive bilingualism supports the notion that two is better than one, that English *plus* other languages can make us stronger individually and as a society.

There are many ways that teachers, even those who do not speak the native languages of their students, can demonstrate an appreciation and support for those languages. Nurturing native language literacy is supported by research that the skills students develop in their native language are usually easily transferred to a second or third language.[37] This being the case, how can we continue to view bilingualism as a deficit?

In their research, María Fránquiz and María de la luz Reyes set out to answer the question, "If I am not fluent in the languages my students speak, how can I effectively teach English language arts to a linguistically diverse class?"[38] They found that teachers do not have to be fluent in the native languages of their students to support its use in the classroom. As a matter of fact, they discovered that encouraging students to use their native languages and cultural knowledge as resources for learning is frequently more important than knowing the students' languages.

What does this mean in practice? In their research, Fránquiz and Reyes provide examples of teachers "who are not paralyzed by their own monolingualism."[39] They document, for example, the positive results of teachers' acceptance of a range of language registers and codes, from standard to more colloquial forms of speech, and from monolingual to more mixed language speech. These language forms are often prohibited in classroom discourse, but allowing them to flourish is a way of using students' current knowledge to build future knowledge. Once again, we return to the metaphor of language as the foundation of a building. In the case study of Yolanda Piedra that follows this chapter, it is clear that staff members' appreciation of her bilingualism motivated Yolanda to succeed academically. Yolanda gives numerous examples of how teachers have done this, from encouraging her use of both languages in school to giving her suggestions for using her bilingualism in selecting a career.

Consciously Fostering Native Language Literacy

As we saw in the previous examples, developing an additive perspective concerning language acquisition counters the assumption that students must forget their native language. Teachers can actively support the native language literacy of their students. In her work with immigrant students, for instance, Cristina Igoa reserves the last period of the day three times a week for students to listen to stories or to read in their native languages. Because she does not speak all the languages of her many students, she recruits college students who are fluent in various languages to help out.[40]

Teachers can also make a commitment to learn at least one of the languages of their students. When they become second language learners, teachers develop a new appreciation for the struggles experienced by language minority students—including exhaustion, frustration, and withdrawal—when they are learning English. This was what happened to Bill Dunn, a doctoral student of mine and a veteran teacher who decided to "come out of the closet as a Spanish speaker." He realized that, after teaching for 20 years in a largely Puerto Rican community, he understood a great deal of Spanish, so he decided to study it formally and to keep a journal of his experiences. Although he had always been a wonderful and caring teacher, putting himself in the place of his students helped him understand a great many things more clearly, from students' grammatical errors in English to their boredom and misbehavior when they could not understand the language of instruction.[41]

The responsibility to create excellent learning environments for language minority students should not rest on individual teachers alone, however. Entire schools can also develop such environments. As you will see in the case study of Yolanda Piedra that follows this chapter, many staff members in her school made a conscious decision to promote their students' native language literacy: They enrolled in the Spanish course offered by the district in large numbers, they attended workshops related to the student population in their school and, in general, they created an environment of cultural and linguistic affirmation. Likewise, Catherine Minicucci and her associates analyzed eight exemplary school reform efforts for language minority students and found the following common characteristics among the schools:

- a school-wide vision of excellence that incorporates students of limited English proficiency;

- the creation of a community of learners engaged in active discovery; and
- well-designed programs to develop both the English and native language skills of language minority students.

Further, they found that the schools made a conscious effort to recruit and hire bilingual staff members, they communicated frequently with parents in their native languages, and they honored the multicultural quality of the student population.[42] The researchers concluded that the success of schools with these attributes severely challenges the conventional assumption that students need to learn English *before* they can learn grade-level content in social studies, math, or anything else.

These examples are based on the assumption that all students come to their learning with skills and talents that can be used as resources. Native language literacy is primary among these, and it is the basis for bilingual education, which we will consider next.

LANGUAGE DIVERSITY AND THE CASE FOR BILINGUAL EDUCATION

The freedom to maintain and use one's native language is thought by some linguists and human rights advocates to be a basic human right. The proposal for a "Declaration of Children's Linguistic Human Rights," for instance, places linguistic rights on the same level as other human rights.[43] This proposal includes the right to identify positively with one's mother tongue, to learn it, and to choose when to use it. Although these rights may be self-evident for language-majority children, they are not so apparent for those who speak a language with a stigma, as is the case with most language minority students in the United States.

Just as racial integration was considered a key civil right for those who were forcibly segregated, bilingual education is viewed by many language-minority communities as equally vital. There is a substantial relationship between bilingual education and equity. Although frequently addressed as simply an issue of language, it can be argued that bilingual education is a civil rights issue because it is the only guarantee that children who do not speak English will be provided education in a language they understand. Without it, millions of children may be doomed to educational underachievement and limited occupational choices in the future.

In 1974, the U.S. Supreme Court recognized the connection between native language rights and equal educational opportunity. Plaintiffs representing 1,800 Chinese-speaking students sued the San Francisco Unified School District in 1969 for failing to provide students who did not speak English with an equal chance to learn. They lost their case in San Francisco, but by 1974 they had taken it all the way to the Supreme Court. In the landmark *Lau v. Nichols* case, the Court ruled unanimously that the civil rights of students who did not understand the language of instruction were indeed being violated. Citing Title VI of the Civil Rights Act, the Court stated, in part,

There is no equality of treatment merely by providing students with the same facilities, textbooks, teachers, and curriculum; for students who do not understand English are effectively foreclosed from any meaningful education. Basic skills are at the very core of what these public schools teach. Imposition of a requirement that, before a child can effectively participate in the educational program he must already have acquired those basic skills is to make a mockery of public education.[44]

Although the decision did not impose any particular remedy, its results were immediate and extensive. By 1975, the Office for Civil Rights and the Department of Health, Education, and Welfare issued a document called "The *Lau* Remedies," which has since then served as the basis for determining whether or not school systems throughout the United States are in compliance with the *Lau* decision. In effect, the document provides guidance in identifying students with a limited proficiency in English, assessing their language abilities, and providing appropriate programs. Bilingual programs are the common remedy of most school systems.

The Equal Educational Opportunities Act (EEOA) of 1974 has also been instrumental in protecting the language rights of students for whom English is not a native language. This law interprets the failure of any educational agency to "take appropriate action to overcome language barriers that impede equal participation by its students in its instructional programs" as a denial of equal educational opportunity.[45] A number of federal cases have resulted in a strong interpretation of this statute. In both the *Lau* decision and the EEOA, bilingual education has emerged as a key strategy to counteract the language discrimination faced by many students in our schools.

There is a dizzying array of program models and definitions of bilingual education.[46] But in general terms, bilingual education can be defined as *an educational program that involves the use of two languages of instruction at some point in a student's school career.* This definition is broad enough to include many program variations. For example, a child who speaks a language other than English, say Vietnamese, may receive instruction in content areas in Vietnamese while at the same time learning ESL. The culture associated with the primary language of instruction is generally part of the curriculum, as is that of the second language. This approach, sometimes called *bilingual/bicultural education,* is based on the premise that the language and culture children bring to school are assets that must be used in their education.

A primary objective of bilingual education is to develop proficiency and literacy in the English language. As such, *ESL,* or English as a Second Language, is an integral and necessary component of all bilingual programs because it goes hand in hand with native language instruction in content areas. When provided in isolation, however, ESL is not bilingual education because the child's native language is not used in instruction. While they are learning English, students in ESL programs may be languishing in their other subject areas because they do not understand the language of instruction. Their education usually consists only of learning English until they can function in the regular English-language environment.

Probably the most common model of bilingual education in the United States is the *transitional bilingual education* approach. In this approach, students receive their content area instruction in their native language while learning English as a second language. As soon as they are thought to be ready to benefit from the monolingual English-language curriculum, they are "exited" or "mainstreamed" out of the program. The rationale behind this model is that native-language services should serve only as a transition to English. Therefore, there is a limit on the time a student may be in a bilingual program, usually three years. This limit was established in 1971 by Massachusetts, the first state to mandate bilingual education, and it has served as a model for other states. The number of states that mandate bilingual education has fluctuated over the years, depending on the political climate in different states at different times.[47]

Developmental or *maintenance bilingual education* is a more comprehensive and long-term model. As in the transitional approach, students receive content area instruction in their native language while learning English as a second language. The difference is that generally no limit is set on the time students can be in the program. The objective is to develop fluency in both languages by using both for instruction. The longer they remain in the program, the more functionally bilingual they become and, therefore, the more balanced is the curriculum to which they are exposed. That is, they can potentially receive equal amounts of instruction in English and in their native language.

Two-way bilingual education is a program model that integrates students whose native language is English with students for whom English is a second language. The goal of this approach is to develop bilingual proficiency, academic achievement, and positive cross-cultural attitudes and behaviors among all students. This approach lends itself to cooperative learning and peer tutoring, because all students have considerable skills to share with one another. There is generally no time limit, although some two-way programs are part of existing transitional programs and therefore have the same entrance and exit criteria, at least for the students who are learning English. Two-way programs hold the promise of expanding our nation's linguistic resources and improving relationships between majority and minority language groups.

A variety of approaches and strategies are used in two-way programs, and these variations are based on the students enrolled, the program design, and the particular community. Most two-way programs use students' native or second language at different stages. For example, in a Spanish/English two-way bilingual program, all students K–2 might study 90 percent of their academic content in Spanish and 10 percent in English. From grades 3 through 6, the same students might have equal instruction in Spanish and English. Results of the two-way model have been very positive. In a study of more than 160 schools with two-way programs (the vast majority of which were Spanish/English), Donna Christian found they were effective in educating both English-speaking students and students who speak languages other than English.[48]

The fact is that bilingual education is generally more effective than other programs such as ESL alone, not only for learning content through the native language but also for learning English. This finding has been reiterated in many studies over the years, most recently in a 1998 summary of research conducted by the Center for Research on Education, Diversity, and Excellence.[49] This apparently contradictory finding can be understood if one considers that students in bilingual programs are given continued education in content areas *along with* structured instruction in English. Students in these programs are building on their previous literacy, but this situation may not be the case in ESL programs that concentrate on English grammar, phonics, and other language features out of context with the way in which real, day-to-day language is used. Even in the antibilingual climate of California in 1998, surprising results were found: Achievement test scores from San Francisco and San Jose found that students who completed bilingual education generally performed better than native English-speaking children in reading, math, language, and spelling. Many of these gains were impressive, and this situation was reported just one month after the passage of Proposition 227, which virtually outlawed the use of bilingual education in the state.[50]

Recent research by Wayne Thomas and Virginia Collier has confirmed once again the superiority of the bilingual education approach. In a comprehensive investigation of the records of 700,000 language minority students in five large school systems from 1982 to 1996, the researchers found that English learners who received bilingual education services finished their schooling with average scores that reached or exceeded the 50th national percentile in all content areas. In contrast, language minority students who received even well-implemented ESL-pull-out instruction—a very common program—typically finished school, if they graduated at all, with average scores between the 10th and 18th national percentiles. Thomas and Collier also found that two-way developmental bilingual education was the most successful program model of all. Unfortunately, this is the least common program model in the United States.[51]

Bilingual programs may have secondary salutary effects. These include motivating students to remain in school rather than dropping out, making school more meaningful, and in general making the school experience more enjoyable. This was certainly true for Manuel Gomes, whose case study follows this chapter. Because of the close-knit relationships between his Crioulo-speaking teachers and their students, Manuel's transition to English was far easier than it might otherwise have been. A related phenomenon may be that bilingual education reinforces close relationships among children and their family members, promoting more communication than would be the case if they were instructed solely in English and lost their native language. This was the finding in a nationwide survey of more than 1,000 families for whom English is a second language: Serious disruptions of family relations occurred when young children learned English in school and lost their native language.[52]

WHY THE CONTROVERSY OVER BILINGUAL EDUCATION?

Bilingual education has always been controversial. Both its proponents and its opponents have long recognized its potential for empowering traditionally powerless groups. Thus the issue is not whether bilingual education works but the *real possibility that it might.* Bilingual education challenges conventional U.S. educational wisdom that native language and culture need to be forgotten in order to be successful students and "real Americans." In spite of its sound pedagogical basis, bilingual education is above all a *political* issue because it is concerned with the relative power or lack of power of various groups in our society.

Bilingual education continues to be controversial because it generally represents the class and ethnic group interests of traditionally subordinated groups and it comes out on the side of education as an emancipatory proposition. As a matter of fact, when English-speaking middle-class children take part in two-way bilingual programs, there is much less controversy. In a study of one two-way program, Barbara Craig found there was great support among English-speaking parents for bilingual education precisely because their children would develop early fluency in Spanish and enhanced career options.[53]

Successful bilingual programs have demonstrated that students can learn through their native language while learning English *and also* achieving academically. This achievement contradicts the conservative agenda, which calls for a return to a largely European American curriculum and pedagogy. Successful bilingual education threatens to explode the myth of the "basics" if the basics means only valuing a Eurocentric curriculum and the English language.

The closer bilingual programs come to using students' language and culture in a liberating way, the more they are criticized. For example, developmental programs tend to be much more controversial than transitional programs; ESL programs, with no bilingual assistance, are viewed as less problematic than either. Understanding the political nature of bilingual education, and of multicultural education in general, is essential if we are to develop effective programs for all our students.

● *CONCLUSION: BEST PRACTICES FOR LANGUAGE MINORITY STUDENTS*

Although bilingual education represents a notable advance over monolingual education, it is unrealistic to expect it to work for all language minority students. It is often perceived as a panacea for all the educational problems of language-minority students, but even with bilingual education, many children are likely to face educational failure. No approach or program can be a panacea for all the problems, educational and otherwise, facing young people. Essential issues such as poverty, discrimination, and structural inequality also need to be faced. Simply substituting one language for another, or books in Spanish with Dick and Jane in brownface, will not guarantee success for language-minority students. Expecting too much of even good programs is counterproductive because in the absence of quick results, the children are again blamed for their failure.

As we have seen, effective pedagogy is not simply teaching subject areas in another language, but instead finding ways to use the language, culture, and experiences of students meaningfully in their education. Even when bilingual programs are more effective than ESL or immersion programs, the pedagogy in such classrooms all too frequently replicates the traditional "chalk and talk" or "transmission" methods found in most classrooms. If bilingual education is to challenge this kind of pedagogy, a far different and more empowering environment needs to be designed.

Another problem with bilingual education has to do with the usual definition of *success* for most bilingual programs. Bilingual programs, particularly those with a transitional focus, are meant to "self-destruct" within a specified time, generally three years. Success in these programs is measured by the rapidity with which they mainstream students. That being the case, their very existence is based on a "compensatory education" philosophy whereby students who enter school knowing little or no English are regarded as needing compensation. Their knowledge of another language is considered a crutch to use until they master what is considered the "real" language of schooling. This is at best a patronizing position and at worst a racist one.

Given this perspective, it is little wonder that many parents do not want their children in bilingual programs or that these programs are often isolated and ghettoized in the schools. This message is not lost on students either. In an ethnographic study of four bilingual students, Commins found that some children are reluctant to speak Spanish because it is perceived to be the language of the "dumb kids."[54] As a result, language minority children may unconsciously jeopardize their own language development by dropping Spanish, a language that benefits their academic achievement by allowing them to use higher level cognitive skills than with their English, which they do not speak as well.

Contrary to the "quick exit" philosophy that undergirds most bilingual programs, research has documented that students generally need a minimum of five to seven years to develop the level of English proficiency needed to succeed academically in school.[55] With most programs permitting students to remain a maximum of only three to four years, only partially positive results can be expected. The research evidence is in direct contrast to program implementation. In spite of this, many programs are successful because they are better than programs that provide no native language support at all.

Equally troublesome for some school districts is that they have numerous language groups in their student population, called *low incidence populations* (i.e., students who speak a particular language for which there may not be sufficient speakers to entitle them legally to a bilingual program. This is often the case with Asian languages and some European languages). In this situation, the most common programmatic practice is some kind of English as a Second Language (ESL) approach. Providing a bilingual program for each of these small groups would be not only impractical but also impossible.

The fact that most bilingual programs are based on the need to separate students is also problematic. Bilingual education has been characterized by some as tracking because students are separated from their peers for instruction. Although the reasons for this separation are legitimate and based on sound research and pedagogy, tracking as a practice flies in the face of equal educational opportunity. This makes it a particularly thorny issue in a democratic society. Add the research evidence suggesting that students should remain in bilingual classrooms until they develop sufficient academic competency in English, and we would be left with some students in segregated language settings for a major part of their schooling. Nevertheless, it must be remembered that a great deal of segregation of language-minority students took place *before* there were bilingual programs (and much of this kind of segregation continues today) in sheltered English and ESL-pullout type programs, and very little criticism was lodged against segregation in those cases.

In fact, Latino students, who represent the highest number in bilingual programs, are now the *most segregated population* in U.S. schools, and bilingual education has nothing to do with this.[56] Instead, "White flight," a retrenchment in busing policies, and segregated residential housing patterns are to blame. We must conclude that sometimes the criticisms that students in bilingual programs are unnecessarily segregated are based more on an ideological opposition to using students' native language than out of a regard for protecting their civil rights.

It is also true, however, that every bilingual program has numerous opportunities for integrating students more meaningfully than is currently the case. Students in the bilingual program can take art, physical education, and other nonacademic classes with their English-speaking peers. The bilingual program can also be more structurally integrated into the school instead of separated in a wing of the building, so that teachers from both bilingual and nonbilingual classrooms can collaborate. This seldom happens because bilingual teachers bear the burden of the "bilingual" label in the same way as their students. These teachers are suspected of being less intelligent, less academically prepared, and less able than non-bilingual teachers—this in spite of the fact that they have generally mastered two languages and developed a wide range of pedagogical approaches for teaching a diverse student body. Because many bilingual teachers are from the same cultural and linguistic backgrounds as the students they teach, they bring a necessary element of diversity into the school. But most schools have not found a way to benefit from their presence.

Two-way bilingual programs provide another opportunity for integration and heightened academic achievement. For example, a recent progress report of a Spanish–English two-way program in the Cambridge, Mass., public schools found that both groups of children were progressing well in all subject matters and neither group was declining in its native language development. Also, children at all grade levels were found to select their best friend without an ethnic or racial bias; the self-esteem of both groups was enhanced; and there was much less segregation than before the program—all worthy social and educational goals.[57]

● *SUMMARY*

There are numerous ways in which language differences may affect students' learning. These differences are not necessarily barriers to learning, but the history of linguicism in our society has resulted in making them so. Language policies and practices in the United States have ranged from a grudging acceptance of language diversity to outright hostility. We have seen the positive impact that recognizing and affirming students' native languages can have on their learning. Even teachers who do not speak the languages of their students can be successful with them, as long as they become familiar with theories and pedagogical approaches to second language acquisition and development, and they have positive attitudes of their language minority students.

We have also pointed out some of the problems that arise when bilingual programs have low status and when students are separated for instruction. Bilingual education certainly is not the sole approach for teaching linguistically diverse students. Even in bilingual programs, for example, when there is an emphasis on low-level rote and drill, traditional classroom practices go unchallenged. The result has been, as Luis Moll claims, that even the major questions addressed in the research (e.g., "How long does it take children to learn English in bilingual classrooms?" or, "Will bilingual education get in the way of students' assimilation?") undermine the role of students' native languages, cultures, and experiences in their learning. Moll believes that this emphasis on low-level skills has given bilingual education a "working-class identity."[58]

Bilingual education cannot completely reverse the history of failure for linguistic minority students; it is both unreasonable and naive to expect it to do so. Nevertheless, bilingual education has proven to be an effective program for students for whom English is a second language because it is based on a fundamental critique of the *assimilation = success* formula on which much of our educational policy and practice are based. The fact that it alone cannot change the achievement of students is an indication of the complexity of factors that affect learning.

● *TO THINK ABOUT*

1. Research the "English Only" movement. Do you consider it an example of linguicism? Why or why not?

2. Why do you think bilingual education has been less controversial at some times than at others? Review the case of California's Proposition 227 in 1998 as an example.

3. The argument that "My folks made it without bilingual education; why give other folks special treatment?" has often been made, particularly by descendants of European American immigrants. Is this a compelling argument? Why or why not?

4. If you were the principal of a school with a large population of language-minority students, how would you address this situation? What if you were a parent of one of those children? A teacher?

5. Some people are offended when the term *English as a second language* is used. They believe that English should be the *first* language of everyone who lives in the United States. Why do people react in this way? What would you say to someone who said this?

Case Study: Manuel Gomes

"It's kind of scary at first, especially if you don't know the language."

The first thing you notice about Manuel Gomes[1] is that he is constantly on the move, as if the engine has started and he is ready to shift to fourth without moving through the other gears. Of slight stature and with a somewhat rumpled look, Manuel has an infectious and lively sense of humor and a generally positive attitude about life. Manuel is 19 years old and will be graduating from high school this year.

In many urban high schools, 19 is no longer a late age to graduate. Many immigrant students graduate quite late. Immigrant and refugee students are more likely to be retained in-grade, inappropriately placed in special education, and at risk of being placed in low academic tracks on the basis of language barriers or slow academic progress. That Manuel has graduated is noteworthy because the dropout rate for foreign-born students is close to 70 percent.[2]

Manuel came to Boston with his family from the Cape Verde Islands when he was 11 years old. Even before its independence from Portugal in 1975, Cape Verde had a huge out-migration of its population. Official documents estimate that close to 180,000 Cape Verdeans emigrated voluntarily between 1970 and 1973, some 20,000 to the United States alone. The process of emigration had begun with the arrival of North American whaling boats from New England in the late seventeenth century. By the end of the nineteenth century, there was already a sizable Cape Verdean community in Massachusetts. Currently, well over twice as many Cape Verdeans reside abroad than live at home. The 325,000 who live in the United States (about equal to the number who reside on the islands) represent the largest Cape Verdean community outside of Cape Verde.[3]

Having suffered from more than 400 years of colonial neglect under Portugal, Cape Verde, an archipelago of 10 large and several smaller islands off the West Coast of Africa, was left in poor economic and social condition. For example, the literacy rate in 1981 was 14 percent, a dramatic indication of the lack of educational opportunities available to the majority of the people. Since independence, the situation has improved remarkably, and the literacy rate in 1987 was over 57 percent.[4] Although the official language of the islands is Portuguese, the lingua franca is Crioulo, an Afro-Portuguese creole.

Most Cape Verdeans in the United States live in New England, particularly Rhode Island and Massachusetts. Manuel's family, like most, came to the United States for economic reasons. Although formerly farmers in Cape Verde, they quickly settled into the urban environment. Manuel's father found a job cleaning offices downtown at night, while his mother stayed home to take care of their many children. They settled in Boston, which has a large Cape Verdean community, and they currently live in a three-decker home with apartments that are occupied by other members of the large family. The neighborhood was once a working-class Irish community and is now multiracial, with a big Catholic church close by and Vietnamese and Cape Verdean restaurants up the street. The older homes, the din on the street, and the crowding all add to the sense of an aging but still vibrant urban community.

Manuel is the youngest of 11 children and the first in his family to graduate from high school. He was in a bilingual program for several years after arriving in Boston. The language of instruction in the program was Crioulo. The State Assembly of Massachusetts passed legislation in 1977 distinguishing Crioulo as a language separate from Portuguese and required that Crioulo-speaking students be placed in separate programs from those for Portuguese-speaking students.[5] The result was a scramble to find Crioulo-speaking teachers and aides and to develop appropriate materials, because few or none existed. The rationale for placing Cape Verdean students in a separate program, notwithstanding the administrative problems it may have created, was pedagogically sound: Students should be taught in the language they speak and understand, not in their second or third language.

Another result of separating the program was that a strong sense of community among teachers, students, and parents developed. Some of the teachers and other staff in the program are intimately involved in the life of the community, and the separation that often exists between school and home, especially for immigrant children, was alleviated. Manuel's participation in the bilingual program proved to be decisive in his education because it allowed a less traumatic transition to the English language and U.S. culture. Nevertheless, he constantly refers to how hard it has been to "fit in," both in school and in society in general.

Boston, like most big cities in the United States, is a highly diverse metropolitan area. It is not unusual to walk from street to street and hear languages from all over the world, smell the foods of different continents, and hear the music of a wide variety of cultures. In spite of this diversity and perhaps in part because of it, the city is not without its tensions, including diverse economic vested interests and interethnic hostility. These tensions are evident in many arenas, including the schools. The attendant problems of court-ordered desegregation, with a long and tumultuous history in the city, are still apparent. The city's schools, for example, have experienced a vast decrease in the percentage of White and middle-class students since desegregation and, although once highly regarded, have lost both resources and prestige.

Manuel's plans for the future are sketchy, but right now he is working in a downtown hotel and would like to use the accounting skills he learned in high school to find a job at a bank. His positive experience in a theater class as a sophomore, along with his great enthusiasm and expressiveness, have sparked a desire to continue in the acting field, perhaps doing commercials. He has begun making inquiries about this possibility. He has also talked of continuing his education and may register at a community college in the near future.

Manuel is excited and proud of graduating from high school but reflects on how difficult it has been to achieve. This is the major theme that characterizes Manuel's experiences, both as a student and as an immigrant to this society. The supportive roles that he and members of his family have played for one another is another key issue. Finally, the mediating role of bilingual education has probably been pivotal in his success as a student. Each of these themes will be explored further.

The Pain and Fear of Immigration

We have a different way of living in Cape Verde than in America. Our culture is totally different, so we have to start a different way of living in America. . . . It's kind of confusing when you come to America, you know.

I liked going to school in Cape Verde, you know, 'cause you know everybody and you have all your friends there.

In our country, we treat people different. There's no crime. You don't have to worry about people jumping you, taking your money. Or walking at night by yourself. There's no fear for that, you know. In Cape Verde, you don't have to worry about something happening to your child, or you don't have to worry about using drugs.

My father and mother used to work on plantations. We used to grow potatoes; we used to grow corn; we used to grow beans and stuff like that. . . . We had a lot of land. Every season, we farmed. We had cows. Me and my brother used to feed the cows and take them to walk and give them water to drink and stuff like that. We used to sell our milk to rich folks and I used to deliver there. It was kinda fun. These rich people, every time I'd go there, they'd feed me, which I liked very much [*laughs*]. They used to give me cake and stuff like that, cookies. I liked that.

We'd have a lot of crops and we'd give some away to poor people, those that don't have any. . . . We had a lot of friends and stuff like that.

When we came to America, it was totally different.

In Cape Verde, they have this rumor that it's easier to make a living up here. So everybody wants to come up here. They have this rumor that once you get here, you find money all around you, you know. So, when you're like coming up here, they make a big commotion out of it. "Oh, you're going to America, rich country," and stuff like that. So they think once you come here, you got it made . . . you're rich. People in our country actually think that *we're* rich here, that we are filthy rich, that money surrounds us, we eat money!

I was disappointed in a lot of ways, especially with the crime, especially with the kids. They don't respect each other, they don't respect their parents. It's very different here. It's very tough.

I was afraid. I had people jumping me a few times, trying to take my wallet and stuff like that. . . . It's a scary situation.

It didn't really bother me, but like what got to me, is if they try to start a fight with you, you go to tell like a teacher, they couldn't do nothing about it. That's what got to me, you know?

It was a few students. I know this kid, this big Black kid, he tried to fight me like three times. Then I had a brother that was going to the same middle school, so he had a fight with my brother, my big brother. After that, it calmed down a little bit, you know?

Kids might try to stab you if you probably step on them. . . . That happened to me once. I stepped on this kid's sneaker once and he tried to fight me. He said, "What you doing?" I said that I'm sorry and he said, "That's not enough," and he tried to punch me. He didn't, but he was very furious.

You gotta get used to it. That's why a lot of Cape Verdean kids, when they get here, they change. They become violent, like some of the kids in America. So, it's sad. It's very hard for the parents. The parents are not used to that, and it's happening a lot with parents in our neighborhood. It's happening to our family. I have a cousin and his mother tried to commit suicide because her son was dealing drugs and hanging with the wrong crowd, with all these hoods. . . . The son almost died because someone beat him up so bad. And it's sad, you know?

They try to be strict about it, you know. But with kids, they try to copy kids that were born here. They try to be like them. They try to go out and do the stuff that *they're* doing. It's like teen pressure, you know? So, it's very hard, you know? You want to fit in. You like to fit in with the crowd.

If you hang with the wrong crowd, you're going to be in big trouble. You just change . . . and you're going to be a person that you don't want to be. . . . You'll probably end up in jail.

I been here eight years and I never hang with the wrong crowd. I've never used drugs in my life. I've never *smelled* cigarettes. So, I really hate when I see other kids doing it. It's sad when you see especially your friends doing it. . . . So I had to say, "Go away. I don't want that life . . . ." So I had to separate from them.

I had a hard time finding friends that wasn't doing that stuff like they were doing. . . . It's very hard if you hate what your friends are doing.

Start learning the language was hard for me. And then start making friends, because you gotta start making new friends. . . . When American students see you, it's kinda hard [to] get along with them when you have a different culture, a different way of dressing and stuff like that. So kids really look at you and laugh, you know, at the beginning.

It was difficult like when you see a girl at school that you like. It's kind of difficult to express yourself and tell her the way you feel about her, you know? When you don't even know the language, it's kind of hard. I had a hard time.

It's kind of scary at first, especially if you don't know the language and like if you don't have friends there.

Some people are slow to learn the language and some just catch it up easy. It wasn't easy for me . . . like the pronunciation of the words and stuff like that. Like in Portuguese and in English, they're different. It's kinda hard, you know?

I don't think I want to be an American citizen. . . . To tell you the truth, I don't like America at all. . . . I like it but I don't like the lifestyles. It's different

from my point of view. What I'm thinking of doing is work in America for
10 years and go back to my country, because America's a violent country. It's
dangerous with crime, with drugs.

Role Reversals within the Family

I took [my father] to the hospital. Then I found out that he had cancer. I didn't
wanna tell him. The doctor told me that he had cancer. I didn't wanna tell
him because he hates to get sick and he hates to die! He hates to die. If you
tell him he's gonna die, he'll kill you before he dies!

This happened when I was in school, so I was missing school a lot . . .
I was the only one that was able to understand the language and stuff like
that. . . . It actually got to the point that *I* had to tell him. It was like sad when
I had to tell him because it's very hard to tell him that he had cancer.

I was worried. And I had to explain to the whole family. And the doctor,
I had to translate for him and stuff like that, tell him what's going on. And I
had to tell the whole family that he was sick and stuff like that. It was really
hard for me, you know?

Because they don't speak English, I have to go places with them to translate and stuff like that. So I'm usually busy. . . . We have a big family, you
know. I have to help them out.

If I felt like I had support from my family, if they only knew the
language. . . . If they were educated, I could make it big, you see what I'm
saying? . . . I would've had a better opportunity, a better chance.

I'm very happy about [graduating]. It means a lot to me. It means that I
did something that I'm very proud [of]. It feels good, you know? And I'd really
like to continue in my education, because you know, I'm the first one. And I
want to be successful with my life.

I just wanted to help them, you know? I wanted to be the one to help
them. . . . They didn't support me, but I wanted to support them.

My mother's proud of me. My father is too. . . .

It was tough for me when I found out that my father had cancer because,
you know, I really wanted to graduate. I just want to show him that I can be
somebody, you know? I actually did this, try to graduate from high school, for
him, you know?

Bilingual Education as Linguistic and Cultural Mediator

A Cape Verdean person is usually, he looks like he's a nice person, educated,
you know? Not all of them, but like 70 percent of Cape Verdeans, they look
educated. . . . They're not violent. . . . You can tell someone is Cape Verdean . . .
if he starts pointing at you. That's a sign that he's Cape Verdean automatic. If
he starts staring at you, he's Cape Verdean.

We have problems when we look at American people. They might think
we are talking about them and stuff like that. So we have to change that

behavior. We have to get used to not pointing at people and not looking at them very much, because American people are not used to people staring at them.

What we do in our country, we *observe* people. It don't mean nothing to us Cape Verdeans. It's just normal. But if we do it to an American person, it makes that American person nervous, I guess, and he would ask you, "What are you looking at?" or, "Why are you looking at me?" and start questioning and probably start trouble with you.

It's normal to us. That's why other people got to understand that not everybody has the same culture; not everybody is the same. So some people don't understand.

Like a Spanish [Hispanic] person, what he usually do, they use their body in a different way. . . . With Spanish, what they do, they point with their lips. They go [*demonstrates puckering of the lips*]. So, that's different. Other cultures, they might use their head; they might use their eyebrows.

It's good to understand other people's culture from different countries. America is made up of different countries, and we all should know a little bit about each one's cultures.

I think [teachers] could help students, try to influence them, that they can do whatever they want to do, that they can be whatever they want to be, that they got opportunities out there. . . . Most schools don't encourage kids to be all they can be.

What they need to do is try to know the student before they influence him. If you don't know a student, there's no way to influence him. If you don't know his background, there's no way you are going to get in touch with him. There's no way you're going to influence him if you don't know where he's been.

You cannot forget about [your culture], you know? It's part of you. You can't forget something like that. . . . You gotta know who you are. You cannot deny your country and say, "I'm an American; I'm not Cape Verdean."

That's something that a lot of kids do when they come to America. They change their names. Say you're Carlos, they say, "I'm Carl . . . ." They wanna be American; they're not Cape Verdean. . . . That's wrong. They're fooling themselves.

I identify myself as Cape Verdean. I'm Cape Verdean. I cannot be an American because I'm not an American. That's it.

[*Describe yourself as a student*] I'm not a genius [*laughing*]! [But] I know that I can do whatever I want to do in life. Whatever I want to do, I know I could make it. I believe that strongly.

COMMENTARY

Manuel's voice is eloquent in expressing the concerns he has had as an immigrant and a student, concerns related to his academic success and his motivation for graduating and possibly continuing his education.

But behind the sometimes forced enthusiasm he displays, Manuel's voice is also tinged with sadness at what might have been. His expression changes when discussing his early experiences in Cape Verde. In spite of the obviously difficult circumstances of going to school, where he was in a crowded, one-room schoolhouse with many other students of all ages and where corporal punishment was a common practice—which made going to school "scary"—over the years Manuel has idealized his experiences there. He seems to have forgotten the harsh life he had there, although he does admit that he did not like farming. In spite of the difficulties, life in Cape Verde was, at least when he reflects on it now, easier and more familiar. Manuel often contrasts the crime and violence in the United States with a now idealized and bucolic childhood in Cape Verde. During his interviews, he also compared child-rearing styles, the respect children learn and show adults, and the priority on making "quick money" in this society with other values in Cape Verde.

Manuel describes, with obvious pain, what it was like being perceived as "different" by his peers. For example, other kids would call him names ("'foreigner' and stuff like that") and ridicule him ("it really gets to a student when other students make fun"). The situation changed after he reached high school, but those first years are indelibly etched in his memory.

The distress caused by immigration is multifaceted. Not only do immigrants leave behind a country that is loved and an existence that is at least familiar, if not comfortable, but they also leave a language and culture that can never find full expression in their adopted country. In addition, they are coming into a situation that may offer many exciting possibilities, but nonetheless is frightening and new. Manuel is ambivalent about his experience in the United States. He does not yet have U.S. citizenship, and he is unsure that he wants it.

Several of the painful incidents described by Manuel focus on interethnic rivalries and violence. This situation is a guarded secret, especially at many urban schools. School officials, perhaps fearful of being labeled racists, are reluctant to confront the prejudicial behaviors and actions of one group of students toward another, whether they involve conflicts between Black and White students or between different students of color. Yet the issue is real and is becoming more apparent all the time. Racial stereotypes and epithets are commonplace and they are evident in the most seemingly sensitive students; for example, Manuel's comment about a "big Black kid" reinforces the negative stereotype of Blacks as frightening and violent. Also, as a result of their low status, most immigrant students are at the very bottom of the social ranking order in high schools.[6]

Many immigrant children experience role reversals with their parents as a result of their parents' lack of English fluency. Manuel carries out the role of "language broker" in his family as his is the public face that interacts with the greater community, whether it be the schools, clinics, or other agencies.[7] Manuel's role as translator was especially vivid when his father developed cancer a couple of years ago. Because his parents speak little English, Manuel was placed in the extraordinary position of being the one to tell him that he had cancer. This experience has had a great impact on him, especially as the cancer was considered terminal. Manuel's words express the great apprehension he felt in telling his father the bad news. Moreover, he also had to tell his father that he needed an operation, not an easy task given his father's memories of the seriousness of surgery in Cape Verde, where it was used only as a last resort and where, according to Manuel, chances of recovery were slim. Although his father seems to have recovered from the cancer against all the odds, the experience left Manuel quite shaken. His grades also suffered during that period.

Other crucial and draining family responsibilities are familiar to young people in Manuel's situation, but not always known by teachers and schools. The role of family interpreter and arbiter is carried out by many immigrant students—resulting in the transfer of authority and status from parents to children, which in turn can lead to further conflicts at home. In addition, it often takes students away from school to attend to family business. Teachers not accustomed to this kind of adult responsibility often interpret students' absences and lateness as a sign that their parents do not care about education or that the students are irresponsible. Frequently, just the opposite is true. That is, it is precisely the most responsible young people who are kept home to attend to important family concerns. Furthermore, the judgment that parents do not care about the education of their children is based on the assumption that schooling is the most serious concern in their lives. For families struggling to survive in a hostile environment, this assumption is questionable.

This does not mean that parents are oblivious to the benefits of education, but rather that they need support in attending to their basic needs. Here is where the school, as an advocate of children and their families, can come in, by helping to find needed services or helping parents devise ways to attend to family needs without keeping their children out of school.

Whereas the role of family arbiter has obviously made Manuel mature beyond his years, on the other side of the coin he has had to count on himself for many things. Because other family members are not fluent in English, they have been unable to give him the help he needs in school. They rarely went to school, for example. Parent involvement in schools in most countries is minimal. The feeling is that once children are in school, it is the school's responsibility to educate them. The parents, in essence, hand over their children to the school in the hope that the school will educate them. To jump to the conclusion that these parents do not care about education is to miss the mark. Rather, most economically oppressed parents see the role of education as extremely important and stress this to their children constantly. Using this belief as the basis for involving parents in their children's education is a more promising approach than simply dismissing the parents as uncaring.

That the bilingual program acted as a linguistic and cultural mediator is evident in many of Manuel's comments. For example, he is extremely perceptive about culture and its manifestations. This happens repeatedly in bilingual programs, where culture and language become a major focus of the curriculum. The description of how his Latino classmates use their lips to point rather than their fingers demonstrates Manuel's sensitivity and sophistication in this area. Few teachers, even those who work with students from different cultures, pick up these sometimes subtle cues.

Manuel has also been able to maintain the cultural meanings attached to particular terms, as seen in his use of *educated* to describe Cape Verdeans. Manuel is referring to the connotation of the word as used by various ethnic groups including Cape Verdeans and Hispanics. That is, besides referring to being schooled, to be educated also means to be respectful and polite; and when used with children, it has the added meaning of being obedient.

By the time he got to high school, Manuel had learned enough English to be able to speak up. He said that the bilingual program at the high school provided a safe environment for him and other Cape Verdean students. It is a rather large program, much larger than the one at the middle school, and most of the teachers and some of the other staff are Cape Verdean as well. Cape Verdean students in the city have a strong identification with this high school and look forward to attending. There is also a close-knit sense of community within the program. In fact, it has always been one of the more constructive and distinguishing characteristics of this particular urban school.

Manuel's bilingual program was a positive one for a number of other reasons as well. For example, the staff is very involved with and connected to the community. Cape Verdean students are usually looked on very positively by all staff members, who consider them well behaved and more serious than other students in the school. The generally high expectations teachers have of them may have an impact on their achievement. Ogbu's theory of "voluntary" and "involuntary" minority status seems to hold some validity in this case.[8] But in recent years, problems similar to those experienced by U.S.-born students have begun to surface in Manuel's school and community. For example, some Cape Verdean staff members in his high school are becoming increasingly concerned with the rising rate of teen pregnancy and intergenerational conflicts in the community. Whether they will affect the academic achievement of the Cape Verdean students in the school remains to be seen but is a source of growing concern.

Manuel speaks fondly of his experiences with the teachers and students in the program. He says that it was "more comfortable" for him there. The program also helped mediate his experiences in the rest of the school and in his community in general. For example, he remembers the theater workshop that he took as a sophomore. Although it was not part of the bilingual program and all the skits were in English, it focused on similar issues. He still recalls with great enthusiasm a monologue he did about a student going to a new school. He could identify with him because it was so reminiscent of his own experiences. The theater class always had a mixture of students of diverse backgrounds and language skills, so it was a place to focus on communication and interpersonal skills in an active way. The performances allowed students to use many different skills and draw on their experiences for content.

The bilingual program helped Manuel retain his language and culture and, with it, his ties to his family and community. It gave him something to hold onto. Even this kind of program, however, is not enough if it is not part of a larger whole that affirms the diversity of all within it. It and other bilingual programs like it become tiny islands in a sea of homogeneity and pressure to conform.

The tension is well expressed by Manuel when he pits being Cape Verdean against being American. The possibility that he could be *both* Cape Verdean and American is not perceived as an option. That is, if he identifies with being American, he is abandoning his culture and country; if he chooses to remain Cape Verdean, his possibilities in this society are limited. These are hard choices for young people to make and are part of the pain of living in a culture that has a rigid definition of "American."

It is obvious that Manuel has not fully come to terms with his experience in the United States. He has had a difficult time "fitting in" but is also uncompromising about keeping his culture and language. This tension is not unusual for students who have gone through the pain of uprooting. The transition, always difficult, may take many years. How much he can assimilate, how far he wants to go in adjusting, how ambivalent or disappointed he feels about his opportunities here are issues for Manuel to resolve. The pain that this balancing act has caused is evident in his conflict over his future in the United States.

One of the ways he has chosen to deal with ambivalence is by joining and becoming very active in a fundamentalist Christian church. As Manuel so eloquently expressed it, "That's the place I belong to. I fit there. I felt that God had moved there. Jesus got hold of me. He said, 'Calm down.'" A number of issues were apparently influential in leading Manuel to this particular church. For example, it was about the time that his father developed cancer and Manuel was immersed in his role as "the man of the family." It was also about the time that he decided to drop some of his friends (as he said, "It's very hard if you hate what your friends are doing"). In looking for something to keep him on track, as the bilingual program and other cultural supports had done previously, he looked toward the community. Although Manuel had been raised a Catholic, the local Catholic church was completely unappealing to him. This, too, became an issue of "fitting in." The Catholic church had made few accommodations to its newest members, many of whom were immigrants who spoke little or no English. His new church, however, seems to have gone to great lengths to welcome Cape Verdeans, and Manuel finally feels he has found a place to fit in.

Throughout his life in the United States, Manuel has had the good sense to follow the sound advice of kin and to seek the kind of support to help him become a successful student. He has overcome many barriers and has now graduated from high school, a tremendous accomplishment when seen in the social and historical context in which he lives. That he has emerged with a few scars is not surprising. Insecurity about his life in the United States, what his future holds for him, and how to resolve the issues of identity and "fitting in" are all problems with which he must continue to cope. Manuel is now at a crossroads. Given his resolve, one clearly has the feeling that he will succeed in life as he has in school.

TO THINK ABOUT

1. Given some of the ways in which Manuel's experience as an immigrant have been frightening and painful, what can teachers and schools do to help?
2. Why do you think Manuel has idealized his former life on the Cape Verde Islands?
3. What can account for Manuel's highly developed sensitivity to cultural differences?
4. Given Manuel's many absences from school during his father's illness, it is probable that school authorities and teachers assumed that his family was wrong in keeping him home to attend to family business. What do you think? What could the school have done to accommodate his family's needs?
5. Why is it important for Manuel to graduate "for" his father?
6. How do you think the bilingual program acted as a *linguistic* and *cultural* mediator for Manuel? What can teachers in nonbilingual programs learn from this?
7. Do you understand why Manuel feels reluctant to identify himself as "American"? How would you approach this issue if he were one of your students?

Case Study: Yolanda Piedra

"Once you get the hang of it, you'll start getting practice with people and teachers, no matter if you talk English or Spanish."

Yolanda Piedra[1] did not learn English until she was 7, but at 13 she is equally comfortable with both Spanish and English. She and her family speak mostly Spanish at home, although according to Yolanda, sometimes they speak English to help her mother "practice." Born in Mexico, Yolanda came to California after having completed kindergarten and part of first grade. In this, she and her family are typical of the immigration wave since the 1980s. The 1990 Census estimated that the foreign-born population in the United States numbered about 15 million. More than a third of these are concentrated in California, by far the most affected of the states.[2] Not surprisingly, by 1992, California had the largest language-minority population in the schools, numbering almost a million students.[3]

Yolanda lives in a midsized, low- to middle-income city in southern California. The primarily one-family houses, most of which are rented, hide the poverty and difficult conditions in which many of the residents live. This is an economically oppressed, largely Mexican and Chicano community, although there are also smaller numbers of White and Black residents in the city.[4] Until a few years ago, it was primarily a rural area, and farm work is one of the main reasons that Mexicans first came here. Gangs were unknown just a few years ago, but spreading from the Los Angeles area they are now involving more and more young people, especially boys, who sometimes join as young as 11 or 12 years of age. The need to deal with the growing gang activity is recognized by residents as their major problem.

Yolanda's parents are separated, and Yolanda lives with her mother, 12-year-old brother, and 3-year-old sister (both of whom she describes as "wild"). Her brother is what she calls a "troublemaker," frequently getting involved in problems at school. He is beginning to get into trouble in the community as well, which may be a sign that further problems, particularly gang activity, will follow. Yolanda's father lives in Mexico, and she rarely sees him. Her mother works in a candy factory. From what Yolanda says, her mother is strict with the children, limiting their social interactions and expecting them all to take on family obligations. She is a single parent struggling to survive with her three children in what can best be described as adverse conditions. Her constant message to all of them concerns the importance of getting an education.

Even though she spoke no English and the transition to a new school and society was difficult, Yolanda recalls mostly positive experiences during her elementary school years. She was in a bilingual program when first entering school and is now in the general education program. Currently an eighth-grader in a primarily Mexican American junior high school, Yolanda is by all accounts a successful student. She is enthusiastic about school and becomes noticeably enlivened when talking about learning and wanting to "make my mind work,"

as she says. She uses English, her second language, in beautifully expressive ways, making unusual and descriptive constructions, probably influenced by her bilingualism. Yolanda consistently gets high grades in most of her subjects. Her favorite class is physical education and her least favorite is English, although she manages to get A's in it as well. Although quite young, Yolanda has narrowed down her future aspirations to two (one not at all consistent with her scholastic success, but very much related to the limiting societal expectations based on gender): She would like to be either a computer programmer or a flight attendant.

Yolanda's city contains one of the largest elementary school districts in California. About 60 percent of the students are Hispanic, Whites making up the majority of the remainder; and the Black community is small but growing. Her junior high school is situated in what is acknowledged to be a tough barrio and is beset with the same kinds of problems of most inner-city schools: gang activity, drugs, and unmet family needs that may interfere with learning. But in both her elementary and junior high schools, there is a feeling of community support. The school is successful with quite a number of its students, but it also faces a great many problems. The school's success may in part be to the credit of the staff, who are attuned to what is going on in the community. Most teachers seem genuinely concerned about their students. This concern is reflected, for example, in the great number of workshops on issues ranging from gangs to cultural diversity. The Spanish class recently given for staff had a full enrollment, including some high-level administrators.

The number of Latino professionals, however, is very low, although an effort is being made to recruit more; a Latino psychologist was hired recently. There is also a Latino community liaison, and the principal has an open-door policy for staff, students, and parents, which helps to create a feeling of engagement and support. Staff members in both of the schools Yolanda has attended have made a conscious effort to include and affirm aspects of the Mexican culture and experience in the curriculum and in extracurricular activities. Yolanda's positive feelings about her school experiences are in part a reflection of the environments these schools have tried to create.

One of the youngest students involved in this project, Yolanda Piedra is nonetheless a mature young woman who is certain about many things: the importance of communication; the benefits of being Mexican and speaking Spanish; and the necessity of surrounding oneself with support from teachers, family, and peers.

Communication

My mom . . . takes really good care of me. . . . She talks to me [about] problems and everything. . . . My mom says that they want me to go to school. That way, I won't be stuck with a job like them. They want me to go on, try my best to get something I want and not be bored . . . to get a job that I like and feel proud of it.

She wants everything kind of like good, perfect, not perfect, but kind of like the best I could do.

I feel proud of myself when I see a [good] grade. And like I see a C, I'm gonna have to put this grade up. And I try my best. . . . When I get a C, my mom doesn't do anything to me 'cause she knows I try my best. . . . Well, she tells me how to work it out.

[*Is your mother involved in school?*] [No], first of all, 'cause she understands English, but she's just embarrassed, shy to talk. . . . And 'cause she's always busy.

Like when it's something important for me, like, "Mom, I'm gonna do this, I want you to be there," she'll be there no matter what. . . . [But] if she takes too much care of me when I'm at home, now at school [too] I'll be dead!

[When I'm older, I want to] take my mom places and just be with my mom all the time.

[*What advice would you give teachers?*] I'd say, "Get along more with the kids that are not really into themselves. . . . Have more communication with them . . . ." I would get along with the students. 'Cause you learn a lot from the students. That's what a lot of teachers tell me. They learn more from their students than from where they go study.

I would help people get along with each other. 'Cause actually what they do around here, is that they see them doing trouble and everything, what they really are is suspending them. . . . They're really pushing them to do it again.

Surrounding Oneself with Success

Actually, there's one friend of mine . . . she's been with me since first grade until eighth grade, right now. And she's always been with me, in bad or good things, all the time. She's always telling me, "Keep on going and your dreams are gonna come true."

Actually, when I got here, I didn't want to stay here, 'cause I didn't like the school. And after a little while, in third grade, I started getting the hint of it and everything and I tried real hard in it.

I really got along with the teachers a lot. . . . Actually, 'cause I had some teachers, and they were always calling my mom, like I did a great job. Or they would start talking to me, or they kinda like pulled me up some grades, or moved me to other classes, or took me somewhere. And they were always congratulating me.

[*What do you remember about Cinco de Mayo?*] That's my favorite month, 'cause I like dancing. And over there, in [elementary school] they had these kinds of dances, and I was always in it. . . . It's kind of like a celebration.

Sometimes you get all tangled up with the grades or school or the teachers, 'cause you don't understand them. But you have to get along with them and you have to work for it.

So, actually, I feel good about it because I like working, making my mind work.

I'm in a folkloric dance. [Teachers] say, "Oh, Yolanda, this is coming up. Do you want to go? I know you dance . . . ."

They brought a show last time, about air and jets. . . . And some lady was working around there. . . . The vice-principal came up to me: "That's a good chance for you, 'cause I know you talk Spanish and English . . . ."

They just really get along with me. They tell what their lives are . . . and they compare them with mine. We really get along with each other. . . . Actually, it's fun around here if you really get into learning.

My social studies class is kind of like really hard for me. But some of the things, I don't know, I find really interesting. . . . I like learning. I like really getting my mind working for that.

[My English teacher] doesn't get along with any of us. She just does the things and sits down.

[Classroom] materials are too low. I mean, they have enough materials and everything, but I mean . . . the kind of problems they have. . . . They're too low.

We are supposed to be doing higher things. And like they take us too slow, see, step by step. And that's why everybody takes it as a joke.

[Education] is good for you. . . . It's like when you eat. It's like if you don't eat in a whole day, you feel weird. You have to eat. That's the same thing for me.

The Benefits of Being Mexican

I feel proud of myself. I see some other kids that they say, like they'd say they're Colombian or something. They try to make themselves look cool in front of everybody. I just say what I am and I feel proud of myself. . . . I don't feel bad like if they say, "Ooh, she's Mexican" or anything. . . . It's like you get along with everything; you're Spanish and English, and you understand both. . . . Once you get the hang of it, you'll start getting practice with people and teachers . . . no matter if you talk English or Spanish.

For me, it's good. For other people, some other guys and girls, don't think it's nice; it's like, "Oh, man, I should've been born here instead of being over there." Not me, it's okay for me being born over there 'cause I feel proud of myself. I feel proud of my culture.

COMMENTARY

Communication emerged as a central theme in Yolanda's interview. Whether discussing family, school, or friends, Yolanda sees communication as crucial for success. Given the primacy of the family in Mexican and Mexican American culture, this consistent communication has had a positive influence. Yolanda sees it as one aspect of her mother's care. She and her mom "communicate," she says, because they talk to each other about many things, including "girl stuff." Grades provide another issue for Yolanda and her mother to communicate about. Grades are meaningful to her, but only in the sense that they motivate her to work harder. "You feel some of your body falling off when you see F's around your grades," she said dramatically during one of her interviews.

Yolanda's mother is typical of other Mexican parents in her desire to have her children succeed in school. She talks to them about the importance of school and supports their accomplishments, but she may be uncertain about how else to help them succeed. This is confirmed by Guadalupe Valdez's research with Mexican immigrant families to determine how they defined success. She found that success was based on how they defined "the good life" in Mexico as well as their desire to prevent their children from experiencing the same kind of oppression they knew. But in the U.S. context, these families were unaware of what was needed for their children to succeed.[6]

Given the great emphasis in middle-class families on developing the kinds of attitudes and behaviors that lead to academic success, families such as Yolanda's are at a distinct disadvantage. Yolanda's mother has been very successful at imparting certain values and goals to her children. The fact remains, however, that European American, middle-class parents, given their own experiences and exposure to the schools, are much more aware of those activities that lead to academic success than are poor and working-class parents from linguistic and cultural backgrounds different from the mainstream. Although Yolanda's mother has been able to give her great motivation and discipline, she has been unable to give her the actual tools or engage her in some of the activities she may need for further success in school. Imbedded in this situation are implications for the responsibility of the schools to assist such parents. The interaction and support between home and school in affirming the messages and activities each values become consequential for ensuring the success of all students. Yet in spite of some families' inability to prepare their children for learning academic skills, communication is at the very least a necessary first step. Yolanda seems to understand and appreciate this fact.

Yolanda also talked about communication in school. She thinks carefully about the advice she would give teachers for providing a better education. She wants teachers to try to understand all their students, but especially those who need extra help, and who hang out in the street, "like people that dress kind of like weird, if you know what I mean."

Gender expectations, including the traditional roles assigned to women in her culture as well as the mainstream culture, have left their imprint on Yolanda in ways that can be considered both limiting and affirming. She is adamant, for instance, about not wanting to get married. This may represent a liberating decision, given her analysis of marriage ("It's cause I've been having so many experiences by my family," she explains). However, she has tentatively selected at least one prospective career (i.e., flight attendant) that reinforces women's role as servers. Interestingly, she herself describes attendants as "kind of maids" on airplanes. She is still young and these plans are likely to change, particularly given Yolanda's great determination and strength of character. In any event, she describes her future as "working, being happy, having fun and freedom," and knowing she is doing the best she can.

Young people succeed when they surround themselves with people and an environment that supports their success. It can almost be described as a cloak for success, keeping out the negative influences and corralling the positive ones. Yolanda has done this in several ways. For example, she talks about her best friend, the one who "helped me grow up," as the most significant person in keeping her motivated. Contrary to conventional wisdom, most adolescents have internalized the values held by the adults who surround them. In looking for friends, therefore, they seek those who voice the same values.

Although the junior high school environment makes her feel both "comfortable and afraid," time and again Yolanda mentioned teachers as pivotal in helping her succeed in school. Teachers who "care" have made the difference. Yolanda's articulation of this factor reinforces what national commissions have been reporting for some time.[7] Teachers' caring makes a difference, for example, when children first enter a new school. Yolanda remembers the trauma of moving to California as a first-grader. It was tremendously difficult adjusting to a new culture, community, and school, although she has always been a good student. Yolanda's positive perceptions about learning are bound to the environment that has been established in her school: one that emphasizes learning. She is enthusiastic about learning, and this eagerness is especially reserved for her challenging classes.

Whereas Yolanda is quick to ascribe her success to teachers, she has also given some thought to what might be holding her back. She cites "problems at home" and not having her father around as two barriers. At school, she believes that teachers create barriers, too. She criticizes attitudes or practices that she feels detract from a positive learning environment. One of these is the low expectations teachers have of some students (materials are "too low"). Yolanda has put her finger on a theme that has emerged in the literature concerning the education of other Mexican American students. In tracking the progress of 100 "at risk" Mexican American students in Austin, Texas, Harriet Romo and Toni Falbo found that many of them dropped out because they correctly perceived that the education they were getting was at such a low level that it would not give them the kind of life they wanted after graduation. None of the students dropped out because they felt the classes were too difficult, but because of boredom or lack of motivation. In one case, the researchers document how a teacher directly told one of the more promising students, "Well, you're not college material."[8]

Yolanda wants teachers to understand that unlike some of the stereotypes about Mexican American students, "they try real hard, that's one thing I know." Yet in spite of the criticisms she has of her school and some teachers, Yolanda clearly loves learning. The metaphor of "education as nutrition" is a good example ("It's good for you. . . . It's like when you eat").

Tied to her positive feeling as a student is an equally positive self-concept. Yolanda is quite certain that being Mexican is a good thing. Her culture is important to her. She compares herself with other Mexican American children who deny their background, and it is clear that she feels sorry for them. Her attitude about the benefits of being Mexican can probably be traced to several sources. One is her family, which reinforces cultural pride in the home. Even when this pride is conscious, however, it often is insufficient to counteract many of the negative messages young people pick up about their devalued status in society.

Frequently, the school is what makes the difference in whether students accept or reject their culture, as seen in research by Iadicola with sixth-grade Hispanic students in selected California schools.[9] He examined the relationship between power differences and curriculum factors in schools to explore the "symbolic violence" suffered by the students. "Symbolic violence," as used by Bourdieu, refers to the maintenance of power relations of the dominant society in the school.[10] It is evident in such concrete factors as the presence or absence of specific people, topics, or perspectives in the curriculum or through the power differences among students, staff, and parents. In the curriculum, for example, how "knowledge" is defined, who are portrayed as "makers of history," which heroes are acknowledged and celebrated, and so on, determine whether groups of people are either valued or devalued in that environment.

Specifically, according to Iadicola, "symbolic violence is performed through curricular choices and pedagogical techniques which impose within the school the power relations of the larger society."[11] Such a process has succeeded when dominated groups learn to view their own culture as unworthy and to regard themselves as "culturally deprived." They begin to identify not with their own group but with the dominant group. Iadicola found that the higher the level of Anglo dominance in the school, the higher the level of symbolic violence as measured by Hispanic students' attitudes toward their own group. In contrast, the higher the level of Hispanic presence in the curriculum, the higher the level of ethnic salience in self-identification. The school is crucial in giving students information, both formally and informally, about what knowledge is of most worth. As a consequence of this information, at least partially, students develop either pride or shame in their background.

The fact that she began her early schooling in Mexico, where her culture was affirmed and valued, cannot be dismissed as a contributing factor in Yolanda's sense of worth and pride. Matute-Bianchi, for example, in an ethnographic study in California, found that many of the Mexican American students who were doing well in school were born in Mexico.[12] Nevertheless, the role of Yolanda's first elementary school and of her current school in accepting and reflecting at least some aspects of Mexican culture is probably a contributing factor in her academic success. The fact that the culture of Hispanic students is at the very least acknowledged in the educational environment seems to have made a difference in how Yolanda and some of her peers react to their ethnicity.

Yolanda Piedra has several more years of schooling to complete. She is a fortunate young woman in the sense that both her elementary school and her junior high school have been affirming of her culture and language. It is unclear whether the high school she attends will be the same but she has gotten a good start: She knows what it is to be a successful student, and her track record may be enough to keep her going in the same path. Also, in spite of many messages in the larger society to the contrary, she has learned the benefits of being Mexican. It is doubtful that she will lose this sense of self in the years to come. Yolanda has also learned to enjoy learning, to make "her mind work." At this point, probably nothing can take away that now ingrained zeal for education.

TO THINK ABOUT

1. Many of Yolanda's teachers are resolved to provide a productive and positive environment for her and the other students in her school. Besides the examples given, think of other ways in which that type of environment could be achieved in this particular school.
2. Yolanda says that when kids are suspended from school, it is "pushing them to do it again." What does she mean? What are the implications for school disciplinary policies?
3. When Yolanda says of her English teacher, "She just does the things and sits down," what does she mean? What can other teachers learn from this?
4. Yolanda has criticized materials in her classes for "being too low." Why do you think she says this? What kinds of practices can schools develop to counteract this perception?
5. Yolanda was selected "Student of the Month" for her academic success. Some would criticize this practice because it alienates and excludes a large number of students; others believe that it helps to motivate good students. What do you think and why? What other approaches might you recommend?
6. Yolanda's decision to be either a computer programmer or a flight attendant sounds like a contradiction. What factors do you think influenced Yolanda in this? What can schools do to help students make good decisions about their future?

• NOTES TO CHAPTER 6

1. Henry T. Trueba, "Culture and Language: The Ethnographic Approach to the Study of Learning Environments." In *Language and Culture in Learning: Teaching Spanish to Native Speakers of Spanish,* edited by Barbara J. Merino, Henry T. Trueba, and Fabián A. Samaniego (Bristol, PA: Falmer Press, 1993), 26–27.
2. An exception is Donna Gollnick and Philip Chinn, who have included linguistic diversity as a separate issue in their conceptualization of multicultural education; see Donna M. Gollnick and Philip C. Chinn, *Multicultural Education in a Pluralistic Society,* 5th ed. (New York: Maxwell Macmillan International, 1998).
3. By *linguicism,* Skutnabb-Kangas means *"ideologies and structures which are used to legitimate, effectuate and reproduce an unequal division of power and resources (both material and nonmaterial) between groups which are defined on the basis of language."* See Tove Skutnabb-Kangas, "Multilingualism and the Education of Minority Children." In *Minority Education: From Shame to Struggle,* edited by Tove Skutnabb-Kangas and Jim Cummins (Clevedon, England: Multilingual Matters, 1988), 13.
4. Dorothy Waggoner, "Language-Minority School-Age Population Now Totals 9.9 Million." *NABE News,* 18, 1 (15 September 1994), 1, 24–26; Roger E. W-B Olsen,

A 1993 Survey of LEP and Adult ESL Student Enrollments in U.S. Public Schools (Atlanta: Symposium on Language Minority Student Enrollment Data, TESOL, 1993).

5. Reynaldo Macías and C. Kelly, *Summary Report of the Survey of the States' Limited English Proficient Students and Available Educational Programs and Services 1994–1995.* (Washington, DC: United States Department of Education, Office of Grants and Contracts Services, George Washington University, 1996).

6. Alejandro Portes and Rubén G. Rumbaut, *Immigrant America: A Portrait,* 2nd ed. (Berkeley, CA: University of California Press, 1996).

7. United States Bureau of the Census, *Statistical Abstract of the United States, 1997, The National Data Book.* (Washington, DC: Bureau of the Census, 1997).

8. Alejandro Portes and Rubén G. Rumbaut, *Immigrant America: A Portrait.*

9. Roger E. W-B Olsen, *A 1993 Survey of LEP and Adult ESL Student Enrollments in U.S. Public Schools; Federal Education Funding: The Cost of Excellence* (Washington, DC: National Education Association, 1990).

10. Joel Spring, *Deculturalization and the Struggle for Equality: A Brief History of the Education of Dominated Cultures in the United States,* 2nd ed. (New York: McGraw-Hill, 1997). See also Meyer Weinberg, *A Chance to Learn: A History of Race and Education in the U.S.* (Cambridge, Mass.: Cambridge University Press, 1977).

11. James Crawford, *Hold Your Tongue: Bilingualism and the Politics of "English Only."* (Reading, MA: Addison-Wesley, 1992).

12. James Crawford, *Hold Your Tongue.*

13. Lowell C. Rose and Alec M. Gallup, "The 30th Annual Phi Delta Kappa/Gallup Poll of the Public's Attitudes Toward the Public Schools." *Phi Delta Kappan,* 80, 1 (September, 1998), 41–56.

14. James Crawford, *Hold Your Tongue,* 11.

15. As quoted in James Crawford, *Hold Your Tongue,* 59.

16. *New York Times,* March 3, 1981.

17. Jim Cummins, *Negotiating Identities: Education for Empowerment in a Diverse Society* (Ontario, CA: California Association for Bilingual Education, 1996), 75.

18. David Corson, *Language, Minority Education and Gender: Linking Social Justice and Power* (Clevedon, England: Multilingual Matters Ltd., 1993).

19. Judith Ortiz Cofer, *Silent Dancing: A Partial Remembrance of a Puerto Rican Childhood* (Houston, TX: Arte Público Press, 1990), 62.

20. Cristina Igoa, *The Inner World of the Immigrant Child* (New York: St. Martins Press, 1995), 50.

21. David Adams, Barbara Astone, Elsa Nuñez-Wormack, and Ivan Smodlaka, "Predicting the Academic Achievement of Puerto Rican and Mexican-American Ninth-Grade Students." *The Urban Review,* 26, 1 (1994), 1–14.

22. Selase W. Williams, "Classroom Use of African American Language: Educational Tool or Social Weapon?" In *Empowerment through Multicultural Education,* edited by Christine E. Sleeter (Albany, NY: State University of New York Press, 1991).

23. Lourdes Díaz Soto, "Native Language School Success." *Bilingual Research Journal,* 17, 1 and 2 (1993), 83–97.

24. Patricia Gándara, *Over the Ivy Walls: The Educational Mobility of Low-Income Chicanos* (Albany, NY: State University of New York Press, 1995).

25. Ana Celia Zentella, *Growing up Bilingual: Puerto Rican Children in New York.* (Malden, MA : Blackwell, 1997).

26. Alejandro Portes and Rubén Rumbaut, *Immigrant America.*

27. Virginia Collier, *Promoting Academic Success for ESL students: Understanding Second Language Acquisition at School* (Elizabeth, NJ: New Jersey Teachers of English to Speakers of Other Languages—Bilingual Educators, 1995), 14.
28. Catherine Snow, "The Myths Around Bilingual Education." *NABE News,* 21, 2 (1997), 29.
29. Luis C. Moll, "Bilingual Classroom Studies and Community Analysis: Some Recent Trends." *Educational Researcher,* 21, 2 (1992), 20–24, 20.
30. Diane August and Kenji Hakuta, eds., *Educating Language-Minority Children.* Commission on Behavioral and Social Sciences and Education, National Research Council, Institute of Medicine. (Washington, D.C.: National Academy Press, 1998).
31. Sonia Nieto, *The Light in Their Eyes: Creating Multicultural Learning Communities* (New York: Teachers College Press, 1999).
32. Jim Cummins, *Negotiating Identities: Education for Empowerment in a Diverse Society* (Ontario, CA: California Association for Bilingual Education, 1996), 73.
33. David Corson, *Language Minority Education,* 179.
34. Stephen Krashen, *Second Language Acquisition and Second Language Learning* (New York: Pergamon Press, 1981).
35. For a more in-depth discussion of this issue, see Sonia Nieto, "Bringing Bilingual Education out of the Basement, and Other Imperatives for Teacher Education." Edited by Zeynep Beykont, *Bilingual Education Works: Linking Research and Practice in Schools* (Cambridge: Harvard Educational Review, 1999).
36. For research on additive and subtractive bilingualism, see Wallace E. Lambert, "Culture and Language as Factors in Learning and Education." In *Education of Immigrant Students,* edited by A. Wolfgang (Toronto: Ontario Institute for Studies in Education, 1975).
37. Stephen Krashen, "Does Literacy Transfer?" *NABE News,* 19, 6 (May 1, 1996), 36–38. See also Barry McLaughlin, *Myths and Misconceptions about Second Language Learning: What Every Teacher Needs To Unlearn* (Santa Cruz, CA: National Center for Research on Cultural Diversity and Second Language Learning, 1992); and Vickie W. Lewelling, *Linguistic Diversity in the United States: English Plus and Official English* (Washington, DC: ERIC Clearinghouse on Literacy Education for Limited-English-Proficient Adults, 1992).
38. María E. Fránquiz and María de la luz Reyes, "Creating Inclusive Learning Communities through English Language Arts: From *Chanclas* to *Canicas.*" *Language Arts,* 75, 3 (March, 1998), 211–220.
39. Ibid., 217.
40. Cristina Igoa, *The Inner World of the Immigrant Child.*
41. For a more extensive discussion of Bill Dunn's experience, see Sonia Nieto, *The Light in Their Eyes.*
42. Catherine Minicucci, Paul Berman, Barry McLaughlin, Beverly McLeod, Beryl Nelson, and Kate Woodworth, "School Reform and Student Diversity." *Phi Delta Kappan,* 77, 1 (September, 1995), 77–80.
43. Tove Skutnabb-Kangas, "Multilingualism and the Education of Minority Children."
44. *Lau* v. *Nichols,* 414 U.S. 563 (1974).
45. Equal Educational Opportunities Act of 1974, 20 U.S.C. 1703 (f).
46. For in-depth descriptions of the many program models and their implications, see Carlos J. Ovando and Virginia P. Collier, *Bilingual and ESL Classrooms: Teaching in Multicultural Contexts,* 2nd ed. (New York: McGraw-Hill, 1998). Also Wayne P.

Thomas and Virginia Collier, *School Effectiveness for Language Minority Students* (Washington, DC: National Clearinghouse for Bilingual Education, 1997).

47. The National Clearinghouse for Bilingual Education, Washington, DC, has current data on bilingual programs throughout the United States. They provide data and documents on students, programs, and policies and can be reached by phone at (800) 321-NCBE.

48. Donna Christian, *Two-Way Bilingual Education: Students Learning through Two Languages* (Santa Cruz, CA: National Center for Research on Cultural Diversity and Second Language Learning, 1994). For a recent review and in-depth profiles of three programs, see Donna Christian, Christopher Montone, Kathryn J. Lindholm, and Isolda Carranza, *Profiles in Two-Way Immersion Education* (McHenry, IL: Delta Systems, 1997).

49. "Findings of the Effectiveness of Bilingual Education." *NABE News* (1 May, 1998), 5.

50. Nanette Asimov, "Bilingual Surprise in State Testing." *The San Francisco Chronicle,* July 7, 1998, A1.

51. Thomas and Collier, *School Effectiveness for Language Minority Students.* See also Christian, et. al., for the number of two-way programs in the United States.

52. This research was reported in "The NABE No-Cost Study on Families." *NABE News* (1 February 1991), 7.

53. Barbara A. Craig, "Parental Attitudes Toward Bilingualism in a Local Two-Way Immersion Program." *The Bilingual Research Journal,* 20, 3 and 4 (Summer/Fall, 1996), 383–410.

54. Nancy L. Commins, "Parents and Public Schools: The Experiences of Four Mexican Immigrant Families," *Equity and Choice,* 8, 2 (1992), 40–45.

55. Thomas and Collier, *School Effectiveness for Language Minority Students,* 1997.

56. Gary Orfield, Gary D. Bachmeier, David R. James, and Tamela Eitle, *Deepening Segregation in American Public Schools* (Cambridge, MA: Harvard Project on School Desegregation, 1997).

57. Mary Cazabon, Wallace E. Lambert, and Geoff Hall, *Two-Way Bilingual Education: A Progress Report on the Amigos Program* (Santa Cruz, CA: National Center for Research in Cultural Diversity and Second Language Learning, 1993).

58. Luis C. Moll, "Bilingual Classroom Studies and Community Analysis: Some Recent Trends." *Educational Researcher,* 21, 2 (March 1992), 20–24.

NOTES TO MANUEL GOMES'S CASE STUDY

1. I am grateful to Carol Shea for the interviews and transcriptions and for many valuable insights in the development of this case study. Carol is a guidance counselor at Madison Park High School in Boston.

2. Laurie Olsen, *Made in America: Immigrant Students in Our Public Schools* (New York: The New Press, 1997).

3. Colm Foy, *Cape Verde: Politics, Economics, and Society* (London: Pinter Publications, 1988).

4. Colm Foy, *Cape Verde;* see also Office of Bilingual Bicultural Education, *A Handbook for Teaching Portuguese-Speaking Students* (Sacramento, CA: California State Department of Education, 1983).

5. Office of Bilingual Bicultural Education, *Handbook for Teaching Portuguese-Speaking Students.*

6. Laurie Olsen, *Made in America.*

7. For a discussion of language brokering among immigrant students, see Lucy Tse, "Language Brokering in Linguistic Minority Communities: The Case of Chinese- and Vietnamese-American Students." *The Bilingual Research Journal*, 20, 3 and 4 (Summer/Fall, 1996), 485–498.

NOTES TO YOLANDA PIEDRA'S CASE STUDY

1. I am grateful to Mac Lee Morante for the interviews and background information for this case study. Dr. Morante is a mental health therapist and a school psychologist in California.
2. Lorraine McDonnel and Paul T. Hill, *Newcomers in American Schools: Meeting the Educational Needs of Immigrant Youth* (Santa Monica, CA: Rand Corporation, 1993).
3. *The Condition of Bilingual Education in the Nation: A Report to the Congress and the President* (Washington, DC: United States Department of Education, Office of the Secretary, 30 June 1992).
4. The terms *Mexican, Mexican American,* and *Chicano* are all used here, depending on the context. For example, Yolanda identifies herself as "Mexicana" or Mexican. Other students may use the term *Mexican American* or *Chicano.* These distinctions usually depend on place of birth, upbringing, social class, language used at home, and other factors.
5. Cinco de Mayo is the celebration of Mexican independence from France. On May 5, 1862, French forces that had invaded Mexico were defeated at Puebla. It is a major Mexican holiday and is celebrated in many schools with Mexican American students.
6. Guadalupe Valdés, *Con Respeto: Bridging the Distance Between Culturally Diverse Families and Schools* (New York: Teachers College Press, 1996).
7. For a review about the importance of caring with Puerto Rican and other Latino students, see Sonia Nieto, "Fact and Fiction: Stories of Puerto Ricans in U.S. Schools." *Harvard Educational Review,* 68, 2 (Summer, 1998), 133–163.
8. Harriet D. Romo and Toni Falbo, *Latino High School Graduation: Defying the Odds* (Austin, TX: University of Texas Press, 1996), 20.
9. Peter Iadicola, "Schooling and Symbolic Violence: The Effect of Power Differences and Curriculum Factors on Hispanic Students' Attitudes toward Their Own Ethnicity." *Hispanic Journal of Behavioral Sciences,* 5, 1 (1983), 21–43.
10. See Pierre Bourdieu, *Outline of Theory and Practice* (Cambridge: Cambridge University Press, 1977).
11. Peter Iadicola, "Schooling and Symbolic Violence," 22.
12. María E. Matute-Bianchi, "Situational Ethnicity and Patterns of School Performance among Immigrant and Nonimmigrant Mexican-Descent Students." In *Minority Status and Schooling: A Comparative Study of Immigrant and Involuntary Minorities,* edited by Margaret A. Gibson and John U. Ogbu (New York: Garland, 1991).

chapter 7

Toward an Understanding of School Achievement

There's so much to learn and that's all I want to do is just learn, try to educate my mind to see what I could get out of it.

Paul Chavez, interviewee

*A*s improbable as it might sound, these are the words of a young man who was suspended and expelled from school on many occasions. A gang member with a difficult family life, Paul had managed to be accepted into an alternative school, where he was experiencing academic success for only the second time in his life. As you will see in his case study, which follows this chapter, Paul is resolute about continuing his education and becoming a teacher or counselor in order to help young people like himself. But given his background and experiences, few people would have believed that he was capable of learning. Conventional theories of academic success or failure do not explain cases such as Paul's.

The simple dichotomy traditionally used to explain the school failure of students, particularly those from culturally diverse and poor backgrounds, presented in the preceding chapters, can be summarized as follows: School failure is the fault either of the students themselves, who are genetically inferior, or of the social characteristics of their communities, which suffer from economic and cultural disadvantages and thus are unable to provide their children with the necessary preparation for academic success.[1] Alternative explanations are that school failure is caused by the structure of schools, which are static, classist, and racist and represent the interests of the dominant classes, or by cultural incompatibilities between the home and the school.[2]

In this chapter we will review a number of theories about the complex conditions that may affect school achievement, then consider how these conditions, acting in tandem, may influence the academic success or failure of students. With this discussion as a basis, case studies of two students who have not been successful in school, Ron Morris and Paul Chavez, will be presented. Both of these young men were written off by their respective schools and teachers as incapable of becoming successful students. Their cases demonstrate that learning can take place even in the most difficult personal and societal circumstances.

DEFICIT THEORIES REVISITED

The theory that genetic or cultural inferiority is the cause of academic failure has been a recurrent theme in U.S. educational history. Throughout the past half century, much of the research on school failure has focused on the inadequacy of students' home environment and culture. In an early review of research concerning the poor achievement of Black children, for instance, Stephen Baratz and Joan Baratz found that most of it was based on the assumption that Black children were deficient in language, social development, and intelligence. This assumption resulted in blaming students' failure to achieve on their so-called deficits; singled out for blame were children's *poorly developed language* (more concretely, the fact that they did not speak standard English); an *inadequate mother* (the assumption being that low-income Black mothers were invariably poor parents); *too little stimulation* in the home (that their homes lacked the kinds of environments that encouraged learning); *too much stimulation* in the home (their homes were too chaotic and disorganized or simply not organized along middle-class norms); and a host of other, often contradictory hypotheses. Baratz and Baratz found that the homes and backgrounds of Black children and poor children in general were classified in the research as "sick, pathological, deviant, or underdeveloped."[3] Such caricatures, which continue to exist, are of little value to teachers and schools who want to provide all children with a high-quality education.

The case studies of Ron Morris and Paul Chavez that follow this chapter are compelling examples of life in difficult circumstances: Both live in poverty with large families headed by single mothers; both have been involved in antisocial and criminal behavior; and both have had negative schooling experiences. One might be tempted to write them off because of these circumstances, but as you shall see in their case studies, both Ron and Paul are now learning successfully in alternative schools. Deficit explanations of school achievement cannot explain their success.

The popularity of deficit theories has waxed and waned during the past three decades as newer and more comprehensive explanations for school underachievement have taken root. But these viewpoints held great sway during the 1960s, and they were responsible for much of the social and educational policy in the following decades. Genetic and cultural inferiority arguments have left a legacy that is still apparent, as we saw in the previous chapter, for example, in the way that bilingual education continues to be conceptualized as a "compensatory" program. The rationale for compensatory education was that children from so-called "deprived homes" needed to be compensated for their genetic, cultural, or linguistic deprivation.

An early critic of deficit theories, William Ryan, turned the argument of cultural deprivation on its head by claiming that it was a strategy to "blame the victim." In a book that had a great impact in challenging the theory of cultural inferiority during its heydey in the 1960s, he stated,

> We are dealing, it would seem, not so much with culturally deprived children as with culturally depriving schools. And the task to be accomplished

is not to revise, amend, and repair deficient children, but to alter and transform the atmosphere and operations of the schools to which we commit these children.[4]

Theories of genetic inferiority and cultural deprivation popularized during the 1960s have left their mark on the schooling of poor children and children of color. These theories are not only classist and racist but also simply inadequate in explaining the failure of so many students. Although the social and economic conditions of their communities and families can be significant contributing factors in the academic failure of students, they alone are not the cause of student failure or success. Moreover, students' home and family situations are seldom subject to change by the school. Since schools cannot change the poverty or living conditions of students, the challenge is to find ways to teach children effectively in spite of the poverty or other disabling conditions in which they may live.

Students' identities—that is, their race, ethnicity, social class, and language, among other characteristics—can also have an impact on their academic success or failure, but it is not these characteristics per se that *cause* failure. Rather, it is the school's *perception* of students' language, culture, and class as *inadequate* and *negative*, and the subsequent devalued status of these characteristics in the academic environment, that help to explain school failure. In Paul Chavez's case study, his early gang affiliation had a decided effect on the academic expectations that teachers had of him.

That the behaviors of middle-class parents of any race or ethnic group tend to be different from those of poor parents is amply documented. Parents living in poverty may be either unaware of the benefits of what middle-class parents know by experience or unable to provide certain activities for their children. Middle-class parents, for example, tend to engage in school-like prereading activities much more regularly than do working-class parents. Schools deem other activities in which middle-class parents and their children participate as essential to educational success: going to the library on a consistent basis, attending museums and other cultural centers, and providing a host of other experiences that schools and society have labeled "enriching."

Whether these activities are in fact enriching is not in question; the problem is that the activities of poor families, some of which may be just as enriching, are not viewed in the same way. For example, many poor families travel either to their original home countries or to other parts of the United States from where they originally came. Children may spend summers "down South" or in Jamaica or Mexico, but what they learn on these trips commonly is ignored by the school in spite of its potentially enriching character. It never occurred to me, for example, that my own experience of visiting family for an entire summer between my fifth and sixth grades might be of interest to my teacher or classmates. Mind you, my teachers never told me this directly, but I had already gotten the message that issues of consequence to my family carried no great weight in school. That I perceived this to be the case is a shame: When I think of the giant tarantula I caught, froze, and brought home, or of the many things I learned about living on a farm, or of how my

Spanish substantially improved that summer, I can only conclude that these things might indeed have been interesting to my teacher and classmates.

Students' ability to develop literacy and other academic skills as traditionally defined by schools is necessary for academic success. But if defined only in this way, academic success is dysfunctional because it encourages students to lose part of their identity in the process. Students' abilities to use the skills, talents, and experiences learned at home and in the community to further their learning must also be included in a definition of academic success.

Shirley Brice Heath's classic research with a Black community that she called "Trackton" is an compelling example. She found that the kinds of questioning rituals in which parents and other adults engaged with children were not preparing the children adequately for school activities.[5] In observing the White middle-class teachers of these children, she found that the questions they asked the students were qualitatively different from the kinds of questions to which the children were accustomed at home. Teachers' questions, for example, concerned pulling attributes of things out of context and naming them (e.g., to identify size, shape, or color). In contrast, in their homes the children were asked questions about whole events or objects as well as about their uses, causes, and effects. The questions their parents asked them often required the children to make analogical comparisons and understand complex metaphors. These questions often were linguistically complex and they required a sophisticated use of language on the part of the children. Often there was no one "right" answer, because answers usually involved telling a story or describing a situation.

The result of the different kinds of questions asked in the different contexts was a perplexing lack of communication in the school: Normally communicative students were silent and unresponsive to teachers' questions, and teachers assumed that their students were deficient in language or unintelligent. There was nothing *wrong* with the questions asked by the families in Trackton; they were simply different from those asked in school and therefore they placed the children at a disadvantage for school success.

Through a research project with Heath, the teachers became aware of the differences in questioning rituals, and they began to study the kinds of questions that adults in Trackton asked. Some of these could be called "probing questions" and teachers began using them in their school lessons. Teachers were then able to use these kinds of questions as a basis for asking more traditional "school" questions, to which children also needed to become accustomed if they were to be successful in school. The results were dramatic: Children became active and enthusiastic participants in these lessons, a dramatic change from their previous passive behavior.

This felicitous example of learning to use the culture of students in their education contradicts the scenario of failure in many schools, where parents are expected to provide help in ways they may be unable. Some parents are unaware of how to give their children concrete support in areas such as homework, but this lack of support in itself does not necessarily produce school failure. For example, in her research with Punjabi students, Margaret Gibson reported that most parents were not able to give their children the kinds of support generally deemed as essential for academic success by schools.[6] Yet the majority of students she studied were academically successful. The parents' articulated support of education, their use of discipline, and the faith they had in the rewards of education were all crucial to the success of their children.

Blaming parents or children for academic failure begs the question, for the role of schools is to educate *all* students from all families, not only the most academically gifted students from economically advantaged, mainstream, English-speaking, European American families. Because schools can do nothing to change a student's social class or home background, it makes sense to focus on what they can change: themselves. As we saw in Chapter 6, schools sometimes think that they must start out with poor children or children of color as if they were blank slates. In effect, this means tearing down the building blocks the children already have in order to start from a middle-class foundation. School-related skills are of course necessary for academic success, but there is no reason why they cannot be built on the linguistic, cultural, or experiential foundation that children already have. The fact that some children come to school with a rich oral tradition is a case in point. Perhaps their parents never read stories to them but instead *tell* them stories. This experience can either be dismissed by schools as trivial or it can be used as the basis for learning.

Genetic and cultural inferiority theories are not a thing of the past. As recently as 1994, Richard Herrnstein and Charles Murray resurrected the argument that genetic inferiority was the root cause of the academic failure among African American students.[7] Although widely discredited by serious scholars as both ethnocentric and scientifically unfounded (see note 16 in Chapter 4), genetic and cultural inferiority theories survive because they provide a simplistic explanation for complex problems. Moreover, by accepting theories of genetic and cultural inferiority, the detrimental effects on student learning of structural inequality, racism, and poverty do not have to be considered.

But we also need to understand the power of what has been called the *cultural capital* of dominant groups. According to Pierre Bourdieu, cultural capital can exist in three forms: dispositions of the mind and body; cultural goods, such as pictures, books, and other material objects; and educational qualifications. In all three forms, transmission of cultural capital is, according to Bourdieu, "no doubt the best hidden form of hereditary transmission of capital."[8] That is, the values, tastes, languages, dialects, and cultures that have most status are invariably associated with the dominant group. As a consequence, the weight of cultural capital cannot be ignored. To do so would be both naïve and romantic because power, knowledge, and resources are located in the norms of dominant cultures and languages. To imply that working-class students and students from dominated groups need not learn the cultural norms of the dominant group is effectively to disempower the students who are most academically vulnerable. But the curriculum should also be relevant to the cultural experiences and values of students from subordinated groups. A complete education needs to include *both* the norms and canon of the dominant *and* of dominated cultures because including culturally relevant curriculum is a valuable way to challenge a mono-cultural canon.

ECONOMIC AND SOCIAL REPRODUCTION REVISITED

The argument that schools reproduce the economic and social relations of society and therefore tend to serve the interests of the dominant classes, articulated first during the 1970s by scholars such as Samuel Bowles, Herbert Gintis, and Joel Spring placed schools squarely in a political context.[9] According to this theory, the role of the schools was to keep the poor in their place by teaching them the proper attitudes and behaviors for becoming good workers, and to keep the dominant classes in power by teaching their children the skills of management and control that would presumably prepare them to manage and control the working class. Schools therefore reproduced the status quo and not only reflected structural inequalities based on class, race, and gender, but also helped to maintain these inequalities.

Economic and social reproduction theorists maintain that the "sorting" function of schools, to use a term coined by Spring, is apparent in everything from physical structure to curriculum and instruction. For example, the schools of the poor are generally factory-like fortresses that operate with an abundance of bells and other controlling mechanisms, whereas the schools of the wealthy tend to be much more "open" physically and emotionally, allowing for more autonomy and creative thinking on the part of students. Likewise, relations between students and teachers in poor communities reflect a dominant–dominated relationship much more so than in middle-class or wealthy communities. The curriculum also differs: More sophisticated and challenging knowledge is generally taught in wealthy schools, whereas the basics and rote memorization are the order of the day in poor schools. The "sorting" function of the schools results in an almost perfect replication of the stratification of society. Although the theories generally concerned the United States, they are true of all societies.

This thinking revolutionized the debate on the purposes and outcomes of schools and placed the success or failure of students in a new light. The benign, stated purpose of U.S. schooling to serve as an "equalizer" is seriously questioned by these theories. For example, that the majority of students in urban schools drop out is not a *coincidence* but actually an *intended outcome* of the educational system. That is, according to reproduction theory, some students are intentionally channeled by the schools to be either fodder for war or a reserve uneducated labor force. Schools do just exactly what is expected of them: They succeed at creating school failure.

The arguments of the social reproduction theorists are compelling and they have had a tremendous impact on educational thinking since the 1970s. But by concentrating on the labor market purpose of schooling, they tend to fall into a somewhat static explanation of school success or failure. School life, according to this analysis, is almost completely subordinated to the needs of the economy, leaving little room for the role that students and their communities have in influencing school policies and practices. Put in its most simplistic form, this analysis assumes that schooling is simply imposed from above and accepted from below. But schools are complex and perplexing institutions and things are not always this neat or apparent.

Economic and social reproduction theories provide a more persuasive analysis of academic failure than either genetic and cultural inferiority or cultural incompatibility theories because they place schools in a sociopolitical context. But these analyses are also incomplete. They can fall into mechanistic explanations of dynamic processes, assuming a simple cause–effect relationship. Such theories fail to explain why students from some culturally dominated communities have managed to succeed in school, or why some schools in poor communities are extraordinarily successful in spite of tremendous odds.

Another problem with economic and social reproduction theories is that, in emphasizing the role of social class, they almost completely neglect gender and race. But social class *alone* cannot explain why schools are also inequitable for females and for students of racially and culturally subordinated communities.

An additional problem is that the lengthy struggles over schooling in which many communities have been historically involved—including the desegregation of schools, bilingual education, multicultural education, and access to education for females and students with special needs—are not taken into account. If education were simply imposed from above, these reforms would never have found their way, even imperfectly, into the school. Some theorists such as Michael Apple have suggested that schools are a product of such conflicts and that the purposes of the dominant class are never perfectly reflected in the schools, but resisted and modified by the recipients of schooling.[10]

Economic and social reproduction theories help explain how academic failure and success are not unintended outcomes but rather logical results of differentiated schooling. They also help remove the complete burden of failure from students, their families, and communities to the society at large, and they provide a *macroanalytic,* or societal, understanding of schooling. But social reproduction theories generally fail to take cultural and psychological issues into account. They are therefore incomplete.

CULTURAL INCOMPATIBILITIES REVISITED

Another explanation for school failure is that it is caused by cultural incompatibilities; that is, because school culture and home culture are often at odds, the result is a "cultural clash" that produces school failure. According to this explanation, it is necessary to consider the differing experiences, values, skills, expectations, and lifestyles with which children enter school and how these differences, in being more or less consistent with the school environment, affect their achievement. The more consistent that home and school cultures are, the reasoning goes, the more successful students will be. The opposite is also true: The more that students' experiences, skills, and values differ from the school setting, the more failure they will experience.

This explanation makes a great deal of sense and it explains school failure more convincingly than simple deficit theories. That some students learn more effectively in cooperative settings than in competitive settings is not a problem per se. What makes it a problem is that many schools persist in providing competitive environments *only*. Given this reality, cultural differences begin to function as a risk factor. This reasoning turns around the popular conception of "children at risk," so that the risk comes not from within the child but develops as a result of particular school policies and practices.

Likewise, the fact that some students enter school without speaking English is not itself a satisfactory explanation for why they fail in school. Rather, the interpretation of their non-English speaking status, and the value or lack of value given to the child's native language are what matter. Whereas in some schools a student might be identified as *non–English-speaking*, in another school that same child might be called *Khmer-speaking*. The difference is not simply a semantic one, for in the first case the child is assumed to be *missing* language, but in the second case, the child is assumed to possess language already. This was the case with my daughter Marisa, as I mentioned at the beginning of Chapter 6. And because language ability is the main ingredient for school success, how schools and teachers perceive children's language is significant.

The cultural mismatch theory is more hopeful than deterministic explanations such as genetic inferiority or economic reproduction theories because it assumes that teachers can learn to create environments in which all students can be successful learners. It also respects teachers as creative intellectuals rather than as simple technicians: Teachers are expected to be able to develop a critical analysis of their students' cultures and use this analysis to teach all their students effectively. Gloria Ladson-Billings, in coining the term "culturally relevant teaching," has suggested that this kind of pedagogy is in sharp contrast to "assimilationist teaching," whose main purpose is to transmit dominant culture beliefs and values in an uncritical way to all students.[11]

Although the cultural mismatch theory is more comprehensive than the cultural or genetic deficit theories, and without their implicit racist and classist overtones, it too is insufficient to explain why some students succeed and others fail. The extraordinarily high dropout rates among American Indian and Alaska Native students, higher than all other racial or ethnic groups in the United States, is a case in point. According to Richard St. Germaine, addressing cultural discontinuities through the curriculum can help, but this strategy alone is only a partial solution because the structural inequality that produces enormous poverty is left untouched.[12]

Olga Vasquez, Lucinda Pease-Alvarez, and Sheila Shannon studied the role of language and culture in an immigrant Mexican community. They recommend that teachers learn to take advantage of students' linguistic and cultural experiences and their families' resources for learning, but their research also led them to conclude that the cultural discontinuities theory alone is inadequate in predicting the school success or failure of an entire group of people. They suggest, for instance, that an emphasis on cultural differences results in overshadowing other conditions that influence learning, including school climate and teaching styles. In their research, they found a good deal of linguistic and cultural flexibility among the children and families they studied. Some used language in ways similar to middle-class homes, others used language that reflects their Mexican heritage, and some used unique speech patterns depending on the situation. According to these researchers, the Mexican culture in the United States exists within "an intersection of multiple cultures and languages rather than isolated and impenetrable to outside influences."[13]

The research by Vasquez, Pease-Alvarez, and Shannon points to a major weakness of the theory of cultural discontinuity: Scanty attention is given to cultural accommodation or biculturation, just to mention two responses to cultural diversity experienced by immigrants. No culture exists in isolation, and a rigid interpretation of the theory of cultural discontinuity presupposes that all children from the same cultural background are the same. As a result, little regard is given to individual and family differences or school conditions that can also influence learning.

Another problem with the cultural discontinuity theory is that it cannot explain why students from some cultural groups are academically successful, even though by all indications they should not be. Margaret Gibson's ethnographic research has documented that although culturally very different from most of their peers, Punjabi students have been quite successful in school.[14] Their grades and high school graduation rates equal or surpass those of their classmates in spite of severe handicaps: Their families are primarily farm laborers and factory workers and many are illiterate and speak little or no English; they generally have to become fluent in English in nonbilingual settings, and very few of them have received any special assistance; and they have been subjected to tremendous discrimination by both peers and teachers. Also, their home values and the values practiced by the school are in sharp contrast. Given this situation, their cultural background should predispose them to school failure. That this is not the case leads us to other explanations, one of which concerns the differences between voluntary and involuntary immigrants.

THE IMMIGRANT EXPERIENCE VERSUS THE "MINORITY" EXPERIENCE

A traditional argument to explain differences in academic achievement is that it will take students who are not doing well in school a generation or two to climb the ladder of success, just as it took all other immigrants to do so. This argument is a specious one because the educational and historical experiences of African Americans, American Indians, Asian Americans, and Latinos are markedly different from those of other ethnic groups. For one, American Indians, African Americans, and many Mexican Americans can hardly be called new immigrants. Many have been here for generations, and some for millenia; furthermore, some Asians have been here for four or five generations and although many do well in school, others are not as successful.

It is clear that certain peoples represent unique cases of subjugation in U.S. history. This is true of American Indians, who were conquered and segregated on reservations; African Americans, who were enslaved and whose families were torn apart; Mexican Americans, whose land was annexed and who were then colonized within their own country; and Puerto Ricans, who were colonized and still live under the domination of the United States. In addition and probably not incidentally, they are all people of color, and the issue of race remains paramount in explaining their experiences.

In an alternative explanation of school failure and success, John Ogbu has suggested that it is necessary to look not only at a group's cultural background but also at its situation in the host society and its perceptions of opportunities available in that society.[15] He classifies most immigrants in the United States as *voluntary immigrants,* and racial minority group immigrants as either *voluntary* or *involuntary minorites,* that is, those who come of their own free will as compared with those who were conquered or colonized. The latter groups have been incorporated into U.S. society against their will: American Indians, Africans, Mexicans, and Puerto Ricans, among others. According to Ogbu, voluntary immigrants include all European and some Southeast Asian, African, and Central American immigrants, among others. The distinction is not always easy to make, because those who appear on the surface to be voluntary immigrants may not be so at all. But it remains a crucial distinction in explaining the present condition of many groups, including their educational experiences.

Ogbu has concluded that students from particular backgrounds experience a great variability in academic performance, and such variabilities often can be explained by the sociopolitical setting in which they find themselves. These students are not always racially different from the dominant group in a society, but they have lower social and political status. Other differences may also help explain their marginal status, especially their social class, gender, and native language. It is not their differences that make them marginal, but rather the *value* placed on those differences by the dominant society. Several extensive reviews have documented that socially and politically dominated groups have experienced the most severe academic disadvantage.[16] In Japan, for instance, students of Korean descent and students from the Buraku caste tend to do quite poorly in Japanese schools because both are perceived in Japan as less valued than the majority population. Yet when they emigrate to the United States, they are equally successful in school as students from the Japanese majority. In addition, their IQ scores, a supposedly immutable indication of intelligence, also rise when these children emigrate to another society. Their dominated and devalued status in their home country seems to be the deciding factor because those who are in minority positions in their own countries are not subject to the same caste-like status in another society and may therefore be more successful in school.

The same phenomenon has been found among Finns, who do poorly in Swedish schools but quite well in schools in Australia. Their history of colonization and subsequent low status in Swedish society seems to be the key ingredient. In New Zealand, the native Maori perform less well in school than immigrant

Polynesians (who share a similar language and culture), and the Samis in Norway and Irish Catholics in Belfast also do less well than their dominant-group peers.

Similar results have been found closer to home. For example, newly arrived immigrants tend to do better in school and have higher self-esteem than those born in the United States.[17] Their self-esteem and school success depend not just on their ethnicity but also on their interaction with U.S. society, and on the strength of the self-concepts they have developed in their home countries, where they are not seen as "minorities." Similarly some research has concluded that American Indian students, especially in urban settings, are almost completely cut off from their tribal roots, and this has negative consequences both for their self-esteem and their staying power in school.[18] Again, the differences in these situations seem to be the sociopolitical context of schooling.

The visions, hopes, dreams, and experiences of voluntary and involuntary minorities also need to be kept in mind. According to Ogbu, most voluntary minorities have a "folk theory" of school success that sees the United States as a land of opportunity, where one gets ahead through education and hard work. According to this view, even a relative newcomer with few skills and little education can succeed economically. Their children can experience even more success if they work hard in school and apply themselves. The fact that they may have to undergo great sacrifices, including racism, economic hardships, and working at several menial jobs at the same time, is understood and accepted.

In the case of the Punjabis studied by Gibson, there were few employment and educational opportunities and sometimes even more discrimination in their home country than in the United States. Given their new situation, immigrants such as the Punjabis are happy to make great sacrifices for what they consider to be certain gains. Gibson found that they were more than willing to play the school game by the established rules.[19] Immigrants coming from war-torn countries or refugee camps, or who have experienced the death of loved ones, may not consider living in an urban ghetto and engaging in backbreaking work to be a severe hardship. Marcelo Suarez-Orozco, for example, documents the extraordinary success of many Central Americans, who go to the same schools and live in the same impoverished and crime-filled neighborhoods as Mexican Americans, who on the contrary have been much more unsuccessful in the schools.[20]

Ogbu claims that the major problem in the academic performance of children from what he calls "castelike" minorities is not that they possess a different language, culture, or cognitive or communication style. The problem lies instead in the nature of the history, subjugation, and exploitation they have experienced *together with* their own responses to their treatment. Caste-like minorities in the United States tend to perceive schooling as providing unequal returns. In their communities, the children do not see their elders getting jobs, wages, or other benefits commensurate with their level of education.

Also, given the long history of discrimination and racism in the schools, involuntary minority children and their families are often distrustful of the educational system. Children in these communities have routinely been subjected to what Cummins calls "identity eradication,"[21] where their culture and language have been stripped away as one of the conditions for school success. These negative experiences result in their perception that equal educational opportunity and the "folk theories" of getting ahead in the United States are myths. The "folk theories," however, are readily accepted by immigrants who have not had a long history of discrimination in this country.

It is not unusual for students from caste-like minorities to engage in what Ogbu calls "cultural inversion," that is, to resist acquiring and demonstrating the culture and cognitive styles identified with the dominant group. These behaviors are considered "White" and include being studious and hardworking, speaking standard English, listening to European classical music, going to museums, getting good grades, and so on. Even extremely bright students from these groups may try just to "get by" because they fear being ostracized by their peers if they engage in behaviors that conform to the mainstream culture. They must cope, in the words of Signithia Fordham and John Ogbu, "with the burden of acting White."[22] They see little benefit in terms of peer relationships in being successful students. Those who excel in school may feel both internal ambivalence and external pressures not to manifest such behaviors and attitudes. In their research in a predominantly African American school, Fordham and Ogbu found that successful students who were accepted by their peers also were either very successful in sports or had found another way to hide their academic achievement. According to Ogbu, involuntary minority parents, who themselves have had a long history of discrimination and negative experiences at school, may subconsciously mirror these same attitudes, adding to their children's ambivalent attitudes about education and success.

Many involuntary minority students choose to emphasize cultural behaviors that *differentiate* them from the majority and are in opposition to it, or what Ogbu calls *oppositional behavior*. Such behaviors include language, speech forms, and other manifestations that help to characterize their group but that are contrary to the behaviors promoted by the schools.

NEW PERSPECTIVES ABOUT THE IMMIGRANT AND "MINORITY" EXPERIENCES

The theories of John Ogbu and other educational anthropologists who were investigating the schooling experiences of immigrant students appeared together for the first time in the *Anthropology and Education Quarterly* journal in 1987, and they have had a profound influence on educational thought since then.[23] These theories have been enormously helpful in explaining the differences in the school experiences of students of various backgrounds. But the theories have also been criticized as being incomplete, ahistorical, and inflexible in allowing for individual differences. For example, Ogbu's theory may result in placing an inordinate responsibility on students and families without taking into account conditions outside their control that also affect learning. In addition, Ogbu's theories do not explain the long struggle of African American people for educational equality and the tremendous faith so many "involuntary minority" communities have had in the promise of education.

His explanation of *oppositional culture* has been criticized as being dangerously close to the old concept of *the culture of poverty*, a deficit theory developed by Oscar Lewis in the 1960s and roundly criticized for its racist and ethnocentric overtones.[24]

In 1997, *Anthropology and Education Quarterly* again addressed the issue of ethnicity and school performance, returning to the theories of Ogbu and others that had been introduced a decade earlier. In this issue, the authors attempt to complicate the immigrant/involuntary minority typology presented in the 1987 issue.[25] According to Margaret Gibson, the editor of the newer issue, recent studies in the United States pose a direct challenge to Ogbu's framework, especially because of its inability to account for intragroup variability: That is, why do some "involuntary" minorities do well in school while others do not? Some scholars and educators have found these theories too dichotomous and deterministic. For example, the typology does not neatly fit all groups, such as Mexican Americans, who share elements of both voluntary and involuntary minorities. Another major criticism discussed in the 1997 issue is the almost complete absence of gender and generational differences in the original theories.

Specifically, the newer issue of the journal compared some countries in Europe to countries such as the United States that are dominated by immigrants in order to determine whether or not Ogbu's model can be applied in other countries. Gibson concludes that Ogbu's typology works better in "new nations," that is, traditional immigrant-receiving countries such as the United States, Canada, and Israel, and less well in the "old nations" of Europe that once were colonizers and now are receiving large numbers of immigrants. But even in the United States, Ogbu's model does not explain generational differences: Recent studies have found that the second generation of "voluntary minorities" is experiencing as much school failure as more established "involuntary minorities" because they do not wholeheartedly accept the "folk theory" of success as did their parents. They are also less likely to perceive the long-term benefits of hard work and study.[26]

Another criticism has to do with the role and influence of oppositional culture. As viewed by Ogbu, oppositional culture is detrimental to academic success because, in rejecting behaviors and attitudes that can lead to success, students are in effect jeopardizing their own futures. The possibility that African American students could be *both* oppositional and academically successful is not presented as a possibility in this theory. In contrast to this viewpoint, in research with six highly successful African American high school students, Carla O'Connor found that a collective orientation had the effect of facilitating a sense of hope and promoting academic achievement. The six students she studied were acutely aware of racism and other injustices and they were oppositional to the extent that they actively resisted injustice. But their opposition did not mean that they rejected the strategies they needed to become successful students.[27]

O'Connor concluded that opposition is not always damaging to students: When it leads to the active resistance of oppression, it can actually motivate students to learn so that they can change. Likewise, David Gillborn, who has studied youths of various backgrounds in Great Britain, suggests that the dichotomy between resistance and conformity is too simplistic because it overlooks the great complexity of students' responses to schooling. That is, accommodation does not guarantee that success will follow, nor is it the only way to be academically successful; similarly, opposition does not necessarily lead to failure.[28]

To understand this process more clearly, we now turn to a consideration of the concept of resistance.

RESISTANCE THEORY

Resistance theory, as articulated by scholars such as Henry Giroux, Jim Cummins, and others adds another layer to the explanation of school failure.[29] According to this theory, *not learning* what schools teach can be interpreted as a form of political resistance. Frederick Erickson maintains that whereas cultural differences may cause some initial school failures and misunderstandings, it is only when they become entrenched over time that *not learning,* a consistent pattern of refusing to learn, becomes the outcome of schooling.[30]

Resistance theory is helpful because it attempts to explain the complex relationship of disempowered communities and their schools. Students and their families are not only victims of the educational system but also actors. They learn to react to schools in ways that make perfect sense, given the reality of the schools, although some of these coping strategies may in the long run be self-defeating and counterproductive. Herb Kohl, in describing what he labels as students who refuse to learn, has concluded, "Over the years I've come to side with them in their refusal to be molded by a hostile society and have come to look upon not-learning as positive and healthy in many situations."[31]

There are numerous examples of students' resistance, and they range from innocuous to dangerous: inattention in class, failure to do homework, negative attitudes toward schoolwork, poor relationships with teachers, misbehavior, vandalism, and violence are all illustrations of students' resistance. We see many of these manifestations of resistance in the case study of Ron Morris that follows this chapter. Ron stated that he would actually decide when he was going to be destructive in school. He did this, he said, because he was not learning anything new, and what he did learn mattered little in his daily life.

The most extreme form of refusing education is dropping out. Michelle Fine's study of a large urban school found two major reasons for students' decisions to leave: a political stance of resistance and disappointment with the "promise of education." Many of the students she spoke with were articulate in their resistance to school; even some of those who stayed were unsure what benefits they would derive from their education.[32]

But what causes students to resist education and otherwise engage in behaviors that might ultimately jeopardize their chances of learning? There is no simple answer to this question, but one probable response is a school climate that rejects students' identities. This is nowhere more evident than in Ron's case study. He was eloquent in describing how he felt the first time he found himself and his people in the curriculum. His reaction was to want to come to school every day because, as he said, "This is real!"

In his research among Yup'ik students and teachers, Jerry Lipka found that resistance was virtually nonexistent, and he concluded that resistance theory "makes much less sense in a classroom where the teacher is your uncle or your aunt and where most of the school employees come from your community."[33] This being the case, what are the implications for students of culturally dominated backgrounds? Does it mean that they always need to be taught by teachers from their own cultural communities? This situation makes sense in some places, but it is untenable and unrealistic in others. A more comprehensive view of students' academic success or failure is needed.

A MORE COMPREHENSIVE VIEW

No simple explanation accounts for student achievement or failure. As we have seen in this chapter, most explanations have been inadequate or incomplete: Some have failed to consider the significance of culture in learning; others have not taken into account the social, cultural, and political context of schooling; and still others have placed all the responsibility for academic failure or success on students and their families. Even the persistence of racism and discrimination, or the presence of unjust policies and practices in schools, or the role that schools play in reproducing existing societal inequities do not by themselves explain school failure.

Underachievement, as Jim Cummins has suggested, is also the result of the interactions between teachers, students, and their families.[34] When teachers respect and affirm the identities and experiences of students and their families, they also change the nature of the interactions they have with them, and this can help promote student achievement. In both the case studies of Ron and Paul, the staff's closeness with students and their families has paid off in the students' growing association with school and learning.

Also, how students and communities *perceive* and *react* to schools is another consideration in explaining school achievement. But in spite of the perceptions and reactions of particular groups to schools, there are always individual exceptions. Not all African American students, even those from economically oppressed communities, fail; some do not see school success as "acting White;" likewise, not all voluntary immigrants are successful in school. Unless we look at individual cases as well as at entire groups, we fall into rather facile but not always accurate explanations of failure. These can lead to stereotypes and inappropriate educational expectations.

But the policies and practices of schools, and the hopes and expectations they have for students, are also key variables in explaining student academic achievement. In Paul's case study, you will see the positive effect that participating in developing the school rules had on him. In the case of Ron, he characterized the curriculum in his former schools as meaningless because it "is not gonna let us know who we really are as people." On the other hand, he described the curriculum in his new school as respecting his identity and experiences.

When teachers and schools believe their students are capable learners and they create appropriate learning environments for them, young people are given a clear and positive message about their worth and abilities. Research on academic behavior among high-achieving African American students, for instance, found that a *combination* of school characteristics *and* individual actions of students together contributed to the achievement differences between high- and low-achieving students.[35] Although African American students with above average reading scores resembled their lower scoring peers in family and school social conditions (including low socioeconomic status, single parent households, and higher rates of segregated schools), the schools attended by higher achievers had a more positive environment and a higher commitment to students. The researchers concluded that *rather than family background*, it was the conditions established by the schools that explained the differences.

Looking beyond just cultural and social class characteristics as determining school achievement can also be empowering because teachers and schools can do something about student learning. School characteristics that have been found to make a positive difference in educational research studies include an enriched and more demanding curriculum, respect for students' languages and cultures, high expectations for all students, and encouragement of parental involvement.[36]

Reforming school structures alone will not lead to substantive improvement in student achievement, however, if such changes are not accompanied by profound changes in what we believe students deserve and are capable of learning. In short, changing policies and practices is a necessary but insufficient condition for improving academic achievement. For example, in research on six high schools that were successful with Latino students, Tamara Lucas, Rosemary Henze, and Rubén Donato found that, in addition to the structural conditions they reviewed, the most significant element in explaining their success was a belief that all students were capable of learning.[37]

Learning environments that may seem at first glance to be totally culturally inappropriate for some children, can in fact be effective. The so-called "Catholic school effect" is a case in point. In some ways, nothing seems more culturally incompatible for African American and Latino students than a Catholic school: Bilingual programs are usually unavailable; classes tend to be overcrowded; and formal environments that stress individual excellence over cooperation are common. Yet Catholic schools have been successful environments for many Latino and African American children, especially those from poor communities. The literature points to the fact that Catholic schools, because of restricted resources, tend to offer all students a less differentiated curriculum, less tracking, and more academic classes. They also have clear, uncomplicated missions and strong social contracts.[38] What may at first glance appear to be incongruous in terms of cultural compatibility is explained by school structures that imply high expectations for all students.

This discussion leads us to the conclusion that school achievement can only be explained by taking into account multiple, competing, and changing conditions: the school's tendency to replicate society and its inequities, cultural and language incompatibilities, the unfair and bureaucratic structures of schools, and the political relationship of particular groups to society and the schools. But it is tricky business to seek causal explanations for school success and failure. How numerous complex conditions are mediated within the school and home settings can also explain students' academic success or failure. All of these conditions help explain in a more comprehensive way the massive school failure of many students. This is the sociopolitical context of multicultural education and it forms the basis for the conceptual framework that has been developed here.

● SUMMARY

In this chapter, we have explored a number of theories regarding conditions that influence school failure and success. The deficit theories popularized in the 1960s were responsible for much of our educational policy during that time and into the present. These theories assumed that children from culturally diverse families or poor neighborhoods were either genetically or culturally inferior to culturally dominant children from the middle class.

An alternative explanation developed during the 1970s was that schools were responsible for school failure because they reproduced the economic and social relations of society and therefore replicated structural inequality. During this time, the cultural mismatch theory was also developed. According to this theory, schools are unsuccessful with a substantial number of students because there is a mismatch between their home cultures and the culture of the school. The argument by John Ogbu and others that there is a crucial distinction between caste-like minorities and immigrant minorities was also developed during the 1970s. This theory argues that cultural differences alone cannot explain the differential school achievement of distinct "minority" groups.

Finally, resistance theory has helped us understand that students and their families are frequently engaged in some form of resistance to the education to which they are exposed. Resistance may be either passive or active and it may have consequences that are counterproductive to the interests of the students who engage in it. Alternatively, resistance can lead to a critical awareness of structural inequality and a desire to succeed academically in order to make change, as we shall see in both case studies that follow this chapter.

I have attempted to develop a comprehensive view of school achievement by providing an analysis and critique of each of these theories. It is clear that no single theory of academic achievement entirely explains why some students succeed in school and others fail. Rather, we need to understand school achievement as a combination of *personal, cultural, familial, interactive, political,* and *societal* issues, and this means understanding the *sociopolitical context* in which education takes place.

● TO THINK ABOUT

1. What does William Ryan mean by "culturally depriving schools"? Can you give some examples?
2. Find out about some of the culturally enriching activities your students are engaged in with their families and communities. How can you use them to create a more culturally affirming classroom?

3. Joel Spring has claimed that our public schools perform a "sorting" role, placing students in school according to their social class. Think about your own experiences and observations, then describe some examples of this "sorting" function.
4. Think of your own students. How accurate do you think John Ogbu's classification of *voluntary* and *involuntary minorities* is? Consider both the advantages and disadvantages of this theory.
5. Think about schools and classrooms with which you are familiar. Have you noticed examples of *student resistance?* If so, what are they and what is their effect?
6. You and a group of your colleagues need to determine why a particular student has been doing poorly in your classes. What will you look at? Why?

Case Study: Paul Chavez

"I don't want to speak too soon, but I'm pretty much on a good road here."

Speaking in an earnest and intense tone, Paul Chavez[1] thinks carefully before sharing his thoughts about the importance of school, the "hood," and his family. Paul is 16 years old and he has already lived a lifetime full of gang activity, drugs, and disappointment. The signs are evident, from his style of dress to the "tag" (tattoo) on his arm, to his reminiscence of "homeboys" who have been killed. Describing himself as Chicano and Mexican American, Paul's is the third generation in his family to be born in Los Angeles. He does not speak Spanish, but says that both his mother and grandmother do even though they too were born and raised here.

Paul lives with his mother, two brothers ages 19 and 9, and two younger sisters. Another brother, 21, does not live at home. His mother is currently trying to obtain her high school equivalency diploma; she failed the test once, but is studying hard to try to pass it next time. She and Paul's father have been separated for about four years, and Paul describes the entire family as "Christian" and says they are all deeply involved in the church except him. His mother is a church leader and his brother is a Bible study leader. Even his father, a recovering alcoholic, who has "lived on the streets" for years and spent time in prison, is now living in what Paul calls a "Christian home," probably a halfway house.

The one-family homes in Paul's East L.A. neighborhood hide the poverty and despair that are easier to see in other urban ghettos, with their high-rise tenements and projects. Here, the mostly Latino families struggle to maintain a sense of community in the well-kept homes on small lots. However, signs of gang activity are apparent in the tags on buildings and walls, and Paul says that an outsider suspected of belonging to another gang is likely to get jumped merely for walking down the street.

School problems began for Paul when he was in third or fourth grade, and he was suspended on numerous occasions for poor behavior. The problem was not lack of ability (his teachers always felt he was smart), but rather lack of interest. He was more interested in belonging to a "school gang," a group of young boys looking for boys in other classes to fight. In spite of the lure of gangs, he remembers fifth grade as the best year he had in school, and he attributes this to Ms. Nelson, the most caring teacher he ever had until now. Paul already wore gang-affiliated attire and he had a reputation as a troublemaker, but she did not let this get in the way of her high expectations of him. It was in her class that he became interested in history, and he still recalls being fascinated by the American Revolution.

By the time he began junior high school, peer pressure, family problems, and street violence brought the situation to a head. Seventh and eighth grades were Paul's worst years, and he did very little schoolwork. He was expelled in eighth grade, and although he was told by school authorities to attend an alternative school in another district, he refused to go and instead stayed home for six months. By ninth grade he was heavily involved in gang activity, joining the 18th Street Gang. Paul says this gang has thousands of members, not only in L.A. but also in other cities and even in other states. Thirteen of his cousins are or have been in the same gang, as has an older brother, so the role of gang as "family" is even more revelant in his case. An uncle and a cousin have both been killed as a result of their gang activity.

Encouraged by his mother, Paul tried to enroll in another program, but again was expelled after a few months. Then he heard about and applied to the Escuela de Dignidad y Orgullo (School of Dignity and Pride), a high school for students who have dropped out of other schools. Heavily Chicano, the school is characterized by a multicultural curriculum with a focus on Chicano history, and it relies on student and staff involvement in its day-to-day operations. The school boasts a variety of services for students, and the staff includes counselors, a psychologist, a probation officer, and several teachers. Paul has not formally been arrested, but because of his previous problems he agreed to a voluntary placement with the probation officer, as he explained during one of his interviews, just to "keep me on the right road."

The road, however, has been far from easy for Paul. He was also expelled from Escuela de Dignidad y Orgullo, and it was only after trying another program and then several months on the street that he realized he wanted to return. All of his friends have quit school, Paul says, and he fears ending up like them. He was accepted once again, although it was not automatic, and he has been doing well since he came back two years ago. Now he spends most of his time at school, doing homework every day when he gets home, and working after school at the local city hall, a job the school found for him. A summer job arranged by the program is also in the works. Paul says that this school is different from any other he has attended because the entire staff cares about and encourages the students, and because Chicano culture and history are central to the curriculum, which makes it a more exciting place to learn.

At this point in his life, Paul even goes to church twice a week with his mother, not because he wants to but because it is one of her rules for living at home. But his philosophy is to take life one day at a time because the lure of gang life is still ever-present. He has not quit the gang, and it is obvious that he is at a crossroads in his life. The next several months may determine which direction his life takes: either an escalating life of crime on the streets or a more promising, albeit less exciting, future of education and work.

Paul's case study highlights two goals he has had for a long time: to be respected and to make something of himself, two goals that are frequently at odds. Another theme that became quickly apparent was the strong influence of his mother and family on his life.

"Everybody's Gotta Get Respect"

I grew up . . . ditching school, just getting in trouble, trying to make a dollar, that's it, you know? Just go to school, steal from the store, and go sell candies at school. And that's what I was doing in the third or fourth grade. . . . I was always getting in the principal's office, suspended, kicked out, everything, starting from the third grade.

My fifth grade teacher, Ms. Nelson . . . she put me in a play and that like tripped me out. Like why do you want *me* in a play? Me, I'm just a mess-up. Still, you know, she put me in a play. And in fifth grade, I think that was the best year out of the whole six years [of elementary school]. I learned a lot about the Revolutionary War, you know. . . . The fifth grade was a grade I'll always remember. Had good friends. We had a project we were involved in. Ms. Nelson was a good teacher. . . . She just involved everyone. We made books, this and that. And I used to like to write, and I wrote two, three books. Was in a book fair and this and that. She did pretty nice things. . . . She got real deep into you. Just, you know, "Come on, you can do it." That was a good year for me, the fifth grade.

I don't know why I got in the gang. I got in just to be in a gang, be somewhere, be known from somewhere. And plus my whole family, I got 13 cousins who are from the 18th Street Gang, so we're pretty much all in it. We're deep in it. . . . We're still there. And I'll be in it forever I guess, 'cause it's my neighborhood and it's just like that over here.

Like you see older cousins going out to parties with girls, you know, talking about the neighborhood [gang] and what happened and this and that. . . . And I remember like two or three years before I got in the neighborhood, I was like . . . "I want to get into the neighborhood. I want to get into 18, get my tag, and this and that." And . . . for that to be a goal for you, that's kind of sick, you know, to be in a gang? And that's the way I thought, you know. . . . It was like, I had a lot of influences on my life . . . more negative than positive, and that's what happened.

My most troubled years was my junior high years. . . . Seventh grade, first day of school, I met this guy and then from there we started to form. And every junior high, you're gonna have a group, okay? You're gonna have a group that you hang around with. . . . And it got to we just started always starting trouble in classes. Whatever period we had, we just started trouble in. And me, I have a great sense of humor, right? I can make people laugh a lot. So then I was always getting kicked out of the classroom. And so what that got me was kind of, I guess popular, right where girls were always around me and . . . I had a big group. . . . But like I was always the one clowning, getting in trouble. So it kind of like set a path for me where I was like all right, so I clown and get popularity. All right, I understand now the program.

I [wasn't] in a gang, but I was dressing pretty still gang affiliated. And so people looked like, "Well, where you from?" "I ain't from nowhere." And that kind of like got me to want to *be* from somewhere so I could tell 'em, "Well, I'm from here . . . ." Those were the years in seventh grade and I was fighting with eighth graders. . . . I'd be in a dance, a little Oriental kid would come up to me and she goes, "I know you, you're Paul" this and that. They would know me. . . . It made me feel good.

I'm into drugs. I'm into weed, marijuana. I like smoking. I always did, you know? Drinking, yes. . . . I've done primos. You know, you get a joint and you put crack inside of primos, smoke it. I don't fuck around with hitting the pipe, freebase, heroin or coke, shooting up slam. None of that shit.

Being in a gang, you think about who you're retaliating, you know, just another Chicano brother. And that's kind of deep. Well, why you're gonna be from a neighborhood, have pride, this and that, and take out your own *raza*, you know?[2] So that kind of always caught me in my mind. . . . You see a lot of your own people just going down because of your neighborhood. And it's a trip. And you got a lot of homeboys that come out from the system, the jails, and it's real segregated in there, you know, the Blacks and Chicanos. And they even got the border brothers, the ones from Mexico who don't speak no English. They're even separated from the Chicanos, the Sureños, that's right from South L.A. . . . Okay, they're paranoid in there, and everybody is like, "What's up with the Blacks? It's on, it's on. We're gonna have a war." And everybody, then they turn little things into big things. . . . So it's really just a race war going on in the inside, and they bring it out to us.

So you get a lot of this negative stuff in the neighborhood, and a lot of it just you either got to take it in, and just dish it out. . . . Like I figure people are just sitting up there watching us killing each other.

See [my gang], we have enemies. See, we're in West L.A., South L.A., Northside and the Eastside, Centralside, and South Centralside. So that's thousands of gang members. So we make enemies everywhere. So we don't get along with nobody. . . . The whole [gang] system is run by youngsters just taking out people for stepping on shoes, you know?

A good time is just where nobody fights, none of your homeboys fight each other. . . . I mean there was a time when we partied and a homey got shot and had to go and, "What happened? Homey is bleeding to death right there." So it's like man, take him to the hospital. That's not a good time. . . . We paint murals for the homeboys, "Rest in Peace." We do all that, you know, barbecues, we have car washes [to raise money] when a homeboy pass away.

It's really hard when you get involved in the neighborhood and you get close to people, and your homeboys pass away. It happened to me already too many, like two times already. . . . Homeboy gets passed away and you get a lot of hate, you know, a lot of hate towards the other neighborhood. And then you get a lot of love towards your neighborhood 'cause you go and you see your homeboys all getting together.

I think right now about going Christian, right? Just going Christian, trying to do good, you know? Stay away from drugs, everything. And every time it seems like I think about that, I think about the homeboys. And it's a trip because a lot of the homeboys are my family too, you know?

It has a great hold on you, and it's like I talk to my cousin. He's still into it real deep. I'm not really. Don't get me wrong: I'm from the neighborhood, but I'm not really deep into it, you know what I mean? . . . But it's like I talk to 'em. "Yeah, we were with the homeboys on the Eastside, blah, blah, blah, this and that," and I'll be like, "Damn," and I think, "I wish I was there getting off on drinking and shit."

I had a cousin, he was 16 in '89 when he passed away. He was my cousin, family, from 18th Street too. And what happened, see, he passed away and that's another tragedy. It's just, you see so much. I'm 16 and I see so much. First his dad passed away and then my cousin, my uncle and my cousin. And you think, "Man, all this because of a gang!" And there's times when you just sit and you think, you sit and you think and you say, "Why? Why? Why? What is this? . . ." But you don't know why, but you have it so much inside of you. . . . It's hard, it's not easy to get rid of. It's something you don't want to get rid of. I don't want to get rid of, but you just got to try to focus on other things right now. . . . I'm from a gang and that's it, and just 'cause I'm from a gang doesn't mean I can't make myself better.

But me, I do care. I have a life and I want to keep it. I don't want to lose it. I have two little sisters and I want to see them grow up too, and I want to have my own family. So, I got the tag, I got a big 18 on my arm where everybody could see it, and that's the way I was about a year ago. You know, man, if you would be talking a year ago I'd be like, "I'm from the neighborhood." I'd be talking to you in slang street all crazy, you know? Now I'm more intelligent.

I try not to get influenced too much, pulled into what I don't want to be into. But mostly, it's hard. You don't want people to be saying you're stupid. "Why do you want to go to school and get a job?" I was talking to my homeboy the other day so [he said] ". . . school? Drop out, like . . . ." "Like, all right, that's pretty good. Thanks for your encouragement" [*laughs*]. See, they trip like that, but they just mess around. That's just a joke but it's like you just think about things like that. I guess your peers . . . they try to pull you down and then you just got to be strong enough to try to pull away.

I got to think about myself and get what I got to get going on. Get something going on, or else nobody else is going to do it. And, yeah, it's true. It is like that. It's where you're starting to think a little different. You sort of know what's happening. All they're thinking about is partying, this and that. Nothing wrong with it, but I got to try to better myself.

Making It Better

I guess in a lot of ways, I am [successful]. A lot of things I'm trying to achieve. Starting something, *already* you're successful, you know? But finishing it, it's gonna make you more complete, successful and complete. Got to have your priorities straight. Get what you got to get done, and get it done, and just be happy when you're doing something.

I came to this school and it was deep here. They got down into a lot of studies that I liked, and there was a lot going on here. But see, I was me, I was just a clown. I always liked to mess around, so they gave me chance after chance. . . . I took it for granted and they kicked me out. They booted me out, right? . . . So I went back to that other school . . . and it was like, "This thing is boring. Nothing going on." And so I called over here and I go, "I need another chance," this and that, to get back into school. So they gave me another chance and that's why I'm here right now, 'cause they gave me a chance.

They get more into deeper Latino history here, and that's what I like. A lot of other, how you say, background, ethnic background. We had even Martin Luther King. We had Cesar Chavez. We had a lot of things.

I never used to think about [being Chicano] before. Now I do . . . being Brown and just how our race is just going out. . . . You know, you don't want to see your race go out like that.

[Chicano], it's what you make it, you know? . . . Let's say I'm Chicano and I dress like a gang member. They're gonna look at you like one of those crazy kids, you know, Mexican kid, Chicano kid. But if you present yourself nice or whatever, it really depends how your outer appears. Like people say it's just *from the inside,* but it's really what's on *the outside,* how you look on the outside, like tattoos and that. So it's like I get discriminated because of a lot of things, and I can't really pinpoint it. So it's like I don't really know if it's 'cause I'm Brown or if it's 'cause of my gang tattoo, so I can't really pinpoint. But for me, as far as me being Chicano, it's prideful, it's pride of your race, of what you are.

[Chicano young people] have some pretty trippy insights of life. It's like they know how to talk to people and they know how to give presentations, you know what I mean? Like what we're doing right now [*referring to the interview*]. . . . A lot of the things they say is pretty deep.

[In this school], they just leave the killings out and talk about how you can make it better, you know what I'm saying? . . . Try to be more of the positive side of being a Brown person, that's what I'm talking about.

A lot of the other alternative schools you can't go because of your gang. It's all gang affiliated. Every single alternative school is gang affiliated. This is the only one where it's all neutral.

[To make school better I would] talk about more interesting things, more things like what *I* would like, students would like. And I would just get more involved, get more people involved. Get things going, not just let them vegetate or . . . on a desk and "Here's a paper," teach 'em a lesson and expect them to do it. You know, get all involved.

Put some music in the school. I mean, put some music and get some like drawings. . . . Get a better surrounding so you feel more like the 'hood, you could learn more, you'll feel more comfortable. This [school] is pretty good, but if you had somebody kicking it, put like a character on the wall of something . . . yeah, like a mural or something, it would be more like a more comfortable setting to work.

Try to find out what *we* think is important. Try to do the best you can to try to get it. The kids want it, they're gonna use it. If they don't want it, they're not, so. . . . I remember the *Diary of Anne Frank.* I was pretty deep into the Nazis and Jews and so that was pretty cool.

There's a lot of different teachers, you know? You can't say really, but [I would want them to have] more patience and more understanding. That's it.

We're not your kids; we're your *students.* You teach us and don't try to control us. I don't know, like a lot of them say, "Oh, my kids . . . you got to obey the rules, face the consequences." Well, how about if we *all* obey the rules and we *all* face the consequences? Why does it always have to be "you guys" face the consequences? Why can't it be like we all do it, you know what I mean?

I think [multicultural education] is important because that goes back to segregating. You got to get to know everybody more better. If you understand them better, you're gonna get along better. So, yeah, I think that would be good.

I'm getting out all I can get out [from his school]. There's so much to learn and that's all I want to do is just learn, try to educate my mind to see what I could get out of it. Anything I can, I'm gonna get out of it.

I try not to expect too much from people. I've been let down a lot, and I just try not to expect too much from people. I just do what I know I can and that's it. . . . No, they didn't let me down *here.* . . . Mostly everybody all encourage me. Like Ms. Falcón right now, you know, "How you doing?" It's all encouragement. Sometimes, I think, "Trip out, like people are always happy [here]."

I was here when they barely opened this school and . . . I brought my mom and my dad and we had a couple of kids here and the staff here. What we did was wrote all the rules, just made an outline of how the school was gonna be. People are gonna get treated right, what you could wear. Everything was done with each other, you know? It wasn't just talked about with the staff and brought to the students, it was the students *and* the staff.

[*What would have made school easier for you?*] If you had asked me that question a year ago, I would have said, "no school!" School would have been made easier if it wasn't so early in the morning [*laughs*]. . . . But school, it will be better if more activities [are] going on. People wouldn't just think of it as a routine, people got into it really where it really meant something. . . . But it's both on the students' part and the teachers' part. It takes both.

The classes [should have] more better learning techniques. It's an advanced age. We got a lot of computer things going on. Get a lot of things going with computers and a lot of things that are going to draw the eye. Catch my eye and I'm gonna be, "oh, all right," and gonna go over there and see what's up.

I think they should get more of these aides, assistants, to be parents, okay? 'Cause the parents, I notice this . . . a parent in a school is more like they got *love.* That's it, they got love and they give it to you. They give it back to more students. I think they should get more like parents involved in the school like to teach this and that. Get more parents involved in the classroom too. Parents have a lot of things to say, I would think, about the schools.

[Teachers should] not think of a lesson as a lesson. Think of it as not a lesson just being taught to students, but a lesson being taught to one of your own family members, you know? 'Cause if it's like that, they get more deep into it, and that's all it takes. Teach a lesson with heart behind it and try to get your kids to understand more of what's going on. And don't lie to your kids, like to your students, saying "Everything is okay and 'just say no to drugs'; it's easy." Let them know what's really going on. Don't beat around the bush. Let them know there's gangs, drugs. "You guys got to get on with that. That's for kids. Do what you got to do and stay in education." They're starting to do that more now. . . . Try to get a dress code going on. I never used to like that but that's a pretty good idea, you know? . . . But not really a strict dress code, but just where you can't wear . . . gang attire.

It just catches up to you later on. It does because when you're in the 10th grade and you sit down to do fractions and you can't do a problem 'cause you didn't really learn the basics, it all catches up. When I was in junior high, I didn't do math the whole seventh and eighth grade. I never did a math paper. Maybe turned one or two in, but it was like, I don't like math and it all catches up to you. . . .

Now I take every chance I get to try to involve myself in something. Now it's like I figure if I'm more involved in school, I won't be so much involved in the gang, you know? . . . It's what you put into it, what you're gonna get out of it. And you know, sometimes I tell myself like accountants are always working with numbers, and I say, I want to be an accountant because I want to do something where I got to work hard to try to get it, and show that I could learn math and do it real good. That's just the kind of person I am, where if I can't do something like just to trip myself up, I want to do this. You know, just so I can learn it more real good and show 'em that I can . . . try to make an example out of myself of everything I do.

[Good grades] make you feel good, getting A's. See this "gang member type man" getting A's. . . . I get pretty good grades. I get A's, B's, and C's. That's better than all F's on report cards that I used to get, all failures in all six subjects.

I could be [a good student]. I am when I want to be, you know? But like if I want to be a clown and mess around I could be a real bad dude, defiant in the classroom. That's what I usually used to get kicked out for. . . . Well, I am right now. I'm a good student.

After when I get my diploma, it's not the end of school, it's the beginning. I still want to learn a lot more after that. I basically want to go to college. . . . That's what I want to do. Get more schooling so I could learn more.

Probably I would want to be either a teacher, a counselor, something like working with youngsters to share my experience with them, you know? 'Cause I know there's a lot of people out there who talk down to youngsters, you know what I'm saying? Instead of talking *with* them. And just try to understand what they're going through.

I mean, you can't get a teacher, put 'em in a classroom with a bunch of kids from the neighborhood, and the teacher lives in [another neighborhood] and expect to understand. I have problems at home, a lot of problems. And to come into school and for a teacher to come with a snotty attitude, I'm gonna give it back. That's the way it is.

I don't want to speak too soon, but I'm pretty much on a good road here. I'm pretty much making it. Trying to make something out of myself. I'm on that way, you know, I'm going that way.

You can't talk about next month, at least at this time. . . . I'm just today, get it done. That's it. The best I can.

And I just, I'm tripping out on myself. I don't believe I'm doing this. But I don't really like to build myself too high . . . because the higher you are the harder you're gonna fall. I don't want to fall.

Family Support: "I Had a Love That Kept Me Home"

I like kids, I like kids a lot. They see me and, "Gee, that guy is scary. He's a gang member . . . ." This experience the other day when I was at work: I was working in [a day care center]. And I walked in and the kids were looking at me like and whispering. . . . And this one kid, this Oriental kid, came up and we started playing. The next thing I know, she was sitting on my lap and all these kids just started coming towards me. And they know, they could feel I love kids.

I don't know why but I love kids, 'cause I look at them and you see, sometimes I look and I pity 'cause I say, "I hope none of the kids go the wrong way." Then I look and I say, "Some of these kids are gonna be something." And when you got to think like that and look at kids and say, "Man, you're gonna grow up in a rough world," it's kind of messed up. You already know this world is kind of destructed out there. It's just sick out there. People, you know, kids killing kids, babies, mothers killing their own babies. It's like animals killing their own young. It's a trip out there. Nah, you can't trust nobody but your mom. Man, that's it, just your mom.

You need to educate your mind. . . . Somebody gets born and throw 'em into the world, you know, they're not gonna make it. You get somebody, you born 'em, you raise 'em, you feed 'em and encourage 'em, and they're gonna make it. That's what the reason for going to school is. A lot of it, of my going to school, is 'cause of my mom. I want her to be proud and her to say that I made it and this and that.

My dad was becoming an alcoholic. He was drinking a lot, and he was basically just partying all the time all week, doing drugs. . . . I didn't really have a father figure, but I had a dad; a dad but not really a father. . . . So my mom basically raised us all alone.

He didn't live with us at all. He lived with us when I was born. He wasn't there because he was always partying with his friends . . . He moved out and then he lived on with his sister. He lived on the streets basically for about four years. And now he decided that ain't the life that he wants to be, living in the streets. So he went in a Christian home trying to better himself, try to make a change for the good.

My mom doesn't curse. She hasn't drank in about six years. She's, you know, good. She used to be a heavy drinker.

My mom used to run with gangs when she was young. My mom and my father both belonged to gangs. . . . They're out of it. . . . They don't mess around no more.

I learned a lot of morals from my mother. Respect, how to respect people. . . . If my mom wasn't in church, she wouldn't be there for us, I don't think. She would be trying to find a way to seek to comfort herself, you know what I mean?

My mom, she's real strong and real understanding. Not strict, but more understanding, you know? She don't really compromise with me. Usually what she says is what she says, that's it. . . . My mom, I wouldn't change nothing, nothing [about her]. My dad, I would . . . just have him be there for me when I was younger. I could have turned out different if he was there, you never know.

It's hard for me to talk to my mom or my dad, but I talk to my mom about a lot of things like girlfriends, things that happen. Like when homeboys die, I don't go talking to nobody else but my mom. My homeboy just passed away about a month ago or two months ago, and I just remember I was in my mom's room. My mom was ironing and I just started crying, and I don't cry a lot. I started crying and I started telling her, "I hurt, Mom. I don't know why, but I hurt so much . . . ." 'Cause I had been trying to, how do you say, run from it, I'd been trying to put it off, like my homeboy's gone, 'cause we were pretty close. . . . So I was like, "It hurts, Mommy." She said, "I know, in your gut," like this and that. So we talked. We get pretty much into it.

She dropped out in the 10th grade and she was pregnant. And she says, "I want you to do good. Don't be like me, going back to school when it's already kind of late, you know." It's never too late but you know what I'm saying. She was like, "Just learn now, Paul. Do it the first time right and you won't have to do it again . . . ."

My mom wants me to go to school basically so I could have a good house and home when I build up my family, and so we won't have to be five people living in a three-bedroom home, with not that much money to live on, you know?

My mom makes a good living, not in money but in moral standards. We're happy with what we've got and that's just the bottom line. So I go to school for my mom, try to help her and try to help me.

My mom, she's not really [involved in school]. She's too busy doing her own thing. She gets out of school, makes dinner, cleans the house, goes to church, comes home, irons for my two sisters. She doesn't really have time for all this. . . . She'll come in and she'll talk to my probation officer, talk to Isabel [*a staff member*], different people, yeah . . . pretty much involved when she can be.

You're gonna realize that you got to learn from day one . . . and education will never end. It's only when you stop it and. . . . I realize that now. . . . But see, me, I never really had somebody to push me. My mother pushed me and my mom, she just got tired. "Paul, you're too much for me." My father, he never really pushed me. . . . He talked to me. That was like, "Education, Paul, education," you know? And getting letters from my dad in jail, "Stay in school," and that's all. He said some pretty deep things, understanding things to me. . . . And my dad always knew the right words to say to me that kind of encouraged me. And my mom, they both encouraged me.

If it wasn't for the family, the love I get from my family, I would look for it in my homeboys. I never had to do that. I just wanted my homeboys to party. . . . A lot of my friends, they go to homeboys to look for just to kick it with somebody. See, me, I had a love that kept me home, that kept me in my place.

I remember I used to just take off from Friday night to Monday morning, come home. My mom be worrying all night, "Where is this guy?" and I was in the street. And that was like every weekend. Till now, I stay home every day and I'm just going to school. . . . I come from work, do my homework, whatever. Go to work, come home, go to church, 'cause I go to church with my mother.

My mom, she's really proud of me. My friend was telling me that she was at church, at Bible study, a gathering at home of church people. And she was crying. She was proud. She said, "Your mom was talking about you and she was crying. She's real proud." And that's my mom, she's real sensitive. I love my mom so much it's even hard to explain. And she thinks, she tells me, "You don't care about me, Paul," this and that, 'cause like it's hard for me. . . . It's hard for me to show my feelings.

COMMENTARY

Luis Rodríguez, author of *Always Running, La Vida Loca: Gang Days in L.A.,* whose experiences parallel Paul's in many ways, describes gangs in this way:

> Gangs are not alien powers. They begin as unstructured groupings, our children, who desire the same as any young person. Respect. A sense of belonging. Protection.[3]

Looking back on his own youth and fearing for the future of his son, who was following the same path, Rodríguez wrote his book to encourage people to understand that gangs, in spite of providing belonging, respect, and protection to their members, represent an unhealthy and self-destructive response to oppression. Gangs emerge when communities are deprived of basic human rights. But according to Rodríguez, few young people would choose gangs if they were given decent education, productive jobs, and positive channels for social recreation.

In an ethnographic study of eight middle school students, all immigrants from Central and South America, Susan Katz came to similar conclusions. The students joined gangs not because of the violence, but because they wanted to affiliate with a group that would provide friendship, support, and cultural identity. In school, the students heard mostly negative messages about Latinos, who were "supposedly stupid, gang members, thieves, prostitutes."[4] Katz concluded that schools may unwittingly contribute to young people's gang involvement by failing to provide the strong cultural identity and support that students need. Although none of the young people she interviewed was in a gang when she began her study, most were by the time she had finished it.

Schools' unintentional complicity in turning students toward gangs was confirmed by Harriet Romo and Toni Falbo. In their research with Mexican American high school students in Texas, they found that although school policies such as "no pass/no play" send the necessary message that academics are more important than extracurricular activities, they also can have a negative effect: Such policies can sever the positive relationships that students at risk of failure have with more wholesome activities.[5]

The yearning for respect, which is after all just another word for a sense of competence, is what Paul described when he talked about joining first what he called a "school gang" and later the full-fledged street gang. Young men and women in desperate economic straits are turning in ever larger numbers to *"la vida loca,"* or the crazy life of gangs. Los Angeles alone is estimated to have 100,000 gang members in 800 gangs, and in 1991, a peak year for gang activity, nearly 600 youths were killed, mostly by other youths.[6]

The rage felt by young people when their dreams are denied or suppressed is turned inward, resulting in such things as drug abuse or suicide, or turned outward, evident in the unspeakably violent actions against their own *raza*, as so poignantly expressed by Paul. Rodríguez describes this violence as emanating too often from the self-loathing that is the result of oppression: "And if they murder, the victims are usually the ones who look like them, the ones closest to who they are—the mirror reflections. They murder and they're killing themselves, over and over."[7]

Latinos are more likely than any other group to report the presence of street gangs in their schools.[8] Yet blame for gangs and for other manifestations of oppression in our society cannot be placed on schools. The issues are simply too complicated for simplistic scapegoating, and they include massive unemployment, a historical legacy of racism and discrimination, and a lack of appropriate housing and health care, among others. In addition, families struggling to survive on a daily basis can seldom do much to counteract the lure of gangs and drugs, with their easy money and instant popularity, that influences so many of their children. As Paul says, his mother, try as she might, just got tired ("Paul, you're too much for me," she said).

Although schools can neither do away with gangs nor put a stop to the violence taking place in communities across the United States every day, they *can* make a difference. Paul was quick to place the responsibility for his past on his own shoulders, rather than blaming teachers. But when he thought more deeply about it, he also recognized that particular teachers and schools *did* make a difference. This is nowhere more evident than in the case of Ms. Nelson or, years later, in his alternative school.

Although Paul has been taught that what's on the inside of people is what counts, he is right to conclude that "it's really what's on the outside" because he has been judged by teachers and others for his style of dress and his tattos. Research by John Rivera and Mary Poplin corroborates Paul's experience: Through interviews with students of diverse backgrounds in four schools in California, they cite the case of a young student who talked about the negative reaction teachers had toward some Chicano students: "Teachers see you as a *cholo,* gangster, lowlife, drug dealer, etc., and that makes them treat you differently than everyone else because they stereotype us and don't give us a chance to show them what we can do."[9]

Chicano parents and their children often have high aspirations, but unless these are somehow incorporated into the culture of schools, they make little difference. For example, using national statistics, Daniel Solorzano found that when social class is controlled, Chicano eighth graders had even higher educational aspirations than did White students.[10] But there is a tremendous mismatch between the high educational aspirations and low educational attainment of Mexican American students. Although Chicanos have one of the highest levels of academic failure in the United States, they also have great faith in education and a history of struggle to secure the benefits of equal educational opportunity for their chidlren.[11]

This finding challenges the conventional wisdom that Chicano youngsters and their families do not care about education, and it shifts the focus to the context and structure of schools. In other words, policies and practices need to be reviewed to make education more engaging and positive for all students. In this regard, Solorzano suggests that schools need to develop strategies that use a "cultural continuities" approach rather than a cultural deficit approach to improve the achievement of students from dominated groups.

Paul's is a good example of how cultural continuities can make a positive difference in education. Aside from Cinco de Mayo festivities, his school experiences until now have been devoid of any mention of Chicano history and culture. His words make clear that studying his culture fascinates and motivates him to learn. He is also thinking critically about what it means to be a Chicano, and he recognizes the importance of including the history of different groups in the curriculum.

There is a notable connection between a positive identity and strong self-esteem: One researcher found that adolescents who have explored and understand the meaning of ethnicity in their lives are more likely to demonstrate better adjustment than those who have not.[12] It is not simply a question of feeling good about themselves; rather, a strong sense of identity is essential for giving young people a sense of their own dignity and worth. Including their experiences in the school's curriculum is one way that Paul and his classmates are given the opportunity to develop this sense of dignity and worth. His statement that Chicano students have "some pretty trippy insights on life" is an acknowledgment of their value.

Paul's suggestion that more Chicano school aides should be hired because they "got love and they give it to you" reminds us of the powerful influence of family on Latino culture. Even families in difficult circumstances want the best for their children, but often they are unaware of how to provide it for them. His father's insistence on "Education, Paul, education," if unaccompanied by structural support to help him stay in school, is of little help. Paul clearly understood this when he said that although his parents supported him, they never really pushed him.

Paul Chavez has been fortunate to be in the alternative school he now attends, and it seems to be acting as a safeguard to keep him at some distance from his gang. The policies and practices of his school are geared toward creating a positive learning environment: There is no tracking; staff interactions with students are positive and healthy; students are involved in the school's governance; there are high expectations and demanding standards of all students; and their languages and cultures are an intrinsic part of the school's curriculum.

One cannot help but remember, however, that Paul is only 16 years old, a tender age with so many difficult situations and easy temptations still facing him. It may take much longer to turn his life around. In spite of his own strong motivation and eloquent insights, his school's caring, his mother's love and strict discipline, and his growing realization that gang life is no solution to the problems facing Chicano youth, he still has a long and hard road ahead of him.

TO THINK ABOUT

1. What can teachers and schools learn from Paul's fifth-grade teacher, Ms. Nelson? Give specific suggestions.
2. What support services do you think are needed in schools such as those in Paul's neighborhood? Why?
3. Take a look at the recommendations that Paul made to improve schools. Which do you think make sense? Why?
4. Why do you think Paul never thought about being Chicano before? What kinds of ethnic studies would be important for students at different levels?
5. How can schools use the tremendously positive feelings about family that Paul and other Latinos have?

Case Study: Ron Morris

"I just felt like the realest person on earth."

Ronald Morris,[1] who describes himself as Afro-American, looks older than his 19 years, not just because of his 6'4" frame, but in temperament as well. He is eloquent, exudes self-confidence, and has a highly expressive face and easy smile. Ron has five siblings and lives with his mother, three sisters, three nieces, and two nephews in a housing development in Boston, Mass., just a few blocks from the Antonia Pantoja Community High School, the alternative school he attends. The school was named for an educational leader in the New York Puerto Rican community who in the 1950s was the major inspiration for Aspira, an agency that promotes education among Puerto Rican and other Latino and inner-city youth. Ron's older brother is in jail and his older sister, whom he describes as "dropping kids," is currently living in a shelter until she finds an apartment. He says his neighborhood is "wild, very wild," because of the constant shootings and drug activity.

Ron's neighborhood was in the news recently because a nine-year-old boy was shot by gang members and several of the students from the school Ron attends were grazed by the bullets. This kind of incident has become almost a daily occurrence in this community, and Ron has not been spared from the ever-present violence.[2] Several months before he was interviewed, Ron was leaving the "T" (subway) station in his neighborhood with his paycheck in his hands when a young man went after him, wrestling him to the ground attempting to get the check. Ron heard shots and suddenly found himself on the ground and wounded. The assailant put the gun to Ron's head, and as Ron got up and ran, he was shot a total of six times. Miraculously, no vital organs were hit and most of the bullets left his body. One, stuck in his hip, is to be removed this month.

A kindergarten teacher's aide who retired four years ago, Ron's mother exerts a strong influence on him and gives him a great deal of support for continuing his studies, urging him to make something of himself. Ron has not seen his father since he was eight or nine years old. Ron's educational history has been a checkered one: He was held back twice, once in fourth grade and once in sixth, and he moved from school to school many times. He was thrown out of one junior high school and sent to another one, where he graduated from eighth grade. After that, he attended two high schools before being expelled and sent to his present school. Coincidentally, the counselor at the school Ron is now attending was the eighth grade teacher he referred to in the interviews as the teacher of "the first real class I ever had."

To graduate from the Boston Public Schools, students need to have accumulated 105 points, but when he began classes at the Pantoja Community High School two years ago, Ron had zero points toward graduation even though he had been in high school for two years. Because this alternative school offers an accelerated program in which students can earn credit for their effort and performance in classes and through individual projects, he has been able to catch up with his points and expects to graduate by the end of this year. The school, a partnership between the Boston Public Schools, the city, and the community, offers a variety of educational, creative, vocational, and cultural opportunities for its 50 students, many of whom had no previously successful experiences in school. In addition to his regular classes, Ron is participating in a small tutorial—an advanced history class offered by a renowned retired professor who taught at Boston University and Harvard. Ron loves this class because students get to examine original documents and tapes about the Cuban Missile Crisis in order to come to their own conclusions about what decision they would have made.

The multicultural curriculum of this alternative school is one of the features that makes it appealing to Ron and the other students. Others include its philosophy of empowerment, democracy, and student and staff collaboration and participation. The school also has an active sports program, and the basketball team won all of its tournaments with other schools throughout the entire Boston area last year. Ron was one of the star basketball players and he hopes to resume playing as soon as his injuries heal completely.

Ron's lack of personal success with education had left him feeling disillusioned about his future, but his experiences at the Pantoja Community High School seem to be turning that around. Although his first goal was to become a professional football player, he has developed more realistic goals and is considering a future as a physical therapist, perhaps for a sports team. Staff at the school are helping him make these consequential decisions by providing him with brochures and information on different professions and colleges. Ron had always thought he could not afford to go to a four-year college and instead had planned on a community college, but his advisers are giving him information on scholarships and they have spoken to him about the possibility of transferring to a four-year college after attending a community college. His future plans also include a nice house and a family.

During the first interview, Ron confided that he was about to become a father with two different young women. Although he said he was willing to take responsibility for the children and he had an ongoing relationship with one of the young women, he also seemed determined to continue his education in spite of his situation. In fact, it was at this point that he talked most fervently about wanting to go to Harvard.

The major themes that emerged from interviews with Ron focused on how schools and his own attitude were complicitous in creating failure, on the key role of the curriculum in teaching young people about who they are, and on his growing sense of responsibility for becoming a better student.

Creating Failure

Depends on how I felt that day [whether I was a good student]. I could come to school and say, "Okay, I'm a do all my work. I ain't gonna mess with nobody." I have this will power. Nobody can make me do what I don't want to do. I do it because I felt like doing it. And sometimes I used to say, "Let me do this work." I come to school, kids be playing. They like, "Come on, Ron, come on, Ron. Let's play, let's go do this, let's go do that." I used to go, "Nah, man, chill . . . [I wanna] do my work."

Teachers used to be like, "Why don't you do this all the time? . . ." And then it was like a habit so the teachers knew it was like okay, one day Ron is gonna come in and do his work. For the rest of the week, he's gonna be destructive. And then it went to, okay, Ron is gonna come and do his work in two days and the rest of the week be destructive. Three days, and so forth, until it was, okay, Ron comes in every day and does the work.

And then the work started getting boring to me 'cause it started getting easier and easier. Then it was getting repeated and repeated. It was like, Ron's gonna come to school now every day and be destructive because he's not learning anything new. And I would have that in my mind. I would actually sleep on that thought: "I'm gonna come to school and I'm gonna destroy it. I will come to school and just mind be gone, just terror, terror." Worst student [that school] ever had for two years. They used to always tell me that. "You are the worst student."

It wasn't that [all] the teachers would tell me. It was this one particular person, the coach of the basketball team. He was Black. He was also either the dean of discipline or the assistant principal. He used to put us down, and then he'll come to us and try to teach this: "You shouldn't be acting like that. You're Black," and stuff like that. And I used to get offended. . . . Me and him used to go at it all the time. Basically I think he's the reason why I got thrown out. He just didn't like me.

The first day [at the new high school] I got into a little problem with kids from the neighborhood, from another neighborhood. And they called me into their office like a couple of days later. And they were basically trying to tell me they didn't want me there because of where I lived and where most of the other kids who went there lived. Like the majority of boys who went there were from this other development.

I didn't really like [school]. I used to always want to skip and go home or smoke or come to class and create ruckus or something. You knew what you was going to class for. You was going to class to get taught really nothing. And I'm not just saying history. All classes are basically boring. Like, Okay, say you learn a new level of math after you pass. Like from the 10th grade down, math is repeated until you take algebra. . . . The problems may get longer, but it's the same thing.

Basically to me, everything is like a repeated pattern. Like science, you learn the same science till you get to high school. Instead of teaching you something different, they give it a new name. They call it biology. It's just earth science. They're just teaching you more about cells. You've learned about cells in earth science. And chemistry is basically an advanced form of biology. They just using elements. Everything repeats itself. . . .

You can get all the good grades in the world. What did you learn? You can take a straight honor roll student and take somebody like a bum off the street who lived life on the street. You can take the straight A student and they can be talking and I done seen this happen. The bum just knows more. You look at the straight A student like them grades don't mean nothing. Like Chinese people aren't smart, they just apply theyself to the work. They come to school on time. They do what they need to achieve that A. Who knows if they're learning anything? You can't say they smarter 'cause they get straight A's. They do what they have to do to get A's. I can get straight D's or straight F's and still know more than half the people in the classroom.

The Boston Public Schools, your reputation follows you. So if you went into one of the guidance counselors and said, "I want to get into college," the guidance counselor went, "Well, I'll talk to you later." And then later would be like too late. You're already graduated, you don't know anything. It's too late.

Two or three years from now, you'll see that same guidance counselor. You may not be what you wanted to be but you didn't sit there and take any old job. You went and got you a nice, good-paying job. You know, probably got a kid now or something. And then the same guidance counselor say, "Well, you've changed a lot." And you look at him and say, "Yeah, I woulda been better. I woulda went to college if you woulda paid me any attention."

When a teacher becomes a teacher, she acts like a teacher instead of a person. She takes her title as now she's mechanical, somebody just running it. Teachers shouldn't deal with students like we're machines. You're a person. I'm a person. We come to school and we all act like people.

[I want teachers to know] that not all of us men are gang members and drug dealers, just a major stereotype. And our women aren't lazy. Things that they say bother us. I want [them] to know that even though we're still going through a little hardship, I'm still proud to be Black and we shouldn't be put down.

[In school], they didn't really teach anything. I went to school. I come in, you sit down, you learn. Like in history, you learn the same thing over and over and over again. I learned some sort of history in the sixth grade and some sort of history in the eighth grade. I get in high school and I'm thinking, "Okay, I'm going to learn a whole new history." I get to high school for the first time, I had the same thing I had in the eighth and sixth grade! You keep asking yourself why they keep doing this? Why they keep doing that? And you see it as "Okay, they don't want you to learn anything."

They talked about Christopher Columbus like he was some great god or something. . . . You went through three different segments of Christopher Columbus. You're saying now, Okay, he's got to be a fake. He's a fictional character. They just keep pumping him up. He's turning from this to this. . . . Then you just get tired. Okay, forget Christopher Columbus. . . . Who cares about Christopher Columbus? He didn't do anything.

You learned about all explorers and Malcolm, a little bit about Malcolm X, a little bit about Martin Luther King. You learned a little bit about slavery, a little bit about this. You learned a little bit about everything. You learned it just so many times.

You just want to say, "Well, isn't it time that we learned something differ-ent?" There's more than just what's in this book, 'cause what's in this book is not gonna let us know who we really are as people. So you have to give us some more, which they wasn't trying to give.

[Teachers should] probably just see what the students like and teach it how they would understand it and so that it's more helpful to them. . . . More discussion instead of more reading, more discussion instead of just letting things be read and then left alone. People read things and then don't under-stand what they read.

Like if school was more, not all fun and games, but it was more realistic than just reading and doing the work and then you leave. You sit there for 45 minutes doing nothing, just reading a whole book and the teacher is doing nothing but letting you read, and she's probably reading the newspaper or eat-ing gum. And that's why the dropout rate is why [it is] because they just come to school and they ain't teaching us nothing, so why am I gonna sit here? I'm a just go somewhere, just drop out. It's the learning style. It's the way they being taught. They feel that they not learning anything so they don't want to be here.

Classes would be like at least an hour, hour and a half. You can't learn anything in 45 minutes. That 45 minutes go by like this [snaps fingers]. Classes need to be like an hour, hour and 45 minutes 'cause you need the time to read and discuss. You just don't need the time to read, give a paper, and leave. . . . These classes, you could take your time and think and talk about things. Then you do the work 'cause you have all the time. Classes have got to be structured like that, more discussion. Not all that sitting there and you read this, do the work.

Like I take Spanish and then after Spanish, I'll take Seymour [the Advanced History tutorial]. Spanish always ends too early. I don't get enough. I'll be dying to learn how to speak Spanish. . . . She'll be right in the middle of something real good and it be 12:15 and I'll be, like, "God!"

I like history and the way [Seymour] teaches it, and it's just that his method and the material that he has to cover the history, it's like the reading is so real. The message here is just so powerful. . . . Instead of just reading, we discuss. We'll read like a certain section and we'll discuss that section. Why was it written like this and what do I think it means? What is the real meaning behind what they're saying? And do I really believe that this could have hap-pened, that could have happened? . . . And he makes sure that you under-stand it fully before he lets you go on.

Curriculum and the Challenge of Identity

My identity as an Afro-American—it's like I can never change that. I can never be anything different. I can never be another race. I'm always going to be Afro-American, and I'll always be looked at differently.

Being Afro-American is a challenge. . . . It's just proving to yourself every day in life. You always prove to yourself, "I can do better than what they want me to do." Knowing that they just threw you out in the jungle just to die anyway.

. . . I don't want to die because I couldn't survive out there. I want to die because I got old and it's time to go. Heart just stopped kicking, of natural causes.

We need more Black people in politics. We don't have no spokespeople in the Senate and City Hall and the Congress. Nobody's up there speaking for us and if there are Black people up there, they're not speaking for us. . . . We don't have no voice. Our voice is just like whispers. They can't hear it. There's too much noise, too much confusion.

Proud to be Afro-American? Well, yeah and no. Yeah, I'm proud to be Afro-American because I'm a Black male and all this and I have so many dreams and so many ways of being, that I come from a great race of kings and queens who went through slavery and our race still survives and all that.

And no, because I have to accept the term Afro-American because I was born in America. I wasn't born where my ancestors come from. I'm not as pure as my ancestors were because your family's been raped and developed these different things. . . . Sometimes that makes me sad when somebody can say, "Well, look at you. You got a White person's nose," or you got this or you got that.

Even though [White students] sit there and White history is the basic history, they don't really know anything about White. They look at it as White people have always been on top, which is not true for about—they don't know about before five, six thousand years ago. Nobody even knew who White people were. To me, that's crazy. Everybody's running around not really knowing who they are. People think they know who they are. . . . They think they know what their history is.

[I felt comfortable in school] once in eighth grade. Just this case, a history class I had. Just made me want to come to school and made me want to say, "Okay, now that I know there are so many false things in the world and that there's so much out there for me to learn, stop bullshitting."

It was a Black African history class. It was titled that. It was just so different from the textbook style. . . . It was no books. It was just documents and papers and commonsense questions and commonsense knowledge. You'd just sit there, be like, "This is real! This is really what it is." And this Black history class, like people was thinking, the school system, at first they wanted him to teach it 'cause it was like okay, he's just trying to make the Black people, pump 'em up and stuff like that. But they was never in the class.

It was basically about Black people, but it showed you all people instead of just Black people. It showed us Latinos. It showed us Caucasians. It showed us the Jews and everything how we all played a part what society in any country is like today. I just sat in that class, and I used to go to that class once a week 'cause it was only a once-a-week class. I'd sit and just be like, I was just so relaxed. I just felt like the realest person on earth.

Taking Responsibility for Becoming a Better Student

My mother wants me to become the best Black man that ever lived on the face of this earth! That is her. She'll start every conversation off with me,

"What are you gonna do now? Go get a job. Go to school." I mean, I could wake up in the morning late for school. . . . "All he does is sleep, hang out all night . . . ." I be upstairs and I wish this woman would shut up! But she's right. I gotta do something. I got to get out now. I have to. It's time for me.

Me and my brother were like the biggest burdens on my mother, 'cause even though my oldest sister was having these kids, but me and my brother were like, he was on the streets. We were doing bad. She knew we was doing bad. Always called, like every other weekend, in jail: "Mom, we're in jail. Come get us out." And things she used to do like she used to leave us in jail. . . . One time I was in jail for like three months. She didn't come visit me. She didn't write. When I called, she didn't even want to speak. I was like 13, 14.

And then . . . . it just popped in my head: I was like, "If we was acting more like men, we wouldn't be in jail doing all this dumb stuff, you idiot!"

The difference between me and my brother, if my brother was sitting here talking to you, the only thing you would notice different between me and him would be the way he looked. Me and him were the same people. We thought the same. We knew what each other wanted.

I go to my brother for advice when things go bad. I like to talk to my brother. . . . Like I could talk to my mother about it, but like she never ran the streets. My brother ran the streets. He sees things how I see it and he can talk to me.

We used to go to court. . . . I used to get up and just say something and they would release me. Personal recons [recognizance]. Then I'd go home. You know, just come back to court. I'd go back to court and just beat the case, period. And then I'd always think about, "Why do I keep going to jail? Why do I always keep . . . doing all this stuff to my mother?"

[My brother] was caught in a deep thing. He was selling drugs. He has two kids like I do from two different women. And he was trying to take care of his kids and sell drugs at the same time, but had little petty cases. And I used to tell him like, "Come on, man, chill out. You got two kids, man. Stop selling drugs. Get a job. The little petty cases are gonna catch up to you." He didn't graduate from high school. He got his GED [general equivalency diploma] in jail.

And my mother used to always, she like, "Y'all two are stressed. Y'all two are killing me." And she used to be like, "When I'm gone, there ain't no other mother in the world. Nobody gonna treat you like Ma did." She used to just say things. It was like she was talking to us as our mother.

I didn't want to be one of the kids who was always living with their mother. I always wanted to show my mother I could survive on my own because those are the things that she taught me. She taught me responsibility. She taught me how to survive. She taught me these things.

I'm trying to get into Harvard. . . . My mother told me I could do it. . . . She'd say things like, "If them women [the two women who were pregnant with his children] really understand what it is for you to be the correct father to your children, they won't burden you. They'll let you become these things, and they'll let these things happen so their kids won't have a typical Black future," as if they're still living in the same house and I'm working making $6 an hour and killing myself and child support is taking all the money. And it's like them women really don't want that type of atmosphere for their kids and stuff, which I don't want, then they got to let you achieve.

[I want] to provide for my kids. I need the education. I have to. I can't just graduate out of high school and stop going to school, to just accept a diploma. It's nothing. . . . I need a real job.

At least I can take one of my kids away from what I lived through. And the other one, I can show the other one to be proud to say, "That's my father, ex-gang member and ex-this and ex-that. He became something in life." So my kid can say, "I'm gonna grow up to become somebody."

I don't want my kid to say, "Okay, my father graduated high school. That's the end of my father's life. He's nothing. He doesn't make enough. I don't get everything I want at Christmas." It's scary sometimes. I don't want my kid to wake up like that.

[Pantoja Community High School] is more out to help you achieve instead of just sitting there doing nothing.

Now I'm not in that, "They're not teaching me nothing, why should I come to school?" type thing. Here, as a difference in Boston Public Schools, it's more direct, it's more learning. You learn more. You learn differently. . . . I'm not learning what the book wants me to learn about Christopher Columbus. I'm learning what, who Christopher Columbus really was, what he really did. I don't want to know what people *thought* he did and what they thought he *should* of did. I was learning a better structured history. . . . [Now I'm studying] the Cuban Missile Crisis and Native Americans in two different history classes.

It's realistic and my beliefs as an Afro-American are respected. If I come to class and don't like the class being taught because it's like that, you're not gonna say, "Well, you got to sit there and learn anyway." At least I had the chance to talk about it. . . . It's not like the Boston Public Schools. . . . "So, you don't want to learn about this class? Who cares? . . ." It's more realistic. If you don't want to learn about that, you have the option of talking about it or not.

[Teachers here] understand my identity and culture. They respect it. . . . When I go to Sandy's class [Humanities] and I'm sitting there sometimes, and like she gets these things and we be reading and discussing it. And then it never ceases to fail. Somebody always has something to say about White people. . . . She's White and we're Blacks and Latinos, and we're just trying to dog her. But she doesn't sit there and get all stressed on it. . . . She respects, she know this is how you feel, and if that's how you feel and that's what you say, say it, okay? You go, "All right," and you just speak about it and she accepted it.

She gives us funny little things. Like she gave us this one thing called "The Day that Wasn't." And at first, I was like, "Come on, now. This is kids' stuff." And I was reading it. And I kept reading it. You know, as you went along, it was like, "Yeah!" 'Cause it was like about identity, 'cause the people kept telling the bear that he wasn't a bear. Finally he just believed that he wasn't a bear. And so the winter came around and then in wintertime he noticed he was always tired. And then he went to sleep in a cave. And then he finally figured out that, "Hey, I'm really a bear!"

That's like some people. Some people don't believe just who they really are. Some people want to be different people. Some Blacks want to be White. Some Whites want to be Black. Why [not] accept what you got? You can't change that. . . . It was like, "Come on, Sandy. Why do you want us to read this?" Then it occurred to me.

I'm learning like in a more accelerated way because not only do I get the opportunity to teach myself because of the material I have to teach myself with, but the teachers are there actually to help you learn too. . . . I may read a book and be like, "Okay, what do they really mean?" And then I talk to one of my teachers and maybe one may not know it, but somebody will be able to tell me. It's not just the teachers. It's the staff, everybody. . . . Everybody's there for each other.

I could be getting a better [education] if it wasn't for me. I'm the only one holding me back, just me. The little things that I do just hold me back. Being late, just little things. The little dumb things that I do hold me back.

I have to just stop all that foolish stuff that I be doing. I have to put that stuff behind me. I'm too old now.

My friend Ernie is like, he's focused. If I could just borrow his head for a couple of months, I would be just like better off than I am now. But since I can't borrow his head, I can like borrow ideas from him. Me and him talk a lot.

[I'm a good student] almost. Not there yet. Have to work on being on time. That's the key thing, being on time. . . . Still very talkative, very talkative. Oh, I could talk a whole class!

When I start college, I'll have to get out of that late mentality. Always wanting to be late. Always knowing, okay, I don't have to go to school today but if I go tomorrow, I know I'm good and fast enough to make up for today's work. But then college isn't like that. . . . It's much like harder, 'cause like college, every day they're teaching you something different. So I'm a know I have to be more on track.

I would have to try to take care of my responsibilities to the fullest, but I know that I don't. So I have to take care of my responsibilities more. And stop being a pain to my mother. I don't think she like that. She's getting tired of that.

I'm not perfect. I wouldn't call myself a good student. I call myself an all right student. I know what's right and what's wrong. I just have to apply [myself] to it.

If you'd asked me about two, three years ago, I'd a told you I didn't have the slightest idea why I came to school. It's stupid, it's boring. They don't teach me nothing. I don't learn anything. I should just stay home. But you're asking me that now in the Pantoja [Community High School]. . . . You'd have to ask me a two-part question: What do I think about school then, and what do I think about it now? Now I think about it differently because I'm not in the Boston public schools. I'm here, I'm learning, I'm learning more from people who know. It's not a book. Boston public schools give you a textbook. Here it's, "I can teach you through experience, through documents, through this, through that."

Once you change like from that childhood atmosphere, 'cause you're older now. You're like, "Okay, I'm 17, 18, think I can still act like a kid and get over in life?" This [school] teaches you that acting like a kid all your life ain't gonna get you over in life unless you're gonna be a comedian. If your goal is not to be a comedian, then why would you want to act like a kid all your life?

Boston public schools didn't train you for life. All they train you for is to know what they want you to know so you can only get so far as what you got. Meaning, if you believe that what they taught you was all real and all this, and went to college and got a degree or something, just went through life thinking what you learned at Boston public schools was right, what you learned in your regular high school was the real deal, you would probably be a confused soul. You'd die wondering why everything is like this.

I'm learning how, instead of planning for the day, like you would normally do, I'm planning for the future.

COMMENTARY

Educational failure is not created by young people alone and is not simply the result of poor academic skills, poor parenting, lack of proper nutrition, or even abject poverty. Nor is educational failure simply the result of disruptive and violent students or overcrowded schools. For African American students, racism and low expectations can also be formidable barriers to school success, and all of these conditions can combine to result in academic failure.[3] Ron seems to understand that failure is created by a multiplicity of conditions, which can include some of those just listed as well as stagnant pedagogy, lack of financial resources and commitment, and a disinterested public, but also include students' own attitudes and behaviors. This understanding helps make Ron's case study a complex and intriguing one that places in bold relief the responsibility that must be borne by all those who claim to care about the educational health of our society.

According to Ron, his failure was created by a boring and irrelevant curriculum, a lack of trust on the part of teachers and guidance counselors of his capability to learn and succeed, the lure of the streets, and his own negative attitude about learning. Especially critical of the curriculum, what he calls "a repeated pattern," Ron feels it is based on myths that prevent students from developing a critical perspective about who they are and what they are learning. His distaste for traditional school curriculum leads him to question the value of grades, and even to suggest that "a bum off the street" might be more intelligent than a straight A student. Ron also criticizes the pedagogy of traditional schools and offers suggestions to help make the curriculum more helpful to students: longer classes, more discussion, and primary sources as the basis of the curriculum. These suggestions are strikingly consistent with the thinking of current educational reformers.[4]

Strongly tied to the irrelevance of the curriculum, in Ron's eyes, is cultural identity. He speaks poignantly about the challenge of being Afro-American, but he also ponders the miseducation received by all students of all backgrounds ("They think they know what their history is," he says of White students). In one of the most telling moments of the interviews, Ron describes the Black African History class he had in eighth grade as "This is real!" and muses, "I just felt like the realest person on earth." The fact that the teacher of this particular class was not only a gifted educator but also African American cannot be underestimated, although Ron quickly points out another Black teacher whom he feels was the reason he was thrown out of one of the schools.[5]

How families contribute to the academic success of their children is the subject of an ongoing study of the Center on Families, Communities, Schools, and Children's Learning Project. Three important and recurring themes have emerged in the preliminary findings that give insight into how families prepare and support their children's academic achievement: African American families of academically successful children provide extended family and community support, provide racial socialization, and act as teachers in the home.[6] Yet extended families in most communities are quickly becoming a relic, and many parents, especially single parents, are forced to cope with the burden of raising their children alone, with few resources and little community support.

Ron's mother raised him, he said, to be responsible and proud of himself. He said, for example, "My mother wants me to become the best Black man that ever lived on the face of this earth!" a good example of what is meant by "racial socialization." Like many African American families, she felt a deep sense of responsibility to prepare her children to face obstacles in the general society by emphasizing pride in their race.

Ron's newfound enthusiasm for school and his emerging educational success is consistent with a recent survey of a large number of young African American men in four cities, which found that caring teachers, appropriate youth programs, and part-time or summer jobs, in conjunction with parent involvement, are conditions that support their high school graduation.[7] Specifically, they found that those who stayed in school were more likely to be in an academic program, and almost three-quarters of those who stayed in school reported that their teachers were interested in how well they were doing in class and gave them hope for the future.

In spite of his mother's guidance and her insistence that he go to school, study, and be serious, Ron ran the streets with his brother and got into trouble for years. He is finally taking responsibility for his life and his education. Ron is doing well in school and planning for the future, and he reflects critically on his past activities and how they held him back. His attitude about school has changed dramatically, and the alternative school he is attending is no doubt at least partly responsible for this change. Staff at the school respect his culture, he says, and they provide stimulating activities, both curricular and extracurricular.

He enjoys this school because he is treated as an adult. Ron is committed to completing his education and has high hopes, some would say even unrealistic expectations, of attending a college such as Harvard.

Ron is also facing formidable challenges in the months and years ahead. He will become a father of two children soon, and he seems somewhat oblivious to how this monumental change will affect his life. Although he says he wants to shoulder some of the responsibility for at least one of the children, it is unclear how he can do so, graduate from high school, go on to college, find some kind of employment, and be on his own, as he says he wants to be. The complex and competing messages that Ron Morris has picked up from his family, schools, peers, and society are evident in his interviews: Be proud, become somebody, trust in yourself, be tough, be a man. How he resolves some of the contradictions he is facing, especially how to become both a good student and a responsible father at such a young age, will certainly be major issues for the decisions he will make in the near future.

TO THINK ABOUT

1. What does Ron's case study teach us about the reasons for students' lack of academic success? How can you apply what you learned through his case to the situation of other students?
2. Why do you think Ron called the Black African history class "the first real class I ever had"? What do you imagine was the content of this class, and how did it differ from other history classes?
3. Culture and identity are major issues for Ron. What implications does cultural identity hold for school curriculum?
4. What do you think about Ron's ideas for the future? What would you tell him if you were his guidance counselor?
5. Before attending this alternative school, Ron had not experienced a great deal of academic success. What features of this school do you think might be useful for other nonalternative schools to know about?

● NOTES TO CHAPTER 7

1. For full expositions of these arguments, see, for example, Carl Bereiter and S. Englemann, *Teaching Disadvantaged Children in the Preschool* (Englewood Cliffs, NJ: Prentice-Hall, 1966); Arthur R. Jensen, "How Much Can We Boost IQ and Scholastic Achievement?" *Harvard Educational Review,* 39 (1969), 1–123; Frank Reissman, *The Culturally Deprived Child* (New York: Harper & Row, 1962).
2. See Samuel Bowles and Herbert Gintis, *Schooling in Capitalist America: Educational Reform and the Contradictions of Economic Life* (New York: Basic Books, 1976); Joel Spring, *The Rise and Fall of the Corporate State* (Boston: Beacon Press, 1972).
3. Stephen S. Baratz and Joan C. Baratz, "Early Childhood Intervention: The Social Science Base of Institutional Racism." In *Challenging the Myths: The Schools, the Blacks, and the Poor,* Reprint Series no. 5 (Cambridge, MA: Harvard Educational Review, 1971).
4. William Ryan, *Blaming the Victim* (New York: Vintage Books, 1972), 61.

5. Shirley Brice Heath, *Ways with Words* (New York: Cambridge University Press, 1983).

6. Margaret A. Gibson, "The School Performance of Immigrant Minorities: A Comparative View." *Anthropology and Education Quarterly,* 18, 4 (December, 1987), 262–275; see also *Minority Status and Schooling: A Comparative Study of Immigrant and Involuntary Minorities,* edited by Margaret A. Gibson and John U. Ogbu (New York: Garland, 1991).

7. Richard J. Herrnstein and Charles Murray, *The Bell Curve: Intelligence and Class Structure in American Life* (New York: Free Press, 1994).

8. Pierre Bourdieu, "The Forms of Capital." In *Handbook of Theory and Research for the Sociology of Education,* edited by John G. Richardson (New York: Greenwood Press, 1986), 246.

9. See Samuel Bowles and Herbert Gintis, *Schooling in Capitalist America;* and Joel Spring, *The Rise and Fall of the Corporate State.*

10. Michael W. Apple, *Teachers and Texts: A Political Economy of Class and Gender Relations in Education* (Boston: Routledge & Kegan Paul, 1986).

11. Gloria Ladson-Billings, "Culturally Relevant Teaching: The Key to Making Multicultural Education Work." In *Research and Multicultural Education: From the Margins to the Mainstream,* edited by Carl A. Grant (Bristol, PA: Falmer Press, 1992).

12. Richard St. Germaine, "Drop-out Rates Among American Indian and Alaska Native Students: Beyond Cultural Discontinuity." *ERIC Digest,* Clearinghouse on Rural Education and Small Schools. (Charleston, WV: Appalachia Educational Laboratory, November, 1995).

13. Olga A. Vasquez, Lucinda Pease-Alvarez, and Sheila M. Shannon, *Pushing Boundaries: Language and Culture in a Mexicano Community* (New York: Cambridge University Press, 1994), 12.

14. Margaret A. Gibson, "School Performance of Immigrant Minorities."

15. John U. Ogbu, "Variability in Minority School Performance: A Problem in Search of an Explanation." *Anthropology and Education Quarterly,* 18, 4 (December 1987), 312–334.

16. For a more extensiive discussion, see Evelyn Jacob and Cathie Jordan, *Minority Education: Anthropological Perspectives* (Norwood, NJ: Ablex, 1993).

17. María E. Matute-Bianchi, "Situational Ethnicity and Patterns of School Performance among Immigrant and Nonimmigrant Mexican-Descent Students." In *Minority Status and Schooling,* edited by Margaret A. Gibson and John U Ogbu. Also, research by Susan Katz with Central American and Mexican immigrants found that those who were born in the United States or who had arrived here before the age of five had the most difficulties at school in terms of both academics and behavior. See Susan Roberta Katz, "Where the Streets Cross the Classroom: A Study of Latino Students' Perspectives on Cultural Identity in City Schools and Neighborhood Gangs." *Bilingual Research Journal,* 20, 3 and 4 (Summer/Fall 1995), 603–631.

18. Donna Deyhle and Karen Swisher, "Research in American Indian and Alaska Native Education: From Assimilation to Self-Determination." In *Review of Research in Education,* vol. 22, edited by Michael W. Apple (Washington, DC: American Educational Research Association, 1997), 113–194.

19. Margaret A. Gibson, "School Performance of Immigrant Minorities."

20. Marcelo M. Suarez-Orozco, "'Becoming Somebody': Central American Immigrants in the U.S." *Anthropology and Education Quarterly,* 18, 4 (December 1987), 287–299.

21. Jim Cummins, *Negotiating Identities: Education for Empowerment in a Diverse Society* (Ontario, CA: California Association for Bilingual Education, 1996).
22. Signithia Fordham and John U. Ogbu, "Black Students' School Success: Coping with the 'Burden of Acting White.'" *Urban Review,* 18, 3 (1986), 176–206.
23. The entire issue of *Anthropology and Education Quarterly,* 18, 4 (December 1987) was devoted to this topic.
24. Gloria Ladson-Billings, "Multicultural Teacher Education: Research, Practice, and Policy." *Handbook of Research on Multicultural Education,* edited by James A. Banks and Cherry A. McGee Banks (New York: Macmillan, 1995); and in the same volume, Clara E. Rodriguez, "Puerto Ricans in Historical and Social Science Research." For Oscar Lewis's theory of *the culture of poverty,* see *La Vida: A Puerto Rican Family in the Culture of Poverty—San Juan and New York* (New York: Random House, 1965).
25. *Anthropology and Education Quarterly,* 28, 3 (September, 1997).
26. Margaret A. Gibson, "Conclusion: Complicating the Immigrant/Involuntary Minority Typology." *Anthropology and Education Quarterly,* 28, 3 (September, 1997), 431–454.
27. Carla O'Connor, "Dispositions Toward (Collective) Struggle and Educational Resilience in the Inner City: A Case Analysis of Six African-American High School Students." *American Educational Research Journal,* 34, 4 (Winter, 1997), 593–629.
28. David Gillborn, "Ethnicity and Educational Performance in the United Kingdom: Racism, Ethnicity, and Variability in Achievement." *Anthropology and Education Quarterly,* 28, 3 (September, 1997), 375–393.
29. Henry A. Giroux, *Theory and Resistance in Education;* see also Jim Cummins, *Negotiating Identities;* and Herbert Kohl, *'I Won't Learn From You' and Other Thoughts on Creative Maladjustment* (New York: New Press, 1994).
30. Frederick Erickson, "Transformation and School Success: The Politics and Culture of Educational Achievement." in Evelyn Jacob and Cathie Jordan, *Minority Education.*
31. Herbert Kohl, *'I Won't Learn From You' and Other Thoughts on Creative Maladjustment* (New York: New Press, 1994), 2.
32. Michelle Fine, *Framing Dropouts: Notes on the Politics of an Urban Public High School* (Albany, NY: State University of New York Press, 1991).
33. Jerry Lipka, "Toward a Culturally-Based Pedagogy: A Case Study of One Yup'ik Eskimo Teacher." In *Transforming Curriculum for a Culturally Diverse Society,* edited by Etta R. Hollins (Mahwah, NJ: Lawrence Erlbaum Associates, 1996).
34. Jim Cummins, *Negotiating Identities: Education for Empowerment in a Diverse Society* (Ontario, CA: California Association for Bilingual Education, 1996).
35. Valerie E. Lee, Linda F. Winfield, and Thomas C. Wilson, "Academic Behaviors Among High-Achieving African-American Students." *Education and Urban Society,* 24, 1 (November 1991), 65–86.
36. See Luis Moll, "Bilingual Classroom Studies and Community Analysis: Some Recent Trends." *Educational Researcher,* 21, 2 (1992), 20–24; Eugene E. García, *Understanding and Meeting the Challenge of Student Cultural Diversity* (Boston: Houghton Mifflin Company, 1994).
37. Tamara Lucas, Rosemary Henze, and Rubén Donato, "Promoting the Success of Latino Language Minority Students: An Exploratory Study of Six High Schools." *Harvard Educational Review,* 60, 3 (1990), 315–340.
38. See, for example, Anthony S. Bryk, Valerie E. Lee, and Peter B. Holland, *Catholic Schools and the Common Good* (Cambridge, MA: Harvard Educational Review

Press, 1993); and Jacqueline Jordan Irvine and Michele Foster, *Growing up African American in Catholic Schools* (New York: Teachers College Press, 1996).

NOTES TO PAUL CHAVEZ'S CASE STUDY

1. I am grateful to Mac Lee Morante for the interview and background information for Paul's case study.
2. *Raza* refers to the people of Mexican and Mexican American origin.
3. Luis J. Rodríguez, *Always Running, La Vida Loca: Gang Days in L.A.* (New York: Simon & Schuster, 1993), 250.
4. Susan Roberta Katz, "Where the Streets Cross the Classroom: A Study of Latino Students' Perspectives on Cultural Identity in City Schools and Neighborhood Gangs." *Bilingual Research Journal,* 20, 3 and 4 (Summer/Fall 1996), 603–631.
5. Harriet D. Romo and Toni Falbo, *Latino High School Graduation: Defying the Odds* (Austin, TX: University of Texas Press, 1996).
6. Luis Rodríguez, *La Vida Loca.*
7. Luis Rodríguez, *La Vida Loca,* 9.
8. One in two Latinos report the presence of school gangs in their schools, compared with one in three Whites and two in five Blacks. See ASPIRA Institute for Policy Research, *Facing the Facts: The State of Hispanic Education, 1994* (Washington, DC: Author, 1994).
9. John Rivera and Mary Poplin, "Multicultural, Critical, Feminine and Constructive Pedagogies Seen through the Lives of Youth," *Multicultural Education, Critical Pedagogy, and the Politics of Difference,* Christine E. Sleeter and Peter L. McLaren, eds. (Albany, NY: State University of New York Press, 1995), 232–233.
10. Daniel Solorzano, "Chicano Mobility Aspirations: A Theoretical and Empirical Note." *Latino Studies Journal,* 3, 1 (January 1992), 48–66.
11. See, for example, Eugene E. García, "Educating Mexican American Students: Past Treatment and Recent Developments in Theory, Research, Policy, and Practice." In James A. Banks and Cherry A. McGee Banks (eds.), *Handbook of Research on Multicultural Education* (New York: Macmillan, 1995); see also Rubén Donato, *The Other Struggle for Equal Schools: Mexican Americans During the Civil Rights Era* (Albany, NY: State University of New York Press,1997).
12. Jean S. Phinney, "A Three-Stage Model of Ethnic Identity Development in Adolescence." In *Ethnic Identity Formation and Transmission among Hispanics and Other Minorities,* edited by Martha E. Bernal and George P. Knight (Albany,NY: State University of New York Press, 1993).

NOTES TO RON MORRIS'S CASE STUDY

1. I want to thank Beatriz McConnie Zapater, director of the Greater Egleston Community High School in Boston. She volunteered to take part in this study, selected Ron, interviewed him, and provided me with many insights and information for developing his case study.
2. A couple of years before this interview took place, homicide was the fourth most common cause of death for Black and Hispanic men of all ages. William P. O'Hare, "America's Minorities: The Demographics of Diversity." *Population Bulletin,* 47, 4 (December 1992).

3. See Jacqueline Jordan Irvine, *Black Students and School Failure: Policies, Practices, and Prescriptions* (Westport, CT: Greenwood Press, 1990); and Kofi Lomotey, *Going to School: The African-American Experience* (Albany, NY: State University of New York Press, 1990).
4. Similar results were found by Patricia Phelan, Ann Locke Davidson, and Hanh Cao Yu in their research with a diverse group of students. See *Adolescents' Worlds: Negotiating Family, Peers, and School* (New York: Teachers College Press, 1998).
5. For an in-depth discussion on the crucial positive role of African American teachers for African American students, see Gloria Ladson-Billings, *The Dreamkeepers* (San Francisco: Jossey-Bass Publishers, 1994); and Michele Foster, *Black Teachers on Teaching* (New York: The New Press, 1997).
6. Josephine A. Bright, "Beliefs in Action: Family Contributions to African-American Student Success." *Equity and Choice,* 10, 2 (Winter 1994), 5–13.
7. Louis Harris and Associates, Inc., *Dropping out or Staying in High School: Pilot Survey of Young African American Males in Four Cities* (New York: Commonwealth Fund, 1994).

part three

Implications of Diversity for Teaching and Learning in a Multicultural Society

———•———

The stories of the students whose voices you have heard in the preceding chapters are striking examples of strength and resilience, of the desire to do well and succeed in spite of sometimes overwhelming odds. They are also stories of defeat and despair when schools provide few structures for success. Students who do poorly and students who do well are equally meaningful sources for discovering how to develop enriching learning environments. They have much to teach us about education in a multicultural society. As Yolanda so perceptively said, teachers "learn more from their students than from where they go study."

Part III analyzes the experiences of the young people in the case studies you have read, and reviews some of the lessons they can teach us by placing their stories in the broader sociopolitical context of schools and society. Students, although rarely consulted, are eloquent in expressing their own needs, interests, and concerns. It is in this spirit that their stories and hopes are presented.

Given the small number of students whose experiences are presented here, a caveat is in order. These young people are not meant to represent all other students of their ethnic, racial, or economic backgrounds. Each of their stories is unique. As case studies, they provide portraits of the lives and experiences of *particular* students because they are examples of the complex interplay of relationships in families, communities, and schools. Although overarching claims for the education of *all* students in U.S. society cannot be made, these case studies can help identify the experiences and viewpoints of specific students who have been successful in school and those who have not. Because they reflect a wide cross section of U.S. school enrollment, they illuminate some key issues about culture and power relationships and schooling for success in a multicultural society. I hope that you will find useful information for learning about students in similar circumstances.

Chapter 8 explores those conditions and experiences that students in the case studies perceive to be central to academic success. This exploration describes how young people, in their own words, define academic success; what they believe has helped them achieve, and what has held them back. The major purpose of this discussion is to explore what teachers and schools can do to provide successful academic environments for all students.

In Chapter 9, a definition of multicultural education is proposed, using seven characteristics: *antiracism and antidiscrimination, basic education, importance for all students, pervasiveness, education for social justice, a process,* and *critical pedagogy.* This definition takes into account the structural, political, cultural, and linguistic contexts presented in Part II.

Chapter 10 concerns three major conditions that promote learning among students: maintaining and affirming cultural connections, supporting extracurricular activities and experiences, and developing positive learning environments in schools. In this chapter, the seven characteristics used to define multicultural education are developed further in a model ranging from *tolerance* to *affirmation, solidarity,* and *critique.*

Chapter 11, the final chapter, gives teachers an opportunity to reflect creatively and critically on their own pedagogy and on the impact of particular policies and practices in schools. Some concrete examples of multicultural education based on the issues considered in Part II are presented and readers are challenged to develop their own examples.

chapter *8*

Learning from Students

*T*he voices of the students in the 12 case studies are testimony to the vitality and spirit of youth and culture. Despite a variety of conditions that might severely test the mettle and aspirations of others in similar circumstances, these youths have demonstrated a staunch determination to succeed in school and in life. Most define themselves as successful students and are proud of this, so understanding the insights of these particular students can be vital for educators interested in providing effective learning environments for all students. Students who have not been as fortunate also have important messages for us, for they challenge us to reconsider prevailing assumptions about learning and teaching.

In this chapter, four major issues that emerged from the case studies are reviewed:

- A redefinition of success and achievement
- A tenacious, although at times conflicted pride in and maintenance of culture and language.
- The key role of activities outside of academics in sustaining students' enthusiasm and motivation for school.
- The central role of family, community, and school in providing environments for success.

THE MEANING OF SUCCESS

Many of the young people in the case studies have a conception of education that is distinct from that commonly held by schools. For some, *being educated* is directly derived from family and cultural definitions of this concept. Marisol, Yolanda, and Manuel all believe that in addition to being good students academically, being educated means being respectful, polite, and obedient, a broader connotation typical of Latinos and others from nonmainstream cultures. Vinh also defines it in much broader terms than U.S. society in general, maintaining that being educated means being, among other things, "nice" and "friendly," as well as listening to your teachers and doing your homework.

The role of hard work in becoming educated was mentioned by most of the students. For them, *intelligence* is not an innate ability or immutable quality, something that one is born with, as it often is defined in U.S. society. On the contrary, intelligence is something that one cultivates, studies hard for, and eventually achieves. Being smart is a goal, not a characteristic. Being smart is also the result of family and community support and the quality of the care shown by teachers and schools. In this sense, intelligence is within everyone's reach.

Grades are a major indicator of academic success in our schools, and their significance holds true for most of the students we interviewed. But contrary to what many teachers and schools may believe, grades may not be as meaningful to academically successful students as are other manifestations of their success. Many of the successful students mentioned being satisfied with a grade for which they worked hard, even if it was not the best grade. On the other hand, Yolanda's or Fern's A's in English are not particularly satisfying to them because the classes were neither engaging nor challenging. Yolanda's social studies class and Fern's science class, both far more demanding and ones in which they did not get as high a grade, were their favorites. Ron, one of the students who has had a problematic educational experience, agreed as well when he said, "I can get straight D's or straight F's and still know more than half the people in the classroom." For many students, grades are not as important as "doing the best you can."

The purposes of education are also much broader and more noble for many of these students than the limited goals schools often set. For example, while teachers often talk in terms of future employment and career goals, many of these students see education as far more. For Vinh, going to school has one purpose: to become educated. A good job is secondary. Yolanda put it most dramatically: Education for her is nourishment, just as necessary as eating.

For Marisol, the purpose of education is also broader. She wants to "be somebody." At present, she has only a vague notion of what this might be, but she does not confuse being educated with preparing for a job. A word should be said, however, about the vague or romantic ideals female students tend to have regarding their future. Marisol, Yolanda, Fern, and Linda all talked about dual and seemingly contradictory career goals. Yolanda wants to be either a computer programmer or a flight attendant; Marisol, a nurse or a model; Fern, a fashion lawyer or U.S. president; and Linda, a teacher or a world famous singer. Particularly for females, the reality of limited choices in the past has had an impact. Most of these young women have chosen to select what to them seem the most glamorous of these choices. Besides culture, language, and social class, gender also mediates what students may consider realistic goals for their future.

But females' ethnic cultures not only *limit* their choices but they also *expand* them. Girls are often subject to limited role expectations and gender stereotyping, but they also receive affirming and powerful messages about being female from their cultures. A study done by Pilar Muñoz and Josette Ludwig, two former graduate students of mine, can illustrate this. They interviewed 10 Puerto Rican women to determine what messages these women had received during their childhood regarding their future role in society. All the women reported that they had been taught to be submissive, quiet, long-suffering, and patient by their mothers and grandmothers. These were the verbal messages they heard. But they also learned, through their mothers' and grandmothers' nonverbal attitudes and behaviors, that women need to be resourceful, intelligent, and stronger than men. These dual and conflicting messages were not lost on the women, all of whom were extraordinarily strong and resilient and had learned to "take care of themselves."[1]

That some of the female students in the case studies have chosen potential careers consistent with restrictive roles does not necessarily mean that these are the only values they have internalized. These young women have also learned to be incredibly determined and to believe in themselves. Young people need to sift through a multitude of values to determine which are the appropriate and more empowering choices to make. Schools have a key role to play in affording all young people a variety of role models and expectations that challenge the limiting roles assigned to them either by their own communities or by society at large. Vivian Lee and Rachel Sing, for instance, found that teachers may assume that the cultural values of female students of nonmainstream cultures inevitably lead to poor academic achievement, low self-esteem, and lack of leadership potential. Instead, Lee and Sing urge educators to encourage immigrant girls to negotiate their way between both cultures and reject the "either-or" choices that are offered.[2]

PRIDE AND CONFLICT IN CULTURE

One of the most consistent, and least expected, outcomes to emerge from these case studies was the resoluteness with which young people maintained pride and satisfaction in their culture and the strength they derived from it. This does not mean that their pride is sustained without great conflict, hesitation, or contradiction. Because the positive sense of cultural identification challenges the messages and models of an essentially assimilationist society, it creates its own internal conflicts. But the fact that almost all of the students mentioned a deep pride in their culture cannot be overlooked. Students volunteered that their culture helped them in many ways, and that they felt proud of who they were. The exception was Vanessa, who was uncomfortable even describing herself in ethnic terms. Vanessa reflected pride and shame in her cultural background, but for different reasons.

The students talked about their culture in a number of ways. Most of them defined themselves naturally in cultural terms, without the embarrassment that one might expect. These young people seem to understand quite intuitively that their heritage informs and enriches them. Strong self-identification is understood as a value. "You gotta know who you are," is how Manuel expressed it.

Conflict and Ambivalence

Pride in culture was neither uniform nor easy for these young people. Marisol, for instance, did not find it necessary to take a course in Puerto Rican history. She did not even seem to think that the school should offer it because, as she put it, she already knew what she should know—although it was clear to me during our interviews that she knew virtually nothing of Puerto Rican history. The experiences of most of the other students in the case studies are similar. Notable exceptions

were Avi and James, who had religious institutions on which to rely for their cultural education.

Pierre Bourdieu's theory of *cultural capital* and of the role of schools in determining what knowledge has greatest status is illuminating here.[3] Because schools
primarily reflect the knowledge and values of economically and culturally dominant groups in society, they validate and reinforce the cultural capital that students
from such groups already bring from home. This validation takes place through the
overt and covert curriculum and the school climate. The confirmation of the dominant culture's supremacy represents a *symbolic violence* against groups that are
devalued. The cultural model held up for all is not within easy reach of all, and only
token numbers of students from less valued groups can achieve it. If those from
dominated groups learn and take on this cultural capital—along the way losing their
own culture, language, and values—they may succeed. In this way, the myth of a
meritocracy is maintained while few students from dominated groups are permitted
to succeed. Given the rules of the game, it is surprising that as many succeed.

Some examples of the symbolic violence suffered by the students will illustrate
this point. James's Lebanese culture is missing from all school activities, although
other, more "visible" cultures are represented. The importance of his culture is
diminished through this absence. Fern's invisibility in her school and in the school's
books and curriculum is another example of the devaluation of knowledge.
Students may perceive that what is not taught is not worthy of learning. In contrast,
the languages and cultures of Yolanda and Manuel are highly evident in their
schools, and teachers often refer to them explicitly, giving them even more status.
The schooling of these two students has more closely reflected their home values,
and in both cases, bilingual programs have been at least partly responsible. Ron and
Paul, although not previously successful in school, have become empowered by the
multicultural curriculum at their alternative schools. For Ron, an eighth grade class
in Black African History that made him feel "like the realest person on earth" was
the only reprieve from an otherwise disempowering and alienating curriculum.

That symbolic violence should cause conflict in students from devalued
groups is hardly surprising. This problem is not unique to the United States but is
evident wherever one group is dominant and held up as the appropriate model.
The Finns in Sweden are a case in point. Formerly colonized by the Swedes, the
Finns who emigrate to Sweden are often perceived in negative and sometimes hostile ways. Neither their culture nor their language is generally valued in Swedish
society. In the words of a young Finn who was educated in Sweden and experienced this firsthand, "When the idea had eaten itself deeply into my soul that it
was despicable to be a Finn, I began to feel ashamed of my origins." The result can
be a conflict that is difficult to resolve. This particular young man concluded that
such conflict was the price he had to pay: "In short, in order to live in harmony
with my surroundings, I had to live in perpetual conflict with myself."[4]

For the students in these case studies, symbolic violence has also worked, but
only partially. For example, Marisol's idea of important school knowledge is only
that which the school has deemed to be so. Only American history, not Puerto
Rican history, is what counts. She also says that Puerto Ricans are "way badder"

than Whites. At the same time and with what may seem to be contradictory feelings, Marisol is very proud of herself, her family, and her people in general. Accordingly, her pride and satisfaction in her culture are conflicted.

The painful alienation from family and culture is not inevitable, although it is a particularly difficult dilemma for the first generation. Even though the task of trying to fit together what are at times contradictory values takes its toll, it need not always result in the complete loss of language and culture. We have seen in our case studies that students struggle to maintain language and culture, in spite of the difficulty of doing so.

Although they have learned to feel proud of themselves for many things, including their culture, their dexterity in functioning in two worlds, and their bilingualism, several of these students have also learned to feel ashamed of their culture and of the people who represent it. They face what they may see as irreconcilable choices: denying or losing their culture if they want to succeed, or keeping it and failing. Sometimes students blame their families and communities for perceived failures while absolving the school of almost all responsibility. After all, they reason, the school cannot be wrong.

Rich sometimes used words to describe his community that either victimized or blamed people for their failure: Blacks are "tacky," "lazy," not "professional," and used to "settling for the easiest way out," some of the very words used by those outside the community to criticize it. Rich used himself as a yardstick with which to measure others of his background. Although demanding accountability from one's own community is necessary, the critical analysis that must accompany it is missing. Rich's case, however, is complex. For instance, he does not place all of the responsibility on his own community. He considers the role schools and teachers play by having low expectations of Black students. He also has learned the hard lesson that "Blacks have to work harder at things."

Vanessa's case is especially notable in this regard. Because she is actively opposed to racism and other forms of discrimination (note her actions beginning in elementary school and her stand against heterosexism), she attempts to distance herself from the privileges she has earned simply as a result of her ethnic background. Vanessa knows that she has benefited because of being White but she does not believe this is fair. Consequently, she has taken the position that one's culture and race are unimportant, accepting color blindness as the ultimate expression of fairness.

Others for whom the conflict is simply too great are expelled or drop out, either physically or psychologically. This was the case with Paul and Ron. For many students who drop out of school, the reason is not that they are incapable of doing the work. Michelle Fine's research in an urban high school found that "successful" students, that is, those who stayed in school, were significantly more depressed, less politically aware, and more conformist than students who had dropped out. Dropouts were more likely to be relatively nondepressed, critical of social injustice, and willing to take initiative. Fine concluded that the price of success for students who remain in school may be silencing one's voice.[5] In a related vein, an ethnographic study by Marietta Saravia-Shore and Herminio Martinez of

Puerto Rican students who had dropped out of school and were currently attending an alternative program found that the clash between conflicting values of their families, peers, and schools were a major impetus for leaving school.[6] Similarly, Donna Deyhle and Karen Swisher, in an extensive review of literature on the education of American Indian students, concluded that the major reason for leaving school was students' perceptions that the school curriculum was not connected to their lives.[7]

Paul and Ron are classic examples of students who leave school not because of their inability to do the work, but rather because of alienating curricula and learning environments combined with difficult conditions in their lives. Now that they find themselves in alternative schools that provide different models of curriculum and pedagogy, they have a second chance.

Another way for young people to resolve the conflict they feel between pride and culture, at least if they are to succeed in school, is to deny the importance of their culture *in the school setting*. At home, the culture may remain vital if they wish to maintain close family relationships. At school, their culture becomes unimportant and superfluous.

As we have seen, most of the young people in the case studies have struggled to remain true to themselves. But the process of fitting into a dominant culture is a complex one and the students are also challenging the dichotomy between being who they are and succeeding academically. This dilemma has been aptly described by Laurie Olsen in her comprehensive study of a highly diverse urban high school in California. One young woman interviewed by Olsen talked about the pressure from peers and teachers to stay within strictly defined cultural borders. She observed, "They want to make you just their culture and if you try to be who you are, and try to be both American and yourself, forget it. It won't work. It's not allowed."[8]

Unfortunately, identity is often viewed as a fixed construct rather than as constantly evolving, shifting, and modified by external contexts and diverse cultures. According to the historian David Tyack,

> Ideologies that stress only similarity or difference do not adequately capture the way social diversity actually operates in American society and public education. By ignoring the interactive nature of cultural exchange and by posing bipolar choices, they also offer questionable guidance about what might be a better approach to social diversity.[9]

The young men and women in the case studies are entangled in the formidable task of defining who they are.

Self-Identification and Conflict

One of the cultural conflicts that some of these students felt was expressed as inability to identify both as "American" and as belonging to their cultural group. Their sense of pride in culture precluded identification with the United States. For some students, claiming both is denying their background or being a traitor to it.

Why young people might make this choice is no mystery: Ethnicity in the United States, according to Stanley Aronowitz, has been "generally viewed as a temporary condition on the way to assimilation."[10] This being the case, it is no surprise that Manuel, for example, is emphatic about saying: "I'm Cape Verdean. I cannot be an American because I'm not an American. That's it."

Manuel did not entertain the possibility that he could be *both* American and also Cape Verdean. Our society has forced many young people to make a choice, and the students in the case studies have usually, although not always, made it in favor of their heritage. Although this is an extraordinarily courageous stand on their part, given their youth and the negative messages about ethnicity around them, it can also be a limiting one. The consequences of such a choice probably affect what they think they deserve and are entitled to in our society. Having no attachment to the dominant society, they may also feel they have no rights. That is, they feel they have no right to claim their fair share of society's power and resources or even to demand equality within it. Exclusive identification as a member of their cultural group may also exacerbate the conflict of being "separate," "different," and consequently powerless.

The way these young people sustain culture is also fascinating to observe. In more than one case, they have maintained their "deep culture," particularly values and worldviews, although they may lose the more superficial aspects such as food and music preferences. These modifications are a function not only of clashing messages from school and home, but also of young peoples' involvement with a peer culture with its own rituals and norms. Although peer culture acts as a primary assimilating structure of our society, we should not assume that individuals have completely abandoned their family's culture simply because they act like other young people their age.

Creating New Cultures

Identity is constantly being negotiated and renegotiated by young people. Even adolescents of similar backgrounds have starkly different senses of their personhood. For instance, in her research among various groups of Asian and Asian American students in an urban high school, Stacey Lee identified one of the groups as "new wavers." Mostly working-class and poor ethnic Chinese, Vietnamese, and Cambodian, these young people challenged the Asian American "model minority" myth: They did not buy into the idea of education as the key to success in the United States. They often had negative and defiant relationships with teachers, and generally did not do well in school. Lee concluded that the new wavers serve as an example of how identities are always mediated through community and school contexts, and this defies easy categorization according to ethnicity.[11] In research with inner-city youths of various backgrounds, Shirley Brice Heath also has suggested that traditional racial and ethnic categories are increasingly inadequate for defining today's youth because such categories present ethnic and cultural communities as homogeneous and static. On the contrary, she found that the racial and ethnic identities of most young people in inner cities are situated and multiple.[12]

Young people are involved in creating new cultures, and this was clear among the case study students. Their native cultures do not simply disappear, as schools and society might expect or want them to. Rather, aspects of the native culture are retained, modified, reinserted into different environments, and recast so that they are workable for a new society. These young people do not totally express the original values of their cultures, nor have they been completely assimilated into the new culture. Marisol, for instance, loves rap and hip hop music, not salsa. Nevertheless, the influence of the Latino culture (as well as other cultures) on these musical forms cannot be denied.

Fashioning a new culture is no easy task. It involves first the difficult and painful experience of learning to survive in an environment that may have values and behaviors at polar extremes from those in the home, for instance, the oft-cited example of Latino children looking down when being reprimanded. Whereas these children have been taught in their homes to look down as a sign of respect, in U.S. mainstream society such behavior is generally interpreted as disrespectful. Children who misbehave are expected to "take their medicine" and "look me straight in the eye." In this case, the behaviors expected at home and at school are diametrically opposed. Even five-year-old children are expected to understand the subtle nuances of these behaviors. They usually do, although their teachers may be completely unaware of the conflicts involved or of the great strains such competing expectations may cause. This example only scratches the surface.

In creating new cultures, young people also need to choose from an array of values and behaviors, selecting those that fit in the new society and discarding or transforming others. The process is neither conscious nor planned. Those whose values and behaviors differ from the mainstream are inevitably involved in this transformation every day. Whether children or adults, students or workers, they are directly engaged in changing the complexion, attitudes, and values of our society. In the process, they may experience the pain and conflict the young people in our case studies demonstrated so well.

The point to remember here is that U.S. society does not simply impose its culture on all newcomers. The process is neither as linear nor as straightforward as those who claim complete success for the process of *Anglo-conformity* might have us believe.[13] But the result has not been a truly pluralistic society either. Although the United States is in fact multicultural, it is so usually in spite of itself; it is not the result of a goal or a desired state. Our society for the most part still reflects and perpetuates European American values and worldviews. But it has always also reflected, albeit at times poorly or stereotypically and against its will, the values of less respected and dominated groups as well. Latino heritage, for instance, can be seen in innumerable ways, from architecture in the Southwest to the myth of the cowboy. Jazz, widely acknowledged to be the greatest authentic U.S. music, is primarily African American in origin rather than Anglo or European American.

What is "American" is neither simply an alien culture imposed on dominated groups nor an immigrant culture transposed indiscriminately to new soil. Neither is it an amalgam of old and new. What is "American" is the result of interactions of old, new, and created cultures. These interactions are neither benign nor smooth.

Often characterized by unavoidable tension and great conflict, the creation of new cultures takes place in the battlefields of the family, the community, and the schools.

But creating new cultures is an exceedingly complex process, made even more complicated by schools, which consciously or not, perceive their role as being to transform all students into a middle-class, European American model. "They want to *monoculture* us," says a student in a video of successful Hispanic students in a Boston high school speaking about their identities and their schooling.[14] As we saw in the case studies, students of diverse backgrounds respond in numerous ways to the pressures of an assimilationist society that is attempting to do away with differences. These young people are involved in the difficult job of creating new alternatives for achieving success in school. By refusing to accept either assimilation or rejection, they force us to look at new ways of defining success. They contradict the road to success that schools and society have traditonally defined, in the process creating new models:

- They have held onto their culture, or at least parts of it, sometimes obstinately so.
- They are often bilingual, even demanding to use their language in school whether or not they are in a bilingual program.
- They are involved with their peers from a variety of backgrounds, with what would be considered typical American teenage activities, tastes, and behaviors.

As a result, they are involved in the process of transforming some of the values of our society.

Identity and Learning

Students pick up competing messages about language and culture from teachers, schools, and society, and this was evident in the case studies. One of the messages to emerge from the case studies can be stated as follows: *Culture is important,* something that most of the students are proud of and maintain. But students also learn that *culture is unimportant* in the school environment.

Recent research corroborates the perspectives of many of the case study students that culture *is* significant, and that it can support learning. In Donna Deyhle's research with Navajo youth, for instance, she found that those students who were able to maintain Navajo and reservation connections gained a firm footing in their own community, and they were also the students who most thrived in the outside world. In comparing a reservation and nonreservation school, she also discovered that the reservation school was more successful in retaining and graduating students. Deyhle concluded that Navajo youths who have a strong traditional culture, or what she termed "cultural integrity," are also the most academically successful students.[15]

A comprehensive portrait of immigrant students in U.S. schools by Alejandro Portes and Rubén Rumbaut reached a similar conclusion: In reviewing numerous studies of the past two decades concerning immigrant students, they found that a positive and enduring sense of cultural heritage—as manifested in strong ties to the ethnic culture and maintainence of native language—is *positively* related to mental health, social well being, and educational achievement. One study that they report on, for instance, determined that students whose bilingualism is limited were far more at risk of dropping out than were fluent bilinguals. Another found a marked relationship between acculturation and risky behaviors associated with poor physical and mental health. In this sense, premature assimilation can act as a risk factor for academic failure and mental illness. They conclude that "selective acculturation," where learning U.S. mainstream ways is combined with sustaining strong cultural bonds, can lead to positive outcomes for many immigrant youth.[16]

Recent research questions the assumption that assimilation is inevitable and healthy. When students themselves are asked, for instance, they generally come out on the side of cultural and linguistic maintenance. Studies on student perspectives join the expanding research that confirms the negative impact of assimilation on students' academic achievement.[17]

One intriguing lesson from the case studies and from the referenced research is this: *The more that students are involved in resisting assimilation while maintaining their culture and language, the more successful they will be in school.* That is, cultural maintenance, even if conflicted, seems to have a positive impact on academic success. This obviously is not true in all cases, as there are many examples of people who have thought that they had to assimilate to succeed in school. But in these cases, we can legitimately ask whether it is necessary to give up part of oneself to be successful. That is the question that these young people are asking themselves and us.

In these particular case studies, students are suggesting an alternative route to academic success. In most cases, maintaining cultural connections seems to have had at least a partially positive influence on academic achievement. Although it is important not to overstate this assertion, it is indeed a real possibility and one that severely challenges the "melting pot" ideology that has dominated U.S. schools and society throughout the twentieth century. As we saw in Chapter 6, similar findings in terms of language maintenance have been consistently reported by researchers in bilingual education. That is, when students' language is used as the basis for their education, when it is respected and valued, students tend to succeed in school.

The notion that assimilation is a prerequisite for success in school or society is contested both by the research reviewed here and by the case studies. The research calls into question the oft-cited claim that students who are not from European American backgrounds have poor self-images and low self-esteem. It is not that simple. The role of schools and society in *creating* low self-esteem in children needs to be considered. That is, students do not simply develop poor self-concepts out of the blue; self-concepts are also the result of policies and practices of schools and society that respect and affirm some groups while devaluing and rejecting others. Although students from dominated groups might partially internalize some of the many negative messages to which they are subjected every day about their culture, race, ethnic group, class, and language, they are not simply passive recipients of such messages. They actively resist negative messages through more positive interactions with peers, family, and even school. The mediating role of families, communities, teachers, and schools helps to contradict detrimental messages and reinforce more affirming ones.

For example, James, in spite of the many negative messages about Arabs to which he has been subjected, has an unshakable confidence in himself, confidence that extends beyond academics: "In a lot of the things that I do, I usually do good." Fern says, "I succeed in everything I do." Yolanda likes "making my mind work." In spite of what she may hear about the supposed ignorance or laziness of Mexicans and Mexican Americans, she is certain that she is intelligent. Even Paul, through his gang activities, is seeking a way to assert his culture and identity. The result may be negative, but the impulse is understandable and a sad statement about a society that has few outlets for positive identification with ethnic cultures and languages.

Students in these case studies also consistently mentioned that their parents taught them to be proud of their culture, that they spoke their native language at home, and that it makes them "feel proud." They also mention schools that reflected their culture and language and helped them to be successful through a bilingual program and other affirming activities. Ron stated that his mother wanted him to be "the best Black man that ever lived on the face of this earth!" Yolanda talked of her teachers' awareness and support of her bilingualism and culture (in this case, the dancing group to which she belongs) in helping her succeed.

The conclusion that sustaining native language and culture nurtures academic achievement turns on its head not only conventional educational philosophy but also the policies and practices of schools that have done everything possible effectively to eradicate students' identities in order, they maintain, for all students to succeed in school. Rather than attempting to erase culture and language, schools should do everything in their power to *use, affirm,* and *sustain* them as a foundation for students' academic success. School policies and practices that stress cultural pride, build on students' native language ability, and emphasize the history and experiences of the students' communities would be the result.

BEYOND ACADEMICS

In nearly all of the case studies of students who have been successful in school, significant involvement in activities beyond academics emerged as a key component. Whether through school-related organizations, hobbies, religious groups, or other activities, students found ways to support their learning. Often, the activities had little to do with academics. Activities had several important roles, both academic and nonacademic: keeping students on track, removing them from negative peer pressure, developing leadership and critical thinking skills, and giving them a feeling of belonging.

Keeping on Track

One way in which activities other than school help is by keeping students "on track." That is, nonschool activities focus students' attention on the importance of school while at the same time providing some relief from it. This finding is consistent with other research. For instance, Jabari Mahiri's research on the literacy activities of 10- to 12-year-old African American males during participation in a neighborhood basketball association found that this sport had immense motivational value in inspiring them to engage in literacy activities. Yet schools too often overlook ways in which the personal interests of youths can enhance their learning.[18] In the case studies, extracurricular activities had a definitive influence, and these extended beyond simply sports.

Marisol, for example, was very involved in the teen clinic. This clinic, located in the high school itself, helps teenagers with information about sexuality, birth control, and parenting. Teenage pregnancy and infant mortality rates in her city are among the highest in the state and provided the impetus for starting the clinic, which is widely acclaimed as innovative and unique. Her involvement in the teen clinic helped Marisol keep her mind on the importance of staying in school.

Extracurricular activities, according to Vanessa, are "a way of releasing energy and feeling good about yourself and being in shape. And working with other people." Fern, too, is quite clear about how she uses her involvement in sports: "I compare it to stuff like when I can't get science, or like in sewing, I'll look at that machine and I'll say, 'This is a basketball; I can overcome it.'"

Shields against Peer Pressure

The negative peer pressure to which most students are subjected can be very difficult to resist. But most of the students in the case studies have been successful in doing so. One reason has been the activities in which they have been involved, which for some act almost like a shield against negative influence. This is described vividly by Paul when he says, "Now it's like I figure if I'm more involved in school, I won't be so much involved in the gang, you know?"

For other students as well, involvement in these school-related and community activities takes up nonschool time, almost acting as a preventive strategy for discouraging less productive, although at times more alluring, activities. This is the reason, for example, that Manuel dropped some of his friends; at just about the same time, he joined a church in which he is deeply involved. Linda's devotion to music and Avi's insistence on honoring the Sabbath can probably be understood in this way as well.

Developing Critical Thinking and Leadership Skills

Extracurricular and out-of-school activities also contribute to the development of important skills, including critical thinking and leadership qualities. Through a theater workshop based on students' experiences and ideas, Manuel was able to analyze critically his own experience as an immigrant to this country. This workshop gave him a place to analyze his experiences more deeply and to articulate consciously and clearly the pain and fear that he felt in his first years here.

James's involvement with bicycle racing, his self-acclaimed first love, consumes both his time and attention. Before his bike accident, he was riding 40 miles per day. But James's involvement extends beyond racing itself: He subscribes to all of the related magazines, has gotten his racing license, and has been actively recruiting others interested in the sport in order to start a biking club. He is also planning to approach local bicycle merchants with the idea of obtaining financial support to sponsor the team.

Avi's work in the synagogue is another powerful example of how extracurricular activities can develop leadership skills. Not only does his involvement in the temple require a great deal of study and sacrifice, but it also makes him a role model for others in his community. Vanessa's work with a peer education group has helped her develop important leadership qualities and a growing critical awareness and sensitivity to issues of exclusion and stratification. In all of these cases, skills related to academic achievement may be developed as a by-product of involvement in extracurricular activities.

Belonging

The feeling of belonging, so important for adolescents, is also a benefit of participating in extracurricular activities. Young people will seek to fit in and belong in any way they can. Some meet this need by joining gangs or taking part in other harmful activities in which they feel part of a "family." For many young people, the satisfaction of belonging is particularly evident in activities related to their ethnic group. Most of the students in the case studies have found positive outlets in sports, clubs, and religious activities. Rich, for example, says he "didn't know there was a place for me" until he became involved in music. Yolanda's mother is strict and does not allow her as much freedom as many of her peers, so her membership in a folkloric Mexican dance group is probably an important outlet for her creative energy. Paul and Ron are notable exceptions to participation in out-of-classroom activities. In both cases, they succumbed to the lure of some of the only "extracurricular" activities in their neighborhoods—gangs and criminal activity. Yet when provided with more positive outlets, they have blossomed: Ron became the star of the football team and Paul is immersed in an after-school job.

Manuel, James, Rich, and Avi have found their niche through, among other things, their church or synagogue. Their religious commitment affirms their ethnicity as well. For Manuel, a Protestant sect is much more in tune with his culture than the Catholic church typically associated with Cape Verdeans. As he so dramatically said during one of his interviews, "I felt that God had moved there," implying that a cultural resonance was missing in the local Catholic church. James's Christian Maronite religion also provides a strong bond with his culture. Rich combines his cultural and religious activities by playing the organ in a local Black church.

These are valuable illustrations of how extracurricular activities in school, activities outside of school including hobbies, and religious and cultural organizations support students in their learning. Rather than detracting from their academic success by taking time away from homework or other school-related activities, such involvement helps young people by channeling their creative and physical energy. In some cases, the activities may also have academic benefits. For example, the development of leadership qualities and critical thinking skills helps students in the classroom as well.

FAMILY, COMMUNITY, AND SCHOOL ENVIRONMENTS FOR SUCCESS

The case studies provide ample and sometimes dramatic evidence of the importance of family, community, and school in supporting and maintaining the academic success of students. Successful students are surrounded by messages that encourage success, including direct and indirect support from family and friends, activities that enhance rather than detract from success, and teachers and other school staff who demonstrate their care.

The Crucial Role of Family

The ways families support children in their learning are complex and sometimes not what one might expect. Non–middle-class families in particular may not have much experience with academic involvement or achievement, but they do what they can to help their children in other ways. One way that families indicate their support for academic success is through high expectations. Education is highly valued by the families of all these students, regardless of their economic background. In fact, in some instances, working-class and poor parents have even *more* hope in education than middle-class parents, for obvious reasons.[19] They cannot always help their children with homework or in learning English, and because they may lack the "cultural capital" valued in the society at large, they may not be able to pass it down to their children. As a result, the ways they manifest high expectations are sometimes indirect. But the messages they verbalize to their children are clear. Vinh says his uncle supports him by saying, "Next time, you should do better." "My mom says that they want me to go to school," says Yolanda. "That way, I won't be stuck with a job like them." Ron jokes that when his mother complains about his staying out all night or hanging out with friends, "I be upstairs, and I wish this woman would shut up!"

Such messages, although powerful, are not always enough. In many of our case studies, the young people had great respect and appreciation for their families and understood the sacrifices that had been made on their behalf. But this appreciation did not always make their school experiences any easier or more tolerable. Because their parents were not always able to give them concrete help and tangible guidance, students sometimes lacked a sense of direction. Manuel put it most poignantly when he said, "If I felt like I had support from my family, if they only knew the language. . . . If they were educated, I could make it big, you see what I'm saying?" Although parents' inability to speak English is not a liability in itself, it can become one if the school does not provide alternative means for student learning through such structures as bilingual programs and homework centers.

Given the kind of help middle-class parents are able to provide for their children, Manuel is absolutely right when he concludes, "I would've had a better opportunity, a better chance." Manuel's perceptions are reinforced by an ethnographic longitudinal research study by Guadalupe Valdés of 10 Mexican immigrant families in the Southwest. In examining what may appear to schools to be indifference to education by Mexican parents, she found just the opposite. That is, she found that working-class Mexican immigrant families bring to the United States goals, life plans, and experiences that, while valuable in their own right, may not help them make sense of what the schools expect of their children.[20]

In spite of a lack of formal education and limited experience with the means for achieving academic success, families often compensate by providing other critical support to their children. In the case of students from different linguistic backgrounds, parents and other family members frequently maintain native language use in the home, despite contrary messages from school and society. The families in most of our case studies have *insisted* on native language use in the home as an important means of maintaining their culture and emotional attachment to their children through family values. Such language use helps students develop literacy and prepares them for school. The more the students were able to use language in a variety of ways and in diverse contexts, the more they replicated the literacy skills necessary for successful schoolwork.

Maintaining native language also implies nurturing cultural connections through such activities as family rituals and traditions, not to mention the even more meaningful underlying cultural values that help form young people's attitudes and behaviors. "Apprenticeship" in their families, and the consequent learning of culture, language, and values, is a primary way in which children receive and internalize the message that they are important.

We have already seen that some of the students in these case studies have assumed a family role of mature and responsible adult. This is particularly true of Manuel, who had to deal with doctors, hospitals, and other agencies during his father's illness. In a curious way, parents' messages about their children's worthiness are reinforced when young people are compelled to take on these responsibilities. Young people develop confidence and self-respect through interactions with the society at large on behalf of their families. This role has probably contributed to the academic success of some of them, even though it may mean that they have to miss school to assist in family matters. But we must also question the need for young people to take on such heavy responsibilities at an early age.

Encouraging communication within the family is another way parents support the academic success of their children. The importance of talking with their parents about issues central to their lives was mentioned by a number of young people. Yolanda, for example, said that she and her mother talk about "girl stuff" as well as about the significance of school. Marisol also emphasized how different her parents are from others because they talk with her and her siblings about "things that are happening nowadays." For Vinh, even long-distance communication is meaningful: He writes to his parents weekly and is in turn revitalized by their messages. Linda's description of shared dinnertime in her family is a beautiful expression of the value of communication.

In numerous ways, academically successful students in these case studies made it clear that they have dedicated their school success to their parents, almost as a way of thanking them for the sacrifices parents have made. Students frequently mentioned that their parents were the motivating force behind their success, even if the parents did not always completely understand or appreciate what it meant. For example, Paul was inspired to return to school by his mother's own return to school. More than one student mentioned making her or his parents *happy*. This focus on parents' happiness, not what one might expect from sophisticated and modern adolescents, is a theme that emerged time and again.

Students in the case studies often describe their parents in remarkably tender and loving ways. From Marisol's "my parents are really beautiful people," to Vanessa's "they're caring and they're willing to go against the norm," students make it clear that their parents have provided warm and close-knit environments, which have had a significant influence on their lives and the formation of values. Rich describes his family as "just a happy-go-lucky family" and says, "It's wonderful being a member of my family." Linda says that her parents are "always there for me, all the time" and even understands the "twisted reasons" for their rules and limits. Fern, in spite of the many problems her family has confronted, says, "I'm gifted to have a family like this." Most of these young people are happy and secure within their families.

This is not to say that parents whose children are not successful in school have *not* provided affirming environments. There are a multitude of complex reasons why students are successful in school, and a close and warm relationship with parents is only one of them. Notwithstanding the caring and loving environments that parents may provide for their children, their children may still be rebellious, alienated, or unsuccessful in school. A good example is Paul, who maintains, "If it wasn't for the family, the love I get from my family, I would look for it in my homeboys. . . . I had a love that kept me home." While earnestly stating this, Paul is still engaged in the gang. Before attending his alternative school, Ron said he continuously asked himself, "Why do I keep going to jail? Why do I always keep . . . doing all this stuff to my mother?"

Other issues intervene in the complex interplay of conditions that influence academic success. What Carlos Cortés calls "the societal curriculum," that is, influences of the general society—including the mass media, gender role expectations, anti-immigrant hysteria, and rampant violence—are another layer of the sociopolitical context that needs to be considered.[21] Other influences may also affect school achievement: rank within family, other family dynamics including relationships among siblings, and simple personality and idiosyncratic differences. It appears, however, that a close and open relationship between children and their parents (or other guardians) is a necessary but incomplete element of school success.

Although parents and other family members are obviously prominent in the success of the case study students, they are for the most part uninvolved according to the traditional definition of parent involvement. There are some exceptions: Fern's father never misses a school activity, and Vanessa's mother was on her local school committee. But most of the students' families do not go to school unless called, do not attend meetings or volunteer in school activities, and are not members of parent organizations. This is somewhat surprising considering the research on the relationship between parent involvement and their children's academic achievement reviewed in Chapter 4. The fact that some of these parents do not speak English, that they themselves have not always had positive experiences in schools, and that they are inhibited by the impersonal and unreceptive nature of many schools may be partial explanations. Other families who are more comfortable with the school environment may have work schedules, child care needs, and other situations that explain their noninvolvement.

Parent involvement as defined by schools is not always imperative for student success. To understand why this is so, the very meaning of *parent involvement* needs to be questioned. Schools generally define involvement as joiniing the PTA, attending meetings, helping their children with homework or taking them to libraries and museums, and other similar activities. But when these young people talked about how their parents helped them, they seldom mentioned involvement in school activities. They *did* mention their parents' role in motivating them to stay in school, being communicative with them, providing an environment of high expectations and loving support, and sacrificing to help their children. This was clearly evident in Rich's case, whose mother had dedicated her life to make certain that he and his siblings got a good education. All three of them would be in college next year, a tough feat for a single mother. It is no wonder that all the case study students have developed such rugged determination to continue, to do well, and to "be someone."

Paul had particularly valuable insights to offer in this regard. Rather than focusing on what the role of parents in school should be, he thought about how schools could use *parent attributes* to make schools more caring places. He urged teachers to "not think of a lesson as a lesson. Think of it as not a lesson just being taught to students, but a lesson being taught to one of your own family members, you know? . . . Teach a lesson with heart behind it."

Teachers, Schools, and Caring

Many of the students in these case studies mention particular teachers, programs, or activities in school that have helped them succeed. The key role teachers play in the achievement of their students is not surprising. The most important characteristic students looked for in their teachers was "caring." Students evaluated their teachers' level of caring by the time they dedicated to their students, their patience, how well they prepared their classes, and how they made classes interesting. For example, in Vinh's favorite class students could work in groups to discuss various themes. James talked about caring when he said that his best teachers took the time to listen to students and to answer all their questions. Interestingly, his favorite teacher also showed her caring by being the faculty adviser for the Helping Hand

Club, which is involved in community service. Avi singled out the math teacher he had in ninth grade as especially helpful. Avi had not really understood math or done well until then, but since this teacher helped him, he has enjoyed math and done well in it.

For Manuel, caring came in the form of an entire program. The bilingual program, in his case, was critical to his eventual school success. It provided a safe environment for him and other Cape Verdean students, who are a minority within a minority. Because several of the teachers were from the same community, there was an important continuity between family and school. The bilingual program also reinforced the importance of home language and values because it included Cape Verdean history and culture.

In case after case, students remembered those teachers who had affirmed them, whether through their language, their culture, or their concerns. Teachers who called on students' linguistic skills or cultural knowledge were named most often, and the alternative schools attended by Paul and Ron were particularly helpful in this regard. Young people could also see through some of the more superficial attempts of teachers to use the student's culture. Vinh explained it best when he said that teachers "understand some things *outside,* but they cannot understand something inside our hearts."

Students are empowered not only by studying about their *own* culture, but also by being exposed to different perspectives through a variety of pedagogical strategies. Although ethnic studies are basic elements of a multicultural perspective, they are far from the entire curriculum. In addition to learning about their own people, students appreciate learning about the histories and perspectives of other people as well. Numerous students mentioned this, including Ron, who loved his "Cuban Missile Crisis" course, and Paul, who was empowered when he read *The Diary of Anne Frank* in elementary school. Moreover, in both instances, it was not only the subject matter, but also how it was taught that made history come alive.

The fact that the teachers and other staff members who understand and call on the students' culture are often from the same background does not mean that only educators from the students' ethnic group can teach them or be meaningful in their lives. Having teachers from students' ethnic backgrounds cannot be underestimated, but students in the case studies also named teachers who were *not* from the same background as they were who had made a difference in their lives. These teachers had either learned the students' language or were knowledgeable about and comfortable with their culture, or they were simply sensitive to the concerns of young people. This was the case with Rich's counselor, who helped him decide to go to pharmacy school. Rich described her as "She was more like you would say a fellow classmate."

What can teachers and other educators learn from these examples? For one, it is apparent that how educators view their role *vis a vis* their students can make a powerful difference in the lives of students. This role definition is not about strategies as much as it is about attitudes. In the words of Jim Cummins, "The interactions that take place between students and teachers and among students are more central to student success than any method for teaching literacy, or science or math."[22]

In a related area, the lesson that *relationships* are at the core of teaching and learning is reinforced through these case studies. Students mentioned teachers who cared about them and how these teachers helped to make them feel that they belonged. When students feel connected to school, they identify as *learners* and they have a far greater chance of becoming successful students. When they feel that they do not belong, identifying as a learner is more difficult.

Finally, educators can learn that there are many ways to show caring. Accepting students' differences is one way; another is to have rigorous and high expectations of them; and becoming what Ricardo Stanton-Salazar has called "institutional agents" who provide social networks for students is equally meaningful. These networks, from information on college admissions, to securing needed tutoring services, are generally unavailable to culturally dominated or poor students, but they can make the difference in achieving academic success.[23]

Whether they are in traditional or alternative schools, whether they are from mainstream or nonmainstream backgrounds, whether they speak students' native languages or not, all teachers can make a significant difference in their students' lives. The young people in our case studies have provided much food for thought in how this can happen.

• SUMMARY

In this chapter, the major themes that emerged in the case studies were reviewed, with particular attention to four themes related to the academic achievement:

- A redefinition of education and success
- Pride and conflict in culture and language
- The role of activities not related to academics in sustaining school success
- The important support of family, community, and teachers

Cultural and in some cases linguistic maintenance play a key role in students' academic success. In most of these cases, language and culture have been reinforced in the home and sometimes in the school as well. When reinforced in both settings, the message that they are valued is clear and powerful. If language and culture are valued only in the home, students may develop conflicted feelings about them.

The larger society also plays a key role in student learning. If young people see their culture devalued in such things as political initiatives (e.g., the proposal to restrict the number of Puerto Ricans coming into Marisol's hometown), they are certain to develop conflicted attitudes concerning their ethnic group. But in spite of sometimes harsh attacks on their culture, successful students have been able to maintain considerable pride in their ethnic group and community. In the process, they reject both the pressure to assimilate and the pressure to give up. They are transforming culture and language in order to fit in, but on their own terms.

The significant role of alternative schools, as we saw in the cases of Ron and Paul, needs to be emphasized. Alternative schools with a strong commitment to innovative, empowering, and inclusive curriculum and pedagogy provide a positive counterpoint to the alienating and disempowering curriculum and pedagogy found in many traditional schools.

Involvement in activities outside of school also plays a part in promoting students' academic achievement. Most successful students were involved successfully in other activities as well. Whether they are sports, social clubs, extracurricular activities in school, religious groups, or other community activities does not seem to matter. Their involvement may develop leadership and other skills that reinforce academic achievement and remove them from possible negative peer pressures.

Finally, families, communities, and school work in different, complementary ways to motivate students to succeed. Although families from culturally dominated and economically poor communities are sometimes unable to give their children the tangible help and support dominant and economically secure families are able to, they serve an indispensable role in their children's school accomplishments. The families of all the successful students we have studied, from those in the middle class to those from low-income families, have provided support in the following ways:

- Maintaining native language and culture in the home
- Having high expectations of their children at all times
- Providing loving and supportive home environments
- Communicating with their children on a consistent basis

Teachers and schools also play an essential role in students' success. We have seen that teachers who care, who take time with students, and who affirm their students' identities, are the most successful. School policies and practices that support students in their learning are also critical. From help after school to small-group work, students were explicit in pointing out the classroom activities and school practices that helped them learn. As the students pointed out, when schools and families work together, school success can become a reality.

● *TO THINK ABOUT*

1. What characteristics do you think define academic success? Do they differ from how you think most teachers define it? Do you think your cultural values influence your definition? How?

2. If it is true that pride in culture and language is important for academic success, what does this mean for school policies and practices? Discuss policies and practices that you think schools should consider to promote educational equity for all students.

3. Engagement in school and community activities emerged as a major support for the academic success of students in the case studies. What can your school do to promote such activities? Be specific, citing concrete examples.

4. The role of families in providing an environment for success was highlighted by many of the students in the case studies but their role was often different from

that which schools traditionally define as "involvement." As a teacher, how might you work with parents to help them develop environments for success?

5. "Caring" on the part of teachers, schools, and parents was highlighted by a number of students. What might schools do to give students the message that they care? How would these practices compare with current practices?

• *NOTES*

1. The research was done for a course I taught on Puerto Rican history and culture at the University of Massachusetts during the Spring 1985 semester. Pilar and Josette interviewed 10 Puerto Rican women who differed in age, social class, marital status, and length of stay in the United States. I am grateful to Josette and Pilar and to the women they interviewed for this example.

2. Vivian W. Lee and Rachel N. Sing, "Gender Equity in Schools for Immigrant Girls." *New Voices,* 3, 2 (1993).

3. Pierre Bourdieu, "The Forms of Capital." In *Handbook of Theory and Research for the Sociology of Education,* edited by John G. Richardson (New York: Greenwood Press, 1986).

4. Antti Jalava, "Mother Tongue and Identity: Nobody Could See that I Was a Finn." In *Minority Education: From Shame to Struggle,* edited by Tove Skutnabb-Kangas and Jim Cummins (Clevedon, England: Multilingual Matters, 1988), 164–165.

5. Michelle Fine, *Framing Dropouts: Notes on the Politics of an Urban Public High School* (Albany,NY: State University of New York Press, 1991).

6. Marietta Saravia-Shore and Herminio Martinez, "An Ethnographic Study of Home/School Role Conflicts of Second Generation Puerto Rican Adolescents." In *Cross-Cultural Literacy: Ethnographies of Communication in Multiethnic Classrooms,* edited by Marietta Saravia-Shore and Steven F. Arvizu (New York: Garland, 1992), 227–251.

7. Donna Deyhle and Karen Swisher, "Research in American Indian and Alaska Native Education: From Assimilation to Self-Determination." In *Review of Research in Education,* vol. 22, edited by Michael W. Apple (Washington, DC: American Educational Research Association, 1997), 113–194.

8. Laurie Olsen, *Made in America: Immigrant Students in our Public Schools* (New York: The New Press, 1997), 55.

9. David Tyack, "Schooling and Social Diversity: Historical Reflections." In *Toward a Common Destiny: Improving Race and Ethnic Relations,* edited by Willis D. Hawley and Anthony W. Jackson (San Francisco: Jossey-Bass Publishers, 1995), 3–38.

10. Stanley Aronowitz, "Between Nationality and Class." *Harvard Educational Review,* 67, 2 (Summer, 1997), 188–207.

11. Stacey J. Lee, *Unraveling the "Model Minority" Stereotype: Listening to Asian American Youth* (New York: Teachers College Press, 1996).

12. Shirley Brice Heath, "Race, Ethnicity, and the Defiance of Categories." In *Toward a Common Destiny: Improving Race and Ethnic Relations in America,* edited by Willis D. Hawley and Anthony W. Jackson (San Francisco: Jossey-Bass Publishers, 1995), 39–70.

13. *Anglo-conformity* refers to the pressures, both expressed and hidden, to conform to the values, attitudes, and behaviors representative of the dominant group in U.S. society.

14. The excellent video *How We Feel: Hispanic Students Speak Out* was developed by Virginia Vogel Zanger and is available from Landmark Films, Inc., Falls Church, VA. Their phone number is (800) 342–4336.

15. Donna Deyhle, "Navajo Youth and Anglo Racism: Cultural Integrity and Resistance." *Harvard Educational Review,* 65, 3 (Fall, 1995), 403–444.

16. Alejandro Portes and Rubén G. Rumbaut, *Immigrant America: A Portrait,* 2nd ed. (Berkeley, CA: University of California Press, 1996).

17. For a review of some of this research, see Sonia Nieto, "Lessons from Students on Creating a Chance to Dream." *Harvard Educational Review,* 64, 4 (Winter, 1994), 392–426.

18. Jabari Mahiri, *Shooting for Excellence: African American and Youth Culture in New Century Schools* (Urbana, IL, and New York: National Council of Teachers of English and Teachers College Press, 1998).

19. See Alejandro Portes and Rubén Rumbaut, *Immigrant America.*

20. Guadalupe Valdés, *Con Respeto: Bridging the Distance between Culturally Diverse Families and Schools* (New York: Teachers College Press, 1996).

21. Carlos E. Cortés, "The Societal Curriculum: Implications for Multiethnic Education." In *Education in the 80's: Multiethnic Education,* edited by James A. Banks (Washington, DC: National Education Association, 1981).

22. Jim Cummins, *Negotiating Identities: Education for Empowerment in a Diverse Society* (Ontario, CA: California Association for Bilingual Education, 1996).

23. Ricardo D. Stanton-Salazar, "A Social Capital Framework for Understanding the Socialization of Racial Minority Children and Youth." *Harvard Educational Review,* 67, 1 (Spring, 1997), 1–40.

chapter 9

Multicultural Education and School Reform

> *"We don't need multicultural education here; most of our students are White."*
> *"I want to include multicultural education in my curriculum, but there's just no time for it."*
> *"Oh, yes, we have multicultural education here: We celebrate Black History Month and there's an annual Diversity Dinner."*
> *"Multicultural education is just therapy for Black students."*
> *"Multicultural education is divisive. We need to focus on our similarities and then everything will be fine."*
> *"I don't see color. All my students are the same to me."*
> *"We shouldn't talk about racism in school because it has nothing to do with learning. Besides, it'll just make the kids feel bad."*
> *"Let's not focus on negative things. Can't we all just get along?"*

*I*n discussing multicultural education with teachers and other educators over many years, I have heard all these comments and more. Statements such as these reflect a profound misconception of multicultural education.

When multicultural education is mentioned, many people first think of lessons in human relations and sensitivity training, units about ethnic holidays, education in inner-city schools, or food festivals. If limited to these issues, the potential for substantive change in schools is severely diminished. On the other hand, when broadly conceptualized, multicultural education can have a great impact on redefining how the four areas of potential school conflict already discussed can be addressed. These are: racism and discrimination, structural conditions in schools that may limit learning, the impact of culture on learning, and language diversity. This chapter focuses on how multicultural education addresses each of these areas.

Schools are part of our communities and as such they reflect the stratification and social inequities of the larger society. As long as this is the case, no school program, no matter how broadly conceptualized, can change things completely and on its own. Moreover, in our complex and highly bureaucratic school systems, no single approach can yield instant and positive results for all students. Thus multicultural education is not a panacea for all educational ills. It will not cure underachievement, remove boring and irrelevant curriculum, or stop vandalism. It will not automatically motivate families to participate in schools, reinvigorate tired and dissatisfied teachers, or guarantee a lower dropout rate.

Despite these caveats, when multicultural education is conceptualized as broad-based school reform, it can offer hope for substantive change. By focusing on major conditions contributing to underachievement, a broadly conceptualized multicultural education permits educators to explore alternatives to a system that leads to failure for too many of its students. Such an exploration can lead to the creation of a richer and more productive school climate and a deeper awareness of the role of culture and language in learning. Multicultural education in a sociopolitical context is both richer and more complex than simple lessons on getting along or units on ethnic festivals. Seen in this comprehensive way, educational success for all students is a realistic goal rather than an impossible ideal.

This chapter proposes a definition of multicultural education based on the conceptual framework developed in the preceding chapters, and it analyzes the seven primary characteristics included in the definition. These characteristics underscore the role that multicultural education can play in reforming schools and providing an equal and excellent education for all students. They address the conditions that contribute to school achievement that have been discussed previously. My definition of multicultural education has emerged from the reality of persistent problems in our nation's schools, especially the lack of achievement among students of diverse backgrounds. A comprehensive definition emphasizes the context and process of education, rather than viewing multicultural education as an add-on or luxury disconnected from the everyday lives of students.

In spite of some differences among major theorists, there has been remarkable consistency over the past quarter century in the field about the goals, purposes, and reasons for multicultural education.[1] But no definition can truly capture all the complexities of multicultural education. The definition I present here reflects my own way of conceptualizing the issues, and it is based on my many years of experience as a student and as an educator of children, youths, and adults. I hope that it will encourage further dialogue and reflection among readers.

Although I have developed seven qualities that I believe are important in multicultural education, you might come up with just three, or with fifteen. The point is not to develop a definitive way to understand multicultural education, but instead to start you thinking about the interplay of societal and school structures and contexts and how they influence learning.

What I believe *is* essential is an emphasis on the sociopolitical context of education and a rejection of multicultural education as either a superficial adding of content to the curriculum, or alternatively, as the magic pill that will do away with all educational problems. I hope that in the process of considering my definition, you will develop your own priorities and your own perspective of multicultural education.

A DEFINITION OF MULTICULTURAL EDUCATION

I define *multicultural education* in a sociopolitical context as follows:

> Multicultural education is a process of comprehensive school reform and basic education for all students. It challenges and rejects racism and other forms of discrimination in schools and society and accepts and affirms the pluralism (ethnic, racial, linguistic, religious, economic, and gender, among others) that students, their communities, and teachers reflect. Multicultural education permeates the schools' curriculum and instructional strategies, as well as the interactions among teachers, students, and families, and the very way that schools conceptualize the nature of teaching and learning. Because it uses critical pedagogy as its underlying philosophy and focuses on knowledge, reflection, and action (*praxis*) as the basis for social change, multicultural education promotes democratic principles of social justice.

The seven basic characteristics of multicultural education in this definition are:

Multicultural education is *antiracist education*.
Multicultural education is *basic education*.
Multicultural education is *important for **all** students*.
Multicultural education is *pervasive*.
Multicultural education is *education for social justice*.
Multicultural education is a *process*.
Multicultural education is *critical pedagogy*.

Multicultural Education Is Antiracist Education

Antiracism, indeed antidiscrimination in general, is at the very core of a multicultural perspective. It is essential to keep the antiracist nature of multicultural education in mind because in many schools, even some that espouse a multicultural philosophy, only superficial aspects of multicultural education are apparent. Celebrations of ethnic festivals are as far as it goes in some places. In others, sincere attempts to decorate bulletin boards or purchase materials with what is thought to be a multicultural perspective end up perpetuating the worst kind of stereotypes. And even where there are serious attempts to develop a truly pluralistic environment, it is not unusual to find incongruencies. In some schools, for instance, the highest academic tracks are overwhelmingly White and the lowest are populated primarily by students of color, or girls are invisible in calculus and physics classes. These are examples of multicultural education *without* an explicitly antiracist and antidiscrimination perspective.

I stress multicultural education as antiracist because many people believe that a multicultural program *automatically* takes care of racism. Unfortunately this is

not always true. Writing about multicultural education almost two decades ago, Meyer Weinberg asserted,

> Most multicultural materials deal wholly with the cultural distinctiveness of various groups and little more. Almost never is there any sustained attention to the ugly realities of systematic discrimination against the same group that also happens to utilize quaint clothing, fascinating toys, delightful fairy tales, and delicious food. Responding to racist attacks and defamation is *also* part of the culture of the group under study.[2]

Being antiracist and antidiscriminatory means paying attention to all areas in which some students are favored over others: the curriculum, choice of materials, sorting policies, and teachers' interactions and relationships with students and their families.

To be more inclusive and balanced, multicultural curriculum must by definition be antiracist. Teaching does not become more honest and critical simply by becoming more inclusive, but this is an important first step in ensuring that students have access to a wide variety of viewpoints. Although the beautiful and heroic aspects of our history should be taught, so must the ugly and exclusionary. Rather than viewing the world through rose-colored glasses, antiracist multicultural education forces teachers and students to take a long, hard look at everything as it was and is, instead of just how we wish it were.

Too many schools avoid confronting in an honest and direct way both the positive and the negative aspects of history, the arts, and science. Michelle Fine calls this the "fear of naming," and it is part of the system of silencing in public schools.[3] To name might become too messy, or so the thinking goes. Teachers often refuse to engage their students in discussions about racism because it might "demoralize" them. Too dangerous a topic, it is best left untouched.

Related to the fear of naming is the insistence of schools on sanitizing the curriculum, or what Jonathon Kozol many years ago called "tailoring" important men and women for school use. Kozol described how schools manage to take the most exciting and memorable heroes and bleed the life and spirit completely out of them. It is dangerous, he wrote, to teach a history "studded with so many bold, and revolutionary, and subversive, and exhilarating men and women." Instead, he described how schools drain these heroes of their passions, glaze them over with an implausible veneer, place them on lofty pedestals, and then tell "incredibly dull stories" about them.[4]

The process of "sanitizing" is nowhere more evident than in current depictions of Martin Luther King, Jr. In attempting to make him palatable to the mainstream, schools have made Martin Luther King a Milquetoast. The only thing most children know about him is that he kept having a dream. Bulletin boards are full of ethereal pictures of Dr. King surrounded by clouds. If children get to read or hear any of his speeches at all, it is his "I Have a Dream" speech. As inspirational as this speech is, it is only one of his notable accomplishments. Rare indeed are allusions to his early and consistent opposition to the Vietnam War; his strong criticism of unbridled capitalism; and the connections he made near the end of his life among racism, capitalism, and war. Martin Luther King, a man full of passion and life, becomes lifeless. He becomes a "safe hero."

Most of the heroes we present to our children are either those in the mainstream or those who have become safe by the process of tailoring. Others who have fought for social justice are often downplayed, maligned, or ignored. For example, although John Brown's actions in defense of the liberation of enslaved people are considered noble by many, in our history books he is presented, if at all, as somewhat of a crazed idealist. Nat Turner is another example. The slave revolt that he led deserves a larger place in our history, if only to acknowledge that enslaved people fought against their own oppression and were not simply passive victims. Yet his name is usually overlooked, and Abraham Lincoln is presented as the "great emancipator," with little acknowledgment of his own inconsistent ideas about race and equality. Nat Turner is not safe; Abraham Lincoln is.

To be antiracist also means to work affirmatively to combat racism. It means making antiracism and antidiscrimination explicit parts of the curriculum and teaching young people skills in confronting racism. It also means that we must not isolate or punish students for naming racism when they see it, but instead respect them for doing so. If developing productive and critical citizens for a democratic society is one of the fundamental goals of public education, antiracist behaviors can help to meet that objective.

Racism is seldom mentioned in school (it is bad, a dirty word) and therefore is not dealt with. Unfortunately, many teachers think that simply having lessons in getting along or celebrating Human Relations Week will make students nonracist or nondiscriminatory in general. But it is impossible to be untouched by racism, sexism, linguicism, heterosexism, ageism, anti-Semitism, classism, and ethnocentrism in a society characterized by all of them. To expect schools to be an oasis of sensitivity and understanding in the midst of this stratification is unrealistic. Therefore, part of the mission of the school becomes creating the space and encouragement that legitimates talk about racism and discrimination and makes it a source of dialogue. This includes learning the missing or fragmented parts of our history.

The dilemma becomes how to challenge the silence about race and racism so that teachers and students can enter into meaningful and constructive dialogue. In the words of Marilyn Cochran-Smith,

> How can we open up the unsettling discourse of race without making people afraid to speak for fear of being naive, offensive, or using the wrong language? Without making people of color do all the work, feeling called upon to expose themselves for the edification of others? Without eliminating conflict to the point of flatness, thus reducing the conversation to platitudes or superficial rhetoric?[5]

A helpful answer to this dilemma, in terms of students, is offered by Henry Giroux. He suggests that although White students may become traumatized by these discussions, bringing race and racism out into full view can become a useful pedagogical tool to help them locate themselves and their responsibilities concerning racism.[6] Beverly Tatum has proposed that discussing racism within the framework of racial and cultural identity theory can help focus on how racism negatively affects all people and provide a sense of hope that it can be changed.[7]

What about teachers? As we saw in Chapter 3, many teachers have had little experience with diversity. Discussions of racism threaten to disrupt their deeply held ideals of fair play and equality. Since most teachers are uneasy with these topics, fruitful classroom discussions about discrimination rarely happen. If this is the case, neither unfair individual behaviors nor institutional policies and practices in schools will change. Students of disempowered groups will continue to bear the brunt of these kinds of inequities.

Multicultural education needs to prepare teachers to confront discrimination of all kinds, and this needs to happen not just in college classrooms but also through inservice education. In one example of the powerful impact that this preparation can have, Sandra Lawrence and Beverly Daniel Tatum described the impact of antiracist professional development on teachers' classroom practice. In their research, they found that many White teachers were apprehensive about engaging in discussions about race with their students because they thought they would degenerate into angry shouting matches. Yet, according to Lawrence and Tatum, after the teachers had participated in an inservice course, most of them took concrete actions in their classrooms and schools that challenged unfair policies and practices, and they were more comfortable in confronting racist behaviors and comments.[8]

The focus on policies and practices makes it evident that multicultural education is about more than the perceptions and beliefs of individual teachers and other educators. Multicultural education is antiracist because it exposes the racist and discriminatory practices in schools discussed in preceding chapters. A school truly committed to a multicultural philosophy will closely examine its policies and the attitudes and behaviors of its staff to determine how these might discriminate against some students. How teachers react to their students, whether native language use is permitted in the school, how sorting takes place, and the way in which classroom organization might hurt some students and help others are questions to be considered. In addition, individual teachers will reflect on their own attitudes and practices in the classroom and how they are influenced by their background as well as by their ignorance of students' backgrounds. This soul searching is difficult, but it is a needed step in developing an antiracist multicultural philosophy.

But being antiracist does not mean flailing about in guilt or remorse. One of the reasons schools are reluctant to tackle racism and discrimination is that these are disturbing topics for those who have traditionally benefited by their race, gender, and social class, among other differences. Because such topics place people in the role of either the victimizer or the victimized, an initial and understandable reaction of European American teachers and students is to feel guilty. Although this reaction probably serves a useful purpose initially, it needs to be understood as only one step in the process of becoming multiculturally literate and empowered. If one remains at this level, then guilt only immobilizes. Teachers and students need to move beyond guilt to a stage of energy and confidence, where they take action rather than hide behind feelings of remorse.

Although the primary victims of racism and discrimination are those who suffer its immediate consequences, racism and discrimination are destructive and demeaning to everyone. Keeping this in mind, it is easier for all teachers and students to face these issues. Although not everyone is directly guilty of racism and discrimination, we are all responsible for it. Given this perspective, students and teachers can focus on discrimination as something everyone has a responsibility to change.

In discussing slavery in the United States, for example, it can be presented not simply as slave owners against enslaved Africans. There were many and diverse roles among a great variety of people during this period: enslaved Africans and free Africans, slave owners and poor White farmers, Black abolitionists and White abolitionists, White and Black feminists who fought for both abolition and women's liberation, people of Native American heritage who stood on the side of freedom, and so on. Each of these perspectives should be taught so that children, regardless of ethnic background or gender, see themselves in history in ways that are not simply degrading or guilt-provoking.

I clearly remember the incident told to me by the father of the only Black child in a class whose teacher asked all the students to draw themselves as a character during the Civil War. This child drew a horse, preferring to see himself as an animal rather than as an enslaved man. We can only imagine the deep sense of pain and emptiness that this child felt. I have also heard teachers talk about White students who, after learning about slavery or the internment of the Japanese in our country during World War II, feel tremendous guilt. This was true of Vanessa Mattison, as you saw in her case study. No child should be made to feel guilt or shame about their background. Providing alternative and empowering roles for all students is another aspect of an antiracist perspective because it creates a sense of hope and purpose.

Multicultural Education Is Basic Education

Given the recurring concern for the "basics" in education, multicultural education must be understood as *basic* education. Multicultural literacy is as indispensable for living in today's world as are reading, writing, arithmetic, and computer literacy.

When multicultural education is peripheral to the core curriculum, it is perceived as irrelevant to basic education. One of the major stumbling blocks to implementing a broadly conceptualized multicultural education is the ossification of the "canon" in our schools. The canon, as understood in contemporary U.S. education, assumes that the knowledge that is most worthwhile is already in place. According to this rather narrow view, the basics have in effect already been defined, and knowledge is inevitably European, male, and upper class in origin and conception. This idea is especially evident in the arts and social sciences. For instance, art history classes rarely leave France, Italy, and sometimes England in considering the "great masters." "Classical music" is another example: What is called classical music is actually *European* classical music. Africa, Asia, and Latin America define their classical music in different ways. This same ethnocentrism is found in our history books, which place Europeans and European Americans as the actors and all others as the recipients, bystanders, or bit players of history. But the canon as it currently stands is unrealistic and incomplete because history is never as one-sided as it appears in most of our schools' curricula. We need to expand what we mean by "basic" by opening up the curriculum to a variety of perspectives and experiences.

The problem that a canon tries to address is a genuine one: Modern-day knowledge is so dispersed and compartmentalized that our young people learn very little that is common. There is no *core* to the knowledge to which they are exposed. But proposing a static list of terms, almost exclusively with European and European American referents, does little to expand our actual common culture.

At the same time, it is unrealistic, for a number of reasons, to expect a perfectly "equal treatment" for all people in the curriculum. A force-fit, which tries to equalize the number of African Americans, women, Jewish Americans, and so on in the curriculum, is not what multicultural education is all about. A great many groups have been denied access in the actual making of history. Their participation has *not* been equal, at least if we consider history in the traditional sense of great movers and shakers, monarchs and despots, and makers of war and peace. But the participation of diverse groups, even within this somewhat narrow view of history, has been appreciable. It therefore deserves to be included. The point is that those who *have* been present in our history, arts, literature, and science should be made visible. Recent literature anthologies are a good example of the inclusion of more voices and perspectives than ever before. Did they become "great writers" overnight, or was it simply that they had been buried for too long?

We are not talking here simply of the "contributions" approach to history, literature, and the arts.[9] Such an approach can easily become patronizing by simply adding bits and pieces to a preconceived canon. Rather, missing from most curricula is a consideration of how generally excluded groups have made history and affected the arts, literature, geography, science, and philosophy *on their own terms*.

The alternative to multicultural education is *monocultural education*. Education reflective of only one reality and biased toward the dominant group, monocultural education is the order of the day in most of our schools. What students learn represents only a fraction of what is available knowledge, and those who decide what is most important make choices that are of necessity influenced by their own limited background, education, and experiences. Because the viewpoints of so many are left out, monocultural education is at best a partial education. It deprives all students of the diversity that is part of our world.

No school can consider that it is doing a proper or complete job unless its students develop multicultural literacy. What such a conception might mean in practice would no doubt differ from school to school. At the very least, we would expect all students to be fluent in a language other than their own; aware of the literature and arts of many different peoples; and conversant with the history and geography not only of the United States but also of African, Asian, Latin American, and European countries. Through such an education, we would expect students to develop social and intellectual skills that would help them understand and empathize with a wide diversity of people. Nothing can be more basic than this.

Multicultural Education Is Important for *All* Students

There is a widespread perception that multicultural education is only for students of color, or for urban students, or for so-called disadvantaged students. This belief is probably based on the roots of multicultural education, which grew out of the civil rights and equal education movements of the 1960s. The primary objective of multicultural education was to address the needs of students who historically had been most neglected or miseducated by the schools, especially students of color. Those who promoted multicultural education thought that education should strike more of a balance, and that attention needed to be given to developing curriculum and materials that reflect these students' histories, cultures, and experiences. This thinking was historically necessary and is understandable even today, given the great curricular imbalance that continues to exist in most schools.

More recently a broader conceptualization of multicultural education has gained acceptance. It is that all students are *miseducated* to the extent that they receive only a partial and biased education. The primary victims of biased education are those who are invisible in the curriculum. Females, for example, are absent in most curricula, except in special courses on women's history that are few and far between. Working-class history is also absent in virtually all U.S. curricula. The children of the working class are deprived not only of a more forthright education but, more important, of a place in history, and students of all social class backgrounds are deprived of a more honest and complete view of our history. Likewise, there is a pervasive and inpenetrable silence concerning gays and lesbians in most schools, not just in the curriculum but also in extracurricular activities. The result is that gay and lesbian students are placed at risk in terms of social well being and academic achievement.[10]

Although the primary victims of biased education continue to be those who are invisible in the curriculum, those who figure prominently are victims as well. They receive only a partial education, which legitimates their cultural blinders. European American children, seeing only themselves, learn that they are the norm; everyone else is secondary. The same is true of males. The children of the wealthy learn that the wealthy and the powerful are the real makers of history, the ones who have left their mark on civilization. Heterosexual students receive the message that gay and lesbian students should be ostracized because they are deviant and immoral. The humanity of all students is jeopardized as a result.

Multicultural education is by definition inclusive. Because it is *about* all people, it is also *for* all people, regardless of their ethnicity, language, sexual orientation, religion, gender, race, class, or other difference. It can even be convincingly argued that students from the dominant culture need multicultural education more than others because they are generally the most miseducated about diversity. For example, European American youths often think that they do not even *have* a culture, at least not in the same sense that clearly culturally identifiable youths do. At the same time, they feel that their ways of living, doing things, believing, and acting are the only acceptable ways. Anything else is ethnic and exotic.

Feeling as they do, these young people are prone to develop an unrealistic view of the world and of their place in it. They learn to think of themselves and their group as the norm and of all others as a deviation. These are the children who learn not to question, for example, the name of "flesh-colored" adhesive strips even though they are not the flesh color of three-quarters of humanity. They do not even have to think about the fact that everyone, Christian or not, gets holidays at Christmas and Easter and that other religious holidays are given little attention in our calendars and school schedules. Whereas children from dominated groups may develop feelings of inferiority based on their schooling, dominant group children may develop feelings of superiority. Both responses are based on incomplete and inaccurate information about the complexity and diversity of the world, and both are harmful.

In spite of this, multicultural education continues to be thought of by many educators as education for the "culturally different" or the "disadvantaged." Teachers in predominantly European American schools, for example, may feel it is not important or necessary to teach their students anything about the civil rights movement. Likewise, only in scattered bilingual programs in Mexican American communities are students exposed to literature by Mexican and Mexican American authors, and it is generally just at high schools with a high percentage of students of color that ethnic studies classes are offered. These are ethnocentric interpretations of multicultural education.

The thinking behind these actions is paternalistic as well as misinformed. Because anything remotely digressing from the "regular" (European American) curriculum is automatically considered soft by some educators, the usual response to making a curriculum multicultural is to water it down. Poor pedagogical decisions are then based on the premise that so-called disadvantaged students need a watered-down version of the "real" curriculum, whereas more privileged children can handle the "regular" or more academically challenging curriculum. But rather than dilute it, making a curriculum multicultural makes it more inclusive, inevitably enriching it. All students would be enriched by reading the poetry of Langston Hughes or the stories of Gary Soto, or by being fluent in a second language, or by understanding the history of Islam.

Multicultural Education Is Pervasive

Multicultural education is not something that happens at a set period of the day, or another subject area to be covered. In some school systems, there is even a "multicultural teacher" who goes from class to class in the same way as the music or art teacher. Although the intent of this approach may be to formalize a multicultural perspective in the standard curriculum, it is in the long run self-defeating because it isolates the multicultural philosophy from everything else that happens in the classroom. Having specialists take complete responsibility for multicultural education gives the impression that a multicultural perspective is separate from all other knowledge. The schism between "regular" and "multicultural" education widens. In this kind of arrangement, multicultural education becomes exotic knowledge that is external to the real work that goes on in classrooms. Given this conception of multicultural education, it is little wonder that teachers sometimes decide that it is a frill they cannot afford.

A true multicultural approach is pervasive. It permeates everything: the school climate, physical environment, curriculum, and relationships among teachers and students and community.[11] It is apparent in every lesson, curriculum guide, unit, bulletin board, and letter that is sent home; it can be seen in the process by which books and audiovisual aids are acquired for the library, in the games played during recess, and in the lunch that is served. *Multicultural education is a philosophy, a way of looking at the world, not simply a program or a class or a teacher*. In this comprehensive way, multicultural education helps us rethink school reform.

What might a multicultural philosophy mean in the way that schools are organized? For one, it would probably mean the end of tracking, which inevitably favors some students over others. It would also mean that the complexion of the school, both literally and figuratively, would change. That is, there would be an effort to have the entire school staff be more representative of our nation's diversity. Pervasiveness probably would also be apparent in the great variety and creativity of instructional strategies, so that students from all cultural groups, and females as well as males, would benefit from methods other than the traditional. The curriculum would be completely overhauled and would include the histories, viewpoints, and insights of many different peoples and both males and females. Topics usually considered "dangerous" could be talked about in classes, and students would be encouraged to become critical thinkers. Textbooks and other instructional materials would also reflect a pluralistic perspective. Families and other community people would be visible in the schools because they would offer a unique and helpful viewpoint. Teachers, families, and students would have the opportunity to work together to design motivating and multiculturally appropriate curricula.

In other less global but no less important ways, the multicultural school would probably look vastly different as well. For example, the lunchroom might offer a variety of international meals, not because they are exotic delights but because they are the foods people in the community eat daily. Sports and games from all over the world might be played, and not all would be competitive. Letters would be sent home in the languages that parents understand. Children would not be punished for speaking their native language; on the contrary, they would be encouraged to do so and it would be used in their instruction as well. In summary, the school would be a learning environment in which curriculum, pedagogy, and outreach are all consistent with a broadly conceptualized multicultural philosophy.

Multicultural Education Is Education for Social Justice

All good education connects theory with reflection and action, which is what Paulo Freire defined as *praxis*.[12] Developing a multicultural perspective means learning how to think in more inclusive and expansive ways, reflecting on what we learn, and applying that learning to real situations. In this regard, John Dewey maintained that "information severed from thoughtful action is dead, a mind-crushing load."[13] Multicultural education invites students and teachers to put their learning into action for social justice. Whether debating a difficult issue, developing a community newspaper, starting a collaborative program at a local senior center, or organizing a petition for the removal of a potentially dangerous waste treatment plant in the neighborhood, students learn that they have power, collectively and individually, to make change.

This aspect of multicultural education fits in particularly well with the developmental level of young people who, starting in the middle elementary grades, are very conscious of what is fair and what is unfair. When their pronounced sense of justice is not channeled appropriately, the result can be anger, resentment, alienation, or dropping out of school physically or psychologically.

Preparing students for active membership in a democracy is the basis of Deweyan philosophy, and it has often been cited by schools as a major educational goal. But few schools serve as a site of apprenticeship for democracy. Policies and practices such as rigid ability grouping, inequitable testing, monocultural curricula, and unimaginative pedagogy mitigate against this lofty aim. The result is that students in many schools perceive the claim of democracy to be a hollow and irrelevant issue. Henry Giroux, for example, has suggested that what he calls "the discourse of democracy" has been trivialized to mean such things as uncritical patriotism and mandatory pledges to the flag.[14] In some schools, democratic practices are found only in textbooks and confined to discussions of the American Revolution, but the chance for students to practice day-to-day democracy is minimal. Social justice becomes an empty concept in this situation.

The fact that power and inequality are rarely discussed in schools should come as no surprise. As institutions, schools are charged with maintaining the status quo, but they are also expected to wipe out inequality. Exposing the contradictions between democratic ideals and actual manifestations of inequality makes many people uncomfortable, and this includes educators. Still, such issues are at the heart of a broadly conceptualized multicultural perspective because the subject matter of schooling is society, with all its wrinkles and warts and contradictions. Ethics and the distribution of power, status, and rewards are basic societal concerns. Education must address them as well.

Although the connection of multicultural education with students' rights and responsibilities in a democracy is unmistakable, many young people do not learn about these responsibilities, the challenges of democracy, or the central role of citizens in ensuring and maintaining the privileges of democracy. Multicultural education can have a great impact in this respect. A multicultural perspective presumes that classrooms should not simply *allow* discussions that focus on social justice, but in fact *welcome* them. These discussions might center on concerns that affect culturally diverse communities—poverty, discrimination, war, the national budget—and what students can do to change them. Because all of these concerns are pluralistic, education must of necessity be multicultural.

Multicultural Education Is a Process

Curriculum and materials represent the *content* of multicultural education, but multicultural education is above all a *process*. First, it is ongoing and dynamic. No one ever stops becoming a multicultural person, and knowledge is never complete. This means that there is no established canon that is frozen in cement. Second, multicultural education is a process because it involves primarily relationships among people. The sensitivity and understanding teachers show their students are more crucial in promoting student learning than the facts and figures they may know about different ethnic and cultural groups. Also, multicultural education is a process because it concerns such intangibles as expectations of student achievement, learning environments, students' learning preferences, and other cultural variables that are absolutely essential for schools to understand if they are to become successful with all students.

The dimension of multicultural education as a process is too often relegated to a secondary position, because content is easier to handle and has speedier results. For instance, developing an assembly program on Black History Month is easier than eliminating tracking. Changing a basal reader is easier than developing higher expectations for all students. The first involves changing one book for another; the other involves changing perceptions, behaviors, and knowledge, not an easy task. As a result, the processes of multicultural education are generally more complex, more politically volatile, and more threatening to vested interests than even controversial content.

Multicultural education must be accompanied by unlearning conventional wisdom as well as dismantling policies and practices that are disadvantageous for some students at the expense of others. Teacher education programs, for example, need to be reconceptualized to include awareness of the influence of culture and language on learning, the persistence of racism and discrimination in schools and society, and instructional and curricular strategies that encourage learning among a wide variety of students. Teachers' roles in the school also need to be redefined, because empowered teachers help to empower students. The role of families needs to be expanded so that the insights and values of the community can be more faithfully reflected in the school. Nothing short of a complete restructuring of curriculum and of the organization of schools is called for. The process is complex, problematic, controversial, and time consuming, but it is one in which teachers and schools must engage to make their schools truly multicultural.

Multicultural Education Is Critical Pedagogy

Knowledge is neither neutral nor apolitical, yet it is generally treated by teachers and schools as if it were. Consequently, school knowledge tends to reflect the lowest common denominator: that which is sure to offend the fewest (and the most powerful) and is least controversial. Students may leave school with the impression that all major conflicts have already been resolved. But history, including educational history, is full of great debates, controversies, and ideological struggles. These controversies and conflicts are often left at the schoolhouse door.

Every educational decision made at any level, whether by a teacher or by an entire school system, reflects the political ideology and worldview of the decision maker. Decisions to dismantle tracking, discontinue standardized tests, lengthen the school day, use one textbook rather than another, study the Harlem Renaissance, or use learning centers rather than rows of chairs—all reflect a particular view of learners and of education.

As educators, all the decisions we make, no matter how neutral they may seem, have an impact on the lives and experiences of our students. This is true of the curriculum, books, and other materials we provide for them. State and local guidelines and mandates may limit what particular schools and teachers choose to teach, and this too is a political decision. What is excluded is often as telling as what is included. Much of the literature taught at the high school level, for instance, is still heavily male, European, and European American. The significance of women, people of color, and those who write in other languages is diminished, unintentionally or not.

A major problem with a monocultural curriculum is that it gives students only one way of seeing the world. When reality is presented as static, finished, and flat, the underlying tensions, controversies, passions, and problems faced by people throughout history and today disappear. But to be informed and active participants in a democratic society, students need to understand the complexity of the world and the many perspectives involved. Using a critical perspective, students learn that there is not just one way of seeing things, or even two or three. I use the number 17 facetiously to explain this: There are at least 17 ways of understanding reality, and until we have learned to do that, we have only part of the truth.

What do I mean by "17 ways of understanding reality"? I mean that there are multiple perspectives on every issue. But most of us have learned only the "safe" or standard way of interpreting events and issues. Textbooks in all subject areas exclude information about unpopular perspectives, or the perspectives of disempowered groups in our society. These are the "lies my teacher told me" to which James Loewen refers in his powerful critique of U.S. history textbooks.[15] For instance, there are few U.S. history texts that assume the perspective of working-class people, although they were and are the backbone of our country. Likewise, the immigrant experience is generally treated as a romantic and successful odyssey rather than the traumatic, wrenching, and often less-than-idyllic situation it was and continues to be for so many. The experiences of non-European immigrants or those forcibly incorporated into the United States are usually presented as if they were identical to the experiences of Europeans, which they have not at all been. We can also be sure that if the perspectives of women were taken seriously, the school curriculum would be altered dramatically. Unless all students develop the skill to see reality from multiple perspectives, not only the perspective of dominant groups, they will continue to think of it as linear and fixed and to think of themselves as passive in making any changes.

According to James Banks, the main goal of a multicultural curriculum is to help students develop decision-making and social action skills.[16] By doing so, students learn to view events and situations from a variety of perspectives. A multicultural approach values diversity and encourages critical thinking, reflection, and action. Through this process, students can be empowered as well. This is the basis of critical pedagogy. Its opposite is what Paulo Freire called "domesticating education," education that emphasizes passivity, acceptance, and submissiveness.[17] According to Freire, education for domestication is a process of "transferring knowledge," whereas education for liberation is one of "transforming action."[18] Liberating education encourages students to take risks, to be curious, and to question. Rather than expecting students to repeat teachers' words, it expects them to seek their own answers.

How are critical pedagogy and multicultural education connected? They are what Geneva Gay has called "mirror images."[19] That is, they work together, according to Christine Sleeter, as "a form of resistance to dominant modes of schooling."[20] Critical pedagogy acknowledges rather than suppresses cultural and linguistic diversity. It is not simply the transfer of knowledge from teacher to students, even though that knowledge may challenge what students had learned before. For instance, learning about the internment of Japanese Americans during World War II is not in itself critical pedagogy. It only becomes so when students critically analyze different perspectives and use them to understand and act on the inconsistencies they uncover.

A multicultural perspective does not simply operate on the principle of substituting one "truth" or perspective for another. Rather, it reflects on multiple and contradictory perspectives to understand reality more fully. In addition, it uses the understanding gained from reflection to make changes. Teachers and students sometimes need to learn to respect even those viewpoints with which they may disagree, not to teach what is "politically correct" but to have students develop a critical perspective about what they hear, read, or see.

Consider the hypothetical English literature book previously mentioned. Let us say that students and their teacher have decided to review the textbook to determine whether it fairly represents the voices and perspectives of a number of groups. Finding that it does not is in itself a valuable learning experience. But if nothing more is done with this analysis, it remains academic; it becomes more meaningful if used as the basis for further action. Ira Shor has proposed that critical pedagogy is more difficult precisely because it moves beyond academic discourse: "Testing the limits by practicing theory and theorizing practice in a real context is harder and more risky than theorizing theory without a context."[21] In this sense, critical pedagogy takes courage.

In the example of the English textbooks, students might propose that the English department order a more culturally inclusive anthology for the coming year. They might decide to put together their own book, based on literature with a variety of perspectives. Or they might decide to write a letter to the publisher with their suggestions. Critical pedagogy, however, does not mean that there is a linear process from *knowledge* to *reflection* to *action*. If this were the case, it would become yet another mechanistic strategy.

A few examples of how the typical curriculum discourages students from thinking critically, and what this has to do with a multicultural perspective, are in order. In most schools, students learn that Columbus discovered America; that the United States was involved in a heroic westward expansion until the twentieth century; that Puerto Ricans were granted U.S. citizenship in 1917; that enslaved Africans were freed by the Emancipation Proclamation in 1863; that the people who made our country great were the financial barons of the previous century; and if they learn anything about it at all, that Japanese Americans were housed in detention camps during World War II for security reasons.

History, as we know, is generally written by the conquerors, not by the vanquished or by those who benefit least in society. The result is history books skewed in the direction of dominant groups in a society. When American Indian people write history books, they generally say that Columbus invaded rather than discovered this land, and that there was no heroic westward expansion but rather an eastern encroachment. Mexican Americans often include references to Aztlán, the legendary land that was overrun by Europeans during this encroachment. Puerto Ricans usually remove the gratuitous word *granted* that appears in so many textbooks and explain that citizenship was instead *imposed,* and it was opposed by even the two houses of the legislature that existed in Puerto Rico in 1917. African Americans tend to describe the active participation of enslaved Africans in their own liberation and they may include such accounts as slave narratives to describe the rebellion and resistance of their people. Working-class people who know their history usually credit laborers rather than Andrew Carnegie with building the country and the economy. And Japanese Americans frequently cite racist hysteria, economic exploitation, and propaganda as major reasons for their evacuation to concentration camps during World War II.

Critical pedagogy is also an exploder of myths. It helps to expose and demystify as well as demythologize some of the truths that we take for granted and to analyze them critically and carefully. Justice for all, equal treatment under the law, and equal educational opportunity, although certainly ideals worth believing in and striving for, are not always a reality. The problem is that we teach them as if they were always real, always true, with no exceptions. Critical pedagogy allows us to have faith in these ideals without uncritically accepting their reality.

Because critical pedagogy is based on the experiences and viewpoints of students, it is by its very nature multicultural. The most successful education is that which begins with the learner and, when using a multicultural perspective, students themselves become the foundation for the curriculum. But a liberating education also takes students beyond their own particular and therefore limited experiences, no matter what their background.

Critical pedagogy is not new, although it has gone by other terms in other times. In our country, precursors to critical pedagogy can be found in the work of African American educators such as Carter Woodson and W. E. B. DuBois.[22] In Brazil, the historic work of Paulo Freire influenced literacy and liberation movements throughout the world. Even before Freire, critical pedagogy was being practiced in other parts of the world. Many years ago, Sylvia Ashton-Warner, teaching Maori children in New Zealand, found that the curriculum, materials, viewpoints, and pedagogy used with them were all borrowed from the dominant culture.[23]

Because Maori children had been failed dismally by New Zealand schools, Ashton-Warner developed a strategy for literacy based on the children's experiences and interests. Calling it an "organic" approach, she taught children how to read by using the words *they* wanted to learn. Each child would bring in a number of new words each day, learn to read them, and then use them in writing. Because her approach was based on what children knew and wanted to know, it was extraordinarily successful. In contrast, basal readers, having nothing to do with their experiences, were mechanistic instruments that imposed severe limitations on the students' creativity and expressiveness.

Other approaches that have successfully used the experiences of students are worth mentioning: the superb preschool curriculum developed by Louise Derman-Sparks and the Anti-Bias Curriculum Task Force is especially noteworthy. Instructional strategies based on students' languages, cultures, families, and communities are also included in wonderful books by Rethinking Schools and NECA. Stephen May's study of the Richmond Road School in New Zealand offers an inspiring example of multicultural education in practice. Catherine Walsh's culturally affirming work with Puerto Rican youngsters is another good example. Ira Shor's descriptions of the work he does in his own college classroom are further proof of the power of critical pedagogy at all levels. Enid Lee, Deborah Menkart, and Margo Okazawa-Rey have developed an exceptional professional development guide for teachers and preservice teachers.[24]

● SUMMARY

In this chapter, we defined multicultural education by these seven characteristics:

Antiracist
Basic
Important for all students
Pervasive
Education for social justice
Process
Critical pedagogy

Multicultural education represents a way of rethinking school reform because it responds to many of the problematic factors leading to school underachievement and failure. When implemented comprehensively, multicultural education can transform and enrich the schooling of all young people. Because multicultural education takes into account the cultures, languages, and experiences of all students, it can go beyond the simple transfer of skills to include those attitudes and critical skills that have the potential to empower students for productive and meaningful lives.

This discussion leads us to an intriguing insight: *In the final analysis, multicultural education as defined here is simply good pedagogy.* That is, all good education takes students seriously, uses their experiences as a basis for further learning, and helps them to develop into critical and empowered citizens. What is multicultural about this? To put it simply, in our multicultural society, all good education needs to take into account the diversity of our student body. Multicultural education is good education for a larger number of our students.

Is multicultural education just as necessary in a monocultural society? We might legitimately ask whether even the most ethnically homogeneous society is truly monocultural, given the diversity of social class, language, sexual orientation, physical ability, and other human and social differences present in all societies. Our world is increasingly interdependent, and all students need to understand their role in a global society and not simply in a nation. Multicultural education is a process that goes beyond the changing demographics in a particular country. It is more effective education for a changing world.

● *TO THINK ABOUT*

1. What do you see as the difference between a *broadly conceptualized multicultural education* and multicultural education as defined in terms of "holidays and heroes"?

2. Do you believe it is important for antiracism and antidiscrimination in general to be at the core of multicultural education? Why or why not?

3. As a proponent of multicultural education, you have been asked by the school board in your city to make a public presentation on its benefits. One of the issues that board members are certain to question you about is the conflict between multicultural education and the "basics." Prepare a presentation in which you answer these critics.

4. Would you say that European American students are miseducated if they are not exposed to a multicultural curriculum? Why?

5. Your school has just hired a "multicultural teacher." Although you and a group of colleagues supportive of multicultural education wanted a more pervasive presence in the school than simply one teacher, you are on the hiring committee and have decided to use your influence to determine the job qualifications and job description. What should these be?

6. Think of a number of curriculum ideas that conform to the definition of multicultural education as social justice. How might students be engaged through the curriculum to consider and act on issues of social justice? Give some specific examples.

7. With a group of colleagues, think about an art, science, or math project that builds on multicultural education as critical pedagogy. How would it do this? In what activities would students be involved? How would these activities motivate them to think critically? to become empowered?

8. How would *you* define multicultural education? What would you include in your definition, and why? Define it for yourself first, and then get together with a group of colleagues for a collective definition. How do your definitions differ? Why? How might your classrooms and schools differ as a result?

● *NOTES*

1. See James A. Banks, "Multicultural Education: Historical Development, Dimensions, and Practice." In *Handbook of Research on Multicultural Education,* edited by James A. Banks and Cherry A. McGee Banks (New York: Macmillan, 1995).
2. Meyer Weinberg, "Notes from the Editor." *A Chronicle of Equal Education,* 4, 3 (November, 1982), 7.
3. Michelle Fine, *Framing Dropouts: Notes on the Politics of an Urban Public High School* (Albany, NY: State University of New York Press, 1991).
4. Jonathan Kozol, "Great Men and Women (Tailored for School Use)." *Learning Magazine* (December, 1975), 16–20.
5. Marilyn Cochran-Smith, "Uncertain Allies: Understanding the Boundaries of Race and Teaching." *Harvard Educational Review,* 65, 4 (Winter, 1995), 541–570.
6. Henry Giroux, "Rewriting the Discourse of Racial Identity: Towards a Pedagogy and Politics of Whiteness." *Harvard Educational Review,* 67, 2 (Summer, 1997), 285–320.
7. Beverly Daniel Tatum, *Why Are All The Black Kids Sitting Together in the Cafeteria? and Other Conversations About Race* (New York: BasicBooks, 1997).
8. Sandra M. Lawrence and Beverly Daniel Tatum, "Teachers in Transition: The Impact of Antiracist Professional Development on Classroom Practice." *Teachers College Record,* 99, 1 (1997), 162–178.
9. For a discussion of different levels of curriculum integration in multicultural education, see James A. Banks, *Teaching Strategies for Ethnic Studies,* 6th ed. (Boston: Allyn & Bacon, 1997).
10. Cathy A. Pohan and Norma J. Bailey, "Opening the Closet: Multiculturalism that is Truly Inclusive." *Multicultural Education,* 5, 1 (Fall, 1997), 12–15.
11. A good example of how a multicultural approach can include educators, students, and families is found in *Teaching and Learning in a Diverse World: Multicultural Education for Young Children,* 2nd ed., by Patricia G. Ramsey (New York: Teachers College Press, 1998).
12. Paulo Freire, *Pedagogy of the Oppressed* (New York: Seabury Press, 1970).
13. John Dewey, *Democracy and Education* (New York: Free Press, 1966; first published 1916), 153.
14. Henry A. Giroux, "Educational Leadership and the Crisis of Democratic Government." *Educational Researcher,* 21, 4 (May 1992), 4–11.
15. James W. Loewen, *Lies My Teacher Told Me: Everything Your American History Textbook Got Wrong* (New York: New Press, 1995).
16. James A. Banks, *Teaching Strategies for Ethnic Studies,* 6th ed. (Boston: Allyn & Bacon, 1997).
17. Paulo Freire, *The Politics of Education: Culture, Power, and Liberation* (South Hadley, MA: Bergin & Garvey, 1985).
18. Paulo Freire, *Pedagogy of the Oppressed.*
19. Geneva Gay, "Mirror Images on Common Issues: Parallels Between Multicultural Education and Critical Pedagogy." In *Multicultural Education, Critical Pedagogy, and the Politics of Difference,* edited by Christine E. Sleeter and Peter L. McLaren (Albany, NY: State University of New York Press, 1995), 155–189.
20. Christine E. Sleeter, *Multicultural Education and Social Activism* (Albany, NY: State University of New York Press), 2.
21. Ira Shor, *When Students Have Power: Negotiating Authority in a Critical Pedagogy* (Chicago: University of Chicago Press, 1996), 3.

22. See, for instance, Carter G. Woodson, *The Miseducation of the Negro* (Washington, DC: Associated Publishers, 1933); W. E. B. DuBois, "Does the Negro Need Separate Schools?" *Journal of Negro Education,* 4, 3 (July 1935), 328–335. For a historical analysis of multicultural education and critical pedagogy, see James A. Banks, "Multicultural Education."

23. Sylvia Ashton-Warner, *Teacher* (New York: Simon & Schuster, 1963).

24. See, for example, Louise Derman-Sparks and the A.B.C. Task Force, *Anti-Bias Curriculum: Tools for Empowering Young Children* (Washington, DC: National Association for the Education of Young Children, 1989); Bill Bigelow, Linda Christensen, Stanley Karp, Barbara Miner, and Bob Peterson (eds.), *Rethinking Our Classrooms: Teaching for Equity and Justice* (Milwaukee, WI: Rethinking Schools, 1994); Catherine E. Walsh, *Pedagogy and the Struggle for Voice: Issues of Language, Power, and Schooling for Puerto Ricans* (New York: Bergin & Garvey, 1991); Stephen May, *Making Multicultural Education Work* (Clevedon, England: Multilingual Matters, 1994); Ira Shor, *When Students Have Power;* Enid Lee, Deborah Menkart, Margo Okazawa-Rey, *Beyond Heroes and Holidays: A Practical Guide to K–12 Anti-Racist, Multicultural Education and Staff Development* (Washington, DC: Network of Educators on the Americas [NECA], 1998).

chapter 10

Affirming Diversity: Implications for Teachers, Schools, and Families

I think [teachers] could help students, try to influence them, that they can do whatever they want to do, that they can be whatever they want to be, that they got opportunities out there . . . Most schools don't encourage kids to be all they can be.

Manuel Gomes, interviewee

*I*n spite of the fact that Manuel Gomes came from a large immigrant family that was struggling to make ends meet and survive in a new country, he had great faith in education. The first of 11 siblings to graduate from high school, Manuel was facing the future with determination and hope. His story can serve as a lesson that students who live in even the most difficult cicumstancees can succeed academically.

The 12 case studies you have read provide concrete evidence that academic success and failure defy the easy categorization and conventional expectations that teachers, schools, and society may have of students from particular backgrounds. The experiences of these young people also point to specific conditions in the home, school, and community that can contribute to learning. Students do not achieve academic success on their own but in conjunction with family, peers, teachers, and schools. This being the case, in this chapter we return to the themes discussed in Chapter 9 with an eye toward understanding how supportive learning environments can be promoted.

This chapter also considers what it means to be an American, and it suggests a model of multicultural education that emerges from the seven characteristics defined in Chapter 9.

LESSONS FROM STUDENTS: MAINTAINING AND AFFIRMING PRIDE IN CULTURE

The racism and other forms of discrimination to which students are subjected in school and society are evident in the case studies. Such discrimination is either overt, as when Marisol was not allowed to speak Spanish in class, or more subtle, as when James's culture was invisible in school activities. But in spite of overpowering and sometimes demoralizing attitudes, behaviors, policies, and practices, most of these students have chosen not to deny or forget their culture or language. Instead, they have tended to rely on them even more firmly, although not necessarily in the school setting and sometimes with contradictory and conflicting attitudes. The young people's reliance on culture and language provides a shield from the devaluation of their identities by schools and society.

A few of the students had supportive school environments that accepted and built on their identities. In Yolanda's case, teachers in both her elementary and junior high schools called on her language and culture as valued resources. Manuel felt that his bilingual program was an oasis of cultural support. Their experiences reinforce the findings of an extensive review of research by Alejandro Portes and Rubén Rumbaut that a pervasive and positive sense of cultural heritage is unmistakably related to mental health and social well-being.[1] The first lesson for schools would seem to be, then, that bilingual and multicultural programs must become integral to the learning environment.

Supporting Native Language Approaches

Bilingual education has been a vital part of the educational landscape for almost three decades and it will probably remain so for the foreseeable future given the growing linguistic diversity in the United States. However, it has always been accompanied by great controversy and less than enthusiastic acceptance, as we saw in Chapter 6. Too often, for example, bilingual programs have been relegated to the space next to the boiler room in the basement or to large unused closets. Such physical placements are a metaphor for the status of these programs.[2] Bilingual teachers have also been segregated programmatically and physically from other staff, making both teachers and students feel isolated from the school community. Even the major goal of bilingual education—to serve as a temporary way station while students learn English to "quick exit" them into an all-English environment—calls into question the viability of such programs.

There needs to be a rethinking of the place of native language use for language minority students. Promoting students' native language—whether through bilingual or ESL programs, or even in nonbilingual settings when teachers encourage students to use it among their peers and in their learning in general—helps make language minority students visible and respected in the school environment. Valuing their language made a difference for the young people in our case studies, as they mentioned time and again. Another example of the power of valuing native language use is found in Margaret Gibson's research among Mexican American high school students, parents, and teachers. Gibson found that successful students and their parents supported additive acculturalism and bilingualism, and that their children's Spanish language maintenance was the topic about which parents were most passionate. Conversely, almost half of the teachers had what Gibson called "English-only attitudes," believing that English monolingualism was the key to success.[3]

Students who do not yet speak English and those who are most proficient in another language have first priority in a bilingual program. But students from homes where a language other than English is spoken, even if they themselves seem fluent in English, should also be given the opportunity to participate in these programs. The seeming conversational English fluency of these students often misleads teachers into believing that they can handle the academic rigors of cognitively demanding work in English. This is not always the case. For example, in one long-term ethnographic study of a Navajo community school in Northeastern Arizona, students in grades K–6 who had the benefit of cumulative, uninterrupted initial literacy experiences in the Navajo language made the greatest gains on local and national measures of achievement.[4]

Bilingualism is also a worthy goal on its own, and a valuable resource that should be supported. Doing away with precisely the kinds of programs needed in a society with growing linguistic and cultural diversity and international interdependence is foolhardy at best. The positive results of maintaining native language fluency in promoting the academic success of students in the case studies is abundantly clear. Even students who are no longer fluent in their native language can benefit from bilingual programs because their pride and self-confidence are promoted.

Space and funds permitting, monolingual speakers of English can and should also be included in bilingual programs. As we saw in Chapter 6, growing available research on two-way programs, in which English speakers and speakers of another language are integrated in one classroom and learn both languages, confirms that it is a powerful way for both groups to develop bilingualism and favorable attitudes toward diversity.

It is unfortunate that most approaches to teaching students of language minority programs have been compensatory in focus. This focus was no more eloquently articulated than by Nathan Glazer who refocused the debate in bilingual education by asserting that the debate would be muted

> . . . if more of it dealt with what the treasures of the Spanish language (and other languages in our increasingly polyglot nation) can offer all of us and less with deficiencies we are trying to overcome in children. Is it not easier to educate the children when we place before them things they enjoy and can profit from, than when we keep reminding them that they are in some way deficient?[5]

Developing Comprehensive Multicultural Programs

Another key lesson from the case studies is that multicultural education should be an integral part of the school experience of all students. This is not to imply that the students themselves recommended multicultural education. On the contrary, if they mentioned it at all, it was usually in the context of fairs, cookbooks, or other more superficial aspects, and certainly not in the comprehensive way it has been defined here. The only exceptions were Ron and Paul, who were specifically asked about multicultural education because their experiences with a multicultural curriculum at alternative schools gave them a more sophisticated understanding of this issue.

Multicultural education in most schools is reduced to making exotic masks, eating ethnic foods, and commemorating selected heroes. Differences in background and language are too often seen as deficits to be corrected rather than strengths on which to build. The students were unaware of what multicultural education might be if it were approached more comprehensively, or how it could help them. But when students are asked specifically about addressing diversity in the schools, they tend to be supportive of such efforts. For instance, a survey among almost 2,500 middle and high school students about multiculturalism in the schools found that a majority were interested in learning more about cultural differences. Among those who were dissatisfied with the extent to which they were learning about multiculturalism in the school, most wanted their school to place *more* emphasis on it rather than less.[6]

There is a need for multicultural education in helping new students adjust to the community and school and in solving issues of interethnic prejudice and hostility. Interethnic hostility and violence are not new to schools. With the influx of large numbers of new immigrants and with few appropriate programs to prepare either communities or schools for their diversity, the problem is becoming more serious. Students' lack of understanding of cultures different from their own, the preconceptions they and their families may have brought from other countries, their internalizing of the negative ways in which differences are treated in our society, and the lack of information provided in the schools all serve to magnify the problem. Add to this the pecking order established in schools among different social and cultural groups and the general reluctance of schools to deal with such knotty issues, and we are left with unresolved but unremitting interethnic hostility.[7]

A growing body of research on multicultural education suggests that only by reforming the entire school environment can substantive changes in attitudes, behaviors, and achievement take place.[8] Most schools have not undertaken such a comprehensive approach. When they do, they find that they need to modify the school culture itself. As a result, they may include in their plans such strategies as conflict resolution, cooperative learning, multicultural curriculum development, parent and community involvement, and the elimination of tracking. Such a comprehensive approach is necessary but also fraught with difficulty because it challenges traditions and conventions that are at the very heart of schooling in the United States.

SUPPORT BEYOND ACADEMICS

When young people are involved in meaningful activities outside of the academic context, whether in the school or community or in a combination of activities including school clubs and sports, religious groups, and out-of-school hobbies, they find support that helps keep them from negative peer pressure and that reinforces their leadership and critical thinking skills. What are the implications of this involvement for schools and communities?

Inclusive and Meaningful Activities

All schools, but particularly those at the secondary level, need to provide inclusive and meaningful activities that attract a wide range of students. Given the renewed emphasis on "the basics" that resulted from the educational reform movement of the 1980s and 1990s, many schools minimized extracurricular activities. Some reforms, particularly those focusing on "raising standards," such as longer school days and fewer "frills" such as music and art, have been felt most profoundly at schools serving poor and culturally subordinated students.

Even in schools that provide extracurricular activities, a majority of students are not involved for many reasons, ranging from lack of funds to schedule conflicts. Some sports programs, although presumably open to all, are in effect restricted to the students most able to afford them. Other programs meet after school and, because they provide no transportation, are available only to those who can get home on their own or who can rely on family or friends for transportation. Students who work after school are also unable to take part in these activities. Some extracurricular activities are restricted by the language and culture of students currently involved or by the perceptions of those not involved that their cultural and language differences are limitations. For example, Cambodian students who are interested in joining the soccer team may feel excluded because there are no other Cambodian students on the team. Or Mexican American students in a bilingual program may want to work on the school newspaper but may not even attempt to join because the newspaper is written entirely in English.

The issue here is equal access. Schools may say that activities are open to all students, but this policy is meaningless unless backed up in practice. Equal conditions of participation need to be established for all students. For instance, if a sports program is costly because of the required equipment, it is reasonable for the school to provide such equipment for those who cannot afford it. The same is true of transportation. If some students are closed off from activities because they do not have the same opportunity to get home from school as others, alternative means of transportation must be provided. There is also something seriously wrong if the newspaper staff in a culturally pluralistic school consists of only European American students. In these cases, broad-based and intentional recruitment of a diversity of students is necessary. This can be done not only by posting announcements but also by making more earnest efforts to involve previously uninvolved students, such as making announcements in every language spoken in the school, having students from various backgrounds involved in the recruiting program, and providing alternative meaningful activities. For the newspaper, for instance, a project in which students interview their families and neighbors concerning a particular issue of importance to the community might be the incentive.

Schools could do a lot more to embrace the interests and experiences of their students than they do currently. Looking for ways in which students can make their voices heard is more likely to result in the participation of a broader range of young people. Neglecting these opportunities will result in the continuation of segregated and restricted school activities.

Implications for Families and Communities

Families and communities also have a responsibility to provide meaningful outlets for young people. This responsibility is carried out by families when they give their children jobs to do in the home. Having family obligations can help students in classroom situations that require behaviors such as diligence, independence, and commitment. Teachers can encourage parents to give their children jobs at home, and then support them when they do.

Communities can use the creative energy and enthusiasm of young people by including them in volunteer work at elementary schools or day care centers, work with the elderly, or activities in social service agencies. Opportunities for after-school work or community service can be provided in much more substantial ways than they currently are. Students can develop cognitive abilities as well as leadership and critical thinking skills through community service because many of them are genuinely interested in the issues affecting their communities. A moving example of this concern is evident in research reported by Carmen Mercado. She and a classroom teacher in a school in New York City helped middle-school students learn to do research so that they could explore problems that were consequential in their own lives and communities. By investigating such issues as homelessness, growing up, relationships with parents, and other subjects close to home, young people learned valuable lessons about these particular topics. They also began to see themselves as empowered and intelligent people capable of doing high-quality research.[9]

Rather than detract from school success, meaningful activities in the home, school, and community that make productive use of students' time support learning. For adolescents, belonging and fitting in are best met with structured activities that at the same time allow for independence and are a vehicle for expression. In other words, students seek environments that support their achievement.

DEVELOPING ENVIRONMENTS FOR SUCCESS

The students in our case studies participated in and sought environments in which they would fit in. These environments are sometimes positive, as in the case of the teen center for Marisol or the synagogue for Avi; or negative, as in the case of gang involvement for Paul. There are several implications concerning what schools and families can do to provide positive environments that promote the achievement of all students. We will first explore what has been called *mutual accommodation*.[10]

Mutual Accommodation

A key question teachers and schools must ask themselves in their interactions with students, particularly those from diverse racial, ethnic, and linguistic backgrounds, is this: *Who does the accommodating?* This question gets to the very heart of how students from nondominant groups experience school every day. Dominant-group students, on the contrary, rarely have to consider learning a new language to communicate with their teachers. They already speak the acceptable school language. The same is true of culture. These students do not generally have to think about their parents' lifestyles and values because their families are the norm, as was seen in Vanessa's case. Students from other groups, however, have to consider such issues *every single day*. Schooling for them is filled with the tension of accommodation.

Some accommodation is, of course, necessary. If students and teachers spoke different languages at all times, operated under different goals and assumptions, and in general had varying expectations from the schools, chaos would result. Students from dominated groups and their families always expect to make some accommodations, which is clear in their willingness to learn English, their eagerness to participate in school life, and their general agreement with the rules of the game implicit in their social contracts with schools.

The problem is that usually only students from dominated groups and their families are asked or forced to do the accommodating. It is noteworthy when the situation is turned around. In one particular school system that experimented with a two-way bilingual program, for example, an evaluation after two years found that English-dominant students and their families were the ones most changed by the program. The trauma of learning a second language was something English-speaking students had to experience firsthand to understand what their Latina and Latino classmates had been going through for years. Because they were learning in Spanish and had to use a different language for the first time in their lives, they developed a healthy respect and compassion for their Spanish-speaking peers. More interaction between the two groups in the classroom, the schoolyard, and the cafeteria was visible. In addition, the English-speaking students began to appreciate the benefits of bilingualism and cited such activities as going to the local *bodega*, or grocery store, and being able to "shop in Spanish." The changes in the attitudes and behaviors of students, and even of their families, were extraordinary.

How then can we address this issue of *who does the accommodating?* In their early research on this question among Mexican American students, Estéban Díaz, Luis Moll, and Hugh Mehan found that when teachers used the students' social and linguistic resources, they helped their students learn. In reading, teachers coordinated aspects of English reading lessons with both English and Spanish. Rather than focus on which language was used, teachers made *comprehension* the lessons' primary goal, and what previously had been a painful and slow process for students was transformed into a successful learning environment. The result was a three-year jump in English reading. Similar findings were reported in a writing group. The researchers concluded that a model of "mutual accommodation" is called for. That is, both teachers and students need to modify their behaviors in the direction of a common goal: "academic success with cultural integrity."[11]

The lesson for teachers and schools is that contrary to conventional wisdom and practice, it is not students and their families who must always do the accommodating. The belief in one-way accommodation explains the tendency among educators to view unsuccessful students as either genetically inferior or culturally deprived. When students do not automatically accommodate to the school (or other) system, their intelligence or ability or that of their families is questioned. The perspective of mutual accommodation allows schools and teachers to use the resources all students already have to work toward academic success. In this model, neither the student nor the teacher expects complete accommodation; rather they work together, using the best strategies at the disposition of each.

In the process of mutual accommodation, teachers and students are equally enriched. For example, using students' language, culture, and experiences as the basis for their learning might mean that teachers have to expand their own repertoires. Also, expanding existing approaches to teaching is an advantage for all students. For one, using various communication styles can result in all students becoming more flexible in their learning. By reorganizing the social structure of classrooms, significant improvements in prosocial development, academic achievement, and race relations can be obtained. Even students' attitudes and behaviors toward one another can be influenced in a positive way. Moreover, providing alternative means for learning is an essentially equitable endeavor, and it strengthens the democratic purposes of schooling.

Mutual accommodation means accepting and building on students' language and culture as legitimate expressions of intelligence and as the basis for learning. On the part of students and families, it means accepting the culture of the school in areas such as expectations about attendance and homework and learning the necessary skills for work in school. Through this process, students, their families, teachers, and schools all benefit. Students and their families, while being respected and accepted, can proceed with learning. Teachers and schools expand their teaching skills and their way of looking at both ability and intelligence.

Teachers' Relationships with Students

Most teachers enter the profession because of a profound belief in young people and an eagerness to help them learn. But many obstacles, including a lack of respect and power for teachers, unresponsive administrators, and the challenges of reaching students from a dizzying variety of backgrounds, make teaching a very difficult job indeed. In spite of these challenges, developing healthy relationships with students is one way to maintain the hope and joy that drew teachers to education in the first place.

Students in our case studies talked at length about teachers who made a difference in their attitudes about school and their engagement with learning. Sometimes these teachers were from the same racial or ethnic background as the students themselves. Linda spoke emphatically about both her first grade teacher, who was Black, and Mr. Benson, who was "mixed," just as she is. Given the absence or invisibility of students' cultures and languages in the school environment, this kind of connection is predictable and healthy. One implication for schools is that more teachers who share the cultural background of students should be recruited.

Teachers from students' racial, cultural, and ethnic background can make a significant contribution to the school, enriching both the environment and the curriculum. But an undue burden is placed on these teachers when they are seen as the representative of their entire racial, ethnic, or linguistic group. Not only are they expected to be role models for students, but they are also increasingly called on to solve problems of cultural misunderstanding, and to translate letters, visit homes, begin the school's multicultural committee, and so on—usually with no extra compensation or recognition. The situation not only is unfair to these teachers, but it may also absolve the school of responsibility for meeting the needs of all its students. Schools have an obligation to aggressively recruit teachers who are as diverse as the student body, something that until now has not been given much of a national priority. When faculty members are from a variety of cultural backgrounds and multilingual, students are more likely to perceive the significance of intellectual pursuits in their own lives.

This does not mean that teachers can only teach students from the same ethnic or racial background. Students in our case studies spoke about teachers of many different backgrounds with whom they established close and meaningful relationships. All teachers, regardless of background, need to develop skills in multicultural communication and understanding. A study by Gloria Ladson-Billings of successful teachers of African American students found that the teachers used culturally congruent pedagogical practices, including students' experiences and cultural roots. Most of the teachers were Black, but a number of them were not.[12] Although teachers' ethnic group membership may have a very powerful impact on student learning, it is this in conjunction with teachers' cultural knowledge and awareness, and their curricular and instructional accommodations, that can make a major difference.

All teachers can become role models for all students as long as they are understanding, caring, and informed. One way in which teachers can build substantial relationships with students is by offering help to those who do not seek their aid. This issue came up numerous times in the case studies: The number of students who had absolutely no guidance in school was astonishing. For students who are the first in their families to go to college, such help is indispensable because their families have no prior experience with which to guide their children. The students who are most vulnerable in terms of having access to college frequently receive the least help in schools, even when they are successful and have high aspirations for their continued schooling. Developing what Ricardo Stanton-Salazar has called "interpersonal networks" of support—including information on college admissions and financial aid, and familiarity with mainstream social and cultural capital—is one way in which teachers can demonstrate their care and high expectations for students, especially for those who have not had access to these networks.[13]

The detrimental role that low expectations play in the school achievement of students, particularly those from dominated groups, was reviewed in Chapter 3. The young people in our case studies brought up this point frequently as a problem in their classrooms and schools. They said that they and their classmates were treated like babies; that the work teachers gave them was undemanding; and that any work, no matter how poor, was accepted. The attitude that students are incapable of performing adequately because they happen to be Black, speak a language other than English, or come from a poor family is widespread. But lowered expectations are not always conscious or based on negative intentions. Sometimes, lowering expectations is a teacher's way of accommodating instruction to student differences. Good intentions, however, do not always lead to positive results. Because such accommodations are based on a presumption that particular students are incapable of high-quality work because of language and cultural differences, they are patronizing at best. Rather than using students' skills and abilities, such accommodations only acknowledge their perceived deficits.

The lesson here is that teachers need to raise expectations and standards for all students. High standards can be achieved in a great variety of ways, and not only through the standardized tests that are increasingly being used as the sole way to measure student learning. Multicultural education means finding and using culturally, multiculturally, and linguistically relevant materials to develop students' cognitive skills. It also means using a variety of approaches in instruction. Raising standards and expectations does not require homogenizing instruction but rather creating new and different opportunities for learning for all students. But in the end, it is students' relationships with their teachers that matter most. All teachers can work to develop relationships that serve to motivate and inspire their students.

Family Environments for Learning

Very few of the parents mentioned in these case studies are involved in school in any but the most superficial way, at least given the way that parent involvement is currently defined. Few of them volunteer their time in school, go to meetings, or even visit the school on a consistent basis. The reasons for this uninvolvement are many, ranging from inability to speak English to limited funds, to lack of previous experience with such activities, to their own negative experiences with schooling.

Consequently, we need to expand what is meant by parent involvement by exploring the activities in which these parents were involved. In so doing, we can develop a more hopeful and democratic model of parent involvement within the reach of all students, despite the level of their parents' schooling, their socioeconomic background, or the language spoken at home. First, most of the parents of the case study students, whether successful or not, stressed the importance of going to school and of going on to college. Many of the students mentioned that their parents wanted them to have a better chance, to do better than they had done, and to have the opportunity for a better job.

How did parents support students' learning? Although most did not help with homework, they monitored it and asked questions that demonstrated an interest in what their children were doing in school. They also provided support in other ways. James talked about how his mother removed his brother from a class because she was unhappy with the way the teacher was treating him. Fern described the time her father had a flat tire and flagged down a car to take him to her school so that he would not miss a class play she was in. Parents were willing to go to great lengths to support their children.

Another way in which parents supported their children's academic success was through their continued use of their native language and reliance on the families' cultural values. When students came from a family who spoke a language other than English, it was always maintained as the language of communication in the home. Although English was also used in most of the homes, the salience of the native language was evident. In all cases, the cultural values of the family were emphasized, whether through religious observance; important family rituals; or deep-seated values such as family responsibility, respect for elders, or high academic aspirations. Rather than obstructing academic success, reliance on native language and culture promoted it.

Home activities as well as school activities need to be considered in an expanded definition of parent involvement. If we perceive parent involvement as simply what occurs in the school, the vital role parents can have in their children's academic success is denied. We are not just concerned with activities traditionally equated with school success, that is, many books and toys in the home, frequent attendance at cultural activities, and so on. What we mean by home activities are intangibles: *consistent communication, high expectations, pride, understanding,* and *enthusiasm* for their children's school experiences.

The view that poor parents and those who speak another language or come from a dominated culture are unable to provide environments that promote learning can lead to condescending practices that reject the skills and resources they already have. Practices such as top-down classes on parenting, reading, nutrition, and hygiene taught by "experts" are the result of this kind of thinking. But when parents are perceived to have skills, strengths, and resources that can aid their children, the results are different. There is nothing wrong with information to help parents with the upbringing and education of their children when it is given with mutual respect, dialogue, and exchange. Parenting is hard work, and any help that teachers and schools can give parents is valuable. But it needs to be a two-way communication that inspires confidence and trust.

Ways to use parents' hope, enthusiasm, and skills need to be explored through school and community activities that accept parents as the first and most important teachers of their children and that use the strengths and resources of families. A powerful example is found in work that Alma Flor Ada did with Mexican American parents and their children. Once a month, a group of parents would meet to discuss children's literature and to read the stories and poems written by their children, and in some cases, by the parents themselves. Most of the parents had very little schooling, but the impact of the project was as significant on them as it was on their children. In the process of dialogue, reading, and writing, parents developed confidence and greater ability in using the resources at their command, particularly their language and culture, to promote the literacy of their children. One mother said, "Ever since I know I have no need to feel ashamed of speaking Spanish, I have become strong."[14]

EXPANDING DEFINITIONS: WHAT IT MEANS
TO BE AMERICAN

As poignantly expressed by students in some of the case studies, a number of young people had great difficulty in accepting a split concept of self (what has commonly been called the "hyphenated American"). In our society, this dichotomy is commmon: one is *either* American *or* foreign, English-speaking *or* Spanish-speaking, Black *or* White. The possibility that one could *at the same time* be Spanish-speaking *and* English-speaking, Vietnamese *and* American, or Black *and* White is hardly considered. A case study of Lowell, Mass. by Peter Kiang quotes a Cambodian who expressed this sentiment with obvious pain: "When they say 'American,' they don't mean us—look at our eyes and our skin."[15]

What does it mean to be an American? This is in many ways the quintessential American dilemma, yet historically it has not invited a deep or sustained critical conversation. Throughout our history with successive generations of newcomers and conflicts with old-timers, either easy speculation or pat answers have been offered. This is because there is in place an unstated assumption of what it means to be an American. Questioning the assumed definition seems almost heretical because a number of troubling contradictions emerge, particularly questions of equality and social justice.[16]

The designation of American is generally reserved for those who are White and English-speaking. Others, even if here for many generations, are still seen as separate. For example, no matter how many generations they have been here and regardless of whether they speak only English and have little contact with their native heritage, Asians are not generally given the designation of American. The same is not usually true for European Americans, even recent arrivals. Even Blacks who have been in this country for hundreds of years are sometimes seen as quite separate. When one is not White, being accepted as a "real" American is far more difficult despite years of residence or even language spoken. Racism has always been implicated in the acceptance or rejection of particular groups in U.S. society.

It is not uncommon to see references to *Americans*, *Blacks*, and *Latinos*, as if they were mutually exclusive. If a text refers to "Americans," whether it is about history, child psychology, geography, or literature, for instance, the cover picture, majority of illustrations, and content is inevitably almost exclusively White. Only if the book concerns what might be considered a deviation from the norm, as would be the case if it were about African American literature or the psychological development of Latino children, do the pictures and content reflect these groups.

Challenging "Heartbreaking Dilemmas"

Self-identification is a very complicated issue because it involves not only cultural but also political questions. As an example, some American Indians prefer not to be called American, given the history of their treatment and abuse by the U.S. government. The same can be said of some Puerto Ricans and Mexican Americans, who may refuse to think of themselves as Americans because of the colonial exploitation of their lands. The result of this refusal may have negative consequences because those who are already disenfranchised may become even more alienated from the sources of power and political change.

As we can see then, for a variety of reasons, the definition of *American* as currently used effectively excludes the least powerful. As such, it legitimates the cultural, economic, and political control and hegemony of those who are already dominant in society. Our present and future diversity demands an expanded and inclusive definition, not hyphenated Americans, implying split and confused identities. *African-American* might imply a bifurcated identity, whereas *African American* signifies that a new definition is possible, one that emphasizes not confusion or denial but the transformation of what it means to be an American.

Americanization in the past has always implied *Angloization.* It meant not only learning English but also forgetting one's native language; not only learning the culture but also learning to eat, dress, talk, and even behave like the European American model. As so movingly expressed by a writer describing the experience of Jews in New York some 80 years ago, "The world that we faced on the East Side at the turn of the century presented a series of heartbreaking dilemmas."[17] To go through the process meant the inevitable loss of a great part of oneself in the bargain.

These heartbreaking dilemmas still exist today, as we have seen in the case studies. At the turn of the century, the choice was generally made in favor of assimilation. The choices, although no less difficult today, are not as limited as they once were. There are two major reasons for this: First, the civil rights and related liberation movements have led to more freedom in maintaining native language and culture and have changed the sociopolitical and historical contexts in which such decisions are made. Second, the number and diversity of immigrants in the United States in the past two decades has been unequaled, except at the beginning of the century (in 1990, the foreign-born population was 19.8 million, or almost 8 percent of the total; in 1910, although the numbers were smaller, the percentage— 14.7 percent—was higher).[18] These changes are having a profound impact on the meaning of assimilation. Americanization can no longer mean assimilation to a homogeneous model. To continue using *American* to refer exclusively to those of European heritage makes little sense.

A Different Approach

The students currently enrolled in our schools are in some ways more fortunate than previous students because they have more freedom in maintaining their language and culture. But the choice is still a painful one. On one hand, if they choose to identify with their culture and background, they may feel alienated from this society; on the other hand, if they identify with U.S. (generally meaning European American) culture, they feel like traitors to their family and community.

As they currently exist, these choices are clear-cut and rigid: One is either true to oneself and family *or* one is an American. This can be compared to what Wallace Lambert has called "subtractive bilingualism," that is, the kind of bilingualism that develops at the expense of one's native language.[19] This kind of bilingualism means that one does not really become bilingual at all, but rather goes from being monolingual in one language to being monolingual in another, although sometimes vestiges of the original language may remain. Multiculturalism too is subtractive if it allows only a transition from being monocultural in one culture to being so in another. Ned Seelye describes this dilemma: "One can escape appearing culturally different by forfeiting one of the two cultures—and there is always considerable pressure on economically and politically subservient groups to make this sacrifice—but trading one brand of monoculturalism for another seems an unnecessarily pallid business."[20]

The opposite of subtractive multiculturalism can be called *additive multiculturalism.* Just as we have seen that children who reach a fuller bilingual development enjoy cognitive advantages over monolinguals, we can speculate that those who reach a state of *additive multiculturalism* also may enjoy advantages over monoculturals, including a broader view of reality, feeling comfortable in a variety of settings, and multicultural flexibility.

Expanding the definition of *American* may help students and others facing the dilemma of fitting into a multicultural society by providing alternatives to self-identification, expanding the choices in making accommodations between cultural and linguistic, and social and national identification. The students in our case studies and others would have more choices than before and would no longer face just "heartbreaking dilemmas." European Americans would no longer be the only "Americans." *E pluribus unum* can no longer mean that cultural differences have to be denied in order to foster a false unity. Complete cultural maintenance is also not a realistic choice, implying as it does that native traditions are preserved in a pure and idealized fashion and without the interdependence with other groups that is so necessary in a pluralistic society.

No longer a choice of whether one *should* assimilate or not, the question now becomes, "How far can society, and the institutions of society such as schools, be pushed to accommodate the changing definition of American?" It is probably the first time in our history that this question has been asked in more than a rhetorical way. The view of the United States as a monolithic, monocultural, and monolingual society is being challenged daily, as seen in the wide use of languages other than English by an increasing percentage of the population, and by the ease and conviction with which growing numbers of people are claiming their heritage as important resources to be nurtured and maintained. The fact that this question can be posed at all places us in a unique historical moment. In the past, such possibilities could not be seriously considered.

The view that schools must be the obligatory assimilators of students needs to be disputed. The boundaries of pluralism, formerly delimited by an Anglocentric definition, are being questioned daily. Given the social and historical context in which we are living, schools must accommodate diversity in more humane and sensitive ways than they have in the past. Formerly, just one major option existed, and it was quickly, if not always eagerly, seized by most immigrants: quick assimilation into the so-called melting pot. In an insightful essay on assimilation written over a quarter of a century ago, William Greenbaum proposed two reasons why it occurred so quickly in the past: one was *hope* and the other was *shame*. Hope contributed in a major way in holding out the promise of equality, economic security, and a safe haven from war and devastation. But, according to Greenbaum, shame was the "main fuel" for the American melting pot: "The immigrants were best instructed in how to repulse themselves; millions of people were taught to be ashamed of their faces, their family names, their parents and grandparents, and their class patterns, histories and life outlooks." [21]

Shame is no longer acceptable to a growing number of people. The students in our case studies, for example, are challenging what it means to be an American. Not content to accept past limitations, they provide evidence that an evolution of meaning is taking place. They are still caught in the conflict and uncertainties of how to expand their possibilities, but these young people are increasingly sure of who they are. They are determined to define their own identities, identities that are different from their parents but not restricted to the static definition of American that has up to now been available.

As long as there are newcomers, as long as there are those who refuse to be included in a definition that denies them both their individual and group identities, the question of becoming American will be with us. The challenge for us as a society is to make room for everyone. Maxine Greene refers to those who are marginalized, both newcomers and old-timers, when she says, "There are always strangers, people with their own cultural memories, with voices aching to be heard."[22]

LEVELS OF MULTICULTURAL EDUCATION AND SUPPORT

If indeed we reject past limits on what it means to be an American, we need to consider how multicultural education can be incorporated in a natural and inclusive way into the curriculum and instruction.

Starting Out

How does a school or a teacher achieve a multicultural perspective in education? To say that multicultural education must be comprehensively defined, pervasive, and inclusive is not to imply that only a full-blown program qualifies. Because multicultural education is a process, it is always changing and never quite finished. Given that multicultural education is critical pedagogy, it is necessarily dynamic. A static "program-in-place" or a slick-packaged program is contrary to the very definition of multicultural education.

Let me illustrate with an example from Susan Barrett, a former student of mine and a talented high school English teacher in a community of European American (primarily Irish, French, and Polish) and Puerto Rican students. When asked how she included a multicultural perspective in her teaching, she replied that she had not yet reached that level. Rather, she said, her classroom had what she called "bicultural moments." As a proponent of multicultural education, she used inclusive curriculum and instructional strategies that emerged from this perspective. But because she felt that the children in her classes did not even know about their own or one another's backgrounds, let alone about the world outside their communities, her curriculum focused on exploring the "little world" of her students' community before venturing beyond it.

An example of a "bicultural moment" in a writing assignment concerned the journals that Susan's students kept. One of the central themes about which they wrote was the family, and their writings were later used as the basis for class discussions. A particularly vivid example involved two adolescent boys, one Irish American and the other Puerto Rican, and their perspectives and feelings toward their baby sisters. The Irish American boy complained about what a brat his little sister was. But the way in which he described her, hidden under the crusty surface of a young man trying to conceal his feelings, was full of tenderness. The Puerto Rican boy's journal, in contrast, was consciously sentimental. He described in great detail just how beautiful and wonderful his baby sister was, and he concluded that everyone in his family was thankful to God for sending her to them. Both of these boys loved their sisters and both were poetic and loving in their descriptions of them, but they expressed their love in widely different ways. Although not claiming that one was an Irish American and another was a Puerto Rican "way" of expression, Susan used their differences as a basis for explaining that the same feelings can be expressed in distinct ways and that different families operate in unique but valid ways. This bicultural moment was illuminating for all her students; it expanded both their literacy and their way of thinking. For Susan, to "begin small" meant to use the experiences and understandings her students bring to class rather than an exotic or irrelevant curriculum.

This is a message worth remembering. In an enthusiasm to incorporate a multicultural philosophy in our teaching, we can sometimes forget that our classrooms are made up of young people who usually know very little about their own culture or that of their classmates. They are a gold mine of resources for teaching and learning. Starting out small, then, means being sensitive to bicultural moments and using them as a beginning for more wide-ranging multicultural education.

Becoming a Multicultural Person

Developing truly comprehensive multicultural education takes many years, in part because of our own monocultural education. Most of us, in spite of our distinct cultural or linguistic backgrounds, were educated in monocultural environments. We seldom have the necessary models for developing a multicultural perspective. We have only our own experiences; and no matter what our background, these have been overwhelmingly Eurocentric and English-speaking.

Becoming a multicultural teacher, therefore, means first becoming a multicultural person. Without this transformation of ourselves, any attempts at developing a multicultural perspective will be shallow and superficial. But becoming a multicultural person in a society that values monoculturalism is not easy. It means reeducating ourselves in several ways.

First, *we simply need to learn more.* We need to be involved in activities that emphasize pluralism. We also need to look for books and other materials that inform us about people and events we may know little about. Given the multicultural nature of our society, those materials are generally available, although sometimes we have learned not to see them.

Second, *we need to confront our own racism and biases.* It is impossible to be a teacher with a multicultural perspective without going through this process. Because we are all products of a society that is racist and stratified by gender, class, and language, among other differences, we have all internalized some of these messages in one way or another. Sometimes, our racism is unconscious, as in the case of a former student of mine who referred to Africans as "slaves" and Europeans as "people" but was horrified when I pointed out what she had said.

Sometimes the words we use convey a deep-seated bias, as when a student who does not speak English is characterized as "not having language," as happened with my daughter when she was three. Our actions also carry the messages we have learned, for example, when we automatically expect that our female students will not do as well in math as our male students. Our own reeducation means not only learning new things but also unlearning some of the old. The process can be difficult and painful but it is a necessary part of becoming multicultural.

Third, *becoming a multicultural person means learning to see reality from a variety of perspectives.* Because we have often learned that there is only one "right answer," we have also developed only one way of seeing things. A multicultural perspective demands just the opposite. Reorienting ourselves in this way can be exhausting and difficult because it means a dramatic shift in our worldview.

Although the transformation of individuals from being monocultural to being multicultural will not by itself guarantee that education will become multicultural, it will lay the groundwork for it. Many years ago, Diane Sweet, a teacher who is thoroughly multicultural in outlook and practice (and the person who interviewed both Avi and James) told me, "Since I've developed a multicultural perspective, I just can't teach in any other way." Diane's philosophical outlook was evident in the content she taught, the instructional strategies she used, the environment in her classroom, the interactions she had with students and their parents, and the values she expressed in her personal life, school, and community.

A Model of Multicultural Education

A monocultural perspective reflects a fundamentally different framework for understanding differences than does a multicultural one. Even multicultural education, however, has a variety of levels of support for pluralism. I would classify them into at least four levels: *tolerance; acceptance; respect;* and *affirmation, solidarity, and critique.* In the process of becoming multicultural, we need to consider these levels of multicultural education and how they might be operationalized in the school.

Whenever we classify and categorize reality, as I do in this model, we run the risk that it will be viewed as static and arbitrary, rather than as messy, complex, and contradictory, which we know it to be. These categories should be viewed as dynamic and as having penetrable borders. My purpose in using them is to demonstrate the various ways in which multicultural education can be revealed in schools. I propose a model ranging from monocultural education to comprehensive multicultural education considered through the seven characteristics of multicultural education I described previously. This model explores how multicultural education pays attention to many components of the school environment and takes different forms in different settings.[23]

Tolerance is the first level. To be tolerant means to have the capacity to bear something, although at times it may be unpleasant. To tolerate differences means to endure them, although not necessarily to embrace them. We may learn to tolerate differences, but this level of acceptance can be shaky because what is tolerated today may be rejected tomorrow. Tolerance therefore represents the lowest level of multicultural education in a school setting. Yet many schools have what they consider very comprehensive mission statements that stress only their *tolerance* for diversity. Although they may believe that this is an adequate expression of support, it does not go far enough. In terms of school policies and practices, tolerance may mean that linguistic and cultural differences are borne as the inevitable burden of a culturally pluralistic society. Programs that do not build on but rather replace differences might be in place, for example, English as a second language (ESL) programs. Other programs or activities would be superficial at best. Black History Month might be commemorated with an assembly program and a bulletin board. The lifestyles and values of students' families, if different from the majority, may be considered by schools to require modification.

Acceptance is the next level of support for diversity. If we accept differences, we at the very least acknowledge them without denying their importance. In concrete terms, programs that acknowledge students' languages and cultures would be visible in the school. These might include a transitional bilingual program that uses the students' primary language at least until they are "mainstreamed" to an English-language environment. It might also mean celebrating some differences through activities such as multicultural fairs and cookbooks. In a school with this level of support for diversity, time might be set aside weekly for "multicultural programs," and parents' native languages might be used for communicating with them through newsletters.

Respect is the third level of multicultural education. Respect means to admire and hold in high esteem. When diversity is respected, it is used as the basis for much of the education offered. It might mean offering programs of bilingual education that use students' native language not only as a bridge to English but also throughout their schooling. Frequent and positive interactions with parents would take place. In the curriculum, students' values and experiences would be used as the basis for their literacy development. Students would be exposed to different ways of approaching the same reality, and as a result they would expand their way of looking at the world. *Additive multiculturalism* would be the ultimate goal for everybody.

Affirmation, solidarity, and critique are based on the premise that the most powerful learning results when students work and struggle with one another, even if it is sometimes difficult and challenging. This means accepting the culture and language of students and their families as legitimate and embracing them as valid vehicles for learning. It also means understanding that culture is not fixed or unchangeable, and that it can be criticized. Because multicultural education is concerned with equity and social justice for all people, and because basic values of different groups are often diametrically opposed, conflict is inevitable. What makes this level different from the others is that conflict is not avoided, but accepted as an inevitable part of learning.

Passively accepting the status quo of any culture is inconsistent with multicultural education. Simply substituting one myth for another contradicts the basic tenets of multicultural education because no group is inherently superior or more heroic than any other. At this level, students not only "celebrate" diversity, but they reflect on and challenge it as well. As expressed by Mary Kalantzis and Bill Cope, multicultural education "needs to consider not just the pleasure of diversity but more fundamental issues that arise as different groups negotiate community and the basic issues of material life in the same space—a process that equally might generate conflict and pain."[24]

Multicultural education without critique keeps cultural understanding at the romantic or exotic stage. If we are unable to transcend our own cultural experience through reflection and critique, then we cannot hope to understand and critique that of others. For students, this process begins with a strong sense of solidarity with others who are different from themselves. When based on deep respect, critique is not only necessary, but in fact healthy. Without critique, the danger that multicultural education might be used to glorify reality into static truth is very real.

In the school, affirmation, solidarity, and critique mean using the culture and language of all students in a consistent, critical, comprehensive, and inclusive way. This goes beyond creating ethnic enclaves that can become exclusionary and selective, although for disenfranchised communities, this might certainly be a step in the process. It means developing *multicultural* settings in which all students feel reflected and visible, for example, through two-way bilingual programs in which the languages of all students are used and maintained meaningfully in the academic setting. The curriculum would be characterized by multicultural sensitivity and inclusiveness, offering a wide variety of content and perspectives. Teachers' attitudes and behaviors would reflect only the very highest expectations for all students. Instructional strategies would also reflect a multicultural perspective and would include a range of means to teach students. Families would be welcomed and supported in the school as students' first and most important teachers. Their experiences, viewpoints, and suggestions would be sought out and incorporated into classroom and school programs and activities. In turn, families would be exposed to a variety of experiences and viewpoints different from their own, which would help them expand their horizons.

Other ways in which these four levels might be developed in schools are listed on the following pages in Table 10.1 . Of course, multicultural education cannot be categorized as neatly as this chart would suggest. This model simply represents a theoretical way of understanding how different levels of multicultural education might be visible in a school. It also highlights how pervasive a philosophy it must be to be effective. Although any level of multicultural education is preferable to the education offered by a monocultural perspective, each level challenges with more vigor a monolithic and ethnocentric view of society and education. As such, the fourth level is clearly the highest expression of support for multicultural education.

The fourth level is also the most difficult to achieve for some of the reasons mentioned previously, including the lack of models of multicultural education in our own schooling and experiences. It is here that we are most confronted by values and lifestyles different from our own, and with situations that severely test the limits of our tolerance. Interacting with people who are different from us in hygienic practices, food preferences, and religious rites can be trying. It is also

TABLE 10.1   Levels of Multicultural Education

		Characteristics of Multicultural Educatio
	Monocultural Education	*Tolerance*
Antiracist/ Antidiscriminatory	Racism is unacknowledged. Policies and practices that support discrimination are left in place. These include low expectations and refusal to use students' natural resources (such as language and culture) in instruction. Only a sanitized and "safe" curriculum is in place.	Policies and practices that challenge racism and discrimination are initiated. No overt signs of discrimination are acceptable (e.g., name calling, graffiti, blatantly racist and sexist textbooks or curriculum). ESL programs are in place for students who speak other languages.
Basic	Defines education as the 3 R's and the "canon." "Cultural literacy" is understood within a monocultural framework. All important knowledge is essentially European American. This Eurocentric view is reflected throughout the curriculum, instructional strategies, and environment for learning.	Education is defined more expansively and includes attention to selected information about other groups.
Pervasive	No attention is paid to student diversity.	A multicultural perspective is evident in some activities, such as Black History Month and Cinco de Mayo, and in some curriculum and materials. There may be an itinerant "multicultural teacher."
Important for All Students	Ethnic and/or women's studies, if available, are only for students from that group. This is a frill that is not important for other students to know.	Ethnic and women's studies are only offered as isolated courses.
Education for Social Justice	Education supports the status quo. Thinking and acting are separate.	Education is somewhat, although tenuously, linked to community projects and activities.
Process	Education is primarily content: who, what, where, when. The "great White men" version of history is propagated. Education is static.	Education is both content and process. "Why" and "how" questions are tentatively broached.
Critical Pedagogy	Education is domesticating. Reality is represented as static, finished, and flat.	Students and teachers begin to question the status quo.

Characteristics of Multicultural Education

Acceptance	Respect	Affirmation, Solidarity, and Critique
Policies and practices that acknowledge differences are in place. Textbooks reflect some diversity. Transitional bilingual programs are available. Curriculum is more inclusive of the histories and perspectives of a broader range of people.	Policies and practices that respect diversity are more evident, including maintenance bilingual education. Ability grouping is not permitted. Curriculum is more explicitly antiracist and honest. It is "safe" to talk about racism, sexism, and discrimination.	Policies and practices that affirm diversity and challenge racism are developed. There are high expectations for all students; students' language and culture are used in instruction and curriculum. Two-way bilingual programs are in place wherever possible. Everyone takes responsibility for challenging racism and discrimination.
The diversity of lifestyles and values of groups other than the dominant one are acknowledged in some content, as can be seen in some courses and school activities.	Education is defined as knowledge that is necessary for living in a complex and pluralistic society. As such, it includes much content that is multicultural. *Additive multiculturalism* is the goal.	Basic education is multicultural education. All students learn to speak a second language and are familiar with a broad range of knowledge.
Student diversity is acknowledged, as can be seen not only in "Holidays and Heroes" but also in consideration of different learning styles, values, and languages. A "multicultural program" may be in place.	The learning environment is imbued with multicultural education. It can be seen in classroom interactions, materials, and the culture of the school.	Multicultural education pervades the curriculum; instructional strategies; and interactions among teachers, students, and the community. It can be seen everywhere: bulletin boards, the lunchroom, assemblies.
Many students are expected to take part in curriculum that stresses diversity. A variety of languages are taught.	All students take part in courses that reflect diversity. Teachers are involved in overhauling the curriculum to be more open to such diversity.	All courses are completely multicultural in essence. The curriculum for all students is enriched.
The role of the schools in social change is acknowledged. Some changes that reflect this attitude begin to be felt: Students take part in community service.	Students take part in community activities that reflect their social concerns.	The curriculum and instructional techniques are based on an understanding of social justice as central to education. Reflection and action are important components of learning.
Education is both content and process. "Why" and "how" questions are stressed more. Sensitivity and cultural diverse understanding of students are more evident.	Education is both content and process. Students and teachers begin to ask, "What if?" Teachers build strong relationships with students and their families.	Education is an equal mix of content and process. It is dynamic. Teachers and students are empowered. Everyone in the school is becoming a multicultural person.
Students and teachers are beginning a dialogue. Students' experiences, cultures, and languages are used as one source of their learning.	Students and teachers use critical dialogue as the primary basis for their education. They see and understand different perspectives.	Students and teachers are involved in a "subversive activity." Decision-making and social action skills are the basis of the curriculum.

extremely difficult and at times impossible to accept and understand cultural practices that run counter to our most deeply held beliefs. For example, if we believe strongly in equality of the sexes and have in our classroom children whose families value males more highly than females, if we need to communicate with parents who believe that education is a frill and not suitable for their children, or if we have children in our classes whose religion forbids them to take part in any school activities except academics—all of these situations test our capacity for affirmation and solidarity. And well they should, for we have all learned to view reality from the vantage point of our own values.

Culture is not static; nor is it necessarily positive or negative. The cultural values and practices of a group of people reflect their best strategies, at a particular historical moment, for negotiating their environment and circumstances. What some groups have worked out as appropriate strategies may be considered unsuitable or even barbaric and uncivilized by others. Because each cultural group has developed in a different context, we can never reach total agreement on the best or most appropriate ways in which to lead our lives.

One way to tackle this dilemma is to emphasize the human and civil rights of all people. These rights guarantee that all human beings are treated with dignity, respect, and equality. Sometimes the values and behaviors of a group so seriously challenge these values that we cannot accept or tolerate them. If the values we as human beings hold most dear are based on extending rather than negating rights, then we must decide on the side of those more universal values.

This brings us to a final consideration: *Multicultural education is not easy. If it were, everyone would be doing it.* Resolving conflicts about cultural differences is difficult, and sometimes impossible. The extent to which our particular cultural lenses may keep us from appreciating differences can be very great. Also, some values are simply irreconcilable, and we need to accept this fact. Usually, however, accommodations that respect both cultural values and basic human rights can be found. Because societies have generally resolved such conflicts in only one way, that is, favoring the dominant culture, few avenues for negotiating differences have been in place. Multicultural education, although at times difficult, painful, and time consuming, can provide one way of attempting such negotiations.

• *CONCLUSION*

Anything less than a program of comprehensive multicultural education will continue to shortchange students in our schools. Our society has promised all students an equal and high-quality education, but educational results have belied this promise. Students most victimized by society, that is, those from economically poor and culturally and linguistically dominated groups, are also the most vulnerable in our schools. Their status tends to replicate the status of their families in society in general. Unless our educational system confronts inequity at all levels and through all school policies and practices, we will simply be proceeding with business as usual.

The case studies in this book underscore the central role of schools in promoting academic success for all students and multicultural education as a promising means to achieve this goal. *Affirming Diversity*, the title of this book, is at the core of multicultural education. It implies that cultural, linguistic, and other differences can and should be accepted, respected, and used as a basis for learning and teaching. Rather than maladies to be cured or problems to be confronted, differences are a necessary starting point for learning and teaching and they can enrich the experiences of students and teachers. Affirming diversity in no way implies that we merely celebrate differences. To the contrary, issues of racism and inequality must be confronted openly in any comprehensive program of multicultural education.

Affirming diversity is not enough unless we also challenge inequitable policies and practices that grant unfair advantages to some students over others. Moreover, simply tackling issues of racism and discrimination at the school level does little to change the broader context. Although improvement in education must take place at the school level, changing the school alone will not lead to substantive changes in society. Schools have often been sites of protest, resistance, and change, and their role in influencing public policy has sometimes been significant. But racism, classism, ethnocentrism, sexism, linguicism, anti-Semitism, handicapism, and other forms of discrimination exist in schools because they exist in society. To divorce schools from society is impossible. Although schools may with all good intentions attempt to provide learning environments free from bias, once students leave the classroom and building they are again confronted with an unequal society.

Teachers, schools, and students engaged in challenging social inequities need an explicit understanding that they are involved in a struggle that critiques and questions the status quo not only of schools but of society. They will inevitably be involved in what Mildred Dickeman over a quarter of a century ago described as "a subversive task" if they are serious about facing issues of cultural pluralism in schools.[25] Her perspective defies the simple definition of multicultural education as celebratory, implying a more complex understanding of difference.

The balance between hope and despair is difficult to maintain, yet that is precisely what is called for. Multicultural education is not a remedy for social inequality, and it cannot guarantee academic success. At the same time, if one of the primary purposes of education is to teach young people the skills, knowledge, and critical awareness to become productive members of a diverse and democratic society, then a broadly conceptualized multicultural education can have a decisive influence. Although racism cannot be wiped out by schools, the role that schools can play should not be underestimated either because, by developing antiracist and affirming policies and practices, schools can make a genuine difference in the lives of many students.

Injustice is multifaceted, and school is but one arena in which it is revealed. Even if a school decides, for example, to do away with standardized tests because it considers them to be discriminatory, the implications of such a radical decision might be far-ranging and counter to its desired goals. How well the school's students do on such tests may determine whether they go to college, what college they will attend, what they will study, and who they can become later in life. In effect, their entire future might depend on knowing how to take tests. This being the case, the school's decision, unless well thought out and followed up by other activities and policies, might in the long run be both a romantic struggle against windmills and detrimental to the students who most need the school's support. Once again we see that schools are not isolated, but rather part of a sociopolitical context that must always be taken into account.

● *SUMMARY*

This chapter reviewed the responsibility of schools to strengthen bilingual and multicultural education. The role of meaningful extracurricular activities was also considered, with examples of what schools and communities can do. Suggestions concerning the role of teachers and families in providing environments for success for all students were presented, specifically, *mutual accommodation, teachers' relationships with students,* and *family environments for learning.*

This chapter also addressed two additional issues that have implications for multicultural education: the definition of *American* and how various levels of multicultural education affect the learning environment. If we begin with the premise that what it means to be an *American* must be continuously renegotiated, then there is ample room for promoting a society characterized by inclusiveness. The expansion of the definition of American also suggests that schools need to be about teaching students, not assimilating them, and that good teaching begins at the level where students are.

● *TO THINK ABOUT*

1. What are schools for? To determine the *function* of schools, investigate the *structure* of schools. Given the following *objectives* of education, work in small groups to design a school for each one.
   a. The purpose of schools is to "Americanize" or assimilate all students to the American way of life.
   b. The purpose of schools is to prepare a few good managers and a lot of good workers.
   c. The purpose of schools is to develop critical thinkers.
   d. The purpose of schools is to prepare citizens for active participation in a democratic society.

   Explore how a school founded on one of these goals might function. Describe the curriculum, materials, administration, community outreach, and structure in the school you design. Working together, compare the differences among the four hypothetical schools. Then compare each of these schools to schools with which you are familiar. What can we learn from these comparisons?
2. Think about some of the ways extracurricular activities in schools you know limit the participation of students. Give examples of what schools can do to become more inclusive. Consider sports, newspaper, student government, and other activities.

3. You are the teacher representative on a search committee for a new teacher for your school. Develop a list of qualities or characteristics you would look for. Would race, ethnicity, gender, or language background make a difference? Why or why not? What if the school were very culturally diverse or monocultural? Would this make a difference?

4. Define *American*.

5. Three different models for understanding pluralism or the lack of it are these:

   • Anglo-conformity: All newcomers need to conform to the dominant European American, middle-class, and English-speaking model.

   • "Melting pot": All newcomers "melt" to form an amalgam that becomes American.

   • "Salad bowl": All newcomers maintain their languages and cultures while combining with others to form a "salad," which is our unique U.S. society.

   In three groups, take one of the previous options and argue that it represents the dominant ideology in U.S. society. Give concrete examples. Afterward, in a large group, decide if one of these ideologies is really the most apparent and successful. Give reasons for your conclusions. How would you critique each of these ideologies? What are the advantages and disadvantages of each?

6. How would you identify a person who has developed what I called *additive multiculturalism?* How might that individual be different from one who is monocultural? Give some examples.

7. Evaluate a school you are familiar with in terms of the model of multicultural education proposed in this chapter. Consider the curriculum; materials; interactions among staff, students, and community; and the entire environment for living and learning in the school.

8. Mildred Dickeman (see note 25) has suggested that teachers are engaged in "a subversive task" if they challenge the monocultural curriculum and other inequities of schools. What does she mean? Do you agree?

● NOTES

1. Alejandro Portes and Rubén Rumbaut, *Immigrant America: A Portrait,* 2nd ed. (University of California Press, 1996).

2. For a further development of this idea, see Sonia Nieto, "Bringing Bilingual Education Out of the Basement, and Other Imperatives for Teacher Education." Edited by Zeynep Beykont *Bilingual Education Works: Linking Research and Practice in Schools* (Cambridge: Harvard Educational Review, 1999).

3. Margaret A. Gibson, "Perspectives on Acculturation and School Performance." *Focus on Diversity* (Newsletter of the National Center for Research on Cultural Diversity and Second Language Learning), 5, 3 (1995), 8–10.

4. Teresa L. McCarty, "Language, Literacy, and the Image of the Child in American Indian Classrooms." *Language Arts,* 70, 3 (March 1993), 182–192.

5. Nathan Glazer, "Where is Multiculturalism Leading Us?" *Phi Delta Kappan,* 75, 4 (December, 1993), 319–323.

6. *Metropolitan Life Survey of the American Teacher 1996.* A survey conducted by Louis Harris and Associates, as cited in *Multicultural Education,* 4, 4 (Summer, 1997), 45.
7. A good example is Laurie Olsen's study of Madison High, *Made in America: Immigrant Students in Our Public Schools* (New York: The New Press, 1997).
8. For a review, see Sonia Nieto, *The Light in Their Eyes: Creating Multicultural Learning Communities* (New York: Teachers College Press, 1999).
9. Carmen I. Mercado, "Caring as Empowerment: School Collaboration and Community Agency." *Urban Review,* 25, 1 (March 1993), 79–104.
10. Stephan Díaz, Luis C. Moll, and Hugh Mehan, "Sociocultural Resources in Instruction: A Context-Specific Approach." In *Beyond Language: Social and Cultural Factors in Schooling Language Minority Students* (Los Angeles: Office of Bilingual Education, California State Department of Education, Evaluation, Dissemination and Assessment Center, 1986).
11. Ibid.
12. Gloria Ladson-Billings, *The Dreamkeepers: Successful Teachers of African American Children* (San Francisco: Jossey-Bass Publishers, 1994).
13. Ricardo D. Stanton-Salazar, "A Social Capital Framework for Understanding the Socialization of Racial Minority Children and Youth." *Harvard Educational Review,* 67, 1 (Spring 1997), 1–40.
14. Alma Flor Ada, "The Pajaro Valley Experience." In *Minority Education: From Shame to Struggle,* edited by Tove Skutnabb-Kangas and Jim Cummins (Clevedon, England: Multilingual Matters, 1988), 235.
15. Peter Nien-Chu Kiang, *Southeast Asian Parent Empowerment: The Challenge of Changing Demographics in Lowell, Massachusetts,* Monograph no. 1. (Boston: Massachusetts Association for Bilingual Education, 1990).
16. For a more complete treatment of this idea, see Sonia Nieto, "On Becoming American: An Exploratory Essay." In *A Light in Dark Times,* edited by William Ayres and Janet L. Miller (New York: Teachers College Press, 1998).
17. Words of Morris Raphael Cohen, quoted in Stephan F. Brumberg, *Going to America, Going to School: The Jewish Immigrant Public School Encounter in Turn-of-the-Century New York City* (New York: Praeger, 1986), 116.
18. As cited by Alejandro Portes and Rubén G. Rumbaut in *Immigrant America: A Portrait.*
19. Wallace E. Lambert, "Culture and Language as Factors in Learning and Education." In *Education of Immigrant Students,* edited by A. Wolfgang (Toronto: OISE, 1975).
20. H. Ned Seelye, *Teaching Culture: Strategies for Intercultural Communication* (Lincolnwood, IL: National Textbook, 1993).
21. William Greenbaum, "America in Search of a New Ideal: An Essay on the Rise of Pluralism." *Harvard Educational Review,* 44, 3 (August 1974), 411–440.
22. Maxine Greene, *The Dialectic of Freedom* (New York: Teachers College Press, 1988), 87.
23. I have expanded this model, providing specific scenarios for each level. See Sonia Nieto, "Affirmation, Solidarity, and Critique: Moving Beyond Tolerance in Multicultural Education." *Multicultural Education,* 1, 4 (Spring 1994), 9–12, 35–38.
24. Mary Kalantzis and Bill Cope, *The Experience of Multicultural Education in Australia: Six Case Studies* (Sydney: Centre for Multicultural Studies, Wollongong University, 1990), 39.
25. Mildred Dickeman, "Teaching Cultural Pluralism." In *Teaching Ethnic Studies: Concepts and Strategies,* 43rd Yearbook, edited by James A. Banks (Washington, DC: National Council for the Social Studies, 1973).

chapter 11

Multicultural Education in Practice

*T*eaching can be a lonely and isolating profession. The myth of the teacher as sole crusader is deeply embedded in our collective psyche. Whether in movies, novels, or autobiographies, the media have reinforced unrealistic portraits of teachers as indefatigable miracle workers or burned out former idealists. Rarely do we see teachers collaborating with or learning from one another. Our most cherished images of teachers reinforce the picture of struggling or heroic individuals on a lonesome journey, whether grading papers late into the night or as charismatic modern-day Pied Pipers of the young people in their care.

Neither of these images is an acceptable alternative because both strengthen the model of teacher as divorced from a historical and sociopolitical context. Although we all learn during our student teaching days that, "once you close the classroom door, you can do anything you want" (and in fact that may be true to some extent), this approach to teaching contradicts the very basis of our lives as social beings who need to interact with and learn from others. The problem has been well articulated by Kenneth Zeichner: "One consequence of this isolation of individual teachers and of the lack of attention to the social context of teaching in teacher development is that teachers come to see their problems as their own, unrelated to those of other teachers or to the structure of schools and school systems."[1]

The one place where teachers do meet and socialize, the teachers' room, is sometimes filled with negative talk about children and their families. As a result, more idealistic and committed teachers learn to stay away from such places to maintain their sense of hope. Although understandable, this may result in isolating from the public discourse precisely those critical voices rarely heard in the great and small debates concerning teaching and learning that go on in schools every day. The other occasion where teachers meet is school meetings, and these are either devoted to deadening announcements and bureaucratic details, or to staff development activities that teachers have had little hand in planning. Clearly, then, other ways to build productive and fulfilling relationships among teachers must be found.

This chapter is based on the assumption that teachers need to work together, as well as with students and their families, to develop approaches that affirm their students and one another. It assumes as well that the ultimate responsibility for developing consequential cooperative relationships rests with teachers, with the support of administrators. The image of the teacher as a knight on a white horse is hopelessly romantic and at the same time ultimately defeating, because it is an illusion that takes too much energy to sustain. I suggest instead that a far more promising approach is to build collaborative relationships that take into account the historical moment and the particular social context in which teachers work, as well as the lives of their students. This means not only that teachers *need* to go into the teachers' room, but also that they must learn to talk with, learn from, and challenge their colleagues in a consistent and constructive manner that reinforces their dual roles as teachers and learners.

In some ways, it is easier to remain isolated, of course. Collaboration demands negotiation, compromise, and sometimes taking a back seat, none of which are necessary when one is working alone. Also, more than one teacher has been seduced by the image of the visionary teacher with his or her adoring students facing a cruel and uncaring world. In real life, however, teachers will find that they can accomplish much more with and for their students if they directly confront alienating conditions for learning, and that this is best done with their colleagues and other allies in and out of school.

Teachers alone are not to blame for lack of experience with collaboration. From education courses to school policies, teachers are expected and even encouraged to work alone. Precious few situations for collective work exist, and teachers must often fight convention and institutional barriers to find the space to work together. Schools that set aside time for collaborative projects on a weekly basis, for example, are rare, and very few teachers have the luxury of meeting and working with their colleagues during the school day. Yet this is exactly one of the school practices that needs to be changed. At the very least, teachers need the freedom to meet for several hours a week for collective work. Even posing this possibility to principals, school boards, teacher unions, and the central administration can eventually lead to changes in the structure of the school day. In the meantime, if teachers begin the process on their own while at the same time demanding structural changes in schools, they will find collaboration to be both personally satisfying and effective.

One of the major problems with developing collaborative relationships is that so few models exist. Teachers might begin by becoming familiar with the growing literature on teacher research and collaborative writing among teacher cohorts.[2] Accounts of teacher research and collaboration provide eloquent testimony to the power of teachers working together, and to the tremendous effect they can have in changing the climate of their classrooms and schools.

Another way of promoting teacher collaboration is by devoting staff meetings primarily to discussions of timely and significant issues rather than to bureaucratic matters. Teachers are more likely to perceive staff meetings as significant to their own context when the meetings center around intellectually stimulating issues that can help teachers with real classroom problems. Otherwise, meetings are seen as just another grind to get through. Mary Cavalier, a middle school principal I know, for example, seeks funds to purchase each staff member copies of books to read and use as the basis of discussion at faculty meetings. They have read and discussed numerous books including Herb Kohl's *I Won't Learn From You and Other Thoughts on Creative Maladjustment*, and *Turning Points: Preparing American Youth for the Twenty-First Century* from the Carnegie Council on Adolescent Development. Both are particularly significant for the middle school setting. Mary also purchased a copy of *Beyond Heroes and Holidays* from Network of Educators on the Americas (NECA) for each of the teams in her school to assist them as they develop curriculum based on the new state curriculum frameworks.

Collective work that builds on student and community strengths and resources also challenges the image of school transformation as simply a bureaucratic endeavor. Jim Cummins, for example, suggests that a reconsideration of the relations of power between teachers and students must take place to effect student learning. He contends that underachievement, particularly of language-minority and other disenfranchised youth, is a result of their subordinate status and the denial of access to power by the dominant group. Cummins therefore concludes that teachers need to develop "collaborative" rather than "coercive relations of power" with their students. That is, the remedy lies not in tinkering with technical or artificial aspects of education, but rather in a redefinition of teachers' and students' roles in the classroom that will challenge students' devaluation. Through collaborative relations of power, teachers and students become engaged in critically studying the historic devaluation of students' cultural identity to reconstruct it in a more equitable and affirming way.[3]

This chapter considers strategies and approaches that teachers and schools can use to affirm and support students in becoming, as Manuel Gomes said, "all that they can be." Because the major goal of any good education is student learning, we will first explore how multicultural education can provide a sound basis for students from all backgrounds to achieve high levels of learning. Collaborative work by teachers is at the center of the suggestions that follow because students learn from the work habits that are modeled for them by teachers. If they see teachers engaged in reading groups, interdisciplinary lesson planning, and collective lobbying to change ability grouping, for example, they will pick up the message that collaborating and sharing can be a powerful way of learning from one another, as well as of changing the world. In this chapter, suggestions for changes in classrooms, schools, and beyond are made, and you are challenged to develop your own collaborative approaches to transforming education so that all students are helped to succeed.

A note of caution: Although collaborative work and planning are essential to school reform, they are not enough, and suggesting that collaboration alone can make schools empowering and exciting places is naïve. For example, in her research of an urban junior high school undergoing restructuring, Pauline Lipman found that although new building-level collaborative structures were developed, most teachers continued to hold onto a deficit model of their students' abilities and backgrounds. As a result, in their team meetings, most teachers focused on the supposed deficits of their individual students—those conditions they had the least power to change—rather than on school-related conditions, over which they actually had more power.[4]

PROBLEM POSING: RECONSIDERING SCHOOL POLICIES AND PRACTICES IN A MULTICULTURAL CONTEXT

As you will recall, the definition of multicultural education in Chapter 9 was derived from an exploration of various conditions that may help explain why some students fail to learn: racism and other forms of discrimination, school structures, and the negative ways in which cultural and linguistic differences are viewed in the school. Using what Paulo Freire called a "problem-posing approach,"[5] this chapter reviews the issues presented in Chapters 3 to 6 of Part II as an organizational framework. We will go back to the following:

- Racism, discrimination, and expectations of students' achievements (Chapter 3).
- Structural and organizational conditions in schools (Chapter 4).
- Culture, identity, and learning (Chapter 5).
- Linguistic diversity (Chapter 6).

In what follows, suggestions for putting multicultural education into practice are made within each of these broad categories. When multicultural education is viewed comprehensively and in a sociopolitical context, conversations that trivialize or otherwise demean cultural, linguistic, social, and other differences are avoided. This approach also challenges the historic tendency to view teachers within the "factory model" as mass production workers unable to develop creative and empowering strategies for their classrooms. In this chapter, your own ideas and experiences are the basis for discussion. Rather than answers or prescriptions for "prejudice reduction" or simple "cultural awareness" lessons, the focus here is on providing a framework for you to reflect on the total educational community in which you work. Specific recommendations should be seen as guidelines for developing an inclusive environment rather than as static recipes for multicultural lessons.

The problem-posing approach rejects the more simplistic but ultimately disrespectful view of teachers as needing specific lessons for "multiculturalizing" the curriculum. By engaging in the process of problematizing and seeking solutions to issues that stand in the way of student learning and empowerment, you can develop a more critical understanding of teaching and learning and the positive or negative influences that school policies and practices, as well as societal attitudes and behaviors, have on students.[6]

It is impossible to become instantly multicultural. Attempts to do so are sometimes comical as well as counterproductive and superficial. However, teachers can do *a little bit every day* and work toward implementing change systematically, which is probably more effective in the long run. Because each school is different in outlook, culture, and especially the nature of the teacher and student body, the emphasis in this chapter is on teachers' and students' development of multicultural approaches that best meet the needs of their particular setting. After a number of suggestions are made in each of the categories in the organizational framework, specific situations and problems for you to work on are presented.

COUNTERING RACISM, DISCRIMINATION, AND LOW EXPECTATIONS

Because racism, discrimination, and low expectations of student abilities are profoundly interconnected, this section considers them together, first exploring several ways in which they interact and then proposing a number of strategies for addressing them.

Our biases are bound up with those of society at large in myriad ways, even in the way we learn to approach differences. The failure to confront children's curiosity about differences in skin color, facial features, or hair textures is a good example. There is a reluctance to address these issues head on because by doing so, we may feel that we are drawing unneeded attention to them. Also, there is resistance to tackle issues of diversity because of the negative ways in which these differences are viewed within the majority culture, and reinforced within dominated cultures. As a result, teachers are inevitably nervous about broaching these turbulent waters.

Children quickly pick up the message that talking about or acknowledging differences is a negative thing. The failure to talk about differences, or about how they are addressed in our society, results in classrooms that are curiously silent about such issues. But these issues *do* get addressed, although generally in secretive and destructive ways. Name-calling, rejection, and other manifestations of hostility can be the result.

Expectations are connected with the biases we have learned to internalize. If we expect children who come from economically poor communities to be poor readers, then we may reflect this belief in the way we teach them. Similarly, if we expect girls to be passive and submissive, we may teach them as if they were. Perhaps our sensitivity to a deaf child's learning needs results in our belief that she cannot learn as quickly as a hearing child. Although our teaching approaches may be either unconscious or developed with the best of intentions, the results can be disastrous. We have seen many vivid examples throughout this book.

Having good intentions or even caring deeply about students is not enough. We need to consider our biases, which even the most enlightened teachers carry with them, every day that we step foot into the classroom. We are sometimes shocked when others point out to us, for instance, that we call on the girls in our class less often than the boys or that we accept slovenly work from some students and not from others. African American and Latino students have often told me that teachers were happy with a C from them in math, say, whereas they expected higher grades from other students in the class. We cannot mandate, of course, that teachers develop high expectations for all students or that schools become antiracist, antisexist institutions overnight, but we can make changes in the educational environment to promote these processes.

Promoting and Actively Working toward Creating a Diverse Staff

Although individual teachers alone cannot generally influence the hiring practices of schools, they can join others to work for a gender-balanced and racially, ethnically, linguistically diverse staff. When positions are available, they can lobby for the inclusion of job qualifications that make it clear that diversity is a key criterion for consideration. This is true for all positions throughout the school and it is particularly crucial for underrepresented groups, such as women in top administrative posts. There is no easy one-to-one correlation between students' self-image and the number of staff or faculty from diverse groups. But schools in which the teaching staff is primarily European American and the administration is heavily male, whereas the student body and kitchen staff are overwhelmingly Mexican American and female, for example, may send a powerful, albeit unintended, message about the second-class status of some students and staff.

Teachers can suggest that aggressive outreach efforts be used to locate a diverse staff. These can include public notices, so that parents and other community members are informed of openings; postings in community centers and local businesses; announcements in local newspapers; and notices sent to local radio stations. These notices should be translated into the major languages spoken in the community.

What Can You Do?
- If the student body in your school is very heterogeneous but the teaching staff is not, what can you do to encourage more diversity on the staff? What if no openings are currently available, but you and others are concerned about the cultural imbalance of students to staff? List some creative ways to make your school more multicultural, using current resources.
- Use the same scenario, but change one condition: Both the teaching staff and student body are quite *homogeneous*. Why is it important to diversify the teaching staff? Create another list of activities to help a largely homogeneous school become multicultural.

Making Differences and Similarities an Explicit Part of the Curriculum

Focusing on human differences and similarities can begin as early as the preschool years, for example, dealing with skin color, hair texture, and other physical differences and similarities. Rather than telling White children that it is not polite to say that Black children have "dirty" skin, the teacher can use this statement as a basis for making skin differences an explicit part of the curriculum. Use individual photographs of the children for a bulletin board on all the beautiful colors of children in the class, pictures from magazines of people from all over the world, stories that emphasize the similarities in human feelings across all groups, and dolls that represent a variety of racial and ethnic groups as well as both sexes.

Patty Bode, a talented art teacher I know, used a color theory lesson to focus attention on skin color. While an elementary art teacher in a public school in Amherst, Mass., (she has since become a middle school teacher), Patty developed a school-wide activity in which every student and staff member in the school was engaged, from cooks to teachers to the principal and custodian. She had everyone mix the primary colors to match their particular skin color and then make hand prints. In the process, they engaged in dialogue about "race," the words we use to describe people of different backgrounds, discrimination and racism, and other issues rarely discussed in most schools. When they were finished, Patty hung all the handprints (over 500) in the halls of the schools. It was a powerful graphic representation of diversity and inclusiveness.

Teachers can work with their students and colleagues to develop a "school culture" so that it is truly a community. For example, some activities and rituals can become school-wide efforts, such as selecting local or national school heroes from a variety of backgrounds; having all students learn songs, poems, or speeches from several cultures; and having all students take part in local history projects that explore the lives, experiences, and accomplishments of many different people. In the classroom, a teacher might develop a *Classtory* (i.e., a history of the class) that includes the pictures and biographies of each member of the class with information about their culture, the languages they speak, and the things they like to do with friends and family. In this way, children learn that history is not simply what has happened in the past to "important" people, but also something that they and their communities are involved in making every day. Activities such as these do not browbeat the concept of similarities and differences into children's heads but develop them as natural outcomes.

With older students, focusing on multicultural literature that depicts the reality of women and men of many groups is an effective strategy (see Appendix for a list of anthologies and professional resources in multicultural literature). Curriculum that discusses the history and culture of particular groups is also helpful, especially when used in an interdisciplinary approach.

From preschool through high school, creating a physical environment that affirms differences is crucial. This environment might include a variety of pictures and posters, wall hangings from different cultures, models made by the students, maps and flags from around the world, bulletin boards of special days that feature multicultural themes, exhibits of art from around the country and the world, and a well-stocked multicultural library in which all manner of differences are evident (see Appendix for a list of resources and places where they can be found). When students are working quietly, music reflecting different cultures can be played. The game corner can include a variety of games, from checkers to Parcheesi to Mankala to dominoes. Different languages can also be used on bulletin boards and posters, with translations in English.

What Can You Do?

- Focus on your specific curriculum. How can you make similarities and differences an explicit part of your curriculum? If you are a subject matter specialist, work with an interdisciplinary group of colleagues and list the topics that you will be teaching in the next month. How can you collaborate on these? If you are an elementary or preschool teacher, work with your colleagues in the same grade to list the themes or topics you will be teaching. How can you make them more explicitly multicultural and antisexist? Or, work across the grades to promote teaching and learning with students of different ages. Write down specific ideas, along with resources for accompanying this task. You may want to develop one or more actual lesson plans in detail as a starting point.

- Think about the resources you already have in your school, classroom, and community. Working with a group of teachers and students, develop an environment that is physically multicultural. Write down concrete ideas or draw the floor plan of your classroom (and school), indicating where and how resources that are multicultural might best be used.

Confronting Racism and Discrimination in the Curriculum

Focusing on similarities and differences alone does not guarantee that racism will disappear. In fact, a focus on similarities and differences can become an excuse for not delving more deeply into racism. Because racism and other biases are generally hushed up or avoided in the curriculum, they become uncomfortable topics of conversation in the school. Making racism and discrimination an explicit part of the curriculum can be a healthy and caring way to address these difficult issues.

Even young children can take part in discussions on racism and discrimination. Although many teachers believe that young children should not be exposed to the horrors of racism at an early age, they overlook the fact that many children suffer the effects of racism or other forms of discrimination every day. Making these discussions an explicit part of the curriculum, for even the youngest children, helps them tackle racism and other biases in productive rather than negative ways.[7]

The name-calling that goes on in many schools provides a tremendous opportunity for teachers and students to engage in dialogue. Rather than addressing these as isolated incidents or as the work of a few troublemakers, as is too often done, making them an explicit part of the curriculum helps students understand these incidents as symptoms of systemic problems in society and schools. Making explicit the biases that are implicit in name-calling can become part of "circle" or "sharing time," or can form the basis for lessons on racism, sexism, ableism, or other biases.

What Can You Do?
- Stereotypes of racial and cultural groups, women, social classes, and disabled people, among others, are all around us. Working with colleagues, create strategies to make these an explicit part of the curriculum. Locate appropriate materials and describe how you would have students counter the stereotypes they see.
- Most teachers have witnessed name-calling and racist and exclusionary behavior in their schools. Recall the last such incident you saw. How was it handled? Would you handle it any differently now? How would you make it an explicit part of the curriculum? What resources might you use to help you? What role should parents and community members have in addressing these issues?

- How might you use stories in the news to bring up issues of racism and other biases? Develop activities related to your subject area and grade level that concern current events in which stereotyping, racism, or exclusion can be found.

CHANGING SCHOOLS: RESTRUCTURE AND RENEWAL

As became abundantly clear in Chapter 4, structural conditions in the schools themselves exacerbate problems of social inequality. Although changing a few structures in the schools cannot guarantee equity, it can set the stage for promoting equal and high-quality education for all students. Let's consider the structures reviewed in Chapter 4 to develop strategies for restructure and renewal in schools.

Tracking

If tracking is generally acknowledged to be a problem in promoting equitable education in a democratic society, then detracking schools is the first step, although it is not enough. The decision to detrack is often made in a top-down manner, with teachers having little or no say in the process. Furthermore, schools are often detracked with little planning or systemic preparation among the staff and student body. Because the large class sizes in many schools make heterogeneous classes unwieldy, teachers may end up regrouping by ability within their classrooms. Also, students often are unaccustomed to the alternatives to tracking, such as cooperative groups and peer tutoring, and may resist these efforts if the transition is not appropriately handled. As a result, the problems associated with tracking often reappear under a different guise.

Most teachers have professional days they can use to attend conferences or meetings or to visit other schools. Visiting schools that have successfully detracked is an effective activity for teachers whose schools are contemplating doing so. Other professional development activities can be used as well. For example, teachers can recommend that staff development sessions address tracking, detracking, and alternative kinds of grouping. A team of interested colleagues might ask for the opportunity to prepare staff seminars in which they share ideas for detracking or for creative grouping in classrooms.

Because tracking also occurs in extracurricular activities, schools need to refocus their efforts to make clubs and other organizations appealing to a wider range of students. The school newspaper, for instance, is generally thought of as an activity for only highly intellectual and academically successful students, whereas sports are seen as the domain of other students. School activities and clubs frequently perpetuate the social class groupings that students develop instead of helping to counter the stereotypes on which they are based. Extracurricular and other activities were significant in the academic success of most of the students in our case studies, as they are to many other students. But often they are seen as exclusive clubs with limited membership. Although the message, "You need not apply" is not purposely given, many students infer that message in the recruitment policies and activities of some clubs and organizations.

What Can You Do?

- Create alternative ways of grouping your students that are not ability based. For example, group students according to their interests, hobbies, native language, birthday month, favorite color, birth order, or alphabetically.
- Work with a group of colleagues to set up interclass groups based on criteria other than ability. Develop relevant and purposeful academic activities for each group.
- Are there classrooms in your school (including special education, bilingual, and ESL) that are substantially separate from the others? With a group of colleagues, develop a plan to collaborate with the teachers and students in those classrooms. You can begin by developing projects of mutual interest to the children. Activities focused on interdisciplinary academic areas with a potential for multicultural learning (e.g., the ecology of the community or the inadequacy of housing and the plight of the homeless) would probably be more successful than those based strictly on cultural awareness, because the students would be exploring specific community problems and attempting to find common solutions. In the process, they would also learn about their differences and similarities.
- With colleagues, develop a staff development session on alternative grouping strategies. How would you present it? How might you use cooperative groups with participants to illustrate your point?

Testing

As we begin the twenty-first century, standardized testing has become more of a mainstay of education in the United States than ever before in our history. Tests are used to place students; assess their progress; remove them from programs; and admit them into top tracks, gifted and talented programs, special education, bilingual classes, and so on. They exert a powerful influence on most educational decisions. Yet, as we have seen, tests correlate more with family income than with intelligence or ability, and the result is that poor students of all backgrounds are unfairly jeopardized in the process.

Given the power they exert, tests and the testing industry need to be monitored closely, evaluated rigorously, and challenged. The specific strategies that each school and school district chooses to engage in may vary, depending on how they use tests, whether the tests are grossly biased or not, and the testing skills that students already have. There are two basic strategies: either challenge the use of tests, or focus attention on test taking and how to use it to the advantage of the students.

Because the effects of testing, particularly standardized testing, are so often negative, particularly for poor students and students of color, one strategy is to challenge the use of tests in the first place. With a group of interested colleagues and parents, you can approach the local school committee and ask that standardized tests be kept to a minimum, that the results be used in more appropriate ways, and that students not be placed at risk because of the results of such tests.

Alternatively, you might decide that given the pervasiveness of testing and the power it exerts on the options of young people, your energy might be better spent in teaching students how to take tests more critically and effectively. In affluent schools and neighborhoods, students learn specific test-taking skills that help them do very well on tests. Poor students do not generally have the same kind of access to learning these skills. For the time being, crucial decisions that affect students' lives are based to a large extent on test results. This fact was brought home quite clearly in the strategy used by Jaime Escalante, the talented calculus teacher in Garfield High School in East Los Angeles, as dramatized in the film *Stand and Deliver*. Escalante's students did so well on the AP calculus tests, in fact, that their scores were questioned by the testing company the first time around. When they retook the tests, they did even better. The fact that poor students of color could excel on these tests was inconceivable to the general public. Because of the test results, many of the young people were given unprecedented access to college and to scholarships that they may have never previously obtained.

What Can You Do?
- Assess the reality of your school and community. Find out how standardized tests are used and how other evaluation criteria may be better employed. Determine which of the strategies described is most appropriate for your school. Get together with colleagues to decide how to proceed.
- Join a local or national group that is demanding major changes in the testing industry and bring the information back to your school. For example, find out what the local teachers' union is doing. FairTest, in Cambridge, Mass., and Rethinking Schools in Milwaukee, Wis. (listed in the *Appendix*), have both been active in this arena.

The Curriculum

Because the curriculum in most schools is skewed toward a European American perspective, it excludes the lives and perspectives of many students. Textbooks and other materials reinforce this bias, making the development of an inclusive curriculum even more difficult. Scrapping the existing curriculum is generally neither feasible nor practical. Several strategies using both the existing curriculum and an emerging one may help to turn this situation around.

Teachers can use the current curriculum as the basis for helping students develop a more critical perspective and better research skills. For example, when studying the Revolutionary War, students can examine the experiences of African Americans, American Indians, women, working people, loyalists, and others whose perspectives have traditionally been excluded from the curriculum. When studying the Industrial Revolution, students can explore the role of the nascent workers' movement, and of children and young women factory workers, as well as the impact of European immigration on the rise of cities. Students can also concentrate on the emergence of scientific discoveries through inventions by African Americans and others during the late nineteenth century.

When teaching different mathematical operations, teachers can ask students to investigate how they are done in other countries. A variety of materials, such as an abacus and other counting instruments, can be demonstrated. If traditional U.S. holidays are commemorated in the curriculum, teachers can try to include other perspectives. For example, for Columbus Day teachers would discuss the concept of "discovery" with students, so that they understand that this was the perspective of the Europeans, not the Indians. Alternative activities would focus on October 12th as the encounter of two worldviews and histories rather than on the "discovery" of one world by another. (*Rethinking Columbus,* from Rethinking Schools, is an excellent publication that includes many lesson plans and other resources for classrooms). Thanksgiving, considered by many Indians to be a day of mourning, is another holiday that can be presented through multiple perspectives.

The tendency to associate holidays from different cultures that happen to fall about the same time as parallel holidays should be avoided. Hanukkah is *not* parallel to Christmas. It has always been a relatively minor holiday that has recently received a lot more attention. The attempt to make it parallel to Christmas uses the Christian holiday as the standard, and is resented by some Jews. In any event, if holidays are commemorated in your school, feedback and suggestions from parents and other community members can make the holiday curriculum as inclusive as possible.

An emerging multicultural curriculum can be created by using the experiences, cultures, and languages of every student. Students should be encouraged to bring their culture into the classroom through a variety of ways, for example, by inviting parents to teach the class about their particular talent, job, or interest. These talents do not have to be culture specific. For instance, a parent who is a seamstress might teach the children how to sew a hem. Although a talent may not be particular to a specific ethnic heritage, it helps students to see that people from all backgrounds have skills and worthwhile experiences.

Activities such as these are particularly effective at the early elementary level, but sometimes they are equally relevant for secondary students studying a specific subject. For example, older students learning calligraphy might invite a local Chinese artist to give them some pointers. Or if they are learning about operating a small business, they can invite a local store owner.

An oral history project could focus on students and their family experiences. For example, for a multicultural library, students can collect stories, poems, and legends from their families, either tape recorded or written down. These can then be illustrated, bound, and placed in the library. More elaborate activities can include dramatizations for the school assembly, videotaping parents and other community members reciting the poems and stories, and readings by older students to children in the younger grades.

What Can You Do?
- With a group of your colleagues, look at the next topic you plan to teach. Think of some ways in which you can make it more inclusive without making it scattered and irrelevant. Develop a number of activities that are reflective of the backgrounds of students in your classroom, school, and

community. Develop a list of resources from the community that can enrich the curriculum.

- Plan a unit that uses the talents and experiences of people in the community as a basis for an oral history curriculum. Teach students how to identify and interview subjects, and how to transcribe the interviews and develop the oral history. Integrate oral history into the rest of your curriculum.

Pedagogy

The case studies in this book highlighted the fact that the standard pedagogy used in many schools is unappealing to most students. The students provided specific suggestions for making schools more interesting.

Although textbooks may be vital teaching and learning tools, they often become the entire curriculum and are used as the only basis of pedagogy in the class, to the exclusion of materials that may be more appealing. Other resources can make the curriculum more inviting for students, including audiovisual materials such as camcorders and cameras, guest speakers, and alternative reading material. For instance, as we saw in Ron's case study, the use of primary documents in the Cuban Missile Crisis curriculum made learning exciting for him.

Even more substantial, however, is to develop a variety of approaches that will interest most students. Although a straight lecture, what has been called "chalk and talk," may be appropriate sometimes, it treats students as passive learners and receptacles of knowledge. It is also culturally inappropriate for many students. To help students become more active learners as well as to provide a multiculturally sensitive learning environment, you can work with other teachers to encourage group work; individualized tasks; collaborative research; peer tutoring; cross-age tutoring; and group reflection, dialogue, and action projects in the school and community. The latter might include volunteer activities at a senior center, working with a local day care center, or a letter-writing campaign about a community issue (e.g., the need for a traffic light at a nearby intersection).

What Can You Do?

- Develop one new teaching strategy weekly to begin using with your class. Start slowly, teaching students how to work in new ways. Often, alternative strategies are unsuccessful simply because students are not taught how to approach them. In addition, we sometimes change the way we do things so radically that chaos ensues. If you add new strategies or approaches to your repertoire on an ongoing and consistent basis, your pedagogy will undergo substantial changes within a year.[8]
- Ask students to give you feedback on your instruction. What do they like? What do they dislike? How would they change the classroom? the materials? What would they do to make it more interesting to them? Just as the students in our case studies were never at a loss for ideas to make learning more "fun" or relevant, your students will have many suggestions as well. Will you hear them?

- Develop a peer evaluation process whereby you and your colleagues visit one another's classrooms to provide help, encouragement, feedback, and ideas on content and approaches. Enlist the help of the principal, parents, and other staff to provide classroom support while you are engaged in these activities.

Physical Structure

There are many things in our physical environment that we can do little about. There are others that we can change, however, both inside our classrooms and out.

Working with parents, students, and colleagues, you can make your classroom inviting and comfortable. In the younger grades, this might mean having interesting activity corners, a cozy place to read, a number of comfortable chairs, and a place for group work. In the older grades, a quiet place for individual work sends the message that learning is an activity that deserves attention and space. Placing seats in a horseshoe arrangement at certain times is an appropriate strategy for involving more students in a discussion. Many teachers in secondary schools feel that decorating the room is unnecessary, yet even older students appreciate a cheerful educational environment where posters, maps, pictures, books, and music are essential.

Outside the classroom, you can inform parents and other community members about some of the policies and practices that make school uninviting so that they can organize to change them. For instance, graffiti and garbage around a school give the message that school is not to be taken seriously. These issues can be brought up at parent–teacher association (PTA), school board, and even city council meetings. Unless demands are made to change these negative messages, children will continue to be the victims.

What Can You Do?
- Look around your classroom. Is it an inviting place? What can you do to make it more so? How can you use children's experiences, interests, and backgrounds to create a good place to work? Think about how they best learn, the languages they speak, and their other talents to build a space that makes them want to come to school.
- Consider your bulletin boards and other places for exhibits or projects. What are they like and how could they be better used? Involve your students in planning and implementing an improved physical space in your classroom.
- Outside your own classroom, work with colleagues to make the entire school a true community. What joint activities can you develop to connect the classrooms, teachers, and grades?

Disciplinary Policies

Disciplinary policies and procedures are commonly developed to provide an atmosphere of purpose and order. Invariably, however, they exclude some students from a meaningful education, for any number of reasons. Insensitivity to cultural, linguistic, and social differences interact with racism, discrimination, and expectations of student achievement to produce an environment in which some students are bound to succeed while others are doomed to fail. Teachers and schools can approach disciplinary policies and practices in creative ways to avoid some of these outcomes.

Whenever possible, students should help determine disciplinary policies and practices. Rather than relying on those who happen to be on the student council, generally a rather limited group of students, a forum can be created in which a broad range of student voices are heard. This forum can include academic classes, assemblies, and other student activities such as sports and clubs.

Schools can determine how disciplinary policies and practices affect some students unfairly by looking at rates of detention, suspension, and assignments to "special" classes or alternative programs for those who have been identified as having behavior problems. If students in these programs are overwhelmingly from one social or racial group or gender, the school needs to take appropriate steps to counteract this tendency.

What Can You Do?

- Create class rules with your students. Think of how rules could be stated in positive rather than negative terms. Focus on privileges rather than on punitive consequences.
- Monitor your own behavior with your students. Do you tend to be more patient with some students than with others? Are you quicker to assign detentions or take other disciplinary measures with certain students? Do you use sarcastic, menacing, or negative language with some students? Ask a colleague to help you identify and change these behaviors.
- Be sensitive to how some students are more negatively affected by particular disciplinary practices than others. For example, if a student is consistently assigned to detention after school and misses work as a result, he or she might be losing needed family income. Think of a number of alternative and more positive strategies for changing their behavior.
- Encourage parents and other community members to participate on committees in which disciplinary policies are discussed. In your own classroom, invite parents to talk about their perceptions of school policies with you.

Limited Role of Students

Students are often uninvolved in decisions affecting their schooling. Involvement in such decisions need not be limited to high school students in the top tracks. Students at all levels, from preschool through high school, can help determine the direction of their schooling in a great many ways. But care needs to be taken to provide real student involvement rather than tokenism. Placing students on committees in which they have little interest and no experience simply to have student involvement can backfire. They soon drop out and in the process learn that they were not valued as significant participants in the first place. Also, teachers' perceptions that students are too young or immature to be involved in decision making is reinforced. The lesson here is that when students feel their input is worthwhile, they will take part.

Students often have hobbies or other interests that are invisible in school. Making them visible is one way of engaging students. For instance, crafts that are familiar and culturally pertinent can be incorporated into the arts curriculum. Students can also be encouraged to tell stories and legends to their classmates.

"Sharing time" with young students, "culture circles" or "problem-posing sessions" with secondary school students, or some other such mechanism can encourage students to participate in dialogue. Such dialogue not only ensures that all students are heard but also helps teachers discover what the students are interested in so that they can develop a more inclusive curriculum.

What Can You Do?

- Set aside a specific time once each week to plan the curriculum with your students. Younger students may only be able to give you very general suggestions, but these can be considered and incorporated whenever possible. Older students may be more articulate in naming issues that they would like to study within the specific subject matter that you teach.
- Ask students to bring in favorite objects or hobbies to use as the basis for lessons. You can help them prepare presentations in which they teach other students in the class or in a small group. Examples of topics they might choose include how to care for a pet gerbil, the fun of stamp collecting, how to make dumplings, how to write some letters in Arabic, some greetings in Japanese, learning to compose music raps, an exhibit of flags from around the world, and so on.
- With colleagues and students, develop a social action project for the school. Working in groups, have students decide on problems or issues in the school or community in which they would like to be engaged (anything from inadequate housing in their neighborhood to not being permitted to chew gum in school) and for which they develop an action plan. Depending on how they are approached, social action projects might take anywhere from a week to an entire academic year and can be interdisciplinary. Using social action projects, the community becomes the primary source of the curriculum.

Limited Role of Teachers

Like students, teachers are often disempowered within the school. Although they usually have some control over the curriculum they implement in their own classrooms, the broad outline is often legislated from a central office. Requirements for testing and other mandated activities may further rob the curriculum of its individualized character. Teachers are not always consulted when decisions about student placement, curriculum, or the purchase of materials are made. As a result, teachers are often treated with little respect.

Teachers can be involved in curriculum design and implementation, through either school or central system curriculum committees. They should also be involved in decisions regarding the purchase of educational materials. Likewise, teachers and other staff members can be consulted when new teachers are to be hired. Serving on interviewing committees, helping to determine job qualifications, and ensuring affirmative action are all crucial functions in which teachers' involvement is fundamental.

Promoting professionalism in teaching is an essential obligation for all school staff at the classroom, department, school, and school system levels. In many cases, released time from the classroom is required for this work to take place.

What Can You Do?
- Develop a support group of teachers and meet weekly to discuss a mutual concern such as disciplinary policies, the role of bilingual education in the school, the nature of the language arts program, or some similar issue. By focusing on a specific problem or issue, teachers can read, discuss, and learn from colleagues and then use this knowledge as a basis for suggestions to change school policies and practices.
- Visit other classrooms and schools that are becoming more multicultural. Share your perceptions of these visits with colleagues.
- Set up a "buddy system" with a trusted colleague to help you grow professionally. Regularly visit each other's classrooms and reflect together on teaching styles, curriculum, and the general climate in your classrooms. Plan to meet at least once each week to review new thoughts, materials, and curricula. Do some team teaching and plan some mutually interesting projects together. Plan on attending relevant conferences with a group from the school.

Limited Family and Community Involvement

Many families are uninvolved in the day-to-day life or in the overall policy development of the school. However, most are involved in the education of their children through the values they have fostered at home and in the implicit and explicit expectations they have of them. All of the ways they are involved need to be fostered by schools and teachers in order to emphasize the essential role that families have in the educational process.

Although families who are not involved in the school in traditional ways should not be penalized, they can be encouraged to become more involved in the day-to-day life of the school. But this is not the only involvement that should be honored. A two-pronged approach in which home and school activities are given equal value is probably best.

Teachers and schools can communicate with families on a consistent basis, through a weekly or monthly newsletter, phone calls, meetings at school or home, or a combination of these methods. When school meetings are to take place, child care, translation into languages spoken by the families, and transportation can be provided. Teachers can encourage family members to bring into the classroom activities and materials that are significant to them and their children. In this way, the curriculum will be more reflective of the students and their communities.

What Can You Do?
- Begin a class newsletter to send home on a regular basis. Include work of all the students. If families speak a language other than English, whenever possible have students work together to translate portions of the newsletter into their home languages.
- Invite families to class to share a particular talent that is related to the curriculum you are teaching. To get a better idea of what these talents are, during the first weeks of class ask parents and other family members to indicate the special skills they have and then plan your curriculum accordingly.
- With colleagues, develop a community-building project to encourage family and community outreach. It might focus on an art project, a health fair, or a "meet the author" night in which a number of local authors (published or not) who reflect the diversity of the community read their stories and poems.

RESPECTING AND AFFIRMING CULTURAL DIFFERENCES

Culture and cultural diversity are at the very core of a multicultural perspective. Although many of the ideas in this chapter have focused on ways to respect and build on cultural differences, several more specific examples of affirming diversity in schools and classrooms can be suggested. We focus on these examples because in far too many cases, teachers leave workshops and other professional development programs without any direct or even indirect information concerning cultural differences. Other than those who happen to major in bilingual education, special education, English as a Second Language (ESL), or at the few places where available, multicultural education, the great majority of teachers are unprepared for the diversity they will face because they have learned little or nothing about it. Teacher education programs for the most part continue to teach as if diversity were either nonexistent or an annoying problem to be overcome.

Learning how to understand cultural differences does not mean simply to learn about culture. Knowing about Cinco de Mayo in the Mexican American community or about health practices among Vietnamese will do little to prepare teachers for day-to-day experiences with students in their classrooms. Furthermore, there simply is not enough time in the teacher education curriculum to cover everything prospective teachers will need to know about all of the cultural groups they will teach in their lifetime. Approaching culture in this way is ineffective because culture is constantly changing, and therefore we can never "teach culture" as if it were static and constant. A more promising approach is to prepare teachers to reflect on how cultural differences *may* affect student learning, and to be open to changing their curriculum and pedagogy accordingly. One way to do this is through practicum experiences in every course taken by prospective teachers, not just in those that focus on diversity. Another is to develop professional development activities for in-service teachers that center on specific issues, dilemmas, and incidents that happen in their classrooms every day.

Because students' cultures may influence how they learn, teachers need to become aware of differences in learning and how these can be accommodated in the classroom. They must always ask the question, *Who does the accommodating? Is it always students from dominated cultures?* To counteract this tendency, it is helpful to plan activities in which the learning preferences of students are reflected. Students who are comfortable working in groups should have the opportunity to do so; so should students who are not used to this style of working. The point is not to segregate students according to their preferences but to have all students develop skills in a broad range of activities.

Teachers can investigate other out-of-school activities in which students are engaged. Some students, for example, love to perform; others like to express themselves through art. Use these activities in the school to motivate students to learn school-related subjects.

What Can You Do?

- Encourage your students to talk about their culture from time to time. Even young students can do so, although in a more limited way than older ones. But students should never be singled out as "experts" about their cultural group, because they may in fact have little knowledge about it. The cultures of students should be made visible in a natural and unobtrusive way. Using culture as a point of reference, they learn that

  Everybody has a culture.

  Their culture is valued in the school.

  Their culture can provide a solid basis for their education.

  Rather than promoting the perception that culture is a source of shame or embarrassment, this approach helps to make it a source of pride and empowerment.

- Encourage students to share their culture with others. Artifacts from home, cultural traditions, books and stories, and notable people in their lives can all be brought into the school to help make the curriculum more inclusive.
- Use interviewing as a teaching strategy. Students can interview one another as well as family and community members. Think of different content areas in which the results of students' interviews can be used to make the curriculum more multicultural.
- Because so many people are first- to third-generation newcomers to the United States, the immigrant experience can be a rich source of

inspiration for the curriculum. Develop a series of interdisciplinary lessons based on the immigration stories of students and their families.

LINGUISTIC DIVERSITY AS A RESOURCE

The languages and dialects that students speak should be made an explicit part of the curriculum if we are to convey the message that language diversity is highly regarded in our schools. Rather than viewing linguistic diversity as a deficit, we need to see it as an asset on which further learning can be built.

Teachers need to learn to say each child's name correctly. They should not make Marisol *Marcy* or Vinh *Vinny*. As simplistic as it may sound, this basic rule of respect is violated daily in classrooms around the nation. Given the pressure to conform that all students face, some of them readily accede to having their names changed so that they can fit in. Although learning many names in different languages may be time consuming for teachers, it is not difficult, and it is a first step in affirming who students are rather than who we may want them to become.

Student language should be accepted without immediate correction, including language from both new speakers of English and those who speak another variety of it. Overcorrecting can intimidate young people. Although all students need to learn standard English, especially those who have been traditionally denied access to higher status learning, it is equally crucial that all teachers learn to accept and value students' native languages or dialects. Rather than directly correcting students' language, teachers can model standard English in their responses or statements. Students soon pick up the message that there are different ways of saying the same thing and that some are more appropriate in certain settings. Linda Howard's case study provides a powerful example of this code switching.

What Can You Do?
- Think about students in your classes who speak a language other than English. Ask them to teach you and the other students some words in the language. Use these words in the classroom context. Put them on bulletin boards and use them in assignments.
- Learn another language. If you have a great many Khmer-speaking students, for example, learning their language would go a long way in showing them you value it. Even just the process of learning another language allows teachers to demonstrate genuine solidarity with students who need to learn a second language. If you have many students who speak diverse languages, learn at least some phrases in each of the languages. As a rule, students are delighted when teachers show a real interest in their language, even if they stumble over words and phrases.
- Even if you do not speak a language other than English, encourage your students to do so. You might, for example, encourage some small-group work and peer tutoring in which students use their native language. You

can also invite family members to volunteer in the classroom by working with a small group of students fluent in the same language.
- Ask students to bring in poems, stories, legends, or songs in their native language. They might want to teach these to their classmates. Have them available (in written form or on tape) for other students to read or listen to.

• SUMMARY

In this chapter, I have tried to encourage teachers to work collaboratively with colleagues, students, and families through a number of problem-posing scenarios that focus on changing school policies and practices. In these ways, developing a multicultural perspective can become a natural outgrowth of the lives of students and teachers.

Multicultural education is not a superficial set of activities, materials, or approaches. I have resisted presenting specific lesson plans because such an approach may overlook or downplay the school conditions that produce unequal academic outcomes in the first place. A prepackaged series of lesson plans is in direct conflict with the goals of a comprehensive multicultural education. If the purpose of education is to prepare young people for productive and critical participation in a democratic and pluralistic society, then the activities, strategies, and approaches we use with them need to echo these concerns. Schools, as currently structured, do little to prepare students for this future because the curriculum and instruction tend to contradict these goals.

The stratification of society likewise cannot be overlooked as profoundly affecting the schooling of students. The cultural and linguistic differences students bring to school, along with how these differences are perceived, also need to be addressed through the curriculum and instruction. To act as if differences of race, social class, ethnicity, native language, and others were immaterial to schooling is disingenuous. It is only by addressing all these issues in a systematic way through the curriculum, instruction, and other practices that real change can happen.

In the final analysis, multicultural education is a moral and ethical issue. The current conditions in our world call for critical thinkers who can face and resolve complex issues—problems such as ethnic polarization, poverty, contamination of our natural resources, and rampant racism—in sensitive and ethical ways. We need all the help we can get to solve these problems, and that means using the talents and strengths of all young people. Our student body is becoming more diverse than ever before, reflecting more racial, cultural, linguistic, and social class differences. But our ability to understand these differences and to use them in constructive ways is still quite limited. If we believe that all students are capable of brilliance, that they can learn at high levels of achievement, and that the cultural and linguistic resources they bring to school are worthy of respect, affirmation, and solidarity, then multicultural education represents a far more principled approach for our schools than does monocultural education.

● *NOTES*

1. Kenneth M. Zeichner, *Connecting Genuine Teacher Development to the Struggle for Social Justice* (East Lansing, MI: National Center for Research on Teacher Learning, Michigan State University, April 1992).

2. Examples of teacher research and collaboration can be found in Sara Warshaeuer Freedman, Elizabeth Radin Simons, Julie Shalhope Kalnin, Alex Casareno, and the M-CLASS Teams, editors, *Inside City Schools: Investigating Literacy in Multicultural Classrooms* (New York: Teachers College Press, 1999); and *Inside/Outside: Teacher Research and Knowledge* edited by Marilyn Cochran-Smith and Susan L. Lytle (New York: Teachers College Press, 1993).

3. Jim Cummins, *Negotiating Identities: Education for Empowerment in a Diverse Society* (Ontario, CA: California Association for Bilingual Education, 1996).

4. Pauline Lipman, *Race, Class, and Power in School Restructuring* (Albany, NY: State University of New York Press, 1998).

5. Paulo Freire, *Pedagogy of the Oppressed* (New York: Seabury Press, 1970).

6. For a good example of how future teachers can learn to problematize school-based conditions, see Jeannie Oakes and Martin Lipton, *Teaching to Change the World* (Boston: McGraw-Hill, 1999).

7. There are a number of excellent resources for developing appropriate early childhood programs with a multicultural perspective. Among these are Louise Derman-Sparks and the A.B.C. Task Force, *Anti-Bias Curriculum: Tools for Empowering Young Children* (Washington, DC: National Association for the Education of Young Children, 1989); Frances E. Kendall, *Diversity in the Classroom: New Approaches to the Education of Young Children,* 2nd ed. (New York: Teachers College Press, 1996); and Patricia G. Ramsey, *Teaching and Learning in a Diverse World: Multicultural Education for Young Children* 2nd ed. (New York: Teachers College Press, Columbia University, 1998).

8. A superb resource for beginning more collaborative approaches is Nancy Schniedewind and Ellen Davidson *Open Minds to Equality: A Sourcebook of Learning Activities To Affirm Diversity and Promote Equity* (Boston: Allyn & Bacon, 1998).

Epilogue

Since *Affirming Diversity* was first published, the most common questions I am asked concern the case study students. These young people's stories were so compelling that readers took a personal interest in their well-being and progress. People ask me, "Where are they now?" or "What are they doing?" "I had never thought about being biracial before I read Linda's case study. Whatever happened to her?" "Paul's case study made me cry. Did he ever graduate? Did he leave the gang?" "I loved Fern. Did she make it?"

Because it is now a decade since some of them were first interviewed, I thought it would be a good time to return to the case study students and find out what had become of them. My intention was to include an update with information about all the interviewees in this new addition.

I contacted my friends and colleagues who had originally conducted the interviews, and asked them to find and interview the young people again. Many of the interviewees had moved and, even when we know their city of residence we were unable to find some of them. (This was the case with Marisol Martínez, whom I interviewed. I made numerous phone calls to Philadelphia, where I had been told her family moved, but to no avail. Manuel Gomes had also moved, and Carol Shea, who interviewed him earlier tried her best to find him but was unsuccessful). In some cases, interviewers were able to get second-hand information about the current status of the person they had interviewed, but couldn't include it because I wanted the interviewee's permission to do so. (This happened with Paul Chavez, who Mac Morante found out about). In other instances, the interviewees were contacted and never returned our phone calls. As a result, we found only three of the twelve interviewees.

Life takes many turns, and not always in the direction that we imagine. Although I was disappointed we had not found more of the original case study students, I include what information we were able to find because I know that readers are interested in knowing what became of them.

Linda Howard

Paula Elliot appreciated the opportunity to follow up with Linda Howard because she welcomed a justification, beyond her own interest and curiosity in how Linda was doing, to find out how similar and different she saw herself since they first met 10 years ago. Paula and Linda met over a leisurely dinner to catch up.

As you will recall, Linda graduated from high school as valedictorian of her class with a four-year scholarship to a prestigious New England university. She started college in Fall of 1989 with the goal of studying early childhood education (she had often spoken about her first grade teacher as her mentor and someone she wanted to emulate). But she dropped out of college just three months after starting. Linda remembers this period of time as a difficult one, saying, "I just didn't fit in. I really felt lost." She described the tremendous sense of social and academic isolation she felt at the university in this way: "I just felt like a pea on a huge pile of rice."

Linda contrasted her overall good health and excellent attendance record in high school with the illness and physical problems she experienced that Fall. She thought these were an indication of her mental state and the sense of hopelessness she felt at the time. Looking back, she wished she had made the decision to go to a smaller school where she would be more likely to enjoy the status of being a "big fish in a small pond." But Linda does not regret what happened because she thinks that the public recognition and support she received in high school had a direct and lasting impact on her lifelong motivation and efforts to excel.

Now 28 years old, Linda has been a senior nursing assistant in a clinic for the past four years, and she held a similar job at a hospital for two years previous. She seems to have taken naturally to this job, perhaps because she had done volunteer and paraprofessional work in her neighborhood hospital while in high school. Linda finds her job personally satisfying because it allows her to provide compassionate support to patients.

Married to an aspiring firefighter, Linda and her husband have two children, a boy aged three and a girl aged 5, who had just started kindergarten. She continues the tradition of reading to her children at bedtime just as her mother read to her. Although she likes her job a great deal, she is pleased that she can devote time outside work to her family and church, and she looks forward to when she can do this full-time.

Linda is very involved in her church. She was baptized as a Jehovah's Witness a few years ago and she refers to herself as a "24/7" Christian: She goes to church three days a week for service, fellowship, and bible study, and she has a strong commitment to leading a life as a missionary. Her church has given her what she was seeking in other religions but had never found: a spiritual life, and acceptance and love from people who do not judge others in negative ways because they are different.

Linda talked about how her ideas about race, difference, and humanity had evolved and become stronger. She read over her original case study and stated that she still feels anger over being labeled. "It's tough to be judged by someone who knows nothing about you. I find that to be very disheartening," she said. Although she identifies very closely with the African American culture, Linda is more adamant that ever about belonging to just the human race.

One reason that she joined her church, Linda said, was because she was impressed with the way people related to one another on a human level. They call each other simply "brother" or "sister," and she has never been asked "What are you?" She mentioned that she was amazed when she first went to an assembly and saw the tremendous diversity among the members of the church and the warm caring relationships they have with one another. "We're all God's children" she said. She added, "When I see that here in America, that really moves me."

Avi Abramson

Diane Sweet found Avi Abramson in the same town he lived in when she first interviewed him 10 years ago. He does not yet have his own family, but he continues to be very involved with his extended family in the temple. Diane writes, "In our conversation, I was amazed to hear that Avi still volunteers to lead the elderly people in the town's little synagogue every Sabbath. 'They would be lost without him,' I heard from one of his buddies. But Avi says they would find a way to carry on without him."

Avi graduated from high school and went on to study at a large comprehensive university where he was able to create his own interdisciplinary major combining photography, lithography, video, computer imagery, and other artistic media. He presently works in the digital media department of a printing company where he does color corrections and retouches images. Besides continuing with his volunteer work, he is very involved with art, music, and writing.

Diane told me that when she met with Avi again, she found out that he had started writing shortly after the time she first interviewed him. As a token of her appreciation for taking the time to be interviewed the first time, she had given Avi a blank journal. That's when he began writing. She was able to read some of his short stories when she met with him recently, and she discovered that many of them chronicle the time spent with the elderly people in the synagogue. Being a writer herself, Diane was impressed with how well Avi captured the nuances of the relationships among the people he writes about.

When Diane asked Avi what might have made his schooling better, he said that in high school, many of the school's requirements did not help him gain any long-term knowledge about the world. He found what he was looking for in college. He graduated, in his words, "on very high spirits, with very creative thoughts, and knowing I accomplished a great deal in terms of my personal growth and my artistic ability."

Fern Sherman

At 13 years of age when Carlie Tartakov first interviewed her, Fern Sherman was one of our youngest interviewees. You will remember Fern as the indomitable young woman who never let anything get in her way. Faced at a tender age with what others might consider insurmountable obstacles—a history of drug and alcohol addiction in her family, being the only Native American student in her school, and having an absent mother—Fern was resolute in wanting to be a successful student and person. Her father loomed large in her interview, and Carlie found that the same was true a decade later.

Carlie located Fern in Springdale, the small city in which she lived when she was first interviewed. Fern graduated from high school a semester early, in 1995, and she married quite young a year later. The son she had shortly thereafter was two years old at the time Carlie interviewed her again. After high school, Fern attended a local community college where she studied fashion merchandising and design. Currently, she is a student at a large state university, majoring in apparel merchandising and design. She also works part time.

Fern is very involved in a number of extra-curricular activities at the university, including the American Indian Rights Organization (AIRO), of which she was president last year, and the United Native American Student Association (UNASA). She also sometimes speaks in university classes about her perspectives and experiences as a Native American. Although Fern has a strong identity and commitment to her Native American community, she also has a social life that includes people of many other ethnic communities.

Fern's devotion to her son is evident. When Carlie asked her to describe herself, Fern wrote, "I am a Native American woman who in life has used the traditions and beliefs taught to me. I have succeeded to the best of my ability and, with the strengths of my beliefs, I hope to raise my child with the kind and loving support that I was raised with." Carlie added "Fern is a complex and interesting person who is hanging on to her dream of being somebody important who makes a difference, while working hard to pass that dream along to her son." When Carlie asked Fern if she still held onto the hope of becoming President of the United States, as she stated during the interview for her first case study, she answered, "Yes, sure."

When Carlie asked what helped her continue despite some of the difficulties she faced, Fern answered,

> My father was the driving force behind a lot of my success in high school. He helped me understand the importance of my education and the benefits of graduating and pursuing my education. In high school, the things that helped me were the support of my family and the knowledge that my future would be much better.

FINAL THOUGHTS

The idea of creating case studies based on extensive interviews with young people of diverse backgrounds came to me when I first contemplated writing *Affirming Diversity* many years ago. Although my editor was very supportive of the idea, the original reviewers of my prospectus had grave doubts about the wisdom of doing so. Most mentioned that, although it might be a good idea in principle, in practice it might result in perpetuating stereotypes about particular ethnic and racial groups. I took their criticisms seriously, but I nevertheless pursued the idea because I knew that case studies of real students portrayed within the cultural and sociopolitical context of their lives could be very powerful. I knew this firsthand because of the tremendous impression the case studies left on me, even though I was the person who put them together! I reasoned that others would be as moved and enlightened as I had been when first crafting the case studies from the students' words. But I never imagined just how powerful they would be, nor the enormous impact they would have on so many people.

Whenever I meet people who have used my book, in almost every instance they first mention how much they have enjoyed and learned from the case studies. Many instructors have asked students to develop case studies of their own using these as a model. The case studies have forced readers to question their assumptions and biases about students, about particular ethnic and racial groups, and about the untapped potential in the young people they teach. If the case studies have managed to shake conventional wisdom and unveil the tremendous complexity of the lives of young people in our classrooms, they have accomplished their aim.

Appendix

RESOURCES FOR COLLABORATION AND EDUCATIONAL TRANSFORMATION

This section includes resources for developing collaborative models that can help break the mold of the teacher as a solitary figure. I have included primarily educational organizations and agencies at the national level. Although teachers may feel that becoming involved in national organizations can do little to change their specific situation, I list them here because I have seen how powerful involvement in such organizations can be for teachers and other educators. The collegial contacts and friendship one can gain from like-minded educators from around the country can be a great support to teachers who feel they are facing insurmountable challenges on their own. Reading timely and critical newspapers and journals, joining progressive organizations, and attending meetings and conferences that focus on school transformation go hand in hand with local actions to change schools.

Because they are more readily available, commercially produced materials are not included here, but I urge you to seek them out as well. A great many more multicultural resources than ever before are currently available, some good and many not very good, so that a critical examination of materials is needed. The book *Beyond Heroes and Holidays,* edited by Enid Lee, Deborah Menkart, and Margo Okazawa-Rey, and published by NECA (listed in the following resources as well as in the bibliography) has an outstanding and comprehensive index of recommended resources, including children's books, professional books, curriculum guides, posters, CD-Roms, journals, tapes, videos, and Internet resources.

The list that follows is not an exhaustive one, but it is meant to support efforts by many teachers and others to bring about substantive and effective change in schools. Phone and fax numbers, as well as e-mail and Web site information, if available, are provided.

California Tomorrow
436 14th Street, Suite 20
Oakland, CA 94612
(415) 441–7631
FAX (510) 496–0220

e-mail: generalinfo@
    californiatomorrow.org
Web site:
    www.californiatomorrow.org

California Tomorrow is an advocacy organization that publishes materials focusing on the tremendous diversity in California's schools, including moving and informative accounts of the experiences of teachers and students.

Clearinghouse for Immigrant Education (CHIME)
  National Coalition of Advocates for Students (NCAS)
  100 Boylston Street, Suite 737
  Boston, MA 02116
  (800) 441–7192
  e-mail: ncasmfe@aol.com
  Web site: ncas1.org
CHIME, a project of NCAS, is a resource center that facilitates access to materials, organizations, and people concerned with the effective education of immigrant students.

Educators for Social Responsibility (ESR)
  23 Garden Street
  Cambridge, MA 02138
  (800) 370–2515
  FAX: (617) 864–5164
  e-mail:
    educators@esrnational.org
A national teachers' organization that offers curricula and professional development, ESR specifically addresses peace education, mediation, and diversity.

Facing History and Ourselves National Foundation (FHAO)
  16 Hurd Road
  Brookline, MA 02146
  (617) 232–1595
  FAX: (617) 232–0281
  Web site:
    http://www.facing.org
FHAO works with teachers around the world to examine ways of bringing important but controversial material into the classroom. Focusing on the Holocaust as a vehicle, FHAO explores issues such as scapegoating, responsibility for others, and how to address the racism and violence faced by many societies today.

FairTest
  342 Broadway
  Cambridge, MA 02139
  (617) 864–4810
  FAX: (617) 497–2224
  e-mail: fairtest@aol.com
  Web site: www.fairtest.org
FairTest is an advocacy organization that works to end the abuses, misuses, and flaws of standardized testing and to make certain that evaluation of students and workers is fair, open, accurate, relevant, accountable, and educationally sound. FairTest has many resources for parents, educators, and others interested in educational reform.

National Association for Bilingual Education (NABE)
  1220 L Street, NW Suite 605
  Washington, DC 20005
  (202) 898–1829
  FAX: (202) 789–2866
  e-mail: NABE@nabe.org
  Web site: www.nabe.org
A professional association founded in 1975, NABE addresses the educational needs of language-minority students. It hosts an annual conference and publishes a newsletter *(NABE News)* and journal *(Bilingual Research Journal)*. It has affiliates in 26 states.

National Association for Multicultural Education (NAME)
  733 15th Street, NW, Suite 430
  Washington, DC 20005
  (202) 628-NAME
  FAX: (202) 628–6264
  e-mail: nameorg@erols.com

A professional organization founded in 1990 to promote multicultural education in the United States, NAME hosts an annual national conference and publishes *Multicultural Perspectives* magazine.

National Clearinghouse for Bilingual Education (NCBE)
Center for Applied Linguistics
1118 22nd Street, NW
Washington, DC 20037
(800) 321-NCBE
e-mail: askncbe@ncbe.gwu.edu
Web site: www.ncbe.gwu.edu
NCBE provides toll-free information on any aspect of bilingual education. It also publishes a free bimonthly newsletter, *Forum.*

National Coalition of Education Activists
P.O. Box 679
Rhinebeck, NY 12572
(914) 876–4580
FAX: (914) 876–4461
e-mail: Rfbs@aol.com
Web site:
Members.aol.com/nceaweb
An organization of teachers, families, and other education activists who focus their efforts on transforming school policies and practices such as tracking, testing, and curriculum. The coalition has a newsletter and hosts an annual conference.

Network of Educators on the Americas (NECA)
1118 22nd Street, NW
Washington, DC 20037
(202) 429–0137
FAX: (202) 429–9766
e-mail: necadc@aol.com
This nonprofit organization seeks to promote peace, justice, and human rights through critical, antiracist, multicultural education. It develops and disseminates valuable classroom resources, including information for teachers and students on Central America and the Caribbean in both English and Spanish. It also publishes a quarterly catalog, *Teaching for Change,* that lists numerous resources. The NECA publication, *Beyond Heroes and Holidays,* is an excellent classroom resource.

Rethinking Schools
1001 East Keefe Avenue
Milwaukee, WI 53212
(800) 669–4192
FAX: (414) 964–9646
e-mail: rfbusiness@aol.com
Web site:
www.rethinkingschools.org
Rethinking Schools is a nonprofit independent newspaper advocating the reform of elementary and secondary public schools, with an emphasis on urban schools and issues of equity and social justice. Published by Milwaukee area teachers and educators with contributing writers from around the United States, it focuses on local and national reform. They have also published *Rethinking Columbus,* a guide to challenge the celebration of the Quincentenary, and *Rethinking Our Classrooms,* a publication that includes creative teaching ideas and hands-on suggestions for bringing issues of justice and equality into classrooms.

Teaching Tolerance
400 Washington Avenue
Montgomery, AL 36104
(334) 264–0286
FAX: (334) 264–3121
Web site:
www.splcenter.org
A publication of the Southern Poverty Law Center, *Teaching Tolerance* is a semiannual magazine mailed at no

charge that provides classroom strategies and curriculum ideas for teachers that focus on diversity and tolerance. The project has also developed a number of teaching resources, including videos and curriculum guides, on the civil rights movement and intolerance in U.S. history.

U.S. Committee for UNICEF
    Education Department
    333 East 38th Street
    New York, NY 10016
    e-mail:
        webmaster@unicefusa.org
This center publishes a wealth of information concerning world development, including books, audiovisual materials, lesson plans, and other resources with an international perspective. Most resources are available for the price of postage, and videos are provided loan-free.

World of Difference Institute
    Anti-Defamation League
    1100 Connecticut Avenue NW,
    #1020
    Washington, DC 20036
An educational agency, the WOD Institute concentrates on professional development and curriculum design with an antiracist focus. They also sponsor an award program for outstanding teachers who exemplify the goals of equity and social justice.

LITERATURE RESOURCES FOR STUDENTS AND TEACHERS ON COMING OF AGE AND THE IMMIGRANT EXPERIENCE

Personal narratives of young people from a variety of ethnic and racial backgrounds are becoming increasingly popular in U.S. literature. Because they reveal the intimate and social experiences of those who feel like "outsiders," novels and short stories can be tremendously powerful in teaching about others who are different from us. Literature also provides an authentic and engaging way to explore issues of inclusion and exclusion, the pain and fear of immigration and racism, and the triumph of the human spirit in the face of obstacles. Gay and lesbian students are often marginalized as well, and fortunately literature is now being written to help both them and their heterosexual peers to face this exclusion honestly.

Much of the literature on diversity and coming of age is appropriate for secondary school students; all of it is helpful for teachers as they explore these issues for their own understanding and as a resource for their curriculum. Literature not only helps to make the curriculum more multicultural, but it also can provide students with examples of experiences that are quintessentially American, although they may be very different from their own. Likewise, a teachers' study group can use novels and short stories about coming of age in a pluralistic society as the content for discussions on diversity, or as a way to propose curriculum transformation.

Although necessarily limited in size, the following list of anthologies and professional resources in multicultural literature can provide helpful insights on the dilemmas of coming of age in a diverse society, and the interconnections among ethnicity, culture, gender, and class. They are a graphic way to learn about the issues faced by many students in U.S. classrooms.

Anthologies About Coming Of Age In A Variety Of Cultures:

Bauer, Marion Dane, ed. *Am I Blue? Coming Out from the Silence.* (New York: Harper Collins, 1994).

Frosch, Mary. *Coming of Age in America: A Multicultural Anthology.* (New York: The New Press, 1994).

King, Laurie. *Hear My Voice: A Multicultural Anthology of Literature from the United States.* (Menlo Park, CA: Addison-Wesley, 1994).

Lewis, Tom J., and Jungman, Robert E., eds. *On Being Foreign: Culture Shock in Short Fiction.* (Yarmouth, ME: Intercultural Press, 1986).

Loughery, John, ed. *First Sightings: Contemporary Stories of American Youth.* (New York: Persea, 1993).

Loughery, John, ed. *Into the Widening World: International Coming-of-Age Stories.* (New York: Persea, 1994).

Mazer, Anne, ed. *America Street: A Multicultural Anthology of Stories.* (New York: Persea, 1993).

Mazer, Anne, ed. *Going Where I'm Coming From: Memoirs of American Youth.* (New York: Persea, 1994).

Singer, Bennett L., ed. *Growing up Gay, Growing up Lesbian: A Literary Anthology.* (New York: The New Press, 1994).

Thomas, Joyce Carol, ed. *A Gathering of Flowers: Stories about Being Young in America.* (New York: Harper & Row, 1990).

Professional Resources In Multicultural Children's Literature:

Barreras, Rosalinda, ed. *Kaleidoscope: A Multicultural Booklist.* (Urbana, IL: National Council of Teachers of English, 1997).

Harris, Violet J., ed. *Teaching Multicultural Literature in Grades K–12,* 2nd ed. (Norwood, MA: Christopher-Gordon Publishers, 1995).

Helbig, Alethea, and Perkins, Agnes Regan. *This Land Is Your Land: A Guide to Multicultural Literature for Children and Young Adults.* (Westport, CT: Greenwood Press, 1994).

Miller, Suzanne M., and McCaskill, Barbara. *Multicultural Literature and Literacies: Making Space for Difference.* (Albany, NY: State University of New York Press, 1993).

Muse, Daphne, ed. *The New Press Guide to Multicultural Resources for Young Readers.* (New York: The New Press, 1997).

Rochman, Hazel. *Against Borders: Promoting Books for a Multicultural World.* (Chicago: American Library Association, 1993).

Rudman, Masha Kabokow. *Children's Literature: An Issues Approach,* 3rd ed. (White Plains, NY: Longman, 1995).

Singer, Bennett L. ed. *Growing Up Gay, Growing Up Lesbian: A Literary Anthology.* (New York: The New Press, 1994).

Willis, Arlette. *Teaching and Using Multicultural Literature in Grades 9–12.* (Norton, MA: Christopher-Gordon Publishers, 1998).

Glossary

Ableism. Discriminatory beliefs and behaviors directed against people with disabilities.

Ageism. Discriminatory beliefs and behaviors directed against people because of their age.

Anti-Arab discrimination. Discriminatory beliefs and behaviors directed against Arabs.

Anti-Semitism. Discriminatory beliefs and behaviors directed against Jews.

Bilingual education. Generally refers to an educational approach that involves the use of two languages of instruction at some point in the student's school career. Other terms associated with bilingual education include: **Bilingual/bicultural education.** The cultures associated with the primary and second languages are also incorporated into the curriculum. **Immersion bilingual education.** Students are immersed in their second language for a year or two before their native language is introduced as a medium of instruction. By their fifth or sixth year of schooling, they may be receiving equal amounts of instruction in both languages. **Maintenance (or developmental) approach.** A comprehensive and long-term method that uses both students' native and second languages for instruction. The primary objective of this approach is to build on and develop students' literacy in their native language and to extend it to their second language as well. **Submersion bilingual education.** Also called "sink or swim," this approach, as used in the United States, places students in a totally English-language environment without using their native language and related literacy experiences as a basis for instruction. **Transitional approach.** Students receive all or most of their content area instruction in their native language while learning English as a second language. As soon as it has been determined that they can benefit from the monolingual English-language curriculum, they are "exited" out of the program. The primary objective of this approach is to teach students English as quickly as possible so that they can continue their education in a monolingual, or "mainstream," program. **Two-way bilingual education.** A program model for integrating students whose native language is English with those for whom English is a second language. The goals of this approach are to develop bilingual proficiency, academic achievement, and positive cross-cultural attitudes and behaviors among all students.

Bilingualism. Two kinds of bilingualism that result from second-language instruction are: **Additive.** Second-language learning that builds on previous literacy in the first language. **Subtractive.** Second-language learning that ignores previous literacy in the first language and thus detracts from developing more extensive literacy in the new language.

Classism. Discriminatory beliefs and behaviors based on differences in social class; generally directed against those from poor and/or working-class backgrounds.

Communication style. How individuals interact with one another and the messages they send, intentionally or not, through their behaviors.

Cultural capital. The knowledge that is associated with the dominant group and that has most status in a society. As defined by Pierre Bourdieu, it can exist in three forms: dispositions of the mind and body; cultural goods such as pictures, books, and other material objects; and educational qualifications. According to him, cultural capital is the best hidden form of the hereditary transmission of capital. See Pierre Bourdieu, "The Forms of Capital." In *Handbook of Theory and Research for the Sociology of Education,* edited by John G. Richardson (New York: Greenwood Press, 1986).

Culture. The values, traditions, social and political relationships, and worldview created, shared, and transformed by a group of people bound together by a a common history, geographic location, language, social class, and/or religion.

Curriculum. The organized environment for learning in a classroom and school. The curriculum includes both expressed elements (usually written down in the form of goals, objectives, lesson plans, and units and included in educational materials such as textbooks) and hidden elements (i.e., the unintended messages, both positive and negative, in the classroom and school environments).

Deficit theories. Explanations that hypothesize that some people are deficient in intelligence and/or achievement either because of genetic inferiority (because of their racial background) or because of cultural deprivation (because of their cultural background and/or because they have been deprived of cultural experiences and activities deemed by the majority to be indispensable for growth and development).

Ebonics. Also called *Black English/Black Language, or African American English/African American Language,* this term refers to the language system characteristically spoken in the African American community. For an in-depth discussion of the controversy surrounding the use of Ebonics in teaching African American children, see *The Real Ebonics Debate: Power, Language, and the Education of African-American Children,* edited by Theresa Perry and Lisa Delpit (Boston: Beacon Press, 1998).

Educational equity. Beyond equal educational opportunity, educational equity is based on fairness and promotes the real possibility of equality of outcomes for a broader range of students.

English as a Second Language (ESL). A systematic and comprehensive approach to teaching English to students for whom it is not a native language. ESL is an essential component of bilingual programs in the United States but can exist by itself as well.

Equal education. Providing the same resources and opportunities for all students.

Ethnocentrism. Discriminatory beliefs and behaviors based on ethnic differences.

Ethnography. Qualitative educational research that uses anthropological methods such as fieldwork, interviewing, and participant/observation to study schools and students.

Eurocentric curriculum. Curriculum that focuses primarily or exclusively on the values, lifestyles, accomplishments, and worldviews of Europeans and/or European Americans.

Heterosexism. Discriminatory beliefs and behaviors directed against gay men and lesbians.

Linguicism. According to Skutnabb-Kangas, this term refers to "ideologies and structures which are used to legitimate, effectuate and reproduce an unequal division of power and resources (both material and non-material) between groups which are defined on the basis of language." See Tove Skutnabb-Kangas, "Multilingualism and the Education of Minority Children." In *Minority Education: From Shame to Struggle,* edited by Tove Skutnabb-Kangas and Jim Cummins (Clevedon, England: Multilingual Matters, 1988), 13.

Low-incidence populations. Legal term to identify a group of speakers of a language other than English too small to be legally entitled to a bilingual program. In most states with mandated bilingual education laws, the minimum number of students who speak a particular language for whom the local school district must have a program is 20.

Multicultural education. A process of comprehensive school reform and basic education for all students. It challenges and rejects racism and other forms of discrimination in schools and society and accepts and affirms the pluralism (ethnic, racial, linguistic, religious, economic, and gender, among others) that students, their communities, and teachers reflect. Multicultural education permeates the schools' curriculum and instructional strategies, as well as the interactions among teachers, students, and families, and the very way that schools conceptualize the nature of teaching and learning. Because it uses critical pedagogy as its underlying philosophy and focuses on knowledge, reflection, and action (*praxis*) as the basis for social change, multicultural education promotes democratic principles of social justice.

Pluralism. There are three basic models for understanding pluralism in our society: **Anglo-conformity.** A model of pluralism based on the concept that all newcomers need to conform to the dominant European American, middle-class, and English-speaking majority. **Cultural pluralism** (alternatively called *salad bowl, mosaic,* or *tapestry*). A model based on the premise that people of all backgrounds have a right to maintain their languages and cultures while combining with others to form a new society reflective of all our differences. **Melting pot.** A model that maintains that differences need to be wiped out to form an amalgam that is uniquely American but without obvious traces of the original cultures.

Praxis. The process of connecting reflection with action in the pursuit of knowledge and social change. See Paulo Freire, *Pedagogy of the Oppressed* (New York: Seabury Press, 1970).

Racism. According to Meyer Weinberg, racism is a system of privilege and penalty based on one's race. It consists of two facets: a belief in the inherent superiority of some people and inherent inferiority of others, and the acceptance of the way goods and services are distributed in accordance with these judgments. See "Introduction." In *Racism in the United States: A Comprehensive Classified Bibliography* (New York: Greenwood Press, 1990).

Resistance theory. As applied to schools, this term refers to the way in which students actively or passively resist learning. Reasons for this resistance may be varied, from cultural or linguistic differences to perceptions that the knowledge taught is meaningless and imposed. It can take a variety of forms, from acting out, to refusing to complete schoolwork or other assignments, to dropping out altogether. Although resistance is rarely intentional, it can be extremely effective either in disrupting or preventing learning or in developing alternative ways of coping within schools.

Self-fulfilling prophecy. Term coined by Robert Merton to refer to the way that students perform based on what teachers expect of them. See Robert Merton, "The Self-Fulfilling Prophecy." *The Antioch Review,* 8, 2 (1948), 193–210.

Sexism. Discriminatory beliefs and behaviors based on one's gender.

Symbolic violence. As used by Pierre Bourdieu, this term refers to the way in which the power relations of the dominant society are maintained in the school primarily through the curriculum. See Pierre Bourdieu, *Outline of Theory and Practice* (Cambridge: Cambridge University Press, 1977).

Tracking (or **Ability Tracking**). The placement of students for instruction with others of equal or matched ability (homogeneous groups).

Voluntary and Involuntary Minorities. The distinctions made between different kinds of minorities by John Ogbu. See his article, "Variability in Minority School Performance: A Problem in Search of an Explanation." *Anthropology and Education Quarterly,* 18, 4 (December 1987), 312–334. *Castelike* or *involuntary minorities* refers to those groups incorporated into a society against their will. In the United States, this term generally refers to American Indians, African Americans, Mexican Americans, and Puerto Ricans, all of whose ancestors were either conquered or enslaved. *Voluntary* or *immigrant minorities* refers to those who have chosen freely to emigrate to the United States.

Bibliography

Abi-Nader, Jeannette. "Meeting the Needs of Multicultural Classrooms: Family Values and the Motivation of Minority Students." In *Diversity and Teaching: Teacher Education Yearbook I.* Edited by Mary John O'Hair and Sandra J. Odell. (Fort Worth, TX: Harcourt Brace Jovanovich, 1993).

Ada, Alma Flor. "The Pajaro Valley Experience." In *Minority Education: From Shame to Struggle.* Edited by Tove Skutnabb-Kangas and Jim Cummins. (Clevedon, England: Multilingual Matters, 1988).

Adams, David, Barbara Astone, Elsa Nuñez-Wormack, and Ivan Smodlaka. "Predicting the Academic Achievement of Puerto Rican and Mexican-American Ninth-Grade Students." *The Urban Review,* 26, 1 (1994), 1–14.

Allport, Gordon W. *The Nature of Prejudice.* (Reading, MA: Addison-Wesley, 1954).

Almeida, Deirdre A. "The Hidden Half: A History of Native American Women's Education." *Harvard Educational Review,* 67, 4 (Winter, 1997), 757–771.

American Behavioral Scientist: Special issue on *The Bell Curve: Laying Bare the Resurgence of Scientific Racism,* 39, 1 (September/October, 1995).

Anglesey, Zoë. "Moving from an Obsolete Lingo to a Vocabulary of Respect." *Multicultural Review,* 6, 3 (September, 1997), 23–28.

Anthropology and Education Quarterly, 28, 3 (September, 1997).

Appiah, Anthony. "Identity, Authenticity, Survival: Multicultural Societies and Social Reproduction." In *Multiculturalism.* Edited by Amy Gutmann. (Princeton, NJ: Princeton University Press, 1994).

Apple, Michael W. *Teachers and Texts: A Political Economy of Class and Gender Relations in Education.* (Boston: Routledge & Kegan Paul, 1986).

Apple, Michael W. "The Text and Cultural Politics." *Educational Researcher,* 21, 7 (October, 1992), 4–11, 19.

Aronowitz, Stanley. "Between Nationality and Class," *Harvard Educational Review,* 67, 2 (Summer, 1997), 188–207.

Aruri, Naseer H. "The Arab-American Community of Springfield, Massachusetts." In *The Arab-Americans: Studies in Assimilation.* Edited by Elaine C. Hagopian and Ann Paden. (Wilmette, IL: Medina University Press International, 1969).

Ascher, Carol. *Testing Students in Urban Schools: Current Problems and New Directions.* (New York: ERIC Clearinghouse for Urban Education, Teachers College, Columbia University, 1990).

Ascher, Carol, and Gary Burnett. *Current Trends and Issues in Urban Education.* (New York: ERIC Clearinghouse for Urban Education, Teachers College, Columbia University, 1993).

Ashton-Warner, Sylvia. *Teacher.* (New York: Simon & Schuster, 1963).

Asimov, Nanette. "Bilingual Surprise in State Testing." *The San Francisco Chronicle,* July 7, 1998, A1.

Aspira Institute for Policy Research. *Facing the Facts: The State of Hispanic Education, 1994.* (Washington, DC: ASPIRA Association, 1994).

Au, Katherine H., and Alice J. Kawakami. "Cultural Congruence in Instruction." In *Teaching Diverse Populations: Formulating a Knowledge Base.* Edited by Etta R. Hollins, Joyce E. King, and Warren C. Hayman. (Albany, NY: State University of New York Press, 1994).

August, Diane, and Kenji Hakuta, eds. *Educating Language-Minority Children.* Commission on Behavioral and Social Sciences and Education, National Research Council, Institute of Medicine. (Washington, D.C.: National Academy Press, 1998).

Azmitia, Margarita, Catherine R. Cooper, Eugene E. García, Angela Ittel, Bonnie Johanson, Edward Lopez, Rebeca Martinez-Chavez, and Lourdes Rivera. *Links Between Home and School Among Low-Income Mexican-American and European-American Families.* (Santa Cruz, CA: National Center for Research on Cultural Diversity and Second Language Learning, 1994).

Banks, James A. "Multicultural Education: Historical Development, Dimensions, and Practice." In *Handbook of Research on Multicultural Education.* Edited by James A. Banks and Cherry A. McGee Banks. (New York: Macmillan, 1995).

Banks, James A. *Teaching Strategies for Ethnic Studies,* 6th ed. (Boston: Allyn & Bacon, 1997).

Baratz, Stephen S., and Joan C. Baratz. "Early Childhood Intervention: The Social Science Base of Institutional Racism." In *Challenging the Myths: The Schools, the Blacks, and the Poor,* reprint no. 5. (Cambridge, MA: Harvard Educational Review, 1971).

Bartolomé, Lilia I. "Beyond the Methods Fetish: Toward a Humanizing Pedagogy." *Harvard Educational Review,* 64, 2 (Summer, 1994), 173–194.

Bennett, Christine I. *Comprehensive Multicultural Education: Theory and Practice,* 4th ed. (Boston: Allyn & Bacon, 1999).

Bennett, Kathleen P. "Doing School in an Urban Appalachian First Grade." In *Empowerment through Multicultural Education.* Edited by Christine E. Sleeter. (Albany, NY: State University of New York Press, 1991).

Bennett, Kathleen P. *The Way Schools Work,* 3rd. ed. (New York: Longman, 1999).

Bereiter, Carl, and Siegfried Englemann. *Teaching Disadvantaged Children in the Preschool.* (Englewood Cliffs, NJ: Prentice-Hall, 1966).

Bigelow, Bill, Linda Christensen, Stanley Karp, Barbara Miner, and Bob Peterson, eds. *Rethinking Our Classrooms: Teaching for Equity and Justice.* (Milwaukee: Rethinking Schools, 1994).

Bigler, Ellen. *American Conversations: Puerto Ricans, White Ethnics, and Multicultural Education.* (Philadelphia: Temple University Press, 1999).

Bloome, David, with Rachel Bloomekatz and Petra Sander. "Literacy, Democracy, and the Pledge of Allegiance." *Language Arts,* 70, 8 (December, 1993), 655–658.

Boateng, Felix. "Combating Deculturalization of the African-American Child in the Public School System: A Multicultural Approach." In *Going to School: The African-American Experience.* Edited by Kofi Lomotey. (Albany, NY: State University of New York Press, 1990).

Bond, Horace Mann. "Two Racial Islands in Alabama." *American Journal of Sociology,* 36, 4 (1930–1931), 554.

Bourdieu, Pierre. "The Forms of Capital." In *Handbook of Theory and Research for the Sociology of Education.* Edited by John G. Richardson. (New York: Greenwood Press, 1986).

Bourdieu, Pierre. *Outline of Theory and Practice.* (Cambridge: Cambridge University Press, 1977).

Bowles, Samuel, and Herbert Gintis. *Schooling in Capitalist America: Educational Reform and the Contradictions of Economic Life.* (New York: Basic Books, 1976).

Braddock, Jomills H., II. "Tracking the Middle Grades: National Patterns of Grouping for Instruction." *Phi Delta Kappan,* 71, 6 (February 1990), 445–449.

Brantlinger, Ellen. *The Politics of Social Class in Secondary School: Views of Affluent and Impoverished Youth.* (New York: Teachers College Press, 1993).

Bright, Josephine A. "Beliefs in Action: Family Contributions to African-American Student Success." *Equity and Choice,* 10, 2 (Winter, 1994), 5–13.

Brophy, Jere E. "Research on the Self-Fulfilling Prophecy and Teacher Expectations." *Journal of Educational Psychology,* 75, 5 (1983), 631–661.

Brumberg, Stephan F. *Going to America, Going to School: The Jewish Immigrant Public School Encounter in Turn-of-the-Century New York City.* (New York: Praeger, 1986).

Bryk, Anthony S., Valerie E. Lee, and Peter B. Holland. *Catholic Schools and the Common Good.* (Cambridge, MA: Harvard Educational Review Press, 1993).

Carnegie Council on Adolescent Development. *Turning Points: Preparing American Youth for the Twenty-First Century.* (Washington, DC: Task Force on the Education of Young Adolescents, 1989).

Carter, Kathy. "The Place of Story in the Study of Teaching and Teacher Education." *Educational Researcher,* 22, 1 (1993), 5–12.

Cazabon, Mary, Wallace E. Lambert, and Geoff Hall. *Two-Way Bilingual Education: A Progress Report on the Amigos Program.* (Santa Cruz, CA: National Center for Research in Cultural Diversity and Second Language Learning, 1993).

"Children of Intermarriage." *New York Times,* June 20, 1984, p. C1.

Children's Defense Fund. *Latino Youths at a Crossroads.* (Washington, DC: Author, 1990).

Christian, Donna. *Two-Way Bilingual Education: Students Learning through Two Languages.* (Santa Cruz, CA: National Center for Research on Cultural Diversity and Second Language Learning, 1994).

Christian, Donna, Christopher Montone, Kathryn J. Lindholm, and Isolda Carranza. *Profiles in Two-Way Immersion Education.* (McHenry, IL: Delta Systems, 1997).

Clark, Christine, Morris Jenkins, and Gwendolyn Stowers, *Fear of Da' Gangsta': The Social Construction, Production, and Reproduction of Violence in Schools for Corporate Profit and the Revolutionary Promise of Multicultural Education.* (Westport, CT: Greenwood, Bergin & Garvey, 1999).

Cochran-Smith, Marilyn. "Uncertain Allies: Understanding the Boundaries of Race and Teaching." *Harvard Educational Review,* 65, 4 (Winter, 1995), 541–570.

Cochran-Smith, Marilyn, and Susan L. Lytle, eds. *Inside/Outside: Teacher Research and Knowledge.* (New York: Teachers College Press, 1993).

Cofer, Judith Ortiz. *Silent Dancing: A Partial Remembrance of a Puerto Rican Childhood.* (Houston: Arte Público Press).

Cohen, Jody. "'Now Everybody Want to Dance': Making Change in an Urban Charter." In *Chartering Urban School Reform: Reflections on Public High Schools in the Midst of Change.* Michelle Fine, ed. (New York: Teachers College Press, 1994).

Collier, Virginia, *Promoting Academic Success for ESL Students: Understanding Second Language Acquisition at School.* (Elizabeth, NJ: New Jersey Teachers of English to Speakers of Other Languages—Bilingual Educators, 1995).

Commins, Nancy L. "Parents and Public Schools: The Experiences of Four Mexican Immigrant Families." *Equity and Choice,* 8, 2 (1992), 40–45.

The Condition of Education . . . Elementary and Secondary Students. http://nces.ed.gov/pubs98/c9843a01.html

The Condition of Bilingual Education in the Nation: A Report to the Congress and the President. (Washington, DC: U.S. Department of Education, Office of the Secretary, 30 June 1992).

Corbett, H. Dickson and Bruce L. Wilson. *Testing, Reform and Rebellion.* (Norwood, NJ: Ablex, 1991).

Corbett, Dick and Bruce Wilson. "Make a Difference *With*, Not *For*, Students: A Plea to Researchers and Reformers." *Educational Researcher*, 24, 5 (June/July, 1995), 12–17.

Corson, David. *Language, Minority Education and Gender: Linking Social Justice and Power.* (Clevedon, England: Multilingual Matters Ltd., 1993).

Cortés, Carlos E. "The Societal Curriculum: Implications for Multiethnic Education." In *Education in the 80's: Multiethnic Education.* Edited by James A. Banks. (Washington, DC: National Education Association, 1981).

Council of the Great City Schools. *National Urban Education Goals: 1992–1993 Indicators Report.* (Washington, DC: Author, 1994).

Craig, Barbara A. "Parental Attitudes Toward Bilingualism in a Local Two-Way Immersion Program." *The Bilingual Research Journal*, 20, 3 and 4 (Summer/Fall, 1996), 383–410.

Crawford, James. *Hold Your Tongue: Bilingualism and the Politics of "English Only."* (Reading, MA: Addison-Wesley Publishing Co., 1992).

Cross, William E., Jr. *Shades of Black: Diversity in African-American Identity.* (Philadelphia: Temple University Press, 1991).

Cruz, Bárbara C. "Stereotypes of Latin Americans Perpetuated in Secondary School History Textbooks." *Latino Studies Journal*, 1, 1 (January, 1994), 51–67.

Cruz-Janzen, Marta I. *Curriculum and the Self-concept of Biethnic and Biracial Persons.* Unpublished doctoral dissertation, College of Education, University of Denver, April, 1997.

Cuban, Larry. *How Teachers Taught: Constancy and Change in American Classrooms, 1880–1990*, 2nd ed. (New York: Teachers College Press, 1993).

Cummins, Jim. *Negotiating Identities: Education for Empowerment in a Diverse Society.* (Ontario, CA: California Association for Bilingual Education, 1996).

Curry, Lynn. *Learning Styles in Secondary Schools: A Review of Instruments and Implications for Their Use.* (Madison, WI: National Center on Effective Secondary Schools, University of Wisconsin, 1990).

Darder, Antonia. *Culture and Power in the Classroom: A Critical Foundation for Bicultural Education.* (New York: Bergin & Garvey, 1991).

Darling-Hammond, Linda. "The Implications of Testing Policy for Quality and Equality." *Phi Delta Kappan*, 73, 3 (November, 1991), 220–225.

Darling-Hammond, Linda. "Performance-Based Assessment and Educational Equity." *Harvard Educational Review*, 64, 1 (Spring, 1994), 5–30.

Darling-Hammond, Linda. *The Right to Learn: A Blueprint for Creating Schools That Work.* (San Francisco: Jossey-Bass Publishers, 1997).

Delpit, Lisa. *Other People's Children.* (New York: The New Press, 1995).

Derman-Sparks, Louise, and the A.B.C. Task Force. *Anti-Bias Curriculum: Tools for Empowering Young Children.* (Washington, DC: National Association for the Education of Young Children, 1989).

Dewey, John. *Democracy and Education.* (New York: Free Press, 1916).

Deyhle, Donna. "Navajo Youth and Anglo Racism: Cultural Integrity and Resistance." *Harvard Educational Review*, 65, 3 (Fall, 1995), 403–444.

Deyhle, Donna and Karen Swisher. "Research in American Indian and Alaska Native Education: From Assimilation to Self-Determination." In *Review of Research in Education*, vol. 22. Michael W. Apple, ed. (Washington, DC: AERA, 1997).

Díaz, Stephan, Luis C. Moll, and Hugh Mehan. "Sociocultural Resources in Instruction: A Context-Specific Approach." In *Beyond Language: Social and Cultural Factors in Schooling Language Minority Students.* (Los Angeles: Office of Bilingual Education, California State Department of Education, Evaluation, Dissemination, and Assessment Center, 1986).

Díaz Soto, Lourdes. "Native Language School Success." *Bilingual Research Journal*, 17, 1 and 2 (1993), 83–97.

Dickeman, Mildred. "Teaching Cultural Pluralism." In *Teaching Ethnic Studies: Concepts and Strategies*, 43rd Yearbook. Edited by James A. Banks. (Washington, DC: National Council for the Social Studies, 1973).

Dilworth, Mary E., ed. *Diversity in Teacher Education: New Expectations.* (San Francisco, CA: Jossey-Bass Publishers, 1992).

Dinnerstein, Leonard. *Anti-Semitism in America.* (New York: Oxford University Press, 1994).

Donaldson, Karen B. McLean. *Through Students' Eyes: Combating Racism in United States Schools.* (Westport, CT: Praeger Publishers, 1996).

Donaldson, Karen B. McLean. "Antiracist Education and a Few Courageous Teachers." *Equity and Excellence in Education,* 30, 2 (September, 1997), 31–38.

Donato, Rubén. *The Other Struggle for Equal Schools: Mexican Americans During the Civil Rights Era.* (Albany, NY: State University of New York Press, 1997).

DuBois, W. E. B. "Does the Negro Need Separate Schools?" *Journal of Negro Education,* 4, 3 (1935), 328–335.

Eccles, Jacquelynne, and Lee Jussim. "Teacher Expectations II: Construction and Reflection of Student Achievement." *Journal of Personality and Social Psychology,* 63, 6 (December, 1992), 947–961.

Eisner, Elliot. "The Promise and Perils of Alternative Forms of Data Representation." *Educational Researcher,* 26, 6, (1997), 4–10.

Ekstrom, Ruth B. "Six Urban School Districts: Their Middle-Grade Grouping Policies and Practices." In *On the Right Track: The Consequences of Mathematics Course Placement Policies and Practices in the Middle Grades.* Report to the Edna McConnell Clark Foundation. (Princeton, NJ, and New York: ETS and the National Urban League, 1992).

El-Badry, Samia. "The Arab-American Market." *American Demographics,* (January, 1994).

Eller-Powell, Rebecca. "Teaching for Change in Appalachia." In *Teaching Diverse Populations: Formulating a Knowledge Base.* Edited by Etta R. Hollins, Joyce E. King, and Warren C. Hayman. (Albany, NY: State University of New York Press, 1994).

Equal Educational Opportunities Act of 1974, 20 U.S.C. 1703 (f).

Erickson, Frederick. "Qualitative Methods in Research on Teaching." In *Handbook of Research on Teaching,* 3rd ed. Edited by Merlin C. Wittrock. (New York: Macmillan, 1986).

Erickson, Frederick. "Transformation and School Success: The Politics and Culture of Educational Achievement." *Anthropology and Education Quarterly,* 18, 4 (December, 1987), 335–356.

Erickson, Frederick. "Culture, Politics, and Educational Practice." *Educational Foundations,* 4, 2 (Spring, 1990), 21–45.

Erickson, Frederick, and Gerald Mohatt. "Cultural Organization of Participant Structures in Two Classrooms of Indian Students." In *Doing the Ethnography of Schooling: Educational Anthropology in Action.* Edited by George D. Spindler. (New York: Holt, Rinehart & Winston, 1982).

Estrin, Elise Trumbull. *Alternative Assessment: Issues in Language, Culture, and Equity.* Knowledge brief no. 11. (San Francisco: Far West Laboratory, 1993).

FairTest, *Tables on State Testing.* (Cambridge, MA: Author, 1997).

Figueroa, Richard A., and Eugene García. "Issues in Testing Students from Culturally and Linguistically Diverse Backgrounds." *Multicultural Education,* 2, 1 (Fall, 1994), 10–19.

"Findings of the Effectiveness of Bilingual Education." *NABE News* (1 May, 1998), 5.

Fine, Melinda. "'You Can't Just Say that the Only Ones Who Can Speak Are Those Who Agree with Your Position': Political Discourse in the Classroom." *Harvard Educational Review,* 63, 4 (1993), 412–433.

Fine, Michelle. *Framing Dropouts: Notes on the Politics of an Urban High School.* (Albany, NY: State University of New York Press, 1991).

Finn, Jeremy, and Charles Achilles. "Answers About Class Size: A Statewide Experiment." *American Educational Research Journal* (Fall, 1990).

Ford, Donna Y. *Reversing Underachievement Among Gifted Black Students: Promising Practices and Programs.* (New York: Teachers College Press, 1996).

Fordham, Signithia, and John U. Ogbu. "Black Students' School Success: Coping with the 'Burden of Acting White.'" *Urban Review,* 18, 3 (1986), 176–206.

Foster, Michele. *Black Teachers on Teaching.* (New York: The New Press, 1997).

Foy, Colm. *Cape Verde: Politics, Economics and Society.* (London: Pinter, 1988).

Fránquiz, María E., and María de la luz Reyes. "Creating Inclusive Learning Communities through English Language Arts: From *Chanclas* to *Canicas.*" *Language Arts,* 75, 3 (March, 1998), 211–220.

Freedman, Sara Warshaeuer, Elizabeth Radin Simons, Julie Shalhope Kalnin, Alex Casareno, and the M-CLASS Teams, eds., *Inside City Schools: Investigating Literacy in Multicultural Classrooms.* (New York: Teachers College Press, 1999).

Freire, Paulo. *Pedagogy of the Oppressed.* (New York: Seabury Press, 1970).

Freire, Paulo. *The Politics of Education: Culture, Power, and Liberation.* (South Hadley, MA: Bergin & Garvey, 1985).

Fruchter, Norm, Anne Galletta, and J. Lynne White. "New Directions in Parent Involvement." *Equity and Choice,* 9, 3 (Spring, 1993), 33–43.

Funderburg, Lise. *Black, White, Other: Biracial Americans Talk about Race and Identity.* (New York: William Morrow & Co., 1994).

Gamoran, Adam, Martin Nystrand, Mark Berends, and Paul Le Pore. "An Organizational Analysis of the Effects of Ability Grouping." *American Educational Research Journal,* 32, 4 (Winter, 1995), 687–715.

Gándara, Patricia. *Over the Ivy Walls: The Educational Mobility of Low-Income Chicanos.* (Albany, NY: State University of New York Press, 1995).

García, Eugene E. *Education of Linguistically and Culturally Diverse Students: Effective Instructional Practices.* (Santa Cruz, CA: National Center for Research on Cultural Diversity and Second Language Learning, 1991).

García, Eugene. "Attributes of Effective Schools for Language Minority Students." *Education and Urban Society,* 20, 4 (August, 1988), 387–398.

García, Eugene. *Understanding and Meeting the Challenge of Student Cultural Diversity.* (Boston: Houghton Mifflin Company, 1994).

García, Eugene. "Educating Mexican American Students: Past Treatment and Recent Developments in Theory, Research, Policy, and Practice." In James A. Banks and Cherry A. McGee Banks, eds. *Handbook of Research on Multicultural Education.* (New York: Macmillan, 1995).

García, Jesús. "The Changing Image of Ethnic Groups in Textbooks." *Phi Delta Kappan,* 75, 1 (September, 1993), 29–35.

Gardner, Howard. *Multiple Intelligences: The Theory in Practice.* (New York: Basic Books, 1993).

Gates, Henry Louis, Jr. *Loose Canons: Notes on the Culture Wars.* (New York: Oxford University Press, 1992).

Gay, Geneva. "Mirror Images on Common Issues: Parallels Between Multicultural Education and Critical Pedagogy." In *Multicultural Education, Critical Pedagogy, and the Politics of Difference.* Edited by Christine E. Sleeter and Peter L. McLaren. (Albany, NY: State University of New York Press, 1995), 155–189.

Gibson, Margaret A. "The School Performance of Immigrant Minorities: A Comparative View." *Anthropology and Education Quarterly,* 18, 4 (December, 1987), 262–275.

Gibson, Margaret A. "Perspectives on Acculturation and School Performance." *Focus on Diversity* (Newsletter of the National Center for Research on Cultural Diversity and Second Language Learning), 5, 3 (1995), 8–10.

Gibson, Margaret A. "Conclusion: Complicating the Immigrant/Involuntary Minority Typology." *Anthropology and Education Quarterly,* 28, 3 (September, 1997), 431–454.

Gibson, Margaret A., and John U. Ogbu, eds. *Minority Status and Schooling: A Comparative Study of Immigrant and Involuntary Minorities.* (New York: Garland, 1991).

Gillborn, David. "Ethnicity and Educational Performance in the United Kingdom: Racism, Ethnicity, and Variability in Achievement." *Anthropology and Education Quarterly,* 28, 3 (September, 1997), 375–393.

Giroux, Henry A. "Educational Leadership and the Crisis of Democratic Government." *Educational Researcher,* 21, 4 (May, 1992), 4–11.

Giroux, Henry A. *Theory and Resistance in Education: A Pedagogy for the Opposition.* (South Hadley, MA: Bergin & Garvey, 1983).

Giroux, Henry. "Rewriting The Discourse of Racial Identity: Towards a Pedagogy and Politics of Whiteness." *Harvard Educational Review,* 67, 2 (Summer, 1997), 285–320.

Glazer, Nathan. "Where is Multiculturalism Leading Us?" *Phi Delta Kappan,* 75, 4 (December, 1993), 319–323.

Goldenberg, Claude. "The Limits of Expectations: A Case for Case Knowledge about Teacher Expectancy Effects." *American Educational Research Journal,* 29, 3 (Fall, 1992), 514–544.

Gollnick, Donna M., and Philip C. Chinn. *Multicultural Education in a Pluralistic Society,* 5th ed. (New York: Maxwell Macmillan International, 1998).

Goodlad, John I. *A Place Called School.* (New York: McGraw-Hill, 1984).

Gould, Stephen Jay. *The Mismeasure of Man.* (New York: Norton, 1981).

Greenbaum, William. "America in Search of a New Ideal: An Essay on the Rise of Pluralism." *Harvard Educational Review,* 44 (August, 1974), 411–440.

Greene, Maxine. *The Dialectic of Freedom.* (New York: Teachers College Press, 1988).

Greene, Maxine. "The Passions of Pluralism: Multiculturalism and the Expanding Community." *Educational Researcher,* 22, 1 (February, 1993), 13–18.

Greenfield, Patricia M., and Rodney R. Cocking, eds. *Cross-Cultural Roots of Minority Child Development.* (Hillsdale, NJ: Lawrence Erlbaum Associates, Publishers, 1994).

Haberman, Martin. "The Pedagogy of Poverty versus Good Teaching." *Phi Delta Kappan,* 73, 4 (December, 1991), 290–294.

Haberman, Martin. "Selecting 'Star' Teachers for Children and Youth in Urban Poverty." *Phi Delta Kappan,* 76, 10 (June, 1995), 777–781.

Hamovitch, Bram A. "Socialization Without Voice: An Ideology of Hope for At-Risk Students." *Teachers College Record,* 98, 2 (Winter, 1996), 286–306.

Harris, Louis, and Associates, Inc. *Dropping out or Staying in High School: Pilot Survey of Young African American Males in Four Cities.* (New York: Commonwealth Fund, 1994).

Harris, Violet J., ed. *Using Multiethnic Literature in the K–8 Classroom* (Norwood, MA: Christopher-Gordon, 1997).

Hartle-Schutte, David. "Literacy Development in Navajo Homes: Does It Lead to Success in School?" *Language Arts,* 70, 8 (December, 1993), 643–654.

Harvard Education Letter, xiii, 1 (January/February, 1997). Special issue on detracking.

Harvard Educational Review, Special Issue on Lesbian, Gay, Bisexual, and Transgender People and Education, 66, 2 (Summer, 1996).

Harvard Educational Review, Special Issue on Puerto Rican Education in the United States, 68, 2 (Summer, 1998).

Heath, Shirley Brice. *Ways with Words.* (New York: Cambridge University Press, 1983).

Heath, Shirley Brice. "Race, Ethnicity, and the Defiance of Categories." In *Toward a Common Destiny: Improving Race and Ethnic Relations in America.* Willis D. Hawley and Anthony W. Jackson, ed. (San Francisco: Jossey-Bass Publishers, 1995), 39–70.

Henderson, Anne T. and Nancy Berla. *A New Generation of Evidence: The Family Is Critical to Student Achievement* (Washington, DC: Center for Law and Education, 1995).

Herbst, Philip H. *The Color of Words: An Encyclopaedic Dictionary of Ethnic Bias in the United States.* (Yarmouth, ME: Intercultural Press, Inc., 1997).

Herrnstein, Richard J., and Charles Murray. *The Bell Curve: Intelligence and Class Structure in American Life.* (New York: Free Press, 1994).

Hidalgo, Nitza M. *"Free Time, School Is Like a Free Time": Social Relations in City High School Classes.* Unpublished doctoral dissertation. Graduate School of Education, Harvard University, 1991.

Hidalgo, Nitza M. "A Layering of Family and Friends: Four Puerto Rican Families' Meaning of Community." *Education and Urban Society,* 30, 1 (November, 1997), 20–40.

Hoffer, Thomas. "Middle School Ability Grouping and Students' Achievement in Science and Math." *Educational Evaluation & Policy Analysis,* 14, 3 (Fall, 1992), 205–227.

Iadicola, Peter. "Schooling and Symbolic Violence: The Effect of Power Differences and Curriculum Factors on Hispanic Students' Attitudes toward Their Own Ethnicity." *Hispanic Journal of Behavioral Sciences,* 5, 1 (1983), 21–43.

Igoa, Cristina. *The Inner World of the Immigrant Child.* (New York: St. Martins Press, 1995).

Institute for Puerto Rican Policy. Puerto Ricans and other Latinos in the United States. *IPR Datanote, 19* (February, 1998).

Irvine, Jacqueline Jordan. *Black Students and School Failure: Policies, Practices, and Prescriptions.* (Westport, CT: Greenwood Press, 1990).

Irvine, Jacqueline Jordan. "Making Teacher Education Culturally Responsive." In *Diversity in Teacher Education: New Expectations.* Edited by Mary E. Dilworth. (San Francisco, CA: Jossey-Bass Publishers, 1992).

Irvine, Jacqueline Jordan. *Critical Knowledge for Diverse Teachers and Learners.* (Washington, DC: American Association of Colleges for Teacher Education, 1997).

Irvine, Jacqueline Jordan, and Michele Foster. *Growing up African American in Catholic Schools.* (New York: Teachers College Press, 1996).

Irvine, Jacqueline Jordan, and Eleanor Darlene York. "Learning Styles and Culturally Diverse Students: A Literature Review." In *Handbook of Research on Multicultural Education.* Edited by James A. Banks and Cherry A. McGee Banks. (New York: Macmillan, 1995).

Jacob, Evelyn, and Cathie Jordan, eds. *Minority Education: Anthropological Perspectives.* (Norwood, NJ: Ablex, 1993).

Jalava, Antti. "Mother Tongue and Identity: Nobody Could See that I Was a Finn." In *Minority Education: From Shame to Struggle.* Edited by Tove Skutnabb-Kangas and Jim Cummins. (Clevedon, England: Multilingual Matters, 1988).

Jensen, Arthur R. "How Much Can We Boost I.Q. and Scholastic Achievement?" *Harvard Educational Review,* 39, 2 (1969), 1–123.

Jervis, Kathe. "'How Come There Are No Brothers on That List?': Hearing the Hard Questions All Children Ask." *Harvard Educational Review,* 66, 3 (Fall, 1996), 546–576.

Jordan, Brigitte. "Cosmopolitan Obstetrics: Some Insights from the Training of Traditional Midwives." *Social Science and Medicine,* 28, 9 (1989), 925–944.

Kaeser, Gigi, and Peggy Gillespie. *Of Many Colors: Portraits of Multiracial Families.* (Amherst, MA: University of Massachusetts Press, 1997).

Kalantzis, Mary, and Bill Cope. *The Experience of Multicultural Education in Australia: Six Case Studies.* (Sydney: Centre for Multicultural Studies, Wollongong University, 1990).

Kaser, Sandy, and Kathy G. Short. "Exploring Culture through Children's Connections." *Language Arts,* 75, 3 (March, 1998), 185–192.

Katz, Michael B. *Class, Bureaucracy, and the Schools: The Illusion of Educational Change in America.* (New York: Praeger, 1975).

Katz, Susan Roberta. "Where the Streets Cross the Classroom: A Study of Latino Students' Perspectives on Cultural Identity in City Schools and Neighborhood Gangs." *Bilingual Research Journal,* 20, 3 and 4 (Summer/Fall, 1995), 603–631.

Kendall, Frances E. *Diversity in the Classroom: New Approaches to the Education of Young Children,* 2nd ed. (New York: Teachers College Press, 1996).

Kiang, Peter Nien-Chu. *Southeast Asian Parent Empowerment: The Challenge of Changing Demographics in Lowell, Massachusetts.* Monograph no. 1. (Boston: Massachusetts Association for Bilingual Education, 1990).

Kiang, Peter Nien-Chu, and Vivian Wai-Fun Lee. "Exclusion or Contribution? Education K–12 Policy." In *The State of Asian Pacific America: Policy Issues to the Year 2020.* (Los Angeles: LEAP Asian Pacific American Public Policy Institute and the UCLA Asian American Studies Center, 1993).

Kim, Heather. *Diversity Among Asian American High School Students.* (Princeton, NJ: Educational Testing Service, 1997).

Kohl, Herbert. *"I Won't Learn from You" and Other Thoughts on Creative Maladjustment.* (New York: The New Press, 1994).

Kozol, Jonathon. "Great Men and Women (Tailored for School Use)." *Learning Magazine* (December, 1975), 16–20.

Kozol, Jonathon. *Savage Inequalities: Children in America's Schools.* (New York: Crown, 1991).

Krashen, Stephen. *Second Language Acquisition and Second Language Learning.* (New York: Pergamon, 1981).

Krashen, Stephen. "Does Literacy Transfer?" *NABE News,* 19, 6 (May 1, 1996), 36–38.

Ladson-Billings, Gloria. "Culturally Relevant Teaching: The Key to Making Multicultural Education Work." In *Research and Multicultural Education: From the Margins to the Mainstream.* Edited by Carl A. Grant. (Bristol, PA: Falmer Press, 1992).

Ladson-Billings, Gloria. *The Dreamkeepers: Successful Teachers of African American Children.* (San Francisco, CA: Jossey-Bass Publishers, 1994).

Ladson-Billings, Gloria. "Multicultural Teacher Education: Research, Practice, and Policy." *Handbook of Research on Multicultural Education.* James A. Banks and Cherry A. McGee Banks, ed. (New York: Macmillan 1995).

Ladson-Billings, Gloria. "Toward a Theory of Culturally Relevant Pedagogy." *American Educational Research Journal,* 33, 3 (Fall, 1995), 465–492.

Lambert, Wallace E. "Culture and Language as Factors in Learning and Education." In *Education of Immigrant Students.* Edited by A. Wolfgang. (Toronto: OISE, 1975).

Lau v. Nichols. 414 U.S. 563. (St. Paul, MN: West Publishing, 1974).

Lawrence, Sandra M., and Beverly Daniel Tatum. "Teachers in Transition: The Impact of Antiracist Professional Development on Classroom Practice." *Teachers College Record,* 99, 1 (1997), 162–178.

Lee, Enid, Deborah Menkart, and Margo Okazawa-Rey. *Beyond Heroes and Holidays: A Practical Guide to K–12 Anti-Racist, Multicultural Education and Staff Development.* (Washington, DC: Network of Educators on the Americas [NECA], 1998).

Lee, Stacey J. *Unraveling the 'Model Minority' Stereotype: Listening to Asian American Youth.* (New York: Teachers College Press, 1996).

Lee, Valerie E., Anthony A. Bryk, and Julia B. Smith. "The Organization of Effective Secondary Schools." In *Review of Research in Education*. 19th Yearbook of the American Educational Research Association. Edited by Linda Darling-Hammond. (Washington, DC: AERA, 1993).

Lee, Valerie E., Linda F. Winfield, and Thomas C. Wilson. "Academic Behaviors Among High-Achieving African-American Students." *Education and Urban Society*, 24, 1 (November, 1991), 65–86.

Lee, Vivian W., and Rachel N. Sing. "Gender Equity in Schools for Immigrant Girls." *New Voices*, 3, 2 (1993).

Levine, Linda. "'Who Says?': Learning to Value Diversity in School." In *Celebrating Diverse Voices: Progressive Education and Equity*. Edited by Frank Pignatelli and Susanna W. Pflaum. (Newbury Park, CA: Corwin Press, 1993).

Lewelling, Vickie W. *Linguistic Diversity in the United States: English Plus and Official English.* (Washington, DC: ERIC Clearinghouse on Literacy Education for Limited-English-Proficient Adults, 1992).

Lewis, Oscar. *La Vida: A Puerto Rican Family in the Culture of Poverty—San Juan and New York.* (New York: Random House, 1965).

Linton, Simi. "Reshaping Disability in Teacher Education and Beyond." *Teaching Education*, 6, 2 (Fall, 1994), 9–20.

Lipka, Jerry. "Toward a Culturally Based Pedagogy: A Case Study of One Yup'ik Eskimo Teacher." In *Transforming Curriculum for a Culturally Diverse Society*. Etta R. Hollins, ed. (Mahwah, NJ: Lawrence Erlbaum Associates, 1996).

Lipman, Pauline. *Race, Class, and Power in School Restructuring* (Albany, NY: State University of New York Press, 1998).

Lipset, Seymour Martin, and Earl Raab. *Jews and the New American Scene.* (Cambridge, MA: Harvard University Press, 1995).

Locked In/Locked Out: Tracking and Placement Practices in Boston Public Schools. (Boston: Massachusetts Advocacy Center, March, 1990).

Loewen, James W. *Lies My Teacher Told Me: Everything Your American History Textbook Got Wrong.* (New York: The New Press, 1995).

Lomawaima, K. Tsianina. "Educating Native Americans." In *Handbook of Research on Multicultural Education*, by James A. Banks and Cherry A. McGee Banks, eds. (New York: Macmillan, 1995).

Lomotey, Kofi, ed. *Going to School: The African-American Experience.* (Albany, NY: State University of New York Press, 1990).

Louis, Karen Seashore, Helen M. Marks, and Sharon Kruse. "Teachers' Professional Community in Restructuring Schools." *American Educational Research Journal*, 33, 4 (Winter, 1996), 757–798.

Lucas, Tamara, Rosemary Henze, and Rubén Donato. "Promoting the Success of Latino Language Minority Students: An Exploratory Study of Six High Schools." *Harvard Educational Review*, 60, 3 (1990), 315–340.

Lundeberg, Mary A., Barbara B. Levin, and Helen Harrington, eds. *Who Learns What From Cases and How? The Research Base for Teaching with Cases.* (Mahwah, NJ: Lawrence Erlbaum Associates, Publishers, 1999).

Macedo, Donaldo P. "Literacy for Stupidification: The Pedagogy of Big Lies." *Harvard Educational Review*, 63, 2 (Summer, 1993), 183–206.

Macías, Reynaldo F., and C. Kelly. *Summary Report of the Survey of the States' Limited English Proficient Students and Available Educational Programs and Services 1994–1995.* (Washington, DC: United States Department of Education, Office of Grants and Contracts Services, George Washington University, 1996).

McCarty, Teresa L. "Language, Literacy, and the Image of the Child in American Indian Classrooms." *Language Arts,* 70, 3 (March, 1993), 182–192.

McCaslin, Mary, and Thomas L. Good. "Compliant Cognition: The Misalliance of Management and Instructional Goals in Current School Reform." *Educational Researcher,* 21, 3 (April, 1992), 4–17.

McDermott, Ray P. "Achieving School Failure: An Anthropological Approach to Illiteracy and Social Stratification." In *Education and Cultural Process: Anthropological Approaches,* 2nd ed. Edited by George D. Spindler. (Prospect Heights, IL: Waveland Press, 1987).

McDermott, Ray P. "Social Relations as Contexts for Learning in School." *Harvard Educational Review,* 47, 2 (May, 1977), 198–213.

McDonnel, Lorraine and Paul T. Hill. *Newcomers in American Schools: Meeting the Educational Needs of Immigrant Youth.* (Santa Monica, CA: Rand Corporation, 1993).

McIntosh, Peggy. *White Privilege and Male Privilege: A Personal Account of Coming To See Correspondences through Work in Women's Studies.* Working paper no. 189. (Wellesley, MA: Wellesley College Center for Research on Women, 1988).

McIntyre, Alice. "Constructing an Image of a White Teacher." *Teachers College Press,* 98, 4 (Summer, 1997), 653–681.

McLaughlin, Barry. *Myths and Misconceptions about Second Language Learning: What Every Teacher Needs to Unlearn.* (Santa Cruz, CA: National Center for Research on Cultural Diversity and Second Language Learning, 1992).

Mahiri, Jabari. *Shooting for Excellence: African American and Youth Culture in New Century Schools.* (Urbana, IL, and New York: National Council of Teachers of English and Teachers College Press, 1998).

Marquez, Roberto. "Sojourners, Settlers, Castaways, and Creators: A Recollection of Puerto Rico Past and Puerto Ricans Present." *Massachusetts Review,* 36, 1 (1995), 94–118.

Matute-Bianchi, María E. "Situational Ethnicity and Patterns of School Performance among Immigrant and Nonimmigrant Mexican-Descent Students." In *Minority Status and Schooling: A Comparative Study of Immigrant and Involuntary Minorities.* Edited by Margaret A. Gibson and John U. Ogbu. (New York: Garland, 1991).

May, Stephen. *Making Multicultural Education Work.* (Clevedon, England: Multilingual Matters, 1994).

Medina, Noe, and D. Monty Neill. *Fallout from the Testing Explosion,* 3rd ed. (Cambridge, MA: FairTest, 1990).

"Meeting the Educational Needs of Southeast Asian Children." *Digest,* ERIC Clearinghouse on Urban Education, 68 (1990).

Mehan, Hugh, and Irene Villanueva. "Untracking Low Achieving Students: Academic and Social Consequences." *Focus on Diversity* (Newsletter of the National Center for Research on Cultural Diversity and Second Language Learning), 3, 3 (Winter, 1993), 4–6.

Meier, Deborah. *The Power of Their Ideas: Lessons for America From a Small School in Harlem.* (Boston: Beacon Press, 1995).

Mercado, Carmen I. "Caring as Empowerment: School Collaboration and Community Agency." *Urban Review,* 25, 1 (March, 1993), 79–104.

Mercado, Carmen I. and Luis Moll. "The Study of Funds of Knowledge: Collaborative Research in Latino Homes." *Centro Bulletin,* ix, 9 (1997), 26–42.

Merriam, Sharan B. *Qualitative Research and Case Study Applications in Education,* 2nd ed. (San Francisco: Jossey-Bass Publishers, 1998).

Merton, Robert. "The Self-Fulfilling Prophecy." *Antioch Review,* 8, 2 (1948), 193–210.

Metropolitan Life Survey of the American Teacher 1996. A survey conducted by Louis Harris and Associates, as cited in *Multicultural Education,* 4, 4 (Summer, 1997), 45.

Miller, Robin Lin, and Mary Jane Rotheram-Borus. "Growing Up Biracial in the United States." In *Race, Ethnicity, and Self: Identity in Multicultural Perspective.* Edited by Elizabeth Pathy Salett and Diane R. Koslow. (Washington, DC: National Multicultural Institute, 1994).

Minicucci, Catherine, Paul Berman, Barry McLaughlin, Beverly McLeod, Beryl Nelson, and Kate Woodworth. "School Reform and Student Diversity." *Phi Delta Kappan,* 77, 1 (September, 1995), 77–80.

Moll, Luis C. "Bilingual Classroom Studies and Community Analysis: Some Recent Trends." *Educational Researcher,* 21, 2 (March, 1992), 20–24.

Murguia, Edward. "On Latino/Hispanic Ethnic Identity." *Latino Studies Journal,* 2, 3 (1991), 8–18.

Murnane, Richard J., and Emiliana Vega. "The Nation's Teaching Force." *Teachers College Record,* 99, 1 (1997), 36–41.

"The NABE No-Cost Study on Families." *NABE News* (1 February 1991).

National Center for Education Statistics. *Dropout Rates in the United States: 1993.* (Washington, DC: Author, 1993).

National Education Association. *Status of the American Public School Teacher, 1995–96.* (Washington, DC: Author, 1997).

National Indochinese Clearinghouse. *A Manual for Indochinese Refugee Education, 1976–1977.* (Arlington, VA: Center for Applied Linguistics, 1976).

Neill, Monty. "Transforming Student Assessment." *Phi Delta Kappan,* 79, 1 (September, 1997), 34–40, 58.

Nelson-Barber, Sharon, and Estrin, Elise Trumbull. "Bringing Native American Perspectives to Mathematics and Science Teaching." *Theory into Practice,* 34, 3 (Summer, 1995), 174–185.

Nieto, Sonia. "We Speak in Many Tongues: Linguistic Diversity and Multicultural Education." In *Multicultural Education for the Twenty-First Century.* Edited by Carlos F. Díaz. (Washington, DC: National Education Association, 1992).

Nieto, Sonia. "Affirmation, Solidarity, and Critique: Moving Beyond Tolerance in Multicultural Education." *Multicultural Education,* 1, 4 (Spring, 1994), 9–12, 35–38.

Nieto, Sonia, guest editor of special issue on the national curriculum standards movement. *Educational Forum,* 58, 4 (Summer, 1994).

Nieto, Sonia. "Lessons from Students on Creating a Chance to Dream." *Harvard Educational Review,* 64, 4 (Winter, 1994), 392–426.

Nieto, Sonia. "A History of the Education of Puerto Rican Students in U.S. Mainland Schools: 'Losers,' 'Outsiders,' or 'Leaders'?" In *Handbook of Research on Multicultural Education.* Edited by James A. Banks and Cherry A. McGee Banks. (New York: Macmillan, 1995).

Nieto, Sonia. "On Becoming American: An Exploratory Essay. In *A Light in Dark Times,* Edited by William Ayres and Janet L. Miller. (New York: Teachers College Press, 1998).

Nieto, Sonia. "Fact and Fiction: Stories of Puerto Ricans in U.S. Schools." *Harvard Educational Review,* 68, 2 (Summer, 1998), 133–163.

Nieto, Sonia. *The Light in Their Eyes: Creating Multicultural Learning Communities.* (New York: Teachers College Press, 1999).

Nieto, Sonia. "Bringing Bilingual Education Out of the Basement, and Other Imperatives for Teacher Education." Edited by Zeynep Beykont. *Bilingual Education Works: Linking Research and Practice in Schools* (Cambridge: Harvard Educational Review, 1999).

Nine-Curt, Carmen. *Nonverbal Communication.* (Cambridge, MA: Evaluation, Dissemination, and Assessment Center, 1984).

Oakes, Jeannie. *Keeping Track: How Schools Structure Inequality.* (New Haven, CT: Yale University Press, 1985).

Oakes, Jeannie. *Multiplying Inequalities: The Effects of Race, Social Class, and Tracking on Opportunities to Learn Mathematics and Science.* (Santa Monica, CA: Rand, 1990), vi.

Oakes, Jeannie. "Can Tracking Research Inform Practice?" *Educational Researcher,* 21, 4 (May, 1992), 12–21.

Oakes, Jeannie, and Gretchen Guiton. "Matchmaking: The Dynamics of High School Tracking Decisions." *American Educational Research Journal,* 32, 1 (Spring, 1995), 3–33.

Oakes, Jeannie, and Martin Lipton. *Teaching to Change the World.* (Boston: McGraw-Hill, 1999).

Oakes, Jeannie, Amy Stuart Wells, Makeba Jones, and Amanda Datnow. "Detracking: The Social Construction of Ability, Cultural Politics, and Resistance to Reform." *Teachers College Record,* 98, 3 (1997), 482–510.

O'Connor, Carla. "Dispositions Toward (Collective) Struggle and Educational Resilience in the Inner City: A Case Analysis of Six African-American High School Students." *American Educational Research Journal,* 34, 4 (Winter, 1997), 593–629.

Ogbu, John U. "Understanding Cultural Diversity and Learning." *Educational Researcher,* 21, 8 (1992), 5–14.

Ogbu, John U. "Variability in Minority School Performance: A Problem in Search of an Explanation." *Anthropology and Education Quarterly,* 18, 4 (December, 1987), 312–334.

O'Hare, William P. *America's Minorities: The Demographics of Diversity,* 47, 2 (Washington, DC: Population Reference Bureau, December 1992).

Olsen, Laurie. *Crossing the Schoolhouse Border: Immigrant Students and the California Public Schools.* (San Francisco: California Tomorrow, 1988).

Olsen, Laurie. *Made in America: Immigrant Students in Our Public Schools.* (New York: The New Press, 1997).

Olsen, Roger E. W-B. *A 1993 Survey of LEP and Adult ESL Student Enrollments in U.S. Public Schools.* (Atlanta: Symposium on Language Minority Student Enrollment Data, TESOL, 1993).

Ordovensky, Pat. "SAT Scores Show Signs of Recovery." *USA Today,* August 27, 1992, p. 1D.

Orfield, Gary, Mark D. Bachmeier, David R. James, and Tamela Eitle. *Deepening Segregation in America's Public Schools.* (Cambridge, MA: Harvard University Project of School Desegregation, 1997).

Ortiz, Flora Ida. "Hispanic-American Children's Experiences in Classrooms: A Comparison Between Hispanic and Non-Hispanic Children." In *Class, Race and Gender in American Education.* Edited by Lois Weis. (Albany, NY: State University of New York Press, 1988).

Ovando, Carlos J. "Teaching Science to the Native American Student." In *Teaching the Indian Child: A Bilingual/Multicultural Approach.* Edited by Jon Reyhner. (Billings, MT: Eastern Montana College, 1992).

Ovando, Carlos J., and Virginia P. Collier. *Bilingual and ESL Classrooms: Teaching in Multicultural Contexts,* 2nd ed. (New York: McGraw-Hill, 1998).

Pang, Valerie Ooka. "Asian Pacific American Students: A Diverse and Complex Population." In *Handbook of Research on Multicultural Education.* James A. Banks and Cherry A. McGee Banks, eds. (New York: Macmillan, 1995).

Persell, Caroline Hodges. "Social Class and Educational Equality." In *Multicultural Education: Issues and Perspectives,* 3rd ed. Edited by James Banks and Cherry A. McGee Banks. (Boston: Allyn & Bacon, 1997).

Pewewardy, Cornel. "Our Children Can't Wait: Recapturing the Essence of Indigenous Schools in the United States." *Cultural Survival Quarterly,* Spring, 1998, 29–34.

Pewewardy, Cornel. "Will the 'Real' Indians Please Stand Up?" *Multicultural Review,* (June, 1998), 36–42.

Phelan, Patricia, Ann Locke Davidson, and Hanh Cao Yu. *Adolescents' Worlds: Negotiating Family, Peers, and School.* (New York: Teachers College Press, 1998).

Philips, Susan Urmston. *The Invisible Culture: Communication in Classroom and Community on the Warm Springs Indian Reservation* (reissued with changes). (Prospect Heights, IL: Waveland Press, 1993).

Phinney, Jean D. "A Three-Stage Model of Ethnic Identity Development in Adolescence." In *Ethnic Identity Formation and Transmission among Hispanics and Other Minorities.* Edited by Martha E. Bernal and George P. Knight. (Albany, NY: State University of New York Press, 1993).

Pohan, Cathy A., and Norma J. Bailey. "Opening the Closet: Multiculturalism That is Truly Inclusive." *Multicultural Education,* 5, 1 (Fall, 1997), 12–15.

Pollard, Diane. "A Profile of Underclass Achievers." *Journal of Negro Education,* 58 (1989), 297–308.

Popham, W. James. "Farewell, Curriculum: Confessions of an Assessment Convert." *Phi Delta Kappan,* 79, 5 (January, 1998), 380–384.

Poplin, Mary, and Joseph Weeres. *Voices from the Inside: A Report on Schooling from Inside the Classroom.* (Claremont, CA: Institute for Education in Transformation, Claremont Graduate School, 1992).

Portes, Alejandro, and Rubén G. Rumbaut. *Immigrant America: A Portrait,* 2nd ed. (Berkeley: University of California Press, 1996).

Quality Education for Minorities Project. Education That Works: An Action Plan for the Education of Minorities. (Cambridge, MA: Massachusetts Institute of Technology Press, January 1990).

Ramirez, Manuel, and Alfredo Castañeda. *Cultural Democracy, Bicognitive Development and Education.* (New York: Academic Press, 1974).

Ramsey, Patricia G. *Teaching and Learning in a Diverse World: Multicultural Education for Young Children,* 2nd ed. (New York: Teachers College Press, Columbia University, 1998).

Reissman, Frank. *The Culturally Deprived Child.* New York: Harper & Row, 1962.

Reyes, María de la luz. "Challenging Venerable Assumptions: Literacy Instruction for Linguistically Different Students." *Harvard Educational Review,* 62, 4 (Winter, 1992), 427–446.

Reyhner, Jon. "Bilingual Education: Teaching the Native Language." In *Teaching the Indian Child: A Bilingual/Multicultural Approach.* (Billings, MT: Eastern Montana College, 1992).

Reyhner, Jon. "Native American Languages Act Becomes Law." *NABE News,* 14, 3 (1 December 1990).

Reyhner, Jon, ed. *Teaching the Indian Child: A Bilingual/Multicultural Approach.* (Billings, MT: Eastern Montana College, 1992).

Ríos, Francisco A. "Teachers' Principles of Practice for Teaching in Multicultural Classrooms." In *Teaching Thinking in Cultural Contexts.* Francisco A. Ríos, ed. (Albany, NY: State University of New York Press, 1996).

Rist, Ray C. "Student Social Class and Teacher Expectations: The Self-Fulfilling Prophecy in Ghetto Education." *Challenging the Myths: The Schools, the Blacks, and the Poor.* Reprint series no. 5. (Cambridge, MA: Harvard Educational Review, 1971).

Rivera, John, and Mary Poplin. "Multicultural, Critical, Feminine and Constructive Pedagogies Seen through the Lives of Youth." *Multicultural Education, Critical Pedagogy, and the Politics of Difference.* Christine E. Sleeter and Peter L. McLaren, ed. (Albany, NY: State University of New York Press, 1995).

Rivera-Batiz, Francisco L., and Carlos E. Santiago. *Island Paradox: Puerto Rico in the 1990s.* (New York: Russell Sage Foundation, 1996).

Rochman, Hazel. *Against Borders: Promoting Books for a Multicultural World.* (Chicago: American Library Association, 1993).

Rodriguez, Clara E. *Puerto Ricans: Born in the U.S.A.* (Boulder, CO: Westview Press, 1991).

Rodriguez, Clara E. "Puerto Ricans in Historical and Social Science Research." *Handbook of Research on Multicultural Education.* James A. Banks and Cherry A. McGee Banks, ed. (New York: Macmillan, 1995).

Rodriguez, Luis J. *Always Running, La Vida Loca: Gang Days in L.A.* (New York: Simon & Schuster, 1993).

Rodriguez, Richard. *Hunger of Memory: The Education of Richard Rodriguez.* (Boston: David R. Godine, 1982).

Romo, Harriet D. and Toni Falbo. *Latino High School Graduation: Defying the Odds.* (Austin, TX: University of Texas Press, 1996).

Rooney, Charles. *Test Scores Do Not Equal Merit.* (Cambridge, MA: FairTest, 1998).

Rose, Lowell C. and Alec M. Gallup. "The 30th Annual Phi Delta Kappa/Gallup Poll of the Public's Attitudes Toward the Public Schools." *Phi Delta Kappan,* 80, 1 (September, 1998), 41–56.

Rosenthal, Robert. "Pygmalian Effects: Existence, Magnitude, and Social Importance." *Educational Researcher,* 16, 9 (December, 1987), 37–41.

Rosenthal, Robert, and Lenore Jacobson. *Pygmalion in the Classroom.* (New York: Holt, Rinehart & Winston, 1968).

Rudman, Masha Kabokow. *Children's Literature: An Issues Approach,* 3rd ed. (White Plains, NY: Longman, 1995).

Rumbaut, Rubén G. *Immigrant Students in California Public Schools: A Summary of Current Knowledge.* (Baltimore: Center for Research on Effective Schooling for Disadvantaged Students, 1990).

Rumbaut, Rubén G. "The Crucible Within: Ethnic Identity, Self-Esteem, and Segmented Assimilation Among Children of Immigrants." In *Origins and Destinies: Immigration, Race, and Ethnicity in America.* Silvia Pedraza and Rubén G. Rumbaut, ed. (Belmont, CA: Wadsworth Publishing Co., 1996).

Ryan, William. *Blaming the Victim.* (New York: Vintage Books, 1972).

Sadker, Myra, and David Sadker. *Failing at Fairness: How America's Schools Cheat Girls.* (New York: Charles Scribner's Sons, 1994).

Sapon-Shevin, Mara. "Ability Differences in the Classroom: Teaching and Learning in Inclusive Classrooms." In *Common Bonds: Anti-Bias Teaching in a Diverse Society.* Edited by Deborah A. Byrnes and Gary Kiger. (Wheaton, MD: Association for Childhood Education International, 1992).

Saravia-Shore, Marietta, and Herminio Martinez. "An Ethnographic Study of Home/School Role Conflicts of Second Generation Puerto Rican Adolescents." In *Cross-Cultural Literacy: Ethnographies of Communication in Multiethnic Classrooms.* Edited by Marietta Saravia-Shore and Steven F. Arvizu. (New York: Garland, 1992).

Schaefer, Richard T. *Racial and Ethnic Groups,* 3rd ed. (Glenview, IL: Scott Foresman, 1988).

Schniedewind, Nancy, and Ellen Davidson. *Open Minds to Equality: A Sourcebook of Learning Activities to Affirm Diversity and Promote Equity,* 2nd ed. (Boston: Allyn & Bacon, 1998).

Seelye, H. Ned. *Teaching Culture: Strategies for Intercultural Communication.* (Lincolnwood, IL: National Textbook, 1993).

Sheets, Rosa Hernandez. "From Remedial to Gifted: Effects of Culturally Centered Pedagogy." *Theory into Practice,* 34, 3 (Summer, 1995), 186–193.

Sheets, Rosa Hernandez. "Urban Classroom Conflict: Student-Teacher Perception." *The Urban Review,* 28, 2 (1996), 165–183.

Shor, Ira. *When Students Have Power: Negotiating Authority in a Critical Pedagogy.* (Chicago: University of Chicago Press, 1996).

Silverman, Rita, William M. Welty, and Sally Lyon. *Multicultural Education Cases for Teacher Problem Solving.* (New York: McGraw-Hill, 1994).

Simon, Rita J., and Howard Alstein. *Transracial Adoptees and Their Families.* (New York: Praeger, 1987).

Sims, Rudine. *Shadow and Substance: Afro-American Experience in Contemporary Children's Fiction.* (Champaign, IL: National Council of Teachers of English, 1982).

Skutnabb-Kangas, Tove. "Multilingualism and the Education of Minority Children." In *Minority Education: From Shame to Struggle.* Edited by Tove Skutnabb-Kangas and Jim Cummins. (Clevedon, England: Multilingual Matters, 1988).

Sleeter, Christine E. "White Racism," *Multicultural Education*, 1, 4 (Spring, 1994), 5–8, 39.

Sleeter, Christine E. *Multicultural Education and Social Activism.* (Albany, NY: State University of New York Press, 1996).

Sleeter, Christine E., and Carl A. Grant. "Race, Class, Gender and Disability in Current Textbooks." In *The Politics of the Textbook.* Edited by Michael W. Apple and Linda K. Christian-Smith. (New York: Routledge & Chapman Hall, 1991).

Snow, Catherine. "The Myths around Bilingual Education." *NABE News*, 21, 2 (1997), 29, 36.

Snow, Richard E. "Unfinished Pygmalion." *Contemporary Psychology*, 14, 4 (1969), 197–200.

Solorzano, Daniel. "Chicano Mobility Aspirations: A Theoretical and Empirical Note." *Latino Studies Journal*, 3, 1 (January, 1992), 48–66.

Solsken, Judith, Jo-Anne Wilson Keenan, and Jerri Willett. "Interweaving Stories: Creating a Multicultural Classroom through School/Home/University Collaboration." *Democracy and Education* (Fall, 1993), 16–21.

Soo Hoo, Suzanne. "Students as Partners in Research and Restructuring Schools." *The Educational Forum*, 57, 4 (Summer, 1993), 386–393.

Spring, Joel. *The Rise and Fall of the Corporate State.* (Boston: Beacon Press, 1972).

Spring, Joel. *The Interaction of Cultures: Multicultural Education in the United States.* (New York: McGraw-Hill, 1995).

Spring, Joel. *Deculturalization and the Struggle for Equality: A Brief History of the Education of Dominated Cultures in the United States*, 2nd ed. (New York: McGraw-Hill, 1997).

St. Germaine, Richard. "Drop-out Rates Among American Indian and Alaska Native Students: Beyond Cultural Discontinuity." *Eric Digest.* (Charleston, WV: Clearinghouse on Rural Education and Small Schools, November, 1995).

Stanton-Salazar, Ricardo D. "A Social Capital Framework for Understanding the Socialization of Racial Minority Children and Youth." *Harvard Educational Review*, 67, 1 (Spring, 1997), 1–40.

Steele, Claude M. "Race and the Schooling of Black Americans." *The Atlantic Monthly* (April, 1992), 68–78.

Suarez-Orozco, Marcelo M. "'Becoming Somebody': Central American Immigrants in U.S. Inner-City Schools." *Anthropology and Education Quarterly*, 18, 4 (December, 1987), 287–299.

Suleiman, Mahmoud F. "Empowering Arab American Students: Implications for Multicultural Teachers." In *1996 Proceedings of the National Association for Multicultural Education Conference.* Carl A. Grant, ed. (San Francisco: Caddo Gap Press, 1997).

Swisher, Karen. "Learning Styles: Implications for Teachers." In *Multicultural Education for the 21st Century.* Edited by Carlos Díaz. (Washington, DC: National Education Association, 1992).

Taeuber, Cynthia (editor and compiler). *The Statistical Handbook on Women in America*, 2nd ed. (Phoenix: Oryx Press, 1996).

Takaki, Ronald. *Strangers from a Different Shore: A History of Asian Americans.* (New York: Penguin Books, 1989).

Tam, Thi Dang Wei. *Vietnamese Refugee Students: A Handbook for School Personnel.* (Cambridge, MA: National Assessment and Dissemination Center, 1980).

Tapia, Javier. "The Schooling of Puerto Ricans: Philadelphia's Most Impoverished Community." *Anthropology and Education Quarterly*, 29, 3 (1998), 297–323.

Tatum, Beverly Daniel. *"Why Are All the Black Kids Sitting Together in the Cafeteria?" and Other Conversations About Race.* (New York: HarperCollins, 1997).

Tatum, Beverly Daniel. "Talking about Race, Learning about Racism: The Application of Racial Identity Development Theory in the Classroom." *Harvard Educational Review,* 62, 1 (Spring, 1992), 1–24.

Taylor, Angela R. "Social Competence and the Early School Transition: Risk and Protective Factors for African-American Children." *Education and Urban Society,* 24, 1 (November, 1991), 15–26.

Taylor, Denny, and Catherine Dorsey-Gaines. *Growing Up Literate: Learning from Inner-City Families.* (Portsmouth, NH: Heinemann, 1988).

Terman, Lewis. *The Measurement of Intelligence.* (Boston: Houghton Mifflin, 1916).

Tharp, Roland G. "Psychocultural Variables and Constants: Effects on Teaching and Learning in Schools." *American Psychologist,* 44, 2 (February, 1989), 349–359.

Thomas, Wayne P., and Collier, Virginia. *School Effectiveness for Language Minority Students.* (Washington, DC: National Clearinghouse for Bilingual Education, 1997).

Tomás Rivera Center Report, 2, 4 (Fall, 1989), Claremont, CA: Tomás Rivera Center.

Torres-Guzmán, María E. "Stories of Hope in the Midst of Despair: Culturally Responsive Education for Latino Students in an Alternative High School in New York City." In *Cross-Cultural Literacy: Ethnographies of Communication in Multiethnic Classrooms.* Edited by Marietta Saravia-Shore and Steven F. Arvizu. (New York: Garland, 1992).

Trueba, Henry T. "Culture and Language: The Ethnographic Approach to the Study of Learning Environments." In *Language and Culture in Learning: Teaching Spanish to Native Speakers of Spanish.* Barbara J. Merino, Henry T. Trueba, and Fabián A. Samaniego, ed. (Bristol, PA: Falmer Press, 1993), 26–44.

Trueba, Henry T., and Pamela G. Wright. "On Ethnographic Studies and Multicultural Education." In *Cross-Cultural Literacy: Ethnographies of Communication in Multiethnic Classrooms.* Edited by Marietta Saravia-Shore and Steven F. Arvizu. (New York: Garland, 1992).

Tse, Lucy. "Language Brokering in Linguistic Minority Communities: The Case of Chinese- and Vietnamese-American Students." *The Bilingual Research Journal,* 20, 3 and 4 (Summer/Fall, 1996), 485–498.

Tyack, David B. *The One Best System: A History of American Urban Education.* (Cambridge, MA: Harvard University Press, 1974).

Tyack, David B. "Schooling and Social Diversity: Historical Reflections." In *Toward a Common Destiny: Improving Race and Ethnic Relations in America.* Edited by Willis D. Hawley and Anthony W. Jackson. (San Francisco: Jossey-Bass Publishers, 1995).

U.S. Bureau of the Census. *Current Population Reports, Series P–60, No. 188.* (Washington, DC: U.S. Government Printing Office, 1995).

U.S. Bureau of the Census. *Statistical Abstract of the United States* (114th ed.). (Washington, DC: U.S. Government Printing Office, 1994), 11.

U.S. Bureau of the Census. *We, the First Americans.* (Washington, DC: U.S. Government Printing Office, 1993).

U.S. Bureau of the Census. *1990 Census of Population and Housing Data Paper Listing.* (Washington, DC: U.S. Government Printing Office, 1990).

United States Bureau of the Census. *Statistical Abstract of the United States, 1997, The National Data Book.* (Washington, DC: Bureau of the Census, 1997).

Valdés, Guadalupe. *Con Respeto: Bridging the Distance Between Culturally Diverse Families and Schools.* (New York: Teachers College Press, 1996).

Valencia, Richard R., ed. *Chicano School Failure and Success: Research and Policy Agendas for the 1990s.* (London: Falmer Press, 1991).

Vasquez, Olga A., Lucinda Pease-Alvarez, and Sheila M. Shannon. *Pushing Boundaries: Language and Culture in a Mexicano Community*. (New York: Cambridge University Press, 1994).

Vogt, Lynn A., Cathie Jordan, and Roland G. Tharp. "Explaining School Failure, Producing School Success: Two Cases." In *Minority Education: Anthropological Perspectives*. Edited by Evelyn Jacob and Cathie Jordan. (Norwood, NJ: Ablex, 1993).

Waggoner, Dorothy. "Language-Minority School-Age Population Now Totals 9.9 Million." *NABE NEWS*, 18, 1 (15 September 1994), 1, 24–26.

Walsh, Catherine E. *Pedagogy and the Struggle for Voice: Issues of Language, Power, and Schooling for Puerto Ricans*. (New York: Bergin & Garvey, 1991).

Wehlage, Gary G., and Robert A. Rutter. "Dropping Out: How Much Do Schools Contribute to the Problem?" In *School Dropouts: Patterns and Policies*. (New York: Teachers College Press, 1986).

Weinberg, Meyer. *Because They Were Jews: A History of Anti-Semitism*. (Westport, CT: Greenwood Press, 1986).

Weinberg, Meyer. *A Chance to Learn: A History of Race and Education in the U.S.* (Cambridge: Cambridge University Press, 1977).

Weinberg, Meyer. "Notes from the Editor." *A Chronicle of Equal Education*, 4, 3 (November, 1982).

Weinberg, Meyer. *Racism in the United States: A Comprehensive Classified Bibliography*. (Westport, CT: Greenwood Press, 1990).

Wellesley College Center for Research on Women. *How Schools Shortchange Girls: The AAUW Report*. (Washington, DC: American Association of University Women Educational Foundation, 1992).

Wheelock, Anne. *Crossing the Tracks: How "Untracking" Can Save America's Schools*. (New York: The New Press, 1992).

Williams, Melvin D. "Observations in Pittsburgh Ghetto Schools." *Anthropology and Education Quarterly*, 12 (1981), 211–220.

Williams, Selase W. "Classroom Use of African American Language: Educational Tool or Social Weapon?" In *Empowerment through Multicultural Education*. Edited by Christine E. Sleeter. (Albany, NY: State University of New York Press, 1991).

Williamson, Joel. *New People: Miscegenation and Mulattoes in the United States*. (New York: Free Press, 1980).

Willis, Arlette, ed., *Teaching and Using Multicultural Literature in Grades 9–12: Moving Beyond the Canon*. (Norwood, MA: Christopher-Gordon, 1998).

Wineburg, Samuel S. "The Self-Fulfillment of the Self-Fulfilling Prophecy: A Critical Appraisal." *Educational Researcher*, 16, 9 (December, 1987), 28–37.

Winfield, Linda, and Michael Woodard. *Assessment, Equity, and Diversity in Reforming America's Schools*. (Los Angeles: National Center for Research on Evaluation, Standards, and Student Testing, UCLA Graduate School of Education, 1994).

Witkin, Herman A. *Psychological Differentiation*. (New York: Wiley, 1962).

Women and Minorities in Science and Engineering. (Washington, DC: National Science Foundation, 1988).

Woodson, Carter G. *The Miseducation of the Negro*. (Washington, DC: Associated Publishers, 1933).

Wollman-Bonilla, Julie E. "Outrageous Viewpoints: Teachers' Criteria for Rejecting Works of Children's Literature." *Language Arts*, 75, 4 (April, 1998), 287–295.

Zanger, Virginia Vogel. "Academic Costs of Social Marginalization: An Analysis of Latino Students' Perceptions at a Boston High School." In *The Education of Latino Students in Massachusetts: Research and Policy Considerations*. Edited by Ralph Rivera and Sonia Nieto. (Boston: Gastón Institute, 1993).

Zanger, Virginia Vogel. *Face to Face: Communication, Culture, and Collaboration,* 2nd ed. (Boston: Heinle & Heinle, 1993).

Zeichner, Kenneth. "Educating Teachers to Close the Achievement Gap: Issues of Pedagogy, Knowledge, and Teacher Preparation." In *Closing the Achievement Gap: A Vision to Guide Changes in Beliefs and Practice* by the Urban Education National Network. (Washington, DC: United States Department of Education, Office of Educational Research and Improvement, 1995).

Zeichner, Kenneth M. *Connecting Genuine Teacher Development to the Struggle for Social Justice.* (East Lansing, MI: National Center for Research on Teacher Learning, Michigan State University, April 1992).

Zentella, Ana Celia. *Growing up Bilingual: Puerto Rican Children in New York.* (Malden, MA : Blackwell, 1997).

Zogby, James J. "When Stereotypes Threaten Pride." *NEA Today* (October, 1982), 12.

Index

Ability grouping. *See* Tracking
Abi-Nader, Jeannette, 150
Abramson, Avi, 8, 110–120, 373
Additive bilingualism, 197–198
Additive multiculturalism, 335–337
African Americans, 41, 147
   academic success, 238–239
   Black dialect, 194
   case studies of, 50–62, 63–72, 262–273
   communication styles, 145–146
   cultural identity, 266–267
   culture-specific teaching, 150
   disciplinary policies and, 104
   gifted programs and, 39
   learning styles and preferences, 184(n9)
   poverty and achievement, 47–48
   relevance of curriculum to, 97
   self-hatred, 70
   teacher expectations of, 45–46
   tracking and, 89–90
   violence among, 276(n2)
Alcohol and alcoholism, 123, 250–251
Allport, Gordon, 34
Always Running, la Vida Loca (Rodríguez), 258–259
Americanization, 333–337
Anglo-conformity, 288, 301(n13)
Angloization, 335
Anglos, 26. *See also* European Americans; Whites
Anthropology and Education Quarterly journal, 241
Anti-Bias Curriculum Task Force, 319
Anti-Semitism, 104, 114
Antonia Pantoja Community High School, 262, 269
Apple, Michael, 100, 236
Arab Americans, 3, 163–171
Ascher, Carol, 41
Ashton-Warner, Sylvia, 318–319
Asian Americans
   academic success, 238–239
   challenging "model minority" myth, 287
   Chinese Americans, 138–139
   differences among groups, 29–30
   Punjabis, 233–234, 238, 240
   Vietnamese Americans, 172–183
Assessment
   equitable alternatives to testing, 92–95
   "Harvard Test of Influenced Acquisition," 43
   as institutional racism, 37
   standardized testing, 37, 43, 92–95, 357–358
Assimilation, 335–337. *See also* Culture, maintaining
   of Arab Americans, 164
   of Jews, 120
   resisting, 290–291
Authentic assessments, 94

Banks, James, 316
Baratz, Joan, 231
Baratz, Stephen, 231
Barrett, Susan, 337
Bennett, Kathleen, 148
Bigler, Ellen, 42–43
Bilingualism, 163
   additive bilingualism, 197–198
   enhancing cognitive development, 194–195
   subtractive bilingualism, 335–336
   supporting, 198–199
Black dialect, 194
Blacks. See African Americans
Bloome, David, 99
Boateng, Felix, 141
Bode, Patty, 354
Bogan, Dan, 150
Bourdieu, Pierre, 234, 284
Bowles, Samuel, 40, 235
Braddock, Jomills, 90
Brantlinger, Ellen, 40
Brown, John, 307
Brumberg, Stephan, 119
Burnett, Gary, 41
Bush, George, 46, 131

Capacidad (Hispanic cultural trait), 162
Cape Verde, 3, 207–216
Career aspirations, 128, 156–157, 160, 175
   ambivalent, 219
   bicycle racer, 166
   educator, 255
   engineering, 163
   failure to attain, 260
   music, 60, 63
   pharmacology, 64
   physical therapist, 263
Carnegie Council on Adolescent Development, 102
Carter, Kathy, 16–17
Case studies, 19–20
   African American, 50–62, 63–72, 262–273
   biracial, 50–62, 371–373
   Cape Verdean, 207–216
   characteristics of, 11–12
   defining success, 281–283
   demographics of students, 13–14
   European American, 73–81
   follow-up interviews, 371–374
   Jewish American, 110–120
   Lebanese American, 163–171
   Mexican American, 218–225, 248–261
   Native American, 122–131
   Puerto Rican, 154–162
   student selection for, 15, 17–19
   theme and format, 15–17

About the Author

Sonia Nieto is Professor of Language, Literacy, and Culture in the School of Education, University of Massachusetts at Amherst. Dr. Nieto's scholarly work focuses on multicultural education, the schooling of language minority and immigrant students, the education of Latinos in the United States, and Puerto Ricans in children's literature. She has written a number of books in addition to *Affirming Diversity*, including *The Light in Their Eyes: Creating Multicultural Learning Communities*, and *Puerto Rican Students in U.S. Schools*. She has also written many book chapters and articles in such journals as *The Harvard Educational Review*, *Theory into Practice*, and *The Educational Forum*. Dr. Nieto has worked extensively with teachers and schools, and she serves on several national boards and commissions that concentrate on educational equity and social justice. She has received numerous awards for her work, including the Human and Civil Rights Award from the Massachusetts Teachers Association in 1989, the Educator of the Year Award from NAME, the National Association for Multicultural Education, in 1997, and the New England Educator of the Year Award from Region One of NAME in 1998, among others. She also received an Annenberg Senior Fellowship for 1998–2000 and she was awarded an honorary doctorate from Lesley College in Cambridge, Massachusetts in 1999. She is married to Angel Nieto, a children's book author and former bilingual teacher. They have two daughters and two granddaughters.